1994 Guide to Literary Agents & Art/Photo Reps

Edited by Kirsten C. Holm

WRITER'S DIGEST BOOKS
CINCINNATI, OHIO

Distributed in Canada by McGraw-Hill,
300 Water Street,
Whitby Ontario L1N 9B6.
Distributed in Australia by Kirby Books, Private
Bag No. 19, P.O. Alexandria NSW2015.

Managing Editor, Market Books Department:
Constance J. Achabal;
Supervisory Editor: Mark Garvey;
Production Editor: Richard D. Muskopf

1994 Guide to Literary Agents & Art/Photo Reps. Copyright © 1994 by Writer's Digest Books.
Published by F&W Publications, 1507 Dana Ave., Cincinnati, Ohio 45207. Printed and bound in the United States of America. All rights reserved. No part of this book may be reproduced in any form or by any electronic or mechanical means including information storage and retrieval systems without written permission from the publisher, except by reviewers who may quote brief passages to be printed in a magazine or newspaper.

International Standard Serial Number
ISSN 1055-6087
International Standard Book Number
0-89879-615-6

Cover illustration by Jack Whitney/AIR Studio Inc.

Pages 23-24 excerpt from How To Be Your Own Literary Agent by Richard Curtis. © 1983 by Richard Curtis. Reprinted by permission of Houghton Mifflin Company. All rights reserved.

Contents

- 1 **From the Editor**
- 3 **How to Use Your Guide to Literary Agents & Art/Photo Reps**

Literary Agents

- 6 **How to Find (and Keep) the Right Agent,** *by Lori Perkins.*
  A comprehensive look at what an agent does and how to get one to do it for you.
- 11 **29 Qualities of a Good Agent,** *by Scott Edelstein.*
- 13 **Write and Wrong: Literary Agents and Ethics,** *by Arnold Goodman.*
  The chairperson of AAR's Committee on Ethics discusses their Canon of Ethics and how to make sure an agent will live up to them.
- 18 **11 Tips on Author-Agent Agreements,** *by Scott Edelstein.*
- 20 **Know What Your Agent Knows About Deal Points,** *by Richard Curtis.*
  Successful contract negotiations need not be a mystery. What to negotiate for (and why).
- 25 **Know Your Rights,** *by B.J. Doyen.*
  A comprehensive article delineating authors' rights and how to protect them.
- 31 **Agents at Large,** *by Pat Matson Knapp.*
  A roundtable of several literary agents operating outside of NYC on their working methods and effectiveness.
- 36 **When the Honeymoon Is Over,** *by Michael Larsen.*
  The warning signs to look for when the relationship with your agent starts turning sour.
- 38 **How to Fire Your Agent Gracefully,** *by Scott Edelstein.*
- 39 **Finding and Working with Literary Agents,** *by Robin Gee.*
  The fundamentals of approaching and working with agents from the former editor of Guide to Literary Agents and Art/Photo Reps.

- 45 **Literary Agents: Nonfee-charging**
- 112 **Literary Agents: Fee-charging**

Script Agents

- 155 **Finding and Working with Script Agents,** *by Kerry Cox.*
  Successful scriptwriter and editor of The Hollywood Scriptwriter, *Cox discusses how to find and what to expect from a script agent.*
- 160 **Script Agents: Nonfee- and Fee-charging**

Art/Photo Reps

181 Finding and Working with Art/Photo Reps, *by Barbara Gordon.*
A former president of the Society of Photographers' and Artists' Reps discusses the rep/talent relationship in this informative article on working with reps.

185 Commercial Art and Photography Reps

225 Fine Art Reps

Resources

233 Recommended Books & Publications

237 Professional Organizations

238 Keys to Symbols and Abbreviations

238 Table of Acronyms

240 Glossary

Indexes

243 Subject Index

268 Children's Book Illustration Index

268 Commercial Art/Photo and Fine Art Reps Geographic Index

270 Agents and Reps Index

280 Listings Index

From the Editor

When I was young, all I could say when asked what my father did was that he talked on the telephone and wrote letters. And actually, that's a pretty apt description of what a literary agent does as well. With this, the third edition of *Guide to Literary Agents & Art/Photo Reps*, we've tried to further demystify what agents and reps do, and show you how to approach them so that they'll do it for you. You may be looking for an agent or rep for the first time, thinking about making a change, or just testing the waters for future reference; this book will help answer the questions you have about building the career you want.

Literary agents

With each edition, we try to accomplish two things with the articles: cover the basics and offer insights you might not get otherwise. Lori Perkins, a New York literary agent for eight years, asks and answers fundamental questions about the author/agent working relationship—what an agent does, whether you need one, how to approach one. Arnold Goodman, chairperson of the Ethics Committee of the Association of Author's Representatives (AAR), discusses issues surrounding agents and professional ethics, along with practical tips on how to make sure your agent is trustworthy. Michael Larsen weighs in with the warning signs to look for when an author/agent relationship is not working.

The technical side of contract negotiations and putting together deals can seem daunting. The agent's job is to represent you in this process and get the best deal for your work, but an author should learn as much as possible about the terms and issues involved. Agent and author Richard Curtis shows how to translate the language of negotiation into plain English, and agent B.J. Doyen provides a comprehensive overview of rights and how to protect them, including the emerging area of commercial merchandising rights.

Until recently, literary agents "had" to be located in New York. With the emergence of modern technology (faxes, computer networks, special phone systems, etc.) proximity is helpful, but not mandatory. Pat Matson Knapp talks with three agents who aren't where you expect them, but who are unexpectedly successful. We've also included several quick checklists on assorted topics that briefly cover the qualities of a good agent, your relationship and how to leave when it's time.

The listings have all been updated, many with important changes, and over 65 new agents have been added.

Art/photo reps

Unlike new writers looking for literary agents, those who seek representation in the areas of fine or commercial art or photography are usually established in their fields. In fact, many reps recommend that artists or photographers first represent themselves to understand exactly what is involved. Reps help expand client lists and handle the paperwork involved in a successful career, finding new work and making sure you get paid for work already completed. With this edition the number of listings for art and photo reps has increased substantially, with over 75 new listings for you to investigate. You'll find specifics on what kind of markets a rep deals in, what types of promotional materials are required, what to send first and what to have in your portfolio.

In addition . . .

The *Guide* also features two additional sections, Script Agents and Fine Art Reps. The section of agents who primarily handle movie and TV scripts has grown by almost 30 new listings this year. The Fine Arts section will help artists seeking galleries, art collectors and other outlets for their work.

Helpful indexes and more

In our experience with other annual directories we've found subject indexes helpful in quickly identifying listings that fit individual readers' specific needs. The *Guide* follows suit. Literary agents and script agents are indexed by fiction and nonfiction subjects, with "horror" added this year. Art/photo and fine art reps are indexed geographically by state. Many agents and reps are also interested in handling work in areas other than their primary focus, and these are cross-referenced in the "Additional" list at the end of each section. A special index is added this year for literary agents and art/photo reps interested in children's book illustration and author/illustrators.

Listings are ranked by levels of openness to submissions, from a new agency (**I**) to an agency "not currently seeking new clients" (**V**). There is a Glossary of words and phrases, a translation Table of Acronyms for various writers' and artists' organizations, and a list of resources including publications and organizations that can be helpful to writers, illustrators and photographers.

We have worked hard this year to make this the best book possible. We're pleased with the number of new and existing listings and the quality of information they contain. Working on the book is a year-round task, and as this book goes off to the printers we're back at work, evaluating the material in this edition, revising questionnaires and updates to send out for the fourth edition. Let me know what you think: What information could you use that isn't provided here? What subjects would you like to see explored in future articles? I look forward to hearing your suggestions.

Wishing you the best of luck and a successful year,

Kirsten Campbell Holm

How to Use Your Guide to Literary Agents & Art/Photo Reps

What do you, as a writer or artist, want to find in an agent or rep? Someone who believes in you? Who wants to help you put together a successful career? Someone who will work full-time to showcase your work to its best advantage? Who will take care of business details, leaving you free to create without distraction?

What does an agent seek in a writer or a rep look for in an artist? Someone whose talent is compelling? Who has the ability and passion that, combined with an agent's knowledge and experience, can achieve success? Someone who is willing to work *hard* until a piece has reached its best, highest form? Who is ready to approach a career professionally?

The objectives are similar. The problem is connecting writer and agent, artist and rep. The *Guide to Literary Agents & Art/Photo Reps* is specifically designed to provide you with the information you need to find the most appropriate person to market your work.

What's in the book

The book is divided into feature articles and listings. Feature articles, written by agents and reps themselves, provide various perspectives on the author/agent relationship as well as information on business details such as contract negotiations and rights. The listings profile individual agencies, what they are interested in seeing and how to present it for their best consideration.

Each chapter contains information on a specific category of agent or rep: nonfee-charging literary agents, fee-charging literary agents, script agents, commercial art and photo reps, and fine art reps. It begins with an introduction on how to approach that type of agent, followed by an explanation of the ranking system we use to designate openness to submissions, and then the listings, full of specific information from the agencies themselves.

Literary and script agents

Nonfee-charging agents earn income from commissions made on the sale of manuscripts. Their focus is selling books, and they do not edit manuscripts or promote books that have already been published. Nonfee-charging agents tend to be highly selective, and prefer to work with established writers and experts in specific fields. While most will accept queries from new writers, many are not looking for new clients. Be sure to check the listing carefully to determine an agent's current needs.

Fee-charging agents charge writers for various services (e.g., reading, critiquing, editing, evaluation, consultation, marketing, etc.), in addition to a commission on sales. Since they are being compensated for additional services, they are generally more receptive to handling the work of new writers. However, reading and other fees can be extremely high, and payment of them rarely ensures that an agent will agree to take you on as a client.

Your best bet is to develop your novel, nonfiction book or script to the point at which it is saleable enough to attract a nonfee-charging agent. If you do choose to approach a fee-charging agent, be sure to research the agency carefully, requesting references and sample critiques. As with any financial transaction, make sure you know what you'll be getting for your money.

Once you've decided to go with a nonfee- or a fee-charging agent, you can further narrow your search for the right agent in one of two ways: read through the listings or use the Subject Index at the back of the book.

You can refer directly to the listings. Nonfee-charging literary agents and fee-charging literary agents are grouped separately. While all script agents are grouped in one section, those that charge fees are clearly indicated with an open box (□) symbol. Reading through the listings gives a more comprehensive idea of who is out there looking for what. And if you're writing on a narrower area that's the way to find your agent.

Another way to work is through the Subject Index. The index is divided into separate sections of nonfee-charging and fee-charging literary agents and script agents. Each section is further divided by fiction and nonfiction subject categories, i.e., romance or child guidance/parenting. Each nonfee-charging agency that indicated they would consider family sagas, for example, is listed in Nonfee-charging agents/Fiction: Family saga. Some agencies did not want to restrict themselves to specific subjects. We have listed them in the subject heading "open to all areas" in both nonfiction and fiction.

Art/photo reps

Commercial art and photography and fine art reps are located in their own sections of the book. Reps handle various types of visual art, including photography, illustration, graphic design and fine art. Most reps require the talent to pay a percentage, and sometimes all, of the advertising costs. Some require payment for special portfolios; a few charge monthly retainers to cover marketing expenses. These listings are designated with a solid box (■) symbol.

Special indexes

Several special indexes in the back of the book expedite your search. An Agents and Reps Index helps you locate individual agents who may be employed by large agencies. Reps have also been indexed geographically by state and province in the back of the book. A small index of agents and reps specializing in children's book illustration area is also included for the first time in this edition.

Targeting agents and reps

With a list of the agents or reps who handle the kind of work you create, read the listings to find the agencies that will be most interested in representing your work.

Check the number code after each listing to determine how receptive the agency is to submissions. Most users of the *Guide* should check three items within the listing: types of work the agency handles; terms, including commission and contract information; and preferred method of submission, found under "Handles" for agents and "How to Contact" for reps.

Writing or art is not "one size fits all" when it comes to representation. Most agents and reps are not likely to consider submissions outside their specific interests or needs. Consider only those agents whose interests correspond with your type of work. Study their terms to determine whether the commission and contract policies (if applicable) are acceptable to you. Recent sales information can also be helpful, as it provides clues to the quality of work and caliber of clients represented by a particular agency.

One reader's method

One reader devised her own successful scheme to find an agent. First, she went through the book carefully, particularly studying the categories of information given: subjects they were interested in; percentage of unpublished writers; sales; etc. She drew up a list of agents who dealt largely in nonfiction, which she was writing. She then made a chart and ranked those agents from a low of 1 to a high of 5. Agents who only took a small percentage of new writers received a 1, those who had been in business for a certain length of time received a 5, an agent that placed her type of nonfiction received a 5, and so on. When she was finished she totaled the points and ranked the agents accordingly. She queried them in that order, and signed with the sixth agent on her list.

When you are confident you have targeted the best agent or rep for your work, submit it according to the procedures outlined in the listing. For more specific information on approaching agents and reps, see Finding and Working with Literary Agents, Finding and Working with Script Agents and Finding and Working with Art/Photo Reps at the beginning of each respective chapter.

Listing Policy and Complaint Procedure

Listings in Guide to Literary Agents & Art/Photo Reps *are compiled from detailed questionnaires, phone interviews and information provided by agents and representatives. The industry is volatile and agencies change addresses, needs and policies frequently. We rely on our readers for information on their dealings with agents and changes in policies or fees that differ from what has been reported to the editor. Write to us if you have new information, questions about agents or if you have any problems dealing with the agencies listed or suggestions on how to improve our listings.*

Listings are published free of charge and are not *advertisements. Although the information is as accurate as possible, the listings are* not *endorsed or guaranteed by the editor or publisher of* Guide to Literary Agents & Art/Photo Reps. *If you feel you have not been treated fairly by an agent or representative listed in* Guide to Literary Agents & Art/Photo Reps, *we advise you to take the following steps:*

- *First try to contact the listing. Sometimes one phone call or a letter can quickly clear up the matter.*
- *Document all your correspondence with the listing. When you write to us with a complaint, provide the name of your manuscript or type of artwork, the date of your first contact with the agency and the nature of your subsequent correspondence.*
- *We will write to the agency and ask them to resolve the problem. We will then enter your letter into our files.*
- *The number, frequency and severity of complaints will be considered in our decision whether or not to delete the listing from our upcoming edition.*

Guide to Literary Agents & Art/Photo Reps *reserves the right to exclude any listing for any reason.*

How to Find (and Keep) the Right Agent

by Lori Perkins

Before I became an agent, I was a journalist, and before that, an aspiring novelist. I tell you this because I, too, wanted to get published. I used to think that New York agents were mystical beings who could change my life with one phone call, if they would only read my query letters.

When I finally decided to leave the news business and became a New York literary agent, I was honestly surprised to find that agents were mere mortals with no super powers, only high-powered Rolodexes and a nearly insane desire to get people published.

As someone who has been on the outside looking in, I am writing this article with the sole purpose of giving you the insider's view on how to get and keep the right agent.

What is an agent?

You'd be surprised at the number of writers who think an agent is an editor, business manager, lawyer, publicist, banker, mother, new best friend, fairy godmother—the list is endless.

A synonym for agent is the term "author's representative," and that really is a perfect definition of the agent's role. An agent is your representative to the publishing industry, who you hire to negotiate in your best interests.

What this entails can differ slightly from agent to agent, but it generally includes the following tasks (assuming your material is ready for submission):

- knowing who to send your work to;
- helping you choose the right publisher/editor (should more than one be interested);
- negotiating the terms of your contract;
- representing the foreign and subsidiary rights (film, magazine, audio, etc.) to your book;
- making sure that your publisher keeps you informed of your book's progress before and after publication;
- preparing your next project for submission and negotiating those terms; and
- keeping on top of the financial and legal aspects of your books after publication.

Do you really need an agent?

Look at the list of things an agent does and tell me you have the time, ability or inclination to handle it all, and won't make mistakes that may set back your career in ways you can't even imagine. Or let me put it to you another way: Only a fool has himself for a client.

That's not to say that authors haven't sold a novel or two themselves, but there's much more to being an agent than making a sale. When an author sells his own book, the editor will often refer him to an agent to guide him through the contract and production process, and fill him in on all the publishing details that she doesn't have the time to go into. Editors edit.

Lori Perkins *is the president of L. Perkins Associates and has been a literary agent for eight years. Prior to that, she was an adjunct professor of journalism at New York University and the publisher of the Manhattan weekly newspaper,* Uptown Dispatch.

Agents know what the industry norms are (such as how much the industry is paying right now for certain kinds of books, what rights are selling, where a house is flexible on contract terms, etc.), they know the history of the publisher with your kind of book, as well as the strengths and weaknesses of your editor.

And agents have clout. When your publisher (and editor) does a deal with your agent, the entire agency roster is on your side. They don't want to upset your agent because it might affect another book they have under contract or their chances of getting one of your agent's really hot writers when her next book comes up.

But, that's not the only reason you need an agent. When I entered the publishing business, I was stunned at the sheer number of books published every year (about 50,000). Only someone who eats (we lunch professionally), sleeps and schmoozes books for a living could possibly keep up with who's buying what for how much and when. Writers write. If you're spending the amount of time necessary to keep up with the publishing business, then you are either working for *Publishers Weekly* or are not as serious about writing as you should be.

What does an agent really do?

When I go to writers' conferences, authors are always amazed that I don't read manuscripts in the office and that I read at the same speed they do. One author actually thought I had some special ability to read manuscripts at super-human speed.

The best way to tell you what agents really do is to describe a typical work day. I start at 10:00 a.m. because editors straggle into their offices late, and I work until 6:00 p.m. The first thing I do is call all the editors who have promised to respond to me by that day to check up on projects on submission. Most of the time I leave a message and the editors get back to me after lunch.

I then prepare the day's multiple submissions to publishers (three to five copies for a novel, five to ten copies for a nonfiction proposal), which includes writing pitch letters, calling all the editors and pitching the book, and then getting everything packaged by 5:00 p.m. for UPS.

Lunch is an extremely important part of my business. It's where I get to know editors' literary tastes, learn what they and their publishing houses are buying right now, hear industry gossip, and pitch my agency for future projects. A good, productive lunch can net me up to ten book sales over a year.

Lunch is therefore sacred, and I do it seriously. I usually have lunch at 12:30 p.m., which means I leave my office at noon to travel. Lunch lasts about two hours, and I'm always back at my desk by 3:00 p.m. I tell you this because you should never call an agent between noon and 3:00 New York time. We should be out to lunch, and if we are in our office answering phone calls, we're not doing our job.

The afternoon I spend getting back to editors who have returned my calls, going through the mail, perhaps reading over a contract or preparing a foreign mailing (I have 11 foreign agents who represent my books throughout the world and I send them monthly bulletins about my books along with a mailing).

From 5:00 p.m. to 6:00 p.m. I call my authors, because I don't have to worry about being interrupted by editors since their work day is over. I can devote full attention to my authors this way. I also return phone calls from the West Coast at this time, because they are just returning from their lunches.

I get home; I have dinner; I put the kid to sleep, unwind, and then try to read at least an hour each weeknight and five hours over the weekend. I average about one novel and four or five proposals a week.

I represent about 50 writers, each of whom writes at least one book a year; some write as many as four. My stable of writers takes up pretty much all of my reading time, which is why I recently took on a partner, who is responsible for fitting the reading of unsolicited manuscripts into his busy day. Right now he represents about 25 writers and I imagine that when he reaches the 50 writer mark, he too will feel that his roster of writers is full.

Most agents can handle about 50-75 writers. If an agent is established, she is quite busy with the authors she has already made a commitment to and will relegate responding to query letters as a lesser priority. Most agents assign this task to the lowliest person in their office, or wait until the pile is so high you can cut it with a scythe.

I used to go through them on Friday afternoon for an hour. If I read each letter carefully (which is the only way to do this), I could go through about 20 an hour. We get at least 30 a week (about 2,000 query letters and partials a year), so they would quickly get backed up. This is why it often takes up to three months to get a form rejection in your self-addressed stamped envelope (SASE). However, without that SASE, you may not receive even that much.

How do I find the right agent?

The best way to get an agent is to be informed, and that doesn't mean clipping the *USA Today* article about how much Scott Turow got for his latest book. It means buying a book like this one (or going to the library) and doing a little research. You will quickly learn that there are about 1,000 literary agents throughout the country and, just like writers, they are all different.

You could do a mass mailing to all agents listed, but that's not a wise investment. The best thing to do is to narrow your field of submission by finding out what areas the agents specialize in and matching them to your type of book.

All books fall into a category or genre and "fiction," "nonfiction," "mainstream" or "best seller" are not specific enough. All agents specialize in some area of publishing. It's impossible nowadays to be a generalist, although most of us are open to new areas. For instance, my areas of interest are horror, thrillers, dark literary fiction, and books about popular culture. My partner specializes in science fiction, fantasy, mysteries and journalistic nonfiction. Recently, I found that the market for adult horror was shrinking, but the young adult market was booming, so I now sell young adult and middle grade horror. I also found that I was becoming interested in Latino issues, and have added that to my areas of representation.

The single most frequent reason I reject query letters is because I don't handle the material I am being queried on. You can save yourself countless postage and aggravation if you do this research ahead of time.

Once you know the kind of book you are writing, you should join a professional organization that supports those writers. All genres have associations (Romance Writers of America, Science Fiction Writers of America, etc.), as do professions (the American Society of Journalists and Authors). You can ask the organization to give you a list of agents who represent your kind of book (you can do this with a phone call to their secretary without even being a member).

Another way to find the right agent is by finding similar published books. Call the publisher of that book and ask to speak to the editor or editorial assistant who handles that book. Ask them who the agent for that title was.

How do I get the right agent to represent me?

Don't try to dazzle or impress a prospective agent. Be direct. In a one-page query letter, tell me what your book is about and who you are. Let your work speak for itself. Don't tell me how your wife, kids, aunt and high school English teacher think you are the next Stephen King. I only want to know if you were a high school track star or Honda Salesman of the Year if it relates directly to your book. The only background I want in a query letter is your relevant publishing history, educational information (writing workshops, who you have studied with, etc.) and maybe some biographical information that relates directly to your book (such as the fact that you're a doctor and have written a medical thriller).

Don't overwhelm me. If you've been writing unpublished for 16 years and have 17 novels in the closet, don't try to pitch all of them to me at once. Just send a query about the one you think is best, with a brief line about how you have other completed manuscripts, should I be interested in seeing something else.

Show me that you've done some research. If you took the time to go to *Guide to Literary Agents*, and chose me from that listing, tell me so in your letter. As a matter of fact, you might even want to start your letter off that way. It will definitely get my attention.

If you've joined a writers' organization, tell me. If they gave you my name, tell me that. If you got my name from one of my clients, tell me that, because if a client of mine asks me to look at something from a new writer, it moves to the top of my pile. If you think your book is similar to a book you know I've represented, tell me that as well.

Below is a basic example of a query letter that would grab my interest:

"Dear Ms. Perkins:
I read your article on agents in the 1994 *Guide to Literary Agents* and I thought you might be interested in seeing an outline and sample chapters of my novel, (title). It's about (brief description).
For your information, I am a member of (professional organization) and I have attended (University writing program). My short stories have appeared in (publications). I've enclosed a SASE for your response."

The only other things you should do is make sure your presentation to me is professional. That means typed, double-spaced on 8½ × 11 paper with a SASE with proper postage. Your query letter should be free of typographical and grammatical errors.

Just as a point of information, because of the sheer volume of queries my agency receives and the hours it takes to go through everything, I prefer to receive a simple query letter first and additional material only if I ask for it. If you really want a quick response, the less material you send, the sooner someone will be able to get back to you.

How does the agent/writer relationship work?

Let's assume you receive a letter from me requesting sample chapters and an outline. Take your time and send me the most polished material you have. Send me the first three chapters of your novel or representative chapters of nonfiction, or your published articles about that topic.

Then be patient. I will endeavor to get back to you within six weeks, but life often gets in the way. For instance, things slow down from Thanksgiving to New Year's, as well as in the summer. If you haven't heard from me in six weeks, feel comfortable in giving me a polite phone call asking for an estimate of when I should be able to get to your work.

Let's assume I like what you've sent and I've read the whole novel or proposal. I might ask you to make some changes that I feel will help sell the book or make it more commercial.

Trust my judgment. I don't get paid until I sell your work, and that's the only reason I'm asking for these changes.

You send me the work and we agree that it's ready to go out. You then become my client, with a verbal handshake over the phone.

Some literary agencies have agency contracts, but I do not. When I sell a book, the publishing contract includes a clause that insures I am the agent of record for that title until the rights revert.

I then go over the terms of our representation, which are pretty standard. We take a 15 percent commission on domestic sales, 20 percent on foreign sales and charge only for photocopying. The older (established prior to 1975) and bigger agencies take a 10 percent commission. Some agencies charge for expenses such as phone calls, faxes, postage, etc., but most charge for copying.

Your material is then sent out to multiple editors and we wait. A sale can be made in a week (more likely for nonfiction) and it has taken me up to three years to sell a novel (rejected by 33 publishers).

If your work is under submission and you haven't heard from me in six weeks, by all means give me a call to ask what's happening. However, if you haven't heard from me it means that no one has gotten back to me, or I've only had rejections. You will definitely hear if I've got an offer for your book. Sometimes I send an author copies of relevant rejection letters (maybe the editor had something to say that was thought-provoking), but it's not a regular procedure.

Once I have an offer for your book, we go over it. We discuss everything from how much money you get and how you get it, to when you will deliver the manuscript. Once the terms of the agreement are made, I usually get the author and editor together over the phone.

It usually takes four to six weeks for me to receive the contract, which I go over with the publisher's contracts department, and then send on to you for your signature. You return it to me, and we wait another four to six weeks for the signing payment.

You then write the book or make the changes the editor requested. All editorial matters go directly to your editor, but keep me informed of your progress on the book, especially if you are having problems with your editor. Sometimes I have to intercede on your behalf.

Let's say you deliver your manuscript on time and your editor loves it. I then write a letter requesting your deliver-and-acceptance payment and we wait at least another six weeks for that.

I then begin asking about your next book. You draw up an outline and sample chapters (fiction or nonfiction) and I send it to your editor. We then wait for her response.

Tips for your author/agent relationship

Be mindful of your agent's schedule. Don't call during lunch hours. Don't call more than once a day. Remember that during the summer many publishers and agents close at noon on Fridays.

Be mindful of your agent's workload. Remember that we have many clients and many books to read. If we don't get to something right away, it is not a comment on our love for you or your work. It just means we are overwhelmed.

Say "Thank You" once in awhile. You can't imagine how nice it is to hear those words, or see them in a letter or card. Yes, it's my job, but it's really nice to know that you think I did it well.

29 Qualities of a Good Agent

A good agent:
1. Knows the market inside and out—including both large and small publishers (and/or production companies).
2. Keeps up with changes and developments in the industry.
3. Knows hundreds of editors, publishers, producers and other industry people; gets along well with most of them; and knows what kinds of material those people appreciate or want to see.
4. Is a good promoter, salesperson and negotiator.
5. Has a good sense of what each of your projects is worth, how much to ask for it, and who is most likely to be interested in it.
6. Has extensive experience as an agent and has made many sales. Ideally, the agent has sold many projects in the same field or genre as your own.
7. Goes to bat for you against publishers or producers whenever necessary.
8. Gets your work out to editors and/or producers promptly, and follows up all submissions when necessary.
9. Sends your work to at least three editors or producers at once (in the case of book proposals, at least four at once); sends a rejected manuscript back out again promptly. (Exception: in TV and film, it is common to send work to only one producer at a time.)
10. Continues to try to sell your work even after it has received some rejections; does not give up until the piece has been rejected at least 15 times.
11. Has a good eye and instinct for what people (editors, publishers, producers, audiences and readers) want.
12. Responds to your work, questions, letters and phone calls promptly.
13. Is honest, straightforward and cordial with you at all times.
14. Is willing to work with you if your material needs a small amount of rewriting, and can give good suggestions for doing that rewriting.
15. Reads and negotiates contracts carefully, thoroughly and shrewdly.
16. Works with you on a project-by-project basis; does not demand exclusive rights to all your work.
17. Lets you know which editors and/or producers have seen and are currently looking at your material.
18. Gets you money, royalty statements and important information promptly; forwards any mail, inquiries and offers promptly.
19. Lets you know promptly when they have stopped trying to sell a piece that has been repeatedly rejected, and immediately permits you to market that piece on your own.
20. Has read extensively; enjoys both popular and literary material and knows the difference between the two.
21. Lives in or near the following city, or visits it frequently:
    a. In the United States: New York (for plays and books); Los Angeles (for television or film)
    b. In Canada: Toronto
22. Earns a commission only on sales in which they were involved; does not expect a percentage of every dollar you earn as a writer.

23. Earns a living almost entirely from commissions, and does not charge fees for reading or submitting manuscripts.
24. Charges reasonable commissions (see "11 Tips on Author-Agent Agreements" on page 18 for details).
25. Does not require potential clients to sign a release before agreeing to read their work.
26. Uses a fair, reasonable author-agent agreement.
27. Supports you in your efforts to write what you wish to write, rather than what is popular this month, or what a publisher or producer has most recently asked for.
28. Believes in you and your ability as a writer.
29. Encourages you to write your best.

From *The Writer's Book of Checklists* by Scott Edelstein, published by Writer's Digest Books. Reprinted by permission of the publisher.

Write and Wrong: Literary Agents and Ethics

by Arnold Goodman

Unlike doctors, lawyers, accountants, engineers, plumbers, electricians, etc., literary agents need not be licensed. Anyone with a telephone, word processor and letterhead is free to call himself a literary agent. Neither references nor experience are required. No governmental agency keeps an eye on the manner in which agents conduct business. There are no rules or regulations. Provided one does not break any laws or commit a crime, virtually anything goes.

So how do you, as a writer, decide whether you should sign with a particular agent? After all, there's a lot at stake. When you turn your manuscript over to an agent, you are entrusting that individual with your writing career, your valuable proprietary rights and your money.

Evaluating an agent

Before signing on the dotted line, some questions will occur to you.

What kind of reputation does that agent have? What kind of relationships does she have in the publishing industry? Does she know the editors who might be receptive to reading (and acquiring) your material? How will your material be presented? Will your agent be accessible to you if you have questions? Will she keep you apprised about submissions and be candid in giving you editors' reactions to your manuscript? How skilled is she at negotiating publishing and other related rights contracts? How aggressive will that agent be in attempting to place film and television rights in your material, or in licensing translation rights to foreign publishers? When the publisher pays monies over to your agent, how soon thereafter will you receive your share? How will you know if you're being properly paid?

Many of these questions deal with the professional competence of an agent; others go to assessing an agent's integrity and honesty. Both areas, of course, are inextricably intertwined, and while it is important for a writer to get answers to all of these questions, I want to focus specifically on how a writer can evaluate the trustworthiness of an agent.

Is an agent trustworthy?

Unfortunately, there simply is no easy or straightforward way to make this kind of assessment.

Certainly, an agent will provide a prospective client with information about his professional background, commission rates, the kind of subject matter that interests him. In some instances, the agent will send a printed brochure or information sheet which addresses these subjects.

But very little of this is helpful in determining whether the agent is, in fact, reputable, honest, and a person of integrity.

Arnold Goodman, a former practicing lawyer in the publishing and entertainment industries, organized Goodman Associates in 1976. The agency represents adult trade fiction and nonfiction. He serves as the chairperson of the Ethics Committee of the Association of Author's Representatives.

Direct interrogation of an agent by a writer about this sensitive area is probably not a worthwhile pursuit. If you are a new writer, you'll probably be so ecstatic at having your work accepted for representation by an agent—any agent—that you won't want to upset the applecart by asking these kinds of questions.

The mere fact that an agent has been in business for a certain number of years is not, in itself, sufficient evidence of trustworthiness. Moreover, an agent is not likely to disclose in a conversation or a printed brochure that several of his (former) clients have lodged complaints about the agent's business practices, that he is *persona non grata* at several publishing houses, that he neglects to keep clients apprised about materials on submission, that he is not easily accessible, or—simply stated—that he just has a bad reputation!

Various lists and directories of agents can only go so far. Using a directory as a starting point, you need to research on your own before you commit yourself to any agent.

Researching an agent further

You may find help by contacting the Authors Guild, the American Society of Journalists and Authors (ASJA), the National Writers Union, Poets & Writers, or other writers' organizations of this kind. If you're not a member it's more difficult, but not impossible, to get assistance and the kind of hard information you are seeking. These organizations are staffed by individuals sympathetic to writers, and it's hard to imagine that your request for information will go unanswered—particularly if you are tactful and diplomatic in your approach.

Since the staffs of these organizations constantly field questions from their members about agents and the agency relationship, and deal with their members' grievances (real or imagined) about agents, they are in an excellent position to know the reputations of various agents. If there has been a history of complaints (rather than one or two isolated incidents) about the business practices of a particular agent, the staff would likely be aware of that. While this kind of information is not generally disseminated, it will be informally provided to any member who takes the trouble to ask.

Neither the ASJA, nor the Authors Guild nor the National Writers Union maintains lists of recommended agents. But ASJA does keep a list of the agents who represent its members. ASJA openly encourages its members to network with one another and share information about agents. In its newsletter, ASJA often alerts its members to specific kinds of problems or grievances which have arisen between its members and agents although specific names are rarely mentioned.

Poets & Writers publishes its own directory of agents. The organization is, however, essentially an information clearinghouse for writers. While Poets & Writers does not have the resources to provide answers to many of the questions posed by writers about agents or to follow up and investigate complaints and grievances, it will refer a writer to people and organizations who can.

The National Writers Union urges its members to complete detailed questionnaires about the agency relationship. The NWU keeps these on file and permits its members to peruse them. The NWU staff uses these completed questionnaires as a resource in counselling its members in this area.

The Authors Guild specifically encourages its members to deal with agents who are members of the Association of Authors' Representatives.

Association of Authors' Representatives (AAR)

AAR is a trade association comprised of more than 275 individual literary and dramatic agents. It is the only trade association in existence in the United States for literary agents.

It holds periodic meetings at which common concerns and problems are addressed. Often, members are briefed by experts about developments and trends in the publishing industry. AAR publishes a newsletter circulated to the AAR membership as well as to the publishing community at large.

Membership in AAR is open to any literary and dramatic agent whose primary business is representing writers and dealing with rights in literary and dramatic material. There are, of course, reputable agents who are not members of AAR. However, to qualify for AAR membership, a certain level of experience must be demonstrated, which assures a degree of competence and professionalism.

AAR was formed in 1991 by the merger of the Society of Authors' Representatives, (SAR), and the Independent Literary Agents Association, (ILAA), two trade associations which had existed side-by-side for a number of years and which decided that one large powerful organization would be more effective than two smaller ones. All AAR agents must subscribe to and agree to be bound by the organization's Canon of Ethics.

AAR's Canon of Ethics

An examination of that Canon reveals what literary agents themselves believe are proper standards of professional behavior; it sheds light on what the agent members believe is the appropriate way to deal with their clients and to conduct their business.

Some basic principles emerge:
- Conflicts of interest are not permitted and are to be scrupulously avoided. An agent's allegiance is solely to his or her client.

Translated into practical terms, this means that an agent's compensation is derived exclusively from the writer-client. An agent cannot accept any form of compensation from a publishing company, or a film company, for example, in return for steering a particular manuscript to that company for a first look.

An agent cannot wear two hats. For example, he cannot act as an agent while at the same time negotiating with his own client to acquire rights in a client's material, and then act as a film or a television producer or as a book packager of that same material. (Book packagers are in the business of adding elements to a manuscript such as editing, graphics, design, etc., and then selling the "package" to a publishing company in return for a royalty or profit participation in which the writer-client does not share.)

- Funds received by the agent which belong to the client are to be safeguarded by depositing them in a special bank account set up solely for that purpose. These funds may not be co-mingled with the agent's other business or personal funds. The client's share of these monies is to be paid over to the client within a specified (brief) period of time. The agent's financial records—insofar as they pertain to transactions involving the client—are open to the client for inspection.

To my knowledge there have not been many instances where an agent has run off with a client's funds, or where the client's funds (co-mingled with the agent's funds) have been attached by the agent's creditors, but it has occurred on occasion. It seems entirely prudent for a writer to have the added protection of having these funds in a special account, out of reach of the agent's creditors.

- If the agent seeks reimbursement from the client for certain expenses (photocopying, messengers, long distance phone calls, etc.), the client must specifically agree in advance to pay these charges; they cannot be billed (or deducted from the client's monies) as an afterthought.
- The agent is required to keep the client up to date regarding the status of submissions

made on behalf of the client. If a writer requests additional information from the agent about her materials, contracts, etc., the agent is required to furnish it.
- The agent is pledged to keep financial and other information about the client confidential.

This is significant for a number of reasons. A writer should be able to rest easy when disclosing to an agent a book idea that has been germinating. There need not be a concern that the agent will reject the idea and then suggest the idea to another client.
- AAR agents are pledged to principles of honorable co-existence, directness and honesty in their relationships with other AAR members. They undertake not to mislead, deceive, dupe, defraud or victimize their clients, their agent colleagues and any other persons with whom they do business.

Practically speaking, AAR agents are required by the Canon to deal openly and honestly with their clients and with the publishers with whom they do business. For example, the Canon would preclude an agent from making misstatements of fact to an editor interested in acquiring rights to a manuscript. While it may seem like a useful sales tactic, the agent cannot tell an editor that he or she has another offer in hand when that is not the case. Dealing in an honest, open, straightforward manner facilitates and dignifies the entire submission and contract negotiating process. Moreover, in the publishing business, where it is commonplace for tens, if not hundreds of thousands of dollars to be committed in the course of a phone call, it's imperative to be able to rely on those with whom you are dealing.

Reading fees are discouraged

The difficult and complex reading fee issue is specifically addressed in the AAR Canon of Ethics. The practice of charging writers a fee to review their work is officially "discouraged." The organization's take on this subject is that the practice too easily lends itself to abuse. From personal experience—first as the Chairperson of the ILAA Ethics Committee and now in a similar position for AAR—I received all too many letters from writers complaining that even though they had paid the fee (hundreds of dollars in many instances), they had not received a useful evaluation of their material. Many had paid the requested fee, received a report and were then invited to pay yet an additional fee for a more detailed analysis. Fortunately, very few of these complaints were directed against our own members but being made aware that this kind of dealing occurs with a degree of regularity was an eye-opening experience for me and my colleagues.

That is not to say that every agent who charges a reading fee is engaging in nefarious practices. There are some fee-charging agents who do render a valuable service to writers. The problem for a writer, of course, is in knowing how to separate the wheat from the chaff.

Nevertheless, AAR frowns on the practice and will not consider for new membership any agent who charges reading fees. It did permit those few members who charged such fees to continue to do so for an interim period following the merger, provided they complied with specific regulations promulgated by the organization.

Know what you'll get for your money

AAR's regulations are helpful guidelines to any writer asked to pay a fee to have material reviewed, for they are designed to insure that the writer is aware of exactly what services will be rendered—and by whom.

AAR requires that any agent-member who charges a reading fee provide to the writer, *prior to the writer making any payment*, a written statement setting forth this information:

- description of the nature and extent of the services to be rendered including a statement as to whether the work will be read in whole or in part;
- whether a written report will be rendered and, if so, the nature and extent of that report;
- statement as to whether the services will be rendered by the agent personally and, if not, the professional background of the person who will render the services;
- a statement as to when the writer will receive the report;
- the amount of the fee, including not only the intial fee but any additional fees which may be requested for additional services;
- an explanation of how the fee is determined, i.e., hourly rate, length of manuscript to be reviewed, length of the report, etc.;
- a statement as to whether and under what circumstances all or any part of the fee is refundable, e.g., if the agent takes on the writer for representation.

Moreover, the agent is required to advise the writer up-front that payment of the reading fee neither guarantees that the agent will take on the writer as a client nor that the work will necessarily be made more saleable to publishers.

I think it's clear that the AAR position is that the writer must know exactly what she is getting into before writing a check.

AAR's Ethics Committee

The AAR bylaws provide for a permanent Ethics Committee charged with promoting observance of the Canon. The Committee investigates all complaints lodged against members and makes a determination as to whether a breach of the Canon has occurred. The Association's bylaws provide for punitive action to be taken against members found in violation, which may be in the form of a reprimand, censure, suspension or even expulsion from the organization. Fortunately, the Ethics Committee has had few occasions to meet — a testament to the professional manner in which the AAR members conduct their business.

A professional, and personal, relationship

While the focus of this article has been on the many things that can go wrong in the writer-agent relationship, the truth is that this kind of thing is the exception rather than the rule. The vast majority of literary agents are dedicated, hardworking professionals of high integrity who care about writers and books and are committed to representing their clients with vigor and enthusiasm. Moreover, clients, for the most part, care about and respect their agents; the relationship often transcends the solely professional to one of friendship.

While AAR does not accept new members who charge reading fees, it permitted those members who charged fees prior to the October 1991 merger of SAR and ILAA to continue for an interim period. This policy will be taken up at the November 1993 Board of Directors meeting, the results of which should be available in January 1994.

11 Tips on Author-Agent Agreements

1. Your agreement with your agent may be either written or oral, but both of you must clearly understand the terms. About half of all agents use written contracts, and half make simple oral agreements.
2. Author-agent agreements are almost always negotiable. Ask for and negotiate any changes that you need to; if the agent will not agree to terms you believe are reasonable, look for another agent.
3. *Do not assume that the terms you are offered are fair or standard.* Author-agent contracts vary widely. *Read any contract very carefully.* Agents (even some of the most effective ones) often protect their interests far more than yours in these agreements.
4. If an agent wants to make an oral agreement, ask for specific terms; if the agent says, "Standard terms" or "Standard commission," ask for details. (If the stated terms are limited to the size of their commission, this is ideal: it means that you and your agent can part ways whenever either of you chooses; that you are not obligated to let the agent handle your next work; and that they are not entitled to any money beyond any commissions.)
5. Do not agree to commissions higher than these:
   a. Material for television and film: 10 percent
   b. Books and other material for print publication: 15 percent; 25 percent for foreign sales; 25 percent for the sale of TV or film rights (15/20/20 percent is the norm)
   c. Plays: 15 percent; 20 percent for sales to stock and amateur companies; 25 percent for foreign sales; 25 percent for the sale of TV or film rights. (Many dramatic agents have lower commissions; 10/15/20/20 percent is not uncommon.)
6. Try to work on a project-by-project basis. Avoid giving an agent the right to represent your entire literary output. This gives the agent the right to do anything with each of your manuscripts, including nothing at all; at the same time, it forbids you from trying to sell anything on your own!
7. Ideally, your agreement should run until either of you wishes to end it (you may be required to give 30 or 60 days' notice, which is fine). Do not let an agent represent your work for a specified period of time (usually one to three years). If an agent you want to work with absolutely insists on a fixed length of time, agree to a maximum of six months or one year.
8. Do not agree to give the agent a commission on every dollar you make from your writing, whether or not they were involved in the sale. A good agent should only want or expect a commission on sales that they made.
9. Do not agree to pay fees of any kind. However, if the agent wants to be reimbursed for reasonable incidental *expenses* (photocopying of manuscripts, overseas airmail postage, long-distance phone charges, etc.) related to selling your work, this is fine.
10. Try to get rid of any provision that requires you to let the agent represent your next project. If the agent insists on this provision and you're otherwise happy with the agreement, try to restrict it as much as possible; change "next project" to "next romance novel," "next nonfiction book for adults," etc.
11. If you make a written agreement, make sure it specifies that the agent will

pay you your share of any money they receive within 30 days (in the case of checks drawn on foreign banks, within 30 days after the check clears). The agent should also agree to forward copies of royalty statements within 30 days.

From *The Writer's Book of Checklists* by Scott Edelstein, published by Writer's Digest Books. Reprinted by permission of the publisher.

Know What Your Agent Knows About Deal Points

by Richard Curtis

When you say you don't understand contract negotiations, what you really mean is, you don't know what your agent is talking about. The terminology is simply less familiar to you than the terminology you use in your everyday negotiations. When it comes to negotiating something as important and sophisticated as a book contract, you cannot legitimately excuse yourself for accepting a bad deal on the grounds that your agent didn't explain to you what was happening. You can understand what goes into a contract and why, what's important to keep and what you can afford to concede.

Of course it's your agent's job to do the actual negotiating for you, but don't let that keep you in ignorance. The more you know, the better off you'll be — literally. If you know how to say, "Please pass the butter," or "Give me a kiss," then you are also capable of telling your agent "If you have to give them translation rights, I want an 80 percent participation with a pass-through on my share." Once the terms of a contract are familiar to you, then negotiations are not some mystical rite only those in the inner sanctum can understand, but the simple application of a process you've been using all your life.

Unfortunately, the new writer is almost invariably on the lighter end of the seesaw when it comes to putting together a deal. Know what options you have when it comes to contracts and you can save your agent and yourself time and aggravation in the attempt to get them. Bone up on your contractual terminology, focusing on a handful of key "deal points" the way most agents do, and you will feel less in the dark and more in control of your career.

Critical deal points

What are those critical deal points on the short list of every agent's negotiation sheet? Too many authors believe the primary item is the size of the advance. This is a very shortsighted approach, because an advance is simply a publisher's prepayment of anticipated revenue your book will earn for you. But if you don't know what kind of revenue the publisher is anticipating, and how much that revenue is worth, the price of your advance becomes meaningless. You might consider saving discussion of the advance for last. If you negotiate the other points wisely, the size of the advance will dictate itself.

So lets discuss those other points.

Foreign rights

The first, believe it or not, is what language your book will be published in. Well, you wrote it in English, right? So unless this is some kind of trick question, English is the language you book will be published in, right? Well, this is in fact a trick question. A potentially important source of revenue for publishers and authors is translation rights. The licensing of publication rights to German, French, Dutch, French, Japanese, Spanish

Richard Curtis has been a literary agent for over 25 years and was the first president of the ILAA. Curtis writes a regular column for Locus, *the magazine for the science fiction field, and is the author of* Beyond the Bestseller: A Literary Agent Takes You Inside the Book Business *and* How to Be Your Own Literary Agent.

and other foreign publishers is a big business, and the issue of who controls those rights—publisher or author—is hot enough to be considered a deal-breaker in many cases. For many authors, money earned from the sale of foreign rights enhances their income considerably, and it is not unusual for foreign revenue to equal or exceed earnings from the American contract.

Distribution

Another bone of contention is the territory in which your publisher is permitted to distribute your English language book. If you assume the territory is everywhere English is spoken, you've just fallen into another trap. The U.S. publishing industry commonly divides the distribution territory into two or more areas, and some are more valuable than others. The principal one of course is the United States, its territories and possessions, and Canada. Another one is the British Commonwealth including Australia, but recently Australia has become a separate and distinct market from the rest of the Commonwealth.

Your publisher has to have the rights for United States and Canada and that's not open for discussion. It would like to have the United Kingdom and its Commonwealth partners including Australia. You may be able to reserve these for yourself, but as that reduces the revenue your publisher expects to earn on your book, expect a reduction in the size of your advance if you do.

If you do concede British Commonwealth and/or translation rights to your publisher, the division of revenue between publisher and yourself will be a minimum of 50-50, but that number is not set in stone and it's worth trying for a 75-25 split in your favor. Whatever your share of these monies, by the way, it will not be paid immediately to you—"passed through" in publisher-speak—but added to the royalties that the U.S. edition of your book is earning and reported to you semiannually.

Subsidiary rights

There are other subsidiary rights—"sub-rights" in the jargon—that are earmarked by your publisher for negotiation. Some of them are seldom negotiable, such as reprint rights and book club rights. Not only does your publisher expect to get these, it expects to retain 50% of the revenue generated by them, and expects you not to bother asking for more. Movie and television adaptation, audio recording, and certain electronic media rights are more subject to negotiation, however. Most publishers will yield movie and television rights to you if you insist. Audio and electronic media are harder to finesse, however. Again, your share of subsidiary rights income goes into your royalty account and is reported every six months.

Royalties

Now, what about those royalties? Some investigation of potential sales, and a little diplomatic questioning of your editor, will yield important numbers enabling you to approach the ballpark in which your advance is calculated. Suppose your publisher says they want to bring your book out in paperback. Every agent knows that the list price of most category paperbacks these days is around $5, that paperback royalties generally range between 6 and 10 percent of list, and that projected sales of most mass market first novels in any category are around 25,000 copies. Like your agent, you have everything you need to estimate the advance, and in the time it takes you to read this sentence, your agent will have done that calculation in his head. Just multiply the $5 list price by the royalty percentage and multiply that by the number of copies your book is expected to sell, and you have a number close to what your publisher is thinking of by way of an advance. Now you know why I suggested you save the advance for last.

Advance

In the above instance, your calculations should yield an advance of approximately $10,000. But tempting as it may be to grab that deal if it's offered to you, hold off for a bit and reflect. For, as we've seen, royalties aren't the whole story. If your publisher is certain your book will sell to a book club and a paperback reprinter, or is confident it will license some of the other rights it has won such as foreign translation, the projected stream of revenue may be more valuable.

An agent can glean some of this information by sounding an editor out, and by studying the performance of similar books in the genre. If, for example, you've written a big, juicy, sexy horror novel, your publisher may well be thinking of publishing it in hardcover and is projecting a lot of subsidiary and foreign rights action on it. Even though there are no guarantees it will be picked up by book clubs or auctioned off for a lot of money to paperback reprinters or foreign publishers, your editor will have more than an inkling about these possibilities. The closer to certainty your editor is about those prospects, the more susceptible she may be to your agent's request for a higher advance than the one first offered.

Not all negotiations are as wide open as the trade press has led you to believe. In many genres, such as category romance, sales figures are uniform from one book to another and advances and royalties are calculated in rigid formulas. You should know what those numbers are when you go into your negotiations. You can learn them by asking authors in the field, reading market reports in writers' publications, and even asking your editor. As your editors have a vested interest in giving you low sales projections, take them with a grain of salt.

If you walk away from the negotiating table feeling you got a lower advance than you deserved—and believe me, you'll find lots of friends who will reinforce that feeling—don't worry. If your book does well, royalties and subsidiary income over and above the advance will raise the book's value to the correct level. And in the next negotiation, you, your agent and your publisher will have a much better idea of what your work is worth.

Option clause

There is one other contractual element I consider so critical that I always try to settle it at the time I negotiate the basic deal. It's not as tangible as such factors as royalties and sub-rights income, but it can have a profound effect on your future. I'm talking about the option clause. The option clause gives your publisher a right of first negotiation on your next book before you show it to another house.

No one disputes that the publisher who buys your work is entitled to first call on your future production. But option clauses are minefields. Read them with extreme caution, so that you don't, for instance, discover that you must wait two years before your publisher has to decide if it will consider buying your next book.

Deals "at-a-glance"

In the accompanying sidebar I've summarized the key elements of three kinds of publishing deals: hardcover, trade paperback and mass market paperback. They are intended for use as handy reference guides when immediate action is called for. I've broken each category of book into three ratings: poor deal, fair deal and good deal. Practice reading these with one hand cupped over the telephone receiver while your family jumps up and down shrieking "They're buying the book! They're buying the book!"

Hardcover

A Poor Deal
Publisher gets world rights in all languages.
Publisher controls movie and television rights.
Advance under $5,000.
Royalties under 10 percent on first 5,000 copies sold, 12½ percent on next 5,000, 15 percent thereafter.
Publisher gets more than 25 percent of British and translation licensing revenue.
Publisher gets more than 10 percent of first-serial, movie and television revenue.
Publisher gets more than 50 percent of reprint, book-club and other primary subsidiary-rights revenue.

A Fair Deal
Publisher gets English-language rights in United States, its territories and possessions, Philippine Islands and Canada.
Publisher does not control movie and television rights.
Publisher may control first-serial, British and foreign-translation rights if author has no agent. Otherwise, these are reserved by author.
Advance between $5,000 and $10,000.
Royalties at least 10 percent on first 5,000 copies sold, 12½ percent on next 5,000, 15 percent thereafter.
If publisher does control first-serial rights, he gets no more than 10 percent of revenue.
If publisher does control British and foreign-translation rights, he gets no more than 25 percent of revenue.
Publisher does not participate in movie and television revenue.
Publisher gets no more than 50 percent of reprint, book-club, and other subsidiary-rights revenue.

A Good Deal
Publisher gets English-language rights in United States, its territories and possessions, Philippine Islands and Canada.
Publisher does not control movie and television rights.
Publisher may control first-serial, British and foreign-translation rights if author has no agent. Otherwise, these are reserved by author.
Advance over $10,000.
Royalties better than 10 percent on first 5,000 copies sold, 12½ percent on next 5,000, 15 percent thereafter.
If publisher does control first-serial rights, he gets no more than 10 percent of revenue, and passes author's share to author upon publisher's receipt.
If publisher does control British and foreign-translation rights, he gets no more

than 25 percent of revenue, and passes author's share to author upon publisher's receipt.

Publisher does not participate in movie and television revenue.

Publisher gets less than 50 percent of reprint, book-club and other primary subsidiary-rights revenue, and passes author's share to author upon publisher's receipt after publisher has recouped advanced.

Trade Paperback

A Poor Deal
Same as poor hardcover deal, except royalties are less than 6 percent on first 10,000 copies sold, 7½ percent thereafter.

A Fair Deal
Same as fair hardcover deal, except royalties are at least 6 percent on first 10,000 copies sold, 7½ percent thereafter.

A Good Deal
Same as good hardcover deal, except royalties are better than 6 percent on first 10,000 copies sold, 7½ percent thereafter.

Mass Market Paperback

A Poor Deal
Same as poor hardcover deal, except royalties are less than 6 percent on first 150,000 copies sold, 8 percent thereafter.

A Fair Deal
Same as fair hardcover deal, except royalties are at least 6 percent on first 150,000 copies sold, 8 percent thereafter.

A Good Deal
Same as good hardcover deal, except royalties are better than 6 percent on first 150,000 copies sold, 8 percent thereafter.

Know Your Rights

by B.J. Doyen

Many authors are so glad to get a contract offer that they sign over their rights without understanding what they are doing. Like marriage, your relationship with your publisher should be regarded as permanent; unlike marriage, it is hard, if not impossible, to get a "divorce" from your publisher once you realize you've made a poor deal.

Both parties bring something to the relationship. The author gives the publisher the exclusive rights to print and sell his or her book, and the publisher gives the author an advance and promises to pay him more in the form of royalties once the upfront cash has been earned back.

Defining your rights

Reprint rights, book club rights and revised editions almost always go with the deal. A writer who insists on retaining these rights may jeopardize the sale as the publisher may count on income from these sources in calculating the potential profitability of a book.

Reprint rights

Reprint rights is a broad term that can mean hardcover, trade paperback and/or mass market paperback rights. If sales take off, the latter can be quite lucrative. In theory, a book coming out in any one of these formats can be reprinted into any other—but in reality, it would be unusual for a paperback book to be reprinted as a hardcover. We've had clients receive a simultaneous hard/soft deal, where the book is published in both hardcover and trade paperback from the first printing. A common procedure is printing first in hardcover or trade paperback and then in mass market paperback. Many books start out as mass market paperbacks, never to be published in the other formats.

Your agent will consider how appealing your book might be to each market, evaluating the way to get the best deal. If a book is of interest to publishers in both hard and soft cover, it will usually come out first in hardcover with the paperback edition (particularly mass market paperbacks) coming out months or years later so that hardcover sales are maximized before the cheaper form is available. Sandra Benitez's *A Place Where the Sea Remembers* was issued by Coffee House Press in hardcover, then reprinted by Simon & Schuster's Touchstone trade paperback line. This works well when the hardcover publisher also does the paperback, but when paperback rights are licensed to another publisher, the hardcover house will want a split of the author's royalties.

Book club rights

Book club rights sales can generate a tidy sum. Your publisher can offer your book to the club "as is" at a discount or it can license a book club "reprint" edition. The publisher should seek out appropriate book club markets as soon as possible because they increase the public's awareness of your book and stimulate retail sales.

B.J. Doyen *is president of Doyen Literary Services, Inc., an agency serving 50 authors. She has written many instructional materials for writers, including an audiotape series endorsed by James Michener. On weekends, B.J. presents intensive* Write to $ell® *seminars with her business partner and husband, Robert H. Doyen.*

Revised edition rights

Somewhere between 10 to 20 percent of the books published in the U.S. are revised or updated editions. If the author makes a few changes to keep the text current, the book is republished as an "update." If at least 30 percent of the text is new material and the book has been republished with a new cover, a new ISBN and new promotion, the book is called a "revised edition." Each update or revision should bring the author another advance.

Updates and revisions extend the life of the book and increase the author's—and the publisher's—profits. The person responsible for the text changes should be the author, but if the publisher requests a revision and the author refuses or is unable to do it, most contracts give the publisher the right to have another writer do the revision, charging the costs of preparing that revision against the original author's earnings.

The publisher may negotiate to retain and exercise excerpt rights in the U.S. and abroad, serial rights, one-time rights, simultaneous rights and syndication rights. Your agent will most likely reserve these rights for you if you are already well-published in major periodicals and have good contacts for your work.

If the publisher retains these rights, it's to your benefit not to be too stingy with the royalty splits (as long as the publisher will indeed aggressively pursue these sales) because the publisher must have a fair profit as an incentive. The splits are negotiable—but the author shouldn't give the publisher more than 50 percent.

If you are offering your work to these markets as a primary sale (that is, not as subsidiary rights to a book contract), be certain you've reserved control of your other rights for possible future use. Why? Your article may later be developed into a film, book or play—as in the case of Budd Schulberg. Based on his newspaper article series, he wrote a screenplay, *On the Waterfront*, that went on to win eight Oscars for best film in 1954. Then he wrote *Waterfront*, the novel, and *On the Waterfront*, the theatrical play, with Stanley Silverman which debuted at the Cleveland Playhouse in 1988.

Excerpt rights

Excerpt (or serial) rights (allowing passages selected from your book, or sometimes the entire text, to be printed in magazines, newspapers or newsletters) should be pursued vigorously because of the tremendous publicity this generates for the book.

At one time, sales of these rights would bring the author more money than from book publication. Serial sales can still be quite lucrative, especially if they involve a celebrity. But even if little or no money is forthcoming, more savvy clients mine their nonfiction books heavily for excerpts, getting in print as extensively as possible—because this sells lots of books.

You should try to suggest ideas for excerpts to the rights director at your publishing house, or to your agent if she's handling these sales. Be specific. If you think your chapter three checklist could be lifted and made into an article titled "How Do I Know If I'm Happy in Love?" which looks just right for *Redbook*, suggest it.

Serial rights

These excerpts can be marketed to American periodicals, or you can offer them abroad, in which case you'd be selling the foreign serial rights. The excerpt can come out either before publication (first serial rights) or after publication (second serial rights).

First North American serial rights are purchased by periodicals which are distributed in both the United States and Canada for simultaneous first appearances of the excerpt in each country. Serial rights can be sold on a nonexclusive basis, that is, excerpts from different parts of the book to different buyers. First Serial Rights sales could involve exclusive rights to the entire book or just to a part of it.

Obviously, you can sell the right to be the first to publish the excerpt only once; this should go to the buyer most likely to pay the highest dollar and give you the best exposure. After that, it could be sold as second serial rights, one-time rights or perhaps as simultaneous rights, probably to periodicals without overlapping circulation; these rights can also bring in good money. For example: after First Serial Rights for Debbie Waterhouse's *Outsmarting the Female Fat Cell* went to *Good Housekeeping* for $20,000, Second Serial Rights for the book went to the *New York Post*, Los Angeles Times Syndicate, *Your Health* and *Women's Health*.

Syndication rights

Newspapers regularly buy and print material they've received from syndicates, which are agencies specializing in these sales. The syndicate is granted exclusive rights to sell your pieces all over the world in first publication and in reprint. Syndicates simultaneously offer their material to many buyers, usually guaranteeing the buyer exclusivity in a particular geographic area.

Books that are to be excerpted in several continuing installments or as columns might be picked up by a syndicate. The value of syndication rights should be more than what the author would get for First Serial sales to one publication. The syndicate takes 50 percent of the earnings. If the author has granted the publisher the right to license syndication, the remaining 50 percent would be split between the author and the publisher as agreed in the publishing contract. If the agent has retained these rights, she can approach a syndicate on the author's behalf. Another option for the author is to self-syndicate.

When selling excerpt rights, it's important to understand what the benefits are to each party in these agreements. We've already mentioned that the author gets good money and, even more important, publicity for his book.

The publication that purchases First Serial Rights gets to "scoop" your book to the world, thus capitalizing on any prepublication publicity your book has generated. The excerpt will require less editing, and it may cost the publication less to buy these rights than it would to commission a freelance writer to do a major piece.

Even though they've lost some of the "scoop" value, Second Serial Rights are attractive because they're cheaper than First Serial Rights. The publication still benefits from the book's publicity and promotion, and the manuscript has already been edited and proofread—a savings in editors' time and energy.

To maximize the effect of the publicity of your book, try to time the publication of excerpts to coincide with your book's availability in bookstores. Keep in mind that the First Serial appearance *must* occur prior to the book's publication date.

Foreign rights

Foreign sales and translations don't always go with the sale of the book. Foreign sales can involve selling the American edition "as is" (in Canada, for example) or it can mean selling the rights to publish another edition in English or translations into other languages. Here again, sales are handled by the publisher or agent, depending on whether these rights were part of the publisher's contract. It is desirable to go with the publisher if they have staff whose only job is to handle these rights, or if they have an international foreign rights department. When the agent has reserved these rights for the author and arranges the sale, the author then gets all of the money instead of giving the publisher a split.

The license for the publication of foreign editions is usually granted for a particular period of time, usually a number of years. When the license expires, it can be renewed by your publisher or agent in your behalf.

Film rights

Publishers feel entitled to a share of your film rights because they believe their publication of your book greatly enhances the chances of the sale; this despite the fact the publisher will be benefitting directly from increased book sales once the movie is out.

Publishers also buy novelization rights to screenplays, which can then go on to become bestsellers. Either way, book into movie or movie into book, the tie-in enhances the sales in each media. Miramax, a film division of Disney, is developing a movie tie-in imprint with Hyperion, the adult trade book line owned by Disney.

With the decline of the networks' power and the proliferation of cable companies and independent producers, more and more original movies are being made expressly for TV. This requires a supply of material—good news to the writer. But you should realize that film sales from books are still a long shot.

Theatrical films (to be released in movie theaters) are the longest shot of all, since roughly 80 or 100 movies are made yearly, and many of these come from original screenplays, not derived from book material. Of those books optioned, dismally few get produced as movies, even among those on the best-seller lists.

The very best time to market film rights is after the book is sold but prior to its publication—that's when it's hottest to the movie people. After publication, it loses its appeal unless the book goes onto best-sellerdom or receives great reviews, which greatly enhances interest. First-time author Rinker Buck's book proposal, tentatively titled *Flight of Passage* and represented by David Black, was acquired by Hyperion. Film rights negotiated by Paradigm for Black with Touchstone went for $85,000 against $450,000, with a $50,000 bestseller bonus.

Film rights sales start out as an option. The author is paid a certain amount of cash for allowing the movie people a certain amount of time to line up the movie's production. Usually the time frame is for six to twelve months and the cash starts in the higher five figures on up, but I know of at least one four-figure deal, and one option purchased with no cash at all. (This is a bad deal for the author. If the option falls through the author will have nothing in return for withdrawing his property from the other film markets.)

At the end of the option's term it can be renewed, in which case you should receive more money, or it expires, and you are free to sell the option to someone else. If "picked up" (that is, purchased), your option has been sold for the already-agreed-upon additional amount of money.

If you're an author with clout, you might be able to swing a percentage of the movie's profits as part of your deal. Usually, however, it's in your best interest to go for as much upfront money as possible.

Two other ways you can benefit from your movie sales are Film Sequel Rights, where a second movie is based on your book, and Remake Rights, where the movie is rewritten and reshot with a different cast. Then there are Television and Cable Film Rights, TV Specials, TV Series based on your work, and Videotapes for direct sale or rental.

Film rights sales should be handled by someone who specializes in this area and has access to the industry. If your literary agent doesn't handle this herself, she will probably have a West Coast affiliate who does.

Electronic media rights

Publishers are including clauses to cover rights you may not even think of. Some of these, like computer and other electronic media rights, may seem worthless when you are selling your book, but may prove to be quite valuable in our high-tech future.

Educational software, computer games and interactive novels for use on home computers, CD-ROM (which will soon be used for home instruction and entertainment), and electronic databases which would be accessed through computer services like CompuServe, are some rights that may be commonly exercised in the future.

Other rights

Other subsidiary rights like filmstrips/AV materials, audio recordings, large type editions and Braille editions for the blind may or may not go along with the book sale. Although budget cuts have forced educational institutions to limit spending in the area of filmstrips/AV materials, it's still a market possibility. If you think your book could profitably be made into filmstrips or other AV materials (like microfiche, microfilm or transparencies) for sale to institutions, organizations or even the general public, discuss this with your agent or publisher. These rights will probably not bring in a lot of money, and with the availability of videoplayers, the markets for filmstrips and transparencies are shrinking.

Audio rights for books on tape, records or compact discs is a growing market more publishers are pursuing. These rights, to the entire book or to excerpts, can be sold separately. They can be divided and sold as direct mail-order rights or as retail rights. These rights can be exercised to sell combination book-tape packages.

Large print editions are appreciated by people with limited vision. Bowker has a directory of these that will help you get a sense of how attractive your book might be to this specialized market. The money isn't terrific, but the markets for these books are increasing as our population ages.

Braille editions and other editions for the physically handicapped are rights usually given away in the copyright application, and I recommend allowing the publisher to grant the right for copies to be made by the Library of Congress' Division for the Blind and Physically Handicapped, with no recompense to the author so long as the publisher also receives no recompense.

Novelties, merchandising rights or product spin-offs to your book could involve things like toys, dolls, stuffed animals or cartoons derived from your children's book character, T-shirts, coffee mugs, coloring books, cocktail napkins, posters, puzzles, calendars, kits, lunch boxes, pencils, games, buttons, greeting cards, stationery, gift wrap, rubber stamps — almost anything that can be derived from your book, its illustrations or its characters.

Commercial rights can accompany either fiction or nonfiction. Examples for fiction are the lunchboxes and the breakfast cereal created from Michael Crichton's *Jurassic Park*; for nonfiction, postcards from *Life's Little Instruction Book* are derived from H. Jackson Brown's book. If you have good ideas that seem appropriate for your book, discuss these with your agent; it may be in your best interest to retain all commercial rights.

Protecting your rights

Allowing your work to be published without a copyright notice can be like allowing squatters to build themselves permanent dwellings on your land. As in real estate, where someone using your property, even without your knowledge, might set a legal precedent for them to continue to do so, so can the author lose or compromise his literary rights by not properly protecting them. And you cannot sell what you do not own.

Copyrights

Although under the Copyright Law of 1978 you do have ownership of your literary material from the time you create it, protecting these rights requires that you be conscientious about filing for copyrights. The copyright should be in the author's name (although it will be the publisher's job to register it) and the copyright notice must appear in the proper form in the published work.

Permissions

If someone wants to use an excerpt of your copyrighted work in his book, he must get permission from you (or your publisher) in writing. Usually, this involves a payment, even if it's just a token amount.

Material that can be used by anyone without permission is said to have entered the Public Domain. It can include material for which copyright protection has not been provided, and material for which the copyright has expired or not been renewed. (The latter applies only to books published before Jan. 1, 1978. Copyright for books published after that date automatically extends to 50 years after the author's death.)

Reversions

Selling the "rights" to use your literary material is separate from selling the actual "ownership" of the material. You are not really selling your property, you are selling the rights to use your property for a period of time. Your agent will see to it that your literary contract will have provisions for your rights to revert back to you.

The publisher should supply the author's agent (or the author) with copies of the licenses entered on the author's behalf, but unfortunately, this is not standard procedure. Even if your publishing contract is later terminated, these licenses remain in force for the time period specified in the license agreement, and the publisher and author each still receive their respective share of the profits.

If you sell the copyright, you lose ownership—at least for 35 years, after which time you may get the property back. But most material has lost its market appeal by then, and who knows if you'll be around to benefit from it anyway?

Work-for-hire

Selling your writing as a work-for-hire is not a good idea, since all rights, as well as the copyright, go to the publisher, usually for one flat sum. Your name won't likely appear anywhere on the published piece, and your work can be altered or used in any manner the buyer pleases. You will not get royalties (the exception being in the case of textbooks), you will not get recognition for your work, nor will you even necessarily know how your material has been used. Think carefully before selling your rights this way.

An author must understand that his literary properties involve a myriad of rights and each right should be given knowledgable consideration when any sale is made. Not only should you understand what rights you are selling, you also should know how you and your publisher will share the earnings from the rights you grant to them—all of which will be spelled out in the publisher's contract.

It's desirable to pursue every possible subsidiary right. Not only does this translate into more earnings for the author, but it greatly enhances the sale of the published book. If the publisher has no interest in pursuing certain rights, these should be retained and marketed by your agent.

Agents at Large
by Pat Matson Knapp

Conventional wisdom says that if you're trying to publish a book, consider New York the center of the universe. If scriptwriting is the path you're pursuing, Hollywood is your Mecca.

It follows, then, that if you want to work with a literary agent to help sell your manuscript and advance your career, a New York or California agent is more likely to "be in the loop" or have his "finger on the pulse" of your chosen market. Right?

Not necessarily, say a legion of successful literary agents who DON'T practice their profession in New York or California, or even anywhere close. Many agents are effectively representing their clients from offices all across the country—from Atlanta, Georgia, to Seattle, Washington, and small towns in between. With telephones, Federal Express, computers and facsimiles in their arsenals, agents can successfully sell their clients' manuscripts from virtually anywhere, and can often work more effectively for their clients by being more geographically accessible to them.

These agents—most of whom are former New York agents, publishers or editors—often serve a regional clientele while maintaining their important contacts at publishing houses in New York and across the country. They stay in tune with the New York scene through these contacts and through strong networks of fellow agents who exchange information and ideas.

To find out how these "agents at large" promote their clients, we talked with three established agents who shared their thoughts and strategies on working outside of New York and Hollywood. Our panel of agents included:

Elizabeth Wales of Levant & Wales Literary Agency, Inc., Seattle, Washington. Wales and partner Dan Levant established their agency in 1988. Before relocating to Seattle in 1983, Levant worked in the sales and marketing departments of Oxford University Press and Viking Penguin in New York, and is a former bookseller and publisher's representative. Levant & Wales specializes in nonfiction and mainstream fiction and represents a variety of clients, from China's bestselling male author to the author of a nonfiction book on interracial love. The agency is a member of the Pacific Northwest Writer's Conference and Book Publishers Northwest, and 60 percent of its clients are from that region.

Oscar Collier of Collier Associates, Seaman, Ohio. Collier has been active in the publishing industry since he started his own agency in the 1960s. He served as president of a small publishing company and later worked in the tradebooks division of Prentice Hall. After returning to his own agency in 1983, Collier moved it from New York to Ohio in 1987. Collier's clients include Harry Brown, author of three bestselling books on financial investment; Frances Spatz Leighton, who has been called the "queen of 'co-authored-with' books;" and a wide range of other authors of fiction and nonfiction. He is author of two books, *How to Write and Sell Your First Novel* and *How to Write and Sell Your First Nonfiction Book*. Collier represents clients nationwide.

Joan Brandt of The Joan Brandt Agency, Atlanta, Georgia. Brandt began her career in 1973 at the Sterling Lord literary agency in New York City. In 1985, she joined the New York City agency Literistic, which merged with Sterling Lord in 1987. She established her

Pat Matson Knapp *is a Cincinnati-based journalist and writer. She is a frequent contributor to* The Artist's Magazine *and* HOW *magazine.*

own agency in 1990 after relocating to Atlanta. Her agency handles an "unbelievably eclectic listing" including novels, nonfiction books and scripts, "from the literary to the mystery and from the nonbook to the erotic." She also handles movie rights for other agents. She is a member of the American Booksellers Association. Her clientele is national, but includes a growing number of Southern writers.

Here's what they had to say.

Many people in the industry still believe it's necessary to have a New York or California agent to be well represented in book publishing or the script market. Is this true?

Wales: No, you don't have to have a New York or California agent to be well represented. My partner likes quotable quotes, and he says we can fax everything to New York except lunch. But not to be glib, we can do this simply because there's a big population here in the Pacific Northwest—a big reading population—and there are lots of fine writers out here. And we can get to them. Unlike agents in New York, we can often support an author where he or she lives. That means not only can we get to them on a personal basis, editorially, but it's a little bit psychological. We are here where they live, and that results in a high trust level.

New York does the deals, but the writers live everywhere. In these days of jet airplanes and electronic mail, faxes and telephones, the distance that perhaps made it harder for agents to make a go of it out here even 10 years ago has been collapsed. Obviously I can't walk out the door and have a drink with an (New York) editor that I'd like to have a drink with; I have to see them later or get on the phone. But I do maintain my contacts in New York, and that's enormously helpful. I go back to New York three or four times a year to keep in touch with editors and add to my contact list.

Collier: When I was working as an agent in New York, this is what I did: I sat in my office and took phone calls from my clients, responded to queries, and when I had something to sell, I'd call up an editor and say, "I have so-and-so..... It looks pretty good. Do you want to see this?" If they said yes and it was urgent, I'd send it over by messenger. If it was routine, I'd put it in the mail. If they liked it, they'd get me on the phone and make an offer, and I'd let my client know and from there, we'd negotiate and make a deal—all on the phone. That's what an agent does.

What I do here is exactly the same. I get queries; I read them and answer them; I take phone calls from my clients and discuss what they're doing; and I call up editors and say, "I have so-and-so, do you want to see it?" If they say yes, I Federal Express it if it's a rush and I mail it if it isn't. If an editor wants to buy, we start negotiations and later wrap up the deal, again mostly on the phone.

When I was in New York, young editors from time to time would want to go out to lunch with me. It was pleasant (and hard on my weight), but for the most part unnecessary. Most of the older, more established editors preferred to just do business on the phone. I can recall people that I did business with for years and never even met in person.

Brandt: The reality is you cannot start out being an agent in Atlanta or Chicago or Detroit or Miami. You cannot learn this business except in New York; you have to have some kind of New York experience or background. You have to put in your years in New York some way or you have to fly into New York at least four or five times a year. This is because the fundamental issue that we're all up against is that it's NOT the material ultimately, it's who you know. You have to know who's who in the New York publishing arena—who the players are and where the bodies are buried. Unless you know the person you're selling to, you really only have as much of a chance of being read and considered seriously as an author getting picked up from the slush pile. Ultimately, my contacts are really the only asset I have to sell to my clients.

A part of my time is spent on a weekly if not a daily basis talking with other agents and editors and picking up information about what's going on in New York. These kinds of contacts help me understand the why's and wherefore's of what's going on.

Do you do anything differently than you would if you were located in New York or California?

Wales: Yes. I guess the most important difference is one of orientation. We face the Asian world here, which is very different from Europe, which New York faces. If you went down my listing, you'd see that it has a different focus, a different preoccupation than New York. We represent China's number one male author, and that came to us because of geographical advantage. Another book on our list, based on an Indian legend, was written by an author who lives in a log cabin up in Alaska.

Some of the more exciting things that are happening in publishing right now are the new voices—new ethnic and cultural groups that have not been published in New York in a large way. So we're here and we have a different focus. We don't worry about the preoccupations of New York. The editors I know expect me to bring them something new and fresh and different, and I do.

Collier: The telephone, naturally, is a very important tool, as it is for every agent. I don't have a fax machine; I think they're just a nuisance. If it's absolutely necessary to conclude a deal in one day, which it has been occasionally, I use a fax machine at a business nearby. I'm glad there's Federal Express; it saves a lot of time. But if I had to, I could do with the regular mail. If I ever have clients who are feeling nervous that I don't "have my finger on the pulse" of the New York publishing industry, I simply talk with them and respond to their concerns. Often I develop a marketing plan that says, "Here are six or seven potentially good publishers for your work. Here's what's going on with them right now." That generally lets them know that I'm in touch with what's going on.

Brandt: I don't use the fax machine at all. I have always claimed, whether I'm working selling movie rights or in the publishing business, that this is not a life and death business. People don't die because you didn't do something five minutes ago. I use UPS. I don't recommend overnight delivery services; it's such a waste of money! The exception is if you talk to someone on the phone about a book and say you're sending it to them, it's best to have it there within the next couple of days so they can remember you talked about it.

As an agent in Atlanta, I think I have to be easier to reach than a New York agent. If I'm not returning my phone calls within 24 or 48 hours (that's way too long), there's no point in my clients having me as an agent. I read extremely fast, and I respond very quickly to material. I'd do this anyway, whether I was here or in New York, but I think it's even more important that I do it here.

Clients always have this perception that you're not in the heart of the business. It's true that I do get information maybe a day late, and I'm not having lunch [with colleagues] on a regular basis, but my network of contacts, including agents and editors, is crucial. Ironically, out of the group of agents that I talk to regularly and exchange information and ideas with, three out of four are not in New York.

Are there advantages to choosing a non-New York or California agent?

Wales: Definitely. As I mentioned earlier, we are here where most of our clients live. That brings a high trust level into the relationship, and it means we can support them more easily. Sixty percent of our clients are from the Pacific Northwest, and we encourage authors from this region to contact us. By working regionally, we can give closer editorial attention to our clients and communicate with them more easily.

We can often identify regional talent earlier than New York agents. For example, if an author writes a beautiful article in a local publication, we see it and can follow up. We're always scouting for local talent. And since we're here, we can take advantage of the network of booksellers and writers out here to hear about good authors. For the same reasons that smart New York editors come out here to scout talent, we have a permanent encampment.

We like to say that we're a good, young, thriving agency first and an agency that's based in Seattle second. We have an entirely different focus than some agencies. We try to run a business that takes time for people, and we try to connect with clients for life.

Collier: I can't say that there are any particular advantages to my being here, because my clientele is national anyway. I suppose I'm more available to my clients by telephone because I'm not out having lunch with editors.

Brandt: I think one advantage is that I'm more accessible to my clients in the South. I have a handful of clients in Atlanta, and a growing number in the South in general. I think it's important to be within "touching distance" if a client needs that.

I think I have an easier life of it because I'm not in the treadmill. I don't have to waste two-and-a-half hours of my work day having lunch with an editor, and that gives me more time to work with my clients.

If location isn't a crucial factor in choosing an agent, what are the most important issues to consider?

Wales: Make sure that what you want from an agent meshes with what she actually has to offer you. Each agency has a different business and content focus, and you want a good fit both in terms of the business and the kinds of books it does.

Collier: The most important thing to find out when you're considering an agent is if he or she has access to major publishers. The easiest way to determine this is to ask what books they've handled in the past, particularly in the past two to three years. Sometimes agents are reluctant to name their clients because of confidentiality issues, but they can give some information, such as if the book was a bestseller. If the agent is relatively new in his practice, find out if he worked in a publishing house and what books he handled there.

Remember that what editors buy is not the agent, it's the material. The agent is just a necessary evil: somebody who screens out bad stuff and who submits stuff that is worth considering. A good agent knows the structure of book publishing companies and the nature of contracts, and has a sense of what something is worth. It's helpful for him to have had experience with some aspect of book publishing, but location doesn't make any difference. After all, there are book publishing companies outside of New York.

Some agents are empathetic, and enjoy talking at length with their clients about the work they're doing, but that isn't strictly necessary. Others are entirely businesslike: They're aggressive salespeople who know how to make a good deal, and they don't think a lot of chitchat is necessary. Finding the right one, of course, is a matter of matching personalities.

Brandt: If you're looking for a literary agent, you should know how long she has been in business and where she has worked before. Rely on your phone contact with the agent to gauge response to your materials and to your concerns and questions. If she is not responding the way you want her to, look for another agent.

Some writers feel they need to have an agent who will hold their hand, who is willing to sit down and talk endlessly about the whiteness of the whale or whatever. Those people, especially, need to have someone within touching distance.

How do you get your clients, and how can an upcoming writer capture your attention?

Wales: Many of our clients come to us through referrals from other clients, booksellers, editors, writers and publishers. Occasionally someone comes in over the transom, which is why all of us pay attention to what comes in, because often the diamond is in the rough.

What this agency looks for is a voice—something that you start reading and know you are in the presence of somebody with a talent for engaging your interest with lovely, well-crafted writing, whatever it may be about. After that we look for a compelling subject, especially something that hasn't been done before. Right now, for example, I'm nursing along a book on interracial love, the first nonfiction book published on that subject.

Collier: Because this agency is a mature one, I have a lot of clients and I have to be super selective about the new writers I choose to work with. I do take on new clients occasionally, but only occasionally. My general advice for a new writer is to find an agent who hasn't been established for that long; new agents tend to be looking for new clients more aggressively.

When an author submits something to me, what helps me the most is when the book is a good one in its category and when the author has already identified an audience for it. The most important factor is knowing the market—knowing who will be interested in reading the book.

Brandt: I often get new clients through recommendations from other clients, but I've also picked up a great number of clients from general queries. I read every query letter I get.

What doesn't get my attention is fancy writing on the envelope and colored envelopes; it's so obvious. Don't quote from the book in your opening paragraph, and don't use the same computer paper for your cover letter that you used for your manuscript; use a proper piece of writing paper. If I find one typographical error or spelling mistake in the query letter, I'm liable to turn you down. I mark those mistakes, and you'd be surprised how many there are. And I will never ever ask anybody to send material who tells me they've written a "fictional novel."

I prefer a straightforward approach: Tell me what you've got, why it's unique and who you are. I'm in a profession, and I assume the people writing to me are trying to break into a professional marketplace. Therefore, you have to have professional material.

When the Honeymoon Is Over

by Michael Larsen

Your working marriage with your agent will go through a period of adjustment, and you may experience the ups and downs that can befall any continuing relationship. But if you both act in a spirit of trust and good faith and have your share of luck, your marriage will succeed.

On the other hand, even the most promising marriage can turn sour. The day may come when you decide that your agent is wrong for you. If that day comes, it's time to think about divorce.

Other than flagrant violations of professional ethics, what reasons justify leaving your agent? The following points indicate you may have a problem with your agent.

Your agent never contacts you. Don't expect an agent to be constantly checking in with you to make sure everything's okay. However, your agent should inform you promptly about significant developments regarding your work. He may only call with good or helpful news, which may be a long time in coming.

At the same time, if you never hear about the progress of your agent's efforts, you may rightly wonder what, if anything, is going on. You can try to avoid this problem by establishing at the outset when you can expect to hear from your agent. If your agent repeatedly fails to abide by the arrangement, find out why and change either the system or the agent.

Your agent is not a mind reader. Call or write if you have a question about your work, but, especially until the agent has sold something for you, don't expect too much in the way of hand-holding.

Your agent fails to respond promptly to letters or phone calls. What would you do if your doctor, lawyer, accountant, or anyone else you hired to work for you didn't return your phone calls? You'd hire someone else.

Agents make their living by mail and by phone. They are extremely sensitive about having their phone calls returned by editors. If your agents likes and respects you and wants to respresent you, your letters and calls will be answered. If your agent won't return your calls or respond to your letters, hire one who will.

However, trust your agent—don't get paranoid if you don't receive an instant response. Find out why. Was the agent ill, very busy, out of town? A responsible agent will have a satisfactory explanation. If not, and poor communication becomes a habit, it's time to move on.

Your agent is not actively pursuing the sale of your work. If your manuscript has become a doorstop in your agent's office, it's not doing either of you any good. Find out what the agent plans to do with the project. Has it been seen by all the likely editors? If you have an agent who is not in New York, is he waiting to discuss the project with editors in person?

Being locked into a long-term contract makes it easier for an agent to slough off, figuring that, no matter what he does or fails to do, the writer's not going anywhere.

Once again, agree at the beginning on the best strategy for selling your book, and if that doesn't work and you or your agent can't come up with a second line of attack, you should

Michael Larsen *is a partner in Michael Larsen/Elizabeth Pomada, the San Francisco Bay Area's oldest literary agency. He has written* Literary Agents: How to Get and Work with the Right One for You, How to Write a Book Proposal *and co-written* How to Write with a Collaborator *with Hal Bennett, all published by Writer's Digest Books.*

be free to pursue the sale of the property yourself or seek another agent.

If we temporarily run out of editors to whom to send a project, we may tell writers to take a shot at selling the book themselves without obligation to us, and if they succeed, they can decide at that time if they want us to negotiate the contract. Meanwhile, if we find a new editor or imprint, or an editor we know changes houses, or we hear about a house needing such a book, we will let the author know we are sending it out.

Keep in mind that sometimes a book only needs time and patience to sell. Whether it's an upswing in handicrafts, a resurgence of interest in category westerns, or a recession, no matter what happens, it's good for somebody and bad for someone else (now, there's a book idea). Even the worst catastrophe can be good for a writer.

Just because your book hasn't sold doesn't inevitably mean that you should switch agents. Writing your next book may be the best course. Time away from it may allow the market for your book to improve, or for you or your agent to come up with a more saleable approach to the subject, or for the success of your next book to make unsold work saleable.

Agents want to represent authors, not books. They're in it for the long run. They know that even if a first book doesn't sell, a second one will probably be more likely to, making the rest of an author's books, including previously unsold work, more marketable.

Your agent is vague about his activities. If your agent doesn't seem to know what's going on with your book or you're not getting definite answers to questions about your work, find out why. If you're not satisfied, find yourself another agent.

Your agent does not want to handle new work. You've written a book or proposal you're very excited about, but your agent either doesn't like it or doesn't think much of its chances. If your agent's arguments about the project's weaknesses don't convince you, what do you do? If it happens once, let your agent continue to handle projects under way and try to sell it yourself. If your agent continues to reject your work, maybe you should be looking for one who's in tune with the direction your work is taking.

Your agent is, despite his best efforts, unable to sell your work. Matching your book with the right time for its publication, the right editor, and the right house may take a phone call or, through no fault of either your book or your agent, years. As long as your agent believes in your book and is trying to sell it, he deserves the right to keep trying. But if it becomes apparent that your agent no longer cares about your book, then it's time to separate the two of them.

Your agent sells your book and it becomes a blockbuster. Suppose you are a new writer represented by a small new agency and, to everyone's surprise, your first book takes off and hits the bestseller list. If the book's success is just a fluke unlikely to repeat itself, consider yourself lucky.

But if you are a novelist who expects to turn out a string of bestsellers, each with a strong movie and foreign-rights potential, then you may have outgrown your agent. Bestselling authors sometimes turn to agents like the prodigiously successful Morton Janklow who are also lawyers and perform both functions for their clients. The decision to change agents will be forced upon you, because if you have a bestseller, agents will start contacting you.

How to Fire Your Agent Gracefully

If you are having a problem with your agent, it is usually best to discuss the problem honestly. If this does not work, or if the agent simply isn't selling your work or is doing a poor job, follow these guidelines:

1. If you have a written agreement with your agent, read it over carefully. Follow its provisions for ending your relationship to the letter. If you have no written agreement, skip to the next step.
2. Write a brief, polite, firm, businesslike letter to your agent. In it state the following:
   a. You no longer think that the relationship is beneficial to you.
   b. You wish to cease to be the agent's (and, if appropriate, the agency's) client.
   c. The agent shall make no more submissions of any of your work.
   d. The agent shall remain your representative on any submissions that are still live, for a period of 60 days.
   e. You wish to receive a list of all organizations (publishers and/or production companies) and people (editors, producers, and/or directors) who have rejected any of your unsold works. Also ask for a list of people and organizations that are still considering your material. Ask the agent to inform you of any offers and/or rejections that result from these submissions.
   f. The agent shall continue to receive royalty statements and money on your behalf for deals already made for you; the agents shall forward all statements and your share of any money to you within 30 days of receipt of such statements and money.
   g. (Optional) All of your manuscripts still in the agent's possession or rejected in the future shall be returned to you.
   h. This shall take effect immediately (or on some specific date noted in your author-agent agreement).
3. *Do not feel guilty.* At worst, the agent will regret losing some potential revenue; you certainly won't leave emotional scars. Clients leave agents, and agents dump clients, all the time. Almost always, it is because neither of them is making any (or enough) money.
4. Look for a new, better agent — or start sending your work out on your own.

From the *Writer's Book of Checklists*, by Scott Edelstein, published by Writer's Digest Books. Reprinted by permission of the publisher.

Finding and Working with Literary Agents

by Robin Gee

The articles included in this book cover a number of very important aspects of the author/agent relationship, including how agents work, what to look for in an agent, and how to know if your agent is behaving professionally. Other articles deal with basic knowledge of rights, as well as insider views on contract negotiation. We're pleased also to offer over 425 detailed listings of literary and script agents. Yet, with all this information, it's still possible to overlook some of the more basic requirements of working with an agent.

We've included this article to make sure these fundamentals are covered. Written especially for those of you looking for an agent for the first time, the information provided here will help you with querying an agent, preparing and presenting your work to an agent, and knowing what you can and cannot expect from your agent. Authors who may be considering changing agents may also find this material helpful.

Thinking about getting an agent

If you've just completed a manuscript or have been sending out your work directly to publishers for awhile without success, you may be thinking of getting an agent. Before you start to query agents, however, you must first have a clear idea of what you want and of what you expect your agent to accomplish.

Many agents complain of writers who expect too much; it's important to note what agents do not do. Agents are not teachers. They may give advice or recommend changes based on their experience and what they know about the market, but no agent is able or willing to try to sell an unsaleable manuscript. Before contacting any agent, you must be certain your work is of publishable quality.

For the most part, agents do not handle short pieces such as magazine articles, poetry or short stories. A few agents will handle short work if they also handle a writer's book-length material, more as a friendly gesture than for profit. The reason is agents' commissions on short work are just too small to make handling such material profitable.

In general you don't need an agent to sell very specialized or experimental work or to sell work to a small or specialized publisher. Most agents work with the big, commercial publishers and look for books with wide appeal, although there are exceptions.

Simply put, an agent's job is to sell your work, help you maximize your earnings from your work, help keep track of your earnings and, thus, advance your career. It is often said agents are one part salesperson, one part business partner.

If you have a book-length manuscript you feel is publishable, and would like someone to manage the marketing of your work, an agent can help. Agents can open doors to publishers who do not take unagented manuscripts. They can put an unsolicited manuscript

---

Robin Gee *is former editor of* Guide to Literary Agents & Art/Photo Reps, *editor of* Novel & Short Story Writer's Market, *a regular contributor to* The Artist's Magazine *and a film reviewer for* Critic's Choice, *a national review syndicate.*

on an editor's desk that on its own might lie buried under the "slush" pile in the outer office.

Looking for an agent

Yet finding the right agent can be almost as hard as finding the right publisher. It's important to put just as much effort into your search. Start by reading all you can about the agent/author process. The articles and introductions in this book were chosen to help answer some of the most frequently asked questions writers have about agents. We've also included within the Resources section a list of books on agents.

Most agents find clients in one of two ways—direct contact or through referrals. One way to make direct contact is to send a query or a proposal package to the agent. Agents list in directories such as this book to let writers know how to get in touch with them. Examine the listings included in this book and check the Subject Indexes (located after the Glossary at the back of the book) to find an agent who handles the type of work you write.

Another way to make direct contact with an agent is to meet one at a writers' conference. Often conferences will invite agents to participate in a panel, give a speech and be the "resident agent" for the conference. Although most agents would not appreciate your just "stopping by" their office for a chat, agents set aside time at conferences to do just that. Writers can sign up to talk with an agent. Some agents will look at material writers send in before the conference, but many just want to meet writers and talk generally about their work. If interested, the agent will ask the writer to send a query and samples after the conference is over.

Many agents find referrals very helpful. A recommendation from an editor, another agent or one of the agent's other clients tells the agent someone else thinks your work is worth considering. Even if you do not know any big-name authors or editors, you can make helpful contacts with them at conferences, readings and any place writers gather. Ask around. Some experienced writers are more than happy to share information and contacts.

Approaching an agent

Most agents will accept unsolicited queries. Many will also look at outlines and sample chapters. Few are interested in seeing unsolicited manuscripts, but those who handle fiction may be more willing to do so. Agents, for the most part, are slow in responding to queries, so they understand the writer's need to contact several at one time. When sending a manuscript, however, it is best to send it to only one agent at a time.

This should go without saying, but submitting to an agent requires the same professional approach you would use when approaching a publisher. Work must be clean, typed, double-spaced and relatively free of cross-outs and typos. If you are sending a computer printout copy, make sure it is printed on at least a near-letter quality printer and the type is dark and easy-to-read. Always include a self-addressed, stamped envelope (SASE) large enough to return your material. To save money, many writers do not want their outlines or manuscripts returned—they just send a self-addressed, stamped envelope or postcard for a reply.

Queries to agents should be brief (one-page) and to-the-point. The first paragraph should quickly state your purpose—you are looking for representation. In the second paragraph you might mention why you are querying this agent and whether you were referred to them by someone. If you chose that agent because of their interest in books like yours, be sure to mention this—in other words, show you have done a little research and are informed about this agent's business.

In the next paragraph or two describe the project. Include the type of book or script it

> WILL I. DREW
> 122 22nd Drive
> Louisville, Colorado 80077
> Telephone: (303)555-5432
>
> Ms. Mary Miller
> The Wilbert Will Agency
> 1776 N. Houston Street
> New York, NY 10077
>
> Dear Ms. Miller:
>
> I have a manuscript I propose to submit for publication some time soon. I do not have an agent at this time, and would like to discuss the possibility of your representing me.
>
> I was referred to you by Dudley Jenkins, one of your clients, who told me of your interest in how-to-books.
>
> I have prepared an outline and two chapters for a book I call, <u>Time-and Trouble-Savers at Home</u>. This book contains 50 time-and energy-saving tips and techniques that would be of interest to homemakers, nursing home managers, hoteliers, health spa managers and others.
>
> I teach home economics at Johnson High School in Louisville. I also teach courses in time and motion studies for corporate clients.
>
> I have had two articles on home care published in <u>Homelife Magazine</u>. I can provide you with copies.
>
> Please let me know if you would like me to send you the outline and chapters for my book. I look forward to hearing from you.
>
> Sincerely,
>
> Will I. Drew

This agent query is concise and direct. The writer mentions a referral from one of the agent's clients, while in the same sentence he demonstrates a knowledge of the type of work the agent handles. He follows with a one-paragraph description of the project, his credentials and background and publishing credits. This sample is from the Writer's Digest Guide to Manuscript Formats, copyright © 1987, Dian Dincin Buchman & Seli Groves. Used with permission of Writer's Digest Books.

is and the proposed audience. If your book fits into a genre or specific category, be sure to mention this. For example, if you have written a private eye detective novel, a cookbook or a movie-of-the-week, be sure to say so. This saves the agent (and yourself) time. You may also want to mention approximate length and any special features.

Follow this with a very short paragraph of personal information relevant to your manuscript. Include some publication credits, if you have any, especially other published books or scripts. For nonfiction, list your professional credentials or experience related to the project. For fiction, you may want to relate something personal that lends credibility to your story. For example, if your novel is about a dentist and you are a dentist, by all means mention this. If it takes place in Mexico City and you once lived there, you want to mention this too. The rule of thumb is to include only that information directly related to your project or what lends credibility.

Close your query with an offer to send either an outline, sample chapters or the complete manuscript. Some agents ask for an outline and/or sample chapters with the query, while some want queries only and will ask for more, if interested. Within this section we've included a sample agent query from *Guide to Manuscript Formats*. This book is also a good source for standard formats for just about any type of material, including scripts, novels, outlines, proposals and cover letters. Script and screen writers will also want to see the article by Kerry Cox on working with script agents featured at the beginning of the Script Agents section.

Making an informed decision

Unfortunately, in most states, agents are not required to have a license or formal training. Basically anyone who can afford a phone can call himself an agent, but there are ways to determine if an agent is legitimate, recognized in the publishing industry and has enough professional experience and potential to sell your work.

Remember you are entering a business agreement. You have the right to ask for references or other information that will help you determine if the agent is the right one for you. Some agents freely give out client names, recent sales or editorial references. Others feel it is an invasion of their client's privacy, but you should ask.

Do some checking by talking to other writers about their experiences with agents. Several writers' clubs have information on agents on file and share this by written request or through their club newsletters.

While some very reputable agents are not affiliated with any agent group, those who do belong to a professional organization are required to maintain certain standards. Agents who are members of the Association of Authors' Representatives (AAR) or signatories of the Writers Guild of America (WGA) East or West have met certain qualifications and have agreed to a code of ethics. We have listed these affiliations within the listings. Be sure to read Arnold Goodman's article Write and Wrong, for an examination of the AAR's code of ethics.

Here's a list of questions you may wish to ask a potential agent. Much of this material is contained in the listings in this book, but it's always good to check if there have been any policy changes.

- How soon do you report on queries? On manuscripts?
- Do you charge a reading fee or a critique fee? If so, how much? If a critique is involved, who will do it? What kind of feedback will I receive? Is the fee nonrefundable? Or will it be credited toward my expenses or refunded, if I become a client?
- Do you offer a written contract? If so, how long is it binding? What projects will it cover? Will (or must) it cover all of my writing?
- What is your commission on domestic, foreign, dramatic and other rights? Will I be responsible for certain expenses? If so, which ones and will they be deducted from earnings, billed directly or paid by an initial deposit?
- How can our agreement be terminated? After termination, what will happen to work already sold, current submissions, etc.?
- Will I receive regular status reports? How often can I expect to receive this information?

Will I receive all information or good news only? Copies of editors' letters?
- Which subsidiary rights do you market directly? Which are marketed through sub-agents? Which are handled by the publisher?
- Do you offer editorial support? How much?
- Do you offer other services such as tax/legal consultation, manuscript typing, book promotion? Which cost extra and which would be covered by the commission?

How agencies make money

The primary way agents make money is by taking a commission on work sold. This is usually a 10 to 20 percent commission taken from a writer's advance and royalties. Most agents charge a slightly higher commission on the sale of foreign rights or other special rights, because they may have to split some of the money with a foreign or specialized agent.

The agents listed in our Nonfee-charging Agents section and many of those listed in the Script Agents section make almost all of their money from commissions earned on sales. Most, however, do deduct some expenses from an author's earnings in addition to the commission. These expenses may include postage costs, long-distance calls, extensive photocopying or express mail fees. Be sure you know exactly what expenses you might be charged before signing an agreement with an agency. Ask your agent to give you prior notification of any large or unusual expenses.

Many agents also charge reading or critique fees. In our book we've put these literary agents into the Fee-charging Agents section. Some script agents also charge for reading and/or critiquing and they are marked with an open box symbol (□) in the Script Agent section.

Reading fees are intended to be used as payment for an outside person to read and report on a manuscript. This saves the agent time and effort. Reading fees can range from $25-$50 on up to $300-$400. Quite often the fee is nonrefundable. Reading fees almost never obligate the agent to agree to represent you, but some agents will refund the fee, if they decide to take you as a client. Others will refund the fee after they sell your work or will credit your account. Some agents also include a report or even a critique with the fee. Before you pay any fees, make sure you have a clear understanding of what the fee will cover.

Many agents also offer critique or editorial services. The fees for these services vary widely as do the quality and extent of the critiques. It's important to ask for a fee schedule and to check the credentials of agents offering these services. Remember, too, while many agents have some editing and writing background, most are unable or unwilling to rewrite entire manuscripts.

Agents may also offer a variety of other services including consultation, publicity and ghostwriting. A few agents are also lawyers and may be available for legal consultation or representation. Keep in mind, however, that if an agent's income is mostly generated by additional services, there is less incentive to sell your book for a commission.

What agencies do

In order to sell your work, an agent must keep up with the market. Agents must maintain constant contact with editors and publishers. They must study the market and know what publishers want. This sounds easier than it really is. Publishing companies are being bought out at a dizzying rate these days and editors change jobs frequently. Until recently, agents near New York (for publishing) and the West Coast (for film) had an advantage of being close to the market. Today, proximity, while still helpful, is less important thanks to modern office technology—faxes, computers, special phone services, etc. Agents at Large, by Pat Matson Knapp, features a roundtable discussion with three regional agents on how they operate.

An agent's job is to get the most money or the best deal for your work. Agents try to help you hold onto your rights so that you can maximize your profits from one piece of work. Depending on your work and the market, an agent may submit your work to various publishers and wait for the best offer. Agents also conduct "auctions" in which publishers are invited to bid for the work at a set time. Work is then sold to the highest bidder.

The agent will represent you in contract negotiations. The final decision is ultimately yours, but the agent will advise you on how to get the best deal, what rights to sell and what rights to try to keep. Richard Curtis's Know What Your Agent Knows About Deal Points helps you understand what the critical deal points are in negotiations. Once you've sold the work, the agent may continue to try to sell additional rights or options to other publishers, movie or television producers, book clubs, audio or video producers, etc. See B.J. Doyen's article, Know Your Rights, for a comprehensive discussion of the various types of rights for sale.

Agents also keep track of your business. Some agents will give you periodic reports about the status of your work. This may include a list of publishers contacted and copies of publishers' letters. Some only report on good news, while others send you copies of rejection letters as well. After the sale, the agent will keep records of your income. Publishers will send the money to the agent for you. Once the agent has deducted the commission and expenses (if any), a check will be forwarded to you.

You can also call on your agent to handle disputes or problems that come up while you are working with an editor or publisher. The agent will check your royalty statements and will ask for an audit, if needed.

Some additional information

For more information on working with agents, see the articles written by agents or other writing professionals in the Literary Agents section. Check also the introductions to each section. These cover material directly related to the entries contained within a section and will help you understand more about each type of agent listed.

We've also included a number of indexes. The Subject Index for each section contains a list of subjects in both nonfiction and fiction. Agencies who have specified interest in handling particular types of material are listed within each subject section. A specialized index is included of agents particularly interested in children's book illustration for author/illustrators. The Agents and Reps Index lists the names of agents and their agency affiliation. This index will be most helpful to writers who have heard or read about a good agent, but do not know the agency for which the agent works.

Literary Agents: Nonfee-charging

As publishing has become costlier and more competitive, agents have become more powerful. The bottom line has convinced many larger publishing houses to eliminate their own reading departments. They rely less on material coming "over the transom" and into the "slush pile," and depend increasingly on material that a literary agent and her staff has culled, submitted on her recommendation and backed by her reputation. While some publishing houses continue to accept unsolicited material, more and more look only at manuscripts submitted through a literary agent. To be effective, then, agents need good contacts in the publishing world.

Access and knowledge

In addition to access to editors, agents also must have an understanding of the markets, of who is buying what, in order to target a manuscript appropriately. Agents know not only which house would be most receptive, but often which editor. This knowledge works to the advantage of the writer, pointing his manuscript in the direction that will most likely bring success. A manuscript submitted by a writer directly to an editor must fit into a specific publishing program's needs. A manuscript submitted to a literary agent has more opportunities. An agency will typically have contacts with a large number of editors who specialize in a variety of genre and mainstream fiction and nonfiction, and might know producers and studios interested in TV and movie scripts.

Finding an agent, especially the first time, however, can be frustrating and difficult. Selling yourself to an agent is just as hard, if not harder, than selling your work to a publisher. Most often, agents seek writers with more than one book in them—a writer with a career. You don't need just one highly polished and well-honed manuscript, you may need two. Or more. You must prove to an agent that you have the ability to earn money from your writing, because if you don't make money she won't either.

This section contains literary agents who do not charge reading or other fees for services such as critiquing, editing or marketing. The agents here derive from 98 to 100 percent of their business from commissions made on the sale of their clients' work. Nonfee-charging agents have a built-in motivation to sell—if they do not sell, they do not make money. These literary agents devote all their time to selling. Their job is to know the market and establish valuable contacts in the field, to know what specific publishing houses are looking for and what individual editors like, and then use that knowledge to make sales.

However, these agents must be selective in what they represent, and often prefer to work with established authors, celebrities or those with professional credentials in a particular field. Almost all will look at queries from new writers, but they are looking for outstanding writing and the competition is fierce.

Study listing information

Before contacting any agency, ascertain that it is open to taking on new clients; listings designated (V) are not currently interested in expanding their rosters. Most of those agencies willing to consider submissions prefer to receive a query letter initially, often with a proposal or outline. Some agents (particularly those dealing largely in fiction) ask for an outline and a number of sample chapters; only send these if they are specified in the listing. Always send a self-addressed stamped envelope (SASE) or postcard for reply. Due to the volume of material they receive, agents tend to take a long time to consider queries, so you may want to send queries to more than one agent at a time. If an agent asks to see the manuscript, however, it is best to let one agent at a time consider the piece.

Commissions range from 10 to 15 percent for domestic sales and usually higher for foreign or dramatic sales, often 20 to 25 percent. The difference goes to the foreign agent or subagent that places the work.

Many of the agents in this section charge for expenses in addition to the commission. Expenses can include foreign postage, fax charges, long-distance phone calls, messenger services, express mail and photocopying. Most of the agents listed charge only for what they consider extraordinary expenses. Make sure you have a clear understanding of what these "extraordinary expenses" are before signing an agency agreement. Most agents will agree to discuss these expenses as they arise and negotiate with their clients on payment.

While most agents deduct expenses from the royalties before passing them on to the author, a few agents included in this section charge a low (no more than $50) one-time-only expense fee. Sometimes these are called "marketing fees." These are fees charged to every client to cover general expenses. Agents charging more than $50 are included in the Literary Agents: Fee-charging section.

Special indexes

To help you with your search for an agent, we've included a number of special indexes in the back of this book. The Subject Index on page 243 is divided into sections for nonfee-charging and fee-charging literary agents and script agents. Each of these sections in the index is then divided by nonfiction and fiction subject categories. If you have written a horror novel and you are interested in nonfee-charging agents, turn to the section of the Subject Index headed Nonfee-charging/Fiction. You will find a subject heading for horror and the names of agencies interested in this type of work. Some agencies did not want to restrict themselves to specific subjects. They have been grouped in the subject heading "open" in both nonfiction and fiction.

We've included an Agents and Reps Index on page 270. Often you will read about an agent, but if he is an employee of a large agency you may not be able to find his business phone or address. We asked agencies to list the agents on their staffs. In the index we list the names in alphabetical order along with the name of their agency. Find the name of the person you would like to contact and then check the agency listing. You will find the page number for the agency's listing in the Listings Index.

Many of the literary agents in this section are also interested in scripts; many script agents will also consider book manuscripts. We have listed agencies whose primary function is selling scripts but will consider some book manuscripts in "Additional Nonfee-charging Agents" at the end of this section. Complete listings for these agents appear in the Script Agent section.

Some art representatives, especially those interested in humor (cartoons and comics) and children's books, also look for writers. Agencies that are primarily art representatives, but are also interested in writers, are included in "Additional Nonfee-charging Agents." The company's complete listing, however, appears in the Commercial Art/Photo Reps section. Finally, a special index on page 268 lists agents and reps looking specifically for children's book illustration and author/illustrators.

For more information on approaching agents and the specifics of the listings, read How

Literary Agents: Nonfee-charging 47

to Use Your Guide to Literary Agents and Art/Photo Reps on page 3, and Finding and Working with Literary Agents. See also the various articles at the beginning of the book for explorations of various aspects of the author/agent relationship.

We've ranked the agencies listed in this section according to their openness to submissions. Below is our ranking system:

I Newer agency actively seeking clients.
II Agency seeking both new and established writers.
III Agency prefers to work with established writers, mostly obtains new clients through referrals.
IV Agency handling only certain types of work or work by writers under certain circumstances.
V Agency not currently seeking new clients. We have included mention of agencies rated V to let you know they are currently not open to new clients. In addition to those ranked V, we have included a few well-known agencies' names who have declined the opportunity to receive full listings at this time. *Unless you have a strong recommendation from someone well respected in the field, our advice is to approach only those agents ranked I-IV.*

ACTON, DYSTEL, LEONE & JAFFE, INC. (II), 79 Fifth Ave., New York NY 10003. (212)647-9500. Fax: (212)647-9506. Contact: M. Perkins. Estab. 1976. Member of AAR. Represents 200 clients. 30% of clients are new/previously unpublished writers. Specializes in commercial nonfiction and fiction; some category fiction; some literary fiction. Currently handles: 50% nonfiction books; 50% novels.
Handles: Nonfiction books, novels. Considers these nonfiction areas: animals; biography/autobiography; business; child guidance/parenting; cooking/food/nutrition; current affairs; ethnic/cultural interests; gay/lesbian issues; government/politics/law; health/medicine; history; military/war; money/finance/economics; music/dance/theater/film; nature/environment; psychology; science/technology; self-help/personal improvement; sports; true crime/investigative; women's issues/women's studies. Considers these fiction areas: action/adventure; contemporary issues; detective/police/crime; ethnic; family saga; glitz; historical; literary; mainstream; mystery/suspense; romance; sports; thriller/espionage. Query. Reports in 2 weeks on queries; 1 month on fiction mss, 3 weeks on nonfiction mss.
Recent Sales: *Funny, You Don't Look Like a Grandmother,* by Lois Wyse (Crown); *Looking for the Light,* by Paul Hendrickson (Knopf).
Terms: Agent receives 15% commission on domestic sales; 19% on foreign sales. Offers written contract. Charges for photocopying and Federal Express.
Tips: Obtains new clients through recommendations from others.

‡ADLER & ROBIN BOOKS INC. (II), 2755 Ordway St. NW, Washington DC 20008. (202)363-7410. Fax: (202)686-1804. Contact: Beth Pratt-Dewey. Estab. 1986. Represents 30 clients. 20% of clients are new/previously unpublished writers. Currently handles: 98% nonfiction books; 2% juvenile books. Member agents: Bill Adler, Jr., Beth Pratt-Dewey.
Handles: Nonfiction books. Considers these nonfiction areas: biography/autobiography; business; cooking/food/nutrition; crafts/hobbies; health/medicine; self-help/personal improvement; women's issues/women's studies. Query with outline/proposal. Reports in 3 weeks on queries.
Terms: Agent receives 15% commission on domestic and foreign sales. Offers written contract.
Tips: Obtains new clients through recommendations.

---

‡ *The double dagger before a listing indicates the listing is new in this edition.*

AGENCY CHICAGO (I), P.O. Box 11200, Chicago IL 60611. Contact: Ernest Santucci. Estab. 1990. Represents 4 clients. 50% of clients are new/previously unpublished writers. Specializes in ghost writing. Currently handles: 40% nonfiction books; 20% scholarly books; 10% novels; 10% movie scripts; 20% TV scripts.
Handles: Nonfiction books, sports books. Considers these nonfiction areas: environment; Afro-American; art/architecture/design; ethnic/cultural interests; music/dance/theater/film; sports. Considers these fiction areas: erotica; experimental; humor/satire; regional. Send outline/proposal, bio and SASE. Reports in 1 month on queries and mss.
Terms: Agent receives 10-15% commission on domestic sales; 15% on foreign sales. Offers written contract, binding for 1 year.
Writers' Conferences: Attends Midwest Writers Conference; International Writers and Translators Conference.
Tips: Obtains new clients through recommendations. "Do not send dot matrix printed manuscripts. Manuscripts should have a clean professional look, with correct grammar and punctuation."

AGENTS INC. FOR MEDICAL AND MENTAL HEALTH PROFESSIONALS (II), P.O. Box 4956, Fresno CA 93744-4956. (209)226-0761. Fax: (209)226-0761 *. Director: Sydney H. Harriet, Ph.D. Estab. 1987. Member of APA. Represents 30 clients. 45% of clients are new/previously unpublished writers. Specializes in "writers who have education and experience in the medical and mental health professions. It is helpful if the writer is licensed, but not necessary. Prior book publication not necessary." Currently handles: 75% nonfiction books; 5% scholarly books; 20% novels.
Handles: Nonfiction books, novels, some scholarly books. Considers these nonfiction areas: child guidance/parenting; nutrition; health/medicine; psychology; science/technology; self-help/personal improvement; sociology; sports; sports medicine/psychology; business communications; mind-body healing; how-to; reference. Considers these fiction areas: contemporary issues; commercial and literary; "suspense, mystery, and science fiction genres acceptable." Query with vita and SASE. Reports in 2 weeks on queries; 1 month on mss.
Recent Sales: *Nobody's Victim,* by Christopher McCullough, Ph.D. (Clarkson Potter); *Say Goodbye to PMS!,* by Cherie Calbom (Berkley Publishing); *DPLA To End Chronic Pain and Depression,* by Arnold Fox, MD and Barry Fox, Ph.D. (Avery Publishing Group); *Breads for Better Health,* by Danielle Chase and Maureen Keane (Prima Publishing).
Terms: Agent receives 15% commission on domestic sales; 20% on foreign sales. Offers written contract, binding for 6-12 months. "After contract with a publisher is signed, office expenses are negotiated."
Writers' Conferences: Attends writers' conferences in California. Willing to attend conferences in other states when requested.
Tips: "Now interested in receiving more novels and business-oriented proposals. Majority of our clients are referred. The rest are obtained from writers using this guide. Our specialty has been to help writers with their manuscripts. If the idea is unique, but the writing needs work, that's where we have done our best work. We rarely receive manuscripts that are contracted immediately. Unfortunately, we cannot respond to queries or proposals without receiving a return envelope and sufficient postage."

THE JOSEPH S. AJLOUNY AGENCY (II), 29205 Greening Blvd., Farmington Hills MI 48334. (313)932-0090. Fax: (313)932-8763. Contact: Joe Ajlouny. Estab. 1987. Signatory of WGA. "Represents humor and comedy writers, humorous illustrators, cartoonists." Member agents: Joe Ajlouny (original humor, how-to); Elena Pantel (music, popular culture); Gwen Foss (general nonfiction).
Handles: "In addition to humor and titles concerning American popular culture, we will consider general nonfiction in the areas of 'how-to' books, history, health, cookbooks, self-help, social commentary, criticism, travel, biography and memoirs." Query first with SASE. Reports in 2-4 weeks.
Recent Sales: *Here Kitty, Kitty . . . ,* by Rich Dommers (Zebra Books); *The Love to Hate Madonna Joke Book,* by Joey West (Pinnacle); *Business Maxims from Dad,* by Richard Rybolt (NAL/Dutton); *Potty Proud,* by Stephanie Olin (Anton Enterprises, Inc.).
Terms: Agent receives 15% commission on domestic sales. Charges for postage, photocopying and phone expenses.
Tips: Obtains new clients "typically from referrals and by some advertising and public relations projects. We also frequently speak at seminars for writers on the process of being published. Just make sure your project is marketable and professionally prepared. We see too much material that is limited in scope and appeal. It helps immeasurably to have credentials in the field or topic being written about."

LEE ALLAN AGENCY (II), P.O. Box 18617, Milwaukee WI 53218. (414)357-7708. Fax: call for number. Contact: Lee Matthias. Estab. 1983. Signatory of WGA. Represents 25 clients. 50% of clients are new/previously unpublished writers. Specializes in suspense fiction. Currently handles: 15% nonfiction books; 75% novels; 5% movie scripts; 5% TV scripts. Member agents: Lee A. Matthias (all types of genre fiction and screenplays, nonfiction); Andrea Knickerbocker (fantasy and science fiction, juvenile fiction, nonfiction); C.J. Bobke (all types); Joanne Erickson (all types); Chris Hill (fantasy).
Handles: Nonfiction books, juvenile books, novels, movie scripts. Considers these nonfiction areas: biography/autobiography; business; child guidance/parenting; computers/electronics; cooking/food/nutrition; current affairs; government/politics/law; health/medicine; history; juvenile nonfiction; military/war; money/finance/economics; music/dance/theater/film; nature/environment; psychology; science/technology; self-help/personal improvement; sports; true crime/investigative. Considers these fiction areas: action/adventure; detective/police/crime; fantasy; historical; humor/satire; juvenile; literary; mainstream; mystery/suspense; psychic/supernatural; romance (contemporary, historical); science fiction; thriller/espionage; westerns/frontier; young adult. Query. Reports in 2-3 weeks on queries; 6 weeks-3 months on mss.
Recent Sales: "Babel," *Star Trek: Deep Space 9*, by Sally Caves (Paramount TV); *The Quests of Winter*, by John Deakins (Roc Fantasy); *Destiny Betrayed: JFK, Cuba And The Garrison Case*, by James Dieugenio (Sheridan Square Press).
Terms: Agent receives 15% commission on domestic sales; 25% on foreign sales. Offers written contract. Charges for "occasional shipping/mailing costs, photocopying, international telephone calls and/or excessive long-distance telephone calls."
Writers' Conferences: Attends World Fantasy Conference, and others.
Tips: Obtains new clients through "recommendations and solicitations, mainly." If interested in agency representation, "read agency listings carefully and query the most compatible. Always query by letter with SASE or IRC with envelope. A very brief, straightforward letter (1-2 pages, maximum) introducing yourself, describing or summarizing your material will suffice. Avoid patronizing or "cute" approaches. We *do not reply* to queries *without* SASE. Do not expect an agent to sell a manuscript which you know is not a likely sale if non-agented. Agents are not magicians; they serve best to find better and more of the likeliest publishers or producers. And they really do their work after an offer by way of negotiating contracts, selling subsidiary rights, administrating the account(s), advising the writer with objectivity, and acting as the buffer between writer and editor."

JAMES ALLEN, LITERARY AGENCY (III), P.O. Box 278, Milford PA 18337. Estab. 1974. Signatory of WGA. Represents 40 clients. 10% of clients are new/previously unpublished writers. "I handle all kinds of genre fiction (except westerns) and specialize in science fiction and fantasy." Currently handles: 2% nonfiction books; 8% juvenile books; 90% novels.
Handles: Novels. Considers these fiction areas: detective/police/crime; fantasy; historical; mainstream; mystery/suspense; romance (historical, regency); science fiction. Query. Reports in 1 week on queries; 2 months on mss. "I prefer first contact to be a query letter with 2-3 page plot synopsis and SASE with a response time of 1 week. If my interest is piqued, I then ask for the first 4 chapters, response time again 1 week. If I'm impressed by the writing, I then ask for the balance of the manuscript, response time about 2 months."
Recent Sales: *Winter in the Heart*, by David Poyer (Tor Books, hardcover); *Always*, by Jeane Renick (HarperMonogram).
Terms: Agent receives 10% commission on domestic print sales; 10% on scripts; 20% on film sales; 20% on foreign sales. Offers written contract, binding for 3 years "automatically renewed. No reading fees or other up-front charges. I reserve the right to charge for extraordinary expenses. I do not bill the author, but deduct the charges from incoming earnings."
Tips: First time at book length need not apply—"*only* taking on authors who have the foundations of their writing careers in place and can use help in building the rest. A cogent, to-the-point query letter is necessary, laying out the author's track record and giving a brief blurb for the book. The response to a mere 'I have written a novel, will you look at it?' is universally 'NO!' "

If you're looking for a particular agent, check the Agents and Reps Index to find at which agency the agent works. Then look up the listing for that agency in the appropriate section.

MARCIA AMSTERDAM AGENCY (II), 41 W. 82 St., New York NY 10024. (212)873-4945. Contact: Marcia Amsterdam. Estab. 1970. Signatory of WGA. Currently handles: 5% nonfiction books; 80% novels; 10% movie scripts; 5% TV scripts.

Handles: Novels, movie scripts, TV scripts. Considers these fiction areas: action/adventure; detective; glitz; historical; horror; humor; mainstream; mystery/suspense; romance (contemporary, historical); science fiction; thriller/espionage; westerns/frontier; young adult. Send outline plus first 3 sample chapters and SASE. Reports in 1 month on queries.

Recent Sales: *Shadow*, by Joyce Sweeney (Dell); *Relentless*, by Kris Franklin (Zebra); *Keepers of the Misty Time*, by Patricia Rowe (Warner); *White Night*, by William Lovejoy (Zebra).

Terms: Agent receives 15% commission on domestic sales; 10% on scripts; 20% on foreign sales. Offers written contract, binding for 1 year, "renewable." Charges for extra office expenses, foreign postage, copying, legal fees (when agreed upon).

Tips: "We are always looking for interesting literary voices."

BART ANDREWS & ASSOCIATES INC. (III), Suite 100, 7510 Sunset Blvd., Los Angeles CA 90046. (213)851-8158. Contact: Bart Andrews. Estab. 1982. Member of AAR. Represents 25 clients. 25% of clients are new/previously unpublished authors. Specializes in nonfiction only, and in the general category of entertainment (movies, TV, biographies, autobiographies). Currently handles: 100% nonfiction books.

Handles: Nonfiction books. Considers these nonfiction areas: biography/autobiography; music/dance/theater/film; TV. Query. Reports in 1 week on queries; 1 month on mss.

Recent Sales: *Roseanne*, by J. Randy Taraborrelli (G.P. Putnam's Sons); *Out of the Madness*, by Rose Books (packaging firm) (HarperCollins).

Terms: Agent receives 15% commission on domestic sales; 15% on foreign sales (after sub-agent takes his 10%). Offers written contract, "binding on a project-by-project basis." Author/client is charged for all photocopying, mailing, phone calls, postage, etc.

Writers' Conferences: Frequently lectures at UCLA in Los Angeles.

Tips: "Recommendations from existing clients or professionals are best, although I find a lot of new clients by seeking them out myself. I rarely find a new client through the mail. Spend time writing a query letter. Sell yourself like a product. The bottom line is writing ability, and then the idea itself. It takes a lot to convince me. I've seen it all! I hear from too many first-time authors who don't do their homework. They're trying to get a book published and they haven't the faintest idea what is required of them. There are plenty of good books on the subject and, in my opinion, it's their responsibility—not mine—to educate themselves before they try to find an agent to represent their work. When I ask an author to see a manuscript or even a partial manuscript, I really must be convinced I want to read it—based on a strong query letter—because I have no intention of wasting my time reading just for the fun of it."

APPLESEEDS MANAGEMENT (II), Suite 302, 200 E. 30th St., San Bernardino CA 92404. (909)882-1667. For screenplays and teleplays only, send to Suite 560, 1870 N. Vermont, Hollywood CA 90027. Executive Manager: S. James Foiles. Estab. 1988. Signatory of WGA, licensed by State of California. Represents 25 clients. 40% of clients are new/previously unpublished writers. Specializes in action/adventure, fantasy, horror/occult, mystery and science fiction novels; also in nonfiction, true crime, biography, health/medicine and self-help; also in materials that could be adapted from book to screen; and in screenplays and teleplays. "We're not accepting unsolicited screenplays and teleplays at this time." Currently handles: 25% nonfiction books; 40% novels; 20% movie scripts; 15% teleplays (movie of the week).

Handles: Nonfiction books, novels, movie scripts, TV scripts (no episodic), teleplays (MOW). Considers these nonfiction areas: biography/autobiography; business; health/medicine; money/finance/economics; music/dance/theater/film; psychology; self-help/personal improvement; true crime/investigative; general nonfiction. Considers these fiction areas: action/adventure; detective/police/crime; fantasy; historical; horror; humor/satire; mainstream; mystery/suspense; psychic/supernatural; science fiction; thriller/espionage; occult/horror novels. Query. Reports in 2 weeks on queries; 2 months on mss.

Terms: Agent receives 10-15% commission on domestic sales; 20% on foreign sales. Offers written contract, binding for 1-7 years.

Tips: "In your query, please describe your intended target audience and distinguish your book/script from similar works."

AUTHORS' LITERARY AGENCY (III), 1707 Donley Dr., P.O. Box 184, Euless TX 76039-0184. Phone and fax: (817)267-1078. Contact: Dick Smith. Estab. 1992. Represents 13 clients. 70% of clients are new/previously unpublished writers. Currently handles: 25% nonfiction books; 75% novels. Member agents: Dick Smith (marketing and promotion); Jim Campise (screening work).
Handles: Nonfiction books, textbooks, novels. Considers these nonfiction areas: biography/autobiography; business; child guidance/parenting; computers/electronics; cooking/food/nutrition; current affairs; government/politics/law; health/medicine; history; juvenile nonfiction; military/war; money/finance/economics; film; nature/environment; self-help/personal improvement; true crime/investigative; women's issues/women's studies. Considers these fiction areas: action/adventure; contemporary issues; detective/police/crime; literary; mainstream; mystery/suspense; thriller/espionage. Query first always. Unsolicited mss will be returned unread. Reports in 1 month on queries; 2 months on mss.
Recent Sales: *Bodysculpting: The Weisbeck Way*, by Chuck Weisbeck and Susan Malone (Eakin Press).
Terms: Agent receives 15% commission on domestic sales; 25% on foreign sales. Offers written contract, binding until cancelled by either party.
Tips: Obtains new clients through recommendations, networking at conferences. "For fiction, always send query letter first with: 1) a synopsis or outline of your work, 2) an author's bio, 3) the first three chapters of your work, and 4) SASE. *Do not send entire ms* until the agency requests it. For nonfiction, submit a query letter first with 1) a bio stating your experience and credentials to write the work, 2) a book proposal (we suggest using Michael Larsen's *How To Write A Book Proposal* as a guideline), and 3) SASE. Always send SASE with all queries. We cannot respond to work submitted without SASE and adequate postage for return to you."

THE AXELROD AGENCY (III), 66 Church St., Lenox MA 01240. (413)637-2000. Fax: (413)637-4725. Estab. 1983. Member of AAR. Represents 30 clients. Specializes in commercial fiction, nonfiction. Currently handles: 40% nonfiction books; 60% fiction.
Handles: Considers these nonfiction areas: art; business; computers; government/politics/law; health/medicine; history; money/finance/economics; music/dance/theater/film; nature/environment; science/technology. Considers these fiction areas: cartoon/comic; detective/police/crime; family saga; historical; literary; mainstream; mystery/suspense; picture book; romance; thriller/espionage. Query. Reports in 10 days on queries; 2-3 weeks on mss.
Terms: Agent receives 10% commission on domestic sales; 20% on foreign sales. Charges for photocopying.
Writers' Conferences: Attends Romance Writers of America and Novelists, Inc. conferences.
Tips: Obtains new clients through referrals.

MALAGA BALDI LITERARY AGENCY (II), P.O. Box 591, Radio City Station, New York NY 10101. (212)222-1221. Contact: Malaga Baldi. Estab. 1985. Represents 40-50 clients. 80% of clients are new/previously unpublished writers. Specializes in quality literary fiction and nonfiction. Currently handles: 60% nonfiction books; 30% novels; 5% novellas; 5% short story collections.
Handles: Nonfiction books, novels, novellas, short story collections. Considers any well-written nonfiction, but do *not* send child guidance, crafts, juvenile nonfiction, New Age/metaphysics, religious/inspirational or sports material. Considers any well-written fiction, but do *not* send confessional, family saga, fantasy, glitz, juvenile, picture book, psychic/supernatural, religious/inspirational, romance, science fiction, western or young adult. Query, but "prefers entire manuscript for fiction." Reports within minimum of 10 weeks. "Please enclose self-addressed jiffy bag with submission and self-addressed postcard for acknowledgement of receipt of manuscript."
Recent Sales: *What Jane Austen Ate and Charles Dickens Knew: From Fox Hunting to Whist—the Facts of Daily Life in 19th Century England*, by Daniel Pool (Simon & Schuster); *House Rules*, by Heather Lewis (Nan Talese/Doubleday); *The Monster Show: A Cultural History of Horror*, by David T. Skal (Norton).
Terms: Agent receives 15% commission on domestic sales; 20% on foreign sales. Offers written contract. Charges "initial $50 fee to cover photocopying expenses. If the manuscript is lengthy, I prefer the author to cover expense of photocopying."
Tips: "From the day I agree to represent the author, my role is to serve as his or her advocate in contract negotiations and publicity efforts. Along the way, I wear many different hats. To one author I may serve as a nudge, to another a confidante, and to many simply as a supportive friend. I am also a critic, researcher, legal expert, messenger, diplomat, listener, counselor and source of publishing information and gossip. I work with writers on developing a presentable submission and make myself available during all aspects of a book's publication."

BALKIN AGENCY, INC. (III), P.O. Box 222, Amherst MA 01004. (413)548-9835. Fax: (413)548-9836. President: R. Balkin. Estab. 1972. Member of AAR. Represents 50 clients. 10% of clients are new/previously unpublished writers. Specializes in adult nonfiction. Currently handles: 85% nonfiction books; 5% scholarly books; 5% reference books; 5% textbooks.
Handles: Nonfiction books, textbooks, reference, scholarly books. Considers these nonfiction areas: animals; anthropology/archaeology; biography; current affairs; health/medicine; history; how-to; language/literature/criticism; music/dance/theater/film; nature/environment; pop culture; science/technology; social science; translations; travel; true crime/investigative. Query with outline/proposal. Reports in 2 weeks on queries; 3 weeks on mss.
Recent Sales: *A Natural History of the Grand Canyon*, by Schmidt (H-M); *A Different Mirror*, by Takaki (Little Brown).
Terms: Agent receives 15% commission on domestic sales; 20% on foreign sales. Offers written contract, binding for 1 year. Charges for photocopying, trans-Atlantic long-distance calls or faxes and express mail.
Tips: Obtains new clients through referrals. "I do not take on books described as bestsellers or potential bestsellers. Any nonfiction work that is either unique, paradigmatic, a contribution, truly witty or a labor of love is grist for my mill."

VIRGINIA BARBER LITERARY AGENCY, INC., 101 Fifth Ave., New York NY 10003. Prefers not to share information.

LORETTA BARRETT BOOKS INC. (II), 101, Fifth Ave., New York NY 10003. (212)242-3420. Fax: (212)727-0280. President: Loretta A. Barrett. Associate: William Clark. Estab. 1990. Represents 70 clients. Specializes in general interest books. Currently handles: 20% fiction; 80% nonfiction.
Handles: Considers all areas of nonfiction and fiction. Query first, then send partial ms and synopsis. Reports in 4-6 weeks on queries and mss.
Terms: Agent receives 15% commission on domestic sales; 20% on foreign sales. Offers written contract. Charges for "all professional expenses."

GENE BARTCZAK ASSOCIATES INC. (II), Box 715, North Bellmore NY 11710. (516)781-6230. Fax: "Available on request only." Vice President: Sue Bartczak. Estab. 1980. Represents 14 clients. 100% of clients are new/previously unpublished writers. Currently handles: 42% nonfiction books; 29% juvenile books; 29% novels.
Handles: Nonfiction books, juvenile books, "No picture books." Considers these nonfiction areas: biography/autobiography; juvenile nonfiction; women's issues/women's studies. Considers these fiction areas: contemporary issues; juvenile (no picture books). Query. Must have SASE. Reports in 2 weeks on queries; 4-6 weeks on mss.
Terms: Agent receives 15% commission on domestic sales; 20% on foreign sales. Offers written contract, binding for 1 year; automatic renewal for 1-year terms unless given 90 days prior written notice to terminate by either party.
Tips: Obtains new clients through recommendations and agency listings. "Be sure to include SASE with any material sent to an agent if you expect to get an answer. If you want the material you sent returned to you, be sure that your SASE has enough postage to take care of that."

‡JOSH BEHAR LITERARY AGENCY (I), Suite 3304, Empire State Bldg., 350 Fifth Ave., New York NY 10118. (212)826-4386. Contact: Josh Behar. Estab. 1993. Represents 12 clients. 90% of clients are new/previously unpublished writers. "I specialize in new and unpublished authors." Currently handles: 10% nonfiction books; 90% novels.
Handles: Nonfiction books, novels. Considers these nonfiction areas: biography/autobiography; business; money/finance/economics; New Age/metaphysics; self-help/personal improvement; women's issues/women's studies. Considers these fiction areas: action/adventure; detective/police/crime; fantasy; literary; psychic/supernatural; romance (contemporary, gothic, historical, regency); science fiction; thriller/espionage. Query. Reports in 1 week on queries; 1 month on mss.

Agents ranked I and II are most open to both established and new writers. Agents ranked III are open to established writers with publishing-industry references.

Literary Agents: Nonfee-charging 53

Terms: Agent receives 15% commission on domestic sales; 20% on foreign sales. Offers written contract, "only after sale has been made."
Writers' Conferences: RWA (NYC), MWA (NYC) SciFi (TBA).
Tips: Obtains new clients through "conferences, editors and former agent I worked for. Tell me a good story."

‡BERNSEN, JAMAIL & GOODSON, L.L.P. (I), Suite 980, 701 Brazos St., Austin TX 78701. (512)476-0005. Fax: (512)476-1513. Contact: Shelly A. Sanford. Estab. 1993. Member of State Bar of Texas; Sports & Entertainment Law Section. Currently handles: 50% nonfiction books; 50% fiction. Member agent: Shelly A. Sanford.
Handles: Nonfiction books, scholarly books, juvenile books, novels, movie scripts. Considers these nonfiction areas: animals; anthropology/archaeology; biography/autobiography; business; computers/electronics; cooking/food/nutrition; crafts/hobbies; ethnic/cultural interests; government/politics/law; health/medicine; history; language/literature/criticism; military/war; music/dance/theater/film; nature/environment; New Age/metaphysics; science/technology; sports; true crime/investigative; Eastern culture and religion; Hinduism; travel. Considers these fiction areas: action/adventure; contemporary issues; detective/police/crime; erotica; ethnic; experimental; fantasy; feminist; gay; historical; juvenile; lesbian; literary; mainstream; mystery/suspense; psychic/supernatural; religous/inspiration; romance (contemporary, gothic, historical, regency); science fiction; sports; thriller/espionage; westerns/frontier; young adult. Query with outline/proposal. Reports in 1 month on queries; 2 months on mss.
Terms: Agent receives 15% commission on domestic and foreign sales. Offers written contract, length of time will vary depending upon client. Charges for office expenses, postage and photocopying only in extreme situations upon prior notice to client and client approval.
Tips: Obtains new clients through solicitation, recommendations from others. "I am interested in writers who view writing as a need or desire rather than a skill. Send query letters and proposals which are concise and direct."

DAVID BLACK LITERARY AGENCY, INC. (II), 156 Fifth Ave., New York NY 10010. (212)242-5080. Fax: (212)924-6609. Associate: Lev Fruchter. Estab. 1990. Member of AAR. Represents 150 clients. Specializes in sports, politics, novels. Currently handles: 80% nonfiction; 20% novels.
Handles: Nonfiction books, novels. Considers these nonfiction areas: politics; sports. Query with outline. Reports in 1 month on queries.
Recent Sales: *Bo*, by Glenn "Bo" Schembechler and Mitch Albom (Warner); *If I Had a Hammer*, by Henry Aaron and Lonnie Wheeler (HarperCollins); *Birdsong Ascending*, by Sam Harrison (HBJ); *There Are No Children Here*, by Alex Kotlowitz.
Terms: Agent receives 15% commission. Charges for photocopying and books purchased for sale of foreign rights.

‡BLASSINGAME SPECTRUM CORP. (II), Suite 1501, 111 Eighth Ave., New York NY 10011. (212)691-7556. Contact: Eleanor Wood. Represents 50 clients. Currently handles: 95% fiction, 5% nonfiction books.
Handles: Considers these nonfiction areas: biography/autobiography; business; child guidance/parenting; health/medicine; history. Considers these fiction areas: contemporary issues; fantasy; historical; literary; mainstream; mystery/suspense; romance; science fiction. Query with SASE. Reports in 2 months on queries.
Terms: Agent receives 10% commission on domestic sales.
Tips: Obtains new clients through recommendations from authors and others.

REID BOATES LITERARY AGENCY (II), P.O. Box 328, 274 Cooks Crossroad, Pittstown NJ 08867. (908)730-8523. Fax: (908)730-8931. Contact: Reid Boates. Estab. 1985. Represents 45 clients. 15% of clients are new/previously unpublished writers. Specializes in general fiction and nonfiction, investigative journalism/current affairs; bios and autobiographies; serious self-help; literary humor; issue-oriented business; popular science; "no category fiction." Currently handles: 85% nonfiction books; 15% novels; "very rarely accept short story collections."
Handles: Nonfiction books, novels. Considers these nonfiction areas: animals; anthropology/archaeology; art/architecture/design; biography/autobiography; business; child guidance/parenting; current affairs; ethnic/cultural interests; government/politics/law; health/medicine; history; language/literature/criticism; nature/environment; psychology; science/technology; self-help/personal improvement; sports; true crime/investigative; women's issues/women's studies. Considers these fiction areas: con-

temporary issues; crime; family saga; mainstream; mystery/suspense; thriller/espionage. Query. Reports in 2 weeks on queries; 6 weeks on mss.
Terms: Agent receives 15% commission on domestic sales; 20% on foreign sales. Offers written contract, binding "until terminated by either party." Charges for photocopying costs above $50.
Tips: Obtains new clients through recommendations from others.

ALISON M. BOND LTD., 171 W. 79th St., New York NY 10024. Prefers not to share information.

GEORGES BORCHARDT INC. (III), 136 E. 57th St., New York NY 10022. (212)753-5785. Fax: (212)838-6518. Estab. 1967. Member of AAR. Represents 200+ clients. 10% of clients are new/previously unpublished writers. Specializes in literary fiction and outstanding nonfiction. Currently handles: 60% nonfiction books; 1% juvenile books; 37% novels; 1% novellas; 1% poetry books. Member agents: Denise Shannon, Cindy Klein, Alexandra Harding.
Handles: Nonfiction books, novels. Considers these nonfiction areas: anthropology/archaeology; biography/autobiography; current affairs; history; women's issues/women's studies. Considers literary fiction. "Must be recommended by someone we know." Reports in 1 week on queries; 3-4 weeks on mss.
Recent Sales: Has sold fiction book by T. Coraghessan Boyle (Viking); nonfiction book by Tracy Kidder (Houghton Mifflin); and *A New Collection of Poems*, by John Ashbery (Knopf).
Terms: Agent receives 10% commission on domestic sales; 15% British sales; 20% on foreign sales (translation). Offers written contract. "We charge cost of (outside) photocopying and shipping mss or books overseas."
Tips: Obtains new clients through recommendations from others.

THE BARBARA BOVA LITERARY AGENCY (II), 207 Sedgwick Rd., West Hartford CT 06107. (203)521-5915. Estab. 1974. Represents 30 clients. Specializes in nonfiction science. Currently handles: 50% nonfiction books; 50% novels.
Handles: Considers these nonfiction areas: science/technology; social sciences. Considers these fiction areas: contemporary issues; mainstream; mystery/suspense; science fiction. Query with SASE. Reports in 1 month on queries.
Terms: Agent receives 15% commission on domestic sales; handles foreign rights.
Tips: Obtains new clients through recommendations from others.

BRANDENBURGH & ASSOCIATES LITERARY AGENCY (III), 24555 Corte Jaramillo, Murrieta CA 92562. (909)698-5200. Contact: Don Brandenburgh. Estab. 1986. Represents 30 clients. "We prefer previously published authors, but will evaluate submissions on their own merits." Works with a small number of new/unpublished authors. Specializes in adult nonfiction for the religious market, limited fiction for religious market and limited nonfiction for the general market. Currently handles: 70% nonfiction books; 20% novels; 10% textbooks.
Handles: Nonfiction books, novels, textbooks. Query with outline. Reports in 2 weeks on queries.
Recent Sales: *Familiar Darknesses*, by Evelyn Minshull (Baker Book House); *The Magic in Aging*, by Ruby MacDonald (Thomas Nelson); *The Living Will and Other Life and Death Medical Choices*, by Dr. Joseph Beltran (Thomas Nelson).
Terms: Agent receives 10% commission on domestic sales; 20% on dramatic sales; 20% on foreign sales. Charges a $35 mailing/materials fee with signed agency agreement.

THE JOAN BRANDT AGENCY (II), 788 Wesley Dr. NW, Atlanta GA 30305. (404)351-8877. Fax: (404)351-0068. Contact: Joan Brandt. Estab. 1990. Represents 100 clients. Also handles movie rights for other agents.
Handles: Novels, nonfiction books, scripts. Considers these fiction areas: contemporary issues; detective/police/crime; literary; mainstream; mystery/suspense; thriller/espionage; "also will consider popular, topical nonfiction." Query with SAE. Reports in 2 weeks on queries.
Terms: Agent receives 15% commission on domestic sales; 20% on foreign sales (co-agents in all major marketplaces). Charges for photocopying and long-distance postage.
Tips: Obtains new clients through recommendations from others and over-the-transom submissions.

BRANDT & BRANDT LITERARY AGENTS INC. (III), 1501 Broadway, New York NY 10036. Contact: Carl Brandt, Gail Hochman, Charles Schlessiger. Estab. 1913. Member of AAR. Represents 200 clients.

Handles: Nonfiction books, scholarly books, juvenile books, novels, novellas, short story collections. Considers these nonfiction areas: agriculture/horticulture; animals; anthropology/archaeology; art/architecture/design; biography/autobiography; business; child guidance/parenting; cooking/food/nutrition; crafts/hobbies; current affairs; ethnic/cultural interests; gay/lesbian issues; government/politics/law; health/medicine; history; interior design/decorating; juvenile nonfiction; language/literature/criticism; military/war; money/finance/economics; music/dance/theater/film; nature/environment; psychology; science/technology; self-help/personal improvement; sociology; sports; true crime/investigative; women's issues/women's studies. Considers these fiction areas: action/adventure; contemporary issues; detective/police/crime; erotica; ethnic; experimental; family saga; feminist; gay; historical; humor/satire; lesbian; literary; mainstream; mystery/suspense; psychic/supernatural; regional; romance; science fiction; sports; thriller/espionage; westerns/frontier; young adult. Query. Reports in 2-4 weeks on queries.
Terms: Agent receives 10% commission on domestic sales; 20% on foreign sales. Charges for "manuscript duplication or other special expenses agreed to in advance."
Tips: Obtains new clients through recommendations from others or "upon occasion, a really good letter. Write a letter which will give the agent a sense of you as a professional writer, your long-term interests as well as a short description of the work at hand."

MARIE BROWN ASSOCIATES INC. (II,III), Room 902, 625 Broadway, New York NY 10012. (212)533-5534. Fax: (212)533-0849. Contact: Marie Brown. Estab. 1984. Represents 100 clients. Specializes in multicultural African-American writers. Currently handles: 50% nonfiction books; 25% juvenile books; 25% other. Member agent: Catherine E. McKinley (Project Editor development; submissions; contract negotiations permissions; PR; submissions; YA).
Handles: Considers these nonfiction areas: art; biography; business; child guidance/parenting; cooking/food/nutrition; ethnic/cultural interests; gay/lesbian issues; history; juvenile nonfiction; money/finance/economics; music/dance/theater/film; New Age; photography; psychology; religious/inspirational; self-help/personal improvement; sociology; women's issues/women's studies. Considers these fiction areas: contemporary issues; ethnic; family saga; feminist; gay; historical; humor/satire; juvenile; literary; mainstream; mystery/suspense; picture book; regional; science fiction. Query with SASE. Reports in 8-10 weeks on queries.
Recent Sales: *Tar Beach*; *Aunt Harriet's Underground Railroad*, by Faith Ringgold (Crown Books); *Conversations with My Sisters*, by Dr. J.B. Cole (Doubleday).
Terms: Agent receives 15% commission on domestic sales; 25% on foreign sales. Offers written contract.
Tips: Obtains new clients through recommendations from others.

CURTIS BROWN LTD. (II), 10 Astor Place, New York NY 10003. (212)473-5400. Member of AAR. Queries: Laura J. Blake. Chairman & CEO: Perry Knowlton. President: Peter L. Ginsberg. Member agents: Emilie Jacobson, Irene Skolnick, Emma Sweeney, Clyde Taylor, Maureen Walters, Timothy Knowlton (film screenplays, plays), Laura J. Blake, Virginia Knowlton, Chris McKerrow (audio rights), Marilyn Marlowe, Jess Taylor, Jeannine Edmunds (film screenplays, plays).
• Perry Knowlton is the current president of AAR.
Handles: Nonfiction books, juvenile books, novels, novellas, short story collections, poetry books, movie scripts, TV scripts, stage plays. All categories of nonfiction and fiction considered. Query. Reports in 3 weeks on queries; 3-5 weeks on mss "only if requested."
Terms: Agent receives 15% on domestic sales; 20% on foreign sales. Offers written contract. Charges for photocopying, some postage, "but only with prior approval of author."
Tips: Obtains new clients through recommendations from others, solicitation, at conferences and query letters.

ANDREA BROWN LITERARY AGENCY, INC. (III, IV), P.O. Box 429, El Granada CA 94018-0429. (415)728-1783. Contact: Andrea Brown. Estab. 1981. Member of AAR, WNBA. 25% of clients are new/previously unpublished writers. Specializes in "all kinds of juveniles—illustrators and authors." Currently handles: 99% juvenile books; 1% novels. Member agent: Donna Blackett (creative executive; picture books, early readers).
Handles: Juvenile books. Considers these nonfiction areas: animals; juvenile nonfiction; science/technology. Considers these fiction areas: juvenile; picture book; young adult. Query. Reports in 2 weeks on queries; 2 months on mss.

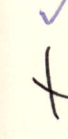

Recent Sales: *Canon the Librarian*, by Mike Thaler (Avon); *Reindeer*, by Caroline Arnold (Scholastic).
Terms: Agent receives 15% commission on domestic sales; 20% on foreign sales.
Writers' Conferences: Attends Jack London Writers Conference; UCLA Writer's Workshop Conference and various SCBWI conferences.

‡HOWARD BUCK AGENCY, Suite 1107, 80 Eighth Ave., New York NY 10011. (212)807-7855. Contact: Howard Buck or Mark Frisk. Estab. 1981. Represents 75 clients. "All-around agency." Currently handles: 75% nonfiction books; 25% novels.
Handles: Nonfiction, novels. Considers all nonfiction and fiction areas. Query with SASE. Reports in 6 weeks on queries.
Terms: Agent receives 15% commission on domestic sales. Offers written contract. Charges for office expenses, postage and photocopying.
Tips: Obtains new clients through recommendations from others.

KNOX BURGER ASSOCIATES LTD., 39½ Washington Square South, New York NY 10012. Prefers not to share information.

JANE BUTLER, ART AND LITERARY AGENT (II, III), P.O. Box 33, Matamoras PA 18336. Estab. 1981. "Prefers published credits, but all queries are welcome; no SASE, no reply." Specializes in fiction. Currently handles: 15% nonfiction books; 80% novels; 5% juvenile books.
Handles: Nonfiction books, novels. Considers these fiction areas: science fiction; fantasy; romantic fantasy; romantic suspense; historical fantasy; dark fantasy; children's fiction; young adult; some horror.
Terms: Agent receives 10% commission on domestic sales; 15% on dramatic sales; 20% on foreign sales.

SHEREE BYKOFSKY ASSOCIATES (IV), Suite 11-D, Box WD, 211 E. 51st St., New York NY 10022. Estab. 1984. Member of AAR. Represents "a limited number of" clients. Specializes in popular reference nonfiction. Currently handles: 80% nonfiction; 20% fiction.
Handles: Nonfiction books. Considers all nonfiction areas. Query with SASE. "No unsolicited manuscripts. No phone calls." Reports in 1 month on queries.
Recent Sales: *International Dictionary of Food & Nutrition*, by Ken and Lois Anderson (Wiley); *Freudulent Encounters for the Jung at Heart*, by Glenn Ellenboyer, Ph.D. (Norton).
Terms: Agent receives 15% commission on domestic sales; 15% on foreign sales. Offers written contract, binding for 1 year "usually." Charges for postage, photocopying and fax.
Tips: Obtains new clients through recommendations from others. "Read the agent listing carefully and comply with guidelines."

CANTRELL-COLAS INC., LITERARY AGENCY (II), 229 E. 79th St., New York NY 10021. (212)737-8503. Contact: Maryanne C. Colas. Estab. 1980. Represents 80 clients. Currently handles: 50% nonfiction books; 25% juvenile books; 25% mainstream.
Handles: Considers these nonfiction areas: anthropology; art; biography; child guidance/parenting; cooking/food/nutrition; current affairs; ethnic/cultural interests; government/politics/law; health/medicine; history; juvenile nonfiction; language/literature/criticism; military/war; money/finance/economics; nature/environment; New Age/metaphysics; psychology; science/technology; self-help/personal improvement; sociology; true crime/investigative; women's issues/women's studies. Considers these fiction areas: contemporary issues; detective/police/crime; ethnic; experimental; family saga; feminist; historical; humor/satire; juvenile; literary; mainstream; mystery/suspense; psychic/supernatural; science fiction; thriller/espionage; young adult. Query with SASE and outline plus 2 sample chapters, and "something about author also." Reports in 2 months on queries.
Recent Sales: *Well and Truly*, by Evelyn Wilde-Mayerson (NAL); *Dade County Pine*, by Evelyn Wilde-Mayerson (Viking); *Bride of the Unicorn*, by Kasey Michaels (Pocket Books); *White Hare's Horses*, by Penina Spinka (Atheneum).
Terms: Agent receives 15% commission on domestic sales; commission varies on foreign sales. Offers written contract. Charges for foreign postage and photocopying.
Tips: Obtains new clients through recommendations from others. "Make sure your manuscript is in excellent condition both grammatically and cosmetically. In other words, check for spelling, typing errors and legibility."

Literary Agents: Nonfee-charging 57

MARIA CARVAINIS AGENCY, INC. (II), Suite 15F, 235 West End Ave., New York NY 10023. (212)580-1559. Fax: (212)877-3486. Contact: Maria Carvainis. Estab. 1977. Member of AAR, Authors Guild, signatory of WGA. Represents 50 clients. 10% of clients are new/previously unpublished writers. Currently handles: 25% nonfiction books; 15% juvenile books; 55% novels; 5% poetry books.
Handles: Nonfiction books, scholarly books, novels, poetry books. Considers these nonfiction areas: biography/autobiography; business; current affairs; government/politics/law; health/medicine; history; military/war; money/finance/economics; psychology; true crime/investigative; women's issues/women's studies; popular science. Considers these fiction areas: action/adventure; detective/police/crime; family saga; fantasy; glitz; historical; humor/satire; juvenile; literary; mainstream; mystery/suspense; romance; thriller/espionage; westerns/frontier; children's; young adult. Query first with SASE. Reports in 2-3 weeks on queries; 3 months on mss.
Recent Sales: *Quality Isn't Enough*, by Joseph H. Boyett and Jimmie T. Boyett (Dutton); *Pumpkin Moon*, by Pamela E. Conrad (Harcourt Brace/Adult); *The Valiant Red Rooster*, by Eric A. Kimmel (Henry Holt & Co.).
Terms: Agent receives 15% commission on domestic sales; 20% on foreign sales. Offers written contract, binding for 2 years "on a book-by-book basis." Charges for foreign postage and bulk copying.
Tips: "75% of new clients derived from recommendations or conferences. 25% of new clients derived from letters of query."

‡MARTHA CASSELMAN LITERARY AGENT (III), P.O. Box 342, Calistoga CA 94515. (707)942-4341. Estab. 1978. Member of AAR. Represents 30 clients. Specializes in "nonfiction, especially food books; limited young adult, children's; fiction. Do not send children's or fiction without query."
Handles: Nonfiction proposals only, food-related proposals and cookbooks. Considers these nonfiction areas: agriculture/horticulture; anthropology/archaeology; biography/autobiography; cooking/food/nutrition; health/medicine; women's issues/women's studies. Send proposal with outline, plus 3 sample chapters. Reports in 2-4 weeks on queries.
Terms: Agent receives 15% commission on domestic sales; 20% on foreign sales (if using subagent). Offers criticism service under special circumstances, on consultation with author. Charges for photocopying, overnight and overseas mailings.
Tips: Obtains new clients through referrals. "No tricky letters; no gimmicks; always include SASE or mailer."

CHADD-STEVENS LITERARY AGENCY (I), 926 Spur Trail, Granbury TX 76049. (817)579-1405. Contact: Lee F. Jordan. Estab. 1991. Represents 15 clients. Specializes in working with previously unpublished authors.
Handles: Novels, novellas, short story collections. Considers these fiction areas: action/adventure; erotica; experimental; fantasy; horror; mystery/suspense; psychic/supernatural; young adult. Send entire ms or 3 sample chapters and SASE. Reports within 6 weeks on mss.
Terms: Agent receives 15% commission on domestic sales; 15% on foreign sales. Offers written contract, binding for 3 months.
Fees: Does not charge a reading fee. Charges a $35 handling fee for entire ms only. Charges for expenses. Payment of handling fee does not ensure agency representation.
Writers' Conferences: Attends several regional (Texas and Southwest) writers' conferences.
Tips: "I'm interested in working with people who have been turned down by other agents and publishers. I'm interested in first-time novelists—there's a market for your work if it's good. Don't give up. I think there is a world of good unpublished fiction out there and I'd like to see it."

‡FRANCINE CISKE LITERARY AGENCY (I, II), P.O. Box 555, Neenah WI 54957. (414)722-5944. Contact: Fran Ciske. Estab. 1993. Member of RWA. Specializes in romance, women's fiction. Currently handles: 100% fiction.
Handles: Considers these nonfiction areas: cooking/food/nutrition; religious/inspirational; true crime; self-help/personal improvement; women's isues/women's studies. Considers these fiction areas: mystery/suspense; religious/inspiration; romance (contemporary, historical, regency, time travel); thriller; westerns/frontier. Query with outline plus 3 sample chapters and SASE. Reports in 1 month on queries; 2 months on mss.

Terms: Agent receives 15% commission on domestic sales; 20% on foreign sales. Offers non-binding terms agreement. Expenses for photocopying will be agreed upon in advance.
Writers' Conferences: RWA National Conference, Wisconsin RWA conferences and workshops.
Tips: Obtains new clients through recommendation, solicitation and conferences. "Written submissions are preferred over a phone query. Agency will work with new writers, and will offer editorial feedback for promising material at no charge. Always include a SASE. Target your material."

SJ CLARK LITERARY AGENCY (IV), 56 Glenwood, Hercules CA 94547. Fax: (510)236-1052. Contact: Sue Clark. Estab. 1982. Represents 10 clients. 90% of clients are new/previously unpublished writers. Specializes in mysteries/suspense, children's books. Currently handles: 35% juvenile books; 65% novels. Member agent: Nichelle Tramble (women writers and commercial novels).
Handles: Juvenile books, novels. Considers these nonfiction areas: New Age/metaphysics. Considers these fiction areas: detective/police/crime; juvenile; mystery/suspense; psychic/supernatural; thriller/espionage; young adult. Query with entire ms. Reports in 1 month on queries; 2 months on mss.
Recent Sales: *Two Points for Murder*, by D.B. Borton (Berkley); *The Changer*, by Tatiana Strelkoff (Rebecca House).
Terms: Agent receives 20% commission on domestic sales. Offers written contract.
Tips: Obtains new clients by word of mouth, listing in *Guide to Literary Agents and Art/Photo Reps*.

CONNIE CLAUSEN ASSOCIATES (II), #16H, 250 E. 87th St., New York NY 10128. (212)427-6135. Fax: (212)996-7111. Contact: Connie Clausen. Estab. 1976. 10% of clients are new/previously unpublished writers. Specializes in true crime, autobiography, biography, health, women's issues, psychology, celebrity, beauty-fashion, how-to, financial. Currently handles: 100% nonfiction books (in New York). Member Agent: Genevieve Field.
Handles: Nonfiction books. Considers these nonfiction areas: biography/autobiography; business; cooking/food/nutrition; current affairs; ethnic/cultural interests; gay/lesbian issues; health/medicine; money/finance/economics; music/dance/theater/film; nature/environment; psychology; self-help/personal improvement; true crime/investigative; women's issues/women's studies. Send outline/proposal. Reports in 3 weeks on queries; 4-6 weeks on mss.
Recent Sales: *Eat Smart, Think Smart*, by Robert Haas (HarperCollins); *What to Do if You Get Breast Cancer*, by Lydia Komarnicky, MD, Anne Rosenberg, MD and Marian Betancourt (Little, Brown); *The Rules*, by Ellen Fein and Sherry Shamoon (Warner); *Born To Be Wild*, by Barry Bowe (Warner).
Terms: Agent receives 15% commission on domestic sales; 20% on foreign sales. Offers written contract, terms vary. Charges for office expenses.
Tips: Obtains new clients through referrals by other clients, publishers, magazine editors and *Writer's Digest*. "Always include SASE. Go to the library and read a book or two on publishing and proposal writing."

DIANE CLEAVER INC. (III), 55 Fifth Ave., New York NY 10003. (212)206-5606. Fax: (212)463-8718. Estab. 1979. Member of AAR. Currently handles: 60% nonfiction books; 40% novels.
Handles: Nonfiction books, novels. Generally open to most nonfiction areas. Considers these fiction areas: mainstream; mystery/suspense; thriller/espionage. Query. Reports in 1-2 weeks on queries.
Terms: Agent receives 15% commission on domestic sales; 19% on foreign sales. Charges for photocopying books for foreign submissions.
Tips: Obtains new clients through recommendations from others.

RUTH COHEN, INC. LITERARY AGENCY (II), P.O. Box 7626, Menlo Park CA 94025. (415)854-2054. Contact: Ruth Cohen or associates. Estab. 1982. Member of AAR, Authors Guild, SCBWI. Represents 75 clients. 20% of clients are new/previously unpublished writers. Specializes in "quality writing in juvenile fiction; mysteries; regency and historical romances, adult women's fiction." Currently handles: 15% nonfiction books; 40% juvenile books; 45% novels.
Handles: Juvenile books, adult novels. Considers these nonfiction areas: ethnic/cultural interests; juvenile nonfiction; true crime/investigative; women's issues/women's studies. Considers these fiction areas: detective/police; ethnic; regencies; family saga; historical; juvenile; literary; mainstream; mystery/suspense; picture books; young adult. Send outline plus 2 sample chapters and SASE. Reports in 1 month on queries. NO UNSOLICITED MSS.
Terms: Agent receives 15% commission on domestic sales; 20% on foreign sales, "if a foreign agent is involved." Offers written contract, binding for 1 year "continuing to next." Charges for foreign postage and photocopying for submissions.

Tips: Obtains new clients through recommendations from others. "A good writer cares about the words he/she uses—so do I. Also, if no SASE is included, material will not be read."

HY COHEN LITERARY AGENCY LTD. (II), #1400, 111 W. 57th St., New York NY 10019. (212)757-5237. Contact: Hy Cohen. "Mail manuscript to P.O. Box 743, Upper Montclair NJ 07043." Estab. 1975. Represents 25 clients. 50% of clients are new/previously unpublished writers. Currently handles: 20% nonfiction books; 5% juvenile books; 75% novels.
Handles: Nonfiction books, novels. All categories of nonfiction and fiction considered. Send 100 pages with SASE. Reports in about 2 weeks (on 100-page submission).
Recent Sales: *The Log of the Jessie Bill*, by Dean Gabbert (M. Evans); *Eye of the Beholder*, by Daniel Hayes (David Godine).
Terms: Agent receives 10% commission.
Tips: Obtains new clients through recommendations from others and unsolicited submissions. "Send double-spaced, legible scripts and SASE. Good writing helps."

COLLIER ASSOCIATES (III), 2000 Flat Run Rd., Seaman OH 45679. (513)764-1234. Contact: Oscar Collier. Estab. 1976. Member of AAR. Represents 75+ clients. 10% of clients are new/previously unpublished writers. Specializes in "adult fiction and nonfiction books only." Currently handles: 50% nonfiction books; 50% novels. Member agents: Oscar Collier (adult fiction, nonfiction). "This is a small agency that rarely takes on new clients because of the many authors it represents already."
Handles: Nonfiction, novels. Query with SASE. Reports in 6-8 weeks on queries; 3-4 months "or longer" on mss.
Recent Sales: *Making Money Outside the Dollar*, by Christopher Weber & Leonard Reiss (Warner Books); *Scripps: The Divided Dynasty*, by Jack Casserly (Donald I. Fine, Inc.); *New Orleans Requiem*, by D.J. Donaldson (St. Martin's Press).
Terms: Agent receives 10-15% commission on domestic sales; 20% on foreign sales. Offers written contract "sometimes." Charges for photocopying and express mail, "if requested, with author's consent, and for copies of author's published books used for rights sales."
Tips: Obtains new clients through recommendations from others. "Send biographical information with query; must have SASE. Don't telephone. Read my books *How to Write and Sell Your First Novel* and *How to Write and Sell Your First Nonfiction Book*."

FRANCES COLLIN LITERARY AGENT, (III), Suite 1403, LAAPR, 110 W. 40th St., New York NY 10018. (212)840-8664. Estab. 1948. Member of AAR. Represents 90 clients. 2% of clients are new/previously unpublished writers. Currently handles: 68% nonfiction books; 1% textbooks; 30% novels; 1% poetry books.
Handles: Nonfiction books, novels. Considers these nonfiction areas: anthropology/archaeology; biography/autiobiography; business; health/medicine; history; nature/environment; true crime/investigative. Considers these fiction areas: detective/police/crime; ethnic; family saga; fantasy; historical; literary; mainstream; mystery/suspense; psychic/supernatural; regional; romance (historical); science fiction. Query with SASE. Reports in 1 week on queries; 6-8 weeks on mss.
Terms: Agent receives 15% commission on domestic sales; 20% on foreign sales. Offers written contract. Charges for overseas postage for books mailed to foreign agents; photocopying of mss, books, proposals; copyright registration fees; registered mail fees; pass along cost of any books purchased.
Tips: Obtains new clients through recommendations from others.

COLUMBIA LITERARY ASSOCIATES, INC. (II,IV), 7902 Nottingham Way, Ellicott City MD 21043. (410)465-1595. Fax: Call for number. Contact: Linda Hayes, Kathryn Jensen. Estab. 1980. Member of AAR, IACP, RWA, WRW. Represents 40 clients. 10% of clients are new/previously unpublished writers. Specializes in women's fiction (mainstream/genre), commercial nonfiction, especially cookbooks. Currently handles: 40% nonfiction books; 60% novels.
Handles: Nonfiction books, novels. Considers these nonfiction areas: cooking/food/nutrition; health/medicine; self-help/personal improvement. Considers these fiction areas: mainstream; commercial women's fiction; suspense; contemporary romance; psychological/medical; thrillers. Reports in 2-4 weeks on queries; 6-8 weeks on mss; "rejections faster."
Recent Sales: *Everywhere That Mary Went*, by Lisa Scottoline (HarperCollins); *100% Pleasure—Low-Fat Cookbook*, by Nancy Baggett and Ruth Glick (Rodale Press).
Terms: Agent receives 15% commission on domestic sales. Offers single- or multiple-book written contract, binding for 6-month terms. "Standard expenses are billed against book income (e.g., books for subrights exploitation, tolls, UPS)."

Writers' Conferences: Attends Romance Writers of America and International Association of Culinary Professionals conferences.
Tips: Obtains new clients through referrals and mail. Submission requirements: "For fiction, send a query letter with author credits, narrative synopsis, first chapter or two, manuscript word count and submission history (publishers/agents); self-addressed, stamped mailer mandatory for response/ms return. (When submitting romances, note whether manuscript is mainstream or category—if category, say which line(s) manuscript is targeted to.) Same for nonfiction, plus include table of contents and note audience, how project is different and better than competition (specify competing books with publisher and publishing date.) Please note that we do *not* handle: historical fiction, westerns, science fiction/fantasy, military books, poetry, short stories or screenplays."

DON CONGDON ASSOCIATES INC. (III), Suite 625, 156 Fifth Ave., New York NY 10010-7002. (212)645-1229. Fax: (212)727-2688. Contact: Don Congdon, Michael Congdon, Susan Ramer. Estab. 1983. Member of AAR. Represents 100+ clients. Currently handles: 50% fiction; 50% nonfiction books.
Handles: Nonfiction books, novels. Considers all nonfiction and fiction areas, especially literary fiction. Query. "If interested, we ask for sample chapters and outline." Reports in 3-4 weeks on manuscript.
Recent Sales: *A Tidewater Morning*, by William Styron (Random House); *Cruel and Unusual*, by Patricia D. Cornwell (Scribner's).
Terms: Agent receives 10% commission on domestic sales.
Tips: Obtains new clients through referrals from other authors. "Writing a query letter is a must."

‡THE DOE COOVER AGENCY (II), 58 Sagamore Ave., Medford MA 02155. (617)488-3937. Fax: (617)488-3153. President: Doe Coover. Agent: Colleen Mohyde. Estab. 1985. Represents 45 clients. Specializes in serious nonfiction and fiction. Currently handles: 80% nonfiction; 20% fiction. Member agents: Doe Coover (cooking, general nonfiction); Colleen Mohyde (fiction, general nonfiction).
Handles: Nonfiction books, fiction. Considers these nonfiction areas: anthropology; biography/autobiography; business; child guidance/parenting; cooking/food; ethnic/cultural interests; health/medicine; history; language/literature/criticism; finance/economics; nature/environment; psychology; religious/inspirational; science/technology; sociology; true crime; women's issues/women's studies. Query with outline. Fiction queries must include SASE and should be addressed to Ms. Mohyde. Reporting time varies on queries.
Recent Sales: *Beating the Street*, by Peter Lynch (Simon & Schuster); *Sword of San Jacinto: A Biography of Sam Houston*, by Marshall DeBruhl (Random House).
Terms: Agent receives 15% commission on domestic sales; 15% on foreign sales.
Tips: Obtains new clients through recommendations from others and solicitation.

BONNIE R. CROWN INTERNATIONAL LITERATURE AND ARTS AGENCY (IV), 50 E. Tenth St., New York NY 10003. (212)475-1999. Contact: Bonnie Crown. Estab. 1976. Represents 8-11 clients. 100% of clients are previously published writers. Specializes in cross-cultural and translations of literary works, American writers influenced by one or more Asian culture. Currently handles: 10% nonfiction books; 70% fiction, 20% poetry (translations only).
Handles: Nonfiction books, novels. Considers these nonfiction areas: animals; ethnic/cultural interests; nature/environment; translations; women's issues/women's studies. Considers these fiction areas: ethnic; family saga; historical; literary. Query with SASE. Reports in 1 week on queries.
Terms: Agent receives 15% commission on domestic sales; 20% on foreign sales. Charges for processing, usually $25, on submission of ms.
Tips: Obtains new clients through "referrals through other authors and listings in reference works. If interested in agency representation, send brief query with SASE."

RICHARD CURTIS ASSOCIATES, INC. (III), 171 E. 74th St., New York NY 10021. (212)772-7363. Fax: (212)772-7393. Contact: Richard Curtis. Estab. 1969. Member of AAR, signatory of WGA. Represents 150 clients. 5% of clients are new/previously unpublished writers. Specializes in genre paperback

---

Check the Literary and Script Agents Subject Index to find the agents who indicate an interest in your nonfiction or fiction subject area.

fiction such as science fiction, women's romance, horror, fantasy, action-adventure. Currently handles: 9% nonfiction books; 1% juvenile books; 90% novels. Member agents: Roberta Cohen, Richard Henshaw.
• Richard Curtis is the current treasurer of AAR.
Handles: Nonfiction books, novels. Considers these nonfiction areas: biography/autobiography; business; child guidance/parenting; history; military/war; money/finance/economics; music/dance/theater/film; science/technology; self-help/personal improvement; sports; true crime/investigative. Considers these fiction areas: action/adventure; detective/police/crime; family saga; fantasy; feminist; historical; horror; mainstream; mystery/suspense; romance; science fiction; thriller/espionage; westerns/frontier. Query. Reports in 2 weeks on queries.
Terms: Agent receives 15% commission on domestic sales; 20% on foreign sales. Charges for photocopying, express, fax, international postage, book orders.
Tips: Obtains new clients through recommendations from others.

DARHANSOFF & VERRILL LITERARY AGENTS (II), 1220 Park Ave., New York NY 10128. (212)534-2479. Fax: (212)996-1601. Estab. 1975. Member of AAR. Represents 100 clients. 10% of clients are new/previously unpublished writers. Specializes in literary fiction. Currently handles: 25% nonfiction books; 60% novels; 15% short story collections. Member agents: Liz Darhansoff, Charles Verrill, Leigh Feldman.
Handles: Nonfiction books, novels, short story collections. Considers these nonfiction areas: anthropology/archaeology; biography/autobiography; current affairs; health/medicine; history; language/literature/criticism; nature/environment; science/technology. Considers literary and thriller fiction. Query letter only. Reports in 2 weeks on queries.
Tips: Obtains new clients through recommendations from others.

‡THE DARK HORSE GROUP, INC. (I, II), P.O. Box 4342, Ann Arbor MI 48106. (313)763-8844. Contact: Lynda Tymensky. Estab. 1993. Represents 8 clients. 40% of clients are new/previously unpublished writers. "We like to develop properties that have multimedia and cross-industry applications." Currently handles 40% nonfiction; 20% juvenile books; 40% syndicated material. Member agents: Lynda Tymensky, Kathleen Wyszaki.
Handles: Nonfiction books, juvenile books, novels, syndicated material. Considers these nonfiction areas: biography/autobiography; business; government/politics/law; history; juvenile nonfiction; New Age/metaphysics; true crime/investigative; self-help/personal improvement; women's issues/women's studies. Considers these fiction areas: action/adventure; cartoon/comic; contemporary issues; detective/police/crime; historical; juvenile; mainstream; mystery/suspense; picture book; psychic/supernatural; science fiction; thriller/espionage. Send outline plus 3 sample chapters. Reports in 2 months on queries.
Terms: Agent receives 15% on domestic sales; 20% on foreign sales. Offers written contract, binding for negotiable time.
Tips: "50% of properties were developed inhouse, 50% were obtained through professional associations. We would like to acquire a few more clients through trade publications. I have an advertising/marketing/journalism background. Dark Horse is looking for a few exceptionally talented authors with material that has multimedia and cross-industry applications. We are willing to spend an enormous amount of energy exploring all possible marketing corridors. We like to take our time and look at all possible options for our clients. We are especially interested in any self-help or how-to book written by a professional in the field it is about. We are also targeting any action/adventure hero book easily given to serialization. We would like to see the work of any children's writer/illustrator who believes they have created a unique character(s) or story concept that is a real kid-pleaser."

ELAINE DAVIE LITERARY AGENCY (II), Village Gate Square, 274 N. Goodman St., Rochester NY 14607. (716)442-0830. President: Elaine Davie. Estab. 1986. Represents 100 clients. 30% of clients are new/unpublished writers. Works with a small number of new/unpublished authors. Specializes in adult fiction and nonfiction, particularly books by and for women and genre/fiction. Currently handles: 30% nonfiction; 60% novels; 10% juvenile books.
Handles: Nonfiction books, novels (no short stories, children's books or poetry). Considers these nonfiction areas: self-help, true crime, women's issues. Considers these fiction areas: genre fiction, history, horror, mystery, romance, western. Query with outline or synopsis and brief description. Reports in 2 weeks on queries.

Recent Sales: *East of Forever*, by Christina Skye (Dell); *Guardian Spirit*, by Marcia Evanick (Bantam); *Twice in a Lifetime*, by Christy Cohen (Bantam).
Terms: Agent receives 15% commission on domestic sales; 20% on dramatic sales; 20% on foreign sales.
Tips: "Our agency specializes in books by and for women. We pride ourselves on our prompt responses to queries and that we never charge a fee of any kind."

THE LOIS DE LA HABA AGENCY INC. (III), Suite 810, 1123 Broadway, New York NY 10010. (212)929-4838. Fax: (212)924-3885. Contact: Lois de la Haba. Estab. 1978. Represents 100+ clients. Currently handles: 55% nonfiction books; 3% scholarly books; ½% textbooks; 10% juvenile books; 23% novels; ½% poetry; ½% short story collections; 3% movie scripts; 2% stage plays; 2% TV scripts; ½% syndicated material. Member agents: Barbara Zitwer, Luna Carne Ross.
Handles: Nonfiction books, scholarly books, juvenile books, novels, movie scripts, TV scripts, stage plays. Considers these nonfiction areas: animals; anthropology/archaeology; art/architecture/design; biography/autobiography; business; cooking/food/nutrition; current affairs; ethnic/cultural interests; gay/lesbian issues; government/politics/law; health/medicine; history; juvenile nonfiction; money/finance/economics; music/theater/dance/film; nature/environment; New Age/metaphysics; psychology/healing; religious/inspirational; self-help/personal improvement; women's issues/women's studies. Considers these fiction areas: contemporary issues; detective/police/crime; erotica; ethnic; experimental; fantasy; feminist; gay; glitz; historical; humor/satire; juvenile; literary; mainstream; mystery/suspense; religious/inspirational; young adult. Send query with outline/proposal and SASE. Reports in 3-5 weeks on queries; 4-8 weeks on mss.
Recent Sales: *Superself*, by Charles J. Givens (Simon & Schuster); *Power Thoughts*, by Dr. Robert Schuller (HarperCollins).
Terms: Agent receives 15% commission on domestic sales; 25% on foreign sales. Offers written contract, binding for 3 years. Charges for "photocopying, long-distance calls, etc."
Writers Conferences: Attends Mystery Writers of America.
Tips: Obtains new clients through recommendations from others.

ANITA DIAMANT, THE WRITER'S WORKSHOP, INC. (II), 310 Madison Ave., New York NY 10017. (212)687-1122. Contact: Anita Diamant. Estab. 1917. Member of AAR. Represents 120 clients. 25% of clients are new/previously unpublished writers. Currently handles: 20% nonfiction books; 80% novels. Member agents: Robin Rue (fiction and nonfiction).
Handles: Nonfiction books, young adults, novels. Considers these nonfiction areas: animals; art/architecture/design; biography/autobiography; business; child guidance/parenting; cooking/food/nutrition; crafts/hobbies; current affairs; government/politics/law; health/medicine; history; juvenile nonfiction; money/finance/economics; nature/environment; New Age/metaphysics; psychology; religious/inspirational; science/technology; self-help/personal improvement; sports; true crime/investigative; women's issues/women's studies. Considers these fiction areas: action/adventure; contemporary issues; detective/police/crime; experimental; family saga; feminist; gay; historical; juvenile; literary; mainstream; mystery/suspense; psychic/supernatural; religious/inspiration; romance; thriller/espionage; westerns/frontier; young adult. Query. Reports "at once" on queries; 3 weeks on mss.
Recent Sales: *Twilight's Child*, by V.C. Andrews (Pocket Books); *The India Exhibition*, by Richard Conroy (St. Martin's); *Miracle of Language*, by Richard Lederer (Pocket).
Terms: Agent receives 15% commission on domestic sales; 20% on foreign sales. Offers written contract.
Writers' Conferences: Attends the Romance Writers of America Annual Conference and the ABA.
Tips: Obtains new clients through "recommendations from publishers and clients, appearances at writers' conferences, and through readers of my written articles."

The publishing field is constantly changing! If you're still using this book and it is 1995 or later, buy the newest edition of Guide to Literary Agents & Art/Photo Reps *at your favorite bookstore or order directly from Writer's Digest Books.*

DIAMOND LITERARY AGENCY, INC. (III), 3063 S. Kearney St., Denver CO 80222. (303)759-0291. Contact: Jean Patrick. President: Pat Dalton. Estab. 1982. Represents 20 clients. 10% of clients are new/previously unpublished writers. Specializes in romance, romantic suspense, women's fiction, thrillers, mysteries. Currently handles: 25% nonfiction books; 70% novels; 3% movie scripts; 2% TV scripts.
Handles: Nonfiction books, novels, scripts. Considers these nonfiction areas with mass market appeal: business; health/medicine; money/finance/economics; nature/environment; photography; psychology; religious/inspirational; self-help/personal improvement; true crime/investigative; women's issues/women's studies. Considers these fiction areas: action/adventure; contemporary issues; detective/police/crime; family saga; feminist; glitz; historical; humor/satire; mainstream; mystery/suspense; religious/inspiration; romance; thriller/espionage. Reports in 1 month on mss (partials).
Recent Sales: *Kiss of Darkness*, by Sharon Brondos (Silhouette).
Terms: Agent receives 10-15% commission on domestic sales; 20% on foreign sales. Offers written contract, binding for 2 years "unless author is well established." Charges a "$15 submission fee for writers who have not previously published/sold the same type of project." Charges for express and foreign postage. "Writers provide the necessary photostat copies."
Tips: Obtains new clients through "referrals from writers, or someone's submitting saleable material. We represent only clients who are professionals in writing quality, presentation, conduct and attitudes—whether published or unpublished. Send a SASE for agency information and submission procedures. People who are not yet clients should not telephone. We consider query letters a waste of time—most of all the writer's, secondly the agent's. Submit approximately first 50 pages and complete synopsis for books, or full scripts, along with SASE and standard-sized audiocassette tape for possible agent comments. Nonclients who haven't sold the SAME TYPE of book or script within five years must include a $15 submission fee by money order or cashier's check. Material not accompanied by SASE is not returned. We are not encouraging submissions from not-yet-published writers at this time."

SANDRA DIJKSTRA LITERARY AGENCY (II), #515, 1155 Camino del Mar, Del Mar CA 92014. (619)755-3115. Contact: Laura Galinson. Estab. 1981. Member of AAR, Authors Guild, PEN West, Poets and Editors, MWA. Represents 80-100 clients. 40% of clients are new/previously unpublished writers. "We specialize in a number of fields." Currently handles: 50% nonfiction books; 5% juvenile books; 35% novels. Member agents: Sandra Dijkstra, president (adult nonfiction, literary and mainstream fiction, selected children's projects, mysteries and thrillers); Laura Galinson, associate agent (adult nonfiction, mystery and thrillers, literary and mainstream fiction, science fiction/fantasy, adventure); Ri Fournier, associate agent (literary and commercial fiction, commerical nonfiction).
Handles: Nonfiction books, novels, some juvenile books. Considers these nonfiction areas: horticulture; anthropology; art/architecture/design; biography/autobiography; business; child guidance/parenting; cooking/food/nutrition; current affairs; ethnic/cultural interests; government/politics; health/medicine; history; literary studies (trade only); military/war (trade only); money/finance/economics; music/dance/theater/film; nature/environment; psychology; science/technology; self-help/personal improvement; sociology; sports; translations; true crime/investigative; women's issues/women's studies. Considers these fiction areas: action/adventure; contemporary issues; detective/police/crime; ethnic; family saga; fantasy; feminist; juvenile; literary; mainstream; mystery/suspense; picture book; science fiction; sports; thriller/espionage; young adult. Send "outline/proposal with sample chapters for nonfiction, synopsis and first 50 pages for fiction and SASE." Reports in 2 weeks on queries; 1-6 weeks on mss.
Recent Sales: *Outsmarting the Female Fat Cell*, by Debra Waterhouse (Hyperion); *Stellaluna*, by Janell Cannon (children's, Harcourt Brace); *Child of Silence*, by Abigail Padgett (Mysterious Press).
Terms: Agent receives 15% commission on domestic sales; 20% on foreign sales. Offers written contract, binding for 2 years. Charges "an expense fee to cover domestic costs so that we can spend time selling books instead of accounting expenses. We also charge for the photocopying of the full manuscript or nonfiction proposal and for foreign postage."
Writers' Conferences: "Has attended Squaw Valley, Santa Barbara, Asilomar, Southern California Writers Conference, Rocky Mt. Fiction Writers, "to name a few. We also speak regularly for writers groups such as PEN West and the Independent Writers Association."
Tips: Obtains new clients "primarily through referrals/recommendations, but also through queries and conferences and often by solicitation. Be professional and learn the standard procedures for submitting your work. Give full biographical information on yourself, especially for a nonfiction project. Always include SASE with correct return postage for your own protection of your work. Query with a 1 or 2 page letter first and always include postage. Nine page letters telling us your life story, or your book's,

are unprofessional and usually not read. Tell us about your book and write your query well. It's our first introduction to who you are and what you can do! Call if you don't hear within a reasonable period of time. Be a regular patron of bookstores and learn what kind of books are being published. Check out your local library and bookstores—you'll find lots of books on writing and the publishing industry that will help you! At conferences, ask published writers about their agents. Don't believe the myth that an agent has to be in New York to be successful—we've already disproved it!"

THE JONATHAN DOLGER AGENCY (II), Suite 9B, 49 E. 96th St., New York NY 10128. (212)427-1853. President: Jonathan Dolger. Contact: Carol Ann Dearnaley. Estab. 1980. Member of AAR. Represents 70 clients. 25% of clients are new/unpublished writers. Writer must have been previously published if submitting fiction. Prefers to work with published/established authors; works with a small number of new/unpublished writers. Specializes in adult trade fiction and nonfiction, and illustrated books.
Handles: Nonfiction books, novels, illustrated books. Query with outline and SASE.
Terms: Agent receives 15% commission on domestic and dramatic sales; 25-30% on foreign sales. Charges for "standard expenses."

DONADIO & ASHWORTH INC. LITERARY REPRESENTATIVES, 231 W. 22nd St., New York NY 10011. Prefers not to share information.

THOMAS C. DONLAN (II, IV), 143 E. 43rd St., New York NY 10017. (212)697-1629. Agent: Thomas C. Donlan. Estab. 1983. Represents 12 clients. "Our agency limits itself to philosophy and theology, mainly, but not exclusively Roman Catholic. No special requirements of earlier publication." Prefers to work with published/established authors. Specializes in philosophical and theological writings, including translations. Currently handles: 2% magazine articles; 90% nonfiction books; 8% textbooks.
Handles: Nonfiction books, textbooks. Considers these nonfiction areas: philosophy, theology, translations. Query with outline. Reports in 2 weeks on queries. *Absolutely no unsolicited mss.*
Terms: Agent receives 10% commission on domestic sales; 6% on foreign sales.

DOYEN LITERARY SERVICES, INC. (II), 19005 660th St., Newell IA 50568-7613. (712)272-3300. President: B.J. Doyen. Associate: Susan Harvey. Estab. 1988. Member of NWC, RWA, HWA, SCBA, SFWA. Represents 50 clients. 20% of clients are new/previously unpublished writers. Specializes in all genre and mainstream fiction and nonfiction mainly for adults (some children's). Currently handles: 54% nonfiction books; 5% juvenile books; 40% novels; 1% poetry books.
Handles: Nonfiction books, juvenile books, novels. Considers most nonfiction areas. No gay/lesbian issues, religious/inspirational, sports or translations. Considers these fiction areas: action/adventure; contemporary issues; detective/police/crime; ethnic; experimental; family saga; fantasy; glitz; historical; humor/satire; juvenile; mainstream; mystery/suspense; picture book; psychic/supernatural; romance; science fiction; thriller/espionage; westerns/frontier; young adult. Query first with SASE. Reports in 1-2 weeks on queries; 6-8 weeks on mss.
Terms: Agent receives 15% commission on domestic sales; 20% commission on foreign sales. Offers a written contract, binding for 1 year.
Tips: "Many writers come to us from referrals, but we also get quite a few who initially approach us with query letters. Do *not* use phone queries unless you are successfully published, a celebrity or have an extremely hot, timely idea that can't wait. Send us a sparkling query letter with SASE. It is best if you do not collect editorial rejections prior to seeking an agent, but if you do, be up-front and honest about it. Do not submit your manuscript to more than one agent at a time—querying first can save you (and us) much time. We're open to established or beginning writers—just send us a terrific manuscript!"

ROBERT DUCAS (II), 350 Hudson St., New York NY 10014. (212)924-8120. Fax: (212)924-8079. Contact: R. Ducas. Estab. 1981. Represents 55 clients. 15% of clients are new/previously unpublished writers. Specializes in nonfiction, journalistic exposé, biography, history. Currently handles: 70% nonfiction books; 1% scholarly books; 28% novels; 1% novellas.
Handles: Nonfiction books, novels, novellas. Considers these nonfiction areas: animals; biography/autobiography; business; current affairs; gay/lesbian issues; government/politics/law; health/medicine; history; military/war; money/finance/economics; nature/environment; science/technology; sports; true crime/investigative. Considers these fiction areas: action/adventure; contemporary issues; detective/police/crime; family saga; historical; literary; mainstream; mystery/suspense; sports; thriller/espionage; westerns/frontier. Send outline/proposal. Reports in 2 weeks on queries; 1 month on mss.

Recent Sales: *Tales of the Earth*, by C. Officer (O.U.P.); *Regret Not a Moment*, by N. McGehee (Little Brown).
Terms: Agent receives 12½% commission on domestic sales; 20% on foreign sales. Charges for photocopying and postage. "I also charge for messengers and overseas couriers to subagents."
Tips: Obtains new clients through recommendations.

DUPREE/MILLER AND ASSOCIATES INC. LITERARY (II), Suite 3, 5518 Dyer St., Dallas TX 75206. (214)692-1388. Fax: (214)987-9654. Contact: Jan Miller. Estab. 1984. Represents 120 clients. 20% of clients are new/previously unpublished writers. Specializes in commercial fiction, nonfiction. Currently handles: 50% nonfiction books; 35% novels. Member agents: Jan Miller, Davis Smith, Dean Williamson, Michael Broussard.
Handles: Nonfiction books, scholarly books, novels, movie scripts, syndicated material. Considers all nonfiction areas. Considers these fiction areas: action/adventure; cartoon/comic; contemporary issues; detective/police/crime; family saga; feminist; gay; glitz; historical; humor/satire; literary; mainstream; mystery/suspense; psychic/supernatural; romance (contemporary, historical); science fiction; sports; thriller/espionage; westerns/frontier. Send outline plus 3 sample chapters. Reports in 1 week on queries; 8-12 weeks on mss.
Terms: Agent receives 15% commission on domestic sales. Offers written contract, binding for "no set amount of time. The contract can be cancelled by either agent or client, effective 30 days after cancellation." Charges $20 processing fee and Federal Express charges.
Writers' Conferences: "Will be attending many national conventions. Also have lectures at colleges across nation."
Tips: Obtains new client through conferences, lectures, clients and "very frequently through publisher's referrals." If interested in agency representation "it is vital to have the material in the proper working format. As agents' policies differ it is important to follow their guidelines. The best advice I can give is to work on establishing a strong proposal that provides sample chapters, an overall synopsis (fairly detailed) and some bio information on yourself. Do not send your proposal in pieces; it should be complete upon submission. Remember you are trying to sell your work and it should be in its best condition."

EDUCATIONAL DESIGN SERVICES, INC. (II, IV), P.O. Box 253, Wantagh NY 11793. (718)539-4107 or (516)221-0995. President: Bertram L. Linder. Vice President: Edwin Selzer. Estab. 1979. Represents 17 clients. 70% of clients are new/previously unpublished writers. Specializes in textual material for educational market. Currently handles: 100% textbooks.
Handles: Textbooks, scholarly books. Considers these nonfiction areas: anthropology/archaeology; business; child guidance/parenting; current affairs; ethnic/cultural interests; government/politics/law; history; juvenile nonfiction; language/literature/criticism; military/war; money/finance/economics; science/technology; sociology; women's issues/women's studies. Query with outline/proposal or outline plus 1-2 sample chapters. Reports in 1 month on queries; 4-6 weeks on mss.
Recent Sales: *New York in U.S. History* (Amsco); *Nueva Historia de Los Estados Unidos* (Minerva Books).
Terms: Agent receives 15% commission on domestic sales; 25% on foreign sales. Offers written contract. Charges for photocopying.
Tips: Obtains new clients through recommendations; at conferences; queries.

VICKI EISENBERG LITERARY AGENCY (II), 929 Fernwood, Richardson TX 75080. (214)918-9593. Fax: (214)918-9976. Contact: Vicki Eisenberg. Estab. 1985. Represents 30 clients. Currently handles: 60% nonfiction books; 40% novels.
Handles: Considers all nonfiction areas. Considers mainstream fiction. Query with SASE. Reports in 6 weeks on queries.
Terms: Agent receives 15% commission on domestic sales. Offers written contract.
Tips: Obtains new clients through referrals from other agencies and authors.

PETER ELEK ASSOCIATES (II, IV), Box 223, Canal Street Station, New York NY 10013. (212)431-9368. Fax: (212)966-5768. Contact: Daniel Goodwin. Estab. 1979. Represents 20 clients. Specializes in children's books—picture books, adult nonfiction and juvenile art. Currently handles: 30% juvenile books. Staff includes Gerardo Greco (Director of Project Development/Multi-Media).
Handles: Juvenile books (fiction, nonfiction, picture books). Considers juvenile nonfiction. Considers juvenile fiction, picture books. Query with outline/proposal and SASE. Reports in 2 weeks on queries; 3 weeks on mss.

Recent Sales: *The Lost Squadron*, by David Hayes (Hyperion); *Wreck of the Lusitania*, by R.D. Ballard (Warner).
Terms: Agent receives 15% commission on domestic sales; 20% on foreign sales. If required, charges for photocopying, typing, courier charges.
Tips: Obtains new clients through recommendations and studying consumer and trade magazines. "No work returned unless appropriate packing and postage is remitted. Actively seeking intellectual property/content, text and images for strategic partnering for multimedia. We are currently licensing series and single projects (juvenile, YA and adult) for electronic platforms such as CD-ROM, and CD-I. Our subsidiary company for this is The Content Company Inc.—contact: Gerardo Greco, at the same address."

ETHAN ELLENBERG LITERARY AGENCY (II), #5-E, 548 Broadway, New York NY 10012. (212)431-4554. Fax: (212)941-4652. Contact: Ethan Ellenberg. Estab. 1983. Represents 70 clients. 25% of clients are new/previously unpublished writers. Specializes in commercial and literary fiction, including first novels, thrillers, mysteries, science fiction, fantasy and horror, all categories of romance fiction, quality nonfiction, including biography, history, health, business and popular science. Currently handles: 25% nonfiction books; 75% novels. Member agent: Steve Seitz (commercial fiction, health, psychology).
Handles: Nonfiction books, novels. Considers these nonfiction areas: biography/autobiography; business; child guidance/parenting; cooking/food/nutrition; crafts/hobbies; current affairs; government/politics/law; health/medicine; history; juvenile nonfiction; military/war; money/finance/economics; nature/environment; new age/metaphysics; psychology; religious/inspirational; science/technology; self-help/personal improvement; sports; true crime/investigative. Considers these fiction areas: action; cartoon/comic; detective/police/crime; family saga; fantasy; glitz; historical; horror; humor/satire; juvenile; literary; mainstream; mystery/suspense; picture book; romance; science fiction; sports; thriller/espionage; westerns/frontier; young adult. Send outline plus 3 sample chapters. Reports in 10 days on queries; 3-4 weeks on mss.
Recent Sales: *Time Flies*, by Eric Rohmann (Crown Children's Books); *Is This the Veternary?*, by John McCormack (nonfiction humor, Crown); *Cut Out* and 2 other thrillers, by Bob Mayer (Presidio); *The Poet*, by Clay Reynolds (Baskerville); *Warstrider 3* and *4*, by Bill Keith (Avon); *Milord Wolf's Bride*, by Diane Stuckert (Zebra); 2 untitled westerns, by Johnny Quarles (Avon); 2 Courtney middle-grade books, by Judi Miller (Minstrel/Pocket).
Terms: Agent receives 15% on domestic sales; 10% on foreign sales. Offers written contract, "flexible." Charges for "direct expenses only: photocopying, postage."
Writers' Conferences: Speaks at Vassar Conference on Children's Publishing, attends a number of other RWA conferences.
Tips: "I obtain clients by client and editor recommendation, active recruitment from magazines, newspapers, etc. and my unsoliciteds. I very seriously consider all new material and have done very well through unsolicited manuscripts. Write a good, clear letter, with a succinct description of your book. Show that you understand the basics and don't make outrageous claims for your book. Make sure you only submit your best material and that it's prepared professionally—perfectly typed with good margins. Find out what any prospective agent will do for you, make sure you have some rapport. Don't be fooled by big names or phony pitches—what will the agent do for you. Good agents are busy, don't waste their time, but don't be afraid to find out what's going on. Besides my professionalism, my greatest skills are editorial—helping novelists develop. We give ample editorial advice for no charge to clients the agency takes."

NICHOLAS ELLISON, INC. (II), 15th Floor, 55 Fifth Ave., New York NY 10003. (212)206-6050. Affiliated with Sanford J. Greenburger Associates. Contact: Elizabeth Ziemska. Estab. 1983. Represents 70 clients. Currently handles: 25% nonfiction books; 75% novels.
Handles: Nonfiction, novels. Considers most nonfiction areas. No biography, gay/lesbian issues or self-help. Considers literary and mainstream fiction. Query with SASE. Reporting time varies on queries.
Recent Sales: *The General's Daughter*, by Nelson De Mille (Warner Books); *Tygers of Wrath*, by Philip Rosenberg (St. Martin's Press); *Bijou*, by Mark Joseph (HarperCollins).
Terms: Agent receives 15% commission on domestic sales; 20% commission on foreign sales.
Tips: Usually obtains new clients from word-of-mouth referrals.

ANN ELMO AGENCY INC. (III), 60 E. 42nd St., New York NY 10165. (212)661-2880, 2881. Fax: (212)661-2883. Contact: Ann Elmo or Lettie Lee. Estab. 1961. Member of AAR, MWA, Authors Guild.

Handles: Nonfiction, novels. Considers these nonfiction areas: cooking/food/nutrition; juvenile nonfiction; women's issues. Considers historical and romance fiction. Query with outline/proposal. Reports in 4-6 weeks "average" on queries.
Terms: Agent receives 15% commission on domestic sales; 20% on foreign sales. Offers written contract (standard AAR contract).
Tips: Obtains new clients through referrals. "Send properly prepared manuscript. A readable manuscript is the best recommendation. Double space."

EMBERS LITERARY AGENCY (V), R 3, Box 173, Spencer IN 47460. Only working with authors it already represents.

‡ESQUIRE LITERARY PRODUCTIONS (I), 1492 Cottontail Lane, La Jolla CA 92037. (619)551-9383. Contact: Sherrie Dixon, Esq. Estab. 1993. Represents 3 clients. 33% of clients are new/previously unpublished writers. Currently handles: 30% nonfiction books; 70% novels.
Handles: Nonfiction books, novels, short story collections. Considers these nonfiction areas: biography/autobiography; child guidance/parenting; military/war; psychology; true crime/investigative; self-help/personal improvement. Considers these fiction areas: action/adventure; contemporary issues; detective/police/crime; ethnic; family saga; fantasy; feminist; gay; glitz; historical; humor/satire; mainstream; mystery/suspense; romance (contemporary); thriller/espionage. Send outline plus 3 sample chapters. Reports in 1 week on queries; 2 weeks on mss.
Terms: Agent receives 15% commission on domestic sales; 15% on foreign sales. Offers written contract.

FELICIA ETH LITERARY REPRESENTATION (II), Suite 350, 555 Bryant St., Palo Alto CA 94301. (415)375-1276. Contact: Felicia Eth. Estab. 1988. Member of AAR. Represents 25-30 clients. Works with established and new writers; "for nonfiction, established expertise is certainly a plus, as is magazine publication – though not a prerequisite. Specializes in provocative, intelligent, thoughtful nonfiction on a wide array of subjects which are commercial and high-quality fiction; preferably mainstream and contemporary. I am highly selective, but also highly dedicated to those projects I represent." Currently handles: 85% nonfiction; 15% novels.
Handles: Nonfiction books, novels. Query with outline. Reports in 3 weeks on queries; 1 month on proposals and sample pages.
Recent Sales: *The Measure of a Man: Becoming the Father You Wish Your Father Had Been*, by Jerrold Shapiro Ph.D. (Dell/Delacorte); *What It's Like to Live Now*, by Meredith Moran (Bantam Books).
Terms: Agent receives 15% commission on domestic sales; 20% on dramatic sales; 20% on foreign sales. Charges for photocopying, Federal Express service – extraordinary expenses.

FARBER LITERARY AGENCY INC. (II), #2E, 14 E. 75th St., New York NY 10021. (212)861-7075. Fax: (212)861-7076. Contact: Ann Farber. Estab. 1989. Signatory of WGA. Represents 30 clients. 84% of clients are new/previously unpublished writers. Currently handles: 65% nonfiction books; 5% scholarly books; 20% stage plays.
Handles: Nonfiction books, textbooks, juvenile books, novels, stage plays. Considers these nonfiction areas: child guidance/parenting; cooking/food/nutrition; music/dance/theater/film; psychology. Considers these fiction areas: action/adventure; contemporary issues; humor/satire; juvenile; literary; mainstream; mystery/suspense; thriller/espionage; young adult. Send outline/proposal plus 3 sample chapters. Reports in 1 week on queries; 1 month on mss.
Terms: Agent receives 15% commission on domestic sales; 20% on foreign sales. Offers a written contract, binding for 2 years.
Tips: Obtains new clients through recommendations from others. "Client must furnish copies of manuscript. Our attorney, Donald C. Farber, is the author of many books. His services are available to the clients of the agency as part of the agency service."

JOHN FARQUHARSON LTD., 250 W. 57th St., New York NY 10107. Prefers not to share information.

‡FLORENCE FEILER LITERARY AGENCY (III), 1524 Sunset Plaza Dr., Los Angeles CA 90069. (213)652-6920/652-0945. Associate: Joyce Boorn. Estab. 1976. Represents 40 clients. No unpublished writers. "Quality is the criterion." Specializes in fiction, nonfiction, screenplays, TV. No short stories.

Handles: Textbooks (for special clients), juvenile books, movie scripts. Query with outline only. Reports in 2 weeks on queries. "We will not accept simultaneous queries to other agents."
Terms: Agent receives 10% commission on domestic sales; 10% on dramatic sales; 20% on foreign sales.

MARJE FIELDS-RITA SCOTT INC.
• Agency charges fees. Declined listing in fee-charging section.

JOYCE A. FLAHERTY, LITERARY AGENT (II, III), 816 Lynda Court, St. Louis MO 63122. (314)966-3057. Contact: Joyce or John Flaherty. Estab. 1980. Member of AAR, RWA, MWA, WWA, Author's Guild. Represents 65 clients. 15% of clients are new/previously unpublished writers. Currently handles: 30% nonfiction books; 70% novels. Member agents: Joyce Flaherty (general fiction and nonfiction, women's fiction); John Flaherty (military fiction and nonfiction thrillers).
Handles: Nonfiction books, novels. Considers these nonfiction areas: collectibles; animals; biography/autobiography; business; child guidance/parenting; crafts/hobbies; health/medicine; history; military/war; money; nature/environment; psychology; self-help/personal improvement; true crime/investigative; women's issues/women's studies; Americana. Considers these fiction areas: contemporary issues; crime; family saga; feminist; historical; literary; mainstream; mystery/suspense; psychic/supernatural; romance; thriller/espionage; frontier; military/aviation/war; women's fiction. Send outline plus 1 sample chapter and SASE. No unsolicited mss. Reports in 6 weeks on queries; 2-3 months on mss unless otherwise agreed on.
Recent Sales: *Targets of Opportunity*, by Joe Weber (Putnam); *The Founders (Book One of The Gairden Legacy)*, by Coleen L. Johnston (St. Martin's Press).
Terms: Agent receives 15% commission on domestic sales; 25-30% on foreign sales. Charges $50 marketing fee for new clients unless currently published book authors.
Writers' Conferences: Attends Romance Writers of America; Missouri Romance Writers Conference; Moonlight and Magnolias; Romantic Times Conference.
Tips: Obtains new clients through recommendations from editors and clients, writers conferences and from queries. "Be concise in a letter or by phone and well focused. Always include a SASE as well as your phone number. If you want an agent to return your call, leave word to call you collect if you're not currently the agent's client. If a query is a multiple submission, be sure to say so and mail them all at the same time so that everyone has the same chance. Know something about the agent beforehand so that you're not wasting each other's time. Be specific about word length of project and when it will be completed if not completed at the time of contact. Be brief!"

‡**FLAMING STAR LITERARY ENTERPRISES (II)**, 320 Riverside Dr., New York NY 10025. Contact: Joseph B. Vallely or Janis C. Vallely. Estab. 1985. Represents 50 clients. 25% of clients are new/previously unpublished writers. Specializes in upscale commercial fiction and nonfiction. Currently handles: 75% nonfiction books; 25% novels.
Handles: Nonfiction books, novels. Considers these nonfiction areas: current affairs; government/politics/law; health/medicine; nature/environment; New Age/metaphysics; science/technology; self-help/personal improvement; sports. Considers these fiction areas: detective/police/crime; glitz; mainstream; mystery/suspense; thriller/espionage. Query with SASE. Reports in 1 week on queries.
Terms: Agent receives 15% commission on domestic sales; 20% on foreign sales. Offers written contract. Charges for photocopying, postage, long distance phone calls only.
Tips: Obtains new clients through over the transom and referrals.

‡**PETER FLEMING AGENCY (IV)**, P.O. Box 458, Pacific Palisades CA 90272. (310)454-1373. Fax: (310)454-4491. Contact: Peter Fleming. Estab. 1962. Represents 17 clients. Specializes in "nonfiction books: innovative, helpful, contrarian, individualistic, pro-free market . . . with bestseller big market potential." Currently handles: 100% nonfiction books.
Handles: Nonfiction books. Considers "any nonfiction area with a positive, innovative, helpful, professional, successful approach to improving the world and abandoning special interests, corruption and patronage." Query with SASE.
Recent Sales: "2 revisions of bestselling *The Living Trust*, by Henry Abts (Contemporary Books—Chicago, Harvey Plotnick-Publisher), over 400,000 sold.
Terms: Agent receives 15% commission on domestic sales; 25% on foreign sales. Offers written contract, binding for 1 year. Charges "only those fees agreed to *in writing*, i.e., NY-ABA expenses shared."

Tips: Obtains new clients "through a *sensational*, different, one of a kind idea for a book usually backed by the writer's experience in that area of expertise."

FOGELMAN LITERARY AGENCY (I), Suite 712, 7515 Greenville Ave., Dallas TX 75231. (214)361-9956. Fax: (214)361-9553. Contact: Evan Fogelman or Linda Diehl. Estab. 1990. Represents 80-85 clients. Specializes in contemporary women's fiction, nonfiction, contemporary women's issues. Currently handles: 30% nonfiction books; 70% novels.
Handles: Considers these nonfiction areas: biography; business; parenting; nutrition; current affairs; government/politics/law; money/finance/economics; self-help/personal improvement; true crime; women's issues/women's studies; gardening. Considers romance fiction (mainstream, contemporary, historical). Query with SASE. Reports in 1-2 working days on 1-page query. Unsolicited mss not accepted.
Terms: Agent receives 15% commission on domestic sales; varying on foreign sales.
Writers' Conferences: St. Louis, Chicago, Phoenix, Houston, Kansas City, Wisconsin, 2nd Miami RWA, National RWA, various multi-genre conferences.
Tips: Obtains new clients through referrals, through writers conferences and through solicited submissions. "If you have any questions, call. All books can't be treated alike."

‡FRONTIER TALENTS (I), Suite 135, 1016 Grand Ave., San Diego CA 92109. Contact: Dennis McAusland. Estab. 1991. Represents 7 clients. 4-7% of clients are new/previously unpublished writers. Specializes in books by border writers or about border life—English and Spanish. Currently handles: 50% nonfiction books, 50% novels and short story collections. Member agents: Dennis McAusland (nonfiction), Ana Maria Corona (Mexican and Spanish-language authors), Linton Robinson (fiction and bilingual).
Handles: Nonfiction books, juvenile books, novels, novellas, short story collections, poetry books. Considers these nonfiction areas: border issues or works by border writers. Considers these fiction areas: action/adventure; cartoon/comic; detective/police/crime; experimental; historical; humor/satire; literary; mainstream; mystery/suspense; thriller/espionage; westerns/frontier. Query. Reports in 1 month on queries; 6 months on mss.
Terms: Agent receives 15% commission on domestic and foreign sales. Offers written contract, length of time depends on contract. Offers criticism service "only to accepted clients."
Writers' Conferences: Attends "most Southern California conferences. We also host conferences in Mexico."
Tips: Obtains new clients through "ads in Mexican magazines, referrals by writers and editors, at conferences and our writing seminars. Note our specialty. Write first. Have good, solid material to show."

CANDICE FUHRMAN LITERARY AGENCY, (II), Box F, Forest Knolls, Forest Knolls CA 94933. (415)488-0161. Fax: (415)488-4335. Contact: Candice Fuhrman. Estab. 1987. Member of AAR. Represents 60 clients. 50% of clients are new/previously unpublished writers. Currently handles: 95% nonfiction books; 5% novels.
Handles: Nonfiction books, novels. Considers these nonfiction areas: animals; anthropology/archaeology; art/architecture/design; biography/autobiography; business; child guidance/parenting; current affairs; ethnic/cultural interests; health/medicine; history; language/literature/criticism; money/finance/economics; music/dance/theater/film; nature/environment; psychology; religious/inspirational; science/technology; self-help/personal improvement; true crime/investigative; women's issues/women's studies. Considers these fiction areas: literary, mainstream. Send outline plus 1 sample chapter. Reports in 1 month on queries.

Agents who specialize in a specific subject area such as children's books or in handling the work of certain writers such as Latino writers are ranked IV.

Recent Sales: *Enduring Grace*, by Carol Flinders (HarperCollins); *Getting Love Right*, by Terrance Gorski (Fireside, Simon & Schuster).
Terms: Agent receives 15% commission on domestic sales; 25% on foreign sales. Offers written contract, binding for 6 months-1 year. Charges postage and photocopying.
Tips: Obtains new clients through recommendations and solicitation. "Please do not call. Send succinct query and well-thought-out proposal. Check out your idea with *Subject Books in Print* and look at the competition to see how your book is different. (This is for nonfiction, of course)."

JAY GARON-BROOKE ASSOC. INC. (II), Suite 5K, 101 W. 55th St., New York NY 10019. (212)581-8300. President: Jay Garon. Vice President: Jean Free. Agent: Nancy Coffey. Estab. 1952. Member of AAR, signatory of WGA. Represents 80 clients. 10% of clients are new/previously unpublished writers. Specializes in mainstream fiction and nonfiction. Currently handles: 15% nonfiction books; 75% novels; 5% movie scripts; 3% TV scripts.
Handles: Nonfiction books, novels, movie scripts, TV scripts, stage plays. Considers these nonfiction areas: biography/autobiography; child guidance/parenting; gay/lesbian issues; health/medicine; history; military/war; music/dance/theater/film; psychology; self-help/personal improvement; true crime/investigative. Considers these fiction areas: action/adventure; contemporary issues; detective/police/crime; family saga; fantasy; gay; glitz; historical; literary; mainstream; mystery/suspense; romance; science fiction. Query. Reports in 3 weeks on queries; 5-8 weeks on mss.
Recent Sales: *The Pelican Brief*, by John Grisham (Doubleday-Dell); *A Time to Kill*, by John Grisham (Dell); *Under Contract*, by Cherokee Paul McDonald (Donald I. Fine Inc.).
Terms: Agent receives 15% on domestic sales; 30% on foreign sales. Offers written contract, binding for 3-5 years. Charges for "photocopying if author does not provide copies."
Tips: Obtains new clients through referrals and from queries. "Send query letter first giving the essence of the manuscript and a personal or career bio with SASE."

MAX GARTENBERG, LITERARY AGENT (II,III), Suite 1700, 521 Fifth Ave., New York NY 10175. (212)860-8451. Fax: (201)535-5033. Contact: Max Gartenberg. Estab. 1954. Represents 30 clients. 5% of clients are new writers. Currently handles: 90% nonfiction books; 10% novels.
Handles: Nonfiction books, novels. Considers these nonfiction areas: agriculture/horticulture; animals; art/architecture/design; biography/autobiography; child guidance/parenting; current affairs; health/medicine; history; military/war; money/finance/economics; music/dance/theater/film; nature/environment; psychology; science/technology; self-help/personal improvement; sports; true crime/investigative; women's issues/women's studies. Considers mainstream and mystery/suspense fiction. Query. Reports in 2 weeks on queries; 6 weeks on mss.
Recent Sales: *Ancient Enemies*, by David Roberts (Simon & Schuster); *Football Fan's Companion*, by Ralph Hickock (Prentice Hall); *Partings and Other Beginnings*, by Ruth Rudner (Crossroad/Continuum); *Choosing to Be Well*, by Carla Cantor with Brian Fallon, M.D. (Houghton Mifflin).
Terms: Agent receives 10% commission on domestic sales; 15% on foreign sales. Offers written contract.
Tips: Obtains new clients "primarily, by recommendations from others, but often enough by following up on good query letters. Take pains in drafting your query letter. It makes the important first impression an agent has of you. Without going on at great length, be specific about what you have to offer and include a few relevant facts about yourself. The most exasperating letter an agent receives is the one which reads, 'I have just completed a novel. If you would like to read the manuscript, please let me know. A SASE is enclosed for your convenience.'"

‡ELLEN GEIGER LITERARY AGENCY (I, II), 3rd Floor, 131 Prince St., New York NY 10012. Mailing address: P.O. Box 178, New York NY 10012. (212)982-6030. Fax: (212)777-8439. Contact: Ellen Geiger. Estab. 1993. Member of Women in Film and TV, associate member of AAR in conjunction with The Charlotte Sheedy Agency. 25% of clients are new/previously unpublished writers. Specializes in adult fiction and nonfiction, journalism, mysteries and thrillers, current events, psychology, history, social issues. "Because I have a background in film and television, I also do film and TV negotiations and companion books to film projects." Currently handles: 65% nonfiction books; 10% scholarly books; 25% novels.
Handles: Nonfiction books, scholarly books, novels. Considers these nonfiction areas: agriculture/horticulture; animals; anthropology/archaeology; art/architecture/design; biography/autobiography; business; computers/electronics; cooking/food/nutrition; current affairs; ethnic/cultural interests; gay/lesbian issues; government/politics/law; health/medicine; history; interior design/decorating; language/literature/criticism; military/war; money/finance/economics; music/dance/theater/film; nature/environ-

Literary Agents: Nonfee-charging 71

ment; photography; psychology; religious/inspirational; science/technology; self-help/personal improvement; sociology; sports; true crime/investigative; women's issues/women's studies; popular culture. No New Age. Considers these fiction areas: action/adventure; contemporary issues; detective/police/crime; erotica; ethnic; family saga; feminist; gay; glitz; historical; humor/satire; lesbian; literary; mainstream; mystery/suspense; regional; thriller/espionage. No romance, science fiction. Query with outline/proposal plus 2 sample chapters. Reports ASAP on queries; 4-6 weeks on mss.
Terms: Agent receives 15% commission on domestic sales; 20% on foreign sales. Offers written contract, cancellable on 30 days notice. Charges for postage, photocopying, international phone calls and faxes, messenger service.
Writers' Conferences: Attends Berkshire Women's History (New England); National Gay and Lesbian Journalists Association (NYC); Malice Domestic (Baltimore); Bouchercon; Organization of American Historians and Buntint Institute (Radcliffe).
Tips: Obtains clients through referrals from editors, clients and other agents. "Referrals from academic and for professional services are a plus too. Conferences are also terrific, as author and agent can meet first. A good query letter is the most important thing! If the author can't write, you'll know by the end of the letter. For nonfiction: credentials of *some* kind are important, as well as membership in professional organizations, as this will help with distribution and marketing."

RONALD GOLDFARB & ASSOCIATES (II), 918-16 St. NW, Washington DC 20036. (202)466-3030. Fax: (202)293-3187. Contact: Ronald Goldfarb. Estab. 1966. Represents "hundreds" of clients. "Minority" of clients are new/previously unpublished writers. Specializes in nonfiction, "books with TV tie-ins." Currently handles: 80% nonfiction books; 1% scholarly books; 1% textbooks; 13% novels; 1% novellas; 1% short story collections; 1% movie scripts; 1% TV scripts; 1% syndicated material. Member agents: Ronald Goldfarb, Joshua Kaufman, Nina Graybill.
Handles: Nonfiction books, textbooks, scholarly books, novels, novellas, short story collections, movie scripts, TV scripts, syndicated material. Considers all nonfiction and fiction areas. Send outline plus 1-2 sample chapters. Reports in 1 month on queries; 2 months on mss.
Recent Sales: *When They Took Away the Man in the Moon*, by Kate Lehrer (Harmony); *Terror in the Night*, by Jack Nelson (Simon & Schuster).
Writers' Conferences: Attends Washington Independent Writers Conference; Medical Writers Conference.
Tips: Obtains new clients mostly through recommendations from others. "We are a law firm which can help writers with related problems, Freedom of Information Act requests, libel, copyright, contracts, etc. We are published writers."

GOODMAN ASSOCIATES (III), 500 West End Ave., New York NY 10024. Contact: Elise Simon Goodman. Estab. 1976. Member of AAR. Represents 100 clients. "Presently accepting new clients on a very selective basis."
• Arnold Goodman is currently chairperson of the AAR's Committee on Ethics.
Handles: Nonfiction, novels. Considers most adult nonfiction and fiction areas. No "poetry, articles, individual stories, children's or YA material." Query with SASE. Reports in 10 days on queries; 1 month on mss.
Terms: Agent receives 15% commission on domestic sales; 20% on foreign sales. Charges for certain expenses: faxes, toll calls, overseas postage, photocopying, book purchases.

IRENE GOODMAN LITERARY AGENCY (II), 17th Floor, 521 Fifth Ave., New York NY 10175. (212)682-2149. Contact: Irene Goodman, president. Estab. 1978. Member of AAR. Represents 45 clients. 10% of clients are new/unpublished writers. Works with a small number of new/unpublished authors. Specializes in genre fiction, popular nonfiction, reference. Currently handles: 20% nonfiction books; 80% novels.
Handles: Novels, nonfiction books. Considers these nonfiction areas: popular; reference. Considers these fiction areas: fantasy; horror; mainstream; mystery; romance (historical); science fiction; suspense; westerns. Query only (no unsolicited mss). Reports in 6 weeks. "No reply without SASE."
Terms: Agent receives 15% commission on domestic sales; 20% on foreign sales.

CHARLOTTE GORDON AGENCY (II), 235 E. 22nd St., New York NY 10010. (212)679-5363. Contact: Charlotte Gordon. Estab. 1986. Represents 30 clients. 10% of clients are new/unpublished writers. "I'll work with writers whose work is interesting to me. Specializes in books (not magazine material, except for my writers, and then only in special situations). My taste is eclectic." Currently handles: 40% nonfiction; 40% novels; 20% juvenile.

Handles: Nonfiction books, novels; juvenile fiction and nonfiction. Must query first with first chapter. No unsolicited mss. Reports in 2 weeks on queries.
Terms: Agent receives 15% commission on domestic sales; 10% on dramatic sales; 10% on foreign sales. Charges writers for photocopying mss.

GOTHAM ART & LITERARY AGENCY INC. (II), Suite 924, 1133 Broadway, New York NY 10010. (212)989-2737. Fax: (212)645-7731. Contact: Anne Elisabeth Suter. Estab. 1983. Currently handles: 10% nonfiction books; 45% juvenile books; 45% novels.
Handles: Considers all nonfiction areas. Considers juvenile, literary and mainstream fiction. Query with SASE. Reports in 2 weeks on queries.
Recent Sales: *A Mass for Arras*, by Andrej Szczypiorski (Grove Press); *The Story of Mr. Summer*, by Patrick Suskind with drawings by Sempé (Knopf); *Happy Birthday, Turk!*, by Jakob Arjouni (Fromm International); *Komodo!*, by Peter Sis (Greenwillow); *Victor and Christabel*, by Petra Mathers (Knopf).
Terms: Agent receives 15% commission on domestic sales; 20% on foreign sales. Offers written contract "on demand." If postage expenses get excessive, will discuss with author.
Writers' Conferences: Attends book fairs in Frankfort and Bologna (International Children Book Fair).

SANFORD J. GREENBURGER ASSOCIATES (II), 55 Fifth Ave., New York NY 10003. (212)206-5600. Fax: (212)463-8718. Contact: Heide Lange. Estab. 1945. Member of AAR. Represents 500 clients. Member agents: Heide Lange, Faith Hamlin, Beth Vesel, Diane Cleaver.
Handles: Nonfiction books, novels. Considers all nonfiction areas. Considers these fiction areas: action/adventure; contemporary issues; detective/police/crime; ethnic; family saga; feminist; gay; glitz; historical; humor/satire; juvenile; lesbian; literary; mainstream; mystery/suspense; picture books; psychic/supernatural; regional; sports; thriller/espionage. Query first. Reports in 1-2 weeks on queries; 1-2 months on mss.
Recent Sales: *Let Me Hear Your Voice*, by Catherine Maurice (Knopf); *Your Money or Your Life*, by Joe Domiguez and Vicki Robin (Viking).
Terms: Agent receives 15% commission on domestic sales; 19% on foreign sales. Charges for photocopying, books for foreign and subsidiary rights submissions.

MAIA GREGORY ASSOCIATES (II), 311 E. 72nd St., New York NY 10021. (212)288-0310. Contact: Maia Gregory. Estab. 1978. Represents 10-12 clients. Currently handles: 98% nonfiction books.
Handles: Considers these nonfiction areas: art; history; language; music/dance/theater/film. Considers literary fiction. Query with outline plus 1 sample chapter and SASE. Reports in 2 weeks on queries.
Terms: Agent receives 15% commission on domestic sales; varies on foreign sales.
Tips: Obtains new clients "through recommendations and queries."

LEW GRIMES LITERARY AGENCY (II), Suite 800, 250 W. 54th St., New York NY 10019-5586. (212)974-9505. Fax: (212)974-9525. Contact: Lew Grimes. Estab. 1991. 50% of clients are new/previously unpublished writers. Currently handles: 40% nonfiction books; 5% scholarly books; 1% textbooks; 50% novels; 2% poetry books; 2% movie scripts.
Handles: Nonfiction books, novels. Query. Reports in 3-4 weeks on queries; 3 months on mss.
Recent Sales: *Don't Speak to Strangers*, by Marion Rosen (St. Martin's); *The Boy, the Devil & Divorce*, by Richard Frede (Pocket).
Terms: Agent receives 15% commission on domestic sales; 20% on foreign sales. Offers written contract. Charges $15 postage and handling for return of ms. "Expenses are reimbursed for unpublished authors and for non-commercial projects."
Tips: Obtains new clients through referral and by query. "Provide brief query and résumé showing publishing history clearly. Always put phone number and address on correspondence and enclose SASE. No faxed queries."

MAXINE GROFFSKY LITERARY AGENCY, 2 Fifth Ave., New York NY 10011. Prefers not to share information.

THE CHARLOTTE GUSAY LITERARY AGENCY (II, IV), 10532 Blythe, Los Angeles CA 90064. (310)559-0831. Fax: (310)559-2639. Contact: Charlotte Gusay. Estab. 1988. Signatory of WGA, member of SPAR. Represents 30 clients. 50% of clients are new/previously unpublished writers. Specializes in fiction, nonfiction, children's (multicultural, nonsexist), children's illustrators, screenplays, books to film. "Percentage breakdown of the manuscripts different at different times."

Literary Agents: Nonfee-charging 73

Handles: Nonfiction books, scholarly books, juvenile books, travel books, novels, movie scripts. Considers all nonfiction and fiction areas. No romance, short stories, science fiction or horror. Query. Reports in 4-6 weeks on queries; 6-10 weeks on mss.
Recent Sales: *Groucho Marx and Other Short Stories and Tall Tales: Selected Writings of Groucho Marx*, edited by Robert Bader (Faber & Faber Pubs).
Terms: Agent receives 15% commission on domestic sales; 10% on dramatic sales; 25% on foreign sales. Offers written contract, binding for "usually 1 year." Charges for out-of-pocket expenses for long distance phone, fax, Federal Express, postage, etc.
Writers' Conferences: Attends Writers Connection, in San Jose, California; Scriptwriters Connection, in Studio City, California; National Women's Book Association, in Los Angeles.
Tips: Usually obtains new clients through referrals, queries. "Please be professional."

THE MITCHELL J. HAMILBURG AGENCY (II), Suite 312, 292 S. La Cienega Blvd., Beverly Hills CA 90211. (310)657-1501. Contact: Michael Hamilburg. Estab. 1960. Signatory of WGA. Represents 40 clients. Currently handles: 75% nonfiction books; 25% novels.
Handles: Nonfiction, novels. Considers all nonfiction areas and most fiction areas. No romance. Send outline plus 2 sample chapters. Reports in 3-4 weeks on mss.
Recent Sales: *A Biography of the Leakey Family*, by Virginia Marrell (Simon & Schuster); *A Biography of Agnes De Mille*, by Carol Easton (Little, Brown).
Terms: Agent receives 10-15% commission on domestic sales.
Tips: Usually obtains new clients through recommendations from others, at conferences or personal search. "Good luck! Keep writing!"

‡**THE HARDY AGENCY (II)**, #204B, 180 Harbor Dr., Sausalito CA 94965. (415)289-1695. Fax: (415)289-1693. Contact: Anne Sheldon, Michael Vidor. Estab. 1990. Represents 4 clients. 75% of clients are new/previously unpublished writers. Specializes in literary fiction with some nonfiction. Currently handles: 20% nonfiction books; 20% juvenile books; 60% novels. Member agents: Anne Sheldon (literary fiction, children's); Michael Vidor (media, marketing and PR).
Handles: Nonfiction books, juvenile books, novels. Considers these nonfiction areas: biography/autobiography; current affairs; government/politics/law; health/medicine; New Age/metaphysics. Considers these fiction areas: contemporary issues; literary. Send outline plus 5 sample chapters. Reports in 1 month on queries and mss.
Terms: Agent receives 15% commission on domestic sales; 20% on foreign sales. Offers written contract, binding for 1 year. Charges for postage, copying. Book editing available ($25 per hour). 85% of business is derived from commissions on mss; 15% from editing fees.
Tips: Obtains new clients from recommendations.

JOHN HAWKINS & ASSOCIATES, INC. (II), 71 W. 23rd St., New York NY 10010. (212)807-7040. Fax: (212)807-9555. Contact: John Hawkins, William Reiss, Sharon Friedman. Estab. 1893. Member of AAR. Represents 100+ clients. 5-10% of clients are new/previously unpublished writers. Currently handles: 40% nonfiction books; 20% juvenile books; 40% novels.
Handles: Nonfiction books, juvenile books, novels. Considers all nonfiction areas except computers/electronics; religion/inspirational; translations. Considers all fiction areas except confessional; erotica; fantasy; romance. Query with outline/proposal. Reports in 1 month on queries.
Terms: Agent receives 15% commission on domestic sales; 20% on foreign sales. Charges for photocopying.
Tips: Obtains new clients through recommendations from others.

THE JEFF HERMAN AGENCY INC. (II), #501C, 500 Greenwich St., New York NY 10013. (212)941-0540. Contact: Jeffrey H. Herman. Estab. 1985. Member of AAR. Represents 100 clients. 10% of clients are new/previously unpublished writers. Specializes in adult nonfiction. Currently handles: 85% nonfiction books; 5% scholarly books; 5% textbooks; 5% novels. Member agent: Deborah Adams (Vice President, nonfiction book doctor).
Handles: Business, popular reference; commercial how-to/self-help; popular psychology; computers; health; spirituality; recovery; history; politics. Query. Reports in 2 weeks on queries; 1 month on mss.
Recent Sales: *The Success Magazine Book Series* (Berkley).
Terms: Agent receives 15% commission on domestic sales. Offers written contract.
Tips: Obtains new clients through referrals and over the transom.

SUSAN HERNER RIGHTS AGENCY (II), P.O. Box 303, Scarsdale NY 10583. (914)725-8967. Contact: Susan Herner or Sue Yuen. Estab. 1987. Represents 50 clients. 25% of clients are new/unpublished writers. Eager to work with new/unpublished writers. Currently handles: 60% nonfiction books; 40% novels. Member agent: Sue Yuen (commercial fiction).
Handles: Nonfiction books, novels. Considers these fiction areas: horror; literary; mystery; mainstream (genre); romance; science fiction; thriller. Query with outline and sample chapters. Reports in 1 month on queries.
Recent Sales: *Outback*, by Joy Chambers (Ballantine); *What You Need to Know About Hispanic-Americans*, by Himilce Novas (Dutton); *The Sports Curmudgeon*, by George Sullivan & Barbara Lagowski (Warner).
Terms: Agent receives 15% commission on domestic sales; 20% on dramatic sales; 20% on foreign sales. Charges for extraordinary postage, handling and photocopying. "Agency has two divisions: one represents writers on a commission-only basis; the other represents the rights for small publishers and packagers who do not have in-house subsidiary rights representation. Percentage of income derived from each division is currently 70-30."

FREDERICK HILL ASSOCIATES, 1325 B, N. Olive Dr., West Hollywood CA 90069. (213)650-4092. Fax: (213)650-4093. Contact: Bonnie Nadell. Estab. 1979. Represents 100 clients. 50% of clients are new/unpublished writers. Specializes in general nonfiction, fiction, young adult fiction.
Handles: Nonfiction books, novels.
Recent Sales: *Wildcatting*, by Shann Nix (Doubleday); *Family Values*, by Phyllis Burke (Random House), untitled thriller, by John Martel (Pocket Books).
Terms: Agent receives 15% commission on domestic sales; 15% on dramatic sales; 20% on foreign sales. Charges for overseas airmail (books, proofs only).

JOHN L. HOCHMANN BOOKS (III, IV), 320 E. 58th St., New York NY 10022. (212)319-0505. Fax: (212)421-8699. President: John L. Hochmann. Estab. 1976. Represents 23 clients. Member of AAR, PEN. Writers must have demonstrable eminence in field or previous publications. Specializes in nonfiction books. Prefers to work with published/established authors. Currently handles: 80% nonfiction; 20% textbooks. Member agent: Theodora Eagle (popular medical and nutrition books).
Handles: Nonfiction trade books, textbooks. Considers these nonfiction areas: anthropology/archaeology; art/architecture/design; biography/autobiography; cooking/food/nutrition; current affairs; gay/lesbian issues; government/politics/law; health/medicine; history; military/war; music/dance/theater/film; sociology. Query with outline, titles of previous books and SASE first. Reports in 1 week on queries; 1 month on mss (solicited).
Recent Sales: *Elaine and Bill: Portrait of a Marriage*, by Lee Hall (HarperCollins); *What Makes a Van Gogh a Van Gogh*, et al, by Richard Mühlberger (Metropolitan Museum of Art); *The Practice of Public Relations*, by David Finn, et al (McGraw Hill).
Terms: Agent receives 15% commission on domestic sales; 25% on foreign sales.
Tips: Obtains new clients through recommendations from authors and editors. "Detailed outlines are read carefully; letters and proposals written like flap copy get chucked. We make multiple submissions to editors, but we do not accept multiple submissions from authors. Why? Editors are on salary, but we work for commission, and do not have time to read ms."

‡**BERENICE HOFFMAN LITERARY AGENCY (III)**, 215 W. 75th St., New York NY 10023. (212)580-0951. Fax: (212)721-8916. Contact: Berenice Hoffman. Estab. 1978. Member of AAR. Represents 55 clients.

The publishing field is constantly changing! If you're still using this book and it is 1995 or later, buy the newest edition of Guide to Literary Agents & Art/Photo Reps *at your favorite bookstore or order directly from Writer's Digest Books.*

Handles: Nonfiction, novels. Considers all nonfiction areas and most fiction areas. No romance. Query with SASE. Reports in 3-4 weeks on queries.
Terms: Agent receives 15% on domestic sales. Sometimes offers written contract. Charges of out of the ordinary postage, photocopying.
Tips: Usually obtains new clients through referrals from people she knows.

HOLUB & ASSOCIATES (II), 24 Old Colony Rd., North Stonington CT 06359. (203)535-0689. Contact: William Holub. Estab. 1967. Specializes in Roman Catholic publications. Currently handles: 100% nonfiction books.
Handles: Nonfiction books. Considers these nonfiction areas: biography; religious/inspirational; spirituality; self-help; theology. Query with outline plus 2 sample chapters and SASE.
Terms: Agent receives 15% commission on domestic sales. Charges for postage and photocopying.
Tips: Obtains new clients through recommendations from others.

HULL HOUSE LITERARY AGENCY (II), 240 E. 82nd St., New York NY 10028. (212)988-0725. Fax: (212)794-8758. President: David Stewart Hull. Associate: Lydia Mortimer. Estab. 1987. Represents 38 clients. 15% of clients are new/previously unpublished writers. Specializes in military and general history, true crime, mystery fiction, general commercial fiction. Currently handles: 60% nonfiction books; 40% novels. Member agents: David Stewart Hull (history, biography, military books, true crime, mystery fiction, commercial fiction by published authors); Lydia Mortimer (new fiction by unpublished writers, nonfiction of general nature including women's studies).
Handles: Nonfiction books, novels. Considers these nonfiction areas: anthropology/archaeology; art/architecture/design; biography/autobiography; business; current affairs; ethnic/cultural interests; government/politics/law; history; military/war; money/finance/economics; music/dance/theater/film; true crime/investigative; sociology. Considers these fiction areas: detective/police/crime; literary; mainstream; mystery/suspense. Query with SASE. Reports in 1 week on queries; 1 month on mss.
Terms: Agent receives 15% commission on domestic sales; 20% on foreign sales, "split with foreign agent." Written contract is optional, "at mutual agreement between author and agency." Charges for photocopying, express mail, extensive overseas telephone expenses.
Tips: Obtains new clients through "referrals from clients, listings in various standard publications such as *LMP*, *Guide to Literary Agents and Art/Photo Reps*, etc. If interested in agency representation, send a single-page letter outlining your project, always accompanied by an SASE. If nonfiction, sample chapter(s) are often valuable. A record of past publications is a big plus."

IMG-JULIAN BACH LITERARY AGENCY (II), (formerly Julian Bach Literary Agency), 22 E. 71 St., New York NY 10021. (212)772-8900. Fax: (212)772-2617. Contact: Julian Bach. Estab. 1956. Member of AAR. Represents 300 clients. Currently handles: 60% nonfiction books; 40% novels. Member agents: Julian Bach, Trish Lande.
Handles: Nonfiction books, novels. Considers these nonfiction areas: anthropology/archaeology; biography/autobiography; business; cooking/food/nutrition; current affairs; government/politics; history; language/literature/criticism; military/war; music/dance/theater/film; nature/environment; psychology; self-help/personal improvement; sports; true crime/investigative; women's issues/women's studies. Considers these fiction areas: detective/police/crime; feminist; literary; mainstream. Query.
Terms: No information provided. Offers written contract.

‡INTERNATIONAL CREATIVE MANAGEMENT (III), 40 W. 57th St., New York NY 10019. (212)556-5600. Fax: (212)556-5665. West Coast office: 8899 Beverly Blvd., Los Angeles CA 90048. (310)550-4000. Member of AAR, signatory of WGA. Member agents: Esther Newberg and Amanda Urban, department heads; Lisa Bankoff; Kristine Dahl; Mitch Douglas; Suzanne Gluck; Sloan Harris; Gordon Kato; Heather Schroder.
Terms: Agent receives 10% on domestic sales; 15% on UK sales; 20% on translations.

If you're looking for a particular agent, check the Agents and Reps Index to find at which agency the agent works. Then look up the listing for that agency in the appropriate section.

INTERNATIONAL PUBLISHER ASSOCIATES INC. (II), 746 W. Shore, Sparta NJ 07871. (201)729-9321. Contact: Joseph De Rogatis. Estab. 1983. Represents 15 clients. Currently handles: 100% nonfiction books.
Handles: Considers all nonfiction areas. Considers mainstream fiction "mostly." Query with SASE. Reports in 3 weeks on queries.
Recent Sales: *The Pocket Pediatrician*, by Dr. David Ziggelman (Doubleday).
Terms: Agent receives 15% commission on domestic sales; 20% on foreign sales. Offers written contract, binding for life of book. Charges for postage and photocopying.
Tips: Obtains new clients through word of mouth and *Guide to Literary Agents and Art/Photo Reps*.

J DE S ASSOCIATES INC. (II), 9 Shagbark Rd., Wilson Point, South Norwalk CT 06854. (203)838-7571. Contact: Jacques de Spoelberch. Estab. 1975. Represents 50 clients. Currently handles: 50% nonfiction books; 50% novels.
Handles: Nonfiction books, novels. Considers these nonfiction areas: biography/autobiography; business; current affairs; ethnic/cultural interests; government/politics/law; health/medicine; history; military/war; New Age; self-help/personal improvement; sociology; sports; translations. Considers these fiction areas: detective/police/crime; historical; juvenile; literary; mainstream; mystery/suspense; New Age; westerns/frontier; young adult. Query with SASE. Reports in 2 months on queries.
Terms: Agent receives 15% commission on domestic sales; 20% on foreign sales. Charges for foreign postage and photocopying.
Tips: Obtains new clients through recommendations from others, authors and other clients.

MELANIE JACKSON AGENCY, Suite 1119, 250 W. 57th St., New York NY 10107. Prefers not to share information.

JANKLOW & NESBIT ASSOCIATES, 598 Madison Ave., New York NY 10022. Prefers not to share information.

JET LITERARY ASSOCIATES, INC. (III), 124 E. 84th St., New York NY 10028. (212)879-2578. President: James Trupin. Estab. 1976. Represents 85 clients. 5% of clients are new/unpublished writers. Writers must have published articles or books. Prefers to work with published/established authors. Specializes in nonfiction. Currently handles: 50% nonfiction books; 50% novels.
Handles: Nonfiction books, novels. No unsolicited mss. Reports in 2 weeks on queries; 1 month on mss.
Recent Sales: *Deeper Thoughts*, by Jack Handey (Hyperion); *How Does Aspirin Find a Headache?*, by David Feldman (HarperCollins).
Terms: Agent receives 15% commission on domestic sales; 15% on dramatic sales; 25% on foreign sales. Charges for international phone and postage expenses.

LLOYD JONES LITERARY AGENCY (II), 4301 Hidden Creek, Arlington TX 76016. (817)483-5103. Fax: (817)483-8791. Contact: Lloyd Jones. Estab. 1988. Represents 32 clients. 40% of clients are new/previously unpublished writers. Currently handles: 100% nonfiction books.
Handles: Nonfiction books. Considers these nonfiction areas: business; current affairs; ethnic/cultural interests; health/medicine; juvenile nonfiction; money/finance/economics; psychology; self-help/personal improvement; sports; true crime/investigative; women's issues/women's studies. Send synopsis. Reports in 2 weeks on queries; 6-8 weeks on mss.
Terms: Agent receives 15% commission on domestic sales; 15% on foreign sales. Offers a written contract "for project only."
Tips: Obtains new clients through recommendations from publishers and writers. "Include a bio on writing projects, and define the target market for the proposed book."

‡LAWRENCE JORDAN LITERARY AGENCY (II), A Division of Morning Star Rising, Inc., Suite 1527, 250 W. 57th St., New York NY 10107. (212)690-2748. Fax: (212)690-5693. President: Lawrence Jordan. Estab. 1978. Represents 50 clients. 25% of clients are new/unpublished writers. Works with a small number of new/unpublished authors. Specializes in general adult fiction and nonfiction. Currently handles: 60% nonfiction; 25% novels; 3% textbooks; 2% juvenile books; 3% movie scripts; 7% stage plays.
Handles: Nonfiction books, novels, textbooks, juvenile books, movie scripts, stage plays. Handles these nonfiction areas: autobiography; business; computer manuals; health; religion; science; self-help; sports. Query with outline. Reports in 3 weeks on queries; 6 weeks on mss.

Recent Sales: *A Way Out of No Way: A Spiritual Memoir*, by Andrew Young (Thomas Nelson); *Southern Journey: A Personal Voyage Through the New South*, by Tom Dent (Harcourt Brace); *Club Grandma: Handbook for Happiness*, by Leslie Lehr Spirson and Claire Lehr (Longmeadow Press).
Terms: Agent receives 15% commission on domestic sales; 20% on dramatic sales; 20% on foreign sales. Charges long-distance calls, photocopying, foreign submission costs, postage, cables and messengers. 99% of income from commissions.

THE KARPFINGER AGENCY (II), Suite 2800, 500 5th Ave., New York NY 10110. Prefers not to share information.

‡THE KELLOCK COMPANY INC. (III), 222 Park Ave. S., New York NY 10003. (212)529-7122. Fax: (212)982-7573. Contact: Alan C. Kellock. Estab. 1990. Represents 75 clients. 10% of clients are new/previously unpublished writers. Specializes in nonfiction only, especially general reference and illustrated books. Currently handles: 75% nonfiction books, 25% juvenile books.
Handles: Nonfiction books. Considers these nonfiction areas: anthropology/archaeology, art/architecture/design, biography/autobiography, business, child guidance/parenting, crafts/hobbies, current affairs, government/politics/law, health/medicine, history, interior design/decorating, juvenile nonfiction, military/war, money/finance/economics, music/dance/theater/film, nature/environment, photography, psychology, self-help/personal improvement, sociology, sports, women's issues/women's studies. Query. Reports in 2 weeks on queries, 1 month on mss.
Terms: Agent receives 15% commission on domestic sales; 25% on foreign sales. Offers written contract. Charges for postage, photocopying.
Tips: Obtains new clients through referrals.

LOUISE B. KETZ AGENCY (II), Suite 4B, 1485 First Ave., New York NY 10021. (212)535-9259. Contact: Louise B. Ketz. Estab. 1983. Represents 25 clients. 15% of clients are new/previously unpublished writers. Specializes in science, business, sports, history and reference. Currently handles: 100% nonfiction books.
Handles: Nonfiction books. Considers these nonfiction areas: anthropology/archaeology; biography/autobiography; business; current affairs; history; military/war; money/finance/economics; science/technology; sports; true crime/investigative. Send outline plus 2 sample chapters. Reports in 4-6 weeks on queries and mss.
Recent Sales: *1001 Things Everyone Should Know About Science*, by James Trefil (Doubleday).
Terms: Agent receives 10-15% commission on domestic sales; 10% on foreign sales. Offers written contract.
Tips: Obtains new clients through recommendations, idea development.

VIRGINIA KIDD, LITERARY AGENT (V), Box 278, Milford PA 18337. Agency not currently seeking new clients.

KIDDE, HOYT & PICARD (III), 335 E. 51st St., New York NY 10022. (212)755-9461. Contact: Katharine Kidde, Wendy Wylegala. Estab. 1980. Member of AAR. Represents 50 clients. Specializes in mainstream fiction. Currently handles: 15% nonfiction books; 5% juvenile books; 80% novels.
Handles: Nonfiction books, novels. Considers these nonfiction areas: African studies; the arts; biography; current events; dance; gay/lesbian issues; history; psychology; women's issues. Considers these fiction areas: detective/police/crime; feminist; gay/lesbian; humor; literary; mainstream; mystery/suspense; romance; thrillers. Query. Reports in a few weeks on queries; 3-4 weeks on mss.
Recent Sales: *The Horses of the Night*, by Michael Cadnum (Carroll & Graf); *Contessa*, by Barrie King (Ballantine).
Terms: Agent receives 10% commission on domestic sales; 10% on foreign sales. Charges for photocopying.
Tips: Obtains new clients through query letters, recommendations from others, "former authors from when I was an editor at NAL, Harcourt, etc.; listings in *LMP*, writers guides."

---

‡ *The double dagger before a listing indicates the listing is new in this edition.*

KIRCHOFF/WOHLBERG, INC., AUTHORS' REPRESENTATION DIVISION (II), #525, 866 United Nations Plaza, New York NY 10017. (212)644-2020. Fax: (212)223-4387. Director of Operations: John R. Whitman. Estab. 1930s. Member of AAP, Society of Illustrators, SPAR, Bookbuilders of Boston, New York Bookbinders' Guild, AIGA. Represents 50 authors. 10% of clients are new/previously unpublished writers. Specializes in juvenile through young adult trade books and textbooks. Currently handles: 5% nonfiction books; 80% juvenile books; 5% novels; 5% novellas; 5% young adult. Member agent: Elizabeth Pulitzer-Voges (juvenile and young adult authors).
Handles: "We are interested in any original projects of quality that are appropriate to the juvenile and young adult trade book markets. Send a query that includes an outline and a sample; SASE required." Reports in 1 month on queries; 6 weeks on mss. Please send queries to the attention of: Liza Pulitzer-Voges.
Recent Sales: *Alvin Ailey*, by Andrea Davis Pinkney (Hyperion); *Nuts to You!*, by Lois Ehlert (Harcourt Brace); *Black Dog, Red House*, by Lizi Boyd (Little, Brown); *Bennie's Pennies*, by Pat Brisson (Doubleday).
Terms: Agent receives standard commission "depending upon whether it is an author only, illustrator only, or an author/illustrator book." Offers written contract, binding for not less than one year.
Tips: "Usually obtains new clients through recommendations from authors, illustrators and editors. Kirchoff/Wohlberg has been in business for over 50 years."

HARVEY KLINGER, INC. (III), 301 W. 53rd St., New York NY 10019. (212)581-7068. Fax: (212)315-3823. Contact: Harvey Klinger. Estab. 1977. Member of AAR. Represents 100 clients. 25% of clients are new/previously unpublished writers. Specializes in "big, mainstream contemporary fiction and nonfiction." Currently handles: 50% nonfiction books; 50% novels. Member agents: Carol McCleary (mysteries, science fiction, fantasy, category fiction), Laurie Liss (politics, women's issues).
Handles: Nonfiction books, novels. Considers these nonfiction areas: biography/autobiography; cooking/food/nutrition; health/medicine; psychology; science/technology; self-help/personal improvement; sports; true crime/investigative; women's issues/women's studies. Considers these fiction areas: action/adventure; detective/police/crime; family saga; glitz; literary; mainstream; mystery/suspense; romance (contemporary); thriller/espionage. Query. Reports in 2 weeks on queries; 6-8 weeks on mss.
Recent Sales: *Blue Crystal*, by Philip Lee Williams (Grove); *Run with the Hunted*, by Charles Bukowski (HarperCollins).
Terms: Agent receives 15% commission on domestic sales; 25% on foreign sales. Offers written contract. Charges for photocopying manuscripts, overseas postage for mss.
Tips: Obtains new clients through recommendations from others.

BARBARA S. KOUTS, LITERARY AGENT (II), P.O. Box 558, Bellport NY 11713. (516)286-1278. Contact: Barbara Kouts. Estab. 1980. Member of AAR. Represent 50 clients. 25% of clients are new/previously unpublished writers. Specializes in adult fiction and nonfiction and children's books. Currently handles: 20% nonfiction books; 40% juvenile books; 40% novels.
Handles: Nonfiction books, juvenile books, novels. Considers these nonfiction areas: biography/autobiography; business; child guidance/parenting; current affairs; ethnic/cultural interests; health/medicine; history; juvenile nonfiction; music/dance/theater/film; nature/environment; psychology; self-help/personal improvement; women's issues/women's studies. Considers these fiction areas: contemporary issues; family saga; feminist; historical; juvenile; literary; mainstream; mystery/suspense; picture book; romance (gothic, historical); young adult. Query. Reports in 2-3 days on queries; 4-6 weeks on mss.
Recent Sales: *Ordinary Time*, by Nancy Mairs (Beacon); *Sukey and the Mermaid*, by Robert San Souci (4 Winds Press).
Terms: Agent receives 10% commission on domestic sales; 20% on foreign sales. Charges for photocopying.
Tips: Obtains new clients through recommendations from others, solicitation, at conferences, etc. "Write, do not call. Be professional in your writing."

LUCY KROLL AGENCY (II,III), 390 W. End Ave., New York NY 10024. (212)877-0627. Fax: (212)769-2832. Agent: Barbara Hogenson. Member of AAR, signatory of WGA. Represents 60 clients. 5% of clients are new/unpublished writers. Specializes in nonfiction, screenplays, plays. Currently handles: 45% nonfiction books; 15% novels; 15% movie scripts; 25% stage plays.

Literary Agents: Nonfee-charging 79

Handles: Nonfiction, movie scripts, TV scripts, stage plays. Query with outline and SASE. No unsolicited mss. Reports in 1 month.
Recent Sales: *Great American Anecdotes*, by John and Claire Whitcomb (Morrow); *Mittel Europa*, by Cliff Slesin, et al. (Clarkson N. Potter).
Terms: Agent receives 10% commission on domestic sales; 10% on dramatic sales; 20% on foreign sales.

EDITE KROLL LITERARY AGENCY (II), 12 Grayhurst Park, Portland ME 04102. (207)773-4922. Fax: (207)773-3936. Contact: Edite Kroll. Estab. 1981. Represents 40 clients. Currently handles: 60% adult books; 40% juvenile books.
Handles: Nonfiction, juvenile books, humor, novels. Considers these nonfiction areas: social and political issues (especially feminist); current affairs. Considers these fiction areas: contemporary issues; feminist; literary; mainstream; mystery/suspense; juvenile; picture books by author/artists. Query in writing only with SASE. For nonfiction, send outline/proposal. For fiction, send outline plus 1 sample chapter or dummy. Reports in 2 weeks on queries; 6 weeks on mss.

PETER LAMPACK AGENCY, INC. (II), Suite 2015, 551 Fifth Ave., New York NY 10017. (212)687-9106. Fax: (212)687-9109. Contact: Peter Lampack. Estab. 1977. Represents 50 clients. 10% of clients are new/previously unpublished writers. Specializes in commercial fiction, male-oriented action/adventure, contemporary relationships, distinguished literary fiction, nonfiction by a recognized expert in a given field. Currently handles: 15% nonfiction books; 85% novels. Member agents: Peter Lampack (psychological suspense, action/adventure, literary fiction, nonfiction, contemporary relationships); Sandra Blanton (contemporary relationships, psychological thrillers, mysteries); Deborah Brown (literary fiction, historical fiction, nonfiction, women's issues).
Handles: Nonfiction books, novels. Considers these nonfiction areas: biography/autobiography; business; current affairs; government/politics/law; health/medicine; history; money/finance/economics; true crime/investigative; women's issues. Considers these fiction areas: action/adventure; contemporary relationships; detective/police/crime; family saga; glitz; historical; literary; mystery/suspense; thriller/espionage. Query. Reports in 2 weeks on queries; 2 months on mss.
Recent Sales: *If I Should Die*, by Judith Kelman (Bantam Books); *Out of the Blue*, by Doris Mortman (Crown/Ballantine); *From Freedom to Slavery*, by Gerry Spence (St. Martin's Press).
Terms: Agent receives 15% commission on domestic sales; 20% on foreign sales. Offers written contract, binding for 1-3 years. "Writer is required to furnish copies of his/her work for submission purposes."
Tips: Obtains new clients from referrals made by clients. "Submit only your best work for consideration. Have a very specific agenda of goals you wish your prospective agent to accomplish for you. Provide the agent with a comprehensive statement of your credentials—educational and professional."

THE ROBERT LANTZ-JOY HARRIS LITERARY AGENCY INC. (II), Suite 617, 156 Fifth Ave., New York NY 10010. (212)924-6269. Fax: (212)924-6609. Contact: Joy Harris. Member of AAR. Represents 150 clients. Currently handles: 50% nonfiction books; 50% novels.
Handles: Considers "adult-type books, not juvenile." Considers all fiction areas except fantasy; juvenile; science fiction; westerns/frontier. Query with outline/proposal and SASE. Reports in 1-2 months on queries.
Terms: Agent receives 15% commission on domestic sales; 20% on foreign sales. Offers written contract. Charges for extra expenses.
Tips: Obtains new clients through recommendations from clients and editors. "No unsolicited manuscripts, just query letters."

MICHAEL LARSEN/ELIZABETH POMADA LITERARY AGENTS (II), 1029 Jones St., San Francisco CA 94109. (415)673-0939. Contact: Mike Larsen or Elizabeth Pomada. Estab. 1972. Member of AAR. Represents 100 clients. 50-55% of clients are new/unpublished writers. Eager to work with new/unpublished writers. "We have very diverse tastes and do not specialize. We look for fresh voices with new ideas. We handle literary, commercial, and genre fiction, and the full range of nonfiction books." Currently handles: 60% nonfiction books; 40% novels. Member agents: Michael Larsen (nonfiction), Elizabeth Pomada (fiction).
Handles: Adult nonfiction books, novels. Query with synopsis and first 30 pages of completed novel. Reports in 2 months on queries. For nonfiction, call first. "Always include SASE. Send SASE for brochure."

Recent Sales: *Montezuma's Pearl*, by David Lee Jones (Avon); *American Quilts*, by Roderick Kiracofe (Clarkson Potter).
Terms: Agent receives 15% commission on domestic sales; 15% on dramatic sales; 20% on foreign sales. May charge writer for printing, postage for multiple submissions, foreign mail, foreign phone calls, galleys, books, and legal fees.

‡**LAZEAR AGENCY INCORPORATED (II)**, Suite 416, 430 First Ave., Minneapolis MN 55401. (612)332-8640. Fax: (612)332-4648. Contact: Susanne Moncur. Estab. 1984. Represents 250 clients. Currently handles: 40% nonfiction books; 20% juvenile books; 29% novels; 1% short story collections; 5% movie scripts; 2.5% TV scripts; 2.5% syndicated material. Member agents: Jonathon Lazear, President; Eric Vrooman (agent); Dennis Cass (Director of Subsidiary Rights); Debra Kass Orenstein, General Counsel.
Handles: Nonfiction books, juvenile books, novels, movie scripts, TV scripts, syndicated material. Considers all nonfiction areas, plus "recovery, heavily illustrated books." Considers all fiction areas. Query with outline/proposal. Reports in 3 weeks on queries; 6-8 weeks on ms.
Terms: Agent receives 15% commission on domestic sales; 20% on foreign sales. Offers written contract, binding "for term of copyright." Charges for "photocopying, international Federal Express."
Tips: Obtains new clients through recommendations from others, "through the bestseller lists, word-of-mouth. The writer should first view himself as a salesperson in order to obtain an agent. Sell yourself, your idea, your concept. Do your homework. Notice what is in the marketplace. Be sophisticated about the arena in which you are writing."

‡**SARAH LAZIN BOOKS**, Suite 300, 126 Fifth Ave., New York NY 10011. Prefers not to share information.

‡**LESCHER & LESCHER LTD. (II)**, 67 Irving Place, New York NY 10003. (212)529-1790. Fax: (212)529-2719. Contact: Robert or Susan Lescher. Estab. 1966. Member of AAR. Represents 150 clients. Currently handles: 75% nonfiction books; 13% juvenile books; 12% novels.
Handles: Nonfiction books, novels. Query with SASE.
Terms: Agent receives 15% commission on domestic sales; 20-25% on foreign sales. Charges for photocopying mss and copyrighting fees.
Tips: Usually obtains new clients through recommendations from others.

LEVANT & WALES, LITERARY AGENCY, INC. (II, IV), 108 Hayes St., Seattle WA 98109. (206)284-7114. Fax: (206)284-0190. Agents: Elizabeth Wales, Dan Levant and Valerie Griffith. Estab. 1988. Member of Pacific Northwest Writers' Conference, Book Publishers' Northwest. Represents 50 clients. We are interested in published and not-yet-published writers. Prefers writers from the Pacific Northwest, West Coast, Alaska and Pacific Rim countries. Specializes in nonfiction and mainstream fiction. Currently handles: 75% nonfiction books; 25% novels.
Handles: Nonfiction books, novels. Considers these nonfiction areas: business; gardening; health; lifestyle; memoir; nature; popular culture; psychology; science—open to creative or serious treatments of almost any nonfiction subject. Considers these fiction areas: mainstream (no genre fiction). Query first. Reports in 3 weeks on queries; 6 weeks on mss.
Recent Sales: *Zen Speaks: Shouts of Nothingness* (Anchor/Doubleday, 1994); *Two Old Women: An Alaska Legend*, by Velma Wallis (HarperCollins, 1994); *Taming the Dragon in Your Child*, by Meg Eastman, Ph.D. (Wiley, 1994).
Terms: Agent receives 15% commission on domestic sales. "We make all our income from commissions. We offer editorial help for some of our clients and help some clients with the development of a proposal, but we do not charge for these services. We do charge, after a sale, for express mail, manuscript photocopying costs, foreign postage and outside USA telephone costs."

ELLEN LEVINE LITERARY AGENCY, INC. (II, III), Suite 1801, 15 E. 26th St., New York NY 10010. (212)889-0620. Fax: (212)725-4501. Contact: Ellen Levine, Diana Finch, Anne Dubuisson. "My two younger colleagues at the agency (Anne Dubuisson and Diana Finch) are seeking both new and established writers. I prefer to work with established writers, mostly through referrals." Estab. 1980. Member of AAR. Represents over 100 clients. 20% of clients are new/previously unpublished writers. Specializes in literary fiction, women's fiction/thrillers, women's issues, books by journalists, current affairs, science, contemporary culture, biographies. Currently handles: 45% nonfiction books; 8% juvenile books; 45% novels; 2% short story collections.
- Ellen Levine is the current secretary of AAR.

Literary Agents: Nonfee-charging 81

Handles: Nonfiction books, juvenile books, novels, short story collections. Query. Reports in 2-3 weeks on queries, if SASE provided; 4-6 weeks on mss, if submission requested.
Terms: Agent receives 15% commission on domestic sales; 20% on foreign sales. Charges for overseas postage, photocopying, messenger fees, overseas telephone and fax, books ordered for use in rights submissions.
Tips: Obtains new clients through recommendations from others.

ROBERT LEWIS (V), 65 E. 96th St., New York NY 10128. Agency not currently seeking new clients. Published writers may query.

RAY LINCOLN LITERARY AGENCY (II), Suite 107-B, Elkins Park House, 7900 Old York Rd., Elkins Park PA 19117. (215)635-0827. Contact: Mrs. Ray Lincoln. Estab. 1974. Represents 34 clients. 35% of clients are new/previously unpublished writers. Specializes in biography, nature, the sciences, fiction in both adult and children's categories. Currently handles: 30% nonfiction books, 20% juvenile books, 50% novels. Member agent: Jerome A. Lincoln.
Handles: Nonfiction books, scholarly books, juvenile books, novels. Considers these nonfiction areas: horticulture; animals; anthropology/archaeology; art/architecture/design; biography/autobiography; business; child guidance/parenting; cooking/food/nutrition; crafts/hobbies; current affairs; ethnic/cultural interests; gay/lesbian issues; government/politics/law; health/medicine; history; interior design/decorating; juvenile nonfiction; language/literature/criticism; money/finance/economics; music/dance/theater/film; nature/environment; psychology; science/technology; self-help/personal improvement; sociology; sports; women's issues/women's studies. Considers these fiction areas: action/adventure; contemporary issues; detective/police/crime; ethnic; family saga; fantasy; feminist; gay; historical; humor/satire; juvenile; lesbian; literary; mainstream; mystery/suspense; psychic/supernatural; regional; romance (contemporary, gothic, historical); science fiction; sports; thriller/espionage; young adult. Query "first, then send outline plus 2 sample chapters with SASE. I send for balance of manuscript if it is a likely project." Reports in 2 weeks on queries; 1 month on mss.
Recent Sales: *Jefferson—a Life,* by Willard Randall (Holt); *Boy, Can He Dance,* by Eileen Rhinelli (Four Winds Press); *School Daze IV,* by Jerry Sfainelli (Scholastic).
Terms: Agent receives 15% commission on domestic sales; 20% on foreign sales. Offers written contract, binding "but with notice, may be cancelled. Charges only for overseas telephone calls. I request authors to do manuscript photocopying themselves. Postage, or shipping charge, on manuscripts accepted for representation by agency."
Tips: Obtains new clients usually from recommendations. "I always look for polished writing style, fresh points of view and professional attitudes."

WENDY LIPKIND AGENCY (II), 165 E. 66th St., New York NY 10021. (212)628-9353. Fax: (212)628-2693. Contact: Wendy Lipkind. Estab. 1977. Member of AAR. Represents 60 clients. Specializes in adult nonfiction. Currently handles: 80% nonfiction books; 20% novels.
Handles: Nonfiction, novels. Considers these nonfiction areas: biography; current affairs; health/medicine; history; science; social history. Considers mainstream and mystery/suspense fiction. No mass market originals. For nonfiction, query with outline/proposal. For fiction, query with SASE only. Reports in 1 month on queries.
Recent Sales: *Where's The Baby* and *Animal's Lullaby,* both by Tom Paxton (Morrow Junior Books).
Terms: Agent receives 15% commission on domestic sales; 20% on foreign sales. Sometimes offers written contract. Charges for foreign postage and messenger service.
Tips: Usually obtains new clients through recommendations from others. "Send intelligent query letter first. Let me know if you sent to other agents."

LITERARY AND CREATIVE ARTISTS AGENCY (III), 3539 Albemarle St. NW, Washington DC 20008. (202)362-4688. Contact: Muriel Nellis, Jane Roberts, Karen Gerwin. Estab. 1982. Member of Authors Guild, associate member of American Bar Association. Represents over 40 clients. "While we prefer published writers, it is not required if the proposed work has great merit." Requires exclusive review of material; no simultaneous submissions. Currently handles: 70% nonfiction books; 15% novels; 10% audio; 5% film/TV.
Handles: Nonfiction, novels, audio, film/TV rights. Considers these nonfiction areas: business; cooking; health; how-to; human drama; lifestyle; memoir; philosophy; politics. Query with outline, bio and SASE. No unsolicited mss. Reports in 2 weeks on queries.

Recent Sales: *Ageless Body, Timeless Mind,* by Dr. D. Chopra (Harmony); *Dancing the Dream,* by M. Jackson (Doubleday); *The One-Room Schoolhouse,* by J. Heynen (Knopf); *Healing Words,* by Dr. L. Dossey (Harper San Francisco); *A Woman's Best Medicine,* by Drs. M. Brown, V. Butler and N. Lonsdorf (Tarcher/Putnam).
Terms: Agent receives 15% commission on domestic sales; 20% on dramatic sales; 25% on foreign sales. Charges for long-distance phone and fax, photocopying and shipping.

THE LITERARY BRIDGE (I, II), Box 196 Alamo C.C., Alamo TX 78516. (210)702-4873. Contact: Genero or Rhobie Capshaw. Estab. 1992. Member of RGV Writers Guild. Represents 15-20 clients. 50% of clients are new/previously unpublished writers. "We specialize in helping authors turn a good idea and good writing into a marketable manuscript." Currently handles: 60% nonfiction books; 40% novels. Member agents: Genero Capshaw, Rhobie Capshaw.
Handles: Nonfiction books, novels, how-to, self-help. Considers these nonfiction areas: animals; anthropology/biography/autobiography; business; government/politics/law; health/medicine; history; juvenile nonfiction; money/finance/economics; nature/environment; new age/metaphysics; psychology; self-help/personal improvement; sports; true crime/investigative; women's issues/women's studies. Considers these fiction areas: action/adventure; contemporary issues; detective/police/crime; family saga; fantasy; feminist; glitz; historical; mainstream; mystery/suspense; psychic/supernatural; science fiction; sports; thriller/espionage; westerns/frontier. Query with 3 sample chapters. Reports in 1-2 weeks on queries; 4-6 weeks on mss.
Terms: Agent receives 10-15% commission on domestic sales; 15-20% on foreign sales; 20% on dramatic sales. Offers written contract, binding for 1 year. "The handling fee includes phone, photocopying and postage and is refunded upon the sale of the manuscript by this agency." 95% of business is derived from commissions on manuscript sales.
Tips: Obtains new clients through solicitation and conferences. "We bridge the gap between writers who know their genre or category and publishers who want quality work."

THE LITERARY GROUP (II), #1505, 270 Lafayette St., New York NY 10012. (212)274-1616. Fax: (212)274-9876. Contact: Frank Weimann. Estab. 1985. Represents 90 clients. 75% of clients are new/previously unpublished writers. Specializes in nonfiction (true crime; biography; sports; how-to). Currently handles: 80% nonfiction books; 20% novels.
Handles: Nonfiction books, novels. Considers these nonfiction areas: animals; biography/autobiography; business; child guidance/parenting; current affairs; gay/lesbian issues; health/medicine; history; music/dance/theater/film; nature/environment; psychology; self-help/personal improvement; sociology; sports; true crime/investigative; women's issues/women's studies. Considers these fiction areas: action/adventure; detective/police/crime; humor/satire; mystery/suspense; sports; thriller/espionage. Query with outline plus 3 sample chapters. Reports in 1 week on queries; 1 month on mss.
Recent Sales: *Back from Tuichi,* by Yossi Ghinsberg (Random House).
Terms: Agent receives 15% commission on domestic sales; 20% on foreign sales. Offers written contract, which "can be cancelled after 30 days."
Writers' Conferences: Attends Florida Suncoast Writers Conference; Southwest Writers Conference; Palm Springs Writers Group.
Tips: Obtains new clients through referrals, writers conferences, query letters.

STERLING LORD LITERISTIC, INC. (III), One Madison Ave., New York NY 10010. (212)696-2800. Fax: (212)686-6976. Contact: Peter Matson. Estab. 1952. Member of AAR, signatory of WGA. Represents 500+ clients. Specializes in "nonfiction and fiction." Currently handles: 50% nonfiction books, 50% novels. Member agents: Peter Matson, Sterling Lord; Jody Hotchkiss (film scripts); Philippa Brophy; Stuart Krichevsky; Elizabeth Grossman.
Handles: Nonfiction books, novels. Considers "mainstream nonfiction and fiction." Query. Reports in 1 month on mss.
Recent Sales: Untitled memoir, by Robert McNamara (Times Books).
Terms: Agent receives 15% commission on domestic sales; 20% on foreign sales. Offers written contract. Charges for photocopying.
Tips: Obtains new clients through recommendations from others.

LOS ANGELES LITERARY ASSOCIATES (II), 6324 Tahoe Dr., Los Angeles CA 90068. (213)464-6444. Contact: Andrew Ettinger. Estab. 1984. Specializes in nonfiction books. Currently handles: 70% nonfiction books; 30% novels.

Handles: Nonfiction books, novels. Considers these nonfiction areas: biography; business; history; money/finance/economics; self-help/personal improvement; inspirational. Considers these fiction areas: contemporary issues; mainstream; thriller/espionage. Not interested in any material on horror; homosexuals/lesbians; science fiction. Query with outline/proposal and SASE. Reports in 1 month on queries.
Terms: Agent receives 10-15% commission on domestic sales; varies on foreign sales.
Writers' Conferences: Attends Santa Barbara Writers Conference.
Tips: Usually obtains new clients by word of mouth and referrals. "Do your grass roots market research, in bookstores and the library. It's important not to forget about your libraries because they'll give you a depth of knowledge that can't be found in cruising a typical bookstore."

NANCY LOVE LITERARY AGENCY (III), 250 E. 65th St., New York NY 10021. (212)980-3499. Fax: (212)308-6405. Contact: Nancy Love. Estab. 1984. Member of AAR. Represents 60 clients. Specializes in adult nonfiction. Currently handles: 90% nonfiction books; 10% novels.
Handles: Nonfiction books, novels. Considers these nonfiction areas: biography/autobiography; child guidance/parenting; cooking/food/nutrition; current affairs; ethnic/cultural interests; government/politics/law; health/medicine; history; nature/environment; psychology; science/technology; self-help/personal improvement; sociology; true crime/investigative; women's issues/women's studies. Considers these fiction areas: action/adventure; contemporary issues; detective/police/crime; ethnic; literary; mainstream; mystery/suspense; thriller/espionage. "For nonfiction, send a proposal, chapter summary and sample chapter. For fiction, send the first 40-50 pages plus summary of the rest (will consider only *completed* novels)." Reports in 2 weeks on queries; 3 weeks on mss.
Recent Sales: *Small Bargains: Children in Crisis and the Meaning of Parental Love*, by William Garrison, Ph.D. (Simon & Schuster); *Wing and a Prayer*, by Harry Crosby (HarperCollins).
Terms: Agent receives 15% commission on domestic sales; 20% on foreign sales. Offers written contract. Charges for photocopying, "if it runs over $20."
Tips: Obtains new clients through recommendations and solicitation. "Many also come through the Writer's Union, where I have a number of clients and a very high rating. I prefer a call to a query letter. That cuts out a step and allows me to express my preference for an exclusive and to discuss the author's credentials. I can also tell a writer that I won't return material without a SASE."

LOWENSTEIN ASSOCIATES, INC. (II), #601, 121 W. 27th St., New York NY 10001. (212)206-1630. President: Barbara Lowenstein. Estab. 1976. Member of AAR. Represents 120 clients. 15% of clients are new/unpublished writers. Specializes in nonfiction—especially science and medical-topic books for the general public—general fiction. Currently handles: 2% magazine articles; 55% nonfiction books; 43% novels. Member agents: Norman Kurz, Nancy Yost.
Handles: Nonfiction books, novels. Considers these nonfiction areas: medicine, science. Considers these fiction areas: romance (historical, contemporary) and "bigger women's fiction," mainstream. Query. No unsolicited mss.
Terms: Agent receives 15% commission on domestic and dramatic sales; 20% on foreign sales. Charges for photocopying, foreign postage, messenger expenses.

LYCEUM CREATIVE PROPERTIES, INC. (I, II), P.O. Box 12370, San Antonio TX 78212. (210)732-0200. President: Guy Robin Custer. Estab. 1992. Signatory of WGA. Represents 18 clients. 60% of clients are new/previously unpublished writers. Currently handles: 20% nonfiction books; 5% scholarly books; 40% novels; 25% movie scripts; 5% stage plays; 5% TV scripts. Member agents: Guy Robin Custer (novels, nonfiction, some screenplays); Dave Roy (novels, screenplays, stage plays); Geoff Osborne (nonfiction, screenplays, stage plays); Caspar Jasso (translations, ethnic/cultural).
Handles: Nonfiction books, textbooks, scholarly books, juvenile books, novels, novellas, movie scripts, stage plays, features for TV (no episodics). Considers these nonfiction areas: anthropology/archaeology; art/architecture/design; biography/autobiography; business; child guidance/parenting; computers/electronics; cooking/food/nutrition; current affairs; ethnic/cultural interests; gay/lesbian issues; government/politics/law; history; juvenile nonfiction; language/literature/criticism; music/dance/theater/film; nature/environment; New Age/metaphysics; psychology; sociology; translations; travel; true crime/investigative; exposé. Considers these fiction areas: action/adventure; cartoon/comic; contemporary issues; detective/police/crime; erotica; ethnic; experimental; fantasy; feminist; gay; historical; humor/satire; juvenile; lesbian; literary; mainstream; mystery/suspense; picture book; psychic/supernatural; romance (gothic, historical); science fiction; thriller/espionage; westerns/frontier; political satire. Query. Reports in 2 weeks on queries; 6-8 weeks on solicited mss.

Terms: Agent receives 10% commission on domestic sales; 20% on foreign sales. Offers written contract, binding for 6 months-2 years. "Some editorial support is available to our signed clients." Writer offsets expenses for long distance tolls, postage, photocopying and any unusual expenses, all agreed upon in advance.
Writers' Conferences: Attends Brown Symposium held at Southwestern University in Georgetown, Texas in February 1994.
Tips: Obtains new clients through well-written queries and referrals. "Always include SASE with your letter of query. All our agents will consider a new writer. We'd rather not read first drafts or unfinished work. Please, no phone queries."

‡**DONALD MAASS LITERARY AGENCY (III)**, Suite 1003, 157 West 57th St., New York NY 10019. (212)757-7755. Contact: Donald Maass. Estab. 1980. Member of AAR. Represents 55 clients. 5% of clients are new/previously unpublished writers. Specializes in commercial fiction, especially science fiction, fantasy, mystery, suspense. Currently handles: 100% novels.
Handles: Novels. Considers these fiction areas: detective/police/crime; family saga; fantasy; historical; literary; mainstream; mystery/suspense; psychic/supernatural; science fiction; thriller/espionage; westerns/frontier. Query with SASE. Reports in 2 weeks on queries, 2-3 months on mss (if requested following query).
Recent Sales: *The Wolf of Winter*, by Paula Volsky (Bantam/Spectra); *A Sudden, Fearful Death*, by Anne Perry (Fawcett Columbine); *Dark Mirror*, by Diane Duane (Pocket Books/Star Trek); *I, Strahd*, by P.N. Elrod (TSR).
Terms: Agent receives 15% commission on domestic sales; 20% on foreign sales. "Manuscript copying for auction charged separately."
Writers' Conferences: Attends World Science Fiction Convention; will attend Malice Domestic, to be held in Bethesda, Maryland from April 23-25.
Tips: "Most new clients are established authors referred by clients, publishers and other writers. We are fiction specialists. Few new clients are accepted, but interested authors should query with SASE. Subagents in all principle foreign countries and Hollywood. No nonfiction or juvenile works considered."

MARGRET MCBRIDE LITERARY AGENCY (II), Suite 225, 4350 Executive Dr., San Diego CA 92121. (619)457-0550. Fax: (619)457-2315. Contact: Winifred Golden or Susan Travis. Estab. 1980. Member of AAR. Represents 40 clients. 10% of clients are new/unpublished writers. Specializes in mainstream fiction and nonfiction.
Handles: Publishing, audio, video film rights. Query with synopsis or outline. Does not read unsolicited mss. Reports in 6 weeks on queries.
Recent Sales: *Let Us Prey*, by Bill Branon (HarperCollins); *Brules*, by Harry Combs (Delacorte); *Don't Fire Them, Fire Them Up*, by Frank Pacetta (Simon & Schuster); *Coffee Will Make You Black*, by April Sinclair (Hyperion); *Technotrends*, by Dan Burnes (Harper Business).
Terms: Agent receives 15% commission on domestic sales; 10% on dramatic sales; 25% on foreign sales.

DONALD MACCAMPBELL INC. (III), 12 E. 41st St., New York NY 10017. (212)683-5580. Editor: Maureen Moran. Estab. 1940. Represents 50 clients. "The agency does not handle unpublished writers." Specializes in women's book-length fiction in all categories. Currently handles: 100% novels.
Handles: Novels. Query; does not read unsolicited mss. Reports in 1 week on queries.
Recent Sales: *Sins of the Children*, by Emilie Richards (Dell); *Alpine* mystery series, by Mary Daheim (Ballentine); *Playhouse Wench*, by Margaret Porter (NAL).
Terms: Agent receives 10% commission on domestic sales; 20% on foreign sales.

‡**GERARD MCCAULEY (III)**, P.O. Box AE, Katonah NY 10536. (914)232-5700. Fax: (914)232-1506. Estab. 1970. Member of AAR. Represents 60 clients. 10% of clients are new/previously unpublished writers. Specializes in history, biography and general nonfiction. Currently handles: 65% nonfiction books; 15% scholarly books; 20% textbooks. "Developing commercial fiction list through Henry O. Houghton. Write 53 Garland Rd., Concord MA 01742."
Handles: Nonfiction books, textbooks, novels ("novels go to Henry Houghton"). Considers these nonfiction areas: biography/autobiography; current affairs; history; military/war; sports. Query. Reports in 1 month on queries; 2 months on mss.

Recent Sales: *Great Good Food*, by Julee Rosso (Crown); *Life Work*, by Donald Hall (Beacon).
Terms: Agent receives 15% commission on domestic sales; 20% on foreign sales. Charges for "postage for all submissions and photocopying."
Tips: Obtains new clients through recommendations. "Always send a personal letter—not a form letter with recommendations from published writers."

ANITA D. MCCLELLAN ASSOCIATES (III), 50 Stearns St., Cambridge MA 02138. Estab. 1988. Member of AAR, Boston Literary Agents' Society. 25% of clients are new/previously unpublished writers. Specializes in general book-length trade fiction and nonfiction.
Handles: Query with SASE only. No computer or technical books, cookbooks, science fiction or horror fiction, or young adult fiction. "No certified mail, no telephone queries, no unsolicited manuscripts." 50-page maximum on sample material. Reports in 3 weeks on queries.
Recent Sales: *The China Bayles Mystery Series*, by Susan Wittig Albert (Scribner's/Berkley PA).
Terms: Agent receives 15% commission on domestic sales; 20% on foreign sales. Charges for photocopying, postage, copies of galleys and books, fax and telephone.
Writers' Conferences: Attends International Feminist Book Fair; National Writers Union Conference.

GINA MACCOBY LITERARY AGENCY (II), Suite 1010, 1123 Broadway, New York NY 10010. (212)627-9210. Contact: Gina Maccoby. Estab. 1986. Represents 30 clients. Currently handles: 33% nonfiction books; 33% juvenile books; 33% novels. Represents illustrators of children's books.
Handles: Nonfiction, juvenile books, novels. Considers these nonfiction areas: biography; current affairs; ethnic/cultural interests; juvenile nonfiction; dance/theater/film; women's issues/women's studies. Considers these fiction areas: literary; juvenile; mainstream; mystery/suspense; thriller/espionage; young adult. Query with SASE. Reports in 4-6 weeks.
Recent Sales: *Snapshot*, by Linda Barnes (Delacorte); *The Old Woman & Her Pig*, by Rosanne Litzinger (Harcourt Brace Jovanovich).
Terms: Agent receives 10% commission on domestic sales; 20-25% on foreign sales. May recover certain costs such as airmail postage to Europe or Japan or legal fees.
Tips: Usually obtains new clients through recommendations from own clients.

RICHARD P. MCDONOUGH, LITERARY AGENT (II), P.O. Box 1950, Boston MA 02130. (617)522-6388. Contact: Richard P. McDonough. Estab. 1986. Represents 30 clients. 50% of clients are new/unpublished writers. Works with unpublished and published writers "whose work I think has merit and requires a committed advocate." Specializes in nonfiction for general contract and fiction. Currently handles: 80% nonfiction books; 10% novels.
Handles: Nonfiction books, novels. Query with outline and SASE or send 3 chapters and SASE. Reports in 2 weeks on queries; 5 weeks on mss.
Recent Sales: *Parents Who Love Reading, Kids Who Don't*, by M. Leonhardt (Crown); *We Will Gather at the River*, by M.R. Montgomery (Simon & Schuster).
Terms: Agent receives 15% commission on domestic sales; 15% on dramatic sales; 15% on foreign sales. Charges for photocopying, phone beyond 300 miles; postage for sold work only.

HELEN MCGRATH (III), 1406 Idaho Ct., Concord CA 94521. (510)672-6211. Contact: Helen McGrath. Estab. 1977. Currently handles: 50% nonfiction books; 50% novels. Member agent: Doris Johnson (fantasy, mystery).
Handles: Nonfiction books, novels. Considers these nonfiction areas: biography; business; current affairs; health/medicine; history; military/war; psychology; self-help/personal improvement; sports; women's issues/women's studies; how-to. Considers these fiction areas: contemporary issues; detective/police/crime; family saga; literary; mainstream; mystery/suspense; psychic/supernatural; science fiction; sports; thriller/espionage; westerns/frontier. Query with proposal and SASE. No unsolicited mss. Reports in 6-8 weeks on queries.
Terms: Agent receives 15% commission on domestic sales. Sometimes offers written contract. Charges for photocopying. $35 processing fee for proposals from authors who have not published a book in past 6 years.
Tips: Usually obtains new clients through recommendations from others.

ROBERT MADSEN AGENCY (I), Suite #1, 1331 E. 34th St., Oakland CA 94602. (510)223-2090. Agent: Robert Madsen. Senior Editor: Kim Van Nguyen. Estab. 1992. Represents 5 clients. 100% of clients are new/previously unpublished writers. Currently handles 25% nonfiction books; 25% fiction books; 25% movie scripts; 25% TV scripts.
Handles: Fiction, nonfiction, film, TV, radio, video, theater. Considers these nonfiction areas: how-to; science; self-help; true crime; history (ancient and myth); political; military; social environment. Considers these fiction areas: action/adventure; humor; mens; mystery; romance; science fiction/fantasy; western. "Willing to look at subject matter that is specialized, controversial, even unpopular, esoteric and outright bizarre. However, it is strongly suggested that authors query first, to save themselves and this agency time, trouble and expense." Query. Reports in 1 month on queries; 2-3 months on mss.
Terms: Agent receives 10% commission on domestic sales; 20% on foreign sales. Offers written contract, binding for 3 years.
Tips: Obtains new clients through recommendations, or by query. "Be certain to take care of business basics in appearance, ease of reading and understanding proper presentation and focus. Be sure to include sufficient postage and SASE with all submissions."

CAROL MANN AGENCY (II,III), 55 Fifth Ave., New York NY 10003. (212)206-5635. Fax: (212)463-8718. Contact: Carol Mann. Estab. 1977. Member of AAR. Represents 100+ clients. 25% of clients are new/previously unpublished writers. Specializes in current affairs; self-help; psychology; parenting; history. Currently handles: 80% nonfiction books; 15% scholarly books; 5% novels. Member agent: Gareth Esersky (contemporary nonfiction).
Handles: Nonfiction books. Considers these nonfiction areas: anthropology/archaeology; art/architecture/design; biography/autobiography; business; child guidance/parenting; current affairs; ethnic/cultural interests; government/politics/law; health/medicine; history; interior design/decorating; money/finance/economics; psychology; self-help/personal improvement; sociology; true crime/investigative; women's issues/women's studies. Considers literary fiction. Query with outline/proposal and SASE. Reports in 3 weeks on queries.
Recent Sales: *Leviathan*, by Paul Auster (Viking/Penguin); *Breaking Blue*, by Tim Egan (Knopf); *Family Affairs*, by Andy Hoffman (Pocket); *Wild Women Don't Wear No Blues*, edited by Marita Golden (Doubleday).
Terms: Agent receives 15% commission on domestic sales; 20% on foreign sales. Offers written contract, binding for 1 year.

MARCH TENTH, INC. (III), 4 Myrtle St., Haworth NJ 07641. (201)387-6551. Fax: (201)387-6552. President: Sandra Choron. Estab. 1982. Represents 40 clients. 5% of clients are new/unpublished writers. "Writers must have professional expertise in the field in which they are writing." Prefers to work with published/established writers. Currently handles: 100% nonfiction books.
Handles: Nonfiction books. Query. Does not read unsolicited mss. Reports in 1 month.
Recent Sales: *U2 Zoo Too*, by B.P. Fallon (Little Brown); *Louie Louie: A Social History Of The Song*, by Dave Marsh (Hyperion); *The College Finder*, by Steven Antonoff (Ballantine).
Terms: Agent receives 15% commission on domestic sales; 20% on dramatic sales; 20% on foreign sales. Charges writers for postage, photocopying, overseas phone expenses.

BARBARA MARKOWITZ LITERARY AGENCY (II), 117 N. Mansfield Ave., Los Angeles CA 90036. (213)939-5927. Literary Agent/President: Barbara Markowitz. Estab. 1980. Represents 14 clients. Works with a small number of new/unpublished authors. Specializes in mid-level and YA; contemporary fiction; adult trade fiction and nonfiction. Currently handles: 25% nonfiction books; 25% novels; 50% juvenile books.
Handles: Nonfiction books, novels, juvenile books. Open to all adult fiction, especially contemporary fiction, detective/mystery/suspense/humor, as well as biography and sports. Query with outline. SASE required for return of any material. Reports in 3 weeks.
Recent Sales: *Sports Headliners*, by Sanford & Green (Crestwood/Macmillan); *Today's Chuckle*, by Paul Collins (Perigee/Putnam).
Terms: Agent receives 15% commission on domestic sales; 15% on dramatic sales; 15% on foreign sales. Charges writers for mailing, postage.
Tips: "We do *not* agent pre-school or early reader books. Only mid-level and YA contemporary fiction and historical fiction. We receive an abundance of pre-school and early reader mss, which our agency returns if accompanied by SASE."

Literary Agents: Nonfee-charging 87

ELAINE MARKSON LITERARY AGENCY (II), 44 Greenwich Ave., New York NY 10011. (212)243-8480. Estab. 1972. Member of AAR. Represents 200 clients. 10% of clients are new/unpublished writers. Specializes in literary fiction, commercial fiction, trade nonfiction. Currently handles: 30% nonfiction books; 40% novels; 20% juvenile books; 5% movie scripts. Member Agents: Geri Thoma, Sally Wofford Girand, Elaine Markson.
Handles: Novels, nonfiction books. Query with outline (must include SASE). SASE is required for the return of any material.
Terms: Agent receives 15% commission on domestic sales; 10% on dramatic sales; 20% on foreign sales. Charges for postage, photocopying, foreign mailing, faxing, long-distance telephone and other special expenses.

MILDRED MARMUR ASSOCIATES LTD. (II), Suite 724, 310 Madison Ave., New York NY 10017. (212)949-6055. Fax: (212)687-6894. Contact: Mildred Marmur. Estab. 1987. Member of AAR. Specializes in serious nonfiction, literary fiction, juveniles, illustrators. Member agents: Mildred Marmur (submissions to book publishers); Jennie Dunham (subsidiary rights for books under contract and juvenile list).
Handles: Nonfiction books, novels. Considers these nonfiction areas: biography/autobiography; business; cooking/food/nutrition; current affairs; ethnic/cultural interests; government/politics/law; health/medicine; history; juvenile nonfiction; military war; money/finance/economics; music/dance/theater/film; nature/environment; religious/inspirational; science/technology; sports; true crime/investigative; women's issues/women's studies. Considers these fiction areas: contemporary issues; detective/police/crime; family saga; feminist; juvenile; literary; mainstream; mystery/suspense; thriller/espionage; young adult. Query with SASE. Reports in 4 weeks on queries.
Terms: Agent receives 15% commission on domestic sales; 20% on foreign sales. Sometimes offers written contract (book-by-book). 100% of business derived from commissions on ms sales.
Tips: Obtains new clients through recommendations from other clients. "Browse in a bookstore or library and look at the acknowledgments in books similar to yours. If an author of a nonfiction book in your general area thanks his or her agent, send your manuscript to that person and point out the link. If you can't figure out who the agent is, try phoning the publisher. At least you'll have a more targeted person. Also, agents are more receptive to written submissions than to pitches over the phone."

THE MARTELL AGENCY (III), Suite 1900, 555 Fifth Ave., New York NY 10017. (212)692-9770. Contact: Bryan Minogue or Alice Fried Martell. Estab. 1984. Represents 75 clients. Currently handles: 65% nonfiction books; 35% novels.
Handles: Nonfiction books, novels. Considers all nonfiction areas. Considers most fiction areas. No science fiction or poetry. Query with outline plus 2 sample chapters and SASE. Reports in 3 weeks on queries, only if interested.
Terms: Agent receives 15% commission on domestic sales; 20% on foreign sales. Offers written contract, binding for 1 year. Charges for foreign postage, photocopying.
Tips: Usually obtains new clients by recommendations from agents and editors.

HAROLD MATSON CO. INC., 276 Fifth Ave., New York NY 10001. Prefers not to share information.

MGA AGENCY INC. (II), Suite 510, 10 St. Mary St., Toronto, ON M4Y 1P9 Canada. (416)964-3302. Fax: (416)975-9209. Contact: Linda McKnight. Estab. 1989. Represents approximately 200 clients. Currently handles: 50% nonfiction books; 40% fiction, 10% juvenile books.
Handles: Nonfiction books, novels. Considers all nonfiction areas. Considers these fiction areas: juvenile; mystery/suspense; picture book; romance; science fiction; young adult. Query with résumé and SASE. Reports in 4-6 weeks on queries.
Recent Sales: *A Song For Arbonne*, by Guy Gauniel Kay (Crown); *You Never Know*, by Isabel Huggan (Viking).
Terms: Agent receives 15% commission on domestic sales; 20% on foreign sales. Offers written contract. Charges for postage, photocopying, fax.
Tips: Usually obtains new clients through recommendations from others and at conferences.

ROBERTA D. MILLER ASSOCIATES (I), 42 E. 12th St., New York NY 10003. Contact: Roberta D. Miller. Estab. 1991. Represents 6 clients. 75% of clients are new/previously unpublished writers. Specializes in literary fiction, young adult. Currently handles: 25% juvenile books; 75% novels. Member agents: Elisabeth Whelan (young adult).

Handles: Nonfiction books, juvenile books, novels. Considers these nonfiction areas: art/architecture/design; biography/autobiography; current affairs; ethnic/cultural interests; language/literature/criticism. Considers these fiction areas: contemporary issues; detective/police/crime; humor/satire; literary; mainstream; young adult. Query with outline plus 1 sample chapter. Reports in 1 month on mss.
Recent Sales: *Kingsland*, by Rosemary Cassata (Vik.).
Terms: Agent receives 15% commission on domestic sales; 25% on foreign sales. Offers written contract. Charges for photocopying, international postage, fax charges. 100% of business derived from commissions on ms sales.
Tips: Obtains new clients from recommendations, agent listings, editors. "US authors only, please."

MOORE LITERARY AGENCY, 4 Dove St., Newburyport MA 01950. (508)465-9015. Fax: (508)465-8817. Contact: Claudette Moore. Estab. 1989. 20% of clients are new/previously unpublished writers. Specializes in trade computer books. Currently handles: 100% computer-related books.
Handles: Computer books only. Send outline/proposal. Reports in 3 weeks on queries.
Recent Sales: *Van Wolverton's Guide to Windows*, by Van Wolverton and Michael Boom (Random House).
Terms: Agent receives 15% commission on all sales. Offers written contract, varies book by book.
Tips: Obtains new clients through recommendations/referrals and conferences.

‡HOWARD MORHAIM LITERARY AGENCY (II), Suite 709, 175 Fifth Ave., New York NY 10010. (212)529-4433. Fax: (212)995-1112. Contact: Howard Morhaim or Allison Mullen. Estab. 1978. Member of AAR. Represents 60 clients. 15% of clients are new/previously unpublished writers. Currently handles: 15% nonfiction books; 5% juvenile books; 75% novels; 2% novellas; 3% short story collections. Member agent: Allison Mullen (women's fiction, romance, mysteries/thrillers).
Handles: Nonfiction books, novels. Considers these fiction areas: detective/police/crime; family saga; glitz; historical; mainstream; mystery/suspense; romance (contemporary, gothic, historical, regency); thriller/espionage. Send outline plus 3 sample chapters. Reports in 1 week on queries; 6 weeks on ms.
Terms: Agent receives 15% commission on domestic sales; 20% on foreign sales. Charges for photocopying only.
Tips: Obtains new clients through recommendations from others; conferences.

WILLIAM MORRIS AGENCY (III), 1350 Avenue of the Americas, New York NY 10019. (212)586-5100. Estab. 1898. Member of AAR. Works with a small number of new/unpublished authors. Specializes in novels, nonfiction.
Handles: Nonfiction books, novels. Query only. Reports in 6 weeks.
Terms: Agent receives 10% commission on domestic sales; 10% on dramatic sales; 20% on foreign sales.

HENRY MORRISON, INC. (II), P.O. Box 235, Bedford Hills NY 10507. "We tend to represent primarily novel-length fiction, in such areas as international thrillers, science fiction and mysteries. We also handle the occasional nonfiction book and screenplay."

MULTIMEDIA PRODUCT DEVELOPMENT, INC. (III), Suite 724, 410 S. Michigan Ave., Chicago IL 60605. (312)922-3063. Fax: (312)922-1905. President: Jane Jordan Browne. Estab. 1971. Member of AAR, RWA, MWA, SCBWI. Represents 100 clients. 5% of clients are new/previously unpublished writers. "We are generalists." Currently handles: 60% nonfiction books; 5% juvenile books; 35% novels.
Handles: Nonfiction books, novels. Considers these nonfiction areas: agriculture/horticulture; animals; biography/autobiography; business; child guidance/parenting; cooking/food/nutrition; current affairs; health/medicine; history; juvenile nonfiction; money/finance; nature; psychology; science/technology; self-help/personal improvement; sociology; true crime/investigative. Considers these fiction areas: detective/police/crime; family saga; glitz; historical; juvenile; mainstream; mystery/suspense; religious/inspirational; romance (contemporary, western historical, regency); thriller/espionage; westerns/frontier. Query "by mail with SASE required. We answer queries with SASE's same or next day, 4-6 weeks on mss."

Recent Sales: *The World of Curries*, by Dave Dewitt Arthur (Little, Brown); *Bengal Rubies*, by Lisa Bingham (Pocket).
Terms: Agent receives 15% commission on domestic sales; 20% on foreign sales. Offers written contract, binding for 2 years. Charges for photocopying, overseas postage, faxes, phone calls.
Tips: Obtains new clients through "referrals, queries by professional, marketable authors. If interested in agency representation, be well informed."

JEAN V. NAGGAR LITERARY AGENCY (III), 1E, 216 E. 75th St., New York NY 10021. (212)794-1082. Contact: Jean Naggar. Estab. 1978. Member of AAR. Represents 100 clients. 20% of clients are new/previously unpublished writers. Currently handles: 30% nonfiction books; 5% scholarly books; 15% juvenile books; 40% novels; 5% short story collections. Member agents: Teresa Cavanaugh, Frances Kuffel. Agent-at-large: Anne Engel (nonfiction).
Handles: Nonfiction books, some juvenile books, novels. Considers these nonfiction areas: biography/autobiography; business; child guidance/parenting; cooking/food/nutrition; current affairs; gay/lesbian issues; government/politics/law; health/medicine; history; interior design/decorating; juvenile nonfiction; money/finance/economics; music/dance/theater/film; New Age/metaphysics; psychology; religious/inspirational; self-help/personal improvement; sociology; true crime/investigative; women's issues/women's studies. "We would, of course, consider a query regarding an exceptional mainstream manuscript touching on any area." Considers these fiction areas: action/adventure; contemporary issues; detective/police/crime; ethnic; family saga; fantasy; feminist; gay; glitz; historical; juvenile; lesbian; literary; mainstream; mystery/suspense; picture book; psychic/supernatural; regional; science fiction; thriller/espionage; young adult. Query. Reports in 24 hours on queries; 2 months on mss.
Recent Sales: *White Man's Grave*, by Richard Dooling (Farrar Straus & Giroux); *Sleep, Baby, Sleep*, by Jessica Auerbach (Putnam's); *Signs of Life, The Language of DNA*, by Robert Pollack (Houghton Mifflin); *The Oracle Glass*, by Judith Merkle Riley (Viking).
Terms: Agent receives 15% commission on domestic sales; 20% on foreign sales. Offers written contract. Charges for overseas mailing; messenger services; book purchases; long-distance telephone; photocopying. "These are deductible from royalties received."
Writers' Conferences: Has attended Willamette Writers Conference; Bread Loaf, Pacific Northwest, Southwest and many others.
Tips: Obtains new clients through "recommendations from publishers, editors, clients and others, and from writers' conferences, as well as from query letters. Use a professional presentation."

RUTH NATHAN (II), Room 706, 80 Fifth Ave., New York NY 10011. Phone and fax: (212)675-6063. Estab. 1980. Member of AAR. Represents 12 clients. 10% of clients are new/previously unpublished writers. Specializes in art, decorative arts, fine art; theater; film; show business. Currently handles: 90% nonfiction books; 10% novels.
Handles: Nonfiction books, novels. Considers these nonfiction areas: art/architecture/design; biography/autobiography; theater/film. Query. Reports in 2 weeks on queries; 1 month on mss.
Recent Sales: *OK Oklahoma*, by Max Wilk (Grove Press); *My Posse Don't Do Homework*, by Lou Anne Johnson (St. Martin's).
Terms: Agent receives 15% commission on domestic sales; 20% on foreign sales. Charges for office expenses, postage, photocopying, etc.
Tips: "Read carefully what my requirements are before wasting your time and mine."

NEW ENGLAND PUBLISHING ASSOCIATES, INC. (II), P.O. Box 5, Chester CT 06412. (203)345-READ and (203)345-4976. Fax: (203)345-3660. Contact: Elizabeth Frost Knappman, Edward W. Knappman, Kathryn Cullen-DuPont. Estab. 1983. Member of AAR. Represents over 100 clients. 15% of clients are new/previously unpublished writers. Specializes in adult nonfiction books of serious purpose.
Handles: Nonfiction books. Considers these nonfiction areas: biography/autobiography; business; child guidance/parenting; government/politics/law; health/medicine; history; language/literature/criticism; military/war; money/finance/economics; nature/environment; psychology; science/technology; self-help/personal improvement; sociology; true crime/investigative; women's issues/women's studies. Send outline/proposal or "phone us to describe your book." Reports in 2 weeks on queries; 3-4 weeks on mss.
Recent Sales: *500 Great Books by Women*, by Dr. Erica Bauermeister, et. al.; *Gay and Lesbian Literary Heritage*, by Claude Summers; *Rebecca West*, by Carl Rollyson; *Atlas of American Battlefields*, by Hubbard Cobb; *Beyond Murder: The Inside Story of the Gainesville Murders*, by John Philpin and John Connelly (all Viking Penguin).

Terms: Agent receives 15% commission on domestic sales; 20% foreign sales (split with overseas agent). Offers a written contract, binding for 6 months.
Tips: "To save time, please call Elizabeth Knappman with adult nonfiction ideas at (203)345-READ. Call Kathryn Cullen-DuPont for fiction or juvenile books at (718)768-8326."

‡**NINE MUSES AND APOLLO (II)**, 2 Charlton St., New York NY 10014. (212)243-0065. Fax: (212)727-3486. Contact: Ling Lucas. Estab. 1991. Represents 50 clients. 50% of clients are new/previously unpublished writers. Specializes in nonfiction. Currently handles: 90% nonfiction books; 10% novels. Member agents: Ling Lucas, Ed Vesneske, Jr.
Handles: Nonfiction books, novels. Considers these nonfiction areas: animals; biography/autobiography; business; current affairs; ethnic/cultural interests; gay/lesbian issues; government/politics/law; health/medicine; history; language/literature/criticism; money/finance/economics; psychology; science/technology; self-help/personal improvement; golf; true crime/investigative; women's issues/women's studies. Considers these fiction areas: commercial; mainstream. Send outline plus 2 sample chapters. Reports in 1 month on mss.
Terms: Agent receives 15% commission on domestic sales; 25% on foreign sales. Offers written contract. Charges for photocopying proposals and manuscripts.
Tips: "Your outline should already be well developed, cogent and reveal clarity of thought about the general structure and direction of your project."

THE BETSY NOLAN LITERARY AGENCY (II), Suite 9W, 50 W. 29th St., New York NY 10001. (212)779-0700. Fax: (212)689-0376. President: Betsy Nolan. Agents: Donald Lehr and Carla Glasser. Estab. 1980. Represents 100 clients. 10% of clients are new/unpublished writers. Works with a small number of new/unpublished authors. Currently handles: 80% nonfiction books; 20% novels.
Handles: Nonfiction books, novels. Query with outline. Reports in 2 weeks on queries; 2 months on mss.
Terms: Agent receives 15% commission on domestic sales; 20% on foreign sales.

‡**EDWARD A. NOVAK III LITERARY REPRESENTATION (II)**, Suite 1, 711 N. Second St., Harrisburg PA 17102. (717)232-8081. Fax: (717)232-7020. Contact: Ed Novak. Estab. 1991. Represents 26 clients. 65% of clients are new/previously unpublished writers. Currently handles: 84% nonfiction books; 16% novels.
Handles: Nonfiction books, novels. Considers these nonfiction areas: art/architecture/design; biography/autobiography; business; child guidance/parenting; current affairs; ethnic/cultural interests; gay/lesbian issues; government/politics/law; health/medicine; history; military/war; money/finance/economics; music/dance/theater/film; nature/environment; science/technology; self-help/personal improvement; sports; true crime/investigative; women's issues/women's studies. Considers these fiction areas: contemporary issues; detective/police/crime; historical; literary; mainstream; mystery/suspense; romance (contemporary, historical); sports; thriller/espionage. Query. Reports in 1 month on queries; 2 months on mss.
Recent Sales: *Our World*, by Michael D. Davis (William Morrow/Avon); *One Up on the Money Managers*, by Anthony R. Gray (Macmillan); *Untitled on Coach Bob Knight*, by Lee Daniel Levine (Simon & Schuster/Pocket Books).
Terms: Agent receives 15% commission on domestic sales; 19% on foreign sales. Offers written contract. Charges for photocopying only.
Tips: Obtains new clients "mostly through referrals, some through my own solicitation, a few through unsolicited queries."

HAROLD OBER ASSOCIATES (III), 425 Madison Ave., New York NY 10017. (212)759-8600. Fax: (212)759-9428. Estab. 1929. Member of AAR. Represents 250 clients. 15% of clients are new/previously unpublished writers. Currently handles: 35% nonfiction books; 15% juvenile books; 50% novels. Member agents: Claire Smith, Phyllis Westberg, Peter Shepherd, Henry Dunow, Wendy Schmalz.

Agents ranked I and II are most open to both established and new writers. Agents ranked III are open to established writers with publishing-industry references.

Literary Agents: Nonfee-charging 91

Handles: Nonfiction books, juvenile books, novels. Considers all nonfiction and fiction subjects. Query lettery *only*. Reports in 1 week on queries; 2-3 weeks on mss.
Terms: Agent receives 10-15% commission on domestic sales; 15-20% on foreign sales. Charges for photocopying for multiple submissions.
Tips: Obtains new clients through recommendations from others.

‡**ALICE ORR AGENCY, INC. (V)**, Suite 1166, 305 Madison Ave., New York NY 10165. Agency not currently seeking new clients, especially not unpublished authors.

‡**FIFI OSCARD AGENCY INC. (II)**, 24 W. 40th St., New York NY 10018. (212)764-1100. Contact: Ivy Fischer Stone, Literary Department. Estab. 1956. Member of AAR, signatory of WGA. Represents 108 clients. 5% of clients are new/unpublished writers. "Writer must have published articles or books in major markets or have screen credits if movie scripts, etc." Specializes in literary novels, commercial novels, mysteries and nonfiction, especially celebrity biographies and autobiographies. Currently handles: 40% nonfiction books; 40% novels; 5% movie scripts; 5% stage plays; 10% TV scripts.
Handles: Nonfiction books, novels, movie scripts, stage plays. Query with outline. Reports in 1 week on queries if SASE enclosed.
Recent Sales: *Tek Secret*, by William Shatner (Putnam's); *Daddy and Me*, by Jeanne Moutoussamy-Ashe (Knopf); *Days of Grace*, by Arthur Ashe and Arnold Rampersad (Knopf); *Star Trek Memories*, by William Shatner with Khris Kreski (HarperCollins).
Terms: Agent receives 15% commission on domestic sales; 10% on dramatic sales; 20% on foreign sales. Charges for photocopying expenses.

‡**OTITIS MEDIA (II)**, 1926 DuPont Ave. S., Minneapolis MN 55403. (612)377-4918. Contact: Richard Boylan or Hannibal Harris. Member of WGA. Currently handles: novels; movie scripts; stage plays; TV scripts. Member agents: B.R. Boylan (novels, nonfiction, screenplays, stage plays); Hannibal Harris (queries, evaluation of proposals, books); Greg Boylan (screenplays, TV scripts, documentaries); Ingrid DiLeonardo (script and ms evaluation, story development).
Handles: Nonfiction books, novels, movie scripts, stage plays, TV scripts. Considers these nonfiction areas: anthropology/archaeology; biography/autobiography; cooking/food/nutrition; ethnic cultural interests; gay/lesbian issues; government/politics/law; health/medicine; history; language/literature/criticism; military/war; music/dance/theater/film; photography; true crime/investigative; self-help/personal improvement; sports; women's issue's/women's studies. Considers these fiction areas: action/adventure; detective/police/crime; fantasy; historical; humor/satire; literary; mainstream; mystery/suspense; picture book; psychic/supernatural; regional; thriller/espionage. Send outline/proposal. Reports in 1-2 weeks on queries.
Terms: Agent receives 10% on domestic sales; negotiable on foreign sales. Offers letter of agreement. "We prefer that the writer pay for his own copying. In drawn out negotiations or auctions, we might charge for postage, phone and fax—but this is unlikely."
Tips: Obtains new clients through recommendations and "also from listings in legit books and with organizations. Talk to one or more reputable agents *before* showing anything to producers or publishers. Beware anyone who asks for free options or token advances. Learn the going minimal rates of payment for books and scripts. Also, don't show your writing to friends or relatives for evaluation. Always try to find someone who has no emotional barriers to giving you an honest opinion."

THE OTTE COMPANY (II), 9 Goden St., Belmont MA 02178. (617)484-8505. Contact: Jane H. Otte or L. David Otte. Estab. 1973. Represents 35 clients. 33% of clients are new/unpublished writers. Works with a small number of new/unpublished authors. Specializes in quality adult trade books. Currently handles: 40% nonfiction books; 60% novels.
Handles: Nonfiction books, novels. "Does not handle poetry, juvenile or 'by-the-number' romance." Query. Reports in 1 week on queries; 1 month on mss.
Terms: Agent receives 15% commission on domestic sales; 7^1/2% on dramatic sales; 10% on foreign sales plus 10% to foreign agent. Charges for photocopying, overseas phone and postage expenses.

THE RICHARD PARKS AGENCY (III), 5th Floor, 138 E. 16th St., New York NY 10003. (212)254-9067. Fax: (212)228-1786. Contact: Richard Parks. Estab. 1988. Member of AAR. Currently handles: 50% nonfiction books; 5% young adult books; 40% novels; 5% short story collections.
Handles: Nonfiction books, novels. Considers these nonfiction areas: horticulture; animals; anthropology/archaeology; art/architecture/design; biography/autobiography; business; child guidance/parenting; cooking/food/nutrition; crafts/hobbies; current affairs; ethnic/cultural interests; gay/lesbian issues;

government/politics; health/medicine; history; language/literature/criticism; military/war; money/finance/economics; music/dance/theater/film; nature/environment; psychology; science/technology; self-help/personal improvement; sociology; true crime/investigative; women's issues/women's studies. Considers these fiction areas: action/adventure; contemporary issues; detective/police/crime; family saga; gay; glitz; historical; lesbian; literary; mainstream; mystery/suspense; psychic/supernatural; thriller/espionage; westerns/frontier; young adult. Query with SASE. "We will not accept any unsolicited material." Reports in 2 weeks on queries.
Recent Sales: *Spidertown*, by Abraham Rodriguez, Jr. (Hyperion); *Gun, with Occasional Music*, by Jonathan Lethen (Harcourt Brace).
Terms: Agent receives 15% commission on domestic sales; 20% on foreign sales. Charges for photocopying or any unusual expense incurred at the writer's request.
Tips: Obtains new clients through recommendations and referrals.

KATHI J. PATON LITERARY AGENCY (II), 19 W. 55th St., New York NY 10019-4907. (212)265-6586. Fax: call first. Contact: Kathi Paton. Estab. 1987. Specializes in adult nonfiction. Currently handles: 65% nonfiction books; 35% fiction.
Handles: Nonfiction, novels, short story collections. Considers these nonfiction areas: business; sociology; psychology; women's issues/women's studies; how-to. Considers literary and mainstream fiction; short stories. For nonfiction, send proposal, sample chapter and SASE. For fiction, send first 40 pages and plot summary or 3 short stories.
Recent Sales: *Total Customer Service*, by Bro Uttal (HarperCollins); *The Myth of the Bad Mother*, by Jane Swigart (Doubleday); *White Trash, Red Velvet*, by Donald Secreast (HarperCollins).
Terms: Agent receives 15% commission on domestic sales; 20% on foreign sales. Offers written contract. Length of time binding is on a per-book basis. Charges for photocopying.
Writers' Conferences: Attends International Womens Writing Guild panels and the Pacific Northwest Writers Conference.
Tips: Usually obtains new clients through recommendations from other clients. "Write well."

RODNEY PELTER (II), 129 E. 61st St., New York NY 10021. (212)838-3432. Contact: Rodney Pelter. Estab. 1978. Represents 10-12 clients. Currently handles: 25% nonfiction books; 75% novels.
Handles: Nonfiction books, novels. Considers all nonfiction areas. Considers most fiction areas. No juvenile, romance, science fiction. For nonfiction, query with SASE. For fiction, send outline, first 50-75 pages and SASE. Reports in 1-3 months.
Terms: Agent receives 15% commission on domestic sales; 20% on foreign sales. Offers written contract. Charges for foreign postage, photocopying.
Tips: Usually obtains new clients through recommendations from others.

L. PERKINS ASSOCIATES (IV), 5800 Arlington Ave., Riverdale NY 10471. (718)543-5344. Fax: (718)543-5355. Contact: Lori Perkins, Peter Rubie. Estab. 1990. Member of AAR, HWA. Represents 100 clients. 15% of clients are new/previously unpublished writers. Perkins specializes in horror, dark thrillers, literary fiction, pop culture. Rubie specializes in science fiction, fantasy, mysteries, history, fiction thrillers, journalistic nonfiction. Currently handles: 40% nonfiction books; 60% novels.
Handles: Nonfiction books, novels. Considers these nonfiction areas: art/architecture/design; current affairs; ethnic/cultural interests; music/dance/theater/film; "subjects that fall under pop culture—TV, music, art, books and authors, film, current affairs etc." Considers these fiction areas: adventure; detective/police/crime; ethnic; horror; literary; mainstream; mystery/suspense; psychic/supernatural; thriller. Query with SASE. Reports immediately on queries "with SASE"; 6-10 weeks on mss.
Recent Sales: *A Darker Shade of Crimson: Memoirs of a Harvard-Chicano* (Bantam); *Burning Down the House*, by Merry McInerny (Tor).
Terms: Agent receives 15% commission on domestic sales; 20% on foreign sales. Offers written contract, only "if requested." Charges for photocopying.
Writers' Conferences: Attends Horror Writers of America Conference; World Fantasy Conference; Necon and Lunacon; Southwest Writers Conference; MidAtlantic Writers Conference; ABA; Cape Cod Writers Conference.

Agents who specialize in a specific subject area such as children's books or in handling the work of certain writers such as Latino writers are ranked IV.

Literary Agents: Nonfee-charging   93

Tips: Obtains new clients through recommendations from others, solicitation, at conferences, etc. "Sometimes I come up with book ideas and find authors (*Coupon Queen*, for example). Be professional. Read *Publishers Weekly* and genre-related magazines. Join writers' organizations. Go to conferences. Know your market."

PERKINS' LITERARY AGENCY (V), P.O. Box 48, Childs MD 21916. Agent not currently seeking new clients, except by referral.

JAMES PETER ASSOCIATES, INC. (III,IV), P.O. Box 772, Tenafly NJ 07670. (201)568-0760. Fax: (201)568-2959. Contact: Bert Holtje. Estab. 1971. Member of AAR. Represents 84 clients. 5% of clients are new/previously unpublished writers. Specializes in nonfiction (history, politics, psychology, health, popular culture, business, biography, reference). Currently handles: 100% nonfiction books.
Handles: Nonfiction books. Considers these nonfiction areas: anthropology/archaeology; art/architecture/design; biography/autobiography; business; crafts/hobbies; current affairs; ethnic/cultural interests; government/politics/law; health/medicine; history; interior design/decorating; military/war; money/finance/economics; psychology; self-help/personal improvement. Send outline/proposal and SASE. Reports in 3-4 weeks on queries.
Recent Sales: *Psychological Symptoms*, by Frank Bruno, Ph.D. (John Wiley & Sons); *What Every American Should Know About American History*, by Alan Axelrod, Charles Phillips (Bob Adams, Inc.).
Terms: Agent receives 15% commission on domestic sales; 20% on foreign sales. Offers written contract; "separate contracts written for each project." Charges for photocopying.
Tips: Obtains new clients through "recommendations from other clients and publishing house editors. I read widely in areas which interest me and contact people who write articles on subjects which could be books. Be an expert in an interesting field, and be able to write well on the subject. Be flexible."

ALISON J. PICARD LITERARY AGENT (II), P.O. Box 2000, Cotuit MA 02635. (508)420-6163. Fax: (508)420-0762. Contact: Alison Picard. Assistant: Janet Burke. Estab. 1985. Represents 60 clients. 25% of clients are new/previously unpublished writers. "Most interested in nonfiction at this time, especially self-help/recovery, pop psychology, how-to, business and current affairs." Currently handles: 40% nonfiction books; 30% juvenile books; 30% novels.
Handles: Considers any general trade nonfiction. Considers any fiction areas except science fiction/fantasy. Query with SASE. Send written query first. No phone/fax queries. Reports in 1 week on queries; 1 month on mss.
Recent Sales: *Proud to Be*, by Amy Dean (Bantam Books); *The King's Shadow*, by Elizabeth Alder (Farrar, Straus and Giroux).
Terms: Agent receives 15% commission on domestic sales; 15% on foreign sales.
Writers' Conferences: Attends Cape Cod Writer's Conference.
Tips: Obtains new clients through recommendations.

AARON M. PRIEST LITERARY AGENCY (II), 23rd Floor, 708 Third Ave., New York NY 10017. (212)818-0344. Contact: Aaron Priest or Molly Friedrich. Currently handles: 50% nonfiction books; 50% fiction.
Handles: Nonfiction books, fiction. Query only (must be accompanied by SASE). Unsolicited mss will be returned unread.
Recent Sales: *Waiting to Exhale*, by Terry McMillan; *A Thousand Acres*, by Jane Smiley; *Day After Tomorrow*, by Allan Folsom.
Terms: Agent receives 15% commission on domestic sales. Charges for photocopying, foreign postage expenses.

SUSAN ANN PROTTER LITERARY AGENT (II), Suite 1408, 110 W. 40th St., New York NY 10018. (212)840-0480. Contact: Susan Protter. Estab. 1971. Member of AAR. Represents 50 clients. 10% of clients are new/unpublished writers. Writer must have book-length project or ms that is ready to be sold. Works with a small number of new/unpublished authors. Currently handles: 30% nonfiction books; 65% novels; 5% magazine articles (for established clients only).
Handles: Nonfiction books, novels. Considers these nonfiction areas: general nonfiction; biography; health/medicine; psychology; science. Considers these fiction areas: mystery; science fiction; thrillers. Send short query with brief description of project/novel. Please include publishing history. "Must include SASE." Reports in 2-3 weeks on queries; 6 weeks on solicited mss. "Please do not call; mail queries only."

94 *Guide to Literary Agents & Art/Photo Reps '94*

Recent Sales: *Peteys,* by Terry Bisson (TOR); *The Hacker and the Ants,* by Rudy Rucker (Morrow/Avonova); *Dr. Nightingale* (mystery series) by Lynn Armistead McKee (Signet); *Walks In Stardust* by Lynn Armistead McKee (Diamond/Berkley); *Electric Revelation,* by David G. Hartwell and Kathryn Kramer (TOR); *Bears Discover Fire and Other Stories,* by Terry Bisson (TOR).
Terms: Agent receives 15% commission on domestic sales; 15% on TV, film and dramatic sales; 25% on foreign sales. Charges for long distance, photocopying, messenger, express mail, airmail expenses.
Tips: "Please send neat and professionally organized queries. Make sure to include an SASE or we cannot reply. We receive up to 100 queries a week and read them in the order they arrive. We usually reply within two weeks to any query. Do not call. If you are sending a multiple query, make sure to note that in your letter."

ROBERTA PRYOR, INC. (II), 24 W. 55th St., New York NY 10019. (212)245-0420. President: Roberta Pryor. Estab. 1985. Member of AAR. Represents 50 clients. Prefers to work with published/established authors; works with a small number of new/unpublished writers. Specializes in serious nonfiction and (tends toward) literary fiction. Special interest in natural history, good cookbooks. Currently handles: 50% nonfiction books; 40% novels; 10% textbooks; 10% juvenile books.
Handles: Nonfiction books, novels, textbooks, juvenile books. Query. SASE required for any correspondence. Reports in 10 weeks on queries.
Recent Sales: *New York, New York: How the Apartment House Transformed the Life of the City,* by Elizabeth Hawes (Knopf); *Strike of the Cobra,* by Timothy Rizzi (techno-thriller, Donald I Fine); *Imaginary Men,* by Enid Shomer (short stories, University of Iowa Press).
Terms: Charges 15% commission on domestic sales; 10% on film sales; 20% on foreign sales. Charges for photocopying, Federal Express service sometimes.
Writer's Conferences: Attends Antioch Writers Conference.

QUICKSILVER BOOKS-LITERARY AGENTS (II), 50 Wilson St., Hartsdale NY 10530. (914)946-8748. Contact: Bob Silverstein. Estab. 1973 as packager; 1987 as literary agency. Represents 50+ clients. 50% of clients are new/previously unpublished writers. Specializes in literary and commercial mainstream fiction and nonfiction (especially psychology, New Age, holistic healing, consciousness, ecology, environment, spirituality). Currently handles: 75% nonfiction books; 25% novels.
Handles: Nonfiction books, novels. Considers these nonfiction areas: anthropology/archaeology; biography; business; child guidance/parenting; cooking/food/nutrition; health/medicine; literature; nature/environment; New Age/metaphysics; psychology; inspirational; self-help/personal improvement; true crime/investigative. Considers these fiction areas: contemporary issues; literary; mainstream. Query, "always include SASE." Reports in up to 2 weeks on queries; up to 1 month on mss.
Recent Sales: *Fed Up! A Woman's Guide to Freedom from the Diet/Weight Prison,* by Terry Nicholetti Garrison (Carroll & Graf); *You Don't Have to Suffer: A Guide to Treating Cancer Pain,* by Susan S. Lang and Richard Patt, M.D. (Oxford University Press); *Cloud Nine: A Dreamer's Dictionary,* by Sandra Thomsen (Avon Books); *Syntonics: The Four Keys to Health and Happiness,* by Dr. Robert Kronemeyer (Simon & Schuster).
Terms: Agent receives 15% commission on domestic sales; 20% on foreign sales. Offers written contract, "only if requested. It is open ended, unless author requests time frame." Charges for postage. Authors are expected to supply SASE for return of mss and for query letter responses.
Writers' Conferences: Attends National Writers Union Conference.
Tips: Obtains new clients through recommendations, listings in sourcebooks, solicitations, workshop participation.

CHARLOTTE CECIL RAYMOND, LITERARY AGENT (III), 32 Bradlee Rd., Marblehead MA 01945. Contact: Charlotte Cecil Raymond. Estab. 1983. Represents 30 clients. 20% of clients are new/previously unpublished writers. Currently handles: 70% nonfiction books; 10% juvenile books; 20% novels.
Handles: Nonfiction books, juvenile books, novels. Considers these nonfiction areas: biography; child guidance/parenting; current affairs; ethnic/cultural interests; gay/lesbian issues; politics; history; juvenile nonfiction; nature/environment; psychology; sociology; translations; women's issues/women's studies. Considers these fiction areas: contemporary issues; ethnic; feminist; gay; lesbian; literary; mainstream; regional; young adult. Query with outline/proposal. Reports in 2 weeks on queries; 6 weeks on mss.
Terms: Agent receives 15% commission on domestic sales. 100% of business derived from commissions on ms sales.

Literary Agents: Nonfee-charging 95

HELEN REES LITERARY AGENCY (II, III), 308 Commonwealth Ave., Boston MA 02116. (617)262-2401. Fax: (617)262-2401. Contact: Joan Mazmamian. Estab. 1981. Member of AAR. Represents 50 clients. 50% of clients are new/previously unpublished writers. Specializes in general nonfiction, health, business, world politics, autobiographies, psychology, women's issues. Currently handles: 60% nonfiction books; 30% novels; 10% syndicated material.
Handles: Nonfiction books, novels. Considers these nonfiction areas: biography/autobiography; business; current affairs; ethnic/cultural interests; government/politics/law; health/medicine; history; New Age/metaphysics; psychology; religious/inspirational; science/technology; self-help/personal improvement; sociology; sports; true crime/investigative; women's issues/women's studies. Considers these fiction areas: contemporary issues; detective/police/crime; family saga; feminist; glitz; historical; humor/satire; mainstream; mystery/suspense; sports; thriller/espionage. Query with outline plus 2 sample chapters. Reports in 1 week on queries; 3 weeks on mss.
Terms: Agent receives 15% commission on domestic sales; 20% on foreign sales.
Tips: Obtains new clients through recommendations from others, solicitation, at conferences, etc.

RENAISSANCE: A LITERARY/TALENT AGENCY, (III), (formerly Joel Gotler Metropolitan Talent Agency), 152 N. La Peer Dr., Los Angeles CA 90048. (310)246-6700. Fax: (310)247-5899. Contact: Joel Gotler. Represents 50 clients. Specializes in selling movies and TV rights from books.
Handles: Nonfiction books, novels. Considers these nonfiction areas: biography/autobiography; history; film; true crime/investigative. Considers these fiction areas: action/adventure; contemporary issue; detective/police/crime; ethnic; family saga; fantasy; historical; humor/satire; literary; mainstream; mystery/suspense; science fiction; thriller/espionage. Query with outline and SASE. Reports in 1 month on queries.
Terms: Agent receives 15% commission on domestic book; 10% on film.
Tips: Obtains news clients through recommendations from others.

RHODES LITERARY AGENCY (II), 140 West End Ave., New York NY 10023. (212)580-1300. Estab. 1971. Member of AAR.
Handles: Nonfiction books, novels (a limited number), juvenile books. Query with outline. Include SASE. Reports in 2 weeks on queries.
Terms: Agent receives 15% commission on domestic sales; 20% on foreign sales.

RIVERSIDE LITERARY AGENCY (I, II), #210, 2840 Broadway, New York NY 10025. (212)666-0622. Fax: (212)749-0858. Contact: Susan Lee Cohen. Estab. 1991. Represents 30 clients. 20% of clients are new/previously unpublished writers. Currently handles: 65% nonfiction books; 30% novels; 5% short story collections.
Handles: Nonfiction books, novels, short story collections. Considers these nonfiction areas: animals; biography/autobiography; business; child guidance/parenting; cooking/food/nutrition; gay/lesbian issues; health/medicine; history; language/literature/criticism; military/war; money/finance/economics; music/dance/theater/film; nature/environment; New Age/metaphysics; psychology; science/technology; self-help/personal improvement; true crime/investigative; women's issues/women's studies. Considers these fiction areas: contemporary issues; detective/police/crime; ethnic; feminist; gay; glitz; historical; lesbian; literary; mainstream; mystery/suspense; psychic/supernatural; science fiction; thriller/espionage. Query. Reports in 1 week on queries; 3 weeks on mss.
Terms: Agent receives 15% commission on domestic sales; 20% on foreign sales. Offers written contract, binding until terminated by either party. Will charge extraordinary expenses (photocopying, foreign postage) to the author's account.
Tips: Usually obtains new clients through recommendations.

THE ROBBINS OFFICE, INC. (II), 866 2nd Ave., New York NY 10017. (212)223-0720. Fax: (212)223-2535. Contact: Kathy P. Robbins, Elizabeth Mackey. Specializes in selling mainstream nonfiction, commercial and literary fiction.
Handles: Nonfiction books, novels, magazine articles for book writers under contract. Does not read unsolicited mss.
Terms: Agent receives 15% commission on all domestic, dramatic and foreign sales. Bills back specific expenses incurred in doing business for a client.

ROCK LITERARY AGENCY (II), P.O. Box 625, Newport RI 02840. (401)849-4442. Fax: (401)849-4442. Contact: Andrew T. Rock. Estab. 1984. Represents 26 clients. Specializes in general adult nonfiction and fiction; business; history; New England. Currently handles: 75% nonfiction books; 25% fiction (package and projects).
Handles: Nonfiction books. Considers these nonfiction areas: general nonfiction (adult); business; history; New England. Considers "only general, adult" fiction areas. Query with SASE. Reports in 10 days on queries.
Terms: Agent receives 15% commission on domestic sales; 20% on foreign sales. Offers written contract.
Tips: Usually obtains new clients through recommendations from others, or "I go out and get people I want to represent."

IRENE ROGERS, LITERARY REPRESENTATIVE (III), Suite 600, 9454 Wilshire Blvd., Beverly Hills CA 90212. (213)837-3511. Estab. 1977. Currently represents 10 clients. 10% of clients are new/previously unpublished authors. "We are currently accepting new clients." Currently handles: 50% nonfiction; 50% novels.
Handles: Nonfiction, novels. Query. Responds to queries in 6-8 weeks.
Terms: Agent receives 10% commission on domestic sales; 5% on foreign sales.

ROSE LITERARY AGENCY (II), Suite 302, 688 Avenue of the Americas, New York NY 10010. (212)242-7702. Fax: (212)242-8947. Contact: Mitchell Rose. Estab. 1986. Represents 60 clients. 25% of clients are new/previously unpublished writers. "We have a broad list, but do have a few areas in which we specialize: film, exposé, history, politics, psychology, nutrition and innovative literary fiction." Currently handles: 80% nonfiction books; 15% novels; 5% short story collections.
Handles: Nonfiction books, novels, short story collections. Considers these nonfiction areas: anthropology/archaeology; art/architecture/design; biography/autobiography; business; child guidance/parenting; cooking/food/nutrition; current affairs; ethnic/cultural interests; gay/lesbian issues; government/politics/law; health/medicine; history; language/literature/criticism; military/war; money/finance/economics; music/dance/theater/film; nature/environment; psychology; science/technology; self-help/personal improvement; sociology; sports; true crime/investigative; women's issues/women's studies. Considers these fiction areas: contemporary issues; ethnic; feminist; gay; humor/satire; literary; thriller/espionage. Query. Reports in 2 weeks on queries; 1 month on mss.
Recent Sales: *Lawrence of Arabia*, by Morris and Raskin (Doubleday); *Kennedy as President*, by Gerald Strober (HarperCollins); *Healing Through Nutrition*, by Melvyn Werbach (HarperCollins); *Consumer's Guide to Today's Health Care*, by Stephen Isaacs and Ava Swartz (Houghton Mifflin).
Terms: Agent receives 15% commission on domestic sales; 20% on foreign sales. Offers written contract. "For projects and authors that show promise, we offer extensive editorial feedback at no charge. Critiques are written by myself and staff project developers." Charges fees "but only for very high volume photocopying. Any expense would be approved by the client before it is incurred."
Tips: Obtains new clients mostly through recommendations of existing clients and from editors. "We have taken on several clients whose initial contacts were through query letters."

JEAN ROSENTHAL LITERARY AGENCY (III), 28 E. 11th St., New York NY 10003. (212)677-4248. Contact: Jean Rosenthal. Estab. 1980. Specializes in "co-productions and series of titles." Currently handles: 60% nonfiction books; 20% juvenile books.
Handles: Nonfiction books, juvenile books. Considers these nonfiction areas: animals; anthropology/archaeology; art/architecture/design; biography; child guidance/parenting; health/medicine; history. Considers mystery/suspense fiction. Query with outline/proposal. Reports in 1 month on queries.
Terms: Agent receives 15% commission on domestic sales; 25% on foreign sales. Offers written contract, binding for "6 months as agent, in perpetuity for sales. I charge postage, fax, telephone and ask that an advance of $50 is sent to me as a draw against expenses if I take on a client."
Tips: Obtains new clients "any way they come. Write a tight proposal, enclose a SASE and indicate if query is being simultaneously sent to lots of agents. Put telephone number on query letter."

THE ROTH AGENCY (II, III), (formerly The Roth Literary Agency), 138 Bay State Rd., Rehoboth MA 02769. (508)252-5818. Contact: Shelley E. Roth. Member of Boston Literary Agents Assoc. Currently handles: 50% fiction; 50% nonfiction books.
Handles: Nonfiction books, novels. Considers these nonfiction areas: biography/autobiography; nutrition; current affairs; gardening; parenting; ethnic/cultural interests; government/politics/law; health/medicine; history; language/literature/criticism; music/dance/theater/film; nature/environment; psy-

chology; self-help/personal improvement; sociology; true crime/investigative; women's issues/women's studies; pop culture. Considers these fiction areas: contemporary issues; ethnic; feminist; literary; mainstream. Fiction: query with first 50 pages of ms, brief synopsis, submission history, author bio and SASE. Nonfiction: query, annotated table of contents, author bio, submission history, 2 chapters, survey of competition and SASE. No phone queries.
Terms: Agent receives 15% commission on domestic sales; 20% on foreign sales. Offers written contract. "Some expenses are charged to the writer, as mutually agreed."
Writers' Conferences: Attends various conferences/workshops throughout the year.
Tips: Obtains new clients mostly through recommendations from others. "The more writers know their market and audience, and the more they've familiarized themselves with the publishing process, the better. This knowledge, plus knowing the competition, is crucial for the new nonfiction writer. Let agents know how you were referred to them, and if you've published before. The concept as well as the execution of the ms must both be excellent, or at least have the potential to be so. Quality writing, a professional attitude, and a sense of humor (you need one in this industry) are important. Credentials and writing credits are a plus."

JANE ROTROSEN AGENCY (II), 318 E. 51st St., New York NY 10022. (212)593-4330. Estab. 1974. Member of AAR. Represents 100 clients. Works with published and unpublished writers. Specializes in trade fiction and nonfiction. Currently handles: 40% nonfiction books; 60% novels.
Handles: Adult fiction, nonfiction. Query with "short" outline. Reports in 2 weeks.
Terms: Receives 15% commission on domestic sales; 15% on dramatic sales; 20% on foreign sales. Charges writers for photocopying, long-distance/transoceanic telephone, telegraph, Telex, messenger service and foreign postage.

PESHA RUBINSTEIN, LITERARY AGENCY, INC. (II), #1D, 37 Overlook Terrace, New York NY 10033. (212)781-7845. Contact: Pesha Rubinstein. Estab. 1990. Member of AAR. Represents 35 clients. 50% of clients are new/previously unpublished writers. Specializes in romance and children's books. Currently handles: 20% juvenile books; 80% novels.
Handles: Genre fiction, juvenile books, picture book illustration. Considers these nonfiction areas: juvenile nonfiction; nature/environment; true crime/investigative. Considers these fiction areas: detective/police/crime; glitz; historical; juvenile; mystery/suspense; picture book; romance. "No science fiction or poetry." Send outline plus 3 sample chapters and SASE. Reports in 2 weeks on queries; 6 weeks on requested mss.
Recent Sales: Three untitled historical romances, by Katharine Kincaid (Zebra Books); *Vatsana's Lucky New Year*, by Sara Gogol (Lerner); *Sagebrush Bride*, by Tanya Anne Crosby (Avon).
Terms: Agent receives 15% commission on domestic sales; 20% on foreign sales. Offers written contract. Charges for photocopying. No collect calls accepted.
Tips: "I advertise with writers' groups, with *Romantic Times*, the RWA and SCBW. For children's book illustrators, I go to galleries, keep an eye on magazine ads. Keep the query letter and synopsis short. The work speaks for itself better than any description can. Never send originals. A phone call after 1 month is acceptable. Always include a SASE covering return of the entire package with the material."

SANDUM & ASSOCIATES (II), 144 E. 84th St., New York NY 10028. (212)737-2011. Fax number on request. Managing Director: Howard E. Sandum. Estab. 1987. Represents 35 clients. 20% of clients are new/unpublished writers. Specializes in general nonfiction—all categories of adult books; commercial and literary fiction. Currently handles: 60% nonfiction books; 40% novels.
Handles: Nonfiction books, novels. Query with proposal, sample pages. Do not send full ms unless requested. Include SASE. Reports in 2 weeks on queries.
Terms: Agent receives 15% commission. Agent fee adjustable on dramatic and foreign sales. Charges writers for photocopying, air express, long-distance telephone/fax.

SCHAFFNER AGENCY, INC. (II), 6625 N. Casas Adobes Rd., Tucson AZ 85704. (602)797-8000. Fax: (602)797-8271. Contact: Timothy Schaffner or Jennifer Powers. Estab. 1948. Represents approximately 40 clients. Specializes in literary fiction and nonfiction, nature and ecology issues, biographies, investigative journalism, Southwestern and Latin American writers, American popular culture and music.

Handles: Nonfiction books, novels. Considers these nonfiction areas: biography/autobiography; nature/environment; conservation issues; popular culture/social commentary; investigative journalism; music. Considers these fiction areas: quality adult fiction; literary. Query with SASE. Reports in 4-6 weeks on queries. Do not query by phone or fax.
Recent Sales: *I Feel Like Hank Williams Tonight*, by Jasen Emmons (Soho Press); *Trust Me: Charles Keating and the Missing Billions*, by Charles Bowden (Random House); *Songbirds, Truffles and Wolves: An American Naturalist in Italy*, by Gary Paul Nabhan (Pantheon).
Terms: Agent receives 15% commission on domestic sales; 20% on foreign sales. Offers written contract, if requested. Charges $15 to cover postage costs.
Tips: "Query first and keep initial presentations concise. Always include SASE."

HAROLD SCHMIDT LITERARY AGENCY (II), #1B, 343 W. 12th St., New York NY 10014. (212)727-7473. Fax: (212)807-6025. Contact: Harold Schmidt. Estab. 1983. Member of AAR. Represents 30 clients. 20% of clients are new/previously unpublished writers. Currently handles: 45% nonfiction books; 5% scholarly books; 50% novels.
Handles: Nonfiction books, scholarly books, novels, short story collections. Considers these nonfiction areas: anthropology/archaeology; art/architecture/design; biography/autobiography; business; current affairs; ethnic/cultural interests; gay/lesbian issues; government/politics/law; health/medicine; history; language/literature/criticism; military/war; money/finance/economics; music/dance/theater/film; nature/environment; New Age/metaphysics; psychology; science/technology; self-help/personal improvement; sociology; translations; true crime/investigative; women's issues/women's studies. Considers these fiction areas: action/adventure; contemporary issues; detective/police/crime; ethnic; family saga; feminist; gay; glitz; historical; horror; lesbian; literary; mainstream; mystery/suspense; psychic/supernatural; science fiction; thriller/espionage; westerns/frontier. Query before sending any material. Endeavors to report 2 weeks on queries; 4-6 weeks on mss.
Recent Sales: *Charlie Chan is Dead*, by Jessica Hagedorn (Viking Penguin); *Heroines*, by Norman Lorre (Goodrich-HarperCollins).
Terms: Agent receives 15% commission on domestic sales; 20% commission on foreign sales. Offers written contract "on occasion—time frame always subject to consultation with author." Charges for photocopying, long distance telephone calls and faxes, ms submission postage costs.
Tips: Obtains new clients through recommendations from others and solicitation. "I cannot stress enough how important it is for the new writer to present a clear, concise and professionally presented query letter. And, please, NEVER send material until requested."

LAURENS R. SCHWARTZ AGENCY (II), Suite 15D, 5 E. 22nd St., New York NY 10010-5315. (212)228-2614. Contact: Laurens R. Schwartz. Estab. 1984. Represents 100 clients. Primarily nonfiction, some adult and juvenile fiction. Within nonfiction, half of authors have doctoral and post-doctoral degress and write for both the academic and crossover (education and trade) markets; other half are general trade (astrology through Zen) and professional/business (real estate, finances, teleconferencing, graphics, etc). Also works with celebrities. Adult fiction: contemporary; fantasy; literary/mainstream. Juvenile: illustrated; series. Currently handles: 60% nonfiction books; 40% fiction (adult and juvenile).
Handles: Everything described above, plus ancillaries (from screenplays to calendars). Does movie tie-in novelizations. "No longer handle screenplays except as tied in to a book, or unless we solicit the screenwriter directly." Does not read unsolicited mss. Reports in 1 month.
Terms: Agent receives 15% commission on domestic sales; up to 25% on foreign sales. "No fees except for photocopying, and that fee is avoided by an author providing necessary copies or, in certain instances, transferring files on diskette—must be IBM compatible." Where necessary to bring a project into publishable form, editorial work and some rewriting provided as part of service. Works with authors on long-term career goals and promotion.
Tips: "Do not like receiving mass mailings sent to all agents. Be selective—do your homework. Do not send *everything* you have ever written. Choose *one* work and promote that. *Always* include an SASE. *Never* send your only copy. *Always* include a background sheet on yourself and a *one*-page synopsis of the work (too many summaries end up being as long as the work)."

LYNN SELIGMAN, LITERARY AGENT (II), 400 Highland Ave., Upper Montclair NJ 07043. (201)783-3631. Contact: Lynn Seligman. Estab. 1985. Represents 32 clients. 15% of clients are new/previously unpublished writers. Currently handles: 75% nonfiction books; 15% novels; 10% photography books.
Handles: Nonfiction books, novels, photography books. Considers these nonfiction areas: anthropology/archaeology; art/architecture/design; biography/autobiography; business; child guidance/parenting; cooking/food/nutrition; current affairs; ethnic/cultural interests; government/politics/law; health/

medicine; history; interior design/decorating; language/literature/criticism; money/finance/economics; music/dance/theater/film; nature/environment; psychology; science/technology; self-help/personal improvement; sociology; translations; true crime/investigative; women's issues/women's studies. Considers these fiction areas: contemporary issues; detective/police/crime; ethnic; fantasy; feminist; historical; humor/satire; literary; mainstream; mystery/suspense. Query with letter or outline/proposal plus 1 sample chapter and SASE. Reports in 2 weeks on queries; 1-2 months on mss.
Recent Sales: *Your Aging Parents*, by Janet Bamford (Consumer Report Books).
Terms: Agent receives 15% commission on domestic sales; 25% on foreign sales. Charges for photocopying, unusual postage or telephone expenses (checking first with the author), Express Mail.
Writers' Conferences: Attends Dorothy Canfield Fisher Conference.
Tips: Obtains new clients usually from other writers or from editors.

THE SEYMOUR AGENCY (II, IV), 7 Rensselaer Ave., P.O. Box 376, Heuvelton NY 13654. (315)344-7223. Contact: Mike Seymour/Mary Sue Seymour. Estab. 1992. Member of RWA, New York State Outdoor Writers, OWAA. 50% of clients are new/previously unpublished writers. Specializes in category romance, some young adult. Member agents: Mary Sue Seymour (category romance, young adult); Mike Seymour (nonfiction, outdoor articles, hunting and fishing and sportsman travel).
Handles: Considers these nonfiction areas: hunting and fishing. Considers these fiction areas: romance (contemporary, gothic, historical, medieval, regency); accepts a few young adult horror or humor or upbeat romance or adventure. Query with first chapter and synopsis. No certified mail, please. Reports in 2 weeks on queries; 1 month on mss.
Terms: Agent receives 15% commission on domestic sales; 15% on foreign sales. Offers written contract, binding for 1 year. Offers criticism service for prospective clients only. Postage fee refundable when/if ms sells. 99% of business derived from commissions on ms sales.
Tips: "We are looking for medieval romance or historicals set in England, Ireland, etc. Will read any category romance. Send query, synopsis and chapter 1. If you don't hear from us, you didn't send SASE. Our critique service is only for works we plan on representing."

CHARLOTTE SHEEDY LITERARY AGENCY, INC. (II), Suite 428, 611 Broadway, New York NY 10012. Prefers not to share information.

THE SHEPARD AGENCY (II), Suite 3, Pawling Savings Bank Bldg., Southeast Plaza, Brewster NY 10509. (914)279-2900 or (914)279-3236. Fax: (914)279-3239. Contact: Jean or Lance Shepard. Specializes in "some fiction; nonfiction: business, biography, homemaking; inspirational; self-help." Currently handles: 75% nonfiction books; 5% juvenile books; 20% novels.
Handles: Nonfiction books, scholarly books, novels. Considers these nonfiction areas: agriculture; horticulture; animals; biography/autobiography; business; child guidance/parenting; computers/electronics; cooking/food/nutrition; crafts/hobbies; current affairs; government/politics/law; health/medicine; history; interior design/decorating; juvenile nonfiction; language/literature/criticism; money/finance/economics; music/dance/theater/film; nature/environment; psychology; religious/inspirational; self-help/personal improvement; sociology; sports; women's issues/women's studies. Considers these fiction areas: contemporary issues; family saga; historical; humor/satire; literary; regional; sports; thriller/espionage. Query with outline, sample chapters and SASE. Reports in 1 month on queries; 2 months on mss.
Recent Sales: *Crane's Wedding Blue Book*, by Steven Feinberg (Simon & Schuster).
Terms: Agent receives 15% on domestic sales. Offers written contract. Charges for extraordinary postage, photocopying and long-distance phone calls.
Tips: Obtains new clients through referrals and listings in various directories for writers and publishers. "Provide info on those publishers who have already been contacted, seen work, accepted or rejected same. Provide complete bio and marketing info."

‡RICHARD R. SHREVES AGENCY (V), P.O. Box 684751, Austin TX 78768-4751. (512)444-1243. Fax: (512)444-4683. Agency not currently seeking new clients.

BOBBE SIEGEL LITERARY AGENCY (II), 41 W. 83rd St., New York NY 10024. (212)877-4985. Fax: (212)877-4985. Contact: Bobbe Siegel. Estab. 1975. Represents 60 clients. 30% of clients are new/previously unpublished writers. Currently handles: 65% nonfiction books; 35% novels.
Handles: Nonfiction books, novels. Considers these nonfiction areas: archaeology; biography/autobiography; child guidance/parenting; nutrition; ethnic; health/medicine; history; literature; nature/environment; psychology; self-help/personal improvement; sports; true crime/investigative; women's is-

sues. Considers these fiction areas: action/adventure; contemporary issues; detective/police/crime; family saga; fantasy; feminist; glitz; historical; literary; mainstream; mystery/suspense; psychic/supernatural; romance (historical); science fiction; thriller/espionage. Query. Reports in 2 weeks on queries; 2 months on mss.
Recent Sales: *The New Untouchables* (Noble Press) and *Making Crime Pay* (Paragon), both by John De Santis.
Terms: Agent receives 15% on domestic sales; 20% on foreign sales. Offers written contract. Charges for photocopying; long-distance or overseas telephone calls or fax messages; airmail postage, both foreign and domestic.
Writers' Conferences: Vermont Writer's Conference.
Tips: Obtains new clients through "word of mouth; editors' and authors' recommendations; through conferences and from people who see my name in publications. Write clear and neat letters of inquiry; always remember to include SASE. Never use dot matrix. In your letter never tell the agent why your book is great. Letters should be spaced and paragraphed so they are easy to read and should not be more than 2 pages."

SIERRA LITERARY AGENCY (II), P.O. Box 1090, Janesville CA 96114. (916)253-3250. Contact: Mary Barr. Estab. 1988. Eager to work with new/unpublished writers. Specializes in contemporary women's novels, mainstream fiction and nonfiction, self-help, self-esteem books.
Handles: Nonfiction books, novels. Query with outline or entire ms. Reports in 2 weeks on queries; 6 weeks on mss.
Recent Sales: *Perfect Just the Way I Am*, by Julie Tamler (St. John's Publishing, Inc.).
Terms: Agent receives 10% commission on domestic sales; 15% on dramatic sales; 20% on foreign sales. Charges writers for photocopying, phone and overseas postage.

EVELYN SINGER LITERARY AGENCY INC. (III), P.O. Box 594, White Plains NY 10602. (914)631-5160/1147. Contact: Evelyn Singer. Estab. 1951. Represents 45 clients. 25% of clients are new/previously unpublished writers. Specializes in nonfiction (adult/juvenile, adult suspense).
Handles: Nonfiction books, juvenile books, novels. Considers these nonfiction areas: anthropology/archaeology; biography; business; child guidance; current affairs; government/politics/law; health/medicine; juvenile nonfiction; money/finance/economics; science; self-help/personal improvement. Considers these fiction areas: contemporary issues; detective/police/crime; historical; mystery/suspense; thriller/espionage. Query. Reports in 2 weeks on queries; 6-8 weeks on mss. "SASE must be enclosed for reply or return of manuscript."
Terms: Agent receives 15% commission on domestic sales; 20% on foreign sales. Offers written contract, binding for 3 years. Charges for long-distance phone calls, overseas postage ("authorized expenses only").
Tips: Obtains new clients through recommendations. "I am accepting writers who have earned at least $20,000 from freelance writing. SASE must accompany all queries and material for reply and or return of ms."

VALERIE SMITH, LITERARY AGENT (III), 1746 Rt. 44/55, Modena NY 12548. (914)883-5848. Contact: Valerie Smith. Estab. 1978. Represents 30 clients. 1% of clients are new/previously unpublished writers. Specializes in science fiction and fantasy. Currently handles: 2% nonfiction books; 96% novels; 1% novellas; 1% short story collections.
Handles: Novels. Considers these fiction areas: fantasy; literary; mainstream; science fiction; young adult. Query. Reports in 2 weeks on queries; 2 months on mss.
Recent Sales: *The Porcelain Dove*, by Delia Sherman (Dutton); *Athyra*, by Steven Brust (Berkley).
Terms: Agent receives 15% commission on domestic sales; 20% on foreign sales. Offers a written contract. Charges for "extraordinary expenses by mutual consent."
Tips: Obtains new clients through recommendations from other clients, various respected contacts.

MICHAEL SNELL LITERARY AGENCY (II), Box 655, Truro MA 02666. (508)349-3718. Contact: Michael Snell. Estab. 1980. Represents 200 clients. 25% of clients are new/previously unpublished authors. Specializes in all types of business and computer books, from low-level how-to to professional and reference. Currently handles: 90% nonfiction books, 10% novels. Member agents: Michael Snell (nonfiction); Patricia Smith (fiction and children's books).
Handles: Nonfiction books, textbooks, scholarly books, juvenile books. Open to all nonfiction categories. Considers these fiction areas: literary; mystery/suspense; thriller/espionage. Query with SASE. Reports in 1 week on queries; 2 weeks on mss.

Recent Sales: *The Heroic Organization,* by Emmitt Murphy (Simon & Schuster); *The Creative Wedding Guide,* by Jacquelin Smith (Adams); *The Teamnet Factor,* by Jessica Lipnack (Oliver Wright); *Women and the Work/Family Dilemma,* by Deborah Swiss (Wiley).
Terms: Agent receives 15% on domestic sales; 15% on foreign sales.
Tips: Obtains new clients through unsolicited mss, word-of-mouth, *LMP* and *Guide to Literary Agents and Art/Photo Reps.* "Send a half- to a full-page query."

ELYSE SOMMER, INC. (II), P.O. Box E, 110-34 73rd Rd., Forest Hills NY 11375. (718)263-2668. President: Elyse Sommer. Estab. 1952. Member of AAR. Represents 20 clients. Works with a small number of new/unpublished authors. Specializes in nonfiction: reference books, dictionaries, popular culture. Currently handles: 90% nonfiction books; 5% novels; 5% juvenile.
Handles: Nonfiction books, novels (some mystery but no science fiction), juvenile (no pre-school). Query with outline. Reports in 2 weeks on queries.
Terms: Agent receives 15% commission on domestic sales (when advance is under 20,000, 10% over); 20% on dramatic sales; 20% on foreign sales. Charges for photocopying, long distance, express mail, extraordinary expenses.

F. JOSEPH SPIELER (V), Room 135, 13th Floor, 154 W. 57th St., New York NY 10019. (212)757-4439. Fax: (212)333-2019. Contact: Joe Spieler or Lisa Ross. Estab. 1981. Represents 47 clients. 2% of clients are new/previously unpublished writers.
Handles: Nonfiction books, novels. Considers these nonfiction areas: biography/autobiography; business; child guidance/parenting; cooking/food/nutrition; current affairs; ethnic/cultural interests; gay/lesbian issues; government/politics/law; history; money/finance/economics; sociology; women's issues/women's studies. Considers these fiction areas: ethnic; family saga; feminist; gay; humor/satire; lesbian; literary; mainstream. Query. Reports in 1-2 weeks on queries; 3-5 weeks on mss.
Recent Sales: *Black Hundred,* by Walter Laqueur (HarperCollins); *Genius in the Shadows,* by William Lanovette (Scribner's).
Terms: Agent receives 15% commission on domestic sales. Charges for long distance phone/fax, photocopying, postage.
Tips: Obtains new clients through recommendations and *Literary Marketplace* listing.

‡GRETCHEN SPIELER LITERARY AGENCY (I, II), 4732 California St., San Francisco CA 94118. (415)668-8162. Contact: Gretchen Spieler. Estab. 1993. Represents 5 clients. 100% of clients are new/previously unpublished writers. Specializes in cookbooks, crafts and hobbies, well-written literature, child-guidance/parenting, self-help/psychology, young adult. Currently handles: 50% nonfiction books; 50% novels.
Handles: Nonfiction books, juvenile books, novels. "I will consider all areas of nonfiction;" specialities in: art/architecture/design; child guidance/parenting; cooking/food/nutrition; crafts/hobbies; history; interior design/decorating; juvenile nonfiction; language/literature/criticism; psychology; self-help/personal improvement; women's issues/women's studies. "I will consider all areas of fiction;" including erotica ("only well-written"); historical; juvenile; literary; mainstream; mystery/suspense; science fiction; thriller/espionage; young adult. Query with outline/proposal or outline plus 2-3 sample chapters. Reports in 2 weeks on queries; 3 weeks on mss." Please send query before sending manuscript."
Terms: Agent receives 15% commission on domestic sales; 20% on foreign sales. Offers written contract, cancellable with notice. Charges for postage, photocopying, fax services, "any other fees that are necessary, always with author's consent."
Tips: Obtains new clients through recommendations from others, word of mouth, writing groups. "Please send queries first. Make sure manuscript or proposal is typed and cleanly photocopied. Always send a SASE."

Agents ranked I-IV are actively seeking new clients. Those ranked V or those who prefer not to be listed have been included to inform you they are not currently looking for new clients.

PHILIP G. SPITZER LITERARY AGENCY (III), 50 Talmage Farm Lane, East Hampton NY 11937. (516)329-3650. Fax: (516)329-3651. Contact: Philip Spitzer. Estab. 1969. Member of AAR. Represents 60 clients. 10% of clients are new/previously unpublished writers. Specializes in mystery/suspense, literary fiction, sports, general nonfiction (not how-to). Currently handles: 50% nonfiction books; 50% novels.
Handles: Nonfiction books, novels. Considers these nonfiction areas: biography/autobiography; business; current affairs; ethnic/cultural interests; government/politics/law; health/medicine; history; military/war; music/dance/theater/film; nature/environment; psychology; sociology; sports; true crime/investigative. Considers these fiction areas: contemporary issues; detective/police/crime; literary; mainstream; mystery/suspense; sports. Send outline plus 1 sample chapter and SASE. Reports in 1 week on queries; 6 weeks on mss.
Terms: Agent receives 15% commission on domestic sales; 20% on foreign sales. Charge for photocopying.
Tips: Usually obtains new clients on referral.

NANCY STAUFFER ASSOCIATES (II,III), Suite 1007, 156 Fifth Ave., New York NY 10010. (212)229-9027. Fax: (212)229-9018. Contact: Nancy Stauffer. Estab. 1989. Member of PEN Center USA West. Represents 50 clients. 10% of clients are new/previously unpublished writers. Currently handles: 50% nonfiction books; 50% fiction.
Handles: Nonfiction books, novels, novellas, short story collections. Considers these nonfiction areas: biography/autobiography; current affairs; ethnic/cultural interests; nature/environment; self-help/personal improvement; sociology; translations; women's issues/women's studies; popular culture. Considers these fiction areas: contemporary issues; literary; mainstream; regional. No unsolicited queries.
Recent Sales: *Woking*, by Billy Mills (Crown Books); *The Lone Ranger and Tonto Fist Fight in Heaven*, by Sherman Alexi (Atlantic Monthly); *Sworn Before Cranes*, by Merrill Gilfilan (Orion).
Terms: Agent receives 15% commission on domestic sales; 20% on foreign sales. Offers written contract. Charges for "long-distance telephone and fax; messenger and express delivery; photocopying."
Writers' Conferences: "I teach a seminar at the UCLA Extension Writers' Program titled 'Getting Published: A One Day Tour Through the World of New York Publishing,' and participate in writers' conferences around the country."
Tips: Obtains new clients primarily through referrals from existing clients.

LYLE STEELE & CO., LTD. (II), Suite 6, 511 E. 73rd St., New York NY 10021. (212)288-2981. Contact: Lyle Steele. Estab. 1985. Signatory of WGA. Represents 125 clients. 20% of clients are new/previously unpublished writers. "In nonfiction we are particularly interested in current events, unique personal stories, biography and autobiography, popular business, true crime, health, parenting, personal growth and psychological self-help. In fiction we are interested in good mysteries not of the hard-boiled type, horror and occult of all types, thrillers and historical novels. We are also open to quality fiction." Currently handles: 70% nonfiction books; 30% novels. Member agents: Jim Kepler (Chicago, nonfiction), Lisa Abercrombie (California, nonfiction).
Handles: Nonfiction books, novels. Considers these nonfiction areas: anthropology/archaeology; biography/autobiography; business; child guidance/parenting; cooking/food/nutrition; current affairs; ethnic/cultural interests; gay/lesbian issues; government/politics/law; health/medicine; history; money/finance/economics; nature/environment; New Age/metaphysics; psychology; science/technology; self-help/personal improvement; sociology; sports; true crime/investigative. Considers these fiction areas: detective/police/crime; family saga; gay; historical; horror; lesbian; literary; mystery/suspense; psychic/supernatural; thriller/espionage. Send outline plus 2 sample chapters. Reports in 10 days on queries; 2 weeks on mss.
Recent Sales: *How to License Your Million Dollar Idea*, by Harvey Reese (Wiley); *The House of Real Love*, by Carla Tomaso (NAL/Dutton).
Terms: Agent receives 15% commission on domestic sales. Offers written contract, binding for 1 year.
Tips: Obtains new clients through recommendations and solicitations. "Our goal is to represent books that provide readers with solid information they can use to improve and change their personal and professional lives. In addition, we take the long view of an author's career. A successful writing career is built step by step, and our goal is to provide the long-term professional management required to achieve it. Be prepared to send your material quickly once an agent has responded. Frequently, we'll have room to take on only a few new clients and a slow response may mean the openings will be filled by the time your material arrives."

‡STEPPING STONE (IV), 59 W. 71st St., New York NY 10023. (212)362-9277. Fax: (212)362-1998. Contact: Sarah Jane Freymann. Member of AAR. Represents 75 clients. 20% of clients are new/previously unpublished writers. Currently handles: 75% nonfiction books; 2% juvenile books; 21% novels; 2% poetry books.

Handles: Nonfiction books, novels, lifestyle-illustrated. Considers these nonfiction areas: animals; anthropology/archaeology; art/architecture/design; biography/autobiography; business; child guidance/parenting; cooking/food/nutrition; current affairs; ethnic/cultural interests; gay/lesbian issues; government/politics/law; health/medicine; history; interior design/decorating; nature/environment; New Age/metaphysics; psychology; religious/inspirational; self-help/personal improvement; true crime/investigative; women's issues/women's studies. Considers these fiction areas: contemporary issues; detective/police/crime; ethnic; literary; mainstream; mystery/suspense; thriller/espionage. Query. Reports in 2 weeks on queries; 6 weeks on mss.

Recent Sales: *Burning Time*, by Leslie Glass (Doubleday); *Water by Design*, by Charles Moore and Jane Lidz (Abrams); *Spiritual Elderin*, by Zalman Schchter Shalomi and Ron Miller (Warner); *Tiger Magic*, by Sy Montgomery (Houghton Mifflin).

Terms: Agent receives 15% commission on domestic sales; 20% on foreign sales. Offers written contract. Offers criticism service. Charges for long distance, overseas postage, photocopying. 99% of business is derived from commissions on ms sales; 1% is derived from criticism services. Payment of a criticism fee does not ensure representation.

Tips: Obtains new clients through recommendations from others. "I love fresh new passionate works by authors who love what they are doing and have both natural talent and carefully honed skill."

GLORIA STERN LITERARY AGENCY (II,III,IV), 2929 Buffalo Speedway, Houston TX 77098. (713)936-8360. Fax: (713)936-8460. Contact: Gloria Stern. Estab. 1976. Member of AAR. Represents 35 clients. 20% of clients are new/previously unpublished writers. Specializes in history, biography, women's studies, child guidance, parenting, business, cookbooks, health, cooking, finance, sociology, true crime. Currently handles: 80% nonfiction books; 5% scholarly books; 15% novels.

• This agency is not affiliated with the Gloria Stern Agency located in California.

Handles: Nonfiction books, scholarly books, novels. Considers these nonfiction areas: anthropology/archaeology; art/architecture/design; biography/autobiography; business; child guidance/parenting; cooking/food/nutrition; current affairs; ethnic/cultural interests; government/politics/law; health/medicine; history; young adult nonfiction; language/literature/criticism; money/finance/economics; psychology; science/technology; self-help/personal improvement; sociology; sports; true crime/investigative; women's issues/women's studies. Considers these fiction areas: contemporary issues; detective/police/crime; ethnic; experimental; family saga; feminist; literary; mainstream; mystery/suspense; romance (contemporary); thriller/espionage; young adult. Query with outline plus 2 sample chapters and SASE. Reports in 1 week on queries; 1 month on mss.

Recent Sales: *Stefan in Love*, by Joseph Machlis (WW Norton); *Breaking the Science Barrier*, by Sheila Tobias and Carl Tomizoka (College Board).

Terms: Agent receives 15% commission on domestic sales; 20% on foreign sales (shared). Offers written contract, binding for 60 days.

Tips: Obtain new clients through editors, previous clients, listings. "I prefer fiction authors that have some published work such as short stories in either commercial or literary magazines or come recommended by an editor or writer. I need a short outline of less than a page, 1-2 chapters and SASE. For nonfiction, I need credentials, an outline, competitive books, 1-2 chapters and SASE. No unsolicited mss."

LARRY STERNIG LITERARY AGENCY (V), 742 Robertson St., Milwaukee WI 53213. Agency not currently seeking new clients.

‡GUNTHER STUHLMANN, AUTHOR'S REPRESENTATIVE (V), P.O. Box 276, Becket MA 01223. Agency not currently seeking new clients.

‡MAYA SWAMY, LITERARY AGENT (I), P.O. Box 9694, Marina Del Rey CA 90295. (310)821-4949. Fax: (310)821-7089. Contact: Maya Swamy. Estab. 1993. Represents 5 clients. 40% of clients are new/previously unpublished writers. "I like words that have been put together well. So even in nonfiction I look for some linguistic style—rather than a dry recital of facts." Currently handles: 40% nonfiction books; 20% scholarly books; 40% novels.

Handles: Nonfiction books, scholarly books, novels, novellas, short story collections. Considers these nonfiction areas: art/architecture/design; biography/autobiography; business; child guidance/parenting; computers/electronics; current affairs; ethnic/cultural interests; government/politics/law; health/medicine; history; language/literature/criticism; military/war; money/finance/economics; music/dance/theater/film; nature/environment; New Age/metaphysics; photography; psychology; religious/inspirational; true crime/investigative; science/technology; self-help/personal improvement; sociology; translations; women's issues/women's studies. Send outline/proposal or outline plus 3 sample chapters. Reports in 2 weeks on queries; 1 month on mss.
Terms: Agent receives 15% commission on domestic sales; 20% on foreign sales. Offers written contract, binding for 1 year.
Writers' Conferences: ABA.
Tips: Obtains new clients through recommendations and solicitations. "Plus I really read the slush pile. I believe gems can be found anywhere. However, manuscripts can only be returned with SASE. Please send me the first 3 chapters—it is impossible to judge the flow of a manuscript unless the chapters are consecutive! Since all writers were once unpublished I think that any unpublished writer is potentially both publishable and as good as any published writer. I am looking to build long-term associations with writers and not one-book deals. However, since my own passion is the language, submitting dry recitals of facts is a waste of your postage and my time. Write about something you feel passionately about—write it so I can feel passionate about it, then let's work together and *sell it*."

ROSLYN TARG LITERARY AGENCY, INC. (III), 105 W. 13th St., New York NY 10011. (212)206-9390. Fax: (212)989-6233. Contact: Roslyn Targ. Original agency estab. 1945; name changed to Roslyn Targ Literary Agency, Inc. in 1970. Member of AAR. Represents approximately 100 clients.
Handles: Nonfiction books, juvenile books, novels, self-help, genre fiction. No mss without queries first. Query with outline, proposal, curriculum vitae, and SASE.
Recent Sales: *Mercy of a Rude Stream: A Star Shines Over Mt. Morris Park*, by Henry Roth (St. Martin's Press); *Coco Grimes*, by Mary Stolz (HarperCollins); *A Case of Rape*, by Chester Himes (Carroll & Graf); *Imagine That!: The Book About Imagination Training*, by Jeffrey L. Brown, M.D. with Julie Davis; *Fractal Resonances*, by Jean Houston (Harper San Francisco).
Terms: Agent receives 10-15% commission on domestic sales; 20% on foreign sales. Charges standard agency fees (bank charges, long distance fax, postage, photocopying, shipping of books, etc.).
Tips: Obtains new clients through recommendations, solicitation, queries. "This agency reads on an exclusive basis only."

PATRICIA TEAL LITERARY AGENCY (III), 2036 Vista Del Rosa, Fullerton CA 92631. (714)738-8333. Contact: Patricia Teal. Estab. 1978. Member of AAR, RWA, Authors Guild. Represents 60 clients. Published authors only. Specializes in category fiction and commercial, how-to and self-help nonfiction. Currently handles: 10% nonfiction books, 90% novels.
Handles: Nonfiction books, novels. Considers these nonfiction areas: biography/autobiography; child guidance/parenting; health/medicine; psychology; true crime/investigative; self-help/personal improvement; women's issues. Considers these fiction areas: glitz, mainstream, mystery/suspense, romance. Query. Reports in 10 days on queries; 6 weeks on requested mss.
Recent Sales: *Past Promises*, by Jill Marie Landis (Berkeley/Jove).
Terms: Agent receives 10-15% commission on domestic sales; 20% on foreign sales. Offers written contract, binding for 1 year. Charges for postage, photocopying.
Writers' Conferences: Attends several Romance Writers of America conferences, Asilomar (California Writers Club) and Bouchercon.
Tips: Usually obtains new clients through recommendations from authors and editors or at conferences. "Include SASE with all correspondence."

‡2M COMMUNICATIONS LTD. (II), #601, 121 W. 27th St., New York NY 10003. (212)741-1509. Fax: (212)691-4460. Contact: Madeleine Morel. Estab. 1982. Represents 40 clients. 20% of clients are new/previously unpublished writers. Specializes in adult nonfiction. Currently handles: 100% nonfiction books.
Handles: Nonfiction books. Considers these nonfiction areas: biography/autobiography; child guidance/parenting; ethnic/cultural interests; gay/lesbian issues; health/medicine; music/dance/theater/film; self-help/personal improvement; women's issues/women's studies. Query. Reports in 1 week on queries, weeks on outlines.

Recent Sales: *Michael Jordan*, by M. Krupel (St. Martin's Press); *Breast Cancer Prevention*, by Epstein and Steinman (Macmillan); *Emergency Baby Care Book*, by Salmans/Phillips (Avon).
Terms: Agent receives 15% commission on domestic sales; 20% on foreign sales. Offers written contract, binding for 2 years. Charges for postage, photocopying, long distance calls and faxes.
Tips: Obtains new clients through recommendations from others, solicitation.

SUSAN P. URSTADT INC. WRITERS AND ARTISTS AGENCY (II), P.O. Box 1676, New Canaan CT 06840. (203)966-6111. Contact: Susan Urstadt. Estab. 1975. Member of AAR. Represents 45 clients. 10% of clients are new/previously unpublished authors. Specializes in illustrated books, popular reference, art, antiques, decorative arts, gardening, travel, horses, armchair cookbooks, business, self-help, crafts, hobbies, collectibles. Currently handles: 95% nonfiction books.
Handles: Nonfiction books. Considers these nonfiction areas: agriculture/horticulture; animals; anthropology/archaeology; art/architecture/design; biography/autobiography; business; child guidance/parenting; cooking/food/nutrition; crafts/hobbies; current affairs; health/medicine; interior design/decorating; military/war; money/finance/economics; music/dance/theater/film; nature/environment; photography; self-help/personal improvement; sports. "No unsolicited fiction please." Send outline plus 2 sample chapters, short author bio and SASE. Reports in 3 weeks on queries.
Recent Sales: *Hearthstrings*, by Carol Pflumm (Viking Studio); *Pleasures of the Garden*, by Emyl Jenkins (Crown).
Terms: Agent receives 15% commission on domestic sales; 20% on foreign sales. Offers written contract.
Tips: Obtains new clients through recommendations from others. "We are interested in building a writer's career through the long term and only want dedicated writers with special knowledge, which they share in a professional way."

VAN DER LEUN & ASSOCIATES (II), 22 Division St., Easton CT 06612. (203)259-4897. Contact: Patricia Van der Leun. Estab. 1984. Represents 30 clients. 50% of clients are new/previously unpublished authors. Specializes in fiction, science, biography. Currently handles: 50% nonfiction books; 40% novels; 10% short story collections.
Handles: Nonfiction books, novels. "Any nonfiction subject OK." Considers these fiction areas: cartoon/comic; contemporary issues; ethnic; historical; literary; mainstream. Query. Reports in 2 weeks on queries; 1 month on mss.
Recent Sales: *Maybe, Maybe Not*, by Robert Fulghum (Villard).
Terms: Agent receives 15% on domestic sales; 25% on foreign sales. Offers written contract.
Tips: "We are interested in high-quality, serious writers only."

MARY JACK WALD ASSOCIATES, INC. (III), 111 E. 14th St., New York NY 10003. (212)254-7842. Contact: Danis Sher. Estab. 1985. Member of Authors Guild, SCBWI. Represents 55 clients. 10% of clients are new/previously unpublished writers. Specializes in literary works, juvenile, TV/film scripts. Currently handles: adult and juvenile fiction and nonfiction, including some original film/TV scripts. Member agents: Danis Sher, Lem Lloyd. Foreign rights representative: Lynne Rabinoff, Lynne Rabinoff Associates. Film/TV rights representative: Monica D. Gilbert, Starfire Productions.
Handles: Nonfiction books, juvenile books, novels, novellas, short story collections, movie scripts, TV scripts. Considers these nonfiction areas: biography/autobiography; current affairs; ethnic/cultural interests; health/medicine; history; juvenile nonfiction; language/literature/criticism; military/war; money/finance/economics; music/dance/theater/film; nature/environment; photography; science/technology; self-help/personal improvement; sociology; sports; translations; true crime/investigative. Considers these fiction areas: action/adventure; contemporary issues; detective/police/crime; ethnic; experimental; family saga; fantasy; feminist; gay; glitz; historical; humor/satire; juvenile; literary; mainstream; mystery/suspense; picture book; thriller; young adult. Query. Reports in 1 month on queries; 2 months on mss.

For explanation of symbols, see the Key to Symbols and Abbreviations. For translation of an organization's acronym, see the Table of Acronyms.

Recent Sales: *The Metamorphosis of Baubo,* by Winifred Milius Lubell (Vanderbilt University Press); 3 book contract, Richie Tankersley Cusick (Pocket Books).
Terms: Agent receives 15% commission on domestic sales; 15-30% on foreign sales. Offers written contract, binding for 1 year.
Tips: Obtains new clients through recommendations from others. "Send a query letter with brief description and credits, if any. If we are interested, we'll request 50 pages. If that interests us, we'll request entire ms, which should be double-spaced. SASE should be enclosed."

‡**WALLACE LITERARY AGENCY, INC. (III),** 177 E. 70 St., New York NY 10021. (212)570-9090. Contact: Lois Wallace/Thomas C. Wallace. Estab. 1988. Member of AAR. Represents 125 clients. 5% of clients are new/previously unpublished writers. Specializes in fiction and nonfiction by good writers. Currently handles: 60% nonfiction books, 35% novels, 5% magazine articles and short stories. "We handle poetry, movie scripts, juveniles and stage plays ONLY if written by clients who write trade books."
Handles: Nonfiction books, novels. Considers these nonfiction areas: anthropology/archaeology, biography/autobiography, current affairs, history, literature, military/war, science; true crime/investigative. Considers these fiction areas: literary, mainstream, mystery/suspense. Send outline plus 1-2 sample chapters, reviews of previously published books, curriculum vitae, return postage. Reports in 2 weeks on queries; 3 weeks on mss.
Terms: Agent receives 10-15% commission on domestic sales; 20% on foreign sales. Offers written contract; binding until terminated with notice. Charges for photocopying, book shipping (or ms shipping) overseas, legal fees (if needed, with writer's approval), galleys and books needed for representation and foreign sales.
Tips: Obtains new clients through "recommendations from editors and writers we respect."

JOHN A. WARE LITERARY AGENCY (II), 392 Central Park West, New York NY 10025. (212)866-4733. Fax: (212)866-4734. Contact: John Ware. Estab. 1978. Represents 60 clients. 40% of clients are new/previously unpublished writers. Currently handles: 75% nonfiction books; 25% novels.
Handles: Nonfiction books, novels. Considers these nonfiction areas: anthropology; biography/autobiography (memoirs); current affairs; history (including oral history, Americana and folklore); investigative journalism; psychology and health (academic credentials required); science; sports; 'bird's eye' views of phenomena. Considers these fiction areas: accessible literate noncategory fiction; mystery/suspense; thriller/espionage. Query by mail first, include SASE. Reports in 2 weeks on queries.
Recent Sales: *Merriwether Lewis: A Biography,* by Stephen E. Ambrose (Simon & Schuster); *Lost in the Wild Beyond: The Tale of Chris McCandless,* by Jon Krakauer (Villard); *The Case for Heaven,* by Mally Cox-Chapman (Putnam); *The Road to My Farm,* by Nora Janssen Seton (Viking).
Terms: Agent receives 15% commission on domestic sales; 15% on dramatic sales; 20% on foreign sales. Charges for messenger service, photocopying, extraordinary expenses.
Tips: "Writers must have appropriate credentials for authorship of proposal (nonfiction) or manuscript (fiction); no publishing track record required. Open to good writing and interesting ideas by new or veteran writers."

HARRIET WASSERMAN LITERARY AGENCY (III), 137 E. 36th St., New York NY 10016. (212)689-3257. Contact: Harriet Wasserman. Member of AAR. Specializes in fiction and nonfiction, some young adult and children's.
Handles: Nonfiction books, novels. Considers "mostly fiction (novels)." Query only. No unsolicited material.
Terms: Information not provided.

WATERSIDE PRODUCTIONS, INC. (II), 2191 San Elijo Ave., Cardiff-by-the-Sea CA 92007. (619)632-9190. Fax: (619)632-9295. President: Bill Gladstone. Estab. 1982. Represents 200 clients. 20% of clients are new/previously unpublished writers. Currently handles: 80% nonfiction; 20% novels. Member agents: Bill Gladstone (trade computer titles, business); Margot Maley (women's issues, serious nonfiction, fiction); Matthew Wagner (trade computer titles, nonfiction, screenplays); Carole McClendon (trade computer titles).
Handles: Nonfiction books, novels. Considers these nonfiction areas: anthropology/archaeology; art/architecture/design; biography/autobiography; business; child guidance/parenting; computers/electronics; ethnic/cultural interests; health/medicine; money/finance/economics; music/dance/theater/film; nature/environment; New Age/metaphysics; psychology; sociology; sports; true crime/investigative; women's issues/women's studies. Considers these fiction areas: action/adventure; contemporary

issues; detective/police/crime; glitz; literary; mainstream; mystery/suspense; romance; thriller/espionage. Query with outline/proposal. Reports in 2 weeks on queries; 6-8 weeks on mss.
Recent Sales: *RIM*, by Sasha Besher (HarperCollins); *DOS for Dummies*, by Dan Gookin (IDG Books); *Online After Dark*, by Rosalin Resnick (Random House).
Terms: Agent receives 15% commission on domestic sales; 25% on foreign sales. Offers written contract. Offers criticism service. Agents write critiques. Charges for photocopying and other unusual expenses. 100% of business is derived from commissions on ms sales.
Tips: Usually obtains new clients through recommendations from others. "Be professional. The more professional a submission, the more seriously it's viewed. Beginning writers should go to a writers workshop and learn how a presentation should be made."

WATKINS LOOMIS AGENCY, INC. (II), Suite 1, 133 E. 35th St., New York NY 10016. (212)532-0080. Contact: Nicole Aragi. Estab. 1908. Represents 120 clients. Specializes in literary fiction, London/UK translations.
Handles: Nonfiction books, novels. Considers these nonfiction areas: art/architecture/design; history; science/technology; translations; journalism. Considers these fiction areas: contemporary issues; literary; mainstream; mystery/suspense. Query with SASE. Reports within 3 weeks on queries.
Terms: Agent receives 10% commission on domestic sales; 20% on foreign sales.

WECKSLER-INCOMCO (III), 170 West End Ave., New York NY 10023. (212)787-2239. Fax: (212)496-7035. Contact: Sally Wecksler. Estab. 1970. Represents 15 clients. 80% of clients are new/previously unpublished writers. Specializes in nonfiction with illustrations (photos and art). Currently handles: 70% nonfiction books; 20% novels. Member agents: Joann Amparan, S. Wecksler (foreign rights/co-editions).
Handles: Nonfiction books, novels. Considers these nonfiction areas: anthropology/archaeology; art/architecture design; biography/autobiography; business; current affairs; history; music/dance/theater/film; nature/environment; photography. Considers these fiction areas: historical; literary; thriller/espionage. Query with outline plus 3 sample chapters. Reports in 6 weeks-2 months on queries; 3 months on mss.
Recent Sales: *Do's & Taboos—Public Speaking*, by Roger Axtell (Wiley); *Making Good*, by Loren Singer (Holt).
Terms: Agent receives 12-15% commission on domestic sales; 20% on foreign sales. Offers written contract, binding for 3 years.
Tips: Obtains new clients through recommendations from others.

THE WENDY WEIL AGENCY, INC. (V), Suite 1300, 232 Madison Ave., New York NY 10016. Agency not currently seeking new clients.

CHERRY WEINER LITERARY AGENCY (III), 28 Kipling Way, Manalapan NJ 07726. (908)446-2096. Fax: (908)446-20963*. Contact: Cherry Weiner. Estab. 1977. Represents 40 clients. 10% of clients are new/previously unpublished writers. Specializes in science fiction, fantasy, westerns, all the genre romances. Currently handles: 2-3% nonfiction books; 97% novels.
Handles: Nonfiction books, novels. Considers self-help/improvement, sociology nonfiction. Considers these fiction areas: action/adventure; contemporary issues; detective/police/crime; family saga; fantasy; glitz; historical; mainstream; mystery/suspense; psychic/supernatural; romance; science fiction; thriller/espionage; westerns/frontier. Query. Reports in 1 week on queries; 6-8 weeks on mss.
Recent Sales: *Maze of Moonlight*, by Gael Baudino (NAL/ROC); *Lady Valient*, by Suzanne Robinson (Bantam/Fanfare).
Terms: Agent receives 15% on domestic sales; 15% on foreign sales. Offers written contract. Charges for extra copies of mss "but would prefer author do it"; 1st class postage for author's copies of books; Express Mail for important document/manuscripts.
Writers' Conferences: Attends Western Writers Convention; Golden Triangle; Fantasy Convention.
Tips: "Meet agents and publishers at conferences. Establish a relationship, then get in touch with them reminding them of meetings and conference."

THE WEINGEL-FIDEL AGENCY (III), #21E, 310 E. 46th St., New York NY 10017. (212)599-2959. Contact: Loretta Fidel. Estab. 1989. Represents 35 clients. 25% of clients are new/previously unpublished writers. Specializes in commercial, literary fiction and nonfiction. Currently handles: 50% nonfiction books; 50% novels.

Handles: Nonfiction books, novels. Considers these nonfiction areas: anthropology/archaeology; art/architecture/design; biography/autobiography; health/medicine; music/dance/theater/film; psychology; science; sociology; true crime/investigative; women's issues/women's studies. Considers these fiction areas: contemporary issues; detective/police/crime; literary; mainstream; mystery/suspense; thriller/espionage. Query with cover letter, résumé and SASE. Reports in 2 weeks on queries; do not send ms.
Recent Sales: *Love Kills*, by Bruce Deitrick Price (Simon & Schuster).
Terms: Agent receives 15% on domestic sales; 20% on foreign sales. Offers written contract, binding for 1 year automatic renewal. Bills back to clients all reasonable expenses such as UPS, Federal Express, photocopying, etc.
Tips: Obtains new clients through referrals. "Be forthcoming about prior representation and previous submissions to publishers."

WESTCHESTER LITERARY AGENCY, INC. (II), Suite 203, 4278 D'Este Court, Lake Worth FL 33467. (407)642-2908. Fax: (407)965-4258. Contact: Neil G. McCluskey. Estab. 1991. Represents 51 clients. 30% of clients are new/previously unpublished writers. Specializes in trade mss and proposals from quality writers with an academic or school background. Currently handles: 65% nonfiction books; 3% juvenile books; 32% novels and novellas. Member agents: Medved Jeffers (ML fiction/adventure); Elaine Jacobs (ML fiction/romance); Arthur Rosenfeld (mystery/western).
Handles: Nonfiction books, juvenile books, novels, novellas, short story collections. Considers these nonfiction areas: biography/autobiography; how-to; business; child guidance/parenting; government/politics; history; juvenile nonfiction; language/literature; military/war; nature/environment; photography; psychology; religious/inspirational; self-help/personal improvement; true crime/investigative. Considers these fiction areas: action/adventure; contemporary/issues; detective/police/crime; family saga; fantasy; historical; humor/satire; juvenile; literary; mainstream; mystery/suspense; religious/inspiration; romance (contemporary, gothic, historical, regency); thriller/espionage; westerns/frontier; young adult. Query with outline/proposal. Reports in 1 month on queries; 6 weeks on mss. "Ordinarily, fiction mss should be submited only after professional editing."
Recent Sales: *Clearwater Summer*, by John E. Keegan (Carroll & Graff); *Live Rent Free Running Your Own Bed & Breakfast Inn*, by Dewey A. Deyer (TAB McGraw Hill).
Terms: Agent receives 15% commission on domestic sales; 20% on foreign sales. Offers written contract, binding for one year and renewable. Client pays for all submission costs.
Tips: Obtains new clients through LMP, stories in WD, recommendations from clients and editors.

RHODA WEYR AGENCY (II, III), 151 Bergen St., Brooklyn NY 11217. (718)522-0480. President: Rhoda A. Weyr. Estab. 1983. Member of AAR. Prefers to work with published/established authors; works with a small number of new/unpublished authors. Specializes in general nonfiction and fiction.
Handles: Nonfiction books, novels. Query with outline, sample chapters and SASE.
Terms: Agent receives 15% commission on domestic sales; 20% on foreign sales.

WIESER & WIESER, INC. (III), 7th Floor, 118 E. 25th St., New York NY 10010. (212)260-0860. Fax: (212)505-7186. Contact: Olga Wieser. Estab. 1975. 30% of clients are new/previously unpublished writers. Specializes in mainstream fiction and nonfiction. Currently handles: 50% nonfiction books; 50% novels. Member agents: Jake Elwell (history, contemporary, sports); George Wieser (contemporary fiction, thrillers, current affairs); Olga Wieser (psychology, fiction, historicals, translations, literary fiction).
Handles: Nonfiction books, novels. Considers these nonfiction areas: business; cooking/food/nutrition; current affairs; health/medicine; history; money/finance/economics; nature/environment; psychology; translations; true crime/investigative. Considers these fiction areas: contemporary issues; detective/police/crime; family saga; historical; literary; mainstream; mystery/suspense; romance (contemporary, historical, regency); thriller/espionage. Query with outline/proposal. Reports in 1 week on queries.
Recent Sales: *The Wall, A Day at the Vietnam Veterans Memorial*, by Peter Meyer and the editors of *Life* (St. Martin's Press); *This Savage Race*, by Douglas C. Jones (Henry Holt & Co.).
Terms: Agent receives 15% commission on domestic sales; 20% on foreign sales. Offers written contract. Offers criticism service. "No charge to our clients or potential clients." Charges for duplicating of ms and overseas mailing of ms or promotional material.
Tips: Obtains new clients through author's recommendations and industry professionals.

‡WITHERSPOON & ASSOCIATES, INC. (II), Suite 700, 157 W. 57th St., New York NY 10019. (212)757-0567. Fax: (212)757-2982. Contact: Kimberly Witherspoon. Estab. 1990. Represents 100 clients. 20% of clients are new/previously unpublished writers. Currently handles: 50% nonfiction books; 45% novels; 5% short story collections.
Handles: Nonfiction books, novels. Considers these nonfiction areas: anthropology/archaeology; biography/autobiography; business; current affairs; ethnic/cultural interests; gay/lesbian issues; government/politics/law; health/medicine; history; money/finance/economics; music/dance/theater/film; science/technology; self-help/personal improvement; true crime/investigative; women's issues/women's studies. Considers these fiction areas: contemporary issues; detective/police/crime; ethnic; family saga; feminist; gay; glitz; historical; humor/satire; lesbian; literary; mainstream; mystery/suspense; romance (contemporary); thriller/espionage. Query. Reports in 1-2 weeks on queries; 6-8 weeks on mss.
Terms: Agent receives 15% commission on domestic sales; 20% on foreign sales. Offers written contract.
Writers' Conferences: Attended Recursos de Santa Fe in Santa Fe, NM; Fishtrap in Oregon.
Tips: Obtains new clients through recommendations from others, solicitation and conferences.

GARY S. WOHL LITERARY AGENCY (II,III), One Fifth Ave., New York NY 10003. (212)254-9126. Estab. 1983. Represents 16 clients. 10% of clients are new/previously unpublished writers. Specializes in textbooks; ESL/bilingual books; how-to books. Currently handles: 30% nonfiction books; 50% textbooks; 10% movie scripts; 10% TV scripts.
Handles: Nonfiction books, textbooks, movie scripts, TV scripts. Considers these nonfiction areas: business; cooking/food/nutrition; crafts/hobbies; sports. Considers these fiction areas: humor/satire; mystery/suspense; romance; sports. Query with outline/proposal. Reports within 2 weeks on mss.
Terms: Agent receives 15% commission on domestic sales; 15% on foreign sales. Offers written contract. 100% of business derived from commissions on ms sales.

RUTH WRESCHNER, AUTHORS' REPRESENTATIVE (II, III), 10 W. 74th St., New York NY 10023. (212)877-2605. Fax: (212)595-5843. Contact: Ruth Wreschner. Estab. 1981. Represents 80 clients. 70% of clients are new/unpublished writers. "In fiction, if a client is not published yet, I prefer writers who have written for magazines; in nonfiction, a person well qualified in his field is acceptable." Prefers to work with published/established authors; works with new/unpublished authors. "I will always pay attention to a writer referred by another client." Specializes in popular medicine, health, how-to books and fiction (no pornography, screenplays or dramatic plays). Currently handles: 5% magazine articles; 75% nonfiction books; 10% novels; 5% textbooks; 5% juvenile books.
Handles: Nonfiction books, textbooks, adult and young adult fiction, magazine articles (only if appropriate for commercial magazines). Particularly interested in mainstream and mystery fiction. Query with outline. Reports in 2 weeks on queries.
Recent Sales: *Columbia-Presbyterian Guide to Osteoarthritis* (Macmillan); *Good Food for Bad Stomachs*, by Henry D. Janowitz, M.D. (Oxford Univ. Press); *The Dirty War*, by Charles Slaughter (YA fiction, Walker & Co.).
Terms: Agent receives 15% commission on domestic sales; 20% on foreign sales. Charges for photocopying expenses. "Once a book is placed, I will retain some money from the second advance to cover airmail postage of books, long-distance calls, etc. on foreign sales. I may consider charging for reviewing contracts in future. In that case I will charge $50/hour plus long-distance calls, if any."

WRITERS HOUSE (III), 21 W. 26th St., New York NY 10010. (212)685-2400. Fax: (212)685-1781. Contact: Albert Zuckerman. Estab. 1974. Member of AAR. Represents 280 clients. 50% of clients were new/unpublished writers. Specializes in all types of popular fiction, nonfiction. No scholarly, professional, poetry and no screenplays. Currently handles: 25% nonfiction books; 35% juvenile books; 40% novels. Member agents: Albert Zuckerman (major novels, thrillers, women's fiction, important nonfiction); Amy Berkower (major juvenile authors, women's fiction, art and decorating, cookbooks, psychology); Merrilee Heifetz (science fiction and fantasy, popular culture, literary fiction); Susan Cohen (juvenile and young adult fiction and nonfiction, Judaism, women's issues); Susan Ginsberg (serious and popular fiction, true crime, narrative nonfiction, personality books, cookbooks); Fran Lebowitz (juvenile and young adult, mysteries, computer-related books, popular culture); Michele Rubin (serious nonfiction).
Handles: Nonfiction books, juvenile books, novels. Considers these nonfiction areas: animals; art/architecture/design; biography/autobiography; business; child guidance/parenting; cooking/food/nutrition; health/medicine; history; interior design/decorating; juvenile nonfiction; military/war; money/finance/economics; music/dance/theater/film; nature/environment; psychology; science/technology;

self-help/personal improvement; true crime/investigative; women's issues/women's studies. Considers any fiction area. "Quality is everything." Query. Reports in 1 month on queries.
Recent Sales: *A Dangerous Fortune,* by Ken Follett (Delacorte); *Black Holes and Baby Universes,* by Stephen Hawking (Bantam); *The Baby Sitters Club,* by Ann Martin (Scholastic).
Terms: Agent receives 15% commission on domestic sales; 20% on foreign sales; 10% on juvenile and young adult books. Offers written contract, binding for 1 year.
Tips: Obtain new clients through recommendations from others. "Do not send manuscripts. Write a compelling letter. If you do, we'll ask to see your work."

WRITERS' PRODUCTIONS (II), P.O. Box 630, Westport CT 06881. (203)227-8199. Contact: David L. Meth. Estab. 1982. Represents 25 clients. Specializes in literary-quality fiction and nonfiction, with a special interest in Asia. Currently handles: 40% nonfiction books, 60% novels.
Handles: Nonfiction books, novels. "Literary quality fiction." Send outline plus 2-3 sample chapters (30-50 pages). Reports in 1 week on queries; 1 month on mss.
Recent Sales: *Night of the Milky Way Railway,* by Miyazawa Kenji (M.E. Sharpe); *Children of the Paper Crane,* by Masamoto Nasu (M.E. Sharpe); *Jinsei Annai: Letters to the Advice Column,* by John and Asako McKinsing (M.E. Sharpe); *Trial by Fire,* by Kathleen Barnes (Thunder's Mouth).
Terms: Agent receives 15% on domestic sales; 25% on foreign sales; 25% on dramatic sales. Offers written contract. Charges for electronic transmissions, long-distance calls, express or overnight mail, courier service, etc.
Tips: Obtain new clients through word of mouth. "Send only your best, most professionally prepared work. Do not send it before it is ready. We must have SASE for all correspondence and return of manuscripts. No telephone calls, please."

WRITERS' REPRESENTATIVES, INC. (II), 25 W. 19th St., New York NY 10011-4202. (212)620-9009. Contact: Glen Hartley or Lynn Chu. Estab. 1985. Represents 100 clients. 5% of clients are new/previously unpublished writers. Currently handles: 90% nonfiction books; 10% novels.
Handles: Nonfiction books, novels. Considers literary fiction. "Nonfiction submissions should include book proposal, detailed table of contents and sample chapter(s). For fiction submissions send sample chapters—not synopses. All submissions should include author biography and publication list. SASE required." No unsolicited mss.
Recent Sales: *The Real Anita Hill,* by David Brock; *The Divorce Culture,* by Barbara DaFoe Whitehead; *The Western Canon,* by Harold Bloom; *The Moral Sense,* by James Q. Wilson.
Terms: Agent receives 15% commission on domestic sales; 20% on foreign sales. "We charge for out-of-house photocopying as well as messengers, courier services (e.g., Federal Express), etc."
Tips: Obtains new clients "mostly on the basis of recommendations from others. Always include a SASE that will ensure a response from the agent and the return of material submitted."

SUSAN ZECKENDORF ASSOC. INC. (II), 171 W. 57th St., New York NY 10019. (212)245-2928. Contact: Susan Zeckendorf. Estab. 1979. Member of AAR. Represents 35 clients. 25% of clients are new/previously unpublished writers. Currently handles: 50% nonfiction books; 50% fiction.
Handles: Nonfiction books, novels, short story collections. Considers these nonfiction areas: art/architecture/design; biography/autobiography; business; child guidance/parenting; health/medicine; history; music/dance/theater/film; psychology; science/technology; sociology; true crime/investigative; women's issues/women's studies. Considers these fiction areas: action/adventure; contemporary issues; detective/police/crime; ethnic; family saga; glitz; historical; literary; mainstream; mystery/suspense; romance (contemporary, gothic, historical); thriller/espionage. Query. Reports in 10 days on queries; 2-3 weeks mss.
Recent Sales: *How to Write a Damn Good Novel, Advanced Techniques,* by James N. Frey (St. Martins); *The History of Fifth Avenue,* by Jerry E. Patterson (Harry Abrams).
Terms: Agent receives 15% commission on domestic sales; 20% on foreign sales. Charges for photocopying, messenger services.
Writers' Conferences: Central Valley Writers Conference, the Tucson Publishers Association Conference, Writer's Connection, Frontiers in Writing Conference (Amarillo), Golden Triangle Writers Conference (Beaumont, Texas).
Tips: Obtains new clients through recommendations, listings in writer's manuals.

Additional Nonfee-charging Agents

The following nonfee-charging agencies have full listings in other sections of this book.

These agencies have indicated that they are *primarily* interested in handling the work of scriptwriters, artists or photographers, but are also interested in book manuscripts. After reading the listing (you can find the page number in the Listings Index), send them a query to obtain more information on their needs and manuscript submission policies.

The Mary Beal Management
Cinema Talent International
Circle of Confusion Ltd.
Client First—A/K/A Leo P. Haffey Agency
The Coppage Company
Diskant & Associates
Douroux & Co.
Dragon Literary, Inc.

Dwyer & O'Grady, Inc.
Paul Kohner, Inc.
Legacies
Helen Merrill Ltd.
Montgomery-West Literary Agency
Jack Scagnetti Talent & Literary Agency
Scribe Agency

Lee Sobel Management Associates
Ellen Lively Steele & Associates
H.N. Swanson Inc.
The Tantleff Office
The Turtle Agency
Erika Wain Agency
Ann Wright Representatives

Nonfee-charging Agents/'93-'94 changes

The following agencies appeared in the last (1993) edition of *Guide to Literary Agents & Art/Photo Reps* but are absent from the 1994 edition. These agencies failed to respond to our request for an update of their listing, or were left out for the reasons indicated in parentheses following the agency name.

A.M.C. Literary Agency (no longer handles unpublished writers)
Linda Allen Literary Agency (out of business)
The Bank Street Literary Agency (out of business)
Helen Barrett Literary Agency (overwhelmed by submissions)
Cole and Lubenow: Books (not currently seeking new clients)
The Fallon Literary Agency (overwhelmed by submissions)
Marje Fields-Rita Scott Inc. (removed per request)
Sharon Jarvis & Co., Inc. (removed per request)
KC Communications (out of business)
M. Sue Lasbury Literary Agency (out of business)
The Lieberman Agency (unable to contact)
Greg Merhige-Merdon Marketing/Promo Co. Inc. (see Literary Agents: Fee-charging section)
Regula Noetzli Literary Agency (joined another agency)
The Norma-Lewis Agency
The Odenwald Connection (no longer a literary agent)
Printed Tree, Inc. (removed per request)
David M. Spatt, Esq. (removed for one year)
Gary S. Wohl Literary Agency

Literary Agents: Fee-charging

The issue of reading fees is as controversial for literary agents as for those looking for representation. While some agents dismiss the concept as inherently unethical and a scam, others see merit in the system, provided an author goes into it with his eyes open. Some writers spend hundreds of dollars for an "evaluation" that consists of a poorly written critique full of boilerplate language that says little, if anything, about their individual work. Others have received the helpful feedback they needed to get their manuscript in shape and have gone on to publish their work successfully.

An agency that charges fees might do so for any of a number of reasons. Many agents start out charging fees until they make some sales and get their businesses off the ground, at which time they can afford to switch to a purely commission-generated status. Some older agencies are feeling the pinch of an economic downturn and have reinstituted small reading fees to cover their costs while riding out the lull in the industry. Some agents enjoy the challenge of specializing in the fresh voices of newer, unpublished writers but have payrolls and expenses to meet in that pursuit. And then again, there are those agents who simply want to make as much money as possible feeding off inexperienced writers and have nothing constructive to offer. The problem, for a new writer particularly, is knowing the difference. This book contains advice and information on how to research an agent in order to avoid this pitfall in your quest for representation.

The cost of doing business has increased and continues to escalate as more writers request consideration of their material and advice in making it more saleable. Some agencies charge reading fees to cover the wages of freelancers hired to read unsolicited material. Some charge "marketing fees" to cover costs such as postage, long-distance telephone charges, travel expenses, legal fees and salaries. Some supplement their income with fees from editing, consulting and public relations services. Because they are compensated for additional services, fee-charging agents are often more open to the work of new writers.

This section lists literary agencies that charge a fee to writers in addition to taking a commission on sales. The sales commissions are the same as those taken by nonfee-charging agents: 10 to 15 percent for domestic sales, 10 to 20 percent for foreign and dramatic sales, with the difference paid to a foreign agent or subagent. Several agencies charge fees only to previously unpublished writers; these are indicated by an asterisk (*). Most agencies will consider you unpublished if you have local or small press publication credits only; check with a prospective agency before sending material to see if you fit their definition of published.

An agent who charges a one-time marketing fee of more than $50 for expenses such as postage, photocopying or long-distance calls will appear in this section. An agent who charges less than $50 for expenses and does not charge for other services appears in the Literary Agents: Nonfee-charging section. There are several types of fees and services, encompassing different activities a literary agency can perform. Confusion sometimes arises when terms are used differently from one agency to the next. Some agencies charge for reading a manuscript, while others charge for reading and evaluation. Some will read manuscripts for free but charge for critiquing and editing, while others offer an abbreviated overall critique for free and charge for more indepth treatment. A few offer consultations

and still others offer translating and typing services for a fee. Here are some of the more frequent terms and their definitions:
- *Reading fee.* This is charged for reading a manuscript (most agents do not charge to look at queries alone). Often the fee is paid to outside readers. It is generally a one-time, nonrefundable fee, but some agents will return the fee or credit it to your account if they decide to take you on as a client.
- *Evaluation fee.* Sometimes a reading fee includes a written evaluation, but many agents charge for this separately. An evaluation may be a one-paragraph report on the marketability of a manuscript or a several-page evaluation covering marketability along with flaws and strengths.
- *Marketing fees.* Usually a one-time charge to offset the costs of handling work, marketing fees cover a variety of expenses and may include initial reading or evaluation.
- *Critiquing service.* Although "critique" and "evaluation" are sometimes used interchangeably, a critique is usually more extensive, with suggestions on ways to improve the manuscript. Many agents offer critiques as a separate service and have a standard fee scale, based on a per-page or word-length basis. Some agents charge fees based on the extent of the service required, ranging from overall review to line-by-line commentary.
- *Editing service.* While we do not list businesses whose primary source of income is from editing, we do list agencies who also offer this service. Many do not distinguish between critiques and edits, but we define editing services as critiques that include detailed suggestions on how to improve the work and reduce weaknesses. Editing services can be charged on similar bases as critiquing services.
- *Consultation services.* Some agents charge an hourly rate to act as a marketing consultant, a service usually offered to writers who are not clients and who just want advice on marketing. Some agents are also available on an hourly basis for advice on a publisher's contract.
- *Other services.* Depending on an agent's background or abilities, the agent may offer a variety of other services to writers including typing, copyediting, proofreading, translating, book publicity and even legal advice.

Payment of a reading or other fee rarely ensures that an agent will take you on as a client. However, if you feel you need more than sales help and would not mind paying for an evaluation or critique from a professional, the agents listed in this section may interest you.

We cannot stress strongly enough, however, the importance of researching these agencies. Be sure to obtain a fee schedule and ask questions about the fees: it's important to clearly understand what fees cover and what you can expect for your money. Do not hesitate to ask any questions that will help you decide. Questions to ask and issues to settle appear in Write and Wrong: Literary Agents and Ethics by Arnold Goodman and Finding and Working with Literary Agents.

To help you with your search for an agent, we've included a number of special indexes in the back of this book. The Subject Index on page 243 is divided into sections for fee-charging and nonfee-charging literary agents and script agents. Each of these sections in the index is then divided by nonfiction and fiction subject categories. If you have written a book on finance and would consider a fee-charging agent, turn to the section of the Subject Index headed Fee-charging/Nonfiction. You will find a subject heading for finance followed by the names of agencies interested in this type of work. Some agencies did not want to restrict themselves to specific subjects. We've grouped them in the subject heading "open" in the nonfiction and fiction categories.

We've included an Agents and Reps Index on page 270. Often you will read about an agent, but since that agent is an employee of a large agency, you may not be able to find that person's business address or phone number. We asked agencies to list the agents on their staffs. In the index we list the names in alphabetical order along with the name of their agency. Find the name of the person you would like to contact and then check the listing for that agency. You will find the page number for the agency's listing in the Listings Index at the end of the book.

Many of the literary agents listed in this section are also interested in scripts; some script agents are also interested in book manuscripts. We have listed agencies whose primary function is selling scripts, but will consider some book manuscripts and charges a reading fee in "Additional Fee-charging Agents" at the end of this section. Complete listings for these agents, however, appear in the Script Agent section.

Some art representatives, especially those interested in humor (cartoons and comics) and children's books, are also looking for writers. Agencies that are primarily art representatives and charge a fee, but are also interested in writers, are included in "Additional Fee-charging Agents." The company's complete listing will appear in the Commercial Art/Photo Representatives section. Finally, a special index on page 268 lists agents and reps specifically interested in children's book illustration and author/illustrators.

For more information on approaching agents and the specifics of our listings, please see How to Use Your Guide to Literary Agents and Art/Photo Reps and Finding and Working with Literary Agents. See also the various articles included at the beginning of this book for the answers to a wide variety of questions concerning the author/agent relationship.

We've ranked the agencies listed in this section according to their openness to submissions. Below is our ranking system:

I Newer agency actively seeking clients.
II Agency seeking both new and established writers.
III Agency prefers to work with established writers, mostly obtains new clients through referrals.
IV Agency handling only certain types of work or work by writers under certain circumstances.
V Agency not currently seeking new clients. We have included mention of agencies rated V to let you know they are currently not open to new clients. In addition to those ranked V, we have included a few well-known agencies' names who have declined the opportunity for full listings at this time. *Unless you have a strong recommendation from someone well respected in the field, our advice is to approach only those agents ranked I-IV.*

*A & R BURKE CORPORATION (II), P.O. Box 11794, Ft. Lauderdale FL 33339-1794. (305)525-0531. Fax: (305)761-1952. Contact: Anna Mae Burke or Robert Burke. Corporation formed 1977, expanded to non-insider writers in 1991. Represents 15 clients. 60% of clients are new/previously unpublished writers. "In addition to adult and young adult fiction, the agency handles technical books, textbooks and computer software among its nonfiction specialties." Currently handles: 5% nonfiction books; 5% scholarly books; 5% textbooks; 10% juvenile books; 60% novels; 15% computer. Member agents: Anna Mae Burke (fiction: adult and young readers; nonfiction: technical); Robert Burke (nonfiction, technical and computer software).
Handles: Nonfiction books, textbooks, scholarly books, juvenile books, novels. Considers these nonfiction areas: art/architecture/design; biography/autobiography; business; computers/electronics; current affairs; psychology; government/politics/law; history; juvenile nonfiction; language/literature/criticism; military/war; money/finance/economics; music/dance/theater/film; science/technology; self-help/personal improvement; sociology; sports; true crime/investigative; women's issues/women's studies. Con-

siders these fiction areas: action/adventure; contemporary issues; detective/police/crime; ethnic; family saga; fantasy; feminist; historical; humor/satire; juvenile; literary; mainstream; mystery/suspense; picture book; romance (contemporary, gothic, historical, regency); science fiction; sports; thriller/espionage; young adult; computer software. Query with outline plus 2 sample chapters. Reports in 2 weeks on queries; 1 month on mss.
Terms: Agent receives 15% commission on domestic sales; 20% on foreign sales. Offers written contract, binding for 1 year.
Fees: Charges $35 reading fee. "The fee is charged to new writers and waived for published writers, and sometimes for those who have made a contact at a writer's meeting and have discussed the work with us and have been encouraged to send a manuscript." Offers criticism service. 85% of business derived from commissions of ms sales; 15% derived from reading fees or criticism service.
Writer's Conferences: North Carolina Writers Conference, Mystery Writers of America (Florida chapter), Florida Freelance Writers Conference.
Tips: "We are always conscious of seeking new clients and may meet one almost anywhere. While we prefer material to be from a published author, unpublished authors have a chance with us. Anna Mae Burke is an attorney and reviews contracts from that perspective at no additional charge to the writer."

ACACIA HOUSE PUBLISHING SERVICES LTD. (II, III), 51 Acacia Rd., Toronto Ontario M4S 2K6 Canada. (416)484-8356. Fax: (416)484-8356. Contact: Frances Hanna. Estab. 1985. Represents 30 clients. "I prefer that writers be previously published, with at least a few articles to their credit. Strongest consideration will be given to those with, say, 3 or more published books. However, I *would* take on an unpublished writer of outstanding talent." Works with a small number of new/unpublished authors. Specializes in contemporary fiction: literary or commercial (no horror, occult or science fiction); nonfiction: all categories but business/economics—in the trade, not textbook area; children's: a few picture books; young adult, mainly fiction. Currently handles: 30% nonfiction books; 50% novels; 20% juvenile books.
Handles: Nonfiction books, novels, juvenile books. Query with outline. Does not read unsolicited mss. Reports in 3 weeks on queries.
Recent Sales: *The Birdwatcher's Companion*, by Barry Kent MacKay (Key Porter); *Kaleidoscope*; *Salamander* (third and fourth of the series) to Constable (UK); *Chicken Little was Right*, by Jean Ruryk (St. Martin's Press).
Terms: Agent receives 15% commission on English language sales; 15% on dramatic sales; and 30% on foreign language sales.
Fees: Charges reading fee on mss over 200 pages (typed, double-spaced) in length; waives reading fee when representing the writer. 4% of income derived from reading fees. Charges $200/200 pages. "If a critique is wanted on a ms under 200 pages in length, then the charge is the same as the reading fee for a longer ms (which incorporates a critique)." 5% of income derived from criticism fees. Critique includes "2-3-page overall evaluation which will contain any specific points that are thought important enough to detail. Marketing advice is not usually included, since most manuscripts evaluated in this way are not considered to be publishable." Charges writers for photocopying, courier, postage, telephone/fax "if these are excessive."

‡ACE CONSULTANTS (I, II), 6261 Dayton Ave., Las Vegas NV 89107. (702)251-8116. Contact: Newton E. Streeter. Estab. 1991. Represents 1 client. 100% of clients are new/previously unpublished writers. Currently handles: 10% nonfiction books; 5% textbooks; 70% novels; 10% movie scripts; 5% stage plays.
Handles: Nonfiction books, novels, movie scripts. Considers these nonfiction areas: biography/autobiography; ethnic/cultural interests; gay/lesbian issues; New Age/metaphysics; sports; true crime/investigative. Considers these fiction areas: action/adventure; erotica; ethnic; gay; humor/satire; lesbian; mainstream; mystery/suspense; psychic/supernatural; thriller/espionage. Query. Reports in 2 days on queries; 1 month on mss.
Terms: Agent receives 15% commission on domestic sales; 20% on foreign sales. Offers written contract, binding for one year, negotiable.
Fees: Charges reading fee. Offers criticism service. Charges other fees.

---

‡ ***The double dagger before a listing indicates the listing is new in this edition.***

ACKERMAN LITERARY SERVICES (I), P.O. Box 1611, Tybee Island GA 31328. (912)786-6174. Contact: Sharon Ackerman. Estab. 1992. Represents 10 clients. 90% of new clients are new/previously unpublished writers. Currently handles: 100% novels. Member agents: Jodi Ceriale, Christine Hoskins.
Handles: Novels, novellas, short story collections, magazine short stories. Considers these nonfiction areas: crafts/hobbies; true crime/investigative. Considers these fiction areas: confessional; detective/police/crime; family saga; glitz; historical; mainstream; mystery/suspense; psychic/supernatural; romance (contemporary, gothic); thriller/espionage. Query with entire ms. Reports in 1 week on queries; 1 month on mss.
Terms: Agent receives 10% commission on domestic sales; 15% on foreign sales.
Fees: Does not charge a reading fee. Criticism service: $50 up to 100,000 words; $75 over 100,000; refundable upon sale of ms. "I prefer to make notations on manuscripts, in addition to a 2-3 page report on marketability, characterization, plot, style, etc. We work with the author on correcting weak points." Charges for postage, photocopying, telephone, etc. "We also offer a manuscript typing service for $2/page."
Writer's Conferences: Attended Romance Writers of America Conference, Savannah GA.
Tips: Obtains new clients through advertising and recommendations. "Manuscripts should have a professional look, correct grammar, no typing errors. We want new writers to know we're here to help. We're interested in long-term career goals. Know the market you're writing for. Don't give up. Make a commitment to writing."

*THE AHEARN AGENCY, INC. (I), 2021 Pine St., New Orleans LA 70118. (504)861-8395. Contact: Pamela G. Ahearn. Estab. 1992. Member of RWA. Represents 17 clients. 33% of clients are new/previously unpublished writers. Specializes in historical romance; also very interested in mysteries and suspense fiction. Currently handles: 10% nonfiction books; 20% juvenile books; 70% novels.
Handles: Nonfiction books, juvenile books, novels, short story collections (if stories previously published), young adult (no picture books). Considers these nonfiction areas: animals; biography; business; child guidance/parenting; current affairs; ethnic/cultural interests; gay/lesbian issues; health/medicine; history; juvenile nonfiction; music/dance/theater/film; self-help/personal improvement; true crime/investigative; women's issues/women's studies. Considers these fiction areas: action/adventure; contemporary issues; detective/police/crime; ethnic; family saga; fantasy; feminist; gay; glitz; historical; humor/satire; juvenile; lesbian; literary; mainstream; mystery/suspense; psychic/supernatural; regional; romance (contemporary, gothic, historical, regency); science fiction; thriller/espionage; westerns/frontier; young adult. Query. Reports in 2-4 weeks on queries; 6-8 weeks on mss.
Recent Sales: *The Ground She Walks Upon*, by Meagan McKinney (Dell); *The Christmas Wish*, by Rexanne Becnel (Dell); *Shinju*, by Laura Jon Rowland (Random House); *The Unwritten Order*, by John Edward Ames (Bantam).
Terms: Agent receives 15% commission on domestic sales; 20% on foreign sales. Offers written contract, binding for 1 year; renewable by mutual consent.
Fees: "I charge a reading fee to previously unpublished authors, based on length of material. Fees range from $125-400. Fee is non-refundable. Offers criticism service. When authors pay a reading fee, they receive a 3-5 single-spaced-page critique of their work, addressing writing quality and marketability." Critiques written by Pamela G. Ahearn. Charges for photocopying. 90% of business derived from commissions; 10% derived from reading fees or criticism services. Payment of reading or criticism fees does not ensure representation.
Writers' Conferences: Attends Midwest Writers Workshop, Moonlight & Magnolias and RWA National conference, Golden Triangle Writers Conference.
Tips: Obtains new clients "usually through listings such as this one and client recommendations. Sometimes at conferences. Be professional! Always send in exactly what an agent/editor asks for, no more, no less. Keep query letters brief and to the point, giving your writing credentials and a very brief summary of your book. If one agent rejects you, keep trying—there are a lot of us out there!"

FAREL T. ALDEN—LITERARY SERVICE (I), 407 Peach St., Washington IL 61571-1929. (309)745-5411. Contact: Farel T. Alden. Estab. 1990. Represents 22 clients. 50% of clients are new/previously unpublished writers. Currently handles: 70% novels; 10% nonfiction books; 20% juvenile books.
Handles: Nonfiction books, juvenile books, novels. Considers these nonfiction areas: animals; history; juvenile nonfiction; New Age/metaphysics; self-help/personal improvement; true crime/investigative. Considers these fiction areas: action/adventure; detective/police/crime; family saga; historical; mainstream; mystery/suspense; psychic/supernatural; thriller/espionage; westerns/frontier. Query first. Reports in 1 month on queries; 2-3 months on mss.

Literary Agents: Fee-charging 117

Terms: Agent receives 15% commission on domestic sales; 20% on foreign sales. Offers written contract, "which can be cancelled with 60 days notice. We use a standard contract compiled by an attorney specializing in the literary field."
Fees: Does not charge a reading fee. Criticism service: "If the writer wishes a critique, he/she may request one. The charge is $1 per double-spaced, manuscript page. We also prefer to make notations on manuscripts in addition to the formal critique. We do them ourselves. They are detailed. We find one of the major problems is an inadequate knowledge of grammar and punctuation! We show the corrections directly on manuscript." Charges for postage, photocopying, telephone. Also offers a ms typing service if the writer has a need. Cost is $1.10/page (double-spaced). 60% of business is derived from commissions on ms sales; 40% derived from criticism service. "We expect to derive most of our income from sales commissions. The critiquing is a service offered our clients." Payment of a criticism fee does not ensure representation.
Tips: Obtains new clients through recommendations from others. "Our agency does not send a publisher a manuscript that is not properly formatted, correctly spelled and properly punctuated. If the writer is not a good typist and lacks in the foregoing areas, we suggest hiring someone to do it; either us or someone locally. Naturally, our emphasis is on content, but appearance is important in a presentation package for a publisher. Please: *no* certified mail submissions!"

JOSEPH ANTHONY AGENCY (II), 15 Locust Court, R.D. 20, Mays Landing NJ 08330. (609)625-7608. Contact: Joseph Anthony. Estab. 1964. Signatory of WGA. Represents 30 clients. 80% of clients are new/previously unpublished writers. "Specializes in general fiction and nonfiction. Always interested in screenplays." Currently handles: 5% juvenile books; 80% novellas; 5% short story collections; 2% stage plays; 10% TV scripts. Member agent: Lena Fortunato.
Handles: Nonfiction books, juvenile books, novels, movie scripts, TV scripts. Considers these nonfiction areas: health/medicine; military/war; psychology; true crime/investigative; science/technology; self-help/personal improvement. Considers these fiction areas: action/adventure; confessional; detective/police/crime; erotica; fantasy; mystery/suspense; psychic/supernatural; romance (gothic, historical, regency); science fiction; thriller/espionage; young adult. Query, SASE required. Reports in 2 weeks on queries; 1 month on mss.
Terms: Agent receives 15% commission on domestic sales; 20% on foreign sales.
Fees: Charges $85 reading fee for novels up to 100,000 words. "Fees are returned after a sale of $3,000 or more." Charges for postage and photocopying up to 3 copies. 10% of business is derived from commissions on ms sales; 90% is derived from reading fees (because I work with new writers). Payment of criticism fee does not ensure representation.
Tips: Obtains new clients through recommendations from others, solicitation. "If your script is saleable, I will try to sell it to the best possible markets. I will cover sales of additional rights through the world. If your material is unsaleable as it stands but can be rewritten and repaired, I will tell you why it has been turned down. After you have rewritten your script, you may return it for a second reading without *any additional fee*. But ... if it is completely unsaleable in our evaluation for the markets, I will tell you why it has been turned down again and give you specific advice on how to avoid these errors in your future material. I do not write on, edit or blue pencil your script. I am an *agent* and an agent is out to sell a script."

‡ASHBY LITERARY AGENCY (I, II), 2840 Walton Creek Dr., Colorado Springs CO 80922. (719)591-9391. Fax: (719)591-5065. Contact: Ed Ashby. Estab. 1992. Represents 18 clients. 60% of clients are new/previously unpublished writers. Specializes in romance/historical romance. Currently handles: 20% nonfiction books; 40% novels; 20% short story collections; 20% articles. Member agent: Tatsue Koyama (history).
Handles: Nonfiction books, novels, novellas. Considers these nonfiction areas: animals; business; computers/electronics; current affairs; government/politics/law; history; military/war; money/finance/economics. Considers these fiction areas: action/adventure; historical; literary; mainstream; mystery/suspense; romance; science fiction; thriller/espionage; westerns/frontier. Query. Reports in 2 weeks on queries; 1 month on mss.
Terms: Agent receives 15% commission on domestic sales; 15% on foreign sales. Offers written contract.
Fees: Reading fee $100/25,000 words or fraction thereof; refundable, depending on author's credentials. Offers a criticism service on arrangement basis, depending on level of difficulty. Critiques comprised of "an overview: what is basically required to make material publishable." 80% of business is derived from commissions on ms sales; 20% is derived from reading fees or criticism services (goal). Payment of a criticism fee does not ensure representation.

Tips: Obtains new clients through recommendations, queries. "Query with proposal."

*AUTHOR AID ASSOCIATES (II), 340 E. 52nd St., New York NY 10022. (212)758-4213; 980-9179. Editorial Director: Arthur Orrmont. Estab. 1967. Represents 150 clients. Specializes in aviation, war, biography, novels, autobiography. Currently handles: 5% magazine fiction; 35% nonfiction books; 38% novels; 5% juvenile books; 5% movie scripts; 2% stage plays; 5% poetry and 5% other. Member agent: Leonie Rosenstiel, vice president, "a musicologist and authority on New Age subjects and nutrition."
Handles: Magazine fiction, nonfiction books, novels, juvenile books, movie scripts, stage plays, TV scripts. Query with outline. "Short queries answered by return mail." Reports within 6 weeks on mss.
Recent Sales: *Play Ball*, by John S. Snyder (Chronicle Books); *Touring America's National Parks*, by Larry Lidamet (Hunter Publishers).
Terms: Agent receives 15% commission on domestic and dramatic sales; 20% on foreign sales.
Fees: Charges a reading fee to new authors, refundable from commission on sale. Charges for cable, photocopying and messenger express. Offers a consultation service through which writers not represented can get advice on a contract. 85% of income from sales of writers' work; 15% of income derived from reading fees.
Tips: Publishers of *Literary Agents of North America*.

AUTHOR AUTHOR LITERARY AGENCY (I, II), P.O. Box 34051, 1200-37 St. SW, Calgary, Alberta T3C 3W2 Canada. (403)242-0226. Fax: (403)242-0226. President: Joan Rickard. Estab. 1992. Member of Writers' Guild of Alberta and CAA. Represents 40 clients. 50% of clients are new/previously unpublished writers. Currently handles: 10% nonfiction books; 5% scholarly books; 5% textbooks; 25% juvenile books; 45% novels; 5% novellas; 5% short story collections.
Handles: Fiction and nonfiction, adult and juvenile, textbooks, scholarly books, novels, novellas, short story collections. No poetry or screenplays. Considers these nonfiction areas: biography/autobiography; business; child guidance/parenting; self-help/personal improvement; true crime/investigative; women's issues/women's studies. Considers these fiction areas: mystery/suspense; science fiction; romance (contemporary). "Responds to all letters of inquiry promptly." Reports in 1 month on queries including ms outlines and/or sample chapters; 2 months on complete mss.
Recent Sales: *Taming the Dragon, Module I: A Preventive Program in Anger Management and Conflict Resolution for Early Childhood Services Programs*, by H.L. Webster and Lorraine Parker (Detselig/Temeron Books).
Terms: Agent receives 15% commission on domestic sales; 20% on foreign sales. Offers written contract.
Fees: "We provide a complete package of reading, editing, evaluating and marketing services." Will read at no charge unsolicited queries and outlines. Reads queries, edits and evaluates outlines and partial mss of up to 3 sample chapters for $75, which is applied toward total reading, editing, evaluating, handling fee if agency agrees to represent author. Complete mss must be accompanied by total handling fee: up to 15,000 words $250; up to 65,000 words $350; up to 85,000 words $450; 85,000+ words flat rate $475 (certified check or money order, please). Manuscripts should rarely exceed 100,000 words. Payment of partial or complete evaluation fee does not ensure representation. "We discuss methods to improve and/or make the manuscripts marketable. Once we place an author's work, there are no further reading-evaluating fees. Charges for additional photocopying of manuscripts submitted to publishers, long-distance telephone/fax to promote sales and express of manuscripts. Consults with and reports promptly to writers on all communications concerning handling and marketing of their manuscripts!"
Tips: "We welcome new, unpublished writers and work closely with clients to assist with honing their writing to as fine a polish as is possible; but the key word is ASSIST. It is not the agent's (or publisher's) job to revise the entire mechanics of formatting, punctuation and literary content/context. Many potentially good stories/novels are rejected by publishers and agents due to improperly, hastily prepared/presented manuscripts. Excellent instructional manuals are available at bookstores or libraries. We provide a *"Crash Course" Kit on Business Letters, Basic Punctuation Guide & Manuscript Formatting* free of charge to clients, or this may be obtained upon request from our agency ($7.95 including postage/handling). Obtains new clients primarily through referrals and writers' manuals. Always enclose SASE for queries/manuscripts."

Literary Agents: Fee-charging 119

THE AUTHORS AND ARTISTS RESOURCE CENTER/TARC LITERARY AGENCY (II), P.O. Box 64785, Tucson AZ 85728-1785. (602)325-4733. Contact: Martha R. Gores. Estab. 1984. Represents 30 clients. Specializes in mainstream adult fiction and nonfiction books. Currently handles: 80% nonfiction books; 20% novels.
Handles: Nonfiction books, novels. Considers all nonfiction areas except essays, autobiography (unless celebrity) and journals. "Especially interested in how-to or self-help books by professionals; parenting books by psychologists or M.D.s." Query with outline. Does not read unsolicited mss. Reports in 2 months if SASE included.
Recent Sales: *Walker of Time* (Harbinger House).
Terms: Agent receives 15% commission on domestic sales; 20% on dramatic sales; 20% on foreign sales.
Fees: Does not charge a reading fee. Criticism service "only if is requested by the author." No set fee. "Each critique is tailored to the individual needs of the writer. We hire working editors who are employed by book publishers to do critiquing, editing, etc." Charges writers for mailing, photocopying, faxing, telephone calls.
Tips: "We do ghosting for professional people. In order to do ghosting, you must be published by a professional, reputable publisher. To be considered, send a business card with your résumé to our Arizona address."

*AUTHORS' MARKETING SERVICES LTD. (II), 217 Degrassi St., Toronto, Ontario M4M 2K8 Canada. (416)463-7200. Fax: (416)469-4494. Contact: Larry Hoffman. Estab. 1978. Represents 17 clients. 25% of clients are new/previously unpublished writers. Specializes in thrillers, romance, parenting and self-help. Currently handles: 65% nonfiction books; 10% juvenile books; 20% novels; 5% other.
Handles: Nonfiction books, novels. Considers these nonfiction areas: biography/autobiography; business; child guidance/parenting; current affairs; military/war; true crime/investigative. Considers these fiction areas: action/adventure; detective/police/crime; mystery/suspense; romance; thriller/espionage. Query. Reports in 1 week on queries; 1-2 months on mss.
Recent Sales: *Coaching for Life*, by Andy Higgins (McClelland & Stewart); *Euromarket Day Finder*, by R.H. Lavers (Pitman).
Terms: Agent receives 15% commission on domestic sales; 20% on foreign sales. Offers written contract, binding for 6-9 months to complete first sale.
Fees: Charges $295 reading fee. "A reading/evaluation fee of $295 applies only to unpublished authors, and the fee must accompany the completed manuscript. Criticism service is included in the reading fee. The critique averages 3-4 pages in length, and discusses strengths and weaknesses of the execution, as well as advice aimed at eliminating weaknesses." 95% of business is derived from commissions on ms sales; 5% is derived from reading fees or criticism service. Payment of a criticism fee does not ensure representation.
Tips: Obtains new clients through recommendations from other writers and publishers, occasional solicitation. "Never submit first drafts. Prepare the manuscript as cleanly and as perfectly, in the writer's opinion, as possible."

MAXIMILIAN BECKER/ALETA M. DALEY, 444 East 82nd St., New York NY 10028. (212)744-1453. Head: Aleta M. Daley. Estab. 1950. Looking for exciting literary and mainstrean fiction, suspense, science fiction. Provocative non-fiction including women's, black and ethnic studies, biography and selected scholarly works. Children's books. Query with sample chapters or a well-developed proposal (nonfiction) with a brief resume. Does not accept unsolicited mss.
- Maximilian Becker died in December, 1992. His associate, Aleta Daley, has taken over the business.

Recent Sales: *The Legend of the Duelist*, by Rutledge Etheridge (Berkley Publishing Group); *Die Pfauenthron Prinzessin*, by Sara Harris (Hestia); *Japan and the Pursuit of a New American Identity*, by Walter Feinberg (Routledge); *Berlin Calling: American Broadcasters in Service To The Third Reich*, by John Carver Edwards (Praeger).
Terms: Agent receives 15% on domestic sales including dramatic and film rights; 20% on foreign sales.
Fees: Does not charge a reading fee. Criticism service: if requested. This includes editorial suggestions. Normal handling fee.

*MEREDITH BERNSTEIN LITERARY AGENCY (II), Suite 503 A, 2112 Broadway, New York NY 10023. (212)799-1007. Fax: (212)799-1145. Contact: Meredith Bernstein. Estab. 1981. Member of AAR. Represents approximately 75 clients. 20% of clients are new/previously unpublished writers. Does not

specialize, "very eclectic." Currently handles: 50% nonfiction books; 50% fiction. Member agents: Elizabeth Cavanaugh and Judy Gittenstein (children's books).
Handles: Fiction and nonfiction books. Query first.
Recent Sales: *What Women Want*, by Patricia Ireland (Dutton/NAL); *Historical Supply Catalogs*, by Alan Wellikoft (Camden House); *When Money Is the Drug*, by Donna Brundy (HarperCollins).
Terms: Agent receives 15% commission on domestic sales; 20% on foreign sales.
Fees: Charges reading fee of up to $100 for unpublished writers only. Charges a $75 disbursement fee per year. 98% of business is derived from commissions on ms sales; 2% is derived from reading or criticism services. Payment of criticism fees does not ensure agency representation.
Tips: Obtains new clients through recommendations from others, solicitation, at conferences; own ideas developed and packaged.

THE BRINKE LITERARY AGENCY (II), 4498 B Foothill Rd., Carpinteria CA 93013. (805)684-9955. Contact: Jude Barvin. Estab. 1988. Represents 24 clients. Currently handles: 25% nonfiction books; 50% novels; 25% movie scripts.
Handles: Considers these nonfiction areas: anthropology; sociology; spiritual; New Age, parapsychology. Considers all fiction areas. Query with SASE.
Recent Sales: *Elvis My Brother*, by Billy Stanley (St. Martins Press).
Terms: Agent receives 15% commissions on domestic sales; 20% on foreign sales. Offers written contract, binding for 1 year.
Fees: Charges reading fee of $125 for novel ms; $100 for screenplays. Criticism service: money deducted from agency expenses or commissions. Charges for office expenses, postage, photocopying.
Writers' Conferences: Attends Santa Barbara Writers Conference.
Tips: Obtains new clients through recommendations from others, queries, mail.

*****PEMA BROWNE LTD. (II)**, HCR Box 104B, Pine Rd., Neversink NY 12765. (914)985-2936. Fax: (914)985-7635. Contact: Perry Browne or Pema Browne. Estab. 1966. Member of SCBWI; signatory of WGA. Represents 50 clients. Handles any commercial fiction, nonfiction, romance, juvenile and children's picture books. Currently handles: 25% nonfiction books; 25% juvenile books; 45% novels; 5% movie scripts.
Handles: Nonfiction books, scholarly books, juvenile books, novels. Considers these nonfiction areas: anthropology/archaeology; art/architecture/design; biography/autobiography; business; child guidance/parenting; cooking/food/nutrition; government/politics/law; health/medicine; juvenile nonfiction; military/war; nature/environment; New Age/metaphysics; psychology; religious/inspirational; true crime/investigative; science/technology; self-help/personal improvement; sports; women's issues/women's studies. Considers these fiction areas: action/adventure, contemporary issues; detective/police/crime; feminist; glitz; historical; humor/satire; juvenile; literary; mainstream; mystery/suspense; picture book; psychic/supernatural; religious/inspiration; romance; science fiction; thriller/espionage; young adult. Query with SASE. Reports in 1 week on queries; 2 weeks on mss.
Recent Sales: *The Great Snake Doctor*, by T. Rantao Ogle (Lothrup Lee & Shepard); *Lady Hope's Rules of Conduct-Regency Romance*, by Cathryn Clare (Avon); *101 Teacher's Résumés*, by Anthony & Roe (Barron's).
Terms: Agent receives 15% commission on domestic sales; 15% on foreign sales.
Fees: Charges reading fee *only* on *selective adult* novels by unpublished authors.
Tips: Obtains new clients through "editors, authors, *LMP*, *Writer's Digest* and as a result of longevity! If writing romance, be sure to receive guidelines from various romance publishers. In nonfiction, one must have credentials to lend credence to a proposal. Make sure of margins, double-space and use clean, dark type."

‡JULIE CASTIGLIA LITERARY AGENCY (II), Suite 510, 1155 Camino Del Mar, Del Mar CA 92014. (619)753-4361. Fax: (619)753-5094. Contact: Julie Castiglia. Estab. 1993. Member of AAR, PEN. Represents 50 clients. 25% of clients are new/previously unpublished writers. Currently handles: 72% nonfiction books, 2% juvenile books, 25% novels, 1% short story collections.

---

* An asterisk indicates those agents who only charge fees to new or previously unpublished writers or to writers only under certain conditions.

Handles: Nonfiction books, juvenile books, novels, short story collections. Considers these nonfiction areas: animals; anthropology/archaeology; art/architecture/design; biography/autobiography; business; child guidance/parenting; cooking/food/nutrition; current affairs; ethnic/cultural interests; health/medicine; history; interior design/decorating; juvenile nonfiction; language/literature/criticism; music/dance/theater/film; nature/environment; New Age/metaphysics; psychology; religious/inspirational; science/technology; self-help/personal improvement; sociology; sports; women's issues/women's studies. Considers these fiction areas: action/adventure; contemporary issues; detective/police/crime; ethnic; family saga; feminist; gay; glitz; literary mainstream; mystery/suspense; picture book; regional; romance (contemporary, gothic, historical, regency); women's fiction especially. Send outline/proposal plus 2 sample chapters; send synopsis with chapters for fiction. Reports in 6-8 weeks on mss.
Recent Sales: *Airwars*, by Barbara Sturken and James Glab (Simon & Schuster); *Spare Change*, by John Peak (St. Martins); *Rebuilding Relationships With Our Adult Children*, by Karen O'Connor (Thomas Nelson); *Devilfish*, by Mike Dunn (Avon); *Hiking Series*, by John McKinney (HarperCollins).
Terms: Agent receives 15% commission on domestic sales; 20% on foreign sales. Offers written contract, binding for 2 months.
Fees: Does not charge a reading fee. Criticism service: $1/page; "a 2-3 page detailed critique on plot, character, story, dialogue, narrative, etc." Charges for excessive postage and copying for first-time authors. Payment of a criticism fee does not ensure representation.
Writers' Conferences: Attends National Writers Club, SDSU Conference, Romantic Times/Booklovers Convention, Bouchecon/Wilamette Writers Conference, Oregon.
Tips: Obtains new clients through solicitations, conferences, referrals. "Be professional with submissions. Attend workshops and conferences before you approach an agent."

THE CATALOG™ LITERARY AGENCY (II), P.O. Box 2964, Vancouver WA 98668. (206)694-8531. Contact: Douglas Storey. Estab. 1986. Represents 50 clients. 50% of clients are new/previously unpublished writers. Specializes in business, health, psychology, money, science, how-to, self-help, technology, parenting, women's interest. Currently handles: 50% nonfiction books; 20% juvenile books; 30% novels.
Handles: Nonfiction books, textbooks, juvenile books, novels. Considers these nonfiction areas: agriculture/horticulture; business; child guidance/parenting; computers/electronics; crafts/hobbies; health/medicine; juvenile nonfiction; money/finance/economics; nature/environment; psychology; science/technology; self-help/personal improvement; women's issues/women's studies. Considers juvenile and mainstream fiction. Query. Reports in 2 weeks on queries; 3 weeks on mss.
Recent Sales: *Applied Ceramics*, by John Klatt (Dekker Publishers); *Kingdom of the Flies*, by Sean Patrick (Amereon House).
Terms: Agent receives 15% on domestic sales; 20% on foreign sales. Offers written contract, binding for about 9 months.
Fees: Does not charge a reading fee. Charges an up-front handling fee from $85-250 that covers photocopying, telephone and postage expense.

COLBY: LITERARY AGENCY (I), 2864-20 Jefferson Ave., Yuba City CA 95993. (916)674-3378. Contact: Pat Colby. Estab. 1990. Represents 15 clients. 93% of clients are new/previously unpublished writers. Specializes in fiction—mystery and comedy. Currently handles: 100% novels. Member agent: Richard Colby.
Handles: Novels, novellas, short story collections. Considers these fiction areas: cartoon/comic; detective/police/crime; humor/satire; mystery/suspense; sports; thriller/espionage; westerns/frontier. Query or send entire ms. Reports within 1 week on queries; 1 month on mss.
Terms: Agent receives 12% commission on domestic sales; 15% commission on foreign sales. Offers written contract, binding for 1 year.
Fees: Charges critiquing fee. Send query or 30 pages of ms for a prompt reply with full explanation of any charges. Critiques are done by Pat or Richard Colby. Charges for editing, photocopying, postage. Payment of critiquing fees does not ensure agency representation.

BRUCE COOK AGENCY (I), P.O. Box 75995, St. Paul MN 55175-0995. (612)487-9355. Estab. 1992. Member of The Loft (writer's organization). 50% of clients are new/previously unpublished writers. Subject areas include romance, mystery, science fiction, juvenile, history, education and religion. Currently handles: 20% nonfiction books; 10% scholarly books; 30% novels; 10% short story collections; 10% movie scripts; 10% TV scripts. Literary Manager: Elizabeth Young (13 years experience with 2 other agencies). Member agent: Edward Young.

Handles: Nonfiction books, textbooks, scholarly books, juvenile books, novels, short story collections, movie scripts, stage plays, TV scripts. Considers these nonfiction areas: biography/autobiography; business; child guidance/parenting; cooking/food/nutrition; health/medicine; history; juvenile nonfiction; language/literature/criticism; music/dance/theater/film; nature/environment; psychology; religious/inspirational; self-help/personal improvement; sociology. Considers these fiction areas: action/adventure; cartoon/comic; family saga; fantasy; historical; humor/satire; juvenile; literary; mystery/suspense; regional; religious/inspiration; science fiction; thriller/espionage; young adult. Query with 1-page outline. Reports in 2 weeks on queries; 1-2 months on mss.
Recent Sales: *Successful Student Teaching*, by F.D. Kreamelmeyer (Sheffield Publishing Company).
Terms: Agent receives 15% commission on domestic sales; 25% on foreign sales. Offers written contract.
Fees: Reading fee for a published author is minimal. Evaluation by qualified professionals based on number of pages to be reviewed and primarily for new authors. Critiques are 5-10 pages long. Charges for out-of-pocket expenses incurred in marketing the ms are charged to the client. Services for marketing are on a contingency basis. 60% of business is derived from commissions on ms sales; 40% is derived from reading fees or criticism services. Payment must be made in advance of service rendered, and is nonrefundable; does not ensure representation.
Writers' Conferences: Lectured at Minneapolis Writers Workshop; Association of PEN Women, Minneapolis.
Tips: Obtains new clients through referrals, networking and advertising. "Make a point of meeting your agent in person. Insist on regular communication. Your manuscript should be legible, typed, double-spaced and with pages marked. Be open to suggestions for improving your manuscripts."

THE CURTIS BRUCE AGENCY (II), P.O. Box 967, 1314 Contractors Blvd., Plover WI 54467-0967. (715)341-3096. Fax: (715)341-3296. President: Bruce W. Zabel. Contact: Curtis H.C. Lundgren. Estab. 1989. Represents approximately 75 clients. 10% of clients are new/previously unpublished writers. Writer must have some published work (no vanity presses or self-published titles) and either a finished novel or proposed nonfiction book. Specializes in novels, commercial fiction of all genres, mainstream fiction and nonfiction. Special interest in *bildungsroman*. Currently handles: 40% fiction; 35% nonfiction; 25% juvenile books.
Handles: Novels, nonfiction books, juvenile books. Considers these nonfiction areas: autobiography/biography; child guidance/parenting; religious/inspirational; self-help/personal improvement. Interested in most all commercial fiction. Willing to look—at no charge—at queries with brief synopsis. Send query with résumé, 1 page synopsis, sample chapter, submission history of the work, return postage and labeled shipper. Reports in 3-5 weeks on queries; 4-6 months on mss.
Recent Sales: *Portofino*, by Frank Schaeffer (Macmillan); *Byzantium*, by Stephen R. Lawhead (HarperCollins); *Hurt People, Hurt People*, by Dr. Sandra Wilson (Nelson).
Terms: Agent receives 15% commission on domestic and dramatic sales; 20% on foreign sales. Offers written contract. Charges for photocopying, purchase of books for subrights sales, cables, fax, overnight airfreight, USPS postage, UPS. Less than 2% of income derived from the following services: Marketability evaluation service available on request with costs to author ranging from $100-200. More in-depth critique service also available with costs to author ranging from $500-1,500.
Tips: Obtains most new clients by referral. "Tell about yourself briefly: your accomplishments and your experiences. Be sure to include your publishing history (even if it is scant) in your résumé. Don't phone query. We have contacts in UK and enjoy working with British authors and publishers."

DORESE AGENCY LTD. (III), 37965 Palo Verde Dr., Cathedral City CA 92234. (619)321-1115. Fax: (619)321-1049. Contact: Alyss Barlow Dorese. Estab. 1977. Represents 30 clients. Currently handles: 65% nonfiction books; 35% novels.
Handles: Considers these nonfiction areas: art; biography/autobiography; business; child guidance/parenting; cooking/food/nutrition; crafts/hobbies; current affairs; gay/lesbian issues; government/politics/law; health/medicine; history; interior design/decorating; language/literature/criticism; military/war; money/finance/economics; music/dance/theater/film; New Age/metaphysics; photography; psychology; true crime/investigative; self-help/personal improvement; sociology; sports; women's issues/women's studies. Considers these fiction areas: action/adventure; contemporary issues; detective/police/crime; ethnic; family saga; feminist; gay; glitz; historical; lesbian; literary; mainstream; mystery/suspense; psychic/supernatural; regional; inspirational; sports; young adult. Send outline/proposal and SASE. Reports in 6 weeks on queries.

Recent Sales: *Rape of Kuwait*, by Jean Sassoon (Knightsbridge); *Get Married Now*, by Hilary Rich (Bob Adams).
Terms: Agent receives 15% commission on domestic sales; 20% on foreign sales. Offers written contract, binding for 2 years.
Fees: Does not charge a reading fee. Criticism service: depends on length of book.
Tips: Obtains new clients through referrals from past clients. "Don't say, 'I've written The Great American Novel.' It's an immediate turnoff."

‡**EASTWIND WRITERS (II)**, P.O. Box 348, Los Angeles CA 90053. (818)951-6609. Fax: (818)951-6609. "For first contact, fax us or send direct mail with your queries." Estab. 1991. Represents 20 clients. 50% of clients are new/previously unpublished writers. Specializes in English, Korean, Japanese translations; copyright registration to the US Library of Congress copyright office. Currently handles: 10% novels; 30% poetry books; 20% short story collections; 30% translations; 10% criticism service. Member agents: Paul Lee, president, and other agents handle translations, editing, proofreading, criticism, foreign rights and copyrights registration.
Handles: Novels, novellas, short story collections, poetry books, translations. Considers these nonfiction areas: biography/autobiography; ethnic/cultural interests; nature/environment; translations for English, Korean, Japanese. Considers these fiction areas: erotica; ethnic; humor/satire; literary; mystery/suspense; picture book; romance (contemporary, gothic, historical, regency); science fiction; westerns/frontier; young adult; translations; criticism. Query with entire ms, outline/proposal or outline. Reports in 2 weeks on queries; 1 month on mss.
Terms: Agent receives 15% commission on domestic sales; 20% on foreign sales. Offers written contract, binding for 5 years.
Fees: Charges $30 for reading fee and no extraordinary expense without written agreement from client. Criticism percent's as in standard commission base. Criticism fee negotiable with critics. Provides one criticism service for poetry, story (novel, short short story, short story) in single or book length, written by professional critics. No office expenses. Marketing, editing, express mail, fax and photocopying considered as extraordinary expenses. 70% of business derived from commissions on ms; 30% derived from reading fees or criticism services. Payment of criticism fee ensures representation.
Tips: Obtains new clients through recommendations from others and direct inquiries, as well as solicitation.

‡**EDEN LITERARY AGENCY (I)**, P.O. Box 11033, Boulder CO 80301. (303)441-7877. Contact: Jodi Jill. Estab. 1992. Represents 26 clients. 75% of clients are new/previously unpublished writers. Currently handles: 25% nonfiction books; 25% juvenile books; 25% novels; 25% puzzles/games. Member agents: Jodi Jill (nonfiction, juvenile), Karen Eden (fiction, special projects).
Handles: Nonfiction books, juvenile books, novels, poetry books, syndicated material. Considers these nonfiction areas: agriculture/horticulture; animals; computers/electronics; cooking/food/nutrition; crafts/hobbies; current affairs; government/politics/law; history; juvenile nonfiction; language/literature/criticism; military/war; money/finance/economics; music/dance/theater/film; nature/environment; photography; science/technology; sports; translations; true crime/investigative; women's issues/women's studies; games and puzzles. Considers these fiction areas: action/adventure; cartoon/comic; confessional; detective/police/crime; experimental; fantasy; historical; humor/satire; juvenile; picture book; romance (contemporary, gothic, historical, regency); science fiction; westerns/frontier; young adult. Query or send entire ms. Reports in 1 month on queries and mss.
Terms: Agent receives 10-25% commission on domestic sales; 14% on foreign sales. Offers written contract, binding for 1-2 years, depending on project.
Fees: Does not charge a reading fee. Criticism service: $50 for clients and nonclients. "Our critique includes a written report plus suggestions for improvements and markets. It is done by our 3 literary agents who together have published 5 books in the last 3 years and over 150 articles." Charges for photocopying, postage and telephone fees. Fees waived if on retainer. 80% of business is derived from commissions on ms sales; 20% is derived from reading fees or criticism services. Payment of criticism fee does not ensure representation.
Tips: "We thrive on recommendations from others; rarely do we go to conferences. We are new, ambitious and would like the opportunity to help you. Send us your manuscripts and SASE with a description on where you want your work at in 2 years. Then we'll see if we can help. Listen to other

writers and you'll know where to send your material for a literary agent."

EXECUTIVE EXCELLENCE (IV), #303, 1 East Center, Provo UT 84606. (801)375-4060. Fax: (801)377-5960. President: Ken Shelton. Agent: Meg McKay. Estab. 1984. Represents 25 clients. Specializes in nonfiction trade books/management and personal development—books with a special focus such as ethics in business, managerial effectiveness, organizational productivity. Currently handles: 100% nonfiction.
Handles: Nonfiction books, magazine articles.
Recent Sales: *Networking Smart*, by Wayne Baker (McGraw-Hill); *Working Alone*, by Murray Felsher (Berkley); *10 Natural Laws of Successful Time and Life Management*, by Hyrum Smith (Warner).
Terms: Agent receives 15% commission on domestic sales. 90% of business is derived from commissions on ms sales; 10% is derived from reading fees or criticism services.
Fees: "We charge a $1 per page ($150 minimum) critical reading and review fee. Waive reading fee if we represent the writer. A $500 deposit is made by the author at the time of signing a contract to cover expenses (calls, mail, etc.)."

THE FILM & FICTION AGENCY (I), Suite 123, 17194 Preston Rd., Dallas TX 75248. (214)380-8392. Contact: Cliff Reed. Estab. 1992. Represents 6 clients. 100% of clients are new/previously unpublished writers. Specializes in screenplays and contemporary fiction. Currently handles: 50% novels; 50% movie scripts. Member agents: Cliff Reed (screenplays), B. Morton (novels).
Handles: Novels, movie scripts. Considers these fiction areas: action/adventure; detective/police/crime; humor/satire; mainstream; mystery/suspense; thriller/espionage; westerns/frontier. Query with outline/proposal. Reports in 2 weeks on queries; 4-6 weeks on mss.
Terms: Agent receives 15% commission on domestic sales; 20% on foreign sales. Offers written contract with 30 day cancellation notice.
Fees: Charges $25 log-in and reading charge with brief critique. Criticism service: $55—novels/screenplays to 50,000 words; $75—novels/screenplays to 75,000 words; $125—novels/screenplays to over 75,000 words. Payment of criticism fee does not ensure representation.
Tips: Obtains new clients through recommendation and ads.

*FRIEDA FISHBEIN LTD. (II), 2556 Hubbard St., Brooklyn NY 11235. (212)247-4398. Contact: Janice Fishbein. Estab. 1928. Represents 30 clients. 50% of clients are new/previously unpublished writers. Currently handles: 10% nonfiction books; 5% young adult; 60% novels; 10% movie scripts; 10% stage plays; 5% TV scripts. Member agents: Heidi Carlson (contemporary); Douglas Michael (play and screenplay scripts).
Handles: Nonfiction books, young adult books, novels, movie scripts, stage plays, TV scripts ("not geared to a series"). Considers these nonfiction areas: animals; biography/autobiography; cooking/food/nutrition; current affairs; juvenile nonfiction; military/war; nature/environment; self-help/personal improvement; true crime/investigative; women's issues/women's studies. Considers these fiction areas: action/adventure; contemporary issues; detective/police/crime; family saga; fantasy; feminist; historical; humor/satire; mainstream; mystery/suspense; romance (contemporary, historical, regency); science fiction; thriller/espionage; young adult. Query letter a must before sending ms or fees. Reports in 2-3 weeks on queries; 4-6 weeks on mss accepted for evaluation.
Recent Sales: *Incident in Iraq*, by Herbert L. Fisher (Avon); *Fat is Not a 4 Letter Word*, by Roy Schroder (Chronamed); *Double Cross*, screenplay (Pathe/MGM).
Terms: Agent receives 10% commission on domestic sales; 15% on foreign sales. Offers written contract, binding for 30 days, cancellable by either party, except for properties being marketed or already sold.
Fees: Charges $75 reading fee first 50,000 words, $1 per 1,000 words thereafter for new authors; $75 for plays, TV, screenplays. Criticism service offered together with reading fee. Offers "an overall critique. Sometimes specific staff readers may refer to associates for no charge for additional readings if warranted." 60% of business is derived from commissions on ms sales; 40% is derived from reading fees or criticism services. Payment of a criticism fee does not ensure representation.

Check the Literary and Script Agents Subject Index to find the agents who indicate an interest in your nonfiction or fiction subject area.

Tips: Obtains new clients through recommendations from others. "*Always* submit a query letter first with an SASE. Manuscripts should be done in large type, double-spaced and one and one-half-inch margins, clean copy and edited for typos, etc."

*FLANNERY, WHITE AND STONE (II), Suite 404, 180 Cook St., Denver CO 80206. (303)399-2264. Fax: (303)399-3006. Contact: Constance Solowiej. Estab. 1987. Represents 45 clients. 40% of clients are new/previously unpublished writers. Specializes in mainstream and literary fiction, unique nonfiction, business and medical books. Currently handles: 40% nonfiction books; 25% juvenile books; 40% fiction. Member agents: Kendall Bohannon (mainstream and literary fiction, juvenile); Constance Solowiej (mainstream and literary fiction, nonfiction, business); Robert FitzGerald (business, medical).
Handles: Nonfiction books, juvenile books; novels; short story collections. Considers these nonfiction areas: business; child guidance/parenting; current affairs; ethnic/cultural interests; gay/lesbian issues; government/politics/law; health/medicine; juvenile nonfiction; money/finance/economics; music/dance/theater/film; nature/environment; psychology; self-help/personal improvement; sociology; sports; women's issues/women's studies. Considers these fiction areas: action/adventure; contemporary issues; ethnic; experimental; family saga; feminist; gay; historical; humor/satire; juvenile; lesbian; literary; mainstream; mystery/suspense; picture book; psychic/supernatural; regional; romance (contemporary, historical); science fiction; thriller/espionage; young adult. Send outline/proposal plus 2 sample chapters. Reports in 1 month on queries; 2 months on mss.
Recent Sales: *The Boy Who Loved Morning*, by Shannon Jacobs (Little, Brown & Co.).
Terms: Agent receives 15% on domestic sales; 20% on foreign sales. Offers written contract.
Fees: "Due to the overwhelming number of mss we receive, FW&S now charges a reading fee for completed mss by new/unpublished authors; $100/100,000 words. The fee includes a 3-5 page overall evaluation report. Charges for photocopying unless author provides copies." 90% of business is derived from commissions; 10% from critiques. Payment of a reading fee does not ensure representation.
Tips: "Make your nonfiction proposals professional and publisher-ready; let your fiction speak for itself."

‡*JOAN FOLLENDORE LITERARY AGENCY (II), 298 Country Club Dr., San Luis Obispo CA 93401. (805)545-9297. Fax: (805)545-9297. Contact: Joan Follendore, adult nonfiction; Mary Howell, adult fiction; Patrick Milburn, children's books; William Brown (art and architecture). Estab. 1988. Member of Book Publicists of Southern California; ABA. Represents 60 clients. 75% of clients are new/previously unpublished writers. Currently handles: 45% nonfiction books; 12% scholarly books; 20% juvenile books; 20% novels; 1% poetry books; 2% short story collections.
Handles: Nonfiction books, textbooks, scholarly books, juvenile books, novels, picture books, poetry, short story collections. Considers all areas, except scripts for stage or screen. Query first. Reports in 1 week on queries.
Recent Sales: *Buttontales* and *Pocketales*, by Ellen V. Mahoney (Putnam).
Terms: Agent receives 15% on domestic sales; 20% on foreign sales. Offers written contract.
Fees: "No fee to authors who've been published in the prior few years by a major house. Other authors are charged a reading fee and our editing service is offered. For nonfiction, we completely edit the proposal/outline and sample chapter; for fiction and children's, we need the entire manuscript. Editing includes book formats, questions, comments, suggestions for expansion, cutting and pasting, etc." Also offers other services: proofreading, rewriting, proposal development, authors' public relations, etc. 65% of business is derived from commissions on ms sales; 35% is derived from reading or editing fees. Payment of fees does not ensure representation unless "revisions meet our standards."
Tips: Obtains new clients through recommendations from others and personal contacts at literary functions. "Study and make your query as perfect and professional as you possibly can."

FORTHWRITE LITERARY AGENCY (II), P.O. Box 922101, Sylmar CA 91392. (818)365-3400. Fax: (818)362-3443. Contact: Wendy L. Zhorne. Estab. 1989. Represents 50 clients. 33% of clients are new/previously unpublished writers. Specializes in fiction, nonfiction, juvenile, "but not limited to those categories." Currently handles: 40% nonfiction books; 20% juvenile books; 40% novels. Sub-agent Bernadette Antle represents 15 clients and handles 30% fiction, 70% screen and teleplays.
Handles: Nonfiction, juvenile fiction and nonfiction, including picture books, novels. Considers these nonfiction areas: agriculture; animals; anthropology; art; biography; business; child guidance; cooking; crafts; health; history; interior design; juvenile nonfiction; economics; theater/film; environment; photography; psychology; inspirational; technology; personal improvement; sociology; women's studies. Considers these fiction areas: action; family saga; historical; juvenile; literary; mainstream; mystery/

suspense; picture book; romance (historical); young adult. Considers scripts for features, TV and cable, all genres *except* horror, "B-movie science fiction;" and pilots for sitcoms. Query. Reports in 3-4 weeks on queries; 4-6 weeks on ms. "No unsolicited manuscripts!"
Recent Sales: *Sorcerer's Guide to Good Health*, by P. Cochrane (Barricade Books); "Deep Space Nine" episode, by Mark Gehred O'Connell (Paramount Studios); "Timescape"—Star Trek: The Next Generation (Paramount).
Terms: Agent receives 15% on domestic sales; 20% on foreign sales. Offers written contract, which is binding for 1 year.
Fees: Charges $75 reading/critique fee "for all materials requested, unless writer has previous serious credits related to topic (same field/genre); $25 for juvenile under 5,000 words. In extreme circumstances we will line critique an exemplary manuscript to aid in improvement so we can represent the writer (fewer than 3 mss/year). Our reading fee includes an overview of major strengths/weaknesses, such as dialogue, plot, flow, characterization for fiction; structure, subject organization, readability, for nonfiction and the 'why' of acceptance or rejection by us.
Writers' Conferences: Attends ABA, Frankfurt Booksellers' Convention, many California conferences and regularly lectures at local colleges and universities on finding an agent or how to write more effectively.
Tips: Obtains new clients through advertising, referrals, conferences, recommendations by producers, chambers of commerce, satisfied authors etc. "Please check your material, including query, for spelling and typing errors before sending. If you are worried whether your material will arrive, send a postcard to return to you dated; don't search area codes for agent's home number; always send a SASE with everything. Never tell an agent, 'All my friends loved it.' Know your subject, genre and competition."

‡**FRAN LITERARY AGENCY (I, II)**, 7235 Split Creek, San Antonio TX 78238-3627. (210)684-1659. Contact: Fran Rathmann. Estab. 1993. Member of WGA, ASCAP. Represents 13 clients. 66% of clients are new/previously unpublished writers. "Very interested in Star Trek novels/screenplays." Currently handles: 15% nonfiction books; 10% juvenile books; 30% novels; 5% novellas; 5% poetry books; 10% movie scripts; 20% TV scripts; 5% how-to and magazine beauty column.
Handles: Nonfiction books, novels, movie scripts, TV scripts. Considers these nonfiction areas: agriculture/horticulture; animals; biography/autobiography; business; cooking/food/nutrition; crafts/hobbies; ethnic/cultural interests; health/medicine; history; juvenile nonfiction; nature/environment; self-help/personal improvement. "Query for others." Considers these fiction areas: action/adventure; cartoon/comic; fantasy; historical; juvenile; mainstream; mystery/suspense; picture book; regional; science fiction; westerns/frontier; young adult. "Query for others." Send outline plus 3 sample chapters. For TV/movie scripts send entire ms. Reports in 2 weeks on queries; 2 months on mss.
Terms: Agent receives 15% commission on domestic sales; 20% on foreign sales. Needs "letter of authorization," usually binding for 6 months.
Fees: Charges $25 processing fee, nonrefundable. Criticism service: $25 for 10 poems, short children's stories, picture books; $50 for novels and screenplays up to 100,000 words. Critiques written by Fran Rathmann. "Indepth critique, discussing style, tone, dialogue, mechanics, etc. as needed. Emphasizes saleability." 80% of business is derived from commissions on mss sales; 20% from reading fees or criticism services. Payment of criticism fee does not ensure representation.
Writers' Conferences: SAWG, San Antonio (Spring '94).
Tips: Obtains clients through recommendations, listing in telephone book. "Please—no phone queries until I have had sufficient time to read your material. Please send SASE or Box!"

‡**GELLES-COLE LITERARY ENTERPRISES (II)**, 12 Tukner Rd., Pearl River NY 10965. (914)735-1913. President: Sandi Gelles-Cole. Estab. 1983. Represents 50 clients. 25% of clients are new/unpublished writers. "We concentrate on published and unpublished, but we try to avoid writers who seem stuck in mid-list." Specializes in commercial fiction and nonfiction. Currently handles: 50% nonfiction books; 50% novels.
Handles: Nonfiction books, novels. "We're looking for more nonfiction—fiction has to be complete to submit—publishers buying fewer unfinished novels." Does not read unsolicited mss. Reports in 3 weeks.
Terms: Agent receives 15% commission on domestic and dramatic sales; 20% on foreign sales.
Fees: Charges reading fee of $100 for proposal; $150/ms under 250 pages; $250/ms over 250 pages. "Our reading fee is for evaluation. Writer receives total evaluation, what is right, what is wrong, is book 'playing' to market, general advice on how to fix." Charges writers for overseas calls, overnight mail, messenger. 5% of income derived from fees charged to writers. 50% of income derived from sales of writer's work; 45% of income derived from editorial service.

‡**THE GISLASON AGENCY (II)**, Suite 600, 5775 Wayzata Blvd., Minneapolis MN 55416. (612)371-9366. Fax: (612)591-0874. Attorney/Agent: Barbara J. Gislason. Estab. 1992. Member of Minnesota State Bar Association, Art & Entertainment Law Section, MIPLA Copyright Committee. 70% of clients are new/previously unpublished writers. Specializes in fiction and nonfiction. Currently handles: 30% nonfiction books; 5% scholarly books; 5% textbooks; 10% juvenile books; 50% novels.
Handles: Nonfiction books, textbooks, scholarly books, juvenile books, novels, short story collections. Considers these nonfiction areas: animals; art/architecture/design; biography/autobiography; child guidance/parenting; current affairs; government/politics/law; music/dance/theater/film; New Age/metaphysics; psychology; self-help/personal improvement; true crime/investigative; women's issues/women's studies. Considers these fiction areas: action/adventure; confessional; contemporary issues; detective/police/crime; experimental; fantasy; feminist; literary; mainstream; mystery/suspense; psychic/supernatural; romance; science fiction; thriller/espionage; law-related; children's books. Query with outline plus 3 sample chapters. Reports in 1 month on queries, 2 months on mss.
Terms: Agent receives 15% commission on domestic sales; 20% on foreign sales. Offers written contract, binding for 1 year with option to renew.
Fees: "$100 deposit to be applied to out-of-pocket expenses, i.e., printing, postage."
Tips: Obtains half of new clients through recommendations from others and half from *Literary Market Place*. "Cover letter should be well written and include a detailed synopsis of the work, and writer's credentials. It is extremely helpful if the writer provides the agent with marketing information and identifies appropriate publishers, as this speeds up the submissions program. With regard to sample chapters, select either the first 3, or 3 that give the agent a good representative sample of the work. In addition to owning an agency, Ms. Gislason practices law in the area of Art and Entertainment and has a broad spectrum of industry contacts."

GLADDEN UNLIMITED (II), P.O. Box 7912, San Diego CA 92167. (619)224-5051. Agent Contact: Carolan Gladden. Estab. 1987. Represents 10 clients. 95% of clients are new/previously unpublished writers. Currently handles: 20% nonfiction; 80% novels.
Handles: Novels, nonfiction. Considers these nonfiction areas: celebrity biography; how-to; self-help; business. Considers these fiction areas: action/adventure; horror; mainstream; thriller. "No romance or children's." Query. Reports in 2 weeks on queries; 2 months on mss.
Recent Sales: *Preventing Crime*, by Robert Y. Thornton (M. Sharpe Co.).
Terms: Agent receives 15% commission on domestic sales; 20% on foreign sales.
Fees: Does not charge a reading fee. Criticism service: $100 (refundable on placement of project) for diagnostic marketability evaluation. Offers "6-8 pages of specific recommendations to turn the project into a saleable commodity. Also include a copy of our handy guide 'The Writer's Simple, Straightforward, Common Sense Rules of Marketability.' Is dedicated to helping new authors achieve publication."

GLENMARK LITERARY AGENCY (I), 5041 Byrne Rd., Oregon WI 53575. (608)255-1812. Contact: Glenn Schaeffer. Estab. 1990. Represents 12 clients. Currently handles: 20% nonfiction books; 80% novels.
Handles: Nonfiction books, novels. Considers all mainstream nonfiction and fiction areas. Query first. Reports in 1 week on queries; 2 weeks on mss.
Terms: Agent receives 15% commission on domestic sales; 15% on foreign sales. Offers written contract, binding for 1 year.
Fees: Charges nonrefundable reading fee of $50 for up to 100,000 words, $100 for over 100,000 words. "The charge is for first-time offerings only. When we receive a query, we tell the client we will thoroughly review the manuscript for $50." Criticism service included in reading fee. "We try to cover all aspects of the writing—presentation, use of language, characterization, plot, dialogue, subject matter and more. My wife, who has a Ph.D. in English literature, and I both review. Outside of the one-time charge, there are no other charges or fees." 30% of business is derived from reading fees. "Eventually, as we mature, we hope 100% of income will come from sales."
Tips: "Generally, writers hear about us through the grapevine . . . discover that there is indeed a literary agency that has time for them, will respond to queries . . . We try to make it clear that writing on a professional level is not easy. It takes a great deal of thought, research, time and effort. A writer can't expect the world to accept, with open arms, anything they decide to write. The subject must appeal to the public. Then they must polish and perfect their manuscript if it is going to make it in today's competitive market."

128 Guide to Literary Agents & Art/Photo Reps '94

‡*CONNIE GODDARD: BOOK DEVELOPMENT (II)**, 203 N. Wabash Ave., Chicago IL 60601. (312)759-5822. (312)759-5823. Contact: Connie Goddard. Estab. 1992. Represents 18 clients. 40% of clients are new/previously unpublished writers. Specializes in Chicago-area writers and projects with Midwest origins. Currently handles: 90% nonfiction books; 10% novels.
Handles: Nonfiction books, novels. Considers these nonfiction areas: agriculture/horticulture; animals; anthropology/archaeology; art/architecture/design; biography/autobiography; business; child guidance/parenting; computers/electronics; cooking/food/nutrition; crafts/hobbies; current affairs; ethnic/cultural interests; government/politics/law; health/medicine; history; interior design/decorating; language/literature/criticism; military/war; money/finance/economics; music/dance/theater/film; nature/environment; photography; psychology; religious/inspirational; science/technology; self-help/personal improvement; sociology; sports; translations; true crime/investigative; women's issues/women's studies. Considers these fiction areas: detective/police/crime; historical; mainstream; mystery/suspense; thriller/espionage. Query with letter or phone call before sending ms or proposal. Reports in 1 month.
Recent Sales: *Fields of Faded Glory*, by Richard Lindberg (Sagamore Publishing).
Terms: Agent receives 10-20% commission on domestic sales. Offers written contract; binding for 3-6 months to begin.
Fees: Charges reading fee. "I charge an evaluation fee of $50-150 to unpublished writers, depending upon amount of material submitted, and I provide an oral or written report, depending upon arrangements made beforehand." Charges for express postage, long distance phone calls, and photocopying; deducted from advance. Payment of a criticism fee does not ensure representation.
Tips: Obtains new clients "mainly by referral. I make frequent appearances, giving "So You Want to Write a Book" talks and speaking frequently about publishing and bookselling in Chicago, Illinois, and Midwest. I want to work with people who want to work; writing books is a business as well as all the other fine things it might be."

LUCIANNE S. GOLDBERG LITERARY AGENTS, INC. (II), Suite 6-A, 2255 W. 84th St., New York NY 10024. (212)799-1260. Editorial Director: Sandrine Olm. Estab. 1974. Represents 65 clients. 10% of clients are new/unpublished writers. "Any author we decide to represent must have a good idea, a good presentation of that idea and writing skill to compete with the market. Representation depends solely on the execution of the work whether writer is published or unpublished." Specializes in nonfiction works, "but will review a limited number of novels." Currently handles: 75% nonfiction books; 25% novels. Member agents: Cyril Hiltebrand (editorial); Jane Moseley (editorial).
Handles: Nonfiction books, novels. Query with outline. Reports in 2 weeks on queries; 3 weeks on mss. "If our agency does not respond within 1 month to your request to become a client, you may submit requests elsewhere."
Recent Sales: *Women Who Kill*, by Tom Kunel (Simon & Schuster); *The Immigrants*, by Dylan Ross (HarperCollins).
Terms: Agent receives 15% commission on domestic sales; 25% on dramatic and foreign sales.
Fees: Charges reading fee on unsolicited mss: $150/full-length ms. Criticism service included in reading fee. 1% of income derived from reading fees. "Our critiques run 3-4 pages, single-spaced. They deal with the overall evaluation of the work. Three agents within the organization read and then confer. Marketing advice is included." Payment of fee does not ensure the agency will represent a writer. Charges for phone expenses, cable fees, photocopying and messenger service after the work is sold. 80% of income derived from commission on ms sales.

THE HAMERSFIELD AGENCY (I,II), 3205 Bunk Knolls Rd., Marianna FL 32446. (904)526-7631. Senior Partner: J.P.R. Ducat. Estab. 1990. Represents 106 clients. 70% of clients are new/previously unpublished writers. Specializes in English and French nonfiction, children's/juvenile literature, photo-travel books and quality photo-journal "table top" books. Currently handles: 70% nonfiction books; 10% photo/travel books; 2% photo-journal books; 18% juvenile books.
Handles: Nonfiction books, novels, juvenile books, photo/travel/journal books. No poetry, lyrics, "absolutely no TV, movie scripts or pornography." Query with outline or send entire ms (if prior arrangement is made). SASE required. Reports within 4-6 weeks on queries.
Terms: Agent receives 15% commission on domestic sales; 20% on foreign sales.
Fees: No reading fee for first reading. Charges a reading fee for a second reading/criticism for new writers. "Reading fee may be waived at our discretion." Charges $150 for 200 pages, $250 for 350 pages, typed, double-spaced mss. Offers critique service and ghostwriting. Charges $75 per hour for contract reviewing. Charges for expenses. 80% of business is derived from commissions on ms sales; 20% from reading fees or criticism service. Payment of fees does not ensure agency representation.

Tips: "Our interest is in a good writer whether he is a new writer or one who has a book previously published—our purpose is to market and promote our client onto the 'bestsellers' list.' "

*ANDREW HAMILTON'S LITERARY AGENCY (II), P.O. Box 604118, Cleveland OH 44104-0118. (216)881-1032. Contact: Andrew Hamilton. Estab. 1991. Represents 15 clients. 60% of clients are new/previously unpublished writers. Currently handles: 50% nonfiction books; 7% scholarly books; 3% juvenile books; 40% novels. Member agent: Andrew Hamilton (music, business, self-help, how-to, sports).
Handles: Nonfiction books, juvenile books, novels, novellas. Considers these nonfiction areas: animals; biography/autobiography; business; child guidance/parenting; cooking/food/nutrition; current affairs; ethnic/cultural interests; government/politics/law; health/medicine; history; juvenile nonfiction; money/finance/economics; music/dance/theater/film; psychology; religious/inspirational; self-help/personal improvement; sociology; sports; true crime/investigative; women's issues/women's studies; minority concerns; pop music. Considers these fiction areas: action/adventure; cartoon/comic; confessional; contemporary issues; detective/police/crime; erotica; ethnic; family saga; humor/satire; juvenile; mystery/suspense; psychic/supernatural; religious/inspiration; romance (contemporary); sports; thriller/espionage; westerns/frontier; young adult. Send entire ms. Reports in 1 week on queries; 3 weeks on mss.
Recent Sales: *Evolution of a Revolution*, by Akida Sababu (Winston-Derek Publishing).
Terms: Agent receives 15% commission on domestic sales; 20% on foreign sales. Offers written contract.
Fees: "Reading fees are for new authors and are nonrefundable. My reading fee is $50 for 60,000 words or less and $100 for ms over 60,000 words. I charge a one time marketing fee of $200 for mss." 70% of business derived from commissions on ms sales; 30% from reading fees or criticism services.
Tips: Obtains new clients through recommendations, solicitation and writing seminars. "Be patient: the wheels turn slowly in the publishing world."

‡ELIZABETH HAYNES LIMITED (I), 3 Willow Court, Cheektowaga NY 14225. (716)832-2702. Contact: Elizabeth Haynes. Estab. 1993. Member of RWA. Represents 20 clients. Specializes in mainstream women's fiction. Currently handles: 100% novels.
Handles: Romance novels (contemporary, gothic, historical, regency). Query with synopsis plus first 3 chapters. Reports in 2 weeks on queries, 1 month on mss.
Terms: Agent receives 15% commission on domestic and foreign sales. Offers written contract, binding for 1 year.
Fees: Does not charge reading fee. Criticism service: $45 line to line edit first 50 pages. "Postage fee not to exceed actual postage cost." 99% of business is derived from commissions on ms sales; 1% is derived from criticism services. Payment of a criticism fee does not ensure representation.
Tips: Obtains new clients through recommendations from others and mail queries. "Keep queries short, synopsis focused and have a great lead."

HEACOCK LITERARY AGENCY, INC. (II), Suite #14, 1523 6th St., Santa Monica CA 90401. (310)393-6227. Fax: (310)451-8524. Contact: Jim or Rosalie Heacock. Estab. 1978. Member of AAR, ATA, SCBWI, signatory of WGA. Represents 60 clients. 30% of clients are new/previously unpublished writers. Currently handles: 85% nonfiction books; 5% juvenile books; 5% novels; 5% movie scripts. Member agents: Jim Heacock (business expertise, parenting, psychology, sports, health, nutrition); Rosalie Heacock (psychology, philosophy, women's studies, alternative health, new technology, futurism, new idea books, art and artists).
Handles: Nonfiction books, juvenile books, novels, movie scripts. Considers these nonfiction areas: anthropology; art/architecture/design; biography (contemporary celebrity); business; child guidance/parenting; crafts/hobbies; current affairs; government/politics; health/medicine (including alternative health); history; military/war; music/dance/theater/film; nature/environment; New Age/metaphysics; psychology; self-help/personal improvement; sociology; sports; true crime; women's issues/women's studies. Considers these fiction areas: contemporary issues; literary; psychic/supernatural. Considers limited selection of top children's book authors. Query with sample chapters. Reports in 2 weeks on queries; 2 months on mss.
Recent Sales: *The Red Racer*, by Audrey Wood (Simon & Schuster); *Wolf Whispers*, by Pauline Ts'o (Sierra Club Books); *The Beginner's Book of Angels*, by David Connolly (Putnam Publishing Group); *Tickeloctopus*, by Audrey Wood, illustrated by Don Wood (Harcourt Brace); *The Arts of Living*, by Wilferd Peterson (Galahad Books); *Adrift*, by Terry Gerritson (CBS Movie-of-the-Week, April 1993).

Terms: Agent receives 15% commission on domestic sales; 25% on foreign sales, "if foreign agent used; if sold directly, 15%." Offers written contract, binding for 1 year.
Fees: Does not charge a reading fee. "We provide consultant services to authors who only need assistance in negotiating their contracts. Charge is $125/hour and no commission charges (10% of our business). Charges for actual expense for telephone, postage, packing, photocopying. We provide copies of each publisher submission letter and the publisher's response." 90% of business is derived from commission on ms sales.
Writers' Conferences: Attends Santa Barbara City College Annual Writer's Workshop; Pasadena City College Writer's Forum; UCLA Symposiums on Writing Nonfiction Books.
Tips: Obtains new clients through "referrals from present clients and industry sources as well as mail queries. Take time to write an informative query letter expressing your book idea, the market for it, your qualifications to write the book, the 'hook' that would make a potential reader buy the book. Always enclose SASE, compare your book to others on similar subjects and show how it is original."

‡*YVONNE TRUDEAU HUBBS AGENCY (II), #101, 32371 Alipaz, San Juan Capistrano CA 92675. (714)496-1970. Contact: Yvonne Hubbs. Estab. 1983; temporarily closed 1990, reopened 1993. Member of RWA. Represents 20 clients. 10% of clients are new/previously unpublished writers. Member agents: Christine Anderson, editor/writer (critiques); Thomas D. Hubbs, journalist (radio broadcasting/public relations); Yvonne Hubbs, agent, lecturer, writer; Christine Anderson (manager, NY office).
Handles: Nonfiction books, novels. Considers these nonfiction areas: current affairs; history; women's issues/women's studies. Considers these fiction areas: action/adventure; contemporary issues; erotica; family saga; fantasy; feminist; glitz; historical; mainstream; mystery/suspense; psychic/supernatural; romance (contemporary, gothic, historical, regency); science fiction; thriller/espionage. Query with outline/proposal plus 1 sample chapter. Reports in 2 weeks on queries, 1 month on mss.
Terms: Agent receives 15% commission on domestic sales; 20% on foreign sales. Offers written contract, binding for one year, but can be cancelled with 30 days notice by both parties.
Fees: Charges $75 reading fee to new writers only; refundable if client is sold within one year. Criticism service included in reading fee. "I personally write the critiques after reviewing the manuscript." Charges for travel expenses (if approved), photocopying, telegraph/fax expenses, overseas phone calls. 60% of business is derived from commissions on ms sales; 40% derived from reading fees or criticism services. Payment of criticism fee does not ensure representation.
Tips: Obtains new clients through recommendations, conferences. "Be professional in your query letter. Always SASE with a query."

INDEPENDENT PUBLISHING AGENCY (I), P.O. Box 176, Southport CT 06490. (203)268-4878. Contact: Henry Berry. Estab. 1990. Represents 25 clients. 30% of clients are new/previously unpublished writers. Especially interested in topical nonfiction (historical, political, social topics) and literary fiction. Currently handles: 50% nonfiction books; 10% juvenile books; 20% novels; 20% short story collections.
Handles: Nonfiction books, juvenile books, novels, short story collections. Considers these nonfiction areas: anthropology/archaeology; art/architecture/design; biography/autobiography; business; child guidance/parenting; cooking/food/nutrition; crafts/hobbies; current affairs; ethnic/cultural interests; government/politics/law; history; juvenile nonfiction; language/literature/criticism; military/war; money/finance/economics; music/dance/theater/film; nature/environment; photography; psychology; religious; science/technology; self-help/personal improvement; sociology; sports; true crime/investigative; women's issues/women's studies. Considers these fiction areas: action/adventure; cartoon/comic; confessional; contemporary issues; crime; erotica; ethnic; experimental; fantasy; feminist; historical; humor/satire; juvenile; literary; mainstream; mystery/suspense; picture book; psychic/supernatural; thriller/espionage; young adult. Send synopsis/outline plus 2 sample chapters. Reports in 2 weeks on queries; 4-6 weeks on mss.
Terms: Agent receives 15% commission on domestic sales; 20% on foreign sales. Offers "agreement that spells out author-agent relationship."
Fees: Does not charge reading fee. Offers criticism service if requested. Charges average $1/page, with $50 minimum for poetry and stories; $100 minimum for novels and nonfiction. Written critique averages 3 pages—includes critique of the material, suggestions on how to make it marketable and advice on marketing it. Charges for postage, photocopying and UPS mailing, legal fees (if necessary). All expenses over $25 cleared with client. 90% of business is derived from commissions on ms sales; 10% derived from criticism services.

Tips: Usually obtains new clients through referrals from clients, notices in writer's publications. Looks for "proposal or chapters professionally presented, with clarification of the distinctiveness of the project and grasp of intended readership."

CAROLYN JENKS AGENCY (II), 205 Walden St., Cambridge MA 02140. Phone and fax: (617)876-6927. Contact: Carolyn Jenks or Elizabeth Tagen. Estab. 1966. 75% of clients are new/previously unpublished writers. "Health care related books and films evolving as specialized interest." Currently handles: 15% nonfiction books; 40% novels; 20% movie scripts; 10% stage plays; 15% TV scripts.
Handles: Nonfiction books, juvenile books, novels, movie scripts, stage plays, TV scripts. Considers these nonfiction areas: animals; art/architecture/design; biography/autobiography; business; cooking/food/nutrition; current affairs; ethnic/cultural interests; gay/lesbian issues; government/politics/law; health/medicine; history; juvenile nonfiction; language/literature/criticism; music/dance/theater/film; New Age/metaphysics; psychology; religious/inspirational; true crime/investigative; self-help/personal improvement; sociology; sports; women's issues/women's studies. Considers these fiction areas: action/adventure; confessional; contemporary issues; detective/police/crime; family saga; fantasy; feminist; gay; lesbian; mystery/suspense; psychic/supernatural; regional; romance (contemporary, historical); science fiction; sports; thriller/espionage. Query. Reports in 4-6 weeks on queries; 3 months on mss.
Terms: Agent receives 15% commission on domestic sales; 20% on foreign sales. Offers written contract, binding for 3 years.
Fee: Charges reading fee of $60 up to 300 pages; $75 over 300. "Sliding scale negotiable."
Tips: "Your first 50, or 35, or even 5 pages have to hook the editor."

LARRY KALTMAN LITERARY AGENCY (II), 1301 S. Scott St., Arlington VA 22204. (703)920-3771. Contact: Larry Kaltman. Estab. 1984. Represents 15 clients. 75% of clients are new/previously unpublished writers. Currently handles: 10% nonfiction books; 75% novels; 10% novellas; 5% short story collections.
Handles: Nonfiction books, novels, novellas, short story collections. Considers these nonfiction areas: health/medicine; science/technology; self-help/personal improvement; sports. Considers these fiction areas: action/adventure; confessional; contemporary issues; detective/police/crime; erotica; ethnic; humor/satire; literary; mainstream; mystery/suspense; romance (contemporary); sports; thriller/espionage; young adult. Query. Reports in 1 week on queries; 2 weeks on mss.
Recent Sales: *Literary Agent Gives Back to the Great Unpublished*, by Larry Kaltman (New Writer's Magazine).
Terms: Agent receives 15% commission on domestic sales; 20% on foreign sales. Offers written contract, binding for 1 year.
Fees: Charges reading fee "for all unsolicited manuscripts; for up to 300 pages, the fee is $250. For each additional page the charge is 50¢/page. The criticism and reading services are indistinguishable. Author receives an approximately 1,500-word report commenting on writing quality, structure and organization and estimate of marketability. I write all critiques." Charges for postage, mailing envelopes and long-distance phone calls.
Writers' Conferences: Attends Washington Independent Writers Spring Conference.
Tips: Obtains new clients through query letters, solicitation. "Plots, synopses and outlines have very little effect. A sample of the writing is the most significant factor. I also sponsor the Washington Prize for Fiction, an annual competition for unpublished works." Awards: $3,000 (1st prize), $2,000 (2nd prize), $1,000 (3rd prize).

*J. KELLOCK & ASSOCIATES LTD. (II), 11017 80th Ave., Edmonton, Alberta T6G 0R2 Canada. (403)433-0274. Contact: Joanne Kellock. Estab. 1981. Member of Writer's Guild of Alberta. Represents 50 clients. 10% of clients are new/previously unpublished writers. "I do very well with all works for children but do not specialize as such." Currently handles: 30% nonfiction books; 1% scholarly books; 50% juvenile books; 19% novels.

Agents ranked I-IV are actively seeking new clients. Those ranked V or those who prefer not to be listed have been included to inform you they are not currently looking for new clients.

Handles: Nonfiction, juvenile, novels. Considers these nonfiction areas: animals; anthropology/archaeology; art/architecture/design; biography/autobiography; business; child guidance/parenting; cooking/food/nutrition; current affairs; government/politics/law; health/medicine; history; juvenile nonfiction; language/literature/criticism; money/finance/economics; music/dance/theater/film; nature/environment; New Age/metaphysics; self-help/personal improvement; sports; true crime/investigative; women's issues/women's studies. Considers these fiction areas: action/adventure; contemporary issues; detective/police/crime; ethnic; experimental; family saga; fantasy; feminist; glitz; historical; horror; humor/satire; juvenile; literary; mainstream; mystery/suspense; picture book; romance; science fiction; sports; thriller/espionage; westerns/frontier; young adult. Query with outline plus 3 sample chapters. Reports in 8-10 weeks on queries; 4-5 months on mss.

Recent Sales: *Please Remove Your Elbow From My Ear*, by M. Godfrey (Avon Books/NY); *Killer Instinct*, by Larry Pike (Zebra Books); *The Reindeer Christmas*, by Moe Price (Harcourt Brace Publishers).

Terms: Agent receives 15% commission on domestic sales (English language); 20% on foreign sales. Offers written contract, binding for 2 years.

Fees: Charges $150 reading fee. "Fee under no circumstances is refundable. *New writers only are charged.* $140 (US) to read 3 chapters plus brief synopsis of any work; $100 for children's picture book material. If style is working with subject, the balance is read free of charge. Criticism is also provided for the fee. If style is not working with the subject, I explain why not; if talent is obvious, I explain how to make the manuscript work. I either do critiques myself or my reader does them. Critiques concern themselves with use of language, theme, plotting—all the usual. Return postage is always required. I cannot mail to the US with US postage, so always enclose a SAE, plus either IRCs or cash. Canadian postage is more expensive, so double the amount for either international or cash. I do not return on-spec long-distance calls, if the writer chooses to telephone, please request that I return the call collect. However, a query letter is much more appropriate." 70% of business is derived from commissions on ms sales; 30% is derived from reading fees or criticism service. Payment of criticism fee does not ensure representation.

Tips: Obtains new clients through recommendations from others, solicitations. "Do not send first drafts. Always double space. Very brief outlines and synopsis are more likely to be read first. For the picture book writer, the toughest sale to make in the business, please study the market before putting pen to paper. All works written for children must fit into the proper age groups regarding length of story, vocabulary level. For writers of the genre novel, read hundreds of books in the genre you've chosen to write, first. In other words, know your competition. Follow the rules of the genre exactly. For writers of science fiction/fantasy and the mystery, it is important a new writer has many more than one such book in him/her. Publishers are not willing today to buy single books in most areas of genre. Publishers who buy science fiction/fantasy usually want a two/three book deal at the beginning."

*NATASHA KERN LITERARY AGENCY (II), P.O. Box 2908, Portland OR 97208-2908. (503)297-6190. Contact: Natasha Kern. Estab. 1986. Member of AAR. Specializes in literary and commercial fiction and nonfiction.

Handles: Nonfiction books, novels. Considers these nonfiction areas: business; child guidance/parenting; cooking/food/nutrition; current affairs; health/medicine; psychology; science/technology; self-help/personal improvement; women's issues/women's studies. Considers these fiction areas: historical; mainstream; mystery/suspense; romance; thriller/espionage; westerns/frontier. "Send a detailed, 1-page query with a SASE, including the submission history, writing credits and information about how complete the project is. For fiction, send a 2-3 page synopsis, in addition to the first 3 chapters. For nonfiction, submit a proposal consisting of an outline, 2 chapters, SASE, and a note describing market and how project is different or better than similar works. Also send a blurb about the author and information about the length of the manuscript. For category fiction, a 5-10-page synopsis should be sent with the chapters." Reports in 5-6 weeks on queries.

---

* *An asterisk indicates those agents who only charge fees to new or previously unpublished writers or to writers only under certain conditions.*

Recent Sales: *Hollywood Be Thy Name*, by Cass Warner (Prima); *Firestar*, by Kathy Morgan (St. Martin's); *Voyage of the Devilfish*, by Mike DiMercurio (D.I. Fine); *Positive Self-Talk for Kids*, by Douglas Bloch (Bantam); *The River's Daughter*, by Vella Munn (TOR/St. Martin's); *Lord Beast*, by Joan Overfield (Avon).
Terms: Agent receives 15% commission on domestic sales; 20% on foreign sales.
Fees: Charges $45 reading fee for unpublished authors. "When your work is sold, your fee will be credited to your account."
Writers' Conference: Attends RWA National Conference; Santa Barbara Writer's Conference; Golden Triangle Writer's Conference.

KEYSER LITERARY AGENCY (II), 663 Hollywood Ave., Salt Lake City UT 84105. "We communicate only by US mail, UPS or Fax." Fax: (801)487-9254. Contact: John O. Keyser. Estab. 1987. Represents 35 clients. 50% of clients are new/unpublished writers. Specializes in "adult manuscripts written by Ph.D's, or college graduates at any level. Also highly specialized in religious Christian texts, New Age and science fiction." Currently handles: 27% nonfiction books; 12% scholarly books; 5% textbooks; 12% juvenile books; 27% novels; 5% novellas; 10% short story collections; 2% TV scripts. Member agents: John O. Keyser (40 yrs. experience teaching at university level and has written religious and scientific texts); Grace R. Keyser (women authors and women's studies).
Handles: Nonfiction books, textbooks, scholarly books, juvenile books, novels, short story collections. Considers these nonfiction areas: biography/autobiography; current affairs; ethnic/cultural interests; politics; history; language/literature/criticism; New Age/metaphysics; psychology; religious/inspirational; science/technology; sociology; women's issues/women's studies. Considers these fiction areas: action/adventure; contemporary issues; ethnic; experimental; family saga; fantasy; feminist; historical; humor/satire; literary; mainstream; medieval; psychic/supernatural; regional; religious/inspiration; historical romance; science fiction with hard science; westerns/frontier. Send entire ms. "Will try to report in 2 weeks on queries; 2 months on manuscripts. After 60 days, if no response—look for another agent."
Recent Sales: *Merlin, Wizard of the Dark Ages*, by Norman L. Koch (Winston/Derek).
Terms: Agent receives 15% commission on domestic sales; 20% on foreign sales. "Offers written contract ONLY after manuscript is accepted by the publisher to publish it; two year initial term STANDARD author/agent contract for the industry, which can be terminated by either party with 30 day written notice."
Fees: "No charge for evaluation of a manuscript. If manuscript is considered publishable and needs editing we will charge $5 per hour per manuscript for correcting spelling, syntax, mechanics of manuscript and overall structure and content if necessary. If manuscript is publishable as is, or after we correct, we will submit to the publisher for $25-50 depending upon size of manuscript. 100-700 pages $25. Over 700 pages $50. Our submission fee includes new white telescoping cardboard boxes, insurance, transportation costs both ways to and from the publisher, cover letters to the editor BUT does NOT guarantee that the publisher will return the manuscript to us. However, few manuscripts have been lost—perhaps 5 or 6 which were involved in unavoidable accidents over the years. Publishers almost always return manuscript if unaccepted. *Agency guarantees representation if we consider manuscript publishable*." 25% of business derived from commission on sales, 75% derived from editing, criticism services or submission fees.
Tips: Obtains new clients by literary agency listing in various publications. "Agency wants manuscripts written by adults only—no juvenile clients. Also, we are highly knowledgeable about literary awards, as well as literary prizes and contests which we keep up on and continually study. We welcome established/published writers who seek an improved human writer/agent relationship and also unpublished authors who believe in quality. We *do* read unsolicited manuscripts. Definitely *no lesbian, gay or porno manuscripts*. We want to engender strong author-agent relationship. We also solicit writers who are producing 'series' books. We are in touch with such publishers and book creators—a popular trend today. Author must exert patience because of time involved in reviewing manuscripts sent to editor. Also, authors invited to send material in the way of ideas to include for the cover letter to the editor, or send excerpts from the manuscript when it is time to submit for possible publication (only at this time). Author may select his own choosing of editor or publisher if he wishes. If we disagree, we will explain why. This is a fluid business and actions are varied on either author's or agent's responsibility and acumen."

‡KLAUSNER INTERNATIONAL LITERARY AGENCY, INC. (II), 71 Park Ave., New York NY 10016. (212)685-2642. Fax: (212)532-8638. Contact: Bertha Klausner. Estab. 1938. Member of Dramatists Guild. Specializes in developing new writers.

Handles: Nonfiction books, textbooks, scholarly books, juvenile books, novels, novellas, short story collections, poetry books, movie scripts, stage plays, TV scripts, syndicated material, foreign literary books. Considers all nonfiction areas. Considers these fiction areas: action/adventure; cartoon/comic; contemporary issues; detective/police/crime; ethnic; experimental; family saga; fantasy; feminist; gay; historical; humor/satire; juvenile; lesbian; literary; mainstream; mystery/suspense; picture book; psychic/supernatural; regional; religious/inspiration; romance (contemporary, gothic, historical, regency); science fiction; sports; thriller/espionage; westerns/frontier; young adult. Query with outline/proposal and author's credits. Reports in 2 weeks on queries.
Recent Sales: Carey Cohen (Prentice Hall); Rosemary Clement (Richard Marek); Will Rogers (B & F Sterling).
Terms: Agent receives 15% commission on domestic sales; 20% on foreign sales. Offers contract only when requested by author.
Fees: Charges reading fee for evaluation of new writers' novels. "No charge for nonfiction, unless subject needs special professional evaluation." Offers criticism service. "Readers are qualified university teachers or editors with qualified experience." Charges other fees only if multiple submissions of 6 copies or more. Payment of criticism fee does not ensure representation.
Tips: Obtains clients mostly through recommendations. "Writers should understand that criticism is one person's evaluation and accept or reject reviews according to their own open mind. It is a continuing education and learning their craft."

LAW OFFICES OF ROBERT L. FENTON PC (II), #390, 31800 Northwestern Hwy., Farmington Hills MI 48334. (313)855-8780. Fax: (313)855-3302. Contact: Robert L. Fenton. Estab. 1960. Member of SAG. Represents 40 clients. 25% of clients are new/previously unpublished writers. Currently handles: 25% nonfiction books; 10% scholarly books; 10% textbooks; 10% juvenile books; 35% novels; 2½% poetry books; 2½% short story collections; 5% movie scripts. Member agents: Robert L. Fenton; Julia Fenton.
Handles: Nonfiction books, novels, short story collections, syndicated material, movie scripts, TV scripts. Considers these nonfiction areas: biography/autobiography; business; child guidance/parenting; computers/electronics; current affairs; government/politics/law; health/medicine; military/war; money/finance/economics; music/dance/theater/film; religious/inspirational; science/technology; self-help/personal improvement; sports; true crime/investigative; women's issues/women's studies. Considers these fiction areas: action/adventure; contemporary issues; detective/police/crime; ethnic; glitz; historical; humor/satire; mainstream; mystery/suspense; romance; science fiction; sports; thriller/espionage; westerns/frontier. Send 3-4 sample chapters (approximately 75 pages). Reports in 2 weeks on queries.
Recent Sales: *Black Tie Only*, by Julia Fenton (Contemporary Books); *Clash of Eagles*, by Leo Rutman (Fawcett); *Blue Orchids*, by Julia Fenton (Berkley).
Terms: Agent receives 15% on domestic sales. Offers written contract, binding for 1 year.
Fees: Charges a reading fee. "To waive reading fee, author must have been published at least 3 times by a mainline New York publishing house." Criticism service: $350. Charges for office expenses, postage, photocopying, etc. 75% of business is derived from commissions on ms sales; 25% derived from reading fees or criticism service. Payment of a criticism fee does not ensure representation.
Tips: Obtains new clients through recommendations from others, individual inquiry.

‡JAMES LEVINE COMMUNICATIONS, INC. (II), 14th Floor, 330 Seventh Ave., New York NY 10001. (212)268-4846. Fax: (212)465-8637. Estab. 1989. Represents 65 clients. 33⅓% of clients are new/previously unpublished writers. Specializes in business, psychology, parenting, health/medicine. Currently handles: 75% nonfiction books; 20% juvenile books; 5% novels.
Handles: Nonfiction books, juvenile books, novels. Considers these nonfiction areas: agriculture/horticulture; animals; art/architecture/design; biography/autobiography; business; child guidance/parenting; computers/electronics; cooking/food/nutrition; gay/lesbian issues; health/medicine; juvenile nonfiction; money/finance/economics; nature/environment; New Age/metaphysics; psychology; religious/inspirational; science/technology; self-help/personal improvement; sociology; sports; true crime/investigative; women's issues/women's studies. Considers these fiction areas: contemporary issues; juvenile; literary; mainstream; young adult. Send outline, proposal plus 1 sample chapter. Reports in 2 weeks on queries; 1 month on mss.
Recent Sales: *The Soul of a Business*, by Tom Chappell (Bantam); *Reconstructing Self, Constructing America: A Cultural History of Psychotherapy*, by Phillip Cushman, Ph.D. (Addison-Wesley); *Best Books, Best Toys, Best Videos for Kids*, by Joanne Oppenheim (HarperCollins).

Literary Agents: Fee-charging 135

Terms: Agent receives 15% commission on domestic sales; 20% on foreign sales. Offers written contract; length of time varies per project.
Fees: Does not charge reading fee. Provides editorial development services; fee depends upon the project. Charges for out-of-pocket expenses—telephone, fax, postage and photocopying—directly connected to the project. 90% of business is derived from commissions on ms sales; 10% derived from editorial development services. Payment of an editorial development fee ensures representation.
Writers' Conferences: Will attend ASJA Annual Conference in New York City (May '94).
Tips: Obtains new clients through client referrals. "We work closely with clients on editorial development and promotion. We work to place our clients as magazine columnists and have created columnists for *McCall's* and *Child*. We work with clients to develop their projects across various media—video, software, and audio."

LITERARY/BUSINESS ASSOCIATES (II), Suite 3, 2000 N. Ivar, Hollywood CA 90068. (213)465-2630. Contact: Shelley Gross. Estab. 1980. Represents 5 clients. 90% of clients are new/previously unpublished writers. Specializes in pop psychology, philosophy, mysticism, Eastern religion, self-help, business, health, contemporary novels. ("No fantasy or SF.") Currently handles: 40% nonfiction; 60% fiction (novels).
Recent Sales: A rock music reference book (Simon & Schuster); a novel (Avon); an anthology (Bantam).
Terms: Agent receives 15% commission on domestic sales; 20% on foreign sales.
Fees: Does not charge a reading fee. Charges $90 critique fee for mss up to 300 pages, $10 each additional 50 pages. "Critique fees are 100% refundable if a sale is made." Critique consists of "detailed analysis of manuscript in terms of structure, style, characterizations, etc. and marketing potential, plus free guidesheets for fiction or nonfiction." Charges $75 one-time marketing fee. 50% of business is derived from commission on ms sales; 50% is derived from criticism and editing services. Payment of a criticism fee does not ensure agency representation. Offers editing on potentially publishable mss.
Tips: Obtains new clients through recommendations from others, solicitation, seminars.

‡*TONI LOPOPOLO LITERARY AGENCY (II), Suite 5, 505 S. Barrington Ave., Los Angeles CA 90049. (310)440-2278. Fax: (310)440-2268. Contact: Toni Lopopolo. Estab. 1990. Represents 40 clients. 85% of clients are new/previously unpublished writers. Specializes in true crime. Currently handles: 75% nonfiction books, 10% scholarly books, 15% novels. Member agent: Toni Lopopolo (mysteries, self-help/how-to).
Handles: Nonfiction books, juvenile books, novels. Considers these nonfiction areas: animals; cooking/food/nutrition; current affairs; ethnic/cultural interests; history; money/finance/economics; nature/environment; psychology; self-help/personal improvement; sociology; true crime/investigative; women's issues/women's studies. Considers these fiction areas: contemporary issues; detective/police/crime; ethnic; family saga; feminist; gay; historical; humor/satire; lesbian; literary; mainstream; mystery/suspense; westerns/frontier. Query. Reports in 1 month on queries; 6 weeks on mss.
Recent Sales: *More Time for Sex: Organization Guide for Couples*, by Harriet Schecter (NAL); *Baby Eats Cookbook*, by Lois Smith (Berkley); *Best of the Cheapskates' Monthly*, by Mary Hunt (SMP).
Terms: Agent receives 15% commission on domestic sales; 10-15% on foreign sales. Offers written contract, binding for 2 years.
Fees: Charges reading fee "for *unrecommended*, first novelists only. Will work with the promising; entire fee refunded upon sale of novel." Offers criticism service: fee depends on length and genre of novel. Charges marketing fee for unpublished writers to cover phone, fax, postage and photocopying only. 95% of business is derived from commissions on ms sales; 5% is derived from reading fees or criticism services. Payment of a criticism fee does not ensure representation.
Writers' Conferences: Speaker and workshop leader at Santa Barbara Writers Conference, California Writers Club Conference.
Tips: Obtains new clients through recommendations from clients, lectures, workshops, conferences, publishers.

M.H. INTERNATIONAL LITERARY AGENCY (I), (formerly Marisa Handaris, Literary Agency), 706 S. Superior St., Albion MI 49224. (517)629-4919. Contact: Mellie Hanke. Estab. 1992. Represents 15 clients. 75% of clients are new/previously unpublished writers. Currently handles 100% novels. Specializes in historical novels. Member agents: Jeff Anderson (detective/police/crime); Martha Kelly (historical/mystery); Costas Papadopoulos (suspense; espionage); Nikki Stogas (confession); Marisa

Handaris (foreign language ms reviewer, Greek); Mellie Hanke (Spanish); Erin Jones Morgart (French).
Handles: Novels. Considers these fiction areas: confession; detective/police/crime; historical; mystery. "We also handle Greek and French manuscripts in the above categories, plus classics." No westerns. Send all material to the attention of Mellie Hanke. Reports in 6 weeks on mss.
Terms: Agent receives 10% commission on domestic sales; 15% on foreign sales.
Fees: Charges reading fee and general office expenses. Offers criticism service, translations from above foreign languages into English, editing, evaluation and typing of mss.
Tips: "We provide translation from Greek and French into English, editing and proofreading."

‡**VIRGINIA C. MCKINLEY, LITERARY AGENCY (I, II),** #4C, 4046 N. Main St., Racine WI 53402. (414)639-7539. Contact: Virginia C. McKinley. Estab. 1992. 100% of clients are new/previously unpublished writers. Currently handles: 30% nonfiction books; 20% juvenile books; 40% novels; 10% poetry books. Member agent: Virginia C. McKinley (religious books, biography/autobiography, fiction).
Handles: Nonfiction books, juvenile books, novels, short story collections, poetry books, movie scripts, stage plays, TV scripts. Considers these nonfiction areas: animals; biography/autobiography; business; child guidance/parenting; ethnic/cultural interests; health/medicine; juvenile nonfiction; military/war; money/finance/economics; music/dance/theater/film; nature/environment; psychology; religious/inspirational; self-help/personal improvement; sociology; sports; women's issues/women's studies. Considers these fiction areas: action/adventure; contemporary issues; detective/police/crime; ethnic; family saga; fantasy; feminist; humor/satire; juvenile; literary; mystery/suspense; religious/inspiration; romance (historical); westerns/frontier. Query with entire ms or 3 sample chapters. Reports in 1 month.
Terms: Agent receives 15% commission on domestic sales; 20% on foreign sales. Offers written contract.
Fees: Criticism service: $125 for 3-page critique. Reports within 2 months. Charges marketing fee—$100 per year for authors under contract; photocopying ms; postage; phone; any unusual expenses. 95% of business is derived from commissions on ms sales; 5% is derived from criticism services. Payment of a criticism fee does not ensure representation.
Tips: Obtains new clients through solicitation. "No multiple submissions. We feel a dynamic relationship between author and agent is essential. SASE must be included with ms or 3 chapters; also query. Will work with writer to develop his full potential."

THE DENISE MARCIL LITERARY AGENCY (II), 685 West End Ave., New York NY 10025. (212)932-3110. Contact: Denise Marcil. Estab. 1977. Member of AAR. Represents 60 clients. 40% of clients are new/previously unpublished authors. Specializes in women's commercial fiction, how-to, self-help and business books. Currently handles: 30% nonfiction books; 70% novels.
Handles: Nonfiction books, novels. Considers these nonfiction areas: business; child guidance/parenting; nutrition; health/medicine; money/finance/economics; music/dance/theater/film; psychology; true crime/investigative; self-help/personal improvement; women's issues/women's studies. Considers these fiction areas: family saga; historical; romance (contemporary, historical, regency). Query with SASE *only*! Reports in 2-3 weeks on queries; "we do not read unsolicited manuscripts."
Recent Sales: *Inside Job: The Looting of America's Savings and Loans*, by Stephen Pizzo, Mary Fricker and Paul Muolo (Dutton); *The Baby Book*, by William Sears, M.D. and Martha Sears, R.N. (Little Brown); *Outlaw Hearts*, by Rosanne Bittner (Bantam); *Border Lord*, by Arnette Lamb.
Terms: Agent receives 15% commission on domestic sales; 20% on foreign sales. Offers written contract, binding for 2 years.
Fees: Charges $45 reading fee for 3 chapters and outline "that we request only." Charges $100 per year for postage, photocopying, long-distance calls, etc. 99.9% of business is derived from commissions on ms sales; .1% is derived from reading fees and criticism.

The publishing field is constantly changing! If you're still using this book and it is 1995 or later, buy the newest edition of Guide to Literary Agents & Art/Photo Reps **at your favorite bookstore or order directly from Writer's Digest Books.**

Writers' Conferences: Has attended University of Texas Conference at Dallas, Southwest Writers Workshop, Pacific Northwest Writers Conference.
Tips: Obtains new clients through recommendations from other authors and "35% of my list is from query letters! Only send a 1-page query letter. I read them all and ask for plenty of material; I find many of my clients this way. *Always* send a SASE."

*THE EVAN MARSHALL AGENCY (III), Suite 216, 22 S. Park St., Montclair NJ 07042. (201)744-1661. Fax: (201)744-6312. Contact: Evan Marshall. Estab. 1987. Member of AAR, RWA. Currently handles: 48% nonfiction books; 48% novels; 2% movie scripts; 2% TV scripts.
Handles: Nonfiction books, novels, movie scripts. Considers these nonfiction areas: biography/autobiography; business; child guidance/parenting; cooking/food/nutrition; current affairs; government/politics/law; health/medicine; history; interior design/decorating; money/finance/economics; music/dance/theater/film; New Age/metaphysics; psychology; self-help/personal improvement; true crime/investigative. Considers these fiction areas: action/adventure; contemporary issues; detective/police/crime; family saga; glitz; historical; mainstream; mystery/suspense; psychic/supernatural; romance; thriller/espionage. Query. Reports in 1 week on queries; 2 months on mss.
Recent Sales: *Highland Love Song*, by Constance O'Banyon (HarperCollins); *Madame Cleo's Girls*, by Lucianne Goldberg (Pocket Books).
Terms: Agent receives 15% on domestic sales; 20% on foreign sales. Offers written contract.
Fees: Charges a fee to consider for representation material by *writers who have not sold a book or script*. "Send SASE for fee schedule. There is no fee if referred by a client or an editor or if you are already published in the genre of your submission."
Tips: Obtains many new clients through referrals from clients and editors.

SCOTT MEREDITH LITERARY AGENCY, LP, (formerly Scott Meredith, Inc.), 845 Third Ave., New York NY 10022.
• Scott Meredith died in February, 1993. The agency was sold the following August.

GREG MERHIGE-MERDON MARKETING/PROMO CO. INC. (II), Suite 203, 1080 E. Indiantown Rd., Jupiter FL 33477. (407)747-9951. Fax: (407)747-6516. Contact: Greg Merhige. Estab. 1989. Signatory of WGA, member of Actors Guild. 90% of clients are new/previously unpublished writers. Currently handles: 5% nonfiction books; 40% juvenile books; 5% novels; 5% novellas; 15% movie scripts; 5% stage plays; 20% TV scripts. Member: Cheryl McCarthy, Account Executive.
Handles: Nonfiction books, juvenile books, novels, novellas, short story collections, poetry books, movie scripts, TV scripts, stage plays. Considers these nonfiction areas: animals; biography/autobiography; child guidance/parenting; cooking/food/nutrition; ethnic/cultural interests; juvenile nonfiction; military/war; music/dance/theater/film; photography; self-help/personal improvement; sociology; sports; true crime/investigative; women's issues/women's studies. Considers these fiction areas: action/adventure; cartoon/comic; confessional; detective/police/crime; ethnic; family saga; fantasy; feminist; humor/satire; juvenile; literary; mainstream; mystery/suspense; picture book; regional; romance; science fiction; sports; thriller/espionage; westerns/frontier; young adult. Send entire ms plus outline. Reports in 12 days on queries; 45 days on mss.
Terms: Agent receives 10% commission on domestic sales; 15% on foreign sales. Offers written contract, binding for 1 or 1½ years.
• This agency charges a marketing fee of $50 per month. In previous editions it was placed in nonfee-charging agents based on the statement that it "charges expenses on special situations."
Tips: Obtains new clients through recommendations from others. "Listen to your agent. Do not try to make your own deal."

*MEWS BOOKS LTD., 20 Bluewater Hill, Westport CT 06880. (203)227-1836. Fax: (203)227-1144. Contact: Sidney B. Kramer. Estab. 1972. Represents 35 clients. Prefers to work with published/established authors; works with small number of new/unpublished authors "producing professional work." Specializes in juvenile (pre-school through young adult), cookery, self-help, adult nonfiction and fiction, technical and medical. Currently handles: 20% nonfiction; 20% novels; 50% juvenile books; 10% miscellaneous. Member agent: Fran Pollak (assistant).
Handles: Nonfiction books, novels, juvenile books, character merchandising and video use of illustrated published books. Query with precis, outline, character description, a few pages of sample writing and author's bio.

Recent Sales: *Dr. Susan Love's Breast Book,* by Susan M. Love, MD, with Karen Lindsey (Addison-Wesley); *It Works for Us!,* by Tom McMahon (Pocket Books/S&S).
Terms: Agent receives 15% commission on domestic sales; 20% on foreign sales.
Fees: Does not charge a reading fee. "If material is accepted, agency asks for $350 circulation fee (4-5 publishers), which will be applied against commissions (waived for published authors)." Charges for photocopying, postage expenses, telephone calls and other direct costs.
Tips: "Principle agent is an attorney and former publisher. Offers consultation service through which writers can get advice on a contract or on publishing problems."

*DAVID H. MORGAN LITERARY AGENCY, INC. (II), P.O. Box 14810, Richmond VA 23221. (804)672-2740. Contact: David Morgan. Estab. 1987. Represents 25-30 clients. Currently handles: 70% nonfiction; 30% novels.
Handles: Nonfiction, novels. Considers all juvenile and adult nonfiction and fiction. Query with SASE. Reports in 1 week on queries.
Recent Sales: *The Love Your Heart Guide for the 1990s,* by Lee Belshin (Contemporary); *Prophecies & Predictions: Everyone's Guide to the Coming Changes,* by Moira Timms Valentine.
Terms: Agent receives 15% commission on domestic sales; 20% on foreign sales. Offers written contract.
Fees: Charges a fee to unpublished authors. "Please query for details." Client must provide photocopies of mss. 95% of business is derived from commissions on ms sales; 5% is derived from reading or criticism fees.
Tips: Obtains new clients through recommendations from others, workshops and advertisements.

‡CHARLES NEIGHBORS LITERARY AGENCY (II), 5907 Main St., Williamsville NY 14221. (716)626-4370. Fax: (716)626-4388. Contact: Charles Neighbors. Estab. 1966. Represents 63 clients. 25% of clients are new/previously unpublished writers. Currently handles: 41% nonfiction books; 44% novels; 5% novellas; 5% short story collections; 5% movie scripts.
Handles: Nonfiction books, textbooks, scholarly books, juvenile books, novels, novellas, short story collections, poetry books, movie scripts, stage plays. Open to all nonfiction and fiction areas. Send minimum 100 pages. Phone or fax before sending. Reports in 2 weeks on queries; 3 weeks on mss.
Terms: Agent receives 10% commission on domestic sales; 15% on foreign sales.
Fees: "We charge $1.50 per double-spaced page for a consideration fee. If we take the person on as a client that fee is refunded regardless of if we sell the book. We also give an overview critique for the fee written by William Appel, who is a former instructor with the WD writing school and author of 6 novels and one nonfiction book." 98% of business is derived from commissions on ms sales; 2% is derived from reading fees. Payment of reading fees does not ensure representation.
Writers' Conferences: Attends Southwest Writers Conference in Houston.
Tips: Obtains new clients through recommendations, queries, conferences. "We agree with John Gardner in *The Art Of Fiction* when he says: 'I assume from the outset that the would-be writer using this book can become a successful writer if he wants to, since most of the people I've known who wanted to become writers knowing what it meant *did* become writers.' We believe that the art of writing cannot be taught, any more than talent or greatness or charisma can. But craft, technique, method and understanding of the medium can most certainly be taught. So can the proper presentation and marketing of writing. We advise new writers to read like professionals. That is, to analyze what they read in order to learn how a writer achieved his/her effect. Above all, don't quit trying to write or get an agent. Tenacity is the ticket."

*BK NELSON LITERARY AGENCY & LECTURE BUREAU (II, III), 84 Woodland Rd., Pleasantville NY 10570. (914)741-1322. Fax: (914)741-1324. Contact: Bonita Nelson, John Benson or Charles Romine. Estab. 1980. Represents 52 clients. 45% of clients are new/previously unpublished writers. Specializes in business/self-help/how-to/computer books. Currently handles: 50% nonfiction books; 5% scholarly books; 5% textbooks; 20% novels; 5% movie scripts; 10% TV scripts; 5% stage plays. Member agents: Bonita Nelson (business books); John Benson (Director of Lecture Bureau); Charles Romine (novels and TV scripts); Dave Donnelly (videos).
Handles: Nonfiction books, textbooks, scholarly books, novels, movie scripts, stage plays, TV scripts. Considers these nonfiction areas: animals; anthropology/archaeology; biography/autobiography; business; child guidance/parenting; computers/electronics; cooking/food/nutrition; crafts/hobbies; current affairs; health/medicine; military/war; money/finance/economics; music/dance/theater/film; nature/environment; psychology; religious/inspirational; science/technology; self-help/personal improvement; sociology; sports; true crime/investigative; women's issues/women's studies. Considers these fiction

areas: action/adventure; contemporary issues; family saga; feminist; literary; mainstream; mystery/suspense; romance; sports; thriller/espionage. Query. Reports in 1 week on queries; 2-3 weeks on ms.
Recent Sales: *Power Reading*, by Phyllis Mindell, Ph.D. (Simon & Schuster); *Power Packed Sales Literature*, by Robert Bly (Wiley & Sons).
Terms: Agent receives 15% on domestic sales; 10% on foreign sales. Offers written contract, exclusive for 6 months.
Fees: Charges $325 reading fee for *new writers' material only*. "It is not refundable. We usually charge for the first reading only. The reason for charging in addition to time/expense is to determine if the writer is saleable and thus a potential client."
Tips: Obtains new clients through referrals and reputation with editors. "We handle the business aspect of the literary and lecture fields. We handle careers as well as individual book projects. If the author has the ability to write and we are harmonious, success is certain to follow with us handling the selling/business."

NEW AGE WORLD SERVICES (II, IV), 62091 Valley View Circle, Joshua Tree CA 92252. (619)366-2833. Owner: Victoria Vandertuin. Estab. 1957. Member of UFO High Desert Research & Report, Academy of Science Fiction, Fantasy & Horror Films and Retailing Alliance and the Institute of Mentalphysics. Represents 45 clients. 100% of clients are new/unpublished writers. Eager to work with new/unpublished writers. Specializes in all New Age fields: occult, astrology, metaphysical, yoga, UFO, ancient continents, para sciences, mystical, magical, political and all New Age categories in fiction and nonfiction. Writer's guidelines for #10 SASE and 4 first-class stamps. Currently handles 40% nonfiction books; 30% novels; 10% poetry.
Handles: Nonfiction books, novels, poetry. Query with outline or entire ms. Reports in 6-8 weeks.
Terms: Receives 15% commission on domestic sales; 20% on foreign sales.
Fees: Charges reading fee of $150 for 300-page, typed, double-spaced ms; reading fee waived if representing writer. Charges criticism fee of $135 for new writers (300-page ms.); 10% of income derived from criticism fees. "I personally read all manuscripts for critique or evaluation, which is typed, double-spaced with about 4 or more pages, depending on the manuscript and the service for the manuscript the author requests. If requested, marketing advice is included. We charge a representation fee if we represent the author's manuscript." Charges writer for editorial readings, compiling of query letter and synopsis, printing of same, compiling lists and mailings.

*****NEW WRITERS LITERARY PROJECT (II)**, Suite 277, 2809 Bird Ave., Miami FL 33133. (305)460-2254. Fax: (305)443-6756. Contact: Robert S. Catz. Estab. 1987. Represents 20 clients. 85% of clients are new/previously unpublished writers. "We specialize in new, unpublished authors." Currently handles: 70% nonfiction books; 30% novels. Member agents: Robert S. Catz, Susan R. Chalker.
Handles: Nonfiction books, novels. Open to all nonfiction and fiction areas. Send outline/proposal or outline plus 3 sample chapters and SASE. Reports in 3 weeks on queries; 7 weeks on mss.
Terms: Agent receives 15% commission on domestic sales; 20% on foreign sales. Offers written contract.
Fees: Charges reading fee. (New writers only. Fee off-set against advances and/or royalties.) 85% of business derived from commission on ms sales; 15% from reading fees or criticism services.
Tips: Obtains new clients through recommendations from others, solicitation, at conferences, etc. "A well-written, thoughtful book proposal is most helpful!"

NEW WRITING AGENCY (I, II), Box 1812, Amherst NY 14226-1812. Estab. 1991. Presently represents few clients. 90% of clients are new/previously unpublished writers. Specializes in "nurturing and representation of new writers." Currently handles: 20% nonfiction books; 60% novels; 5% novellas; 5% poetry books; 5% short story collections; 5% other. Member agents: Richard Lynch (literary, short story, poetry); Sam Meade (science fiction, western, action/adventure); Mason Deitz (nonfiction); Rita Howard (romance).

If you're looking for a particular agent, check the Agents and Reps Index to find at which agency the agent works. Then look up the listing for that agency in the appropriate section.

Handles: Nonfiction books, scholarly books, novels, novellas, short story collections, poetry books, movie scripts, stage plays. Open to all fiction and nonfiction areas. Reports in 1 week on queries; 2-3 weeks on mss. Send SASE.
Terms: Agent receives 12.5% commission on domestic sales; 17.5% on foreign sales and sub agents. Offers written contract, binding for 1 year (options).
Fees: Charges "$35 for unsolicited manuscripts seeking representation (rejections include 1-2 page critique). Developmental editing or reading critique fee is $1/page (4-8 page single-spaced critique addresses content, form, writing problems and successes and offers suggestions). Line editing fee based on free sample edit. Workshops by mail available, developed individually to meet the needs of participants. Submissions for all services are considered for representation. Active marketing fees limited by agreement with author. Payment of fee does not ensure representation."
Tips: "We often obtain clients from workshop or reading/critiquing service as we work to achieve proper standards in the writing. We accept only exceptional work for representation, but are willing to work with those who can take our criticism and use it in improving a text. Criticism is based on our knowledge of the market, and our replies to writers reflect marketability."

*NORTHEAST LITERARY AGENCY (II), 69 Broadway, Concord NH 03301. (603)225-9162. Contact: Victor A. Levine. Estab. 1973. Represents 15 clients. 50% of clients are new/previously unpublished writers. Specializes in popular fiction, children's picture books. Currently handles 75% nonfiction books; 25% novels. Member agents: Don Emmons (nonfiction); Dale Harrington (fiction).
Handles: Novels, nonfiction books, juvenile books, short story collections, poetry books, movie and TV scripts. Considers all nonfiction subjects. Considers all fiction, especially mystery and suspense, contemporary romance and science fiction. Query. Reports in 5 days on queries; 10 days on mss.
Recent Sales: *Signature Macros,* by Art Campbell (TAB/McGraw Hill).
Terms: Agent receives 15% commission on domestic sales; 25% on foreign sales. Offers a written contract cancellable on 3-months' notice.
Fees: Charges a reading fee to unpublished writers, "refundable following a sale." Criticism service: costs depend on type of criticism and whether conducted by mail or in a seminar or workshop setting. Charges for extraordinary expenses, such as express mail, long-distance phone calls, extensive photocopying but not for marketing or ordinary office expenses."
Writers' Conferences: Underwrites Wells Writer's Workshop, which meets twice yearly in Wells, Maine.
Tips: Obtains new clients through classes, workshops, conferences, advertising in *Writer's Digest*, referrals. "Please be very specific about writing background, published credits and current project(s)." Always include SASE.

NORTHWEST LITERARY SERVICES (II), 9-2845 Bellendean Rd. RR1, Shawnigan Lake, British Columbia V0R 2W0 Canada. (604)743-8236. Contact: Brent Laughren. Estab. 1986. Represents 20 clients. 75% of clients are new/previously unpublished writers. Specializes in working with new writers. Currently handles: 25% nonfiction books; 10% juvenile books; 55% novels; 10% short story collections. Member agent: Jennifer Chapman (juvenile books).
Handles: Nonfiction books, juvenile books, novels, movie scripts, stage plays, TV scripts. Considers these nonfiction areas: agriculture/horticulture; animals; art/architecture/design; biography/autobiography; child guidance/parenting; cooking/food/nutrition; crafts/hobbies; health/medicine; history; juvenile nonfiction; language/literature/criticism; music/dance/theater/film; nature/environment; New Age/metaphysics; photography; self-help/personal improvement; sports; translations; true crime/investigative; women's issues/women's studies. Considers these fiction areas: action/adventure; confessional; contemporary issues; detective/police/crime; erotica; ethnic; experimental; family saga; fantasy; feminist; historical; humor/satire; juvenile; literary; mainstream; mystery/suspense; picture book; psychic/supernatural; regional; romance; science fiction; sports; thriller/espionage; westerns/frontier; young adult. Query with outline/proposal. Reports in 1 month on queries; 2 months on mss.
Terms: Agent receives 15% on domestic sales; 20% on foreign sales. Offers written contract.
Fees: Does not charge a reading fee. Charges criticism fee: $100 for book outline and sample chapters up to 20,000 words. Charges 75¢-$1/page for copyediting and content editing; $1/page for proofreading; $10-20/page for research. "Other related editorial services available at negotiated rates. Critiques are 2-3 page overall evaluations, with suggestions. All fees, if charged, are authorized by the writer in advance." 95% of business is derived from commissions on ms sales; 5% is derived from reading fees or criticism service. Payment of criticism fee doesn't ensure representation.

Literary Agents: Fee-charging 141

Tips: Obtains new clients through recommendations. "Northwest Literary Services is particularly interested in the development and marketing of new and unpublished writers, though not exclusively, since this can be a long-term project without monetary reward. We are also interested in literary fiction, though again not exclusively."

*OCEANIC PRESS (II), Seaview Business Park, Unit #106, 1030 Calle Cordillera, San Clemente CA 92673. (714)498-7227. Fax: (714)498-2162. Contact: Peter Carbone. Estab. 1956. Represents 35 clients. 15% of clients are new/previously unpublished writers. Specializes in celebrity interviews. Currently handles: 20% nonfiction books; 20% novels; 60% syndicated material. Member agent: Katherine Singer (child development, family relations).
Handles: Nonfiction books, novels, syndicated material, biographies. Considers these nonfiction areas: biography/autobiography; business; child guidance/parenting; computers/electronics; health/medicine; money/finance/economics; music/dance/theater/film; New Age/metaphysics; psychology; science/technology; self-help/personal improvement; sports; true crime/investigative; women's issues/women's studies; movies. Considers these fiction areas: detective/police/crime; erotica; experimental; family saga; mainstream; mystery/suspense; psychic/supernatural; romance (contemporary, gothic, regency); science fiction; sports; thriller/espionage; westerns/frontier; young adult. Send outline/proposal and list of published work. Reports in 1 month on queries; 6 weeks on mss.
Terms: Agent receives 15% commission on domestic sales; 20% on foreign sales; "50% syndication only if wanted." Offers written contract, binding for 1 year.
Fees: Charges a $350 reading fee to new writers only. Criticism service included in reading fee. Criticism done by professional readers. 98% of business is derived from commissions on ms sales; 2% is derived from reading fees or criticism service. Payment of a criticism fee ensures representation, if marketable.
Tips: Obtains new clients through recommendations. "Do good writing and good research. Study the market."

*OCEANIC PRESS SERVICE, Seaview Business Park, Unit #106, 1030 Calle Cordillera, San Clemente CA 92672. (714)498-7227. Fax: (714)498-2162. Manager: Helen J. Lee. Estab. 1940. Represents 100 clients. Prefers to work with published/established authors; will work with a small number of new/unpublished authors. Specializes in selling features of worldwide interest; romance books, mysteries, biographies, nonfiction of timeless subjects, reprints of out-of-print titles. Currently handles: 20% nonfiction books; 30% novels; 10% juvenile books; 40% syndicated material.
Handles: Magazine articles, nonfiction books, novels, juvenile books, syndicated material. Will read—at no charge—unsolicited queries and outlines. Reports in 2 weeks on queries.
Recent Sales: *400 Crosswords* (Landoll); *60 Second Shiatzu*, by Eva Shaw (Heyne and 6 foreign publishers).
Terms: Agent receives 15% commission on domestic sales; 20% on foreign sales.
Fees: Charges reading fee: $350/350 pages for unpublished writers. Reading fee includes detailed critique. "We have authors who published many books of their own to do the reading and give a very thorough critique." 2% of income derived from reading fees.

ANDREA OLESHA AGENCY (I, II), P.O. Box 243, Wood Village OR 97060. (503)667-9039. Contact: Andrea Olesha. Estab. 1992. Member of Willamette Writer's. Represents 2 clients. 100% of clients are new/previously unpublished writers. Specializes in nonfiction. Currently handles: 50% nonfiction books; 50% fiction.
Handles: Nonfiction books, juvenile books, novels. Considers these nonfiction areas: cooking/food/nutrition; ethnic/cultural interests; gay/lesbian issues; interior design/decorating; language/literature/criticism; music/dance/theater/film; nature/environment; self-help/personal improvement; women's issues/women's studies. Considers these fiction areas: action/adventure; contemporary issues; ethnic; experimental; family saga; fantasy; feminist; gay; glitz; humor/satire; juvenile; lesbian; literary; mainstream; mystery/suspense; psychic/supernatural; regional; religious/inspiration; science fiction; young adult. Query with sample chapters. Reports in 2 months on queries; 1 month on mss. "I do not return any material without an SASE."
Terms: Agent receives 10% commission on domestic sales; 15% on foreign sales. Offers written contract, binding for 1 year.
Fees: Charges reading fee "to new authors, refundable upon sale." Charges for postage.
Writers' Conferences: Attends Willamette Writers Conference held in Portland, OR in August.
Tips: Obtains new clients through advertising and listings in literary circles. "We have the contacts."

142 Guide to Literary Agents & Art/Photo Reps '94

*WILLIAM PELL AGENCY (II), Suite 8D, 300 E. 40th St., New York NY 10016. (212)490-2845. Contact: William Pell. Estab. 1990. Represents 6 clients. 95% of clients are new/previously unpublished writers. Member agent: Fran Russo (novels).
Handles: Novels. Considers photography nonfiction. Considers these fiction areas: detective/police/crime; humor/satire; thriller/espionage. Query with 2 sample chapters. Reports in 1 month on queries; 3 months on mss.
Terms: Agent receives 15% commission on domestic sales; 20% on foreign sales. Offers written contract, binding for 1 year.
Fees: Charges reading fee of $100 for new writers. 90% of business is derived from commission on ms sales; 10% is derived from reading fees or criticism services. Payment of criticism fees does not ensure representation.

‡PEN & INK LITERARY AGENCY (I, II), 2867 Silvercliff Dr., Dayton OH 45449. (513)434-0686. Contact: Theresa Freed. Estab. 1993. Member of RWA, Golden Triangle Writers Guild. Represents 5 clients. 100% of clients are new/previously unpublished writers. "We specialize in new, unpublished authors." Currently handles: 30% nonfiction books; 10% juvenile books; 60% novels.
Handles: Nonfiction books, juvenile books, novels, poetry books, movie scripts, TV scripts. Considers these nonfiction areas: agriculture/horticulture; art/architecture/design; biography/autobiography; business; child guidance/parenting; computers/electronics; cooking/food/nutrition; crafts/hobbies; gay/lesbian issues; health/medicine; history; interior design/decorating; juvenile nonfiction; military/war; money/finance/economics; nature/environment; photography; psychology; religious/inspirational; self-help/personal improvement; sociology; true crime/investigative; know-how books. Considers these fiction areas: action/adventure; cartoon/comic; confessional; contemporary issues; detective/police/crime; family saga; fantasy; gay; glitz; historical; humor/satire; juvenile; lesbian; mainstream; mystery/suspense; picture book; psychic/supernatural; religious/inspiration; romance (contemporary, gothic, historical, regency); science fiction; thriller/espionage; young adult. Send entire ms. Reports in 2 weeks on queries; 4-6 weeks on mss.
Terms: Agent receives 15% commission on domestic sales; 20% on foreign sales. Offers written contract, binding for 1 year.
Fees: Reading fee: $90, refundable upon receipt of advance. Criticism service included in reading fee upon request. Critique includes 2-3 page evaluation of author's work. Charges office expenses—postage, phone calls, photocopying; marketing expenses; editing fee—upon request. 70% of business is derived from commissions on ms sales; 30% is derived from reading fees or criticism services. Payment of a criticism fee does not ensure representation.
Writers' Conferences: Attends Antioch Writers' Workshop, Antioch College; Romance Writers of America, Golden Triangle Writers Guild Writers Conference.
Tips: Obtains new clients through queries, recommendations, conferences, advertising in *Writer's Digest*. "Please submit manuscript in proper form. This will save everyone time and money."

PMA LITERARY AND FILM MANAGEMENT, INC., Suite 501, 220 W., 19th St., New York NY 10011. (212)929-1222. Fax: (212)206-0238. President: Peter Miller. Associate Agents: Jennifer Robinson, Anthony Schneider, Lory Manrique. Estab. 1975. Represents 80 clients. 50% of clients are new/unpublished writers. Specializes in commercial fiction and nonfiction, thrillers, true crime and "fiction with *real* motion picture and television potential." Writer's guildelines for 5×8½ SASE and 2 first-class stamps. Currently handles: 50% fiction; 25% nonfiction; 25% screenplays.
Recent Sales: *Interest of Justice* and *Mitigating Circumstances*, by Nancy Taylor Rosenberg (Dutton); *Body of a Crime*, by Michael Eberhardt (Dutton).
Handles: Fiction, nonfiction, film scripts. Considers these nonfiction areas: history; science; biographies. Considers these fiction areas: thrillers; adventure; suspense; horror; women's issues. Query with outline and/or sample chapters. Reports in 1 week on queries; 2-4 weeks on ms.
Terms: Agent receives 15% commission on domestic sales; 20-25% on foreign sales.
Fees: Does not charge a reading fee. Paid reading evaluation service available upon request. "The evaluation, usually 4-7 pages in length, gives a detailed analysis of literary craft and commercial potential as well as further recommendations for improving the work." Charges for photocopying expenses.

JULIE POPKIN (II), #204, 15340 Albright St., Pacific Palisades CA 90272. (310)459-2834. Fax: (310)459-4128. Estab. 1989. Represents 26 clients. 40% of clients are new/unpublished writers. Specializes in selling book-length mss including fiction—all genres—and nonfiction. Especially interested in social issues. Currently handles: 50% nonfiction books; 50% novels; some scripts. Sub-agents: Ray-

Literary Agents: Fee-charging 143

Güde Merton (Badhamburg, Germany); Strarz-Kánska (Krakow, Poland); Eulama (Rome, Italy).
Recent Sales: *Love Match: Nelson vs. Navratilova*, by Sandra Faulkner and Judy Nelson (Birch Lane); *Woman In Residence*, by Dr. Michelle Harrison (Fawcett); *Six Roads from Newton*, by Edward Speyer (John Wiley); *Time Off for Murder, Rendezvous Nachladenschluss*, by Zelda Popkin (mystery, published in French and German).
Handles: Nonfiction books, novels. Considers these nonfiction areas: art; criticism; feminist; history; politics. Considers these fiction areas: juvenile; literary; mainstream; mystery; romance; science fiction. Reports in 1 month on queries; 2 months on mss.
Terms: Agent receives 15% commission on domestic sales; 10% on dramatic sales; 25% on foreign sales.
Fees: Does not charge a reading fee. Charges $100/year for photocopying, mailing, long distance calls.

*SIDNEY E. PORCELAIN (II,III), 414 Leisure Loop, Milford PA 18337-9568. (717)296-6420. Manager: Sidney Porcelain. Estab. 1952. Represents 20 clients. 50% of clients are new/unpublished writers. Prefers to work with published/established authors; works with a small number of new/unpublished authors. Specializes in fiction (novels, mysteries and suspense) and nonfiction (celebrity and exposé). Currently handles: 2% magazine articles; 5% magazine fiction; 5% nonfiction books; 50% novels; 5% juvenile books; 2% movie scripts; 1% TV scripts; 30% "comments for new writers."
Recent Sales: *Steve McQueen*, by Marshall Terrill.
Handles: Magazine articles, magazine fiction, nonfiction books, novels, juvenile books. Query with outline or entire ms. Reports in 2 weeks on queries; 3 weeks on mss.
Terms: Agent receives 10% commission on domestic sales; 10% on dramatic sales; 10% on foreign sales.
Fees: Does not charge a reading fee. Offers criticism service to new writers. 50% of income derived from commission on ms sales.

PUDDINGTONSTONE LITERARY AGENCY (II), Affiliate of SBC Enterprises Inc., 11 Mabro Dr., Denville NJ 07834-9607. (201)366-3622. Contact: Alec Bernard and Eugenia Cohen. Estab. 1979. Represents 25 clients. 80% of clients are new/previously unpublished writers. Currently handles: 10% nonfiction books; 70% novels; 20% movie scripts.
Handles: Nonfiction books, novels, movie scripts. Query first with SASE. Reports immediately on queries; 1 month on mss "that are requested by us."
Recent Sales: *Maximizing Cash Flow*, by Emery Toneré (John Wiley); *Manbirds*, by Marlys Wills (Prentice-Hall).
Terms: Agent receives 10-15% sliding scale (decreasing) on domestic sales; 20% on foreign sales. Offers written contract, binding for 1 year with renewals.
Fees: Reading fee charged for unsolicited mss over 20 pages. Negotiated fees for market analysis available.
Tips: Obtains new clients through referrals and listings.

QCORP LITERARY AGENCY (I), P.O. Box 8, Hillsboro OR 97123-0008. (800)775-6038. Contact: William C. Brown. Estab. 1990. Represents 14 clients. 75% of clients are new/previously unpublished writers. Currently handles: 40% nonfiction books; 60% fiction books. Member agent: William C. Brown.
Handles: Fiction and nonfiction books, including textbooks, scholarly books, novels, novellas, short story collections, poetry. Considers all nonfiction areas. Considers all areas of fiction, excluding cartoon/comic books. Query through critique service. Reports in 2 weeks on queries; 1 month on mss.
Recent Sales: *Served Cold*, by Edward Goldberg (West Coast Crime).
Terms: Agent receives 10% commission on domestic sales; 20% on foreign sales. Offers written contract, binding for 6 months, automatically renewed unless cancelled by author.
Fees: "No charges are made to agency authors if no sales are procured. If sales are generated, then charges are itemized and collected from proceeds up to a limit of $200, after which all expenses are absorbed by agency." Offers critique service.

Agents ranked I-IV are actively seeking new clients. Those ranked V or those who prefer not to be listed have been included to inform you they are not currently looking for new clients.

Tips: Obtains new clients through recommendations from others and from critique service. "New authors should use our critique service and its free, no obligation first chapter critique to introduce themselves. Call or write for details. Our critique service is serious business, line by line and comprehensive. Established writers should call or send résumé. We are admittedly new but very attentive and vigorous."

RHODES LITERARY AGENCY (II), P.O. Box 89133, Honolulu HI 96830-9133. (808)947-4689. Director: Fred C. Pugarelli. Agent: Ms. Angela Pugarelli. Estab. 1971. Represents 50 clients. 99% of clients are new/previously unpublished writers. Specializes in novels and screenplays. Currently handles: 10% nonfiction books; 70% novels; 20% movie scripts.
Handles: Nonfiction books, textbooks, scholarly books, juvenile books, novels, novellas, short story collections, poetry books, movie scripts, stage plays, TV scripts, syndicated material. Considers all fiction and nonfiction areas, including science fiction and fantasy. Query or send entire ms, outline/proposal and bio or send outline plus sample chapters and bio. Reports in 2-4 weeks on queries; 1-2 months on mss.
Recent Sales: *Sleep Mastery*, by H. Vafi M.D. and Pamela Vafi (Bob Adams). "In addition, over the years we have sold over 120 manuscripts to *Travel & Leisure, Mature Years, Signature, Millionaire Magazine, The Saint Mystery Magazine, The Saint Mystery Library, Fantastic Universe, 77 Sunset Strip, Men's Digest, Rascal, Opinion, The Mendocino Robin, Hyacinths and Biscuits* and other national periodicals."
Terms: Agent receives 10% commission on domestic sales; 20% on foreign sales.
Fees: Charges $155 reading fee for books up to 45,000 words; $165 for books over 45,000 words; $155 for screenplays. Charges for photocopying and some unusual office expenses. 10% of business is derived from commissions on ms sales at present; 90% is derived from reading fees or criticism services.
Tips: Obtains new clients through listings in various market guides and recommendations. "Send a one or two-page query first with bio and a SASE."

‡ROSE AGENCY (I), 2033 Ontario Circle, Ft. Wayne IN 46802. (219)432-5857. Contact: Lynn Clough. Estab. 1993. Currently handles: 50% nonfiction books; 25% juvenile books; 25% novels.
Handles: Nonfiction books, juvenile books, novels. Considers these nonfiction areas: business; child guidance/parenting; juvenile nonfiction; religious/inspirational; self-help/personal improvement. Considers these fiction areas: action/adventure; contemporary issues; historical; humor/satire; juvenile; mainstream; mystery/suspense; religious/inspiration; romance (contemporary); young adult. Send entire ms. Reports in 4-6 weeks on mss.
Terms: Agent receives 15% commission on domestic sales; 20% on foreign sales. Offers written contract, binding for 1 year.
Fees: Does not charge reading fee. Offers criticism service; "fees vary." Charges "$35 handling fee for complete manuscript submissions." Payment of a criticism fee does not ensure representation.
Tips: "If you have come this far, you probably have what it takes to be a published author. We want to see your best stuff, because we find that writers are dreamers driven by some inner compulsion to put words on paper. Just because you aren't published doesn't mean you aren't a writer. We'd like to read your work."

***RUSSELL-SIMENAUER LITERARY AGENCY INC. (II)**, P.O. Box 43267, Upper Montclair NJ 07043. (201)746-0539. Fax: (201)746-0754. Contact: Jacqueline Simenauer or Margaret Russell. Estab. 1990. Member of Authors Guild, Authors League, NASW. Represents 35 clients. 75% of clients are new/previously unpublished writers. Specializes in psychiatry/psychology, self-help, how-to, human sexuality. Currently handles: 77% nonfiction books; 5% juvenile books; 10% novels; 3% movie scripts; 5% TV scripts. Member agents: Jacqueline Simenauer, (ms/outline critiques); Margaret Russell, (restructuring, editing, rewriting, ghosting, ms appraisal).
Handles: Nonfiction books, juvenile books, novels, movie scripts, TV scripts. Considers these nonfiction areas: child guidance/parenting; health/medicine; juvenile nonfiction; money/finance/economics; psychology; religious/inspirational; self-help/personal improvement; sociology; true crime/investigative; women's issues/women's studies; human sexuality; psychiatry. Considers these fiction areas: detective/police/crime; family saga; feminist; juvenile; mainstream; mystery/suspense; psychic/supernatural; romance (contemporary); thriller/espionage. Query with outline/proposal. Reports in 2-3 weeks on queries; 3-4 weeks on mss.

Recent Sales: *Your Body Never Lies*, by Masdin Rush (Simon & Schuster); *Children and Violence*, by Janice Cohn (William Morrow).
Terms: Agent receives 15% commission on domestic sales; 25% on foreign sales.
Fees: "There is no charge for reading an outline/proposal. If a client, however, wants a complete manuscript critique, the fee is $1.25/page. Criticism service involves analysis of originality of ideas (marketability), effectiveness, organization of information and writing. Reading fees will be refundable upon sale of the ms. There are no fees for published writers." Charges for postage, photocopying, phone, fax, if sale is made. 90% of business is derived from commissions on ms sales; 10% is derived from reading fees or criticism services.
Tips: Obtains new clients through recommendations from others; advertising in various journals, newsletters, etc. and professional conferences.

SUSAN SCHULMAN, A LITERARY AGENCY (III), 454 W. 44th St., New York NY 10036. (212)713-1633/4/5. Fax: (212)586-8830. President: Susan Schulman. Estab. 1979. Member of AAR. 10-15% of clients are new/unpublished writers. Prefers to work with published/established authors; works with a small number of new/unpublished authors. Currently handles: 70% nonfiction books; 20% novels; 10% stage plays.
Handles: Nonfiction, fiction, plays, especially contemporary women's fiction and genre fiction such as mysteries and women's interests, including politics, business, health and psychology. Query with outline. Reports in 2 weeks on queries; 6 weeks on mss. SASE required.
Recent Sales: *Why Me? Why This? Why Now?*, by Robin Norwood (women's self-help) (Random House, Inc., Crown Publishers); *The Afterlife of George Cartwright*, by John Steffer (literary fiction) (Henry Holt & Co.).
Terms: Agent receives 15% commission on domestic sales; 10-20% on dramatic sales; 7½-10% on foreign sales (plus 7½-10% to co-agent).
Fees: Offers criticism service: $50, only if detailed analysis requested; fee will be waived if representing the writer. Less than 2% of income derived from reading fees. Charges for foreign mail, special messenger or copying services.

SEBASTIAN LITERARY AGENCY (III), Suite 708, 333 Kearny St., San Francisco CA 94108. (415)391-2331. Fax: (415)391-2377. Owner Agent: Laurie Harper. Estab. 1985. Represents approximately 50 clients. Specializes in business, sociology and current affairs. Currently handles: 75% nonfiction books; 25% fiction (novels).
Handles: Nonfiction books, select novels. "No children's or YA." Considers these nonfiction areas: anthropology/archaeology; art/architecture/design; biography/autobiography; business; child guidance/parenting; computers/electronics; current affairs; ethnic/cultural interests; government/politics/law; health/medicine; history; money/finance/economics; nature/environment; psychology; science/technology; self-help/personal improvement; sociology; sports; true crime/investigative; women's issues/women's studies. Considers these fiction areas: detective/police/crime; ethnic; family saga; gay; glitz; historical; literary; mainstream; mystery/suspense; thriller/espionage. No romance, science fiction or horror. Query with outline, author bio plus 3 sample chapters. Reports in 3 weeks on queries; 4-6 weeks on mss.
Recent Sales: *Jump Start Parenting*, by Beverly Deadmond (Thomas Nelson Publishing); *Real Numbers: Analyzing Income Properties For a Profitable Investment*, by Joseph Sinclair (Business One Irwin).
Terms: Agent receives 15% commission on domestic sales; 20% on foreign sales. Offers written contract.
Fees: Charges a $100 annual administration fee for clients and charges for photocopies of ms for submission to publisher. No reading fees.
Tips: Obtains new clients through "referrals from authors and editors, some at conferences and some from unsolicited queries from around the country. If interested in agency representation, for *fiction*, "know the category that your novel belongs in, according to market study, and be sure that you have made it conforming to that category. Too many novels fall in-between categories, and are unsaleable as a result. For *nonfiction*, it is important to convey more than the facts and statistics about the subject of your book—you need to convey its *relevance* to us, and your fascination or enthusiasm for it."

*****SINGER MEDIA CORPORATION (III)**, Seaview Business Park, Unit #106, 1030 Calle Cordillera, San Clemente CA 92672. (714)498-7227. Fax: (714)498-2162. Contact: Kurt Singer. Estab. 1940. Represents 100+ clients for books, features, cartoons. 15% of clients are new/previously unpublished writers. Specializes in romance, business, self-help, dictionaries, quiz books, cartoons, interviews. Currently handles: 25% nonfiction books; 35% novels; 40% syndicated material. Member agents: Helen

146 Guide to Literary Agents & Art/Photo Reps '94

J. Lee (general novels); Kurt Singer (business books); Katherine Han (self-help); Peter Carbone (Asia department); Janice Hawkridge (romance books); Kristy Lee (cartoons and comic strips).
Handles: Nonfiction books, syndicated material, business titles, cartoons. Considers these nonfiction areas: biography/autobiography; business; child guidance/parenting; computers/electronics; health/medicine; money/finance/economics; psychology; self-help/personal improvement; translations; true crime/investigative; women's issues/women's studies; cartoons; dictionaries; juvenile activities; interviews with celebrities. Considers these fiction areas: cartoon/comic; detective/police/crime; erotica; fantasy; glitz; mystery/suspense; picture book; psychic/supernatural; romance (contemporary); science fiction; thriller/espionage; westerns/frontier; teenage romance. Query. "Give writing credits." Reports in 3 weeks on queries; 4-6 weeks on mss.
Recent Sales: "De Grassi TV series books," Vols. 11 and 12 (Bertelsmann); *Bible of Management*, by C. Northcote Parkinson (Jaman's Manufacturer's Association).
Terms: Agent receives 15% commission on domestic sales; 20% on foreign sales.
Fees: Charges $350 reading fee "only to unpublished writers. Criticism service is part of our reading fee. Our readers are published authors or ghostwriters." 97% of business is derived from commissions on ms and book sales; 3% is derived from reading fees or criticism service. Payment of a criticism fee ensures representation "unless it is not saleable to the commercial market."
Writers' Conference: Attends Romance Writers of America.
Tips: "We have been in business for 52 years and are known. If interested in agency representation, books are not written, but rewritten and rewritten. Syndication is done on a worldwide basis, and must be of global interest. Hollywood's winning formula is God/inspiration, sex and action. Try to get reprints of books overseas and in the USA if out of print."

*SOUTHERN LITERARY AGENCY (III), 16411 Brookvilla Dr., Houston TX 77059. (713)780-9443. Contact: Michael Doran. Estab. 1980. Represents 58 clients. 20% of clients are new/previously unpublished writers. "We are most interested in popular financial, professional and technical books." Currently handles: 70% nonfiction books; 20% novels; 10% movie scripts. Member agents: Michael Doran (nonfiction), Patricia Coleman (mainstream novels, some nonfiction).
Handles: Nonfiction books, novels, movie scripts. Considers these nonfiction areas: anthropology/archaeology; biography/autobiography; business; child guidance/parenting; health/medicine; history; money/finance/economics; psychology; self-help/personal improvement. Considers these fiction areas: action/adventure; detective/police/crime; humor/satire; mainstream; mystery/suspense; thriller/espionage. Telephone query. Reports in 1 month on mss.
Recent Sales: *Sharp Dressed Men*, by David Blayneg (Hyperion); *Real Choices in Cancer Surgery*, by Richard Evans (Avery).
Terms: Agent receives 15% commission on domestic sales; 20% on foreign sales. Offers written contract.
Fees: "There is a $350 fee on unpublished new novelists, returnable if their manuscript is publishable and we do the selling of it. Refund on first royalties. Offers multi-page critique on manuscripts which can be made marketable; 1-page remarks and suggestions for writing improvements otherwise. Charges cost-per on extraordinary costs, pre-agreed." 90% of business derived from commissions on ms sales; 10% from reading fees or criticism services.
Writers' Conferences: ABA; Texas and other Southern regional.
Tips: Obtains new clients through conferences, yellow pages—mainly referrals. "Learn about the book business through conferences and reading before contacting the agent."

STATE OF THE ART LTD. (II), 4267 W. Florida Ave., Denver CO 80219. (303)936-1978. Fax: (303)936-1770. Contact: C.J. Ficco. Estab. 1983. Represents 10 clients. Currently handles: 50% nonfiction books, 50% novels. Member agents: Hary Fleenor (Sr. Editor); C.J. Ficco (Jr. Editor); Aleita S. Currier (Secretary).
Handles: Nonfiction, novels. Considers these nonfiction areas: art; self-help/personal improvement; women's studies; also open to new topics. Considers these fiction areas: contemporary issues; feminist; mystery/suspense/detective; science/speculative fiction—no experimental fiction. Query with SASE or by phone. "If we agree to review work, prepare first and last chapters plus a full, detailed outline plus synopsis." Reports in 2 weeks on written queries.

Recent Sales: *Walking on Air*, by Helen McLaughlin (State of the Art, Ltd.); *Snowbound in the High Rockies*, by Louis C. Farmer (State of the Art, Ltd.).
Terms: Agent receives 10% and up commission on domestic sales. Offers written contract upon acceptance.
Fees: Charges a reading fee for unsolicited mss (minimum $150). Offers detailed literary and market evaluation.
Tips: Usually obtains new clients from directory listings and phone/mail queries. Typed work only. No hand-written submissions unless you are willing to pay to have it typed.

MICHAEL STEINBERG LITERARY AGENCY (III), P.O. Box 274, Glencoe IL 60027. (708)835-8881. Contact: Michael Steinberg. Estab. 1980. Represents 27 clients. 5% of clients are new/previously unpublished writers. Specializes in business and general nonfiction, mysteries, science fiction. Currently handles: 75% nonfiction books, 25% novels.
Handles: Nonfiction books; novels. Considers these nonfiction areas: biography; business; child guidance; computer; current affairs; ethnic/cultural interests; government/politics/law; history; money/finance/economics; nature/environment; psychology; self-help/personal improvement. Considers these fiction areas: action/adventure; contemporary issues; detective/police/crime; erotica; mainstream; mystery/suspense; science fiction; thriller/espionage. Query for guidelines. Reports in 2 weeks on queries; 6 weeks on mss.
Terms: Agent receives 15% on domestic sales; 15-20% on foreign sales. Offers written contract, which is binding, "but at will."
Fees: Charges $75 reading fee for outline and chapters 1-3; $200 for a full ms to 100,000 words. Criticism service included in reading fee. Charges actual phone and postage, which is billed back quarterly. 95% of business is derived from commissions on ms sales; 5% is derived from reading fees or criticism services.
Tips: Obtains new clients through unsolicited inquiries and referrals from editors and authors. "We do not solicit new clients. Do not send unsolicited material. Write for guidelines and include SASE. Do not send generically addressed, photocopied query letters."

‡GLORIA STERN AGENCY (II), #3, 1235 Chandler Blvd., North Hollywood CA 91607. (818)508-6296. Contact: Gloria Stern. Estab. 1984. Member of IWOSC, SCW. Represents 14 clients. 80% of clients are new/unpublished writers. Specializes in consultation, writer's services (ghost writing, editing, critiquing, etc.). Currently handles: 79% fiction; 19% nonfiction books; 8% movie scripts; 2% reality based. Member agent: Gloria Stern (romance, detective, science fiction).
• This agency is not affiliated with the Gloria Stern Literary Agency located in Texas.
Handles: Novels, movie scripts, short story collections. Considers these nonfiction areas: business; cooking; current affairs; ethnic/cultural interests; health/medicine; money/finance/economics; New Age/metaphysical; psychology (pop); self-help/personal improvement; sociology; true crime/investigative; women's issues/women's studies. Considers these fiction areas: action/adventure; contemporary issues; detective/police/crime; erotica; fantasy; feminist; glitz; mainstream; romance (contemporary, gothic, historical, regency); science fiction; thriller/espionage; western/frontier. Query with short bio, credits. Reports in 3-4 weeks on queries; 3-5 weeks on mss.
Terms: Agent receives 12% commission on domestic sales; 20% on foreign sales. Offers written contract, binding for 1 year.
Fees: Charges reading fee, by project (by arrangement), $35/hour for unpublished writers. Criticism service: $35/hour. Critiques are "detailed analysis of all salient points regarding such elements as structure, style, pace, development, publisher's point of view and suggestions for rewrites if needed." Charges for long-distance, photocopying and postage. 38% of income derived from sales, 29% from reading fees, 26% from correspondence students, 7% from teaching. Payment of reading fee does not insure representation.
Writer's Conferences: Pasadena Writer's Forum (Spring '94).
Tips: Obtains new clients from book (*Do the Write Thing: Making the Transition to Professional*), classes, lectures, listings, word of mouth. "To a writer interested in representation: Be sure that you have researched your field and are aware of current publishing demands. Writing is the only field in which

---

Agents who specialize in a specific subject area such as children's books or in handling the work of certain writers such as Latino writers are ranked IV.

all the best is readily available to the beginning writer. Network, take classes, persevere and most of all, write, write and rewrite."

*MARK SULLIVAN ASSOCIATES (II), Suite 1700, 521 Fifth Ave., New York NY 10175. (212)682-5844. Contact: Mark Sullivan. Estab. 1989. 50% of clients are new/previously unpublished writers. Currently handles: 20% nonfiction books; 5% textbooks; 60% novels; 5% poetry books; 10% movie scripts. Specializes in science fiction, women's romance, detective/mystery/spy, but handles all genres.
Handles: Nonfiction books, textbooks, scholarly books, novels, novellas, short story collections, poetry books, movie scripts. Considers these nonfiction areas: anthropology/archaeology; biography/autobiography; business; cooking/food/nutrition; crafts/hobbies; current affairs; health/medicine; interior design/decorating; language/literature/criticism; military/war; money/finance/economics; music/dance/theater/film; nature/environment; New Age/metaphysics; photography; psychology; religious/inspirational; science/technology; sports. Considers all fiction areas. Query or send query, outline plus 3 sample chapters. Reports in 2 weeks on queries; 3-4 weeks on mss.
Recent Sales: *Mutual Funds,* by Lyle Allen (Avon).
Terms: Agent receives 10-15% commission on domestic sales; 20% on foreign sales. Offers written contract.
Fees: Charges $95 reading fee for new writers. Critique is provided with reading fee. Charges for photocopying and long-distance telephone calls. 90% of business is derived from commissions on ms sales; 10% of business is derived from reading fees or criticism services. Payment of fees does not ensure agency representation. "However, the firm's offer to read an entire manuscript is a reflection of our strong interest."
Tips: Obtains new clients through "advertising, recommendations, conferences. Quality of presentation of query letter, sample chapters and manuscript is important. Completed manuscripts are preferred to works in progress."

‡TARC LITERARY AGENCY (II), P.O. Box 64785, Tucson AZ 85728-4785. (602)325-4733. Contact: Martha Gore. Represents 50 clients. Specializes in fiction and nonfiction books only. Currently handles: 80% nonfiction books, 20% novels.
Handles: Nonfiction, novels. Considers these nonfiction areas: pop psychology; self-help; true crime. Considers these fiction areas: mainstream; mystery/suspense. Query. Reports in 1 month on queries, 3 months on mss.
Terms: Agent receives 15% commission on domestic sales. Offers written contract.
Fees: Does not charge a reading fee. Criticism service is not solicited, only if requested by writer; fee varies. Critiques are private or telephone consultations. 80% of business is derived from commissions on ms sales; 20% is derived from reading fees or criticism service. Payment of reading or criticism fees does not ensure representation.
Tips: Obtains new clients through recommendations from others.

DAWSON TAYLOR LITERARY AGENCY (II), 4722 Holly Lake Dr., Lake Worth FL 33463. (407)965-4150. Contact: Dawson Taylor, Attorney at Law. Estab. 1974. Represents 21 clients. 80% of clients are new/previously unpublished writers. Specializes in nonfiction, fiction, sports, military history. Currently handles: 80% nonfiction; 5% scholarly books; 15% novels.
Handles: Nonfiction books, textbooks, scholarly books, novels, nonfiction on sports, especially golf. Query with outline. Reports in 5 days on queries; 10 days on mss.
Recent Sales: *The Man Who Killed Boys,* by C. Linedecker (St. Martin's).
Terms: Agent receives 15% or 20% commission "depending upon editorial help." Offers written contract. Indefinite, but cancellable on 60 days notice by either party.
Fees: "Reading fees are subject to negotiation, usually $100 for normal length manuscript . . . more for lengthy ones. (Includes critique and sample editing.) Criticism service subject to negotiation . . . from $100. Critiques are on style and content, include editing of ms, and are written by myself." 90% of business is derived from commissions on ms sales; 10% is derived from reading fees or criticism services. Payment of reading or criticism fees does not ensure representation.
Tips: Obtains new clients through "recommendations from publishers and authors who are presently in my stable."

*JEANNE TOOMEY ASSOCIATES (II), 95 Belden St., Falls Village CT 06031. (203)824-0831/5469. Fax: (203)824-5460. Contact: Jeanne Toomey. Estab. 1985. Represents 10 clients. 50% of clients are new/previously unpublished writers. Specializes in "nonfiction; biographies of famous men and women; history with a flair—murder and detection. No children's books, no poetry, no Harlequin-

type romances." Currently handles: 45% nonfiction books; 20% novels; 35% movie scripts.
Handles: Nonfiction books, novels, short story collections, movie scripts. Considers these nonfiction areas: agriculture/horticulture; animals; anthropology/archaeology; art/architecture/design; biography/autobiography; government/politics/law; history; interior design/decorating; money/finance/economics; nature/environment; true crime/investigative. Considers these fiction areas: detective/police/crime; psychic/supernatural; thriller/espionage. Send outline plus 3 sample chapters. "Query first, please!" Reports in 1 month.
Recent Sales: *A Woman Named Jackie*, by C. David Heymann (Lyle Stuart); *Llantarnam*, by Muriel Maddox (Sunstone Books).
Terms: Agent receives 15% commission on domestic sales.
Fees: Charges $100 reading fee for unpublished authors; no fee for published authors. "The $100 covers marketing fee, office expenses, postage, photocopying. We absorb those costs in the case of published authors."

‡*VISIONS PRESS (II), P.O. Box 4904, Valley Village CA 91617. (805)273-4718. Contact: Allen Williams Brown. Estab. 1991. Represents 9 clients. 60% of clients are new/previously unpublished writers. "We prefer to support writers who incorporate African-American issues in the storyline. Will handle adult romance novels, children's books and consciousness-raising pieces." Currently handles: 20% nonfiction books; 50% novels; 30% magazine pieces. Member agents: Carrie Brown (consciousness-raising pieces for magazines such as *UPSCALE* and *Emerge*); Christopher Brown (romance novels with African-American women as heroines); Elizabeth Brown (nonfiction).
Handles: Nonfiction books, novels, magazine pieces. Considers these nonfiction areas: ethnic/cultural interests; gay/lesbian issues; religious/inspirational; self-help/personal improvement; women's issues/women's studies. Considers these fiction areas: confessional; contemporary issues; erotica; ethnic; gay; lesbian; mainstream; romance (contemporary); young adult. Send outline plus 2 sample chapters and author bio or description of self. Reports in 2 weeks on queries; 1 month on mss.
Terms: Agent receives 10% commission on domestic sales; 15% on foreign sales. Offers written contract, specific length of time depends on type of work—novel or magazine piece.
Fees: Charges reading fee. "Reading fees are charged to new writers only. Fee is refunded if agency decides to represent author. Fees are based on length of manuscript ($100 for up to 300 pages; $150 for any length thereafter.)" Offers criticism service. "Same as for the reading fee. Both the reading fee and the criticism fee entitle the author to a critique of his/her work by one of our editors. We are interested in everyone who has a desire to be published . . . to hopefully realize their dream. To that end, we provide very honest and practical advice on what needs to be done to correct a manuscript." Additional fees "will be negotiated with the author on a project by project basis. Often there is a one-time fee charged that covers all office expenses associated with the marketing of a manuscript." 90% of business is derived from commissions on ms sales; 10% is derived from reading fees or criticism services. Payment of a criticism fee does not ensure representation.
Writers' Conferences: "We do not usually attend writing conferences. Most of our contacts are made through associations with groups such as NAACP, Rainbow Coalition, Urban League and other such groups that promote consciousness-raising activities by African-Americans. We look for talent among African-American scholars and African-American "common folk" who can usually be found sharing their opinions and visions at an issues-related conference and town hall type meeting."
Tips: Obtains new clients through recommendations from others and through inquiries. "We believe the greatest story ever told has yet to be written! For that reason we encourage every writer to uninhibitedly pursue his/her dream of becoming published. A no from us should simply be viewed as a temporary setback that can be overcome by another attempt to meet our high expectations. Discouraged, frustrated, and demoralized are words we have deleted from our version of the dictionary. An aspiring writer must have the courage to press on and believe in his/her talent."

BESS WALLACE LITERARY AGENCY (II), P.O. Box 972, Duchesne UT 84021. (801)738-2317. Contact: Bess D. Wallace. Estab. 1978. Represents 30 clients. 90% of clients are new/previously unpublished writers. Currently handles 90% nonfiction books; 5% scholarly books; 5% textbooks. Specializes in criminal psychology.
Handles: Nonfiction books, textbooks, scholarly books. Considers these nonfiction areas: agriculture/horticulture; animals; anthropology/archaeology; current affairs; government/politics/law; history; military/war; psychology; true crime/investigative. Considers science fiction. Query with outline/proposal. Reports in 3 weeks on queries; 6 weeks on mss.

Terms: Agent receives 15% commission on domestic sales; 10% commission on foreign sales. Offers written contract if author wishes it, binding for 2 years.
Fees: Offers criticism service. "Usually $150 for any size ms." Letter which explains errors in plot, sentence structure etc. by Bess D. Wallace. Other fees charged only if requested to edit and/or retype. $1.50 per page to edit; $2 per page to edit and retype. 80% of business derived from commission on ms sales. 20% derived from reading fees or criticism services. Payment of criticism fee does not ensure representation.
Tips: Obtains new clients through *Guide to Literary Agents and Art/Photo Reps*, *LMP*, etc. Send query first or call.

*THE GERRY B. WALLERSTEIN AGENCY (II), Suite 12, 2315 Powell Ave., Erie PA 16506. (814)833-5511. Fax: (814)833-6260. Contact: Ms. Gerry B. Wallerstein. Estab. 1984. Member of Authors Guild, Inc., ASJA. Represents 40 clients. 25% of clients are new/previously unpublished writers. Specializes in nonfiction books and "personalized help for new novelists." Currently handles: 52% nonfiction books; 2% scholarly books; 2% juvenile books; 35% novels; 2% short story collections; 2% TV scripts; 2% short material. (Note: juvenile books, scripts and short material marketed for *clients only*!)
Handles: Nonfiction books, scholarly trade books, novels, short story collections. Considers all nonfiction areas provided book is for general trade ("no textbooks"). Considers these fiction areas: action/adventure; contemporary issues; detective/police/crime; family saga; glitz; historical; humor/satire; literary; mainstream; mystery/suspense; romance; thriller/espionage; westerns/frontier; young adult. To query, send entire ms for fiction; proposal (including 3 chapters) for nonfiction books. "No manuscripts are reviewed until writer has received my brochure." Reports in 1 week on queries; 2 months on mss.
Recent Sales: *Satanic Panic: The Creation of a Contemporary Legend*, by Jeffrey S. Victor (Open Court Publishing Co.); *Dancing In The Dark*, by Susan P. Teklits (HarperPaperbacks/Monogram); *Cat Killer* and *Mouse Trapped*, by Sandy Dengler (Victor Books/Scripture Press Publications).
Terms: Agent receives 15% on domestic sales; 20% on foreign sales. Offers written contract, which "can be cancelled by either party, with 60 days' notice of termination."
Fees: "To justify my investment of time, effort and expertise in working with newer or beginning writers, I charge a reading/critique fee based on length of manuscript, for example: $350 for each manuscript of 105,000 to 125,000 words." Critique included as part of reading fee. "Reports are 1-2 pages for proposals and short material; 2-4 pages for full-length mss; done by agent." Charges clients $20/month postage/telephone fee; and if required, ms photocopying or typing, copyright fees, cables, attorney fees (if approved by author), travel expense (if approved by author). 50% of business is derived from commissions on ms sales; 50% is derived from reading fees and critique services. Payment of a critique fee does not ensure representation.
Writers' Conferences: Westminster College Conference; Midwest Writers' Conference; National Writers' Uplink, Writer's Center at Chautauqua.
Tips: Obtains new clients through recommendations; listings in directories; referrals from clients and publishers/editors. "A query letter that tells me something about the writer and his/her work is more likely to get a personal response."

‡JAMES WARREN LITERARY AGENCY (II), 13131 Welby Way, North Hollywood CA 91606. (818)982-5423. Agent: James Warren. Editor: Michael Hofstein. Estab. 1969. Represents 60 clients. 60% of clients are new/unpublished writers. "We are willing to work with select unpublished writers." Specializes in fiction, history, textbooks, professional books, craft books, how-to books, self-improvement books, health books and diet books. Currently handles 40% nonfiction books; 20% novels; 10% textbooks; 5% juvenile books; 10% movie scripts; 15% TV scripts and teleplays.
Handles: Juvenile books, historical romance novels, movie scripts (especially drama and humor), TV scripts (drama, humor, documentary). Query with outline. Does not read unsolicited mss. No reply without SASE. Brochure available for SASE. Reports in 1 week on queries; 1 month on mss.
Recent Sales: *Madame President* (New Saga Press); *Witty Words* (Sterling Press).
Terms: Agent receives 10% commission on domestic sales; 20% on foreign sales.
Fees: Charges reading fee of $2.50/1,000 words; refunds reading fee if material sells. 20% of total income derived from fees charged to writers; 80% of income derived from commission on ms sales. Payment of fee does not ensure representation.

*SANDRA WATT & ASSOCIATES (II), Suite 4053, 8033 Sunset Blvd., Hollywood CA 90046. (213)653-2339. Contact: Davida South. Estab. 1977. Signatory of WGA. Represents 55 clients. 15% of clients are new/previously unpublished writers. Specializes in scripts: film noir, romantic comedies; books:

women's fiction, mystery, commercial nonfiction. Currently handles: 40% nonfiction books, 35% novels, 25% movie scripts. Member agents: Sandra Watt (scripts, nonfiction, novels); Davida South (scripts).
Handles: Nonfiction books, novels, movie scripts. Considers these nonfiction areas: animals; anthropology/archaeology; New Age/metaphysics; self-help/personal improvement; sports; true crime/investigative; women's issues/women's studies. Considers these fiction areas: detective/police/crime; glitz; mainstream; mystery/suspense; thriller/espionage. Query. Reports in 1 week on queries; 2 months on mss.
Recent Sales: *Lessons in Survival*, by Laramie Dunaway (Warner); *The Lemurs Legacy: The Evolution of Power, Sex and Love*, by Jay Russell Ph.D. (Putnam); *One of Their Own*, CBS and Citadel (M.O.W.)
Terms: Agent receives 15% commission on domestic sales; 25% on foreign sales. Offers written contract, binding for 1 year.
Fees: Does not charge reading fee. Charges a one-time nonrefundable marketing fee of $100 *for unpublished authors.*
Tips: Obtains new clients through recommendations from others, referrals and "from wonderful query letters. Don't forget the SASE!"

WEST COAST LITERARY ASSOCIATES (II), Suite 151, 7960-B Soquel Dr., Aptos CA 95003. (408)685-9548. Contact: Acquisitions Editor. Estab. 1986. Member of Authors League of America. Represents 60 clients. 75% of clients are new/previously unpublished clients. Currently handles: 20% nonfiction books; 80% novels.
Handles: Nonfiction books, novels. Considers these nonfiction areas: biography/autobiography; current affairs; ethnic/cultural interests; government/politics/law; history; language/literature/criticism; music/dance/theater/film; nature/environment; psychology; true crime/investigative; women's issues/women's studies. Considers these fiction areas: action/adventure; contemporary issues; detective/police/crime; experimental; historical; literary; mainstream; mystery/suspense; regional; romance (contemporary and historical); science fiction; thriller/espionage; westerns/frontier. Query first. Reports in 2 weeks on queries; 1 month on mss.
Terms: Agent receives 10% commission on domestic sales; 20% commission on foreign sales. Offers written contract, binding for 6 months.
Recent Sales: *High Roller*, by Jan Welles (New Horizon Press); *Carnival of Saints*, by George Herman (Ballantine); *The Ballad of Rocky Ruiz*, by Manuel Ramos (St. Martin's).
Fees: Does not charge a reading fee. Charges an agency marketing and materials fee between $75 and $95, depending on genre and length. Fees are refunded in full upon sale of the property.
Tips: "Query with SASE for submission guidelines before sending material."

WILDSTAR ASSOCIATES (II), (formerly The Adele Leone Agency, Inc.), 26 Nantucket Place, Scarsdale NY 10583. (914)901-2965. Fax: (914)337-0361. Contact: Ralph Leone. Estab. 1978. Represents 50 clients. 20% of clients are new/previously unpublished writers. Specializes in women's fiction, romance (historical, contemporary), horror, science fiction, nonfiction, hard science, self-help, parenting, nutrition. Currently handles: 40% nonfiction books; 60% novels. Member agents: Ralph Leone (crime, romance, nonfiction); Richard Monaco (horror, fantasy, science fiction, nonfiction); Matt Jorgensen (graphics, comics, art).
Handles: Nonfiction books, novels. Considers these nonfiction areas: biography/autobiography; business; child guidance/parenting; cooking/food/nutrition; crafts/hobbies; current affairs; ethnic/cultural interests; gay/lesbian issues; government/politics/law; health/medicine; history; interior design/decorating; language/literature/criticism; military/war; money/finance/economics; music/dance/theater/film; nature/environment; new age/metaphysics; psychology; true crime/investigative; science/technology; self-help/personal improvement; sports; women's issues/women's studies. Considers these fiction areas: action/adventure; detective/police/crime; family saga; fantasy; glitz; historical; horror; literary; mainstream; mystery/suspense; psychic/supernatural; romance; science fiction; thriller/espionage; westerns/frontier. Query. Reports in 2 weeks on queries.
Recent Sales: *Animals*, by Skipp/Spector (Bantam Books); *Fractals*, by John Briggs (St. Martin's).
Terms: Agent receives 15% commission on domestic sales; 15% on foreign sales, "unless foreign agent is used, then 10%." Offers written contract, binding "no less than 1 year."
Fees: Charges $50 reading fee.
Writers' Conferences: PEN Writers Conference; World Horror, World Fantasy, ABA.
Tips: Obtains new clients through recommendations from others, at conferences. "Send simple clear queries and return postage."

*STEPHEN WRIGHT AUTHORS' REPRESENTATIVE (III), P.O. Box 1341, F.D.R. Station, New York NY 10150-1341. (212)213-4382. Authors' Representative: Stephen Wright. Estab. 1984. Prefers to work with published/established authors. Works with a small number of new/unpublished authors. Specializes in fiction, nonfiction, screenplays. Currently handles: 20% nonfiction; 60% novels; 10% movie scripts; 10% TV scripts.
Handles: Nonfiction books, novels, young adult and juvenile books, movie scripts, radio scripts, stage plays, TV scripts, syndicated material. Query first; do *not* send ms. Include SASE with query. Reports in 3 weeks on queries.
Terms: Agent receives 10-15% commission on domestic sales; 10-15% on dramatic sales; 15-20% on foreign sales.
Fees: "When the writer is a beginner or has had no prior sales in the medium for which he or she is writing, we charge a reading criticism fee; does not waive fee when representing the writer. Charges $600/300 pages; or $100/50 pages (double-spaced). We simply do not 'read' a manuscript, but give the writer an in-depth criticism. If we like what we read, we would represent the writer. Or if the writer revises manuscript to meet our professional standards and we believe there is a market for said manuscript, we would also represent the writer. We tell the writer whether we believe his/her work is marketable. I normally provide the critiques."

‡WRITE DESIGNS LITERARY AGENCY (I), P.O. Box 191554, Atlanta GA 31119. (404)634-5874. Contact: Judy Strickland. Estab. 1993. Represents 3 clients. 65% of clients are new/previously unpublished writers. Specializes in travel (guidebooks, travelogues, picture books), spy and WWI adventure novels, reference books on consumer and general interest topics. Currently handles 70% nonfiction books; 30% novels.
Handles: Nonfiction books, novels. Considers these nonfiction areas: art/architecture/design; biography/autobiography; business; computers/electronics; cooking/food/nutrition; crafts/hobbies; health/medicine; history; military/war; money/finance/economics; nature/environment; photography; religious/inspirational; sports; travel; southern topics. Considers these fiction areas: action/adventure; detective/police/crime; historical; literary (Southern writers); mainstream; mystery/suspense; religious/inspiration; thriller/espionage. "Will not accept works with overt sex, profanity. No occult/horror." Query with outline/proposal and SASE for nonfiction; query with outline plus 3-5 sample chapters of no more than 50 pages and SASE for fiction. Reports in 2-4 weeks on queries; 5-10 weeks on mss.
Recent Sales: *Paris for Free* by Mark Beffart (Mustang Publishing).
Terms: Agent receives 15% commission on domestic sales; 20% on foreign sales. Offers written contract.
Fees: Does not charge a reading fee. Criticism service: $1.00 per page. Written critique with suggestions. Charges for excessive postage, telephone calls, "which may be waived, depending on status of book (% of advance, sales, etc.)." 95% of business is derived from commissions on ms sales; 5% from reading or critique fees.
Tips: Obtains new clients from recommendations. "We have wide-ranging tastes, but take a look at what sells before sending us a proposal. Convince us that your work is worth selling. Send concise, clear and well thought out queries and proposals. Prefer experienced writers (magazines, technical work, etc.); send clips with proposals and queries."

‡THE WRITER'S ADVOCATE (I), 1st Floor, 1400 Market St., Denver CO 80202. (303)592-1233. Fax: (303)629-7689. Contact: Maria Melillo. Estab. 1992. Represents 15 clients. 90% of clients are new/previously unpublished writers. "We actively seek fiction and film scripts with strong female roles as well as other 'nontraditional' character/plot treatments." Currently handles: 15% nonfiction books; 10% scholarly books; 15% juvenile books; 30% novels; 10% short story collections; 15% movie scripts; 5% TV scripts. Member agents: Maria Melillo (nonfiction); Jane Curtis (film and TV); Kendall Bohannon (fiction).

• This editorial service company recently expanded to include agenting services. Kendall Bohannon is also editorial director of the literary agency Flannery White & Stone, in this section.

Handles: Nonfiction books, scholarly books, juvenile books, novels, novellas, short story collections, movie scripts, TV scripts. Considers these nonfiction areas: animals; anthropology; art/architecture/design; biography/autobiography; business; child guidance/parenting; cooking/food/nutrition; crafts/hobbies; current affairs; ethnic/cultural interests; gay/lesbian issues; government/politics/law; health/medicine; history; interior design/decorating; juvenile nonfiction; language/literature/criticism; military/war; money/finance/economics; music/dance/theater/film; nature/environment; New Age/metaphysics; photography; psychology; religious/inspirational; self-help/personal improvement; sociology; sports; translations; true-crime/investigative; women's issues/women's studies. Considers these fiction

areas: action/adventure; confessional; contemporary issues; detective/police/crime; erotica; ethnic; experimental; family saga; fantasy; feminist; gay; glitz; historical; humor/satire; juvenile; lesbian; literary; mainstream; mystery/suspense; picture book; psychic/supernatural; regional; religious/inspiration; romance (contemporary, gothic, historical, regency); science fiction; sports; thriller/espionage; westerns/frontier; young adult. Query. Reports in 2 weeks on queries; 6-8 weeks on mss.
Terms: Agent receives 15% commission on domestic sales; 20% on foreign sales. Offers written contract, for open period of time, cancellable by either part with 30 days notice.
Fees: Charges a reading fee. Criticism service included in reading fee: screenplays $150; ms analysis (3-5 pages) $200, over 100,000 words $300; works-in-progress $300, over 100,000 words $450. "All editorial work is done by professional editors and widely published authors." Charges for photocopying and postage.
Writers' Conferences: Aspen Writers Conference, Aspen CO.
Tips: Obtains new clients through recommendations, guide listings, conferences, meetings/workshops. "We are a new agency (formerly an editorial service) specializing in new writers. We offer various editorial services for a fee to our writers and are interested in working with serious writers and potential writers to develop saleable projects. We also offer referral services for freelance writers."

*WRITER'S CONSULTING GROUP (II, III), P.O. Box 492, Burbank CA 91503. (818)841-9294. Director: Jim Barmeier. Estab. 1983. Represents 10 clients. "We will work with both established and unestablished writers. We welcome unsolicited queries." Currently handles: 40% nonfiction books; 20% novels; 40% movie scripts.
Handles: True stories of men and women overcoming adversities or challenges in their lives (the author must have the legal rights to pitch the story); true stories of unusual survival; true stories about women who have overcome major obstacles in their lives; topical true stories out of the news for which the author can obtain the rights; stories about historical women; stories with irony; unusual family stories; off-beat mother-daughter, wife-husband, sister-sister stories; death row or prison stories; true crime (especially if the villain is a female); novels (women's, mainstream, contemporary thrillers); movie scripts (comedies, love stories, thrillers, women's stories). Query or send proposal. Include SASE. Reports in 1 month on queries; 3 months on mss.
Recent Sales: "Witness Against My Mother." (CBS Movie of the Week). *Moment to Moment.* (Medical Consumers Publishing).
Terms: "We will explain our terms to clients when they wish to sign. We receive a 10% commission on domestic sales."
Fees: Sometimes charges reading fee. "Additionally, we offer ghostwriting and editorial services, as well as book publicity services for authors. Mr. Barmeier is a graduate of Stanford University's Master's Degree in Creative Writing Program."
Tips: "We will help an author from concept to final product—if need be, designing the proposal, creating the package, doing rewrites on the manuscript. We are on the lookout for controversial women's stories that can be turned into movies-of-the-week. These usually involve women who take risks, are involved in challenging or ironic situations, and have happy endings."

TOM ZELASKY LITERARY AGENCY (II), 3138 Parkridge Crescent, Chamblee (Atlanta) GA 30341. (404)458-0391. Contact: Tom Zelasky. Estab. 1986. Represents 5 clients. 60% of clients are new/previously unpublished writers. Specializes in detectives and westerns, Vietnam, others (depending on quality and marketability). Currently handles: 10% nonfiction books; 80% novels.
Handles: Nonfiction books, novels, novellas, short story collections, movie scripts, stage plays. Considers these nonfiction areas: biography/autobiography; current affairs; government/politics; military/war; self-help/personal improvement; true crime/investigative; women's issues/women's studies. Considers these fiction areas: confessional; contemporary issues; detective/police/crime; family saga; feminist; historical; literary; mainstream; mystery/suspense; romance (contemporary); science fiction; thriller/espionage; westerns/historical; young adult. Query first, then send entire ms with synopsis. Reports in 1-2 weeks on queries; 1-2 months on mss.
Recent Sales: *Alone In The Valley*, by Ken Bohr (Second Chance/Permanent Press).
Terms: Agent receives 10-15% commission on domestic sales; 20-25% on foreign sales. Offers written contract, binding for 1 year and "renewed automatically by 30 days after end of year."
Fees: "A reading fee of $100 is charged. The reading fee is for reviewing and reading a manuscript. A 1-page critique is sent if the manuscript is rejected by the agency. My readers and I write the critique, which covers basic writing concerns, the physical format presentation of the manuscript and especially the technique. Postage and photocopying is deducted from the reading fee or after the royalty commission is earned." 50% of business is derived from commissions on ms sales; 50% is

derived from reading fees and criticism services. Payment of a reading fee ensures representation, if ms is acceptable.

Writers' Conferences: Attends the Florida Suncoast Writers' Conference, Tennessee Mountain Writers Conference, Council Authors' and Journalists' Conference, South Eastern Writers Conference and other conferences. "I don't attend these conferences every year, but use the scatter theory."

Tips: Obtains new clients through query letters, phone queries, conferences, directories, "publishers from everywhere. Know the mechanics and techniques of the art of writing. Practice and produce. Don't rely on past laurels. Use writing knowledge at all facets of writing. Go where the writing is done to acquaint oneself about the writing/publishing profession. And, set a daily pattern of writing as a laboring job, 8 hours or what hours preferable, depending upon a job-for-living necessity. You will be successful in the long run but it may take years, decades. Who knows?"

Additional Fee-charging Agents

The following fee-charging agencies have full listings in other sections of this book. These agencies have indicated they are *primarily* interested in handling the work of scriptwriters, artists or photographers, but are also interested in book manuscripts. After reading the listing (you can find the page number in the Listings Index), send them a query to obtain more information on their needs and manuscript submission policies.

The Chandelyn Literary Agency
Dykeman Associates Inc.

Alice Hilton Literary Agency
L. Harry Lee Literary Agency
Raintree Agency

Silver Screen Placements
A Total Acting Experience

Fee-charging Agents/'93-'94 changes

The following agencies appeared in past editions of *Guide to Literary Agents & Art/Photo Reps* but are absent from the 1994 edition. These agencies failed to respond to our request for an update of their listing, or were left out for the reasons indicated in parentheses following the agency name.

Argonaut Literary Agency
The Blake Group Literary Agency
Brady Literary Management
Ruth Hagy Brod Literary Agency
Linda Chester Literary Agency
Connor Literary Agency
Bill Cooper Assoc., Inc.
Creative Concepts Literary Agency (complaints)
Dorothy Deering Agency (complaints)
Larney Goodkind
Gary F. Iorio, Esq. (removed per request)
JLM Literary Agents

Leon Jones Literary Agency (complaints)
Lee Shore
Lighthouse Literary Agency
Literary Representation South
Living Faith Literary Agency (complaints)
March Media Inc.
David H. Morgan Literary Agency, Inc.
The Panettieri Agency (complaints)
Pegasus International Literary & Film Agents (complaints)
Penmarin Books
Peterson Associates (unable to contact)

Arthur Pine Associates, Inc.
D. Radley-Regan & Associates
Renaissance Literary Agency (complaints)
Rights Unlimited
Rising Sun Literary Agency
Sherry Robb Literary Properties
Richard H. Roffman Associates
Shoestring Press
Southern Writers
Marianne Strong
Tiger Moon Enterprises
Carlson Wade (complaints)
The Wilshire Literary Agency

Script Agents

Finding and Working with Script Agents

by Kerry Cox

As editor and publisher of a newsletter targeted solely at aspiring and professional scriptwriters, I've talked to dozens of agents and hundreds of writers, all embroiled in a daily search for each other. Each wants what the other has to offer: The agent needs material to sell and the writer needs someone to sell material. Seems like it should be a piece of cake to find the right match and start making money, right?

Of course, the reality is that it's not easy at all. The reason? According to writers, it's "They don't recognize my talent; they read my stuff and send it back." Talk to an agent, though, and the story you'll hear is, "Ninety-five percent of what I receive is garbage. When I find a truly talented writer, I fall all over myself to sign that writer right away!"

So there's the clue. If you, the writer, want to attract and land an agent, you have to concentrate your efforts not on finding the agent, but on writing top-notch scripts. The simple fact is, if you can write an outstanding script, you can find an outstanding agent.

Now, there are some basic rules to follow in bringing that script to the agent's attention. But before we go into that, let's answer the question that's probably uppermost in your mind as you begin your Agent Quest.

Do I really need an agent?

Nope. If you want, you can approach production companies on your own, and try to convince them to let you submit your script with a release form. The smaller companies will probably let you do that. The larger ones, studios included, might possibly let you do it too, although it's becoming less and less likely. Television producers will almost invariably ignore, if not prohibit, unagented submissions.

So, if you really want to give your script the best shot possible, yes, you should very, very seriously consider getting an agent. For one thing, production companies and studios are plagued by "nuisance" lawsuits, where a writer claims that his or her script has been stolen. To protect themselves from these legal hassles, producers have come to rely on agents to provide a kind of safety screen and keep things on a professional level.

Additionally, producers have no time to wade through the oceans of scripts that get sent to Hollywood every day by prospective writers. They rely on the agent to handle that,

---

Kerry Cox *is a scriptwriter who has over two dozen television credits with Aaron Spelling Productions, The Disney Channel and others. He has had a play produced in New York, written a feature film on assignment and co-authored* Successful Scriptwriting *by Writer's Digest Books. He is the editor and publisher of* The Hollywood Scriptwriter.

and perform a quality control function in weeding out the bad and circulating only the worthwhile scripts.

All right, so you need an agent to submit your script for you. Is that all an agent does?

What they do

In an interview with *The Hollywood Scriptwriter*, one agent refers to her function as a "yenta" for writers. "My job is to introduce writers to producers, and hope they'll build a business relationship. I find work for my writers, and negotiate the deals for them." An agent will act, on any given day, as a negotiator, mediator, troubleshooter, critic, advisor and salesperson. And most of them do all of this for the standard ten percent off the top.

Let's talk a minute about commissions and fees, because script agents differ somewhat from their "literary" counterparts in this regard. First, there's the matter of reading fees. The Writers Guild of America specifically prohibits signatory agents from charging reading fees. Period. Now, there is no rule that says that an agent has to be a Guild-signatory, but this goes back to the question of respectability and credibility. Producers are more likely to seriously consider material sent by recognized professionals, and *all* the top agencies (and the vast majority of mid-size and small agencies, for that matter) are Guild-signatory agencies.

On the other hand, there is no rule that prohibits an agency from offering a critique service, and there are a number of agencies that do so. Be careful, however, of agencies who will (for a fee) "develop" your work until it is ready for representation—most likely this "development" will go on a mighty long time, and be quite expensive.

Finally, a script agent customarily gets ten percent of the "deal." For example, if you were hired to write a single television episode, your agent would be entitled to ten percent of the writing fee. It is not mandatory to pay an agent's commission on residuals (money you get for reruns of the episode), although some writers choose to do so.

In the case where an agent has had to cut another agent in on the deal, such as a foreign sale, the writer might have to pay a 15% commission. In all cases, the commission is well worth the time, trouble, and expense a good agent puts forth in marketing your work.

What they don't do

An agent can't guarantee you will have a successful career. They are not the end—they are the means to an end. Keep in mind that once you have an agent, you are still the one who is responsible for your career, and will be expected to write, and try to make professional contacts, and write some more.

An agent won't necessarily represent everything you write. If you turn in something they honestly feel they can't sell, they will explain to you that the work is not up to your usual standards, and feel it would be harmful to your reputation to send it out. If you insist, they will either send it to a few friends in the business for an objective opinion, or they will refuse to put it on the market. Obviously, at that point you have a decision to make.

An agent won't give you a daily update on how your material is doing. There simply isn't enough time. The best thing to do is check in with your agent about once every two weeks.

Unless your agent is also a lawyer, he or she cannot represent you in court. Generally speaking, an agent provides no legal protection or resources, although most have a working relationship with at least one entertainment attorney and can recommend one when necessary.

An agent's job is to sell your work, and/or find you writing work. That's all.

So how do I get one?

A successful agent once told us, "An agent doesn't like to be 'got' any more than anyone else." Instead, she likened the process to something more akin to a "romance" where there is a courtship period and eventual commitment.

The courtship begins with you, the writer, taking the initiative. If you have a friend or acquaintance who has an agent and might be willing to recommend your work, that's the best way to go. If you have attended a seminar or workshop in which an agent was a guest speaker or panelist, and you are able to make some personal contact, that's another good avenue.

If, however, you're coming in from the cold, like the majority of writers are, your approach needs to begin with a query letter. This letter isn't all that different from the query letters you may have sent to magazines or book publishers in the past, and the goals are the same: a) demonstrate to the agent that you are a relatively sane, competent professional who understands the craft; and b) pique the agent's personal and professional interest enough to request a look at your work.

When you write your query letter, consider the fact that the agent will probably get about a dozen others that day, along with an assortment of scripts, business mail, and the junk mail we all get. Your job is to make your letter practically jump out of that pile, excite the reader and encourage a fast response.

Start by making sure the letter and even the envelope you mail it in are professional in appearance. Get some decent letterhead. It doesn't have to be fancy, but it should look like you take your writing career seriously. Listings for agents in directories such as this usually give contact names. If not, call an agency, and talk to the receptionist, a secretary, or even an agent, and get the name of someone specific to whom you can address the letter. Addressing the letter to "Dear Sir/Madam" just doesn't cut it.

Third step: plan the letter. You don't want it to take up more than one page if at all possible. Leave out any information that isn't absolutely necessary. Avoid hardsell, glittering claims about the abundance of money your script will make the agent, or the sheer genius you demonstrated in crafting this masterpiece. Instead, you'll want to include two things: a) Your credentials, if any (and not just writing credentials. For instance, if your script is a detective drama, and you're a detective, by all means mention that fact); b) A brief summary of your script—"brief" meaning no more than a paragraph or two.

Some other items that might be important would be related to the type of script you've written. If it's an historical drama, for instance, you might note that you have spent x number of years researching the period, especially if your story is based upon true events. You might also want to mention that you have written a number of other spec scripts, too (assuming you have—and you should), which shows the agent that you are not sending out your first effort, but have been earnestly working at this a while.

When summarizing your story in the letter, you may feel reluctant to tell the whole tale, and give away the ending. There are no rules about this. A good generalization would be to craft your query letter in such a way that it leaves the agent wanting more—whether wanting to find out the ending, or find out how you managed to create the ending you've described.

Once you've written the letter, be sure to include a SASE for response, send it off to as many agents as you'd like, and get to work on your next script.

What if they say yes?

Writers are so preconditioned for—and often experienced with—failure, that a positive response tends to induce sudden euphoria and a subsequent lack of judgment.

If an agent expresses an interest in seeing your material, stop and think for a moment. First, is your script already being considered by another agent, one who responded more promptly? If so, it's generally considered poor etiquette to circulate your script to more than one prospective agent at a time (although it's not necessarily an uncommon practice).

Second, are you absolutely sure your script is ready to be seen? This could represent a very important moment in your career, and you don't want to blow it by being overeager. Even though you were positive it was ready when you sent out the query letter, take an hour or so and read the script one more time, keeping as objective a frame of mind as possible. If any part of it feels weak to you, or bothers you in some way—if you even find a typo or two—don't send it out until it's *perfect*.

Assuming you send the script and the agent likes it, several things might happen. You might be asked, "What else have you got?" This is pretty common, and usually means that your script showed some real writing talent, but the agent doesn't feel quite ready to invest the time and effort necessary to develop a new client without first determining if you are a "One-Script Wonder." An agent is interested not only in selling your first script, but wants to know that you have long-term potential as well. This is a very crucial stage of the "romance" and this next point can't be stressed enough: *Don't send another script if it's not just as good as the first one.* Presumably, you have already sent what you consider to be your best work; but it should have been a tough call, because you weren't sure if your second one was really your best. If you have a second script that's good, send it. If you don't, tell the agent you're working on one, and will be happy to submit it once you're finished. If you panic, and send one of your earlier scripts that isn't quite as good, but it's all you've got—you'll lose your chance with that agent, who will probably send both scripts back to you, most likely with one of those highly personal form rejection letters.

Now, let's say the agent calls, and wants to represent you. In fact, she wants you to sign a one-year, or even (less common) a two-year contract. Do you do it? What if it turns out you don't like this agent after six months—are you stuck with her for two years?

Thanks to the Writers Guild, you aren't stuck. There is a 90-day clause built in to the contract of every Guild-signatory agent, which states, roughly speaking, that either you or the agent can exercise the right to sever the relationship if the agent hasn't found you above-scale work within a 90-day period. (The term "scale" refers to minimum fees set by the WGA.) Of course, it isn't *mandatory* that you call it quits within that period, and in fact it would be a little unrealistic for a new writer to expect his or her agent to make a sale or find work that quickly; however, it does offer an "escape" for those who feel they need it. (If you are not dealing with a signatory agent, you may want to consider asking for such a clause in your contract.)

Are there agents for scriptwriters who don't write for TV or movies?

Yes, although they are usually the same agents who do handle movie and television writers. Playwrights, for instance, can greatly benefit from an agent. Naturally, there is more action on the East Coast than the West for a playwright, but Hollywood agencies tend to either have a New York office or work closely with a New York agent.

The way for a playwright to get an agent is to invite several to a performance, or even a staged reading, of the play. Not all agents want to represent playwrights, for one reason or another, so be sure to call and ascertain if there is any interest before sending out the invitations. Notice too that it's up to you, the playwright, to get yourself produced at the local level before approaching an agent. That's not the case for television and movie writers.

Interested in writing for animation? There are a limited number of agencies that handle that type of work, and a couple of them who specialize almost exclusively in cartoon writers. The fact is, however, it's not necessary for an animation writer to have an agent. The animation houses and producers are much more accessible than their live-action counterparts, and bring new writers on-board all the time.

Ancillary scriptwriting markets, such as industrials, corporate films or video, marketing, radio, etc. are generally not handled by literary agents. There has been some movement within the Writers Guild to bring educational and informational scriptwriting into the fold in terms of fee schedules and so forth, but it's been a half-hearted effort at best. For the time being, educational and informational scriptwriters remain on their own in terms of finding work and negotiating fees.

Some final advice

Stay informed. There are a number of trade publications and specialty newsletters that should be regular reading for aspiring scriptwriters. *Daily Variety* and *The Hollywood Reporter* are the daily business papers of the entertainment industry. *The Hollywood Scriptwriter* is my newsletter targeted specifically for aspiring and professional scriptwriters, and features agency updates throughout the year, along with an Annual Agency Issue every summer that surveys open agencies. Addresses for these publications appear in Resources near the back of this book.

Know your craft. Invest in some scriptwriting books. *Successful Scriptwriting*, Writer's Digest Books, offers an instructional overview of each type of scriptwriting, and includes a chapter on finding an agent, along with a standard release form you can use when submitting material. Some other books: *Making a Good Script Great*, by Dr. Linda Seger; *How to Sell Your Screenplay*, by Carl Sautter; *Writing Screenplays That Sell*, by Michael Hauge; and of course *Adventures in the Screen Trade*, by William Goldman, which isn't exactly an instructional book but is required reading for all screenwriters.

Be professional. Understand and follow the correct format for whatever type of script you're writing (just about any of the books mentioned will provide you with detailed format specifications). Always include a SASE with any correspondence. Keep phone calls brief and to the point. Send only your best work. Continue to perfect your skills as you search for and after you find an agent. Treat your writing not as a hobby or a dream, but as a chosen career.

Keep the faith. Remember, everyone, even the most successful writers, began their careers without an agent. As a top agent once said, "(An agent) is always looking for writing that has a spark, that shows imagination, that has vision . . . and style."

If that's you she's talking about, then keep at it. Persevere. As Jim Cash ("Top Gun," "Dick Tracy") put it in one interview, "There's only one way to succeed: accept failure as a temporary state, however long that state may be, and simply outlast it."

Good luck.

Script Agents: Nonfee-charging and Fee-charging

A script agent is not a luxury now; it's almost a necessity, since most studios and networks return unsolicited manuscripts unopened and unread. In an industry that prides itself on connections, on who you know and who knows you, a single, solitary writer can feel very isolated. Success requires good writing *and* good connections. That's what a script agent does: make her connections work for a client's writing. So how do you connect with an agent?

Agents look for one of two things in a potential client: someone who has been making a living off his writing, or someone they believe has the ability to do so. It may seem that, as with a loan, you can't get an agent unless you don't need one. But good writing, presented well, will find an agent that is willing to throw her reputation and connections behind it.

The ideal script agent understands what a writer writes, is able to explain it to others, and has credibility with individuals who are in a position to make decisions. An agent sends out material, advises what direction a career should take and makes the financial arrangements. Beyond those seemingly straightforward tasks there lies a new breed of agents in Hollywood. "Packaging agents," acting as small studios, combine stories, stars, writers, even directors, and shop the whole around town looking for a buyer, a studio or production company interested in the project. This trend increases the odds that a script will actually be produced, and often keys the writer into other potential projects.

There are two sides to an agent's representation of a scriptwriter: finding work on an existing project and selling original scripts. Most writers break in with scripts written on "spec," that is, for free. A spec script is a calling card that demonstrates skills and gets your name and abilities before influential people. It can be based either on an existing idea or an original concept. Script agents try to match writers they represent and projects they hear about in the first case, or try to get a writer's own project made in the second.

A spec script for television can be based on a current show. This demonstrates knowledge of the format and ability to create believable dialogue in established voices. It's best to choose a show you like; you will be better able to create plot and dialogue between characters you enjoy. Current hot shows for writers include *Northern Exposure*, *NYPD Blue*, *Law and Order*, *Seinfeld* and *Murphy Brown*. Half-hour shows generally have a writing staff and only occasionally buy freelance scripts. Hour-long shows are more likely to pick up scripts written on spec.

To write a script for an original television show, you must first write a "treatment," an outline of plot and description of characters that is approximately ten pages long. A treatment is basically a sales tool for the agent to use in shopping the idea around. Keep in mind, however, that this presents only the concept and does not demonstrate screenwriting talents. A pilot and a few samples of future episodes will probably be required for any serious consideration. Most studios and networks will not back a new television show with an untried writer. While they may buy your concept, they may not hire you to write. Screenwriters will usually get a few drafts tied to the sale before the producers bring in more experienced writers.

Script Agents: Nonfee-charging and Fee-charging

Scriptwriting is an art, as well as a business, and the craft comes first. That's something that can only be achieved through individual work, although writer's groups, workshops and seminars can be invaluable in targeting your energies and efforts in the right direction. Writing must come before marketing: If you have nothing to say, you have nothing to sell. The business of presenting your writing, however, is simple and basic. Keep your query letter succinct. Never send a script unless it is requested. Always include a SASE with a query letter or script. Since different types of scripts require different formats, make sure you know how to present your script properly. The *Writer's Digest Guide to Manuscript Formats*, by Dian Dincin Buchman and Seli Groves and *The Complete Book of Scriptwriting*, by J. Michael Straczynski are good sources for script formats.

Always approach a screen agent well-informed. For starters, read Finding and Working with Script Agents by Kerry Cox on page 155 and check our Resources section on the subject. Read books on the industry. A good primer is *Successful Scriptwriting*, by Jurgen Wolff and Kerry Cox. For an insider's view on what sells in Hollywood, read *Getting Your Script Through the Hollywood Maze*, by Linda Stuart. Check trade publications such as *Variety*, *The Hollywood Reporter* or *Dramalogue*, and newsletters such as the WGA West's or *The Hollywood Scriptwriter* to keep current on trends and directions. Magazines such as *American Film Magazine* or *Writer's Digest* offer insights into the industry and tips on improving your writing. Take a look at the listings in the scriptwriting section in *Writer's Market* to see what different markets are looking for.

This section contains information on agents who will pitch screenplays, teleplays or stage plays to television and film producers or theatrical companies. Many of the agencies in the literary agents' sections of this book also handle scripts, but agencies that *primarily* sell scripts are represented here.

Many of the agents listed are signatories to the Writers Guild of America Artists' Manager Basic Agreement. You can contact this organization for more information on specific agencies. Agents who are affiliated with this group are not permitted to charge for reading scripts, but can charge for critiques and other services. The WGA also offers a registration service; it's smart to register your script with the group before sending it out. Write the Guild for more information on this and on membership (see the Resources section).

Help with your search

To help you with your search for an agent, we've included a number of special indexes in the back of this book. The Subject Index on page 243 is divided into sections for fee-charging and nonfee-charging literary agents and script agents. Each of these sections in the index is then divided by nonfiction and fiction categories. This will tell you what subject area an agency is interested in seeing, but specific script types (TV episode, movie-of-the-week, documentary, stage play) are mentioned in the script agent's listing. We've included an Agents and Reps Index on page 270. Often you will read about an agent, but if that agent is an employee of a large agency, you may not be able to find his business number. We asked agencies to list the agents on their staffs. In the index we list the agents' names in alphabetical order along with the name of their agencies. Find the name of the person you would like to contact and then check the listing for that agency.

Many of the nonfee- and fee-charging literary agents are also interested in scripts. If the agency's primary function is selling books, but is interested in seeing some scripts, we've included it in "Additional Script Agents" at the end of this section.

About the listings

The listings in this section differ slightly from those in the literary agent sections. A breakdown of the types of scripts each agency handles is included in the listing. Nonfee-charging and fee-charging agencies are not listed separately. As noted above, WGA signatories are not permitted to charge reading fees, but many agencies do charge for a variety of other services—critiques, consultations, promotion, marketing, etc. Those agencies who charge some type of fee have been indicated with a box (□) symbol by their name. The heading "Recent Sales" is also slightly different. Often scripts are untitled at the time of sale, so we asked for the production company's name. We've found the film industry is very secretive about sales, but you may be able to get a list of clients or other references upon request.

We've ranked the agencies listed in this section according to their openness to submissions. Below is our ranking system.

I Newer agency actively seeking clients.
II Agency seeking both new and established writers.
III Agency prefers to work with established writers, mostly obtains new clients through referrals.
IV Agency handling only certain types of work or work by writers under certain circumstances.
V Agency not currently seeking new clients. We have included mention of agencies rated V to let you know they are currently not open to new clients. In addition to those ranked V, we have included a few well-known agencies' names who have declined the opportunity for full listings at this time. *Unless you have a strong recommendation from someone well respected in the field, our advice is to approach only those agents ranked I-IV.*

‡AGAPE PRODUCTIONS (IV, V), P.O. Box 147, Flat Rock IN 47234. Agency not currently seeking new clients.

AGENCY FOR THE PERFORMING ARTS (II), Suite 1200, 9000 Sunset Blvd., Los Angeles CA 90069. (310)273-0744. Fax: (310)275-9401. Contact: Stuart M. Miller. Estab. 1962. Signatory of WGA. Represents 50+ clients. Specializes in film and TV scripts.
Handles: Movie scripts, TV scripts. Considers all nonfiction and fiction areas. Query must include SASE. Reports in 2-3 weeks on queries.
Terms: Agent receives 10% commission on domestic sales. Offers written contract.
Tips: Obtains new clients through recommendations from others.

□**ALLIED ARTISTS (II)**, 811 W. Evergreen, Chicago IL 60522. (312)482-8488. Fax: (312)482-8371. Contact: Coleen Gallagher. Estab. 1984. Member of SAG/AFTRA. Represents 80 clients. 10% of clients are new/previously unpublished writers. Specializes in "comedy, and character driven scripts." Currently handles: 20% TV scripts; 20% syndicated material; 60% movie scripts.
Handles: Movie scripts, TV scripts. Considers these nonfiction areas: government/politics/law; music/dance/theater/film. Considers these fiction areas: action/adventure; comic; detective/police/crime; erotica; psychic/supernatural; romance (contemporary, gothic, historical, regency); science fiction; sports. Query with outline. Reports in 1 month on queries.
Recent Sales: "Dick Gibson Show," by Peter Amster (Lippitz Productions); "Dumping Ground," by Tom Towles (New Line).
Terms: Agent receives 10% commission on domestic sales; 10% on foreign sales.
Fees: Charges a reading fee "for new writers only." Offers a criticism service "for new writers only." Critiques are written by Coleen Gallagher. 90% of business is derived from commissions on ms sales; 10% is derived from reading or criticism fees.

Tips: Obtains new clients through recommendations from others.

ALL-STAR TALENT AGENCY (I), 7834 Alabama Ave., Canoga Park CA 91304. (818)346-4313. Contact: Robert Allred. Estab. 1991. Signatory of WGA. Represents 2 clients. 100% of clients are new/previously unpublished writers. Specializes in film, TV. Currently handles: movie scripts, TV scripts, 4 books.
Handles: Novels, movie scripts, stage plays, TV scripts. Considers these fiction areas: action/adventure; cartoon/comic; contemporary issues; detective/police/crime; family saga; fantasy; historical; humor/satire; mainstream; mystery/suspense; psychic/supernatural; romance (contemporary); science fiction; sports; thriller/espionage; westerns/frontier; "any mainstream film or TV ideas." Query. Reports in 3 weeks on queries; 2 months on mss.
Terms: Agent receives 10% commission on domestic sales; 10% on foreign sales with foreign agent receiving additional 10%. Offers written contract, binding for 1 year. 100% of business derived from commissions on ms.
Tips: Obtains new clients through recommendations and solicitation. "A professional appearance in script format, dark and large type and simple binding go a long way to create good first impressions in this business; as does a professional business manner."

MICHAEL AMATO AGENCY (II), 1650 Broadway, New York NY 10019. (212)247-4456-57. Fax: (212)247-4456. Contact: Susan Tomkins. Estab. 1970. Signatory of WGA, member of SAG, AFTRA, Equity. Represents 6 clients. 2% of clients are new/previously unpublished writers. Specializes in TV and theater. Currently handles nonfiction books; stage plays.
Handles: Nonfiction books, juvenile books, novels, movie scripts, stage plays, TV scripts. Considers these nonfiction areas: cooking/food/nutrition; current affairs; health/medicine; women's issues/women's studies. Considers these fiction areas: action/adventure; juvenile; young adult. Query. Reports "within a month" on queries.
Tips: Obtains new clients through recommendations.

□**AMERICAN PLAY CO., INC. (II),** Suite 1204, 19 W. 44th St., New York NY 10036. (212)921-0545. Fax: (212)869-4032. President: Sheldon Abend. Estab. 1889. Century Play Co. is subsidiary of American Play Co. Specializes in novels, plays, screenplays and film production.
Handles: Novels, movie scripts, stage plays. Considers all nonfiction and fiction areas. Send entire ms, "double space each page." Reports as soon as possible on ms.
Terms: Agent receives 15% commission on domestic sales; 15% on foreign sales.
Fees: Charges $100-150 reading fee, which includes a 2-3 page critique. Criticism service: $100.
Tips: Obtains new clients through referrals, unsolicited submissions by authors. "Writers should write novels before screenplays. They need to know what's going on behind the camera. Before they write a play, they need to understand stage and sets. Novels need strong plots, fully developed characters."

‡**BDP & ASSOCIATES TALENT AGENCY (IV),** 10637 Burbank Blvd., North Hollywood CA 91601. (818)506-7615. Fax: (818)506-4983. Vice President, Literary: Samuel W. Gelfman. Estab. 1980. Signatory of WGA, member of SAG. Specializes in theatrical motion pictures and long-form TV.
Terms: Agent receives 10-15% commission on domestic sales. Charges for postage, photocopying, any other expenses entailed in sale (legal fees, etc.).
Tips: Obtains new clients through "recommendations from known professionals in the entertainment industry only!"

□**THE MARY BEAL MANAGEMENT CO. (III),** 144 North Pass Ave., Burbank CA 91505. (818)846-7812. Estab. 1988. Currently handles: 50% movie scripts; 50% TV scripts.
Handles: Nonfiction books, movie scripts, TV scripts. Considers these nonfiction areas: gay/lesbian issues; government/politics/law; psychology; true crime/investigative. Considers these fiction areas: detective/police/crime; erotica; feminist; gay/lesbian; literary; mainstream; mystery/suspense; psychic/

☐ *An open box indicates script agents who charge fees to writers. WGA signatories are not permitted to charge for reading manuscripts, but may charge for critiques or consultations.*

supernatural; science fiction; thriller/espionage. Query with SASE. Reports in 6 weeks on queries; 3 months on mss.
Fees: Charges $280 reading fee or $85 for first act only. "If script is commendable, will refer to agents and producers."
Tips: Obtains new clients through referrals mainly. "Be sure that a script is the best it can be before seeking representation."

LOIS BERMAN, WRITERS' REPRESENTATIVE (III), 21 W. 26th St., New York NY 10010. (212)684-1835. Contact: Lois Berman or Judy Boals. Estab. 1972. Member of AAR. Represents about 25 clients. Specializes in dramatic writing for stage, film, TV.
Handles: Movie scripts, TV scripts, plays. Query first.
Terms: Agent receives 10% commission.
Tips: Obtains new clients through recommendations from others.

THE MARIAN BERZON AGENCY (II), 336 E. 17th St., Costa Mesa CA 92627. Also: #110, 1614 Victory Blvd., Glendale CA 91201. (818)548-1560, 548-1565. Literary Agent: Mike Ricciardi. Estab. 1979. Signatory of WGA. "We are also a talent agent and signatory of SAG, AFTRA, Equity and AGVA." 88% of clients are new/previously unpublished writers. Specializes in screenplays of all genres, especially comedy (must be honest), inspirational and thrillers. Currently handles: 5% juvenile books, 2% novels, 70% movie scripts, 6% stage plays, 12% TV scripts, 5% songs for movies and musical theater (cassettes only). Member agents: Mike Ricciardi (literary/screenplay, comedy, action romantic comedy); Chris Bannister (comedy sitcom); David Beavers (character driven and drama screenplay); Mark Amador (dramatic TV and social issue screenplay). "We also have an office in NYC."
Handles: Movie scripts, stage plays, TV scripts. Considers these screenplay areas: action/adventure; contemporary issues; feel-good romantic comedies; family saga; fantasy; juvenile comedy/drama; romantic comedy/drama; juvenile; mainstream; mystery/suspense; religious/inspiration; romance (contemporary); thriller/espionage; young adult; screen stories about real people. "No slasher or serial killers!" Query with bio, small photo, cover letter and one-page summary. SASE. "Unsolicited scripts will be returned unread C.O.D." Reports in 45 days or sooner on queries. "We will not answer any query without SASE. *Please* inquiry telephone calls only between the hours of 4:00-6:30 p.m. M-F (Pacific Time)."
Recent Sales: *Hostile Environment*, by Jacque Buntrock (BU West Productions); *Manhattan Transfer*, by John E. Stith (Allied Stars/Bettina Vivianno); *Final Vow*, by jacque Buntrock (Ace Productions); *Sweet Tooth*, by Mark Troy (Arnold Schwarzenegger as the Tooth Fairy).
Terms: Agent receives 10% commission on domestic sales; 15% on foreign sales (short fiction and plays 15%; advances 15% on novels). Offers written contract and WGA rider with agreement. "Never charges a reading fee. We give a detailed and complete breakdown for free. We charge only for postage, fax, long distance and postal insurance directly related to the client for writers who are not established or members of the guild and only until the writer's first sale. No charges after that." 100% of business derived from commissions on ms sales. "We offer some probationary representations to film students who demonstrate outstanding potential, even before their screenplay is finished."
Tips: Obtains new clients through recommendations from others and known producers. "If you really want to be represented, take note of the old saying 'you never get a second chance to make a first impression.' Be sure your queries intrigue us. Forget your ego. Include a photo and #10 envelope with sufficient postage. Write us a personal cover letter. No computer draft or mimeographed correspondence. Write to us like you really want to be considered. Include short creative bio. Read and absorb *The Complete Guide to Standard Script Format* (parts 1 & 2) by Cole and Haag and Margaret Mehring's *The Screenplay: A Blend of Film Form & Content* before submitting. Screenplays should never be longer than 115 pages. They must be visual and not dialogue heavy. Structure, character development and narrative drive are the most important elements we look for. Screenplay description must be visually and actually alive. Make certain the opening of your screenplay is a 'grabber.' We believe in the new writer and will even spend time and effort by appointment (in person) in our offices in California. Don't be in love with words when you write a screenplay—think images. Today's big market is 'PG'—feel-good stories with kids, old-fashioned romantic comedies and fantasy. Don't fill the page with words—make your script a comfortable and wonderful read. As Robert Browning once proclaimed, 'less is more!' "

Script Agents: Nonfee-charging and Fee-charging 165

*BETHEL AGENCY (II), Suite 16, 641 W. 59th St., New York NY 10019. (212)664-0455. Contact: Lewis R. Chambers. Estab. 1967. Represents 25+ clients.
Handles: Movie scripts, TV scripts. Considers these nonfiction areas: agriculture/horticulture; animals; anthropology/archaeology; art/architecure/design; biography/autobiography; business; child guidance/parenting; cooking/food/nutrition; crafts/hobbies; current affairs; ethnic/cultural interests; gay/lesbian issues; government/politics/law; health/medicine; history; interior design/decorating; juvenile nonfiction; language/literature/criticism; military/war; money/finance/economics; music/dance/theater/film; nature/environment; photography; psychology; religious/inspirational; science/technology; self-help/personal improvement; sociology; space; sports; translations; true crime/investigative; women's issues/women's studies. Considers these fiction areas: action/adventure; cartoon/comic; confessional; contemporary issues; detective/police/crime; ethnic; family saga; fantasy; feminist; gay; glitz; historical; humor/satire; juvenile; lesbian; literary; mainstream; mystery/suspense; picture book; psychic/supernatural; regional; religious/inspiration; romance (contemporary, gothic, historical, regency); sports; thriller/espionage; westerns/frontier; young adult. Query with outline plus 1 sample chapter and SASE. Reports in 1-2 months on queries.
Terms: Agent receives 15% commission on domestic sales; 20% on foreign sales. Offers written contract, binding for 6 months to 1 year.
Fees: Charges reading fee only to unpublished authors; writer will be contacted on fee amount.
Tips: Obtains new clients through recommendations from others. "Never send original material."

DON BUCHWALD AGENCY (III), 10 E. 44th St., New York NY 10017. (212)867-1070. Contact: Kristin Miller or Michael Traum. Estab. 1977. Signatory of WGA. Represents 50 literary clients. Talent and literary agency.
Handles: Screenplays, stage plays, TV scripts. Considers these nonfiction areas: biography/autobiography; current affairs; history; science/technology; sports. Considers these fiction areas: action/adventure; family saga; mainstream; romance (contemporary, gothic, historical, regency); science fiction; thriller/espionage; westerns/frontier. Query with SASE only.
Tips: Obtains new clients through other authors, agents.

‡KELVIN C. BULGER AND ASSOCIATES (I), Suite 905, 123 W. Madison, Chicago IL 60602. (312)280-2403. Fax: (312)922-4221. Contact: Kelvin C. Bulger. Estab. 1992. Signatory of WGA. Represents 25 clients. 90% of clients are new/previously unpublished writers. Currently handles: 75% movie scripts; 25% TV scripts.
Handles: Movie scripts, TV scripts, syndicated material. Considers these nonfiction areas: current affairs; ethnic/cultural interests; history. Considers these fiction areas: cartoon/comic; contemporary issues; family saga; historical; humor/satire. Query. Reports in 2 weeks on queries; 2 months on mss. "If material is to be returned writer must enclose SASE."
Recent Sales: *The Playing Field* (documentary), by Darryl Pitts (CBS).
Terms: Agent receives 10% commission on domestic sales; 10% on foreign sales. Offers written contract, binding from 6 months-1 year.
Tips: Obtains new clients through solicitations and recommendations. "Proofread before submitting to agent."

□THE MARSHALL CAMERON AGENCY (II), Rt. 1 Box 125, Lawtey FL 32058. (904)964-7013. Fax: (904)964-6905. Contact: Margo Prescott. Estab. 1986. Signatory of WGA. Specializes in feature films and TV scripts and true story presentations for MFTS. Currently handles: 70% movie scripts; 30% TV scripts. Member agents: Margo Prescott; Ashton Prescott.
Handles: Movie scripts, TV scripts. Has suspended representation of books. Considers: action/adventure; detective/police/crime; romantic comedies; drama (contemporary); mystery/suspense; thriller/espionage. Query. Reports in 1 week on queries; 1-2 months on mss.
Terms: Agent receives 10% commission on domestic sales; 20% on foreign sales. Offers written contract, binding for 1 year.
Fees: No reading fee for screenplays. Charges $85 to review all true story material for TV or film ("maybe higher for extensive material"). Offers criticism service, overall criticism, some on line criticism. "We recommend changes, usually 3-10 pages depending on length of the material (on request only)." Charges nominal marketing fee which includes postage, phone, fax, Federal Express. 90% of business is derived from commissions on sales; 10% is derived from reading fees or criticism services. Payment of a criticism fee does not ensure representation.
Tips: "Often professionals in film and TV will recommend us to clients. We also actively solicit material. Always enclose SASE with your query."

MARGARET CANATELLA AGENCY (V), P.O. Box 674, Chalmette LA 70044-0674. Agency not currently seeking new clients.

‡□THE CHANDELYN LITERARY AGENCY (II), P.O. Box 50162, 7750 Maryland, Clayton MO 63105. Fax: (314)531-2627. President: T. Patrick Miller (Tim). Estab. 1991. Signatory of WGA. Represents 5 clients. 50% of clients are new/previously unpublished writers. Currently handles: 10% nonfiction books; 10% juvenile books; 10% novels; 50% movie scripts; 10% stage plays; 10% TV scripts. Member agents: T. Patrick Miller (picture books, novels, plays, screenplays, teleplays), N. Rochelle Collins (children's books).
Handles: Nonfiction books, scholarly books, juvenile books, novels, movie scripts, TV scripts. Considers these nonfiction areas: agriculture/horticulture; animals; anthropology/archaeology; art/architecture/design; biography/autobiography; business; child guidance/parenting; cooking/food/nutrition; crafts/hobbies; current affairs; ethnic/cultural interests; health/medicine; history; interior design/decorating; juvenile nonfiction; language/literature/criticism; money/finance/economics; music/dance/theater/film; nature/environment; photography; psychology; religious/inspirational; science/technology; self-help/personal improvement; sociology; sports; women's issues/women's studies. Considers these fiction areas: action/adventure; cartoon/comic; contemporary issues; ethnic; family saga; fantasy; historical; humor/satire; juvenile; literary; mystery/suspense; picture book; religious/inspiration; romance (contemporary); science fiction; young adult. Query with entire ms or outline/proposal and 3 sample chapters. Reports in 4-6 weeks on queries; 4-6 months on mss. Include SASE with all submissions.
Recent Sales: *The Strawberry Fox* and *The Christmas Toy Welcome*, all by Prentiss Van Daves (Jordan Enterprises Publishing Company); *Tony L.*, Erica Hughs.
Terms: Agent receives 10% commission on domestic sales; 20% on foreign sales (using subagent). Offers written contract; binding for 3 months-1 year.
Fees: Criticism service: $25 for ms under 100 pages. "We provide writers with a written critique of their work submitted to me. We charge writers for postage, photocopying and there is a $150 initial marketing fee." 80% of business is derived from commissions on ms sales; 20% derived from editorial or consultation services. Payment for critique does not ensure representation.
Tips: Obtains new clients through recommendations from editors, publishers and clients. "Professional or enthusiastic new/unpublished writers must be inspired and determined to work with their agents by contributing their time to promote their published works to build their writing career."

CINEMA TALENT INTERNATIONAL (II), Suite 808, 8033 Sunset Blvd., West Hollywood CA 90046. (213)656-1937. Contact: George Kriton and George N. Rumanes. Estab. 1976. Represents approximately 23 clients. 3% of clients are new/previously unpublished writers. Currently handles: 1% nonfiction books; 1% novels; 95% movie scripts; 3% TV scripts. Member agents include: George Kriton and George N. Rumanes.
Handles: Nonfiction books, novels, movie scripts, TV scripts. Query with outline/proposal plus 2 sample chapters. Reports in 4-5 weeks on queries; 4-5 weeks on ms.
Terms: Agent receives 10% on domestic sales; 20% on foreign sales. Offers written contract, binding for 2 years.
Tips: Obtains new clients through recommendations from others.

CIRCLE OF CONFUSION LTD. (II), 131 Country Village Lane, New Hyde Park NY 11040. (212)969-0653. Contact: Rajeev K. Agarwal, Lawrence Mattis. Estab. 1990. Signatory of WGA. Represents 60 clients. 80% of clients are new/previously unpublished writers. Specializes in screenplays for film and TV. Currently handles: 10% novels; 5% novellas; 80% movie scripts; 5% TV scripts.
Handles: Nonfiction books, novels, novellas, short story collections, movie scripts, stage plays, TV scripts. Considers these nonfiction areas: biography/autobiography; business; current affairs; gay/lesbian issues; government/politics/law; health/medicine; history; juvenile nonfiction; true crime/investigative; women's issues/women's studies. Considers all fiction areas. Send entire ms. Reports in 1 week on queries; 1 month on mss.
Terms: Agent receives 10% commission on domestic sales; 10% on foreign sales. Offers written contract, binding for 1 year.
Tips: Obtains new clients through queries, recommendations and writing contests. "We pitch books, scripts, short stories and plays for film/TV."

‡CLIENT FIRST—A/K/A LEO P. HAFFEY AGENCY (II), P.O. Box 795, White House TN 37188. (615)325-4780. Contact: Charlene Adams. Estab. 1990. Signatory of WGA. Represents 11 clients. 70% of clients are new/previously unpublished writers. Specializes in movie scripts. Currently handles: 5% novels;

95% movie scripts. Member agent: Leo P. Haffey Jr. (attorney/agent to the motion picture industry).
Handles: Novels, novellas, short story collections, movie scripts. Considers these fiction areas: action/adventure; cartoon/comic; contemporary issues; detective/police/crime; family saga; historical; humor/satire; mystery/suspense; romance (contemporary, historical); science fiction; sports; thriller/espionage; westerns/frontier. Query. Reports in 1 week on queries; 2 months on mss.
Terms: Offers written contract, binding for a negotiable length of time.
Tips: Obtains new clients through referrals. "The motion picture business is a numbers game like any other. The more you write the better your chances of success."

‡□**COAST TO COAST TALENT AND LITERARY (II)**, Suite 200, 4942 Vineland Ave., North Hollywood CA 91601. (818)762-6278. Fax: (818)762-7049. Estab. 1986. Signatory of WGA. Represents 20 clients. 35% of clients are new/previously unpublished writers. Specializes in "true stories and true crime books that can be packaged into movies/scripts." Currently handles: 25% nonfiction books; 50% movie scripts; 25% TV scripts.
Handles: Nonfiction books, novels, movie scripts, TV scripts, syndicated material, true stories, humor books. Considers these nonfiction areas: Music/dance/theater/film; mystery; New Age/metaphysics; self-help/personal improvement; true crime/investigative; women's issues/women's studies. Considers these fiction areas: action/adventure; detective/police/crime; erotica; humor/satire; literary; mystery/suspense; psychic/supernatural; romance (historical); thriller/espionage. Query. Reports in 2 months on queries; 6 months on mss.
Recent Sales: "Deep Space 9," by Hilary Rader (Paramount); *Tales from the Cryptkeeper*, by Larry Black (Donner/Nelvana); *The Melinda Mason Story*, movie of the week (Alexander/Enright); *Veronica's Room*, by Brad Mendelson (original screenplay based on Ira Levin play) (Hemdale Entertainment).
Terms: Agent receives 10% commission on domestic sales; 15% on foreign sales. Offers written contract, binding for 1 year.
Fees: Does not charge a reading fee. Criticism service: for mss only, not screenplays.
Tips: Obtains new clients through recommendations, query letter. "Be concise in what you're looking for. Don't go on and on in your query letter, get to the point."

COMEDY INK (II), #243, 8070 La Jolla Shores Dr., La Jolla CA 92037. (619)525-7916. Contact: Brian Keliher. Estab. 1986. Signatory of WGA. Represents 10 clients. 70% of clients are new/previously unpublished writers. Specializes in movie scripts. "Our specialty is comedy, but we also accept dramatic works." Currently handles: 10% nonfiction books; 10% TV scripts; 80% movie scripts.
Handles: Movie scripts. Query or send entire script.
Terms: Agent receives 10% commission on domestic sales. Offers written contract.
Tips: Obtains new clients at conferences and through recommendations from others. "Remember two important words: patience and persistence. They are not mutually exclusive!"

‡**THE COPPAGE COMPANY (III)**, 11501 Chandler Blvd., North Hollywood CA 91601. (818)980-1106. Fax: (818)509-1474. Estab. 1984. Signatory of WGA, member of DGA, SAG. Represents 25 clients. Specializes in "literary novels; writers who do other jobs, i.e., producing, directing, acting."
Handles: Novels, novellas, movie scripts, stage plays, TV scripts.
Terms: Agent receives 10% commission on domestic sales; 10% on foreign sales. Offers written contract, binding for 2 years.
Tips: Obtains new clients through recommendation only.

‡**CYBERSTORM! (II)**, P.O. Box 6380, Reno NV 89513. Fax: (702)322-7529. Contact: James L'Angelle. Estab. 1991. Signatory of WGA. Represents 6 clients. 100% of clients are new/previously unpublished writers. Specializes in movie scripts. Currently handles: 100% movie scripts. Member agent: James L'Angelle.

---

‡ *The double dagger before a listing indicates the listing is new in this edition.*

Handles: Movie scripts. Considers these fiction areas: action/adventure; detective/police/crime; humor/satire. Query with SASE. Reports in 1 week on queries; 2 weeks on mss.
Terms: Agent receives 10% commission on domestic sales; 10% on foreign sales. Offers written contract, any time length.
Tips: Obtains new clients through WGA listing; *Hollywood Scriptwriter* listing.

‡DIAMOND LITERARY (IV), Box 48114, 35 Lakewood Blvd., Winnipeg, Manitoba R2J 4A3 Canada. Contact: Bryan. Estab. 1990. Signatory of WGA. Represents 1 client. "We will screen song demos for submissions. We submit screenplays as well."
Handles: Movie scripts, TV scripts, song demos. Query.
Tips: "90% of received work is imperfect. Proofread better."

DISKANT & ASSOCIATES (III), Suite 202, 1033 Gayley Ave., Los Angeles CA 90024. (310)824-3773. Contact: George Diskant. Estab. 1983. Represents 12 clients. Currently handles: 40% nonfiction books; 20% movie scripts; 20% TV scripts. Considers these nonfiction areas: biography/autobiography; current affairs; history. Considers these fiction areas: contemporary issues; historical; mystery/suspense; young adult. "Won't accept any unsolicited manuscripts at this time. Telephone query only."
Terms: Agent receives 15% commission on domestic sales.
Tips: "We deal with teleplays and screen plays mostly."

‡DOUROUX & CO. (II), Suite 310, 445 S. Beverly Dr., Beverly Hills CA 90212. (310)552-0900. Fax: (310)552-0920. Contact: Michael E. Douroux. Estab. 1985. Signatory of WGA, member of DGA. 20% of clients are new/previously unpublished writers. Currently handles: 5% novels; 40% movie scripts; 5% stage plays; 40% TV scripts. Member agents: Michael E. Douroux (chairman/CEO); Steve Doran (associate).
Handles: Novels, movie scripts, stage plays, TV scripts. Considers these fiction areas: action/adventure; detective/police/crime; family saga; fantasy; historical; humor/satire; mainstream; mystery/suspense; romance; science fiction; thriller/espionage; westerns/frontier. Query. Reports in 1 week on queries; 3 weeks on mss.
Terms: Agent receives 10% commission on domestic sales. Offers written contract, binding for 2 years. Charges for photocopying only.

‡DRAGON LITERARY, INC. (II), P.O. Box 16290, Salt Lake City UT 84116-0290. Contact: Theron Wood. Estab. 1991. Signatory of WGA. Currently represents 19 clients. 100% of clients are new/previously unpublished writers. Currently handles: 4% juvenile books; 10% novels; 66% movie scripts; 20% TV scripts. Member agents: Bruce D. Richardson, CEO; Theron B. Wood.
Handles: Novels, movie scripts, TV scripts ("Star Trek"). Open to all nonfiction areas on a case-by-case basis. Open to all fiction areas on a case-by-case basis. "We'll look at anything; if it's too entertaining to put down, it'll get a good read." Send entire ms with reference to writer's guide. Reports in approximately 1 week on queries, 3 months on mss.
Terms: Agent receives 10% commission on domestic sales; 10% on foreign sales (depending on circumstances). Offers written contract, binding for 1 year; 90-day "no sale" clause. Free critique with review. "Reader (agent) writes critique during review with respect to: development/format, page by page issues, premise, characterization, dialogue, story, overall effect and climax."
Tips: Obtains most new clients through inquiries, referrals from WGA. Approximately 150 submissions per year. Don't be overanxious or annoying; we're all busy and being overbearing won't help. Writing exceptional material is the best way to find an agent."

□DYKEMAN ASSOCIATES INC. (III), 4115 Rawlins, Dallas TX 65219. (214)528-2991. Fax: (214)528-0241. Contact: Alice Dykeman. Estab. 1988. 20% of clients are new/previously unpublished writers. Currently handles: 20% novels; 20% business and other; 60% TV scripts.
Handles: Novels, short story collections, movie scripts, TV scripts. Considers these nonfiction areas: biography/autobiography; business; money/finance/economics; religious/inspirational. Considers these fiction areas: action/adventure; contemporary issues; detective/police/crime; fantasy; mystery/suspense; religious/inspiration; science fiction; thriller/espionage. Query with outline/proposal or outline plus 3 sample chapters. Reports in 1 week on queries; 1 month on mss.

Terms: Agent receives 15% commission on domestic sales; 15% on foreign sales. Offers written contract.
Fees: Charges $250 reading fee. Criticism service is included in reading fee. Critiques are written by readers and reviewed by Alice Dykeman. Charges for postage, copies, long distance phone calls. Payment of criticism fees does not ensure representation.
Tips: Obtains new clients through listings in directories and word of mouth.

□**EARTH TRACKS AGENCY (I, II),** Suite 286, 4809 Ave. N, Brooklyn NY 11234. Contact: David Krinsky. Estab. 1990. Signatory of WGA. Represents 5 clients. 50% of clients are new/previously unpublished writers. Specializes in "movie and TV script sales of original material." Currently handles: 20% novels; 50% movie scripts; 10% stage plays; 20% TV scripts. Member agent: David Krinsky (movie scripts).
Handles: Movie scripts, TV scripts ("no Star Trek"), TV movie scripts. Considers these fiction areas: action/adventure; cartoon/comic; contemporary issues; detective/police/crime; erotica; humor/satire; romance (contemporary); thriller/espionage; young adult. Query with SASE. Reports in 4-6 weeks on queries; 6-8 weeks on mss ("only if requested").
Terms: Agent receives 10-12% commission on domestic sales; 10-12% on foreign sales. Offers a written contract, binding for 6 months to 2 years.
Fees: "There is no fee if I accept to read a TV/movie script. For plays and books I charge $100 a book or $75 a stage play, nonrefundable. Criticism service: $25 per item (treatment or manuscript) submitted. I personally write the critiques. Critique not provided on scripts. An author *must* provide *proper* postage (SASE) if author wants material returned. If no SASE enclosed, material is not returned." 90% of business is derived from commissions on ms sales; 10% is derived from reading fees or criticism service. Payment of a criticism fee does not ensure representation.
Tips: Obtains new clients through recommendations and letters of solicitations by mail. "Send a one-page letter describing the material the writer wishes the agency to represent. Do not send anything other than query letter with SASE. Unsolicited scripts will not be returned. Do not 'hype' the material—just explain exactly what you are selling. If it is a play, do not state 'screenplay.' If it is a movie script, do not state 'manuscript,' as that implies a book. Be specific, give description (summary) of material."

‡**F.L.A.I.R. or FIRST LITERARY ARTISTS INTERNATIONAL REPRESENTATIVES (II, IV),** P.O. Box 666, Coram NY 11727. Contact: Jacqulin Chambers. Estab. 1991. Signatory of WGA. Represents 15 clients. Specializes in sitcoms, screenplays, movie of the weeks. Member agents: Ruth Schulman, Jacqulin Chambers.
Handles: Movie scripts, TV scripts. Considers these nonfiction areas: animals; archaeology; child guidance/parenting; health/medicine; juvenile; money/finance/economics; film; nature/environment; psychology; inspirational; true crime/investigative; personal improvement; women's isues. Considers these fiction areas: action/adventure; comic; detective/police/crime; erotica; family saga; fantasy; humor/satire; juvenile; mystery/suspense; psychic/supernatural; inspiration/contemporary; thriller/espionage; young adult. Query with synopsis. Reports in 2 weeks on queries; 6 months on mss.
Recent Sales: *Witness to Murder,* by Bill Johnston (Stuart Benjamin Productions).
Terms: Agent receives 10% commission on domestic sales; 10% on foreign sales. Offers written contract, binding for 1 year. Criticism service: screenplays $120; sitcoms $50. "I give a complete listing of what can be improved within their script, as well as suggested changes. I have compiled an at-home workshop for screen and sitcom writers: screenwriters $10; sitcom writers $5." Charges marketing fee, office expenses, postage, photocopying and phone calls. 70% of business is derived from commissions on ms sales; 30% from reading fees or criticism service. Payment of criticism fee does not ensure representation.
Tips: "Become a member of the Writer's Digest Book Club and you will learn a lot. Learning the format for screenplays and sitcoms is essential. Register all your work with either the copyright office or the WGA. You must send a query letter and synopsis of your script with a SASE. Please do not call."

ROBERT A. FREEDMAN DRAMATIC AGENCY, INC. (II, III), Suite 2310, 1501 Broadway, New York NY 10036. (212)840-5760. President: Robert A. Freedman. Vice President: Selma Luttinger. Estab. 1928. Member of AAR, signatory of WGA. Prefers to work with established authors; works with a small number of new authors. Specializes in plays, movie scripts and TV scripts.
• Robert Freedman is the current vice president of the dramatic division of AAR.

Handles: Movie scripts, stage plays, TV scripts. Query. Does not read unsolicited mss. Usually reports in 2 weeks on queries; 3 months on mss.
Terms: Agent receives 10% on dramatic sales; "and, as is customary, 20% on amateur rights." Charges for photocopying mss.
Recent Sales: "We will speak directly with any prospective client concerning sales that are relevant to his/her specific script."

SAMUEL FRENCH, INC. (II, III), 45 W. 25th St., New York NY 10010. (212)206-8990. Editors: William Talbot and Lawrence Harbison. Estab. 1830. Member of AAR. Represents plays which it publishes for production rights.
Handles: Stage plays. Query or send entire ms. Replies "immediately" on queries; decision in 2-8 months regarding publication. "Enclose SASE."
Terms: Agent usually receives 10% professional production royalties; 20% amateur production royalties.

‡**THE GARDNER AGENCY (III)**, 4952 New Ross Ave., Richmond VA 23228-6335. (804)742-1821. Fax: (804)649-0475. Contact: Charles G. Meyst. Estab. 1981. Signatory of WGA. 85% of clients are new/previously unpublished writers. Currently handles: 50% movie scripts, 50% TV scripts.
Handles: Movie scripts, TV scripts. Considers these nonfiction areas: business; music/dance/theater/film; New Age/metaphysics. Considers these fiction areas: action/adventure; detective/police/crime; erotica; experimental; fantasy; humor/satire; mainstream; psychic/supernatural; science fiction; thriller/espionage. Send outline/proposal. Reports in 2 months on queries.
Terms: Agent receives 10% commission on domestic sales; 10% on foreign sales. Offers written contract. Charges for unusual expenses.
Tips: Obtains new clients through recommendations from others.

□**THE GARY-PAUL AGENCY (II)**, #17, 84 Canaan Court, Stratford CT 06497-4538. (203)336-0257 or (203)831-2894. Contact: Gary Maynard or Chris Conway. Estab. 1989. Represents 78 clients. Specializes in client representation and ms/product marketing. Most clients are freelance writers/designers/producers. Member agents: Gary Maynard, Christopher Conway, Miguel Valenti, Lesley Roy, Paul Caravatt.
Handles: Movie scripts, TV scripts, educational and technical publications, films/videos, products. Query with letter of introduction. Reports in 10 days on requested submissions.
Terms: Agent receives 10-20% commission on mss; 25-35% on products.
Fees: No charge for client representation. Charges $300-800 for ms marketing, $2$2,000-6,000 for film/video and product marketing. "All promotional and marketing costs are the responsibility of the client."
Writers' Conferences: NBC Writers' Workshop (Burbank, CA), Script Festival (Los Angeles, CA), Yale University Writers' Workshop, Media Art Center Writers' Workshop (New Haven, CT), Fairfield University "Industry Profile Symposium" (Fairfield, CT).
Tips: "There is no such thing as a dull story, just dull story telling. Give us a call."

‡**GEDDES AGENCY (IV)**, #200, 8457 Melrose Place, Los Angeles CA 90069. (213)651-2401. Fax: (213)653-0901. Contact: Ann Geddes. Estab. 1983 in L.A., 1967 in Chicago. Signatory of WGA, member of SAG, AFTRA. Represents 10 clients. 100% of clients are new/previously unpublished writers. "We are mainly representing actors—writers are more 'on the side.' " Currently handles: 100% movie scripts.
Handles: Movie scripts. Query with synopsis. Reports in 2 months on mss only if interested.
Terms: Agent receives 10% commission on domestic sales. Offers written contract, binding for 1 year. Charges for "handling and postage for a script to be returned—otherwise it is recycled."
Tips: Obtains new clients through recommendations from others and through mailed-in synopses. "Send in query—say how many scripts available for representation. Send synopsis of each one. Mention something about yourself."

THE GERSH AGENCY (II, III), 232 N. Canon Dr., Beverly Hills CA 90210. (310)274-6611. Contact: Ron Bernstein. Estab. 1962. Signatory of WGA. Less than 10% of clients are new/previously unpublished writers. Special interests: "mainstream—convertible to film and television."

Script Agents: Nonfee-charging and Fee-charging 171

Handles: Movie scripts, TV scripts. Send entire ms. Reports on ms in 4 weeks.
Recent Sales: *Hot Flashes*, by Barbara Raskin (Penny Marshall); *Donato & Daughter* (Universal).
Terms: Agent receives 10% commission on domestic sales. "We strictly deal in *published* manuscripts in terms of potential film or television sales, on a strictly 10% commission—sometimes split with a New York literary agency or various top agencies."

GRAHAM AGENCY (II), 311 W. 43rd St., New York NY 10036. (212)489-7730. Owner: Earl Graham. Estab. 1971. Represents 35 clients. 35% of clients are new/unproduced playwrights. Willing to work with new/unproduced playwrights. Specializes in full-length stage plays.
Handles: Stage plays, musicals. "We consider on the basis of the letters of inquiry." Writers *must* query before sending any material for consideration. Reports "as soon as possible on queries."
Terms: Agent receives 10% commission.

‡▫GIL HAYES & ASSOC. (III), P.O. Box 63333, Memphis TN 38163. Contact: Gil Hayes. Estab. 1992. Signatory of WGA. Represents 8 clients. 10% of clients are new/previously unpublished writers. Specializes in children's films, art or B grade, no action-adventure. Currently handles: 50% novels; 50% movie scripts. Member agent: Gil Hayes (art, avant garde and children's films).
Handles: Movie scripts. Considers these nonfiction areas: biography/autobiography; current affairs; health/medicine. Considers these fiction areas: literary, mainstream, mystery/suspense, regional. Query. Reports in 1 month on queries, 8-10 weeks on mss.
Terms: Agent receives 10% commission on domestic sales; 15-20% on foreign sales. Offers written contract, length of time varies, normally 2 years.
Fees: Charges reading fee: $50 script/ms in advance, $100 if return and notes are requested; new writers only. 100% refundable if representing writer. Criticism service: $50 for script in advance, $100 if requesting written notes. "Gil Hayes writes and reviews all critiques. Some major input from writers I already represent if area is appropriate. Writers must provide bound copies usually 5 to 10 at a time if I represent them. I pay postage, handling, Federal Express to studios, producers, etc." 90% of business is derived from commission on ms sales; 10% derived from reading fees or criticism services. Payment of a criticism fee does not ensure representation.
Tips: Obtains new clients through "recommendations from others—contacts at tape and film commission offices around the nation. Always register with WGA or copyright material before sending to anyone."

▫ALICE HILTON LITERARY AGENCY (II), 13131 Welby Way, North Hollywood CA 91606. (818)982-2546. Estab. 1986. Eager to work with new/unpublished writers. "Interested in any quality material, although agent's personal taste runs in the genre of 'Cheers.' 'L.A. Law,' 'American Playhouse,' 'Masterpiece Theatre' and Woody Allen vintage humor."
Handles: Book length mss (fiction and nonfiction), juvenile, movie scripts, TV feature-length scripts.
Terms: Agent receives 10% commission. Brochure available with SASE. Preliminary phone call appreciated.
Fees: Charges evaluation fee of $2.50/1,000 words. Charges for phone, postage and photocopy expenses.
Recent Sales: *Jihad*, by Kurt Fischel (New Saga Press); *Tax Free America*, by Boris Isaacson (Tomorrow Now Press).

‡CAROLYN HODGES AGENCY (III), 1980 Glenwood Dr., Boulder CO 80304. (303)443-4636. Contact: Carolyn Hodges. Estab. 1989. Represents 12 clients. 90% of clients are new/previously unpublished writers. "Represents only screenwriters for film and television movies of the week." Currently handles: 80% movie scripts; 20% TV scripts (movies of the week).
Handles: Movie scripts, TV scripts. Considers these fiction areas: action/adventure; contemporary issues; detective/police/crime; ethnic; experimental; fantasy; feminist; gay; glitz; historical; juvenile; lesbian; literary; mainstream; mystery/suspense; psychic/supernatural; regional; romance (contemporary, historical); science fiction; thriller/espionage. Query with 1-page synopsis. Reports in 1 week on queries; 4-6 weeks on mss.
Terms: Agent receives 10% on domestic sales; foreign sales "depend on each individual negotiation." Offers written contract, standard WGA. No charge for criticism. "I always try to offer concrete feedback, even when rejecting a piece of material. I do request that writers supply me with copies of their screenplays. I pay all other expenses."

Writers' Conferences: Will attend Writers In The Rockies TV and Film Screenwriting Conference, held in Boulder CO in August '94.
Tips: Obtains new clients via WGA agency list or by referral. "Become proficient at your craft. Attend all workshops accessible to you. READ all the books applicable to your area of interest. READ as many 'produced' screenplays as possible. Live a full, vital and rewarding life so your writing will have something to say. Get involved in a writer's support group. Network with other writers."

‡MICHAEL IMISON PLAYWRIGHTS LTD. (III, IV), 28 Almeida St., Islington London N1 1TD England. 071-354-3174. Fax: 071-359-6273. Contact: Michael Imison or Sarah McNair. Estab. 1944. Member of PMA. 10% of clients are new/previously unpublished writers. Specializes in stage plays including plays in translation—especially Russian and Italian. Currently handles: 10% movie scripts; 80% stage plays; 10% TV scripts.
• North American writers should send SAE with IRCs for response, available at most post offices.
Handles: Stage plays. Query first. Reports in 1 week on queries; 2 months on mss.
Terms: Agent receives 10-15% commission on sales. Charges for photocopying. 100% of business is derived from commissions on ms sales.
Tips: Obtains new clients through personal recommendation. "Biographical details can be helpful. Generally only playwrights whose work has been performed will be considered."

INTERNATIONAL LEONARDS CORP. (II), 3612 N. Washington Blvd., Indianapolis IN 46205-3534. (317)926-7566. Contact: David Leonards. Estab. 1972. Signatory of WGA. Currently handles: 50% movie scripts; 50% TV scripts.
Handles: Movie scripts, TV scripts. Considers these nonfiction areas: anthropology/archaeology; biography/autobiography; business; current/affairs; history; money/finance/economics; music/dance/theater/film; new age/metaphysics; psychology; religious/inspirational; science/technology; self-help/personal improvement; sports; true crime/investigative. Considers these fiction areas: action/adventure; cartoon/comic; contemporary issues; detective/police/crime; family saga; fantasy; historical; humor/satire; mainstream; mystery/suspense; religious/inspiration; romance (contemporary, gothic, historical, regency); science fiction; sports; thriller/espionage. Query. Reports in 1 month on queries; 6 months on mss.
Terms: Agent receives 10% commission on domestic sales; 10% on foreign sales. Offers written contract, "WGA standard," which "varies."
Tips: Obtains new clients through recommendations and queries.

‡CHARLENE KAY AGENCY, Suite 6, 901 Beaudry St., St. Jean/Richelieu, Quebec J3A 1C6 Canada. (514)348-5296. Estab. 1992. Signatory of WGA. 100% of clients are new/previously unpublished writers. Specializes in teleplays and screenplays. Currently handles: 50% TV scripts; 50% movie scripts.
Handles: Movie scripts, TV scripts. Considers these fiction areas: action/adventure, biography/autobiography; family saga; romance (contemporary); thriller/espionage. Query with outline/proposal. Reports in 1 month on queries with SASE or IRCs; 8-10 weeks on mss.
Terms: Agent receives 10% commission on domestic sales; 10% on foreign sales. Offers written contract binding for 1 year. Returns Canadian scripts if SASE provided; does not return scripts from US.
Tips: "My agency is listed on the WGA lists and query letters arrive by the dozens every week. I don't even have to advertise in any magazine. As my present clients understand, success comes with patience. A sale rarely happens overnight, especially when you are dealing with totally unknown writers. Many top agencies don't want to deal with unsolicited materials because they know how hard it is to make someone unknown known to the industry. I like the challenge of breaking down doors for new talents: they are the giants of tomorrow!"

THE JOYCE KETAY AGENCY, Suite 1910, 1501 Broadway, New York NY 10036. (212)354-6825. Fax: (212)354-6732. Contact: Joyce Ketay or Carl Mulert, agents. Member of AAR.
Handles: Theater and film scripts. Playwrights and screenwriters only. No novels.

‡KICK ENTERTAINMENT (I), 1934 E. 123rd St., Cleveland OH 44106. (216)795-2515. Fax: same. Contact: Sam Klein. Estab. 1992. Represents 5 clients. 100% of clients are new/previously unpublished writers. Currently handles: 100% movie scripts.

Handles: Movie scripts. Considers these nonfiction areas: military/war; true crime/investigative. Considers these fiction areas: action/adventure; detective/police/crime; family saga; fantasy; mystery/suspense; psychic/supernatural; science fiction; thriller/espionage; westerns/frontier. Query. Reports in 2 weeks on queries; 6-8 weeks on mss.
Terms: Agent receives 10% commission on domestic sales; 10% on foreign sales. Offers written contract, binding for 2 years.
Tips: "Always send a query letter first, and enclose a SASE."

PAUL KOHNER, INC. (IV), 9169 Sunset Blvd., West Hollywood CA 90069. (310)550-1060. Contact: Gary Salt. Estab. 1938. Member of ATA. Represents 150 clients. 10% of clients are new/previously unpublished writers. Specializes in film and TV rights sales and representation of film and TV writers.
Handles: Nonfiction books, movie scripts, stage plays, TV scripts. Considers these nonfiction areas: history; military/war; music/dance/theater/film; true crime/investigative. Query with SASE. Reports in 2 weeks on queries.
Recent Sales: Has sold scripts to 20th Century Fox, Warner's, Disney.
Terms: Agent receives 10% commission on domestic sales; 10% on foreign sales. Offers written contract, binding for 1-3 years. "We charge for copying manuscripts or scripts for submission unless a sufficient quantitiy is supplied by the author. All unsolicited material is automatically returned unread."

☐**L. HARRY LEE LITERARY AGENCY (II)**, Box #203, Rocky Point NY 11778. (516)744-1188. Contact: L. Harry Lee. Estab. 1979. Signatory of WGA, member of Dramatists Guild. Represents 285 clients. 65% of clients are new/previously unpublished writers. Specializes in movie scripts. "Comedy is our strength, both features and sitcoms, also movie of the week, science fiction, novels and TV. Currently handles 30% novels; 50% movie scripts; 5% stage plays; 15% TV scripts. Member agents: Mary Lee Gaylor (episodic TV, feature films); Charles Rothery (feature films, sitcoms, movie of the week); Katie Polk (features, mini-series, children's TV); Patti Roenbeck (science fiction, fantasy, romance, historical romance); Frank Killeen (action, war stories, American historical, westerns); Hollister Barr (mainstream, feature films, romantic comedies); Ed Van Bomel (sitcoms, movie of the week, mysteries, adventure stories); Colin James (horror, Viet Nam, war stories); Judith Faria (all romance, fantasy, mainstream); Charis Biggis (plays, historical novels, westerns, action/suspense/thriller films); Stacy Parker (love stories, socially significant stories/films, time travel science fiction); Jane Breoge (sitcoms, after-school specials, mini-series, episodic TV); Cami Callirgos (mainstream/contemporary/humor, mystery/suspense); Vito Brenna (action/adventure, romantic comedy, feature films, horror); Anastassia Evereaux (feature films, romantic comedies).
Handles: Novels, movie scripts, stage plays, TV scripts, humor, sitcoms. Considers these nonfiction areas: history; military/war. Considers these fiction areas: action/adventure; detective/police/crime; erotica; family saga; fantasy; historical; horror; humor/satire; literary; mainstream; mystery/suspense; romance (contemporary, gothic, historical, regency); science fiction; sports; thriller/espionage; westerns/frontier; young adult. Query "with a short writing or background résumé of the writer. A SASE is a must. No dot matrix, we don't read them." Reports in "return mail" on queries; 3-4 weeks on mss. "We notify the writer when to expect a reply."
Recent Sales: *Twisted*, by Hollister Barr (Leisure Books); *Golden Conquest*, by Patricia Roenbeck (Leisure Books).
Terms: Agent receives 15% commission on domestic sales; 20% on foreign sales; 10% on movie/TV scripts and plays. Offers written contract "by the manuscript which can be broken by mutual consent; the length is as long as the copyright runs."
Fees: Does not charge a reading fee. Criticism service: $195 for screenplays; $150 for movie of the week; $95 for TV sitcom; $195 for a mini-series; $1 per page for one-act plays. "All of the agents and readers write the carefully thought-out critiques, 3-page checklist, 2 to 4 pages of notes, and a manuscript that is written on, plus tip sheets and notes that may prove helpful. It's a thorough service, for which we have received the highest praise." Charges for postage, handling, photocopying per submission, "not a general fee." 90% of business is derived from commissions on ms sales. 10% is derived from criticism services. Payment of a criticism fee does not ensure representation.
Tips: Obtains new clients through recommendations, "but mostly queries. If interested in agency representation, write a good story with interesting characters and that's hard to do. Learn your form and format. Take courses, workshops. Read *Writer's Digest*; it's your best source of great information."

‡**LEGACIES (I)**, 501 Woodstock Circle, Perico Bay, Bradenton FL 34209. Phone and fax: (813)792-9159. Executive Director: Mary Ann Amato. Estab. 1993. Signatory of WGA, member of Florida Motion Picture & Television Association, Board of Talent Agents, Dept. of Professional Regulations License No. TA 0000404. 50% of clients are new/previously unpublished writers. Specializes in screenplays. Currently handles 10% nonfiction books; 5% poetry books; 75% movie scripts; 10% stage plays.
Handles: Movie scripts, TV scripts. Considers these fiction areas: contemporary issues; ethnic; family saga; feminist; historical; humor/satire. Query, then send entire ms. Enclose SASE. Reports in 2 weeks on queries; 4-6 weeks on mss.
Terms: Agent receives 15% commission on domestic sales; 20% on foreign sales (WGA percentages on member sales). Offers a written contract.

HELEN MERRILL LTD. (II), Suite 1 A, 435 W. 23rd St., New York NY 10011. (212)691-5326. Contact: Lourdes Lopez or Helen Merrill. Estab. 1975. Member of AAR. Represents 100 clients. Currently handles 30% nonfiction books; 70% stage plays.
Handles: Stage plays, fiction, nonfiction. Considers biographies. Considers these fiction areas: contemporary issues; literary; mainstream. Query with SASE. Reports in 3 weeks on queries.
Terms: Agent receives 15% commission on domestic sales. Charges for postage, photocopies.
Tips: Usually obtains new clients through recommendations from others.

MONTGOMERY-WEST LITERARY AGENCY (IV), 7450 Butler Hills Dr., Salt Lake City UT 84121. Contact: Carole Western. Estab. 1989. Signatory of WGA. Represents 30 clients. 80% of clients are new/previously unpublished writers. Specializes in movie and TV scripts, contemporary fiction and nonfiction books. Currently handles: 30% novels; 60% movie scripts. Member agents: Carole Western (movie and TV scripts); Nancy Gummery (novel, consultant and editor).
Handles: Novels, movie scripts, TV scripts. Considers these fiction areas: action/adventure; detective/police/crime; mystery/suspense; romance (contemporary, historical, regency); science fiction; thriller/espionage. Query with outline, 1 sample chapter and SAE. Reports in 6-8 weeks on queries; 8-10 weeks on mss. "We have editing and critiquing branch for reasonable fee."
Terms: Agent receives 15% commission on domestic sales for novels, 10% on movie scripts; 15% on foreign sales for books. Charges for telephone, postage and consultations.
Writers' Conferences: Attends 3 workshops a year; WGA West Conference.
Tips: "Send in only the finest product you can and keep synopses and treatments brief and to the point. Have patience and be aware of the enormous competition in the writing field."

‡**DOROTHY PALMER (III)**, 235 W. 56 St., New York NY 10019. Phone and fax: (212)765-4280. Estab. 1990. Signatory of WGA. Represents 12 clients. 90% of clients are new/previously unpublished writers. Specializes in screenplays, TV. Currently handles: 70% movie scripts, 30% TV scripts.
Handles: Movie scripts, TV scripts. Considers these nonfiction areas: cooking/food/nutrition; current affairs; health/medicine; true crime/investigative; women's issues/women's studies. Considers these fiction areas: detective/police/crime; humor/satire; mystery/suspense; romance (contemporary); thriller/espionage. Send entire ms with outline/proposal.
Recent Sales: "Startek," by Manuel Garcia (Paramount).
Terms: Agent receives 10% commission on domestic sales; 10% on foreign sales. Offers written contract, binding for 1 year.
Tips: Obtains new clients through recommendations from others. "Do *not* telephone. When I find a script that interests me, I call the writer. Calls to me are a turn-off because it cuts into my reading time."

PANDA TALENT (II), 3721 Hoen Ave., Santa Rosa CA 95405. (707)576-0711. Fax: (707)544-2765. Contact: Audrey Grace. Estab. 1977. Signatory of WGA, member of SAG, AFTRA, Equity. Represents 10 clients. 80% of clients are new/previously unpublished writers. Currently handles: 5% novels; 5% stage plays; 40% TV scripts; 50% movie scripts.
Handles: Movie scripts, TV scripts. Considers these nonfiction areas: animals; military/war; psychology; sports; true crime/investigative. Considers these fiction areas: action/adventure; confessional; detective/police/crime; family saga; humor/satire; juvenile; mystery/suspense; sports; thriller/espionage. Query with treatment. Reports in 3 weeks on queries; 2 months on mss.

Script Agents: Nonfee-charging and Fee-charging 175

Terms: Agent receives 10% commission on domestic sales; 10% on foreign sales.
Fees: "We sometimes make suggestions. There is no fee."

‡**PANETTIERE & CO. (I, II),** 1841 N. Fuller Ave., Los Angeles CA 90046. (213)876-5984. Fax: (213)876-5076. Contact: Vincent Panettiere. Estab. 1992. Signatory of WGA, member of DGA. Represents 40 clients. 40% of clients are new/previously unpublished writers. Currently handles: 80% movie scripts; 20% TV scripts.
Handles: Movie scripts, TV scripts. Query. Reports in 1 month.
Terms: Agent receives 10% commission on domestic sales. Offers written contract, binding for 1 year. "We bill client for copies of scripts that are distributed."
Tips: Obtains new clients through recommendations from others and solicitation. "A gifted writer needs no advice. An untalented writer will heed no advice."

□**RAINTREE AGENCY (II),** 360 W. 21 St., New York NY 10011. (212)242-2387. Contact: Diane Raintree. Estab. 1977. Represents 6-8 clients. Specializes in novels, film and TV scripts, plays, poetry and children's books.
Handles: Considers all fiction areas and some nonfiction. Phone first.
Terms: Agent receives 10% on domestic sales.
Fees: May charge reading fee. "Amount varies from year to year."

STEPHANIE ROGERS AND ASSOCIATES (III), #218, 3855 Lankershim Blvd., Hollywood CA 91604. (818)509-1010. Owner: Stephanie Rogers. Estab. 1980. Represents 33 clients. 20% of clients are new/unproduced writers. Prefers that the writer has been produced (movies or TV), his/her properties optioned or has references. Prefers to work with published/established authors. Specializes in screenplays—dramas (contemporary), action/adventure, romantic comedies and suspense/thrillers for movies and TV. Currently handles: 10% novels; 50% movie scripts; 40% TV scripts.
Handles: Novels (only wishes to see those that have been published and can translate to screen), movie scripts, TV scripts (must be professional in presentation and not over 125 pages). Query. Does not read unsolicited mss. SASE required.
Terms: Agent receives 10% commission on domestic sales; 10% on dramatic sales; 20% on foreign sales. Charges for phone, photocopying and messenger expenses.
Tips: "When writing a query letter, you should give a short bio of your background, a thumbnail sketch (no more than a paragraph) of the material you are looking to market and an explanation of how or where (books, classes or workshops) you studied screenwriting." Include SASE for response.

JACK SCAGNETTI TALENT & LITERARY AGENCY (III), #210, 5330 Lankershim Blvd., North Hollywood CA 91601. (818)762-3871. Contact: Jack Scagnetti. Estab. 1974. Signatory of WGA. Represents 40 clients. 50% of clients are new/previously unpublished writers. Specializes in film books with many photographs. Currently handles: 10% nonfiction books; 80% movie scripts; 10% TV scripts. Member agents: Jack Scagnetti (nonfiction and screenplays) and Lynne Pembroke (fiction).
Handles: Considers these nonfiction areas: health; military/war; self-help/personal improvement; sports; true crime/investigative. Considers these fiction areas: mainstream; mystery/suspense; sports; thriller/espionage. Query with outline/proposal. Reports in 1 month on queries; 6-8 weeks on mss.
Recent Sales: *Successful Car Buying,* (Stackpole Books).
Terms: Agent receives 10% commission on domestic sales; 15% on foreign sales. Offers written contract, binding for 6 months-1 year. Charges for postage and photocopies.
Tips: Obtains new clients through "referrals by others and query letters sent to us. Write a good synopsis, short and to the point and include marketing data for the book."

SCRIBE AGENCY (IV), P.O. Box 580393, Houston TX 77258-0393. (713)333-1094. Contact: Marta White or Carl Sinclair. "Please call before sending material." Estab. 1988. Signatory of WGA. Represents 20 clients. 40% of clients are new/previously unpublished writers. Specializes in book-length literary fiction for adults, movie and TV scripts. Currently handles: 40% novels; 40% movie scripts; 20% TV scripts. Member agents: Marta White; Carl Sinclair; Robert Fannin.

For explanation of symbols, see the Key to Symbols and Abbreviations. For translation of an organization's acronym, see the Table of Acronyms.

Handles: Novels, movie scripts, TV scripts. Does not want to see "horrors/thrillers or other material promoting violence and/or sexual abuse." Considers these fiction areas: contemporary issues; literary; mainstream. No science fiction. Query with SASE. Reports in 3-4 weeks on queries; 1 month on mss.
Recent Sales: *Family Values* (Advantage Press).
Terms: Agent receives 25% commission on domestic and foreign sales. Offers written contract, binding time is negotiable.
Tips: Obtains new clients through recommendations. "Call, and submit query with SASE first."

KEN SHERMAN & ASSOCIATES, 9507 Santa Monica Blvd. Beverly Hills CA 90210. Agency not currently seeking new clients.

‡SILVER SCREEN PLACEMENTS (I), 602 65th St., Downers Grove IL 60516. (708)963-2124. Fax: (708)963-1998. Contact: William Levin. Estab. 1991. Signatory of WGA. Represents 3 clients. 100% of clients are new/previously unpublished writers. Currently handles: 5% juvenile books; 5% novels; 80% movie scripts; 10% TV scripts.
Handles: Juvenile books, novels, movie scripts, TV scripts. Considers these fiction areas: action/adventure; cartoon/comic; contemporary issues; detective/police/crime; family saga; fantasy; historical; humor/satire; juvenile; mainstream; mystery/suspense; science fiction; thriller/espionage; young adult. Query with outline/proposal and SASE. Reports in 1 week on queries, 6 weeks on mss.
Terms: Agent receives 10% commission on domestic sales; 10% on foreign sales. Offers written contract, binding for 2-4 years.
Tips: Obtains new clients through "recommendations from other parties, as well as being listed with WGA."

‡LEE SOBEL MANAGEMENT ASSOCIATES (II, IV), Suite 2C, 123 W. 93 St., New York NY 10025. (212)865-8356. Contact: Lee Sobel. Estab. 1992. Represents 20 clients. 85% of clients are new/previously unpublished writers. Specializes in "development, creation and marketing of commercial screenplays and novels, with an emphasis on high-quality genre material, especially crime fiction and mystery novels." Currently handles: 5% juvenile books; 45% novels; 50% movie scripts.
Handles: Primarily novels; movie scripts. Considers these nonfiction areas: biography; true crime/investigative. Considers these fiction areas: action/adventure; fantasy; horror; mainstream; mystery/suspense; science fiction; thriller/espionage. Query with synopsis and SASE. Reports in 1 month on mss "if not sooner (I am very fast and very selective)."
Recent Sales: *Kiss Them Goodbye*, by Joseph Eastburn (Wm. Morrow); *Midnight Blue* (screenplay), by Douglas Brode (optioned by Wildsmith Entertainment).
Terms: Agent receives 15% commission on domestic sales; 20% on foreign sales. "25% on projects created by Lee Sobel." Offers written contract. "While I did not charge initially, the costs of photocopying and postage have become prohibitive and I am now asking that expenses such as these be deducted from sales."
Tips: Obtains new clients in "the usual ways. Be respectful of the agent's time. Always enclose a SASE, and when an agent turns you down, do not call to ask why. Move on or keep in touch by mail. I also prefer all new prospective clients to communicate by mail—a good letter will indicate writing ability—a phone call will not. Unlike most agents, I also create, develop and package my own original ideas and work very closely with the writer through the entire creative process."

‡CAMILLE SORICE AGENCY (II), #1, 7540 Balboa Blvd., Van Nuys CA 91406. (818)995-1775. Contact: Camille Sorice. Estab. 1988. Signatory of WGA. Represents 3 clients. 100% of clients are new/previously unpublished writers.
Handles: Nonfiction books, novels, movie scripts. Considers these nonfiction areas: psychology; self-help/personal improvement. Considers these fiction areas: feminist; mystery/suspense. Send entire ms. Reports in 6 weeks on mss.
Tips: Obtains clients through solicitation.

---

‡ The double dagger before a listing indicates the listing is new in this edition.

Script Agents: Nonfee-charging and Fee-charging 177

‡**STANTON & ASSOCIATES INTERNATIONAL LITERARY AGENCY (II)**, 4413 Clemson Dr., Garland TX 75042. (214)276-5427. Fax: (214)348-6900. Contact: Henry Stanton/Harry Preston. Estab. 1990. Signatory of WGA. Represents 36 clients. 90% of clients are new screenwriters. Specializes in screenplays only. Currently handles: 50% movie scripts; 50% TV scripts.
Handles: Movie scripts, TV scripts. Query. Reports in 1 week on queries; 1 month on screenplays (review).
Recent Sales: *Splintered Image* (Hearst Entertainment); *Belle and Her Boys* (Bob Banner Associates); *The Body Shop* and *Sisters Revenge* (Esquivel Entertainment).
Terms: Agent receives 15% commission on domestic sales. Offers written contract, binding for 2 years on individual screenplays. Returns scripts with reader's comments.
Tips: Obtains new clients through WGA listing, *Hollywood Scriptwriter*, word of mouth (in Dallas). "We have writers available to edit or ghostwrite screenplays. Fees vary dependent on the writer. All writers should always please enclose a SASE with any queries."

ELLEN LIVELY STEELE & ASSOCIATES (III), P.O. Drawer 447, Organ NM 88052. (505)382-5449. Fax: (505)382-9821. Contact: Ellen Lively Steele or Harold Servis. Estab. 1980. Signatory of WGA. Represents 20 clients. 30% of clients are new/previously unpublished writers. Specializes in New Age, occult, cookbooks, screenplays, children's. Currently handles: 20% nonfiction books; 1% textbooks; 5% juvenile books; 25% novels; 55% movie scripts; 35% TV scripts; 28% New Age.
Handles: Nonfiction and juvenile books, novels, movie scripts, TV scripts, New Age. Considers these nonfiction areas: cooking/food/nutrition; New Age/metaphysic; self-help/personal improvement; true crime/investigative; women's issues/women's studies; men's issues. Considers these fiction areas: action/adventure; detective/police/crime; family saga; glitz; humor/satire; mainstream; mystery/suspense; psychic/supernatural; thriller/espionage. Query with outline and 3 sample chapters. Reports in 6 weeks on queries; 2-3 months on ms.
Terms: Agent receives 10% commission on domestic sales; splits percentage on foreign sales. Offers written contract, binding for 2 years. Charges for postage, fax, copies, phone calls. "Charges no extraordinary expense without written agreement from client. No office expenses. Marketing and editing expenses would fall into above list, usually."
Tips: Obtains new clients through recommendations from other clients, producers and editors, "very few from queries."

H.N. SWANSON INC. (III), 8523 Sunset Blvd., Los Angeles CA 90069. President: Thomas J. Shanks. Estab. 1934. Signatory of WGA. Represents over 100 clients. 10% of clients are new/previously unpublished writers. Currently handles: 60% novels; 40% movie and TV scripts. Member agents: Steven Fisher, Michele Wallerstein, Gail Barrick, David Murphy.
Handles: Novels, novellas, movie scripts, TV scripts (episodic, long form and sit-com). Considers these nonfiction areas: current affairs; sports. Considers these fiction areas: action/adventure; detective/police/crime; historical; humor/satire; mainstream; mystery/suspense; sports; thriller/espionage. Query. Reports within 3-4 weeks on queries. Queries must be accompanied by SASE.
Terms: Agent receives 10% commission on domestic sales; varies on foreign sales. Offers written contract.
Tips: Obtains new clients through recommendations "from respected individuals within the writing and development community. For the most part, we co-agent with publishing agents, representing the motion picture and television sales of their clients. We do represent the publishing interests of a few clients."

□**THE TALENT BANK AGENCY (III)**, #721, 1680 Vine St., Los Angeles CA 90048. (213)735-2636. Estab. 1990. Signatory of WGA. Represents 23 clients. "Seeking established writers: few additional authors are being added now." 99% of clients are new/previously unpublished writers. Currently handles: 73% movie scripts; 2% stage plays; 25% TV scripts. Member agent: Bill Lee, owner (talent).
Handles: Movie scripts, stage plays, TV scripts. Considers these areas: action/adventure; contemporary issues; detective/police/crime; ethnic; family saga; fantasy; feminist; gay; historical; humor/satire; juvenile; lesbian; mainstream; mystery/suspense; science fiction; thriller/espionage; westerns/frontier. Query. Reports in 2 weeks on queries; 6-8 weeks on mss.

Terms: Agent receives 10% commission on domestic sales. Offers written contract, binding for 1-2 years.
Fees: Does not charge a reading fee now. Will offer a criticism service at a later date.
Tips: Obtains new clients through recommendations and solicitations. "Be sure your letter of inquiry is grammatical and well-spelled. Avoid arrogance and modesty. Be forthright and business-like; get to your point succinctly. Pitch your work in a two-paragraph format. Treatment depends on length of piece. When submitting a screenplay, be sure it is correctly formatted. Have a 'hook' in the first 10 pages or figure no one will read beyond that. Give me a reason to want to continue."

THE TANTLEFF OFFICE (II), Suite 700, 375 Greenwich St., New York NY 10013. (212)941-3939. President: Jack Tantleff. Agents: John B. Santoianni and Jill Bock. Estab. 1986. Signatory of WGA, member of AAR. Specializes in television, theater, film, fiction and nonfiction. Currently handles 15% movie scripts; 70% stage plays; 15% TV scripts. Query with outline. Member agents: John Santoianni (theater); Jill Bock (TV and film); Anthony Gardner (fiction, nonfiction books); Alan Willig (talent); Jay Kane (talent).
Terms: Agent receives 10% commission on domestic sales; 10% on dramatic sales; 10% on foreign sales.

□**A TOTAL ACTING EXPERIENCE (II)**, Suite 206, Dept. N.W., 14621 Titus St., Panorama City CA 91402. (818)901-1044. Contact: Dan A. Bellacicco. Estab. 1984. Signatory of WGA. Represents 30 clients. 50% of clients are new/previously unpublished writers. Specializes in "quality instead of quantity." Currently handles 5% nonfiction books; 5% juvenile books; 10% novels; 5% novellas; 5% short story collections; 50% movie scripts; 5% stage plays; 10% TV scripts; 5% how-to books and videos.
Handles: Nonfiction books, textbooks, juvenile books, novels, novellas, short story collections, poetry books, movie scripts, stage plays, TV scripts, syndicated material, how-to books, videos. "No heavy violence or drugs." Considers these nonfiction areas: animals; art/architecture/design; biography/autobiography; business; child guidance/parenting; computers/electronics; cooking/food/nutrition; crafts/hobbies; current affairs; ethnic/cultural interests; gay/lesbian issues; government/politics/law; health/medicine; history; juvenile nonfiction; language/literature/criticism; military/war; money/finance/economics; music/dance/theater/film; nature/environment; new age/metaphysics; photography; psychology; religious/inspirational; true crime/investigative; science/technology; self-help/personal improvement; sociology; sports; translations; women's issues/women's studies; "any well-written work!" Considers all fiction areas. Query with outline plus 3 sample chapters. Reports in 3 months on mss. "We will respond *only* if interested, material will *not* be returned."
Terms: Agent receives 10% on domestic sales; 10% on foreign sales. Offers written contract, binding for 2 years or more.
Fees: Offers criticism service (for our clients only at no charge.) 60% of business is derived from commission on ms sales.
Tips: Obtains new clients through mail and conferences. "We seek new sincere, quality writers for long-term relationships. We would love to see film, television, and stage material that remains relevant and provocative 20 years from today; dialogue that is fresh and unpredictable; and story, theme and characters that are intelligent, enlightening, humorous, witty, creative, inspiring, and, most of all, entertaining. Please keep in mind quality not quantity. Your character must be well delineated and fully developed with high contrast."

‡**THE TURTLE AGENCY (III)**, 12456 Ventura Blvd., Studio City CA 91604. (818)506-6898. Fax: (818)506-1723. Contact: Cindy Turtle, Beth Bohn. Estab. 1985. Signatory of WGA, member of SAG, AFTRA. Represents 45 clients. Specializes in network TV, features, interactive. Currently handles: 5% novels; 25% movie scripts; 70% TV scripts.
Handles: Movie scripts, TV scripts. Considers these fiction areas: action/adventure; detective/police/crime; erotica; fantasy; historical; mainstream; mystery/suspense; psychic/supernatural; romance; science fiction; thriller/espionage; westerns/frontier; young adult. Query. Reports in 2 weeks on queries; 1 month on mss. "If writer would like material returned, enclose SASE."
Terms: Agent receives 10% commission on domestic sales. Offers written contract, binding for 2 years.
Tips: Obtains new clients through recommendations, usually—on *rare* occassions through query letters.

ERIKA WAIN AGENCY (II), #102, 1418 N. Highland, Hollywood CA 90028. (213)460-4224. Contact: Erika Wain. Estab. 1979. Signatory of WGA, member of SAG-AFTRA, Authors Guild. 50% of clients are new/previously unpublished writers. Currently handles: 5% juvenile books; 80% movie scripts; 15% TV scripts.
Handles: Juvenile books, movie scripts, TV scripts. Considers these nonfiction areas: animals; military/war; science/technology; true crime/investigative; women's issues/women's studies. Considers these fiction areas: action/adventure; detective/police/crime; family saga; fantasy; feminist; humor/satire; juvenile; mystery/suspense; science fiction; thriller/espionage. Query. Reports immediately if interested on queries and ms.
Terms: Agent receives 10% commission on domestic sales. Offers written contract.
Tips: Obtains new clients through recommendation from others, solicitation.

‡JULIUS WINDERMERE AGENCY (I, II), P.O. Box 1901, Independence MO 64855. (816)252-7276. Contact: Mr. Prince. Estab. 1993. Signatory of WGA. 100% of clients are new/previously unpublished writers. Currently handles: 50% movie scripts; 50% TV scripts.
Handles: Movie scripts, TV scripts. "Looking in particular for romance, with strong female leads." Query. Reports in 1 month on queries; 2-3 months on mss.
Terms: Agent receives 10% commission on domestic sales; 10% on foreign sales. Offers written contract, binding for 1 year with 4 month clause (standard contract used by all signatory agencies in WGA). "Clients who have signed must supply agency with clean, crisp copies of manuscript for submissions to studios, etc."
Tips: Obtains new clients through recommendation, solicitation. "Send query with SASE envelope for approval; manuscripts must be accompanied by SASE as well. Send to the attention of Submissions Dept."

ANN WRIGHT REPRESENTATIVES (II, III), 9J, 136 E. 56th St., New York NY 10022-3619. (212)832-0110. Head of Literary Department: Dan Wright. Estab. 1963. Signatory of WGA. Represents 50 clients. 25% of clients are new/unpublished writers. "Writers must be skilled and have superior material for screenplays, stories or novels that can eventually become motion pictures or television properties." Prefers to work with published/established authors; works with a small number of new/unpublished authors. "Eager to work with any author with material that we can effectively market in the motion picture business worldwide." Specializes in themes that make good motion pictures. Currently handles 20% novels; 60% movie scripts; and 20% TV scripts.
Recent Sales: *Yuppie Scum*, by Sean Breckenridge (St. Martin's); *Vengeance*, by Bob Mendes (Manteau).
Handles: Query with outline—does not read unsolicited mss. Reports in 3 weeks on queries; 2 months on mss. "All work must be sent with a SASE to ensure its return."
Terms: Agent receives 10% commission on domestic sales; 10% on dramatic sales; 10% on foreign sales; 20% on packaging. Critiques only works of signed clients. Charges for photocopying expenses.

‡WRITERS & ARTISTS AGENCY (III), Suite 1000, 19 W. 44th St., New York NY 10036. (212)391-1112. Fax: (212)398-9877. Contact: Scott Hudson or William Craver. West Coast location: Suite 900, 924 Westwood Blvd., Los Angeles CA 90024. (310)824-6300. Fax: (310)824-6343. Estab. 1970. Signatory of WGA, member of AAR. Represents 100 clients.
Handles: Movie scripts, TV scripts, stage plays. Query with brief description of project, bio and SASE. Reports in 2-4 weeks on queries.
Recent Sales: *M Butterfly*, David Henry Hwang (Tony Award play for 1989).
Terms: Agent receives 10% commission on domestic sales; varies on foreign sales. Offers written contract (required).

Additional Script Agents

The following agencies have full listings in other sections of this book. These agencies have indicated they are *primarily* interested in handling book manuscripts, but are also interested in scripts. After reading the listing (you can find the page number in the Listings Index), send a query to obtain more information on their needs and script submission policies.

Allan Agency, Lee
Amsterdam Agency, Marcia

Anthony Agency, Joseph
Appleseeds Management

Bernsen, Jamail & Goodson, L.L.P.

Brandt Agency, The Joan
Brinke Literary Agency, The
Brown Ltd., Curtis
Browne Ltd., Pema
Cook Agency, Bruce
de la Haba Agency Inc., The Lois
Diamond Literary Agency, Inc.
Farber Literary Agency Inc.
Feiler Literary Agency, Florence
Film And Fiction Agency, The
Fishbein Ltd., Frieda
ForthWrite Literary Agency
Fran Literary Agency
Garon-Brooke Assoc. Inc., Jay
Goldfarb & Associates, Ronald
Grimes Literary Agency, Lew
Gusay Literary Agency, The Charlotte
Heacock Literary Agency, Inc.
Jenks Agency, Carolyn
Jordan Literary Agency, Lawrence
Keyser Literary Agency
Klausner International Literary Agency, Inc.
Kroll Agency, Lucy
Law Offices of Robert L. Fenton PC
Lazear Agency Incorporated
Literary and Creative Artists Agency
Lyceum Creative Properties, Inc.
McBride Literary Agency, Margret
McKinley, Literary Agency, Virginia C.
Madsen Agency, Robert
Markson Literary Agency, Elaine
Marshall Agency, The Evan
Merhige-Merdon Marketing/Promo Co. Inc., Greg
Morris Agency, William
Neighbors Literary Agency, Charles
Nelson Literary Agency & Lecture Bureau, BK
New Writing Agency
Northeast Literary Agency
Northwest Literary Services
Oscard Agency, Inc., Fifi
Otitis Media
Popkin, Julie
Puddingtonstone Literary Agency
Rhodes Literary Agency
Roth Agency, The
Russell-Simenauer Literary Agency Inc.
Schulman, A Literary Agency, Susan
Southern Literary Agency
Stern Agency, Gloria
Sullivan Associates, Mark
Toomey Associates, Jeanne
Wald Associates, Inc., Mary Jack
Wallace Literary Agency, Inc.
Warren Literary Agency, James
Watt & Associates, Sandra
Wohl Literary Agency, Gary S.
Wright Authors' Representative, Stephen
Writer's Advocate, The
Writer's Consulting Group
Zelasky Literary Agency, Tom

Script Agents/'93-'94 changes

The following agency appeared in the last (1993) edition of *Guide to Literary Agents & Art/Photo Reps* but is absent from the 1994 edition. This agency failed to respond to our request for an update of their listing.

Peregrine Whittlesey Agency
(unable to contact)

Art/Photo Reps

Finding and Working with Art/Photo Reps

by Barbara Gordon

There seems to be a lack of information as well as a lot of misinformation on the function and role of artists' and photographers' representatives. Whether or not to get a rep is a major career decision, so it's important to understand first what a representative is, what they can and cannot do for you and how they work.

A good definition of a representative is one who is the marketing and selling arm of a talent. First of all, if comparisons are to be made, an artists' and photographers' representative is comparable to a literary agent or talent agent in some respects. A rep does not employ artists and photographers, but acts as their agent in obtaining assignments from advertisers, publishers, corporations and others.

The representative is responsible for packaging the product (art and photography) by getting the portfolio in selling condition. This involves editing of the portfolio as well as advising the talent on what needs to be added to fill in the missing gaps. The representative must then take the product to market. This is done through sales calls and advertising, promotion and public relations channels. To do this effectively a good representative must obviously have a thorough working knowledge of what clients are prospects for the talent's work as well as the knowledge of what advertising and promotion mediums will most effectively reach those clients at the most efficient cost.

On the practical side the representative negotiates the best prices and working conditions for the talent while keeping the talent competitive in the marketplace. The rep must have a knowledge of current market trends, prices and job situations and enough experience to talk knowledgeably about the product he/she is selling and pricing.

In addition to payment received for completing the assignment, the representative will negotiate expenses, usages, terms of payment, deadlines, royalties, licensing and other rights where applicable. The representative will check out the credit worthiness of the new client, do the billing, collecting of invoices, and collect and pay sales taxes when necessary. A representative will also develop publicity programs for the talent, handle agency shows and presentations, service current business, open new markets and expand existing markets.

On a personal level a rep should have the health, energy and flexibility to flow with the ups and downs of the freelancing business, as well as enough financing to stay in business during the down times. It goes without saying that a good representative should be honest,

Barbara Gordon *operates Barbara Gordon Associates in New York City, representing both illustrators and photographers. She is a past president of the Society of Photographers and Artists Representatives, has written for both art and photography publications, and co-authored (with her husband, Elliott)* How to Sell Your Photographs and Illustrations.

trustworthy, in tune with the talent and their aspirations and believe in the work of the talent.

Talents reps handle, talents they don't

Most representatives primarily handle commercial photographers and artists. A few handle designers, but since designers have a different buying audience than artists and photographers it is not as common. Designers usually have to search longer and harder for a representative.

Commercial reps do not handle fine artists (by fine artists I mean those who are looking for gallery affiliation). If a fine artist has a commercial style and is interested in doing commercial assignments however, a commercial representative may be interested in handling him. However, there are a few fine art representatives, and interested artists will find them in the Fine Art Reps section in this book.

Commercial reps also do not handle craftspeople, primarily because most commercial assignments involve the buying of flat art or photography. Occasionally there is a craftsperson who can make models or do something that applies to the commercial marketplace, but this is a rare situation and craftspeople looking for representation may be better served by a fine art rep or a crafts gallery. Reps, however, often handle photo-retouchers and hair and make-up people, simply because these skills are very compatible with a representative who is handling photographers.

Finding a representative

How does one go about finding a representative? One of the best places to start is to get the names and addresses of people in the field. This directory and the directories of professional organizations are probably the best sources with which to start. I also suggest that a prospective talent ask art directors and art buyers to give them recommendations, since these are the people that the client deals with and obviously you want a representative who clients feel has knowledge and integrity.

With your list in hand send either a promotion sheet or slides of your work to the representative in question, explaining that you are looking for representation. *Never* send original artwork. If you want something returned, send a self-addressed stamped envelope for that purpose. Always label your slides with your name and address just in case the slides become detached from your letter. Indicate "up" and "front" on your slides as well. Most reps ask for 10-15 slides. Plastic slide sleeves are available at most art and photography supply stores.

Since the representative is primarily interested in the saleability of your work and must *see* it, this is the best way to approach a prospective representative. Unless a representative specifically requests them, phone calls and résumés are not recommended for first contacting reps since it's the work they are concerned with.

If a representative expresses an interest in you and your work, your next step is to check out the rep. Ask questions. Find out about the talent they currently handle and what type of clients they work with.

Be sure you have a clear understanding of the rep's policies. You might ask a rep:
- Do you handle competitive talents? If yes, do you have a large enough client base to handle talents with similar work?
- Will you share promotion and advertising costs? What is the split?
- What advertising and promotion would you do for my work?

- How long have you been in business?
- How broad is your client base?

You might also want to speak with art directors and buyers in the field about the representative, especially if they deal with the rep on a regular basis:
- Does the rep seem to have heavy talent turnover?
- Does the rep have consistent follow-through or does he have an assistant handle the job after the sale is made?
- Is the rep fair, honest, thorough?

One final tip—trust your instincts. If everything checks out and you are getting "bad vibes" from the rep in question anyway, trust those instincts and move on. Conversely, if your instincts are telling you "this is the rep for me," go with those feelings too.

How does a representative work?

Ths most common arrangement, and the one most sought by talent, is the "exclusive" relationship. In this situation the representative will represent a talent "exclusively." That means the representative will not represent a competing talent. In return for this exclusive arrangement, the representative will get a percentage of the creative fee on all assignments, usually 25 percent on in-town situations and 30 percent for out-of-town.

Under the exclusive arrangement the talent covers all of his own expenses, including portfolio costs (shooting transparencies, prints, laminates, etc.) on the theory that the portfolio is the permanent possession of the talent no matter who represents him/her. The representative covers the cost of running an office, making sales calls, etc. On advertising and promotion costs, the talent and representative split them on the same basis as the commission with the representative paying 25-30 percent of the costs and the talent paying 70-75 percent of the costs.

Some other representative-talent relationships include representatives who work on a straight salary. This usually occurs with a very large photography or design studio or television production house. Brokering is another situation. A representative represents a large group of competing talents and does not get a percentage on all of the assignments. Because the representative does not get a regular commission on all assignments, the rep will "broker" assignments, taking anywhere from 25-60 percent per assignment. In this case the representative usually does not pay for any part of the advertising and promotion costs involved.

When we talk about sharing expenses of advertising and promotion, what kinds of advertising and promotion are we referring to? The most common forms of advertising and promotion include: sending direct mail pieces to a specialized list of prospective clients; taking out advertising pages in one of the directories specifically for this purpose; arranging showings of the talent's work; and a variety of public relations efforts such as doing press releases on the talent's accomplishments.

All representatives have a "termination" clause in their contracts allowing them compensation after the talent and representative split. The reasoning behind this is that often it can take a representative years to establish a talent and the representative gets no compensation for this effort. The feeling is the rep is entitled to some part of the talent's compensation after termination based on earlier efforts. The termination compensation is very involved and can range from commissions on assignments for a period of six months or more after termination or sometimes a percentage of the last year's earnings.

As you can gather, the termination and other financial aspects of an agreement between an artist and representative are very complex and all that can be given here are some of the highlights of some of the arrangements. A talent seeking representation should do his own research and confer with several representatives before making a final determination.

Do you really need a representative?

This is a very personal question that needs a very personal, individual answer. However, let me counter with another question. With so many legal and medical books around, does one really need a lawyer or doctor? And the answer is that sometimes all you need is a legal form from a stationery store or a remedy from the health food store, and sometimes you need the real thing.

There are artists and photographers who want to totally control their careers and have the high energy level and determination to promote and sell themselves. They do an excellent job of it without any outside assistance. There are also artists and photographers who are too busy doing assignments to handle the selling and promoting of their works. They want and need representation. Some artists simply like the support and interaction they get from a representative in this isolated world of freelancing.

Practically speaking, there are not enough representatives for the people seeking representation so, initially, many artists and photographers may find they have no choice but to represent themselves. As a working representative myself, I feel it's very good experience for a talent to represent himself sometime in his career. It gives him some insight to his buying audience and some familiarity and appreciation of how a representative functions.

One last word of advice: If you can't get a representative at first, keep trying. Representatives' situations change, and while they may be "booked" up in the beginning of the year, as the months go on they may find they have different needs and will be more receptive to your work at a later time.

For more information on artists' and photographers' reps contact SPAR, the Society of Photographers and Artists Representatives, Suite 1166, 60 E. 42nd St., New York NY 10165. This is a nonprofit organization of photographers' and artists' reps who sponsor educational programs for members and provide members with mailing lists and other educational materials. The group publishes a directory of their members with the types and names of talent they represent.

Commercial Art and Photography Representatives

For a successful professional relationship with a commercial art or photography representative, you must be prepared to invest both time and money in your career. Having a rep does not mean you will spend less time or money marketing your work, but you will spend it differently. A rep will still require you to prepare promotional materials such as fliers and brochures, well-organized multiple portfolios and even national advertising in various sourcebooks--and these are expensive. In return, however, a representative can help you earn back this investment many times over. In fact, having someone else act as your business manager and sales staff can give you more time for creating your work.

A rep can be a good deal. The commission paid may be more than offset by income from additional work. But getting a rep is a serious career move. In addition to getting your portfolio and self-promotion pieces in shape, you must also be ready to approach your career as a business. Your professionalism will mean as much to a rep (and your clients) as your talent.

Taking yourself seriously

It's a rep's job to present a client's artwork to the right people and places so that it sells. An artist has the responsibility to assist her rep as much as possible in that effort. The most important way to help a rep is to have a professional attitude towards the business of your art.

For the most part a representative will require you to have a well-developed portfolio. Some have specific requirements for uniformity, but most just expect you to include your best work in a neat format. Before approaching a rep, take a good look at your portfolio. Is only your best work included? (Remember your portfolio is only as strong as your weakest piece or image.) Is your work mounted neatly on a page or are your slides labeled and secured in sleeves?

Since your rep may be sending out more than one portfolio at a time, you may need copies of many of your pieces (or slides). It's easy to see you will need to spend money—depending on the requirements, perhaps several hundred dollars—getting your portfolio ready. Once you have invested this money, however, your portfolio will be the key your rep uses to unlock many doors.

Most reps also require a direct mail piece or participation in a group package with other talents the rep handles. This, too, can be a big investment. You may be asked to take out your own ad in one of the creative directories, such as *American Showcase* or *The Creative Black Book*, but in return your work will be seen by hundreds of art directors. One nice bonus for taking out an ad—most of these books provide you with tearsheets of your page that can be used as direct mail pieces. Advertising costs usually are a shared expense, generally split on the same proportion as the commission. Most reps receive a 25-30 percent commission and will absorb an equal percentage of advertising costs.

You may be asked to share expenses also, but most reps absorb the usual office and marketing expenses. Though some reps now ask for a monthly fee to cover unusual expenses, this does not seem to be a trend.

Most important, you must develop a professional attitude. A representative's job is to find you more and better assignments. Yet more assignments mean more deadlines. In this business you must deliver, and on time. Art directors at magazines and ad agencies trust the rep to present to them only those talents willing and able to follow through on assignments.

Approaching art or photo reps

Start by approaching a rep with a brief query letter and a direct mail piece, if you have one. If you do not have a flier or brochure, send some other representation of your work, such as photocopies or (duplicate) slides along with a self-addressed, stamped envelope. Since this can be costly, check the rep's listing here and call to make sure the rep is open to queries at this time.

This should go without saying, but never send original work with a query. We hear too many horror stories about originals lost or damaged en route. Later (when showing your portfolio) you may be asked to send originals, but this is only after the rep has shown strong interest in your work.

When sending slides, be sure to label them. Your name and phone number (and/or address) should appear on each slide in case they are separated from your other material. Also label "up" and "front" and any other information that might prove helpful.

In your query letter be as brief as possible, but let the rep know a little about your background and career goals. Tell the rep about any established clients and what you have been doing for them. Although most reps prefer an exclusive arrangement, if you have another rep in a different part of the country, be sure to mention this too.

Help with your search

To help with your search for representation, we've included a Geographic Index on page 268, divided by state and province. There also is an Agents and Reps Index on page 270 to help you locate individual reps. Often you will read about a rep, but if that rep is an employee of a large agency, you may not be able to find his business number. We asked agencies to list representatives on their staffs. In the index we list the names in alphabetical order along with the name of their agency. Find the name of the person you would like to contact and then check the listing for that agency.

Some of the literary agencies and a few of the fine art reps are also interested in commercial illustrators or photographers. This is especially true of agents who deal with children's book publishers. If an agency's *primary* function is selling manuscripts for writers or the work of fine artists, but is also interested in handling some illustrators or photographers, it is listed in "Additional Commercial Art/Photo Reps." Finally, we've added an index on page 268 that lists agents and reps looking specifically for children's book illustration and author/illustrators.

In addition to the listings in this section, word-of-mouth and referrals are still an important way to find representation. You may also be able to meet a rep at a show or workshop. Artist and photographer organizations provide information on reps to members through newsletters and meetings. For other information on the business of art, see *Artist's Market*; for photographers' organizations and information on the business, see *Photographer's Market* (both by Writer's Digest Books).

For more information on working with art and photo reps, see Barbara Gordon's article, Finding and Working with Art/Photo Reps. See also Resources for a list of other books on the art and photography business.

The Society of Photographers and Artists Representatives (SPAR) is an organization for professional representatives. The group sponsors educational programs for members

Commercial Art and Photography Representatives 187

and publishes a directory of their membership (including the talent each represents). While some reputable reps do not belong to any organization, SPAR members are required to maintain certain standards and follow a code of ethics. They have also developed a standard rep/artist agreement. For more information on the group, write to SPAR, Suite 1166, 60 E. 42nd St., New York NY 10165.

About the listings

Many of the representatives listed in this section handle both illustration and photography. Some also handle graphic designers, story board artists, photographer's models and set people. Although most reps like to handle a variety of work, some specialize in fashion or other specific fields.

Many representatives do not charge for additional expenses beyond those incurred in preparing your portfolios or other advertising materials. A handful also charge monthly retainers to cover marketing expenses. Where possible, we've indicated these listings with a solid box (■) symbol.

We've ranked the agencies listed in this section according to their openness to submissions. Below is our ranking system:

I   Newer representative actively seeking clients.
II Representative seeking both new and established artists and photographers.
III Representative prefers to work with established artists and photographers, mostly through referrals.
IV Representative handling only certain types of work or work by artists and photographers under certain circumstances.
V   Representative not currently seeking new clients. We have included mention of agencies rated V only to let you know they are currently not open to new clients. In addition to those ranked V, we have included a few well-known agencies' names who have declined listings. *Unless you have a strong recommendation from someone well respected in the field, our advice is to approach only those agents ranked I-IV.*

‡ANNE ALBRECHT AND ASSOCIATES (V), #1609, 1749 N. Wells, Chicago IL 60614. Representative not currently seeking new talent.

‡■AMERICAN ARTISTS, REP. INC. (III), #1W, 353 W. 53rd St., New York NY 10019. (212)582-0023. Fax: (212)582-0090. Commercial illustration representative. Estab. 1930. Member of SPAR. Represents 30 illustrators. Markets include: advertising agencies; corporations/client direct; design firms; editorial/magazines; paper products/greeting cards; publishing/books; sales/promotion firms.
Handles: Illustration, design.
Terms: Rep receives 30% commission. "All portfolio billed to artist." Advertising costs are split: 70% paid by talent; 30% paid by representative. "Promotion is encouraged; portfolio must be presented in a professional manner—8×10, 4×5, tearsheets, etc." Advertises in *American Showcase, Creative Black Book, RSVP, The Workbook,* Medical and Graphic Artist Guild publications.
How to Contact: For first contact, send query letter, direct mail flier/brochure, tearsheets. Reports in 1 week if interested. After initial contact, drop off or mail in appropriate materials for review. Portfolio should include tearsheets, slides.
Tips: Obtains new talent through recommendations from others, solicitation, at conferences.

‡JERRY ANTON, INC. (III, V), Studio 203, 119 W. 23rd St., New York NY 10011. Representative not currently seeking new talent.

‡APRIL & WONG (III), Suite 1151, 41 Sutter St., San Francisco CA 94104. (415)668-4719. Contact: John Wong. Commercial illustration, commercial photography and graphic design representative. Estab. 1984. Member of Society of Illustrators, ASMP, Art Directors Club, Ad Club. Represents 10 illustrators, 3 photographers and 1 designer. Markets include: advertising agencies; corporations/client direct; design firms; editorial/magazines.
Handles: Illustration, photography, design.
Terms: Rep receives 25% commission. Exclusive area representation is required. Advertising costs are split: 50% paid by talent; 50% paid by representative. For promotional purposes, talent must provide tearsheets, mailers or overruns. Advertises in *American Showcase*, *Creative Black Book* and *The Big Book*.
How to Contact: For first contact, send query letter, résumé, tearsheets. Reports in 2 weeks if interested. Portfolio should include transparencies, mounted, double black museum board.
Tips: "Point out your strengths; no one does everything well, no one."

‡ARTIST DEVELOPMENT GROUP (II), 27 Circuit Dr., Edgewood RI 02905-3712. (401)785-2770. Fax: (401)785-2773. Contact: Rita Campbell. Estab. 1982. Member of Rhode Island Women's Advertising Club. Represents photography, fine art, graphic design, as well as performing talent to advertising agencies, corporate clients/direct. Markets include: advertising agencies; corporations/client direct. Staff includes Rita Campbell, Marvin Lerman.
Handles: Illustration, photography.
Terms: Rep receives 20-25% commission. Advertising costs are split: 50% paid by talent; 50% paid by representative. For promotional purposes, talent must provide direct mail promotional piece; samples in book for sales meetings.
How to Contact: For first contact, send résumé, bio, direct mail flier/brochure. Reports in 3 weeks. After initial contact, drop off or mail in appropriate materials for review. Portfolios should include tearsheets, photographs.
Tips: Obtains new talent through "referrals as well as inquiries from talent exposed to agency promo."

‡ARTISTS ASSOCIATES (II), 211 E. 51st St., New York NY 10022. (212)755-1365. Fax: (212)755-1987. Contact: Bill Erlacher. Commercial illustration representative. Estab. 1964. Member of Society of Illustrators, Graphic Artists Guild, AIGA. Represents 11 illustrators. Markets include: advertising agencies; corporations/client direct; design firms; editorial/magazines; paper products/greeting cards; publishing/books; sales/promotion firms.
Handles: Illustration, fine art, design.
Terms: Rep receives 25% commission. Advertises in *American Showcase*, *RSVP*, *The Workbook*, *Society of Illustrators Annual*.
How to Contact: For first contact, send direct mail flier/brochure.

ARTISTS INTERNATIONAL (III), 320 Bee Brook Rd., Washington CT 06777-1911. (203)868-1011. Fax: (203)868-1272. Contact: Michael Brodie. Commercial illustration representative. Estab. 1970. Represents 20 illustrators. Specializes in children's books. Markets include: advertising agencies; design firms; editorial/magazines; licensing.
Handles: Illustration only.
Terms: Rep receives 30% commission. No geographic restrictions. Advertising costs are split: 70% paid by talent; 30% paid by representative. For promotional purposes, talent must provide 2 portfolios. Advertises in *American Showcase*. "We also have our own full-color brochure, 24 pages."
How to Contact: For first contact, send slides, photocopies and SASE. Reports in 1 week. After initial contact, drop off or mail in appropriate materials for review. Portfolio should include slides, photostats.
Tips: Obtains new talent through recommendations from others, solicitation, at conferences, *Literary Market Place* etc. "SAE with example of your work; no résumés required."

---

‡ *The double dagger before a listing indicates the listing is new in this edition.*

Commercial Art and Photography Representatives 189

ASCIUTTO ART REPS., INC. (II, IV), 1712 E. Butler Circle, Chandler AZ 85225. (602)899-0600. Fax: (602)899-3636. Contact: Mary Anne Asciutto. Children's illustration representative. Estab. 1980. Member of SPAR, Society of Illustrators. Represents 20 illustrators. Specializes in children's illustration for books, magazines, posters, packaging, etc. Markets include: publishing/packaging/advertising.
Handles: Illustration only.
Recent Sales: *Black Beauty* (Hugh Lauter, Levin Associates); *At Your Fingertips* (series of 8 books) (McClanahan & Co.).
Terms: Rep receives 25% commission. No geographic restrictions. Advertising costs are split: 75% paid by talent; 25% paid by representative. For promotional purposes, talent should provide "prints (color) or originals within an 11 × 14 size format."
How to Contact: Send a direct mail flier/brochure, tearsheets, photocopies and SASE. Reports in 2 weeks. After initial contact, send in appropriate materials if requested. Portfolio should include original art on paper, tearsheets, photocopies or color prints of most recent work. If accepted, materials will remain for assembly.
Tips: In obtaining representation "be sure to connect with an agent that handles the kind of accounts you (the artist) *want*."

‡CAROL BANCROFT & FRIENDS (II, IV), P.O. Box 959, Ivy Hill Rd., Ridgefield CT 06877. (203)438-8386. Fax: (203)438-7615. Owner: Carol Bancroft. Promotion Manager: Chris Tuqeau. Illustration representative for children's publishing. Estab. 1972. Member of SPAR, Society of Illustrators, Graphic Artists Guild. Represents 25 illustrators. Specializes in illustration for children's publishing—text and trade; any children's-related material.
Handles: Illustration for children of all ages. Looking for multicultural artists and fine artists wishing to get into publishing.
Terms: Rep receives 25% commission. Advertising costs are split: 75% paid by talent; 25% paid by representative. For promotional purposes, talent must provide "flat copy (not slides), tearsheets, promo pieces, good color photocopies, etc. Ten pieces or more is best; narrative scenes and children interacting." Advertises in *RSVP*.
How to Contact: For initial contact, "call Chris for information or send samples and SASE." Reports in 1 month.
Tips: Obtains new talent through solicitation and recommendation.

‡SAL BARRACCA ASSOC. INC. (II), 381 Park Ave. S., New York NY 10016. (212)889-2400. Fax: (212)889-2698. Contact: Sal Barracca. Commercial illustration representative. Estab. 1988. Represents 23 illustrators. "90% of our assignments me book jackets." Markets include: advertising agencies; publishing/books.
Handles: Illustration.
Terms: Rep receives 25% commission. Exclusive area representation is required. Advertising costs are split: 75% paid by talent; 25% paid by representative. For promotional purposes "portfolios must be 8 × 10 chromes that are matted. We can shoot original art to that format at a cost to the artist. We produce our own promotion and mail out once a year to over 16,000 art directors."
How to Contact: For first contact, send direct mail flier/brochure, tearsheets and SASE. Reports in 1 week; 1 day if interested. After initial contact, drop off or mail in appropriate materials for review. Portfolio should include tearsheets, slides.
Tips: Obtains new talent from artists sending samples of their work. "Make sure you have at least 3 years of working on your own so that you don't have any false expectations from an agent."

‡CECI BARTELS ASSOCIATES (III), 3286 Ivanhoe, St. Louis MO 63139. (314)781-7377. Fax: (314)781-8017. Contact: Ceci Bartels. Commercial illustration and photography representative. Estab. 1980. Member of SPAR, Graphic Artists Guild, ASMP. Represents 20 illustrators and 3 photographers. "My staff functions in sales, marketing and bookkeeping. There are 7 of us. We concentrate on advertising agencies and sales promotion." Markets include advertising agencies; corporations/client direct; design firms; publishing/books; sales/promotion firms.
Handles: Illustration, photography. "Illustrators capable of action with a positive (often realistic) orientation interest us."
Terms: Rep receives 30% commission. Advertising costs are split: 70% paid by talent; 30% paid by representative "after sufficient billings have been achieved. Artists pay 100% initially. We need direct mail support and advertising to work on the national level. We welcome 6 portfolios/artist. Artist is advised not to produce multiple portfolios or promotional materials until brought on." Advertises in *American Showcase, Creative Black Book, RSVP, The Workbook, CIB*.

How to Contact: For first contact, send query letter, direct mail flier/brochure, tearsheets, slides, SASE, portfolio with SASE or promotional materials. Reports if SASE enclosed. After initial contact, drop off or mail in appropriate materials for review. Portfolio should include tearsheets, slides, photographs, 4×5 transparencies. Obtains new talent through recommendations from others; "I watch the annuals and publications."

BARBARA BEIDLER INC. (III), #506, 648 Broadway, New York NY 10012. (212)979-6996. Fax: (212)505-0537. Contact: Barbara Beidler. Commercial illustration and photography representative. Estab. 1986. Represents 1 illustrator, 4 photographers, 3 fashion stylists. Specializes in fashion, home furnishings, life style, portraits. Markets include: advertising agencies; catalog agencies; corporations/client direct; design firms; editorial/magazines; publishing/books; sales/promotion firms.
How to Contact: For first contact, send direct mail flier/brochure. After initial contact, write for appointment to show portfolio of tearsheets, slides.
Tips: Obtains new talent through recommendations from others.

BERENDSEN & ASSOCIATES, INC. (III), 2233 Kemper Lane, Cincinnati OH 45206. (513)861-1400. Fax: (513)861-6420. Contact: Bob Berendsen. Commercial illustration, photography, graphic design representative. Estab. 1986. Member of SPAR, Art Directors Club of Cincinnati AAF (Advertising Club of Cincinnati). Represents 24 illustrators, 4 photographers, 4 designers. Specializes in "high-visibility consumer accounts." Markets include: advertising agencies; corporations/client direct; design firms; editorial/magazines; paper products/greeting cards; publishing/books; sales/promotion firms.
Handles: Illustration, photography. "We are always looking for illustrators that can draw people, product and action well. Also, we look for styles that are unique."
Terms: Rep receives 25% commission. Charges "mostly for postage but figures not available." No geographic restrictions. Advertising costs are split: 75% paid by talent; 25% paid by representative. For promotional purposes, "artist must co-op in our direct mail promotions, and sourcebooks are recommended. Portfolios are updated regularly." Advertises in *RSVP*, *Creative Illustration Book*, *The Ohio Source Book* and *American Showcase*.
How to Contact: For first contact, send query letter, résumé, tearsheets, slides, photographs, photocopies and SASE. Reports in weeks. After initial contact, drop off or mail in appropriate materials for review. Portfolios should include tearsheets, slides, photographs, photostats, photocopies.
Tips: Obtains new talent "through recommendations from other professionals. Contact Bob Berendsen, president of Berendsen and Associates, Inc. for first meeting."

BERNSTEIN & ANDRIULLI INC. (III), 60 E. 42nd St., New York NY 10165. (212)682-1490. Fax: (212)286-1890. Contact: Sam Bernstein. Commercial illustration and photography representative. Estab. 1975. Member of SPAR. Represents 54 illustrators, 16 photographers. Staff includes Tony Andriulli; Howard Bernstein; Fran Rosenfeld; Judy Miller; Leslie Nusblatt; Molly Birenbaum; Craig Haberman; Natalie Ortiz, Helen Goon; Libby Edwards. Markets include: advertising agencies; corporations/client direct; design firms; editorial/magazines; paper products/greeting cards; publishing/books; sales/promotion firms.
Handles: Illustration and photography.
Terms: Rep receives a commission. Exclusive career representation is required. No geographic restrictions. Advertises in *American Showcase*, *Creative Black Book*, *The Workbook*, *New York Gold*, *Creative Illustration Book*.
How to Contact: For first contact, send query letter, direct mail flier/brochure, tearsheets, slides, photographs, photocopies. Reports in 1 week. After initial contact, drop off or mail in appropriate materials for review. Portfolio should include tearsheets, slides, photographs.

CAROLYN BRINDLE INC. (II,IV), 203 E. 89th St., New York NY 10128. (212)534-4177. Fax: (212)996-9003. Contact: Carolyn Brindle. Commercial illustration and fine art representative. Estab. 1974. Represents 5 illustrators, 1 fine artist. Specializes in fashion-oriented work. Markets include: advertising agencies; corporations/client direct; design firms; editorial/magazines; paper products/greeting cards; publishing/books; corporate and private collections; interior decorators; museums.

If you're looking for a particular rep, check the Agents and Reps Index to find at which agency the rep works. Then look up the listing for that agency in this section.

Commercial Art and Photography Representatives   191

Handles: Illustration. Looks for "unusual or new technique."
Terms: Rep receives 25% commission. Exclusive representation is required. No geographic restrictions. Advertising costs are split: 75% paid by talent; 25% paid by representative. For promotional purposes, "we require a well-organized portfolio. We create promotional pieces with the artist that we both feel represents their work." Advertises in *RSVP, Creative Illustration*.
How to Contact: For first contact, send query letter and direct mail flier/brochure, tearsheets, photocopies and SASE. Reports in 5 days-1 month, if interested. After initial contact, drop off or mail in appropriate materials for review. Portfolio should include original art, tearsheets, "examples of work that has not been published."
Tips: Usually obtains new talent through "recommendations from others in the fashion field, advertising agency art directors, magazine art directors, illustrators that are friends of artists already represented. If possible, before contacting a representative, look at the advertising annuals, e.g., *Creative Illustration* or *RSVP*, and see the kind of work the representative shows. See if your work would fit in with what you see. The promotional pages usually reflect the representative's way of thinking and taste."

SAM BRODY, ARTISTS & PHOTOGRAPHERS REPRESENTATIVE (III), 15 W. Terrace Rd., Great Neck NY 11021-1513. (212)758-0640; (516)482-2835. Fax: (212)697-4518. Contact: Sam Brody. Commercial illustration and photography representative and broker. Estab. 1948. Member of SPAR. Represents 4 illustrators, 3 photographers, 2 designers. Markets include: advertising agencies; corporations/client direct; design firms; editorial/magazines; publishing/books; sales/promotion firms.
Handles: Illustration, photography, design, "great film directors."
Terms: Rep receives 25-30% commission. Exclusive area representation is required. Advertising costs are split: 75% paid by talent; 25% paid by representative. For promotional purposes, talent must provide 8×10 transparencies (dupes only) with case, plus back-up advertising material, i.e., cards (reprints—*Black Book*, etc.) and self-promos. Advertises in *Creative Black Book*.
How to Contact: For first contact, send bio, direct mail flier/brochure, tearsheets. Reports in 3 days or within 1 day if interested. After initial contact, call for appointment or drop off or mail in appropriate materials for review. Portfolio should include tearsheets, slides, photographs.
Tips: Obtains new talent through recommendations from others, solicitation. In obtaining representation, artist/photographer should "talk to parties he has worked with in the past year."

BROOKE & COMPANY (II), 4323 Bluffview, Dallas TX 75209. (214)352-9192. Fax: (214)350-2101. Contact: Brooke Davis. Commercial illustration and photography representative. Estab. 1988. Represents 10 illustrators, 2 photographers. "Owner has 18 years experience in sales and marketing in the advertising and design fields."
Terms: No information provided.
How to Contact: For first contact, send bio, direct mail flier/brochure, "sample we can keep on file if possible" and SASE. Reports in 2 weeks. After initial contact, write for appointment to show portfolio or drop off or mail in portfolio of tearsheets, slides or photographs.
Tips: Obtains new talent through referral or by an interest in a specific style. "Only show your best work. Develop an individual style. Show the type of work that you enjoy doing and want to do more often. Must have a sample to leave with potential clients."

‡PEMA BROWNE LTD. (II), HCR Box 104B, Pine Rd., Neversink NY 12765. (914)985-2936. Fax: (914)985-7635. Contact: Pema Browne or Perry Browne. Commercial illustration representative. Estab. 1966. Represents 12 illustrators. Specializes in general commercial. Markets include: advertising agencies; editorial/magazines; all publishing areas; children's picture books.
Handles: Illustration. Looking for "professional and unique" talent.
Terms: Rep receives 30% commission. Exclusive area representation is required. For promotional purposes, talent must provide color mailers to distribute. Representative pays mailing costs on promotion mailings.
How to Contact: For first contact, send query letter, direct mail flier/brochure and SASE. Reports in 2 weeks if interested. After initial contact, drop off or mail in appropriate materials for review. Portfolios should include tearsheets and transparencies or good color photocopies.
Tips: Obtains new talent through recommendations. "Be familiar with the marketplace."

BRUCK AND MOSS ASSOCIATES (IV), 333 E. 49th St,. New York NY 10017. (212)980-8061 or (212)982-6533. Fax: (212)832-8778 or (212)674-0194. Contact: Eileen Moss or Nancy Bruck. Commercial illustration representative. Estab. 1978. Represents 12 illustrators. Markets include: advertising

agencies; corporations/client direct; design firms; editorial/magazines; publishing/books; sales/promotion firms; direct marketing.
Handles: Illustration.
Terms: Rep receives 30% commission. Exclusive area representation is required. No geographic restrictions. Advertising costs are split: 70% paid by talent; 30% paid by representative. For promotional purposes, talent must provide "4×5 transparencies mounted on 7×9 black board. Talent pays for promotional card for the first year and for trade ad." Advertises in *American Showcase and Workbook*.
How to Contact: For first contact, send tearsheets, "if sending slides, include an SASE." After initial contact, drop off or mail in appropriate materials for review. Portfolios should include tearsheets. If mailing portfolio include SASE or Federal Express form.
Tips: Obtains new talent through referrals by art directors and art buyers, mailings of promo card, source books, art shows, *American Illustration* and *Print Annual*. "Make sure you have had experience repping yourself. Don't approach a rep on the phone, they are too busy for this. Put them on a mailing list and mail samples. Don't approach a rep who is already repping someone with the same style."

‡**KATHY BRUML/ARTISTS REPRESENTATIVE (III),** 303 N. Monroe, Ridgewood NJ 07450. (201)444-4271. Commercial photography representative. Estab. 1981. Represents 3 photographers. Markets include: corporations/client direct; design firms; art publishers.
Handles: Photography, fine art.
Terms: Rep receives 25% commission.

■**TRICIA BURLINGHAM/ARTIST REPRESENTATION (III),** 2330 Broadway, Santa Monica CA 90404. (310)998-9176. Office Manager: Tiffany Bowne. Commercial photography representative. Estab. 1979. Member of APA. Represents 7 photographers. Markets include: advertising agencies; corporations/client direct; design firms; editorial/magazines.
Handles: Photography.
Terms: Rep receives 25-30% commission. Charges for Federal Express, messengers. Exclusive area representation is required. Advertising costs are paid by talent. For promotional purposes, "we require all artists to provide promotional material with a mailing piece (envelope/tube, etc.) We require at least 2 portfolios and a shipping case." Advertises in *The Workbook*.
How to Contact: For first contact, send direct mail flier/brochure. Reports in 3 weeks, only if interested. Portfolio should include tearsheets, slides, photographs, "all promotional material/direct mail pieces."
Tips: Obtains new talent through "recommendations from others and our solicitations and research. All promotional material sent in is viewed by Tricia Burlingham. Please send only nonreturnable items."

‡**MARILYN CADENBACH ASSOCIATES (II),** 149 Oakley Rd., Belmont MA 02178. (617)484-7437. Fax: (617)484-5305. Contact: Marilyn Cadenbach. Commercial photography representative. Estab. 1988. Represents 5 photographers. Markets include: advertising agencies; design firms; editorial/magazines.
Handles: Photography.
Terms: Discussed directly with photographer. Advertises in *Creative Black Book*, *The Workbook*, *Lurzer's International Archive*.
How to Contact: For first contact, send letter with samples of work—follow up with phone call.

‡**MARIANNE CAMPBELL (III),** Pier 9 Embarcadero, San Francisco CA 94111. (415)433-0353. Fax: (415)433-0351. Contact: Marianne Campbell. Commercial photography representative. Estab. 1990. Member of APA. Represents 3 photographers. Markets include: advertising agencies; corporations/client direct; design firms; editorial/magazines.
Handles: Illustration, photography.
Terms: Rep receives 25% commission. Charges a percentage for FedEx charges. Advertising costs are split: 75% paid by talent; 25% paid by representative. For promotional purposes, talent must provide direct mail pieces "in which we share cost. Portfolio must consistently be updated with new, fresh work."

■ *A solid box indicates reps who charge a fee for expenses or who charge special fees in addition to commission and advertising costs.*

How to Contact: For first contact, send direct mail flier/brochure, printed samples of work. Reports in 2 weeks, only if interested. Call for appointment to show portfolio of tearsheets, slides, photographs.
Tips: Obtains new talent through recommendations from others, outstanding promotional materials. "Be considerate of rep's time. Be persistent but not pushy."

STAN CARP, INC. (III, IV), 2166 Broadway, New York NY 10024. (212)362-4000. Contact: Stan Carp. Commercial photography representative and director. Estab. 1959. Member of SPAR. Represents 3 photographers. Markets include: advertising agencies; corporations/client direct; design firms; editorial/magazines; paper products/greeting cards; publishing/books; sales/promotion firms.
Handles: Photography and "commercial directors."
Terms: Rep receives 25% commission. Exclusive area representation is required. No geographic restrictions. Advertising costs are split: 75% paid by talent; 25% paid by representative. Advertises in *Creative Black Book, The Workbook*, and other publications.
How to Contact: For first contact, send photographs. Reporting time varies. After initial contact, call for appointment to show a portfolio of tearsheets, slides, photographs.
Tips: Obtains new talent through recommendations from others.

‡CHIP CATON ARTIST REPRESENTATIVE (III), 15 Warrenton Ave., Hartford CT 06105. (203)523-4562. Fax: (203)231-9313. Contact: Chip Caton. Commercial illustration, commercial photography representative. Estab. 1986. Member of SPAR, Graphic Artists Guild. Represents 24 illustrators and 5 photographers. Markets include: advertising agencies; corporations/client direct; design firms; editorial/magazines; sales/promotion firms.
Handles: Illustration, photography.
Terms: Rep receives 25% commission. Exclusive area representation is required. Advertising costs are split: 75% paid by talent; 25% paid by representative. For promotional purposes, talent must provide portfolio case and appropriate representation of work. Advertises in *American Showcase, The Workbook, California Image*.
How to Contact: For first contact, send query letter, tearsheets, slides, photographs, photocopies and SASE. Reports in 2 weeks if interested. After initial contact, call for appointment.
Tips: Obtains new talent through referrals from clients, artist's queries.

CAROL CHISLOVSKY DESIGN INC. (II), 853 Broadway, New York NY 10003. (212)677-9100. Fax: (212)353-0954. Contact: Carol Chislovsky. Commercial illustration representative. Estab. 1975. Member of SPAR. Represents 20 illustrators. Markets include: advertising agencies; design firms; editorial/magazines; publishing/books.
Handles: Illustration.
Terms: Rep receives 30% commission. Advertising costs are split: 70% paid by talent; 30% paid by representative. For promotional purposes, talent must provide direct mail piece. Advertises in *American Showcase, Creative Black Book* and sends out a direct mail piece.
How to Contact: For first contact, send direct mail flier/brochure. Portfolio should include tearsheets, slides, photostats.
Tips: Obtains new talent through solicitation.

WOODY COLEMAN PRESENTS INC. (II), 490 Rockside Rd., Cleveland OH 44131. (216)661-4222. Fax: (216)661-2879. Contact: Woody. Creative services representative. Estab. 1978. Member of Graphic Artists Guild. Represents illustration, photography, models and talent. Markets include: advertising agencies; corporations/client direct; design firms; editorial/magazines; paper products/ greeting cards; publishing/books; sales/promotion firms; public relations firms.
Handles: Illustration, photography, models and talent through a full-color, modem-accessible database open 24 hours every day.
Terms: Rep receives 25% commission. Advertising costs are split: 75% paid by talent; 25% paid by representative. For promotional purposes, talent must provide "all portfolios in 4×5" transparencies." Advertises in *American Showcase, Creative Black Book, The Workbook*, other publications.
How to Contact: For first contact, send query letter, tearsheets, slides, SASE. Reports in 1 week, only if interested. Portfolio should include tearsheets, 4×5 transparencies.
Tips: "Solicitations are made directly to our agency. Concentrate on developing 8-10 specific examples of a single style exhibiting work aimed at a particular specialty, such as fantasy, realism, Americana or a particular industry such as food, medical, architecture, transportation, film, etc." Specializes in "quality service based on being the 'world's best listeners.' We know the business, ask good questions and simplify an often confusing process. We are truly representative of a 'service' industry."

JAN COLLIER REPRESENTS (III), P.O. Box 470818, San Francisco CA 94147. (415)552-4252. Contact: Jan. Commercial illustration representative. Estab. 1978. Represents 12 illustrators. Markets include: advertising agencies; design firms.
Handles: Illustration, photography.
Terms: Rep receives 25% commission. Exclusive area representation is required. Advertising costs are split: 75% paid by talent; 25% paid by representative. Advertises in *American Showcase*, *Creative Black Book*, *The Workbook*, *The Creative Illustration Book*.
How to Contact: For first contact, send tearsheets, slides and SASE. Reports in 5 days, only if interested. After initial contact, call for appointment to show portfolio of slides.

DANIELE COLLIGNON (II), 200 W. 15th St., New York NY 10011. (212)243-4209. Contact: Daniele Collignon. Commercial illustration representative. Estab. 1981. Member of SPAR, Graphic Artists Guild, Art Director's Club. Represents 12 illustrators. Markets include: advertising agencies; corporations/client direct; design firms; editorial/magazines; publishing/books.
Handles: Illustration.
Terms: Rep receives 30% commission. Exclusive area representation is required. No geographic restrictions. Advertising costs are split: 75% paid by talent; 25% paid by representative. For promotional purposes, talent must provide 8 × 10 transparencies (for portfolio) to be mounted, printed samples, professional pieces. Advertises in *American Showcase*, *Creative Black Book*, *The Workbook*.
How to Contact: For first contact, send direct mail flier/brochure, tearsheets. Reports in 3-5 days, only if interested. After initial contact, drop off or mail in appropriate materials for review. Portfolio should include tearsheets, transparencies.

CONRAD REPRESENTS . . . (II), (formerly James Conrad & Associates), #5, 2149 Lyon St., San Francisco CA 94185. (415)921-7140. Contact: James Conrad. Commercial illustration and photography representative. Estab. 1984. Member of SPAR, Society of Illustrators, Graphic Artists Guild. Represents 25 illustrators, 6 photographers. Markets include: advertising agencies; corporate art departments; graphic designers and publishers of books; magazines, posters; calendars and greeting cards.
Handles: Illustration, photography.
Terms: Rep receives 25% commission. Exclusive regional or national representation is required. No geographic restrictions. For promotional purposes, talent must provide a portfolio "and participate in promotional programs."
How to Contact: For first contact, send samples. Follow up with phone call.

‡**CORNELL + MCCARTHY (II, IV)**, 2-D Cross Hwy., Westport CT 06880. (203)454-4210. Fax: (203)454-4258. Contact; Merial Cornell. Children's book illustration representative. Estab. 1989. Member of SCBWI. Represents 30 illustrators. Specializes in children's books
Handles: Illustration. Looking for children's book illustrators.
Terms: Rep receives 25% commission. Advertising costs are split: 75% paid by talent; 25% paid by representative. For promotional purposes, talent must provide 10-12 strong portfolio pieces relating to children's publishing.
How to Contact: For first contact, send query letter, direct mail flier/brochure, tearsheets, photocopies and SASE. Reports in 1 month. After initial contact, call for appointment or drop off or mail in appropriate materials for review. Portfolio should include original art, tearsheets, photocopies.
Tips: Obtains new talent through recommendations, solicitation, at conferences. "Work hard on your portfolio."

CREATIVE ARTS OF VENTURA (V), P.O. Box 684, Ventura CA 93002. Representative not currently seeking new talent.

‡**CREATIVE FREELANCERS MANAGEMENT, INC. (II, III)**, 25 W. 45th St., New York NY 10036. (212)398-9540. Fax: (212)398-9547. Contact: Marilyn Howard. Commercial illustration representative. Estab. 1988. Represents 30 illustrators. "Our staff members have art direction, art buying or illustration backgrounds." Specializes in children's book, advertising, architectural, conceptual. Markets include: advertising agencies; corporations/client direct; design firms; editorial/magazines; paper products/greeting cards; publishing/books; sales/promotion firms.

Handles: Illustration. Artists must have published work.
Terms: Rep receives 30% commission. Exclusive area representation is preferred. Advertising costs are split: 70% paid by talent; 30% paid by representative. For promotional purposes, talent must provide "printed pages to leave with clients. Co-op advertising with our firm could also provide this. Transparency portfolio preferred if we take you on but we are flexible." Advertises in *American Showcase, Creative Black Book*.
How to Contact: For first contact, send tearsheets or "whatever best shows work. We also have a portfolio drop off policy on Wednesdays." Reports only if interested. After initial contact, drop off or mail in appropriate materials for review. Portfolios should include tearsheets, slides, photographs, photostats, photocopies.
Tips: Obtains new talent through "word of mouth and from our advertising."

CREATIVE PRODUCTIONS, INC. (III), 12703 Crystal, Grandview MO 64030. (816)761-7314. Contact: Linda Pool. Commercial photography representative. Estab. 1982. Represents 2 illustrators, 4 photographers. Markets include: advertising agencies; corporations/client direct; design firms.
Handles: Photography.
Terms: Rep receives 30% commission. Advertising costs are negotiable. For promotional purposes, talent must provide transparencies. "I complete promo pieces, but we share the cost." Advertises in *American Showcase, The Workbook*.
How to Contact: For first contact, send "sample of his/her favorite piece, what he enjoyed completing." Reports in 2 weeks, only if interested. After initial contact, call for appointment to show portfolio.

‡CVB CREATIVE RESOURCE, (II), 1856 Elba Circle, Costa Mesa CA 92626. (714)641-9700. Fax: (714)641-9700. Contact: Cindy Brenneman. Commercial illustration, photography and graphic design representative. Estab. 1984. Member of SPAR, ADDOC. Specializes in "high-quality innovative images." Markets include: advertising agencies; corporations/client direct; design firms.
Handles: Illustration. Looking for "a particular style or specialized medium."
Terms: Rep receives 30% commission. Exclusive area representation is required. Advertising costs are split: 70% paid by talent; 30% paid by representative, "if reps name and number appear on piece." For promotional purposes, talent must provide promotional pieces on a fairly consistent basis. Portfolio should be laminated. Include transparencies or cibachromes. Images to be shown are mutually agreed upon by talent. Advertises in *The Workbook*.
How to Contact: For first contact, send slides or photographs. Reports in 2 weeks, only if interested. After initial contact, call for appointment to show portfolio of tearsheets, slides, photographs, photostats.
Tips: Obtains new talent through referrals. "You usually know if you have a need as soon as you see the work. Be professional. Treat looking for a rep as you would looking for a freelance job. Get as much exposure as you can. Join peer clubs and network. Always ask for referrals. Interview several before settling on one. Personality and how you interact will have a big impact on the final decision."

LINDA DE MORETA REPRESENTS (II), 1839 Ninth St., Alameda CA 94501. (510)769-1421. Fax: (510)521-1674. Contact: Linda de Moreta. Commercial illustration and photography representative; also portfolio and career consultant. Estab. 1988. Represents 4 illustrators, 4 photographers. Markets include: advertising agencies; corporations/client direct; design firms; editorial/magazines; paper products/greeting cards; publishing/books; sales/promotion firms.
Handles: Illustration, photography.
Terms: Rep receives 25% commission. Exclusive representation requirements vary. Advertising costs are split: 75% paid by talent; 25% paid by representative. Materials for promotional purposes vary with each artist. Advertises in *The Workbook, The Creative Black Book, Bay Area Creative Sourcebook*.
How to Contact: For first contact, send direct mail flier/brochure, tearsheets, slides, photocopies, photostats and SASE. "Please do *not* send original art. SASE for any items you wish returned." Responds to any inquiry in which there is an interest. Portfolios are individually developed for each artist and may include tearsheets, photostats, transparencies.
Tips: Obtains new talent through client and artist referrals, primarily, some solicitation. "I look for a personal vision and style of illustration or photography combined with professionalism, maturity and a willingness to work hard."

‡SHARON DODGE AND ASSOCIATES (II), #202, 1201 First Ave. S., Seattle WA 98132. (206)622-7035. Fax: (206)622-7041. Contact: Kathy. Commercial illustration and photography representative. Estab. 1985. Member of Graphic Artists Guild. Represents 16 illustrators, 4 photographers. Special-

izes in advertising primarily, with some publishing work. Markets include: advertising agencies; corporations/client direct; design forms; editorial/magazines; publishing/books.
Handles: Illustration, computer illustration. "Interested in artists on the edge of the above technology."
Terms: Rep receives 25-30% commission. Exclusive area representation is required. For promotional purposes, talent must provide 11×14 transparencies "or flat art mounted in cases furnished by us." Advertises in *American Showcase*, *Creative Black Book*, *The Workbook* and *Archive*.
How to Contact: For first contact, send tearsheets. Reports in 1 month, only if interested.
Tips: Obtains new talent through recommendations from others, solicitation, at conferences. "Make direct phone contact after sending materials."

DODGE CREATIVE SERVICES INC. (III), 301 N. Water St., Milwaukee WI 53202. (414)271-3388. Fax: (414)347-0493. Contact: Tim Dodge. Commercial illustration, photography and graphic design. Estab. 1982. Represents 15 illustrators, 2 photographers, 6 designers. Specializes in "representation to the Midwest corporate and advertising agency marketplace." Markets include: advertising agencies; corporations/client direct; design firms; sales/promotion firms.
Handles: Illustration, photography, design. Looking for "absolutely outstanding and unique work only."
Terms: Rep receives 30% commission. Exclusive area representation is required. Advertising costs are split: 70% paid by talent; 30% paid by representative. For promotional purposes, talent must provide "portfolios provided as slides/transparencies (at least 3 complete sets)."
How to Contact: For first contact, send query letter, tearsheets, slides. Reports in 2 weeks. After initial contact, write for appointment to show portfolio of thumbnails, tearsheets, slides.
Tips: Obtains new talent generally through recommendations and direct inquiries. "Make the presentation meticulous, keep the work focused. Show a desire to build a business and make a commitment."

‡KAREN DONALDSON REPRESENTS (I, II), 954 W. Washington, Chicago IL 60607. (312)733-5657. Fax: (312)733-7691. Commercial photography representative. Estab. 1992. Member of CAR (Chicago Artist Representatives). Markets include: advertising agencies; corporations/client direct; design firms.
Handles: Illustration, photography. "Looking for unique illustrators. Style doesn't matter."
Terms: Rep receives 25% commission. Advertising costs are split: 80% paid by talent; 20% paid by representative. For promotional purposes, talent must provide "3-5 portfolios at least. In one national book as well." Advertises in *Creative Black Book*.
How to Contact: For first contact, send query letter, tearsheets. Reports in 2 weeks. After initial contact, call for appointment to show portfolio of thumbnails, roughs, original art, tearsheets.
Tips: Obtains new talent through "recommendations or just work that I see that I'm interested in. If you are in a national book ask your rep if they know of any reps currently looking to add talent. Often they deal with reps and know who's interested etc."

‡DW REPRESENTS (IV), Suite 1161, 870 Market St., San Francisco CA 94102. (415)989-2023. Fax: (415)989-6265. Contact: David Wiley. Commercial illustration and photography representative. Estab. 1984. Member of AIP (Artists in Print). Represents 6 illustrators, 1 photographer. Specializes in "reliability!"
Terms: No information provided.
How to Contact: For first contact, send direct mail flier/brochure, tearsheets, slides, photographs, and SASE ("very important"), "whatever communicates what they enjoy doing!" Reports in 3 days. After initial contact, call for appointment or drop off or mail in appropriate materials. Portfolio should include, roughs, original art, tearsheets.

The needs of art and photography reps are constantly changing! If you are using this book and it is 1995 or later, buy the newest edition of Guide to Literary Agents and Art/Photo Reps *at your favorite book or art supply store or order directly from Writer's Digest Books.*

Tips: Obtains new clients through creative directory listings and referrals. "Write down you goals and state points to achieve. Present portfolios filled with direct relationships to one's business. In selling yourself to art reps or clients who buy art, talk so they can be inspired, included and heard."

‡DWYER & O'GRADY, INC. (IV), P.O. Box 239, Mountain Rd., East Lempster NH 03605. (603)863-9347. Fax: (603)863-9346. Contact: Elizabeth O'Grady. Agents for children's picture book artists and writers. Estab. 1990. Member of Society of Illustrators, Graphic Artists Guild, SCBWI, ABA. Represents 20 illustrators and 12 writers. Staff includes Elizabeth O'Grady, Jeffrey Dwyer. Specializes in children's picture books and occasionally young adult novels. Markets include: publishing/books.
Handles: Illustrators and writers of children's books. "Favor realistic and representational work for the older age picture book. Artist must have full command of the figure and facial expressions."
Terms: Rep receives 15% commission. Additional fees are negotiable. Exclusive area representation is required (world rights). Advertising costs are paid by representative. For promotional purposes, talent must provide both color slides and prints of at least 20 sample illustrations depicting the figure with facial expression.
How to Contact: When making first contact, send query letter, slides, photographs and SASE. Reports in 1½ month. After initial contact, call for appointment and drop off or mail in appropriate materials for review. Portfolio should include slides, photographs.
Tips: Obtains new talent through "referrals from people we trust and personal search."

‡STEVEN EDSEY & SONS, (III), 520 N. Michigan, Chicago IL 60611. (312)527-0351. Fax: (312)527-5468. Contact: Steve Edsey. Commercial illustration and photography representative. Estab. 1985. Represents 30 illustrators, 3 photographers and 2 designers. "We have 6 reps in Chicago." Specializes in illustration. Markets include: advertising agencies; corporations/client direct; design firms; paper products/greeting cards; publishing/books; sales/promotion firms.
Handles: Illustration.
Terms: Rep receives 70% commission. Exclusive area representation is required. Advertising costs are split: 70% paid by talent; 30% paid by representative. Advertises in *Sourcebook*.
How to Contact: For first contact, send query letter, tearsheets. "Follows up with a call." After initial contact, call for appointment to show portfolio of original art.
Tips: Obtains new talent through recommendations from others. "They find us. Have a great book! Be on time!"

‡ELLIOTT/OREMAN ARTISTS' REPRESENTATIVES, (I, III), 265 Westminster Rd., Rochester NY 14607. (716)244-6956. Fax: (716)244-0307. Contact: Shannon Elliott. Commercial illustration, photography and animation representative. Estab. 1983. Represents 10 illustrators, 1 photographer and 1 animator. Markets include: advertising agencies; corporations/client direct; design firms; editorial magazines; paper products/greeting cards; publishing/books; architectural firms.
Handles: Illustration. Looking for artists specializing in computer illustration, architectural illustration, comps.
Terms: Advertising costs are split: 75% paid by talent; 25% paid by representative. For promotional purposes, talent must have a tearsheet, which will be combined with others in a sample folder. Printed samples are mounted and laminated for portfolio. Advertises in *American Showcase, Creative Black Book*.
How to Contact: For first contact, send query letter, tearsheets, slides, "whatever they have." Reports in 1 month. After initial contact, drop off or mail in appropriate materials for review. "I will call to schedule an appointment, if interested." Portfolio should include photocopies, printed samples.
Tips: Obtains new talent through recommendations from others, solicitation.

‡RHONI EPSTEIN/PHOTOGRAPHER'S REPRESENTATIVE (III), 3814 Franklin Ave., Los Angeles CA 90027. (213)663-2388. Fax: (213)662-0035. Contact: Rhoni Epstein. Commercial photography representative. Estab. 1983. Member of APA. Represents 8 photographers. Staff includes Frolic Taylor (marketing); Annie Consoletfi (design/advertising). Specializes in advertising/entertainment photography. Markets include advertising agencies; music industry.
Handles: Photography.
Terms: Rep receives 30% commission. Fees negotiable with individual artist. Exclusive representation required. No geographic restrictions. Advertising costs are paid by talent. For promotional purposes, talent must have a spread in a national book, portfolio to meet requirements of photographer. Advertises in *The Workbook*.

How to Contact: For first contact, send direct mail flier/brochure. Reports in 1 week, only if interested. After initial contact, call for appointment or drop off or mail in appropriate materials for review. Portfolio should demonstrate own personal style.
Tips: Obtains new talent through recommendations. "Research the rep and her agency the way you would research an agency before soliciting work!"

‡■RANDI FIAT & ASSOCIATES (II), 1727 S. Indiana, Chicago IL 60616. (312)464-0964. Fax: (312)464-0969. Contact: Randi Fiat. Commercial illustration and photography representative. Estab. 1980. Member of SPAR and CAR. Represents 4 illustrators and 6 photographers. "We represent talent with a strong fine art orientation in the commercial arena." Markets include: advertising agencies; corporations/client direct; design firms; editorial/magazines; paper products/greeting cards; publishing books; sales/promotion firms.
Handles: Illustration, photography.
Terms: Rep receives 25% commission. "We have a nominal 'per job' fee ($50) to cover incidentals." Tries to represent talent nationally. Advertising costs are split: 75% paid by talent; 25% paid by representative. "We work with talent to create portfolio and promotional look." Advertises in *American Showcase*, *Creative Black Book*, *The Workbook*, *AR 100*.
How to Contact: For first contact, send query letter, bio, tearsheets, photocopies and SASE. Reports in 1 week if interested. After initial contact, call for appointment.
Tips: Obtains new talent through recommendations from others. "Send the best work only."

PAT FORBES INC. (V), 11459 Waterview Cluster, Reston VA 22090-4315. Representative not currently seeking new talent.

(PAT) FOSTER ARTIST REP. (II), 22 E. 36th St., New York NY 10016. (212)685-4580. Fax: same. Contact: Pat Foster. Commercial illustration representative. Estab. 1981. Member of SPAR, Graphic Artists Guild. Represents 10 illustrators. Markets include: advertising agencies; corporations/client direct; sales/promotion firms.
Handles: Illustration.
Terms: Rep receives 25% commission. "No additional charge for my services, i.e., shooting, obtaining pix ref/costumes." No geographic restrictions. Advertises in *American Showcase*.
How to Contact: For first contact, send direct mail flier/brochure, tearsheets, slides, and SASE.
Tips: Obtains new talent through recommendations mostly from associates in the business. "Work must look fresh; good design sense incorporated into illustration."

FRANCISCO COMMUNICATIONS, INC. (II, III), 419 Cynwyd Rd., Bala Cynwyd PA 19004. (215)667-2378. Fax: (215)667-4308. Contact: Carol Francisco. Commercial illustration representative. Estab. 1983. Represents 7 illustrators. Markets include: advertising agencies; corporations/client direct.
Handles: Illustration.
Terms: Rep receives 25% commission. Advertising costs are split: 75% paid by talent; 25% paid by representative. For promotional purposes, talent must provide "promo samples, originals or same size copies of some samples."
How to Contact: For first contact, send query letter, direct mail flier/brochure, tearsheets. Reports in 2 weeks only if interested. After initial contact, call for appointment to show portfolio of tearsheets, photographs, photostats, photocopies.

‡FREELANCE HOTLINE, INC. (IV), Suite 405, 311 First Ave. N., Minneapolis MN 55401. (612)341-4411. Fax: (612)341-0229. Contact: Elisa Soper. Commercial illustration, graphic design, desktop and keyline artists representative. Estab. Chicago 1986, Minneapolis 1992. Member of AIGA. Specializes in desktop and keyline artists. Markets include: advertising agencies; corporations/client direct; design firms; sales/promotion firms.
Handles: Illustration, design, desktop publishing/graphic arts. Artists should have "2 years professional desktop and/or keylining experience (Mac, IBM platforms)."
Terms: Have set fee and pay rate. Independent contractor pays no fees. "All talent have their own portfolios, etc. Freelance Hotline also has a portfolio." Advertises in *Creative Black Book*, *Gold Book*, magazines, newspapers, MacChicago, Computer User, etc.
How to Contact: For first contact, send query letter, résumé, bio, direct mail flier/brochure (samples not necessary). Reports in 2 weeks (always contacted, qualified or not). After initial contact, Freelance Hotline calls to set up appointment to show portfolio of thumbnails, roughs, original art, tearsheets, slides, photographs, photostats, photocopies (variety of materials, concept to print).

Commercial Art and Photography Representatives 199

Tips: Obtains new talent through Yellow Pages, magazines, newspapers, conferences, seminars, Macshows, Gold/Black books, etc. "Call! (612)341-4411."

JEAN GARDNER & ASSOCIATES, Suite 108, 444 N. Larchmont Blvd., Los Angeles CA 90004. (213)464-2492. Fax: (213)465-7013. Contact: Jean Gardner. Commercial photography representative. Estab. 1985. Member of APA. Represents 6 photographers. Specializes in photography. Markets include: advertising agencies; design firms.
Handles: Photography.
Terms: Rep receives 25% commission. Exclusive representation is required. No geographic restrictions. Advertising costs are paid by the talent. For promotional purposes, talent must provide promos, *Workbook* advertising, a quality portfolio. Advertises in *The Workbook*.
How to Contact: For first contact, send direct mail flier/brochure.
Tips: Obtains new talent through recommendations from others.

†GIANNINI & TALENT (III, IV, V), 803 Malcolm Dr., Silver Spring MD 20901-3747. (301)439-0103. Fax: (301)439-0104. Contact: Judi Giannini. Commercial illustration and photography representative. Estab. 1987. Represents 1 illustrator, 6 photographers. Specializes in talent that works in fine art and commercial arenas, or "who have singular personal styles that stand out in the market place." Markets include: advertising agencies; corporations/client direct; design firms; editorial/magazines; publishing/books; art consultants. Clients include private collections.
Handles: Illustration, photography.
Terms: Rep receives 25% commission. Charges for out-of-town travel, messenger and FedEx services, newsletter. Exclusive East Coast and Southern representation is required. Advertising costs are paid by talent. For promotional purposes, talent must provide leave-behinds and "at least have a direct mail campaign planned, as well as advertising in local and national sourcebooks. Portfolio must be professional." Advertises in *American Showcase*, *Creative Black Book*, *The Workbook* and *Creative Sourcebook*.
How to Contact: For first contact, talent should send query letter, direct mail flier/brochure. Reports in 1 week, only if interested. Call for appointment to show portfolio of slides, photographs.
Tips: Obtains new talent through recommendations from others. "Learn to be your own best rep while you are getting established. Then consider forming a co-op with other artists of non-competitive styles who can pay someone for six months to help them get started. Candidates for good reps have an art and sales background."

STEPHEN GILL (II), #904, 37 E. 28th St., New York NY 10016. (212)889-2365. Fax: (212)889-1946. Contact: Stephen Gill or Anne Gill. Commercial illustration, commercial photography and fine art representative. Estab. 1975. Represents 2 illustrators, 1 photographer and 5 fine artists. Specializes in conceptual. Markets include: corporations/client direct; art publishers; private collections.
Handles: Illustration, photography, fine art, fashion.
Terms: Rep receives 50% commission. No geographic restrictions. "All artists pay for their own promotional materials. A direct mail piece is helpful but not necessary." Advertises in Yellow Pages.
How to Contact: For first contact, send résumé, direct mail flier/brochure, slides and SASE. All materials needed to be returned must be accompanied by SASE. Reports in 1 month. After initial contact, drop off or mail in appropriate materials with SASE. Portfolio should include slides with SASE.
Tips: Obtains new clients through recommendations and direct mail. "At this time we need 3-5 fashion illustrators."

MICHAEL GINSBURG & ASSOCIATES, INC. (II, III), Suite 24E, 240 E. 27th St., New York NY 10016. (212)679-8881. Fax: (212)679-2053. Contact: Michael Ginsburg. Commercial photography representative. Estab. 1978. Represents 5 photographers. Specializes in advertising and editorial photographers. Markets include advertising agencies, corporations/client direct, design firms, editorial/magazines, sales/promotion firms.

A IV ranking indicates reps who specialize in a particular type of illustration or photography such as fashion illustration or food photography.

Handles: Photography.
Terms: Rep receives 25% commission. Charges for messenger costs, Federal Express charges. Exclusive area representation is required. Advertising costs are split: 75% paid by talent; 25% paid by representative. For promotional purposes, talent must provide a minimum of 5 portfolios—direct mail pieces 2 times per year—and at least 1 sourcebook per year. Advertises in *Creative Black Book* and other publications.
How to Contact: For first contact, send query letter, direct mail flier/brochure. Reports in 2 weeks, only if interested. After initial contact, call for appointment to show portfolio of tearsheets, slides, photographs.
Tips: Obtains new talent through personal referrals and solicitation.

‡**DENNIS GODFREY REPRESENTING ARTISTS (III)**, Suite 6E, 231 W. 25th St., New York NY 10001. Phone and fax: (212)807-0840. Contact: Dennis Godfrey. Commercial illustration representative. Estab. 1985. Represents 6 illustrators. Specializes in publishing. Markets include: advertising agencies; corporations/client direct; design firms; publishing/books.
Handles: Illustration.
Terms: Rep receives 25% commission. Prefers exclusive area representation in NYC/Eastern US. Advertising costs are split: 75% paid by talent; 25% paid by representative. For promotional purposes, talent must provide mounted portfolio (at least 20 pieces), as well as promotional pieces. Advertises in *The Workbook*.
How to Contact: For first contact, send tearsheets. Reports in 2 weeks, only if interested. After initial contact, write for appointment to show portfolio of tearsheets, slides, photographs, photostats.
Tips: Obtains new talent through recommendations from others, occasionally by solicitation.

‡**DAVID GOLDMAN AGENCY (II)**, #918, 41 Union Square W., New York NY 10003. (212)807-6627. Contact: David Goldman. Commercial illustration representative. Estab. 1980. Staff includes Norm Bendell, Keith Bendis, Mitch Rigie (humorous illustration); Michelle Barnes, Kazushige Nitta, Steve Dininno, James Yang (conceptual art); Mazemaster David Anson Russo (author/mazes, alphabet lettering), Rose Fox (decorative). Specializes in "finding unique, highly stylized talents for exclusive North American representation, emphasizing licensing markets." Markets include: advertising agencies; corporations/clients direct; design firms; editorial/magazines; paper products/greeting cards; publishing/books; sales/promotion firms; apparel; puzzles; mugs; CD-ROMs; TV production companies.
Handles: Illustration. Looking for "unique conceptual illustrators not working on computers who are serious about building a long-term career in illustration."
Terms: Rep receives 25% commission. Exclusive area representation is required in North America. "I look for a wonderful person behind the art, and a dedicated hard working team player. I must like the person, the rest will always follow..." Advertises in *American Showcase*, *Corporate Showcase*, *Eurolink*.
How to Contact: "I prefer to meet illustrator personally when in New York. We do not answer queries." After initial contact, call for appointment to show portfolio of best representation of illustrator's body of work.
Tips: Obtains new talent through "recommendations, magazines (where I'll like a style and locate the illustrator) and appointments in our office. I look for a great person behind the work, someone art directors and designers will enjoy communicating with."

‡**GWEN WALTERS GOLDSTEIN (II)**, 50 Fuller Brook Rd., Wellesley MA 02181. (617)235-8658. Commercial illustration representative. Estab. 1976. Member of Graphic Artists Guild. Represents 17 illustrators. "I lean more toward book publishing." Markets include: advertising agencies; corporations/client direct; editorial/magazines; paper products/greeting cards; publishing/books; sales/promotion firms.
Handles: Illustration.
Terms: Rep receives 30% commission. Charges for color photocopies. Advertising costs are split: 70% paid by talent; 25% paid by representative. For promotional purposes, talent must provide direct mail pieces. Advertises in *American Showcase* (sometimes), *Creative Black Book*, *RSVP*.
How to Contact: For first contact, send résumé, bio, direct mail flier/brochure. After initial contact, representative will call. Portfolio should include "as much as possible."
Tips: Obtains new talent "from all directions."

Commercial Art and Photography Representatives 201

‡TOM GOODMAN INC. (II), 626 Loves Lane, Wynnewood PA 19096. (215)649-1514. Fax: (215)649-1630. Contact: Tom Goodman. Commercial photography and electronic/computer imaging and illustration representative. Estab. 1986. Represents 5 photographers. Specializes in commercial photography, electronic imaging. Markets include: advertising agencies; corporations/client direct; design firms; editorial/magazines; sales/promotion firms.
Handles: Photography, electronic imaging.
Terms: Rep receives 25% commission. Exclusive area representation is required. Advertising costs are split: 80% paid by talent; 20% paid by representative. For promotional purposes, representative requires portfolio of transparencies and printed samples. Requires direct mail campaigns. Optional: sourcebooks. Advertises in *American Showcase.*
How to Contact: For first contact, send query letter, direct mail flier/brochure. Reports in 2 weeks if interested. After initial contact, call for appointment to show portfolio of tearsheets, large transparencies.

BARBARA GORDON ASSOCIATES LTD. (II), 165 E. 32nd St., New York NY 10016. (212)686-3514. Contact: Barbara Gordon. Commercial illustration and photography representative. Estab. 1969. Member of SPAR, Society of Illustrators, Graphic Artists Guild. Represents 9 illustrators, 1 photographer. "I represent only a small select group of people and therefore give a great deal of personal time and attention to the people I represent."
Terms: No information provided. No geographic restrictions in continental US.
How to Contact: For first contact, send direct mail flier/brochure. Reports in 2 weeks. After initial contact, drop off or mail in appropriate materials for review. Portfolio should include tearsheets, slides, photographs; "if the talent wants materials or promotion piece returned, include SASE."
Tips: Obtains new talent through recommendations from others, solicitation, at conferences, etc. "I have obtained talent from all of the above. I do not care if an artist or photographer has been published or is experienced. I am essentially interested in people with a good, commercial style. Don't send résumés and don't call to give me a verbal description of your work. Send promotion pieces. *Never* send original art. If you want something back, include a SASE. Always label your slides in case they get separated from your cover letter. And always include a phone number where you can be reached."

T.J. GORDON/ARTIST REPRESENTATIVE (II), P.O. Box 4112, Montebello CA 90640. (213)887-8958. Contact: Tami Gordon. Commercial illustration, photography and graphic design representative; also illustration or photography broker. Estab. 1990. Member of SPAR. Represents 8 illustrators, 3 photographers. Markets include: advertising agencies; corporations/client direct; design firms; editorial/magazines.
Handles: Illustration, photography, design.
Terms: Rep receives 30% commission. Advertising costs are paid by talent (direct mail costs, billable at end of each month). Represents "illustrators from anywhere in US; designers and photographers normally LA only, unless photographer can deliver a product so unique that it is unavailable in LA." For promotional purposes, talent must provide "a minimum of 3 pieces to begin a 6-month trial period. These pieces will be used as mailers and leave behinds. Portfolio is to be professional and consistent (pieces of the same size, etc.) At the end of the trial period agreement will be made on production of future promotional pieces."
How to Contact: For first contact, send bio, direct mail flier/brochure. Reports in 2 weeks, if interested. After initial contact, call for appointment to show portfolio of tearsheets.
Tips: Obtains new talent "primarily through recommendations and as the result of artists' solicitations. Have an understanding of what it is you do, do not be afraid to specialize. If you do everything, then you will always conflict with the interests of the representatives' other artists. Find your strongest selling point, vocalize it and make sure that your promos and portfolio show that point."

‡ANITA GRIEN—REPRESENTING ARTISTS (V), 155 E. 38th St., New York NY 10016. Representative not currently seeking new talent.

CAROL GUENZI AGENTS, INC. (II), 1863 S. Pearl St., Denver CO 80210. (303)733-0128. Contact: Carol Guenzi. Commercial illustration, film and animation representative. Estab. 1984. Member of Denver Advertising Federation and Art Directors Club of Denver. Represents 23 illustrators, 3 photographers, 1 computer designer. Specializes in a "wide selection of talent in all areas of visual communications." Markets include: advertising agencies; corporations/client direct; design firms; editorial/magazine, paper products/greeting cards, sales/promotions firms.

Handles: Illustration, photography. Looking for "unique style application."
Terms: Rep receives 25% commission. Exclusive area representative is required. Advertising costs are split: 75% paid by talent; 25% paid by the representative. For promotional purposes, talent must provide "promotional material after 6 months, some restrictions on portfolios." Advertises in *American Showcase*, *Creative Black Book*, *The Workbook*, "periodically."
How to Contact: For first contact, send direct mail flier/brochure. Reports in 2-3 weeks, only if interested. Call or write for appointment to drop off or mail in appropriate materials for review, depending on artist's location. Portfolio should include tearsheets, slides, photographs.
Tips: Obtains new talent through solicitation, art directors' referrals, an active pursuit by individual. "Show your strongest style and have at least twelve samples of that style, before introducing all your capabilities. Be prepared to add additional work to your portfolio to help round out your style."

PAT HACKETT/ARTIST REPRESENTATIVE (III), Suite 502, 101 Yesler Way, Seattle WA 98104-2552. (206)447-1600. Fax: (206)447-0739. Contact: Pat Hackett. Commercial illustration and photography representative. Estab. 1979. Represents 25 illustrators, 2 photographers. Markets include: advertising agencies; corporations/client direct; design firms; editorial/magazines.
Handles: Illustration.
Terms: Rep receives 25-33% commission. Exclusive area representation is required. No geographic restrictions, but sells mostly in Washington, Oregon, Idaho, Montana, Alaska and Hawaii. Advertising costs are split: 75% paid by talent; 25% paid by representative. For promotional purposes, talent must provide "standardized portfolio, i.e., all pieces within the book are the same format. Reprints are nice, but not absolutely required." Advertises in *American Showcase*, *Creative Black Book*, *The Workbook*, *Creative Illustration*, *Medical Illustration Source Book*.
How to Contact: For first contact, send direct mail flier/brochure. Reports in 1 week, only if interested. After initial contact, drop off or mail in appropriate materials: tearsheets, slides, photographs, photostats, photocopies.
Tips: Obtains new talent through "recommendations and calls/letters from artists moving to the area. We prefer to handle artists who live in the area unless they do something that is not available locally."

HALL & ASSOCIATES (III), #10, 1010 S. Robertson Blvd, Los Angeles CA 90035. (310)652-7322. Fax: (310)652-3835. Contact: Marni Hall. Commercial illustration and photography representative. Estab. 1983. Member of SPAR, APA. Represents 10 illustrators and 5 photographers. Markets include: advertising agencies; design firms. Member agent: Christie Deddens (Artist Representative).
Handles: Illustration, photography.
Terms: Rep receives 25-28% commission. Exclusive area representation is required. No geographic restrictions. Advertising costs are paid by talent. For promotional purposes, talent must advertise in "1 or 2 source books a year (double page), provide 2 direct mail pieces and 1 specific, specialized mailing. No specific portfolio requirement except that it be easy and light to carry and send out." Advertises in *Creative Black Book*, *The Workbook*.
How to Contact: For first contact, send direct mail flier/brochure. Reports in 5 days. After initial contact, drop off or mail in appropriate materials for review. Portfolios should include tearsheets, transparencies, prints (8×10 or larger).
Tips: Obtains new talent through recommendations from others or artists' solicitations. "Don't show work you think should sell but what you enjoy shooting. Only put in tearsheets of great ads, not bad ads even if they are a highly visible client."

BARB HAUSER, ANOTHER GIRL REP (V), P.O.Box 421543, San Francisco CA 94142-1443. (415)647-5660. Fax: (415)285-1102. Estab. 1980. Represents 10 illustrators and 1 photographer. Markets include: primarily advertising agencies and design firms; corporations/client direct.
Handles: Illustration.
Terms: Rep receives 25-30% commission. Exclusive representation in the San Francisco area is required. No geographic restrictions.
How to Contact: For first contact, send direct mail flier/brochure, tearsheets, slides, photographs, photocopies and SASE. Reports in 3-4 weeks. Call for appointment to show portfolio of tearsheets, slides, photographs, photostats, photocopies.

HK PORTFOLIO (III), 666 Greenwich St., New York NY 10014. (212)675-5719. Contact: Harriet Kasak. Commercial illustration representative. Estab. 1986. Member of SPAR. Represents 30 illustrators. Specializes in children's book illustration. Markets include: advertising agencies; editorial/magazines; publishing/books.

Commercial Art and Photography Representatives 203

Handles: Illustration.
Terms: Rep receives 25% commission. No geographic restrictions. Advertising costs are split: 75% paid by talent; 25% paid by representative. Advertises in *American Showcase, RSVP*.
How to Contact: No geographic restrictions. For first contact, send query letter, direct mail flier/brochure, tearsheets, slides, photographs, photostats and SASE. Reports in 1 week. After initial contact, drop off or mail in appropriate materials for review. Portfolio should include tearsheets, slides, photographs, photostats, photocopies.
Tips: Leans toward a highly individual, more tradebook look, rather than one that is more mass market or commercial.

RITA HOLT & ASSOCIATES, INC. (II,III), 920 Main St., Fords NJ 08863 (908)738-5258. Contact: Rita Holt. Commercial photography representative. Estab. 1976. Member of SPAR. Represents 4 photographers. Specializes in automotive and location photography. Markets include: advertising agencies; corporations/client direct; design firms; sales/promotion firms.
Handles: Photography, especially automotive.
Terms: Commission taken by rep varies. Charges for all expenses. Advertising costs are paid by talent. For promotional purposes, talent must provide direct mail piece or package and portfolio—"specifics depend on market." Advertises in *Creative Black Book, The Workbook* ("depends on the market").
How to Contact: For first contact, send direct mail flier/brochure, photographs, portfolio with a return Federal Express air bill. Reports only if interested (time varies). After initial contact, drop off or mail in appropriate materials.
Tips: Obtains new talent through recommendations from others. "Sell a rep the same way you would sell a client."

SCOTT HULL ASSOCIATES (III), 68 E. Franklin S., Dayton OH 45459. (513)433-8383. Fax: (513)433-0434. Contact: Scott Hull or Frank Sturges. Commercial illustration representative. Estab. 1981. Represents 20 illustrators.
Terms: No information provided.
How to Contact: Contact by sending slides, tearsheets or appropriate materials for review. Follow up with phone call. Reports in 2 weeks.
Tips: Obtains new talent through solicitation.

‡JEDELL PRODUCTIONS, INC. (II), 370 E. 76th St., New York NY 10021. (212)861-7861. Contact: Joan Jedell. Commercial photography representative. Estab. 1969. Member of SPAR. Specializes in photography. Markets include: advertising agencies.
Handles: Photography, fine art.
How to Contact: After initial contact, drop off or mail in portfolio of photographs. For returns, include SASE or Federal Express number.

‡KASTARIS & ASSOCIATES (II, III), 3301a S. Jefferson, St. Louis MO 63118. (314)773-2600. Fax: (314)773-6406. Commercial illustration representative. Estab. 1987. Represents 16 illustrators and 2 photographers. Markets include: advertising agencies; design firms; editorial/magazines; publishing/books; sales/promotion firms.
Handles: Illustration.
Terms: Rep receives 25% commission. Exclusive area representation is negotiable. Advertising costs are split: 75% paid by talent; 25% paid by representative. Talent "must have at least 3,000 promotional tearsheets; must advertise with my firm; must provide 4×5 transparencies for portfolio." Advertises in *American Showcase, The Workbook*.
How to Contact: For first contact, send direct mail flier/brochure, tearsheets and SASE if you want sampler back. Reports in 1 month if interested. After initial contact, call for appointment.
Tips: "Show one style only. Have a strong portfolio that includes images of people, products, animals, food and typography."

Reps ranked I and II are most open to new, as well as established, talents. Those ranked III prefer established talent with references from others in the art or photography field.

PEGGY KEATING (III, IV), 30 Horatio St., New York NY 10014. (212)691-4654. Contact: Peggy Keating. Commercial illustration representataive. Estab. 1969. Member of Graphic Artists Guild. Represents 7 illustrators. Specializes in fashion illustration (men, women, children, also fashion-related products). Markets include: advertising agencies; corporations/client direct; editorial/magazines; sales/promotion firms; "mostly pattern catalog companies and retail."
Handles: "Fashion illustration, but only if top-drawer."
Terms: Rep receives 25% commission. Exclusive area representation is required. For promotional purposes, talent must provide "strong sample material that will provide an excellent portfolio presentation." Advertises by direct mail.
How to Contact: For first contact, send tearsheets, photocopies. Reports in days, only if interested. After initial contact, drop off or mail in appropriate materials for review. Portfolio should include thumbnails, roughs, original art, tearsheets, slides, photographs, photostats, photocopies. "It might include all or one or more of these materials. The selection and design of the material are the important factor."
Tips: Obtains new talent through "recommendations from others, or they contact me directly. The talent must be first-rate. The field has diminished and the competition if fierce. There is no longer the tolerance of not yet mature talent, nor is there a market for mediocrity."

‡KELLOGG CREATIVE SERVICES (V), 525 E. Flower, Phoenix AZ 85012. (602)241-1828. Fax: (602)265-7353. Contact: Mollie Cirino.

RALPH KERR (II), 239 Chestnut St., Philadelphia PA 19106. (215)592-1359. Fax: (215)592-7988. Contact: Ralph Kerr. Commercial illustration and photography representative. Estab. 1987. Represents 1 photographer. Markets include: advertising agencies; corporations/client direct; design firms; editorial/magazines; paper products/greeting cards; publishing/books.
Handles: Illustration, photography.
Terms: Rep receives 20% commission. Exclusive area representation is required. Advertising costs are split: 50% paid by talent; 50% paid by representative. For promotional purposes, portfolio required. Advertises in *Creative Black Book*.
How to Contact: For first contact, send query letter. Reports in 1 week. After initial contact, call for appointment to show portfolio of tearsheets, slides, photographs.

‡KESWICK HAMILTON (III), 3519 W. Sixth St., Los Angeles CA 90020. (213)380-3933. Fax: (213)380-2906. Contact: Maggie Hamilton. Commercial photography and graphic design representative. Estab. 1990. Member of AIGA, APA. Represents 16 photographers, 2 designers. Specializes in entertainment, editorial, automotive. "Graphic design is not merely repped. It is an actual part, i.e., we are a photo/design agency." Markets include: advertising agencies; corporations/client direct; design firms; editorial/magazines.
Handles: Illustration, photography, design.
Terms: Rep receives 25% commission. Charges for messengers or FedEx if photographer has requested sending. Exclusive area representation required. Advertising costs are paid by talent. For promotional materials, talent must provide current portfolios (2-4 books), mailing pieces and open to sourcebooks. Advertises in *American Showcase*, *Creative Black Book*, *The Workbook* and *California Sourcebook* (Black Book Publishing).
How to Contact: For first contact, send query letter with direct mail flier/brochure. Reports in 1 week. Call for appointment to show portfolio of tearsheets, slides, photographs.
Tips: Obtains new talent through my own awareness and recommendations from others. "Think about if you were a rep, what you would want in a photographer? Portfolio—2-4 books; material—mailers, etc.; and a good sense of how hard it is to accomplish success without vision and commitment."

KIRCHOFF/WOHLBERG, ARTISTS REPRESENTATION DIVISION (II), #525, 866 United Nations Plaza, New York NY 10017. (212)644-2020. Fax: (212)223-4387. Director of Operations: John R. Whitman. Estab. 1930s. Member of SPAR, Society of Illustrators, AIGA, Assn. of American Publishers, Book Builders of Boston, New York Bookbinders' Guild. Represents over 50 illustrators. Artist's Representative: Elizabeth Ford (juvenile and young adult trade book and textbook illustartors). Specializes in juvenile and young adult trade books and textbooks. Markets include: publishing/books.

Commercial Art and Photography Representatives 205

Handles: Illustration and photography (juvenile and young adult). Please send all correspondence to the attention of Elizabeth Ford.
Terms: Rep receives 25% commission. Exclusive representation to book publishers is usually required. Advertising costs paid by representative ("for all Kirchoff/Wohlberg advertisements only"). "We will make transparencies from portfolio samples; keep some original work on file." Advertises in *American Showcase*, *Art Directors' Index*; *Society of Illustrators Annual*, children's book issue of *Publishers Weekly*.
How to Contact: For first contact, send query letter, "any materials artists feel are appropriate." Reports in 4-6 weeks. "We will contact you for additional materials." Portfolios should include "whatever artists feel best represents their work. We like to see children's illustration in any style."

BILL AND MAURINE KLIMT (II), 7-U, 15 W. 72nd St., New York NY 10023. (212)799-2231. Contact: Bill or Maurine. Commercial illustration representative. Estab. 1978. Member of Society of Illustrators, Graphic Artists Guild. Represents 14 illustrators. Specializes in paperback covers, young adult, romance, science fiction, mystery, etc. Markets include: advertising agencies; corporations/client direct; design firms; editorial/magazines; paper products/greeting cards; publishing/books; sales/promotion firms.
Handles: Illustration.
Terms: Rep receives 25% commission, 30% commission for "out of town if we do shoots. Supplying reference on jobs. The artist is responsible for only their own portfolio. We supply all promotion and mailings other than the publications." Exclusive area representation is required. No geographic restrictions. Advertising costs are split: 75% paid by talent; 25% paid by representative. For promotional purposes, talent must provide 4×5 or 8×10 mounted transparencies. Advertises in *American Showcase*, *RSVP*.
How to Contact: For first contact, send direct mail flier/brochure, and "any image that doesn't have to be returned unless supplied with SASE." Reports in 5 days. After initial contact, call for appointment to show portfolio of professional, mounted transparencies.
Tips: Obtains new talent through recommendations from others and solicitation.

‡ELLEN KNABLE & ASSOCIATES, INC. (II, III), 1233 S. LaCienega Blvd., Los Angeles CA 90035. (310)855-8855. (310)657-0265. Contact: Ellen Knable, Kathee Toyama. Commercial illustration, photography and production representative. Estab. 1978. Member of SPAR, Graphic Artists Guild. Represents 6 illustrators, 5 photographers. Markets include: advertising agencies; corporations/client direct; design firms.
Terms: Rep receives 25-30% commission. Exclusive West Coast/Southern California representation is required. Advertising costs split varies. Advertises in *The Workbook*.
How to Contact: For first contact, send query letter, direct mail flier/brochure and tearsheets. Reports within 2 week. Call for appointment to show portfolio.
Tips: Obtains new talent from creatives/artists. "Have patience and persistence!"

CLIFF KNECHT–ARTIST REPRESENTATIVE (II, III), 309 Walnut Rd., Pittsburgh PA 15202. (412)761-5666. Fax: (412)261-3712. Contact: Cliff Knecht. Commercial illustration representative. Estab. 1972. Represents 15 illustrators, 1 design firm, 2 fine artists. Markets include: advertising agencies; corporations/client direct; design firms; editorial/magazines; paper products/greeting cards; publishing/books; sales/promotion firms.
Handles: Illustration.
Terms: Rep receives 25% commission. No geographic restrictions. Advertising costs are split: 75% paid by the talent; 25% paid by representative. For promotional purposes, talent must provide a direct mail piece. Advertises in *American Showcase* and *Graphic Artists Guild Directory of Illustration*.
How to Contact: For first contact, send résumé, direct mail flier/brochure, tearsheets, slides. Reports in 1 week. After initial contact, call for appointment to show portfolio of original art, tearsheets, slides, photographs.
Tips: Obtains new talent directly or through recommendations from others.

‡KORMAN & COMPANY (III), PHA, 135 W. 24th St., New York NY 10011. (212)727-1442. Fax: (212)727-1443. Contact: Alison Korman. Commercial photography representative. Estab. 1984. Member of SPAR. Represents 3 photographers. Markets include: advertising agencies; corporations/client direct; editorial/magazines; publishing/books; sales/promotion firms.

Handles: Photography.
Terms: Rep receives 25-30% commission. "Talent pays for messengers, mailings, promotion." Exclusive area representation is required. Advertising costs are paid by talent "for first 2 years, unless very established and sharing house." For promotional purposes, talent must provide portfolio, directory ads, mailing pieces. Advertises in *Creative Black Book, The Workbook, Gold Book*.
How to Contact: For first contact, send direct mail flier/brochure. Reports in 1 month if interested. After initial contact, write for appoinment or drop off or mail in portfolio of tearsheets, photographs.
Tips: Obtains new talent through "recommendations, seeing somebody's work out in the market and liking it. Be prepared to discuss how you can help a rep to help you."

‡**ELAINE KORN ASSOCIATES, LTD. (III),** 372 Fifth Ave., New York NY 10018. (212)760-0057. Fax: (212)465-8093. Commercial photography representative. Estab. 1981. Member of SPAR. Represents 6 photographers. Specializes in fashion. Markets include: advertising agencies; editorial/magazines.
Handles: Photography.
How to Contact: For first contact, send promotional pieces. After initial contact, write for appointment to show portfolio.

PETER KUEHNEL & ASSOCIATES (III), Suite 2108, 30 E. Huron Plaza, Chicago IL 60611-2717. (312)642-6499. Fax: (312)642-0377. Contact: Peter Kuehnel. Marker illustration, photography and film representative. Estab. 1984. Member of SPAR. Represents 5 illustrators, 2 photographers, 3 directors and an animation production company. Staff includes Lily Stefanski. Markets include: advertising agencies; corporations/client direct; design firms; editorial/magazines; sales/promotion firms.
Handles: Illustration, photography, film production.
Terms: Rep receives 25% commission. "Any and all expenses billed to artist involved on a 75/25 basis." Exclusive area representation is required. Sells in the Midwest. Advertising costs are split: 75% paid by talent; 25% paid by representative. Materials talent must provide for promotion vary case by case. Advertises in *Creative Black Book, The Workbook, Chicago Sourcebook*.
How to Contact: For first contact, send query letter, direct mail flier/brochure and SASE. Reports in 2 weeks. After initial contact, call for appointment to show portfolio.
Tips: Obtains new talent through "recommendations from buyers, etc." To obtain representation, "work hard, practice, practice, practice."

‡**SHARON KURLANSKY ASSOCIATES (IV),** 192 Southville Rd., Southborough MA 01772. (508)872-4549. Fax: (508)460-6058. Contact: Sharon Kurlansky. Commercial illustration representative. Estab. 1978. Represents 9 illustrators. Staff includes John Gamache, Bruce Hutchison, Colleen (calligraphy); Fran O'Neill, Julia Talcott, Mary Anne Lloyd, Geoffrey Hodgkinson (typographic design); Peter Harris, John Avakian (informational graphics). Markets include: advertising agencies; corporations/client direct; design firms; editorial/magazines; paper products/greeting cards; publishing/books; sales/promotion firms.
Handles: Illustration.
Terms: Rep receives 25% commission. Exclusive area representation is required. Advertising costs are split: 75% paid by talent; 25% paid by representative. "Will develop promotional materials with talent. Portfolio presentation formatted and developed with talent also." Advertises in *American Showcase, The Creative Illustration Book* under artist's name.
How to Contact: For first contact, send direct mail flier/brochure, tearsheets, slides and SASE. Reports in 1 month if interested. After initial contact, call for appointment to show portfolio of tearsheets, photocopies.
Tips: Obtains new talent through various means.

‡**MARY LAMONT (V),** 56 Washington Ave., Brentwood NY 11717. Representative not currently seeking new talent.

‡**SHARON LANGLEY REPRESENTS! (III),** A-129, 4300 N. Narragansett, Chicago IL 60634. (708)670-0912. Fax: (708)670-0926. Contact: Sharon Langley. Commercial illustration and photography representative. Estab. 1988. Member of CAR (Chicago Artists Representatives). Represents 6 illustrators and 2 photographers. Markets include: advertising agencies; corporations/client direct; design firms; editorial/magazines; publishing/books; sales/promotion firms.

Commercial Art and Photography Representatives 207

Handles: Illustration, photography. Although representative prefers to work with established talent, "I am always receptive to reviewing illustrators' work."
Terms: Rep receives 25% commission. Exclusive area representation is preferred. Advertising costs are split: 75% paid by talent; 25% paid by representative. For promotional purposes, talent must provide printed promotional piece, well organized portfolio. Advertises in *Creative Black Book, The Workbook, Chicago Source Book, Creative Illustration*.
How to Contact: For first contact, send printed promotional piece. Reports in 2 weeks if interested. After initial contact, call for appointment to show portfolio of tearsheets, transparencies.
Tips: Obtains new talent through art directors, clients, referrals. "When an artist just starts freelancing it's a good idea to represent yourself for a while. Only then are you able to appreciate and respect a professional agent. Don't be discouraged when one rep turns you down. Contact the next one on your list!"

FRANK & JEFF LAVATY & ASSOCIATES (II), Suite 212, 217 E. 86th St., New York NY 10028-3617. (212)355-0910. Commercial illustration and fine art representative. Represents 15 illustrators.
Handles: Illustration.
Terms: No information provided.
How to Contact: For first contact, send query letter, direct mail flier/brochure, tearsheets, slides and SASE. Reports in 1 week. After initial contact, call for appointment to show portfolio of tearsheets, 8×10 or 4×5 transparencies.
Tips: Obtains new talent through solicitation. "Specialize! Your portfolio must be focused."

‡**LEE + LOU PRODUCTIONS INC. (II, III)**, #108, 8522 National Blvd., Culver City CA 90232. (310)287-1542. Fax: (310)287-1814. Commercial illustration and photography representative, digital and traditional photo retouching. Estab. 1981. Represents 10 illustrators, 5 photographers. Specializes in automotive. Markets include: advertising agencies.
Handles: Photography.
Terms: Rep receives 25% commission. Charges shipping, entertainment. Exclusive area representation required. Advertising costs are paid by talent. For promotional purposes, talent must provide direct mail advertising material. Advertises in *Creative Black Book, The Workbook* and *Single Image*.
How to Contact: For first contact, send direct mail flier/brochure, tearsheets. Reports in 1 week. Call for appointment to show portfolio of photographs.
Tips: Obtains new talent through recommendations from others, some solicitation.

‡**LEIGHTON & COMPANY (III)**, 4 Prospect St., Beverly MA 01915. (508)921-0887. Fax: (508)921-0223. Contact: Leighton O'Connor. Commercial illustration and photography representative. Estab. 1986. Member of Graphic Artists Guild, ASMP. Represents 8 illustrators and 3 photographers. Staff includes Jodie Sinclair (fashion and lifestyle photography), Daniel Walsh (location photography), Jeffrey Coolidge (still life photography). Markets include: advertising agencies; corporations/clients direct; design firms; editorial/magazines; publishing/books.
Handles: Illustration, photography. "Looking for photographers and illustrators who can create their work on computer."
Terms: Rep receives 25% commission. Advertising costs are split: 75% paid by talent; 25% paid by representative. For promotional purposes, "talent is required to supply me with 6×9 color mailer(s). Photographers and illustrators are required to supply me with laminated portfolio as well as 2 4×5 color transparency portfolios." Advertises in *Creative Illustration, Graphic Artist Guild Directory of Illustration*.
How to Contact: For first contact, send query letter, direct mail flier/brochure, tearsheets and SASE. Reports in 1 week if interested. After initial contact, drop off or mail in appropriate materials with SASE for review. Portfolio should include tearsheets, slides, photographs.
Tips: "My new talent is almost always obtained through referrals. Occasionally, I will solicit new talent from direct mail pieces they have sent to me. It is best to send work first, i.e., tearsheet or direct mail pieces. Only send a portfolio when asked to. If you need your samples returned, always include a SASE. Follow up with one phone call. It is very important to get the correct spelling and address of the representative. Also, make sure you are financially ready for a representative, having the resources available to create a portfolio and direct mail campaign."

‡**LEVIN•DORR (II)**, Suite 1015, 1123 Broadway, New York NY 10010. (212)627-9871. Fax: (212)243-4036. Contact: Bruce Levin or Chuck Dorr. Commercial photography representative, Estab. 1982. Member of SPAR. Represents 6 photographers. Markets include: advertising agencies; design firms; editorial/magazines; sales/promotion firms.
Handles: Photography.
Terms: Rep receives 25% commission. Exclusive area representation is required. Advertising costs are split: 75% paid by talent; 25% paid by representative. For promotional purposes, "talent must have a minimum of 5 portfolios which are lightweight and fit into Federal Express boxes." Advertises in *Creative Black Book*, *The Workbook*, *Gold Book*.
How to Contact: For first contact, send "portfolio as if it were going to advertising agency." After initial contact, call for appointment to show portfolio of tearsheets, slides, photographs.
Tips: Obtains new talent through recommendations, word-of-mouth, solicitation. "Don't get discouraged."

‡**JIM LILIE ARTIST'S REPRESENTATIVE (III)**, #706, 110 Sutter St., San Francisco CA 94104. (415)441-4384. Fax: (415)395-9809. Commercial illustration and photography representative. Estab. 1977. Represents 7 illustrators, 1 photographer. Markets include: advertising agencies; design firms.
Handles: Illustration.
Terms: Rep receives 25% commission. Exclusive area representation is required. Advertising costs are split: 75% paid by talent; 25% paid by representative. For promotional purposes, talent must provide portfolio of either transparencies or laminated pieces: 8×10. Advertises in *American Showcase*, *Creative Black Book* and *The Workbook*.
How to Contact: For first contact send direct mail flier/brochure, tearsheets and SASE. Portfolio should include tearsheets, photocopies.
Tips: Obtains new talent through recommendations from others.

‡**LINDGREN & SMITH (III)**, 41 Union Square, New York NY 10003. Commercial illustration representative. Estab. 1986. Represents 20 illustrators.
How to Contact: For first contact, send "sample of artwork not to be returned unless SASE is included. Reports back with SASE in 1 day, or suggest phone call to us after we receive sample. We usually don't interview unless we call them." Portfolio should include tearsheets, 4×5 or 8×10 transparencies.
Tips: Obtains new talent through recommendations. "Know the artists that the rep handles before you contact them."

‡**JOHN LOCKE STUDIOS, INC. (IV)**, 15 E. 76th St., New York NY 10021. (212)288-8010. Fax: (212)288-8011. Associate Representative: Eileen McMahon. Commercial illustration representative. Estab. 1943. Represents 21 illustrators. "Noted for representing high profile European and American artists—New Yorker cartoonists—Folon, Gorey, Searle, Francois, Sis, etc." Markets include: advertising agencies; corporations/client direct; design firms; editorial/magazines; paper products/greeting cards; publishing/books; sales/promotion firms.
Handles: Illustration. "When we look for new talent, which is rare, it must be work that is extremely individualistic, not totally realistic, humorous—the work of a mature artist."
Terms: Rep receives 25% commission. Exclusive area representation is required. Advertising costs are split: 50% paid by talent; 50% paid by representative. For promotional purposes, talent must send "tearsheets for portfolio using 11×14 sheets, any published books or specialty packages/pieces to include with portfolio; slides." Advertises in *American Showcase*, *The Workbook*, *New York Gold*; "rarely advertise in directories—most promotion-direct mail, now."
How to Contact: For first contact, send query letter. Reports in 2 weeks. After initial contact, call for appointment to show portfolio of original art (if possible), tearsheets, slides.
Tips: Obtains new talent through "recommendations and our own solicitation; watch European publications for artists who are making their mark. With us, not pushing too hard is the best advice. Recommendation from known art director, designer, editor extremely helpful. Show a small sample of really first-rate work."

PETER & GEORGE LOTT (II), 60 E. 42nd St., New York NY 10165. (212)953-7088. Commercial illustration representative. Estab. 1958. Member of Society of Illustrators, Art Directors Club. Represents 15 illustrators. Markets include: advertising agencies; corporations/client direct; design firms; editorial/magazines; publishing/books; sales/promotion firms; "all types fashion and beauty accounts (men's, women's, children's, still life and accessories).

Handles: Illustration. "We are currently looking for romance novel illustrators. As a general rule, we're interested in any kind of saleable commercial art."
Terms: Rep receives 25% commission. No geographic restrictions. Advertises in *American Showcase*, *Creative Black Book*, *The Workbook* and other publications.
How to Contact: For first contact, "call to drop off portfolio."
Tips: "Check with us first to make sure it is a convenient time to drop off a portfolio. Then either drop it off or send it with return postage. The format does not matter, as long as it shows what you can do and what you want to do."

‡**MCCONNELL MCNAMARA & CO. (III)**, 182 Broad St., Wethersfield CT 06109. (203)563-6154. Fax: (203)563-6159. Contact: Paula B. McNamara. Commercial illustration, photography and fine art representative. Estab. 1975. Member of SPAR, Graphic Artists Guild, ASMP, ASPP. Represents 1 illustrator, 1 photographer and 1 fine artist. Staff includes Paula B. McNamara (photography, illustration and fine art). Specializes in advertising and annual report photography. Markets include: advertising agencies; corporations/client direct; design firms; editoral/magazines; paper products/greeting cards; publishing/books; sales/promotion firms; stock photography-travel; corporate collections; galleries.
Handles: Photography. "Looking for photographers specializing in stock photography of New England."
Terms: Rep receives 25-30% commission. Exclusive area representation is required. Advertising costs are split: 75% paid by talent; 25% paid by representative. For promotional purposes, talent must provide "professional portfolio and tearsheets already available and ready for improving; direct mail piece needed within 3 months after collaborating."
How to Contact: For first contact, send query letter, résumé, direct mail flier/brochure, tearsheets. Reports in 1 month if interested. "Unfortunately we don't have staff to evaluate and investigate new talent or offer counsel." After initial contact, write for appointment to show portfolio of tearsheets, slides, photographs.
Tips: Obtains new talent through "recommendations by other professionals, sourcebooks and industry magazines—who's who stuff. Prefer to follow our own leads rather than receive unsolicited promotions and inquiries. It's best to have repped yourself for several years to know your strengths and be realistic about your marketplace. The same is true of having experience with direct mail pieces, developing client lists, and having a system of follow up. We want our talent to have experience with all this so they can properly value our contribution to their growth and success—otherwise that 25% becomes a burden and point of resentment."

COLLEEN MCKAY PHOTOGRAPHY (III), #2, 229 E. Fifth St., New York NY 10003. (212)598-0469. Fax: (212)598-0762. Contact: Colleen McKay. Commercial editorial and fine art photography representative. Estab. 1985. Member of SPAR. Represents 4 photographers. Staff includes Cara Sadownick. "Our photographers cover a wide range of work from location, still life, fine art, fashion and beauty." Markets include: advertising agencies; design firms; editorial/magazines; stores.
Handles: Commercial and fine art photography.
Terms: Rep receives 25% commission. Exclusive area representation is required. Advertising costs are split: 75% paid by talent; 25% paid by representative. "Promotional pieces are very necessary. They must be current. The portfolio should be established already." Advertises in *Creative Black Book*, *Select*, *New York Gold*.
How to Contact: For first contact, send query letter, résumé, bio, direct mail flier/brochure, tearsheets, slides, photographs. Reports in 2-3 weeks. "I like to respond to everyone but if we're really swamped I may only get a chance to respond to those we're most interested in." Portfolio should include tearsheets, slides, photographs, transparencies (usually for still life).
Tips: Obtains talent through recommendations of other people and solicitations. "I recommend that you look in current resource books and call the representatives that are handling the kind of work that you admire or is similar to your own. Ask these reps for an initial consultation and additional references. Do not be intimidated to approach anyone. Even if they do not take you on, a meeting with a good rep can prove to be very fruitful! Never give up! A clear, positive attitude is very important."

MARTHA PRODUCTIONS, INC. (III, IV), 4445 Overland Ave., Culver City CA 90230. (310)204-1771. Fax: (310)204-4598. Contact: Martha Spelman. Commercial illustration and graphic design representative. Estab. 1978. Member of Graphic Artists Guild. Represents 25 illustrators, 1 designer (studio). Staff includes Jennifer Ehlers (assignment illustration), Martha Spelman (artist representative), Caroline Beghin (artist representative). Specializes in b&w and 4-color illustration. Markets include: adver-

tising agencies; corporations/client direct; design firms; editorial/magazines; paper products/greeting cards.
Handles: Illustration.
Terms: Rep receives 30% commission. Exclusive area representation is required. No geographic restrictions. Advertising costs are split: 70% paid by talent; 30% paid by representative. For promotional purposes, talent must provide "a minimum of 12 images, 3 4×5 transparencies of each. (We put the transparencies into our own format.) In addition to the transparencies, we require 4-color promo/tearsheets and participation in the biannual Martha Productions brochure." Advertises in *The Workbook*, *Single Image*.
How to Contact: For first contact, send query letter, direct mail flier/brochure, tearsheets, slides and SASE (if materials are to be returned). Reports only if interested. After initial contact, drop off or mail in appropriate materials for review. Portfolio should include tearsheets, slides, photographs, photostats.
Tips: Obtains new talent through recommendations and solicitation.

MATTELSON ASSOCIATES LTD. (II), 37 Cary Road, Great Neck NY 11021. (212)684-2974. Fax: (516)466-5835. Contact: Judy Mattelson. Commercial illustration representative. Estab. 1980. Member of SPAR, Graphic Artists Guild. Represents 2 illustrators. Markets include: advertising agencies; corporations/client direct; design firms; editorial/magazines; paper products/greeting cards; publishing/books; sales/promotion firms.
Handles: Illustration.
Terms: Rep receives 25-30% commission. Exclusive area representation is required. No geographic restrictions. Advertising costs are split: 75% paid by talent; 25% paid by representative. For promotional purposes, talent must provide c-prints and tearsheets, custom-made portfolio. Advertises in *American Showcase*, *Creative Black Book*, *RSVP*, *New York Gold*.
How to Contact: For first contact, send direct mail flier/brochure, tearsheets and SASE. Reports in 2 weeks, if interested. After initial contact, call for appointment to show portfolio of tearsheets, c-prints.
Tips: Obtains new talent through "recommendations from others, solicitation. Illustrator should have ability to do consistent, professional-quality work that shows a singular direction and a variety of subject matter. You should have a portfolio that shows the full range of your current abilities. Work should show strong draftsmanship and technical facility. Person should love their work and be willing to put forth great effort in each assignment."

MENDOLA ARTISTS (II), Penthouse, 420 Lexington Ave., New York NY 10170. (212)986-5680. Fax: (212)818-1246. Contact: Tim Mendola. Commercial illustration representative. Estab. 1961. Member of Society of Illustrators, Graphic Artists Guild. Represents 60 or more illustrators, 3 photographers. Markets include: advertising agencies; corporations/client direct; design firms; editorial/magazines; sales/promotion firms.
Handles: Illustration. "We work with the top agencies and publishers. The calibre of talent must be in the top 5%."
Terms: Rep receives 25% commission. Artist pays for all shipping not covered by client and 75% of promotion costs. Exclusive area representation is sometimes required. Advertising costs are split: 75% paid by talent; 25% paid by representative. For promotional purposes, talent must provide 8×10 transparencies and usually promotion in at least one sourcebook. Advertises in *American Showcase*, *Creative Black Book*, *RSVP*, *The Workbook*.
How to Contact: For first contact, send direct mail flier/brochure, tearsheets, slides. Reports in 1 week. After initial contact, drop off or mail in appropriate materials for review. Portfolio should include original art, tearsheets, slides, photographs.

‡SUSAN MILLER REPRESENTS (II), Suite 29A, 1641 Third Ave., New York NY 10128. (212)427-9604. Fax: (212)427-7777. Contact: Susan Miller. Commercial photography representative. Estab. 1983. Member of SPAR. Represents 1 illustrator and 10 photographers. "Firm deals mainly in advertising photography." Markets include: advertising agencies; sales/promotion firms.
Handles: Illustration, photography. "Interested in seeing humorous cartoon illustration."
Terms: Rep receives 25-30% commission in US; 33% in Europe. Advertising costs are paid by talent. "Talent must be able to self-promote in a directory page and possibly other mailers if possible." Advertises in *Creative Black Book*, *The Workbook*, *New York Gold*.

Commercial Art and Photography Representatives 211

How to Contact: For first contact, send query letter, direct mail flier/brochure, photocopies and SASE. Reports in 2 weeks. After initial contact, call for appointment to show portfolio of slides, photographs.
Tips: "New talent comes to us through a variety of means. Recommendation from art buyers and art directors is one way, solicitation is another way. Photographers and illustrators sending portfolis must pay courier both ways. Talent should please check directory ads to see if we have conflicting talent before contacting us. Most people calling us do not take the time to do any research, which is not wise."

MONTAGANO & ASSOCIATES (II), #1606, 405 N. Wabash, Chicago IL 60611. (312)527-3283. Fax: (312)527-9091. Contact: David Montagano. Commercial illustration, photography and television production representative and broker. Estab. 1983. Represents 7 illustrators, 2 photographers. Markets include: advertising agencies; corporations/client direct; design firms; editorial/magazines; paper products/greeting cards.
Handles: Illustration, photography, design.
Terms: Rep receives 25-30% commission. No geographic restrictions. Advertises in *American Showcase*, *The Workbook*.
How to Contact: For first contact, send direct mail flier/brochure, tearsheets, photographs. Portfolio should include original art, tearsheets, photographs.
Tips: Obtains new talent through recommendations from others.

VICKI MORGAN ASSOCIATES, (III), 194 Third Ave., New York NY 10003. (212)475-0440. Contact: Vicki Morgan. Commercial illustration representative. Estab. 1974. Member of SPAR, Graphic Artists Guild, Society of Illustrators. Represents 12 illustrators. Markets include: advertising agencies; corporations/client direct; design firms; editorial/magazines; paper products/greeting cards; publishing/books; sales/promotion firms.
Handles: Illustration. "Full-time illustrators only."
Terms: Rep receives 25-30% commission. Exclusive area representation is required. No geographic restrictions. Advertising costs are split: 75% paid by talent; 25% paid by representative. "We can develop an initial direct mail piece together. We require samples for 3 duplicate portfolios; the presentation form is flexible." Advertises in *American Showcase*.
How to Contact: For first contact, send any of the following: direct mail flier/brochure, tearsheets, slides with SASE. "If interested, we keep on file and consult these samples first when considering additional artists. No drop-off policy."
Tips: Obtains new talent through "recommendations from artists I represent and mail solicitation."

‡**MICHELE MORGAN/ARTIST REPRESENTATIVE (V)**, #20-425, 2646 DuPont Dr., Irvine CA 92715. Representative not currently seeking new talent.

THE NEIS GROUP (II), 11440 Oak Dr., Shelbyville MI 49344. (616)672-5756. Fax: (616)672-5757. Contact: Judy Neis. Commercial illustration and photography representative. Estab. 1982. Represents 30 illustrators, 7 photographers. Markets include: advertising agencies; design firms; editorial/magazines; publishing/books.
Handles: Illustration, photography.
Terms: Rep receives 25% commission. Advertising costs are split: 75% paid by talent; 25% paid by representative. Advertises in *The American Showcase*.
How to Contact: For first contact, send direct mail flier/brochure, tearsheets, photographs. Reports in 5 days. After initial contact, drop off or mail in appropriate materials for review. Portfolio should include tearsheets, photographs.
Tips: "I am mostly sought out by the talent. If I pursue, I call and request a portfolio review."

‡**THE NEWBORN GROUP (III)**, 135 E. 54th St., New York NY 10022. (212)421-0050. Fax: (212)421-0444. Owner: Joan Sigman. Commercial illustration representative. Estab. 1964. Member of SPAR, Society of Illustrators, Graphic Artists Guild. Represents 10 illustrators. Markets include: advertising agencies; design firms; editorial/magazines; publishing/books.
Handles: Illustration.
Terms: Rep receives 25% commission. Exclusive area representation is required. Advertising costs are split: 75% paid by talent; 25% paid by representative. Advertises in *American Showcase*, *The Workbook*, *Directory of Illustration*.

How to Contact: For first contact, send query letter, direct mail flier/brochure. Reports in 2-3 weeks. Do not sent portfolio.
Tips: Obtains new talent through recommendations from other talent or art directors.

‡**OZ NEW YORK INC. (III)**, 7th Floor, 9 E. 37th St., New York NY 10016. (212)686-5277. Fax: (212)545-7167. Contact: Timothy Priano. Commercial photography representative, hair, makeup and fashion stylists. Estab. 1981. Represents 6 photographers. Staff includes Sally Harlor (hair and makeup), Mari Faucher (photography), Boda (fashion stylist). Markets include: advertising agencies; corporations/client direct; design firms; editorial/magazines; sales/promotion firms.
Handles: Photography.
Terms: Rep receives 25% commission. Charges for messengers and freight. Exclusive area representation is required, Advertising costs are split: 75% paid by talent; 25% paid by representative. For promotional purposes, talent must provide a minimum of 4 portfolios and a business card.
How to Contact: For first contact, send direct mail flier/brochure. Reports in 5 days, only if interested. After initial contact, drop off or mail in appropriate materials for review. Portfolio should include original art, tearsheets, personal work.
Tips: Obtains new talent through referrals only, "When you are ready for a rep make sure that you need the person. It is really hard to rep someone who is out looking for work in the same places that you are. Clients do not like an overlap of promotion."

JACKIE PAGE (III), 219 E. 69th St., New York NY 10021. (212)772-0346. Commercial photography representative. Estab. 1987. Member of SPAR and Ad Club. Represents 10 photographers. Markets include: advertising agencies.
Handles: Photography.
Terms: "Details given at a personal interview." Advertises in *The Workbook*.
How to Contact: For first contact, send direct mail flier/brochure. After initial contact, call for appointment to show portfolio of tearsheets, slides, photographs.
Tips: Obtains new talent through recommendations from others and mailings.

JOANNE PALULIAN (III), 18 McKinley St., Rowayton CT 06853. (203)866-3734 or (212)581-8338. Fax: (203)857-0842. Commercial illustration representative. Estab. 1976. Member of SPAR. Represents 7 illustrators. Markets include: advertising agencies; corporations/client direct; design firms; editorial/magazines; sales/promotion firms.
Handles: Illustration.
Terms: Rep receives 30% commission. Exclusive area representation is required. Advertising costs are split: 75% paid by talent; 25% paid by representative. For promotional purposes, talent must provide portfolio and promotional materials. Advertises in *American Showcase, Creative Black Book, Workbook, Graphic Artist Guild Illustration Book, Single Image.*
How to Contact: For first contact, send direct mail flier/brochure. Reports in 2 days, only if interested. After initial contact, drop off or mail in appropriate materials for review. Portfolio should include tearsheets, transparencies (4×5 or 8×10) of original art.
Tips: "Talent usually contacts me, follows up with materials that I can keep. If interest is there, I interview. Do not send materials without my consent. Include return packaging with necessary postage. Be courteous and friendly. You are asking someone to give you his or her time and attention for your benefit."

■**RANDY PATE & ASSOCIATES (III, IV)**, P.O. Box 2160, Moorpark CA 93021. (805)529-8111. Fax: (805)529-2171. Commercial illustration representative. Estab. 1979. Member of Society of Illustrators, Graphic Artists Guild. Represents 9 illustrators, 2 designers. Specializes in entertainment. Markets include: advertising agencies; corporations/client direct; design firms; sales/promotion firms.
Handles: Illustration.
Terms: Rep receives 25% commission. Occasionally charges other fee; "this varies." Exclusive area representation is required. Advertising costs are split: 75% paid by talent; 25% paid by representative. For promotional purposes, talent should provide "a full page in *The Workbook*, and at least 2 portfolios (8×10 transparencies or 11×14 print/tearsheets preferred)." Advertises in *The Workbook*.
How to Contact: For first contact, send query letter, direct mail flier/brochure, tearsheets and SASE. Reports in 2 weeks, only if interested. After initial contact, call for appointment to show portfolio of tearsheets, transparencies (4×5 or 8×10).
Tips: Obtains new talent through recommendations from others.

Commercial Art and Photography Representatives 213

‡■THE PENNY & STERMER GROUP (II), 19 Stuyvesant Oval, New York NY 10009-2021. (212)505-9342. Fax: (212)505-1844. Contact: Carol Lee Stermer. Commercial illustration representative. Estab. 1975. Member of Graphic Artists Guild. Represents 9 illustrators, animation artist. Specializes in illustration for packaging. Markets include: advertising agencies; corporations/client direct; design firms; editorial/magazines; paper products/greeting cards; publishing/books; sales/promotion firms.
Handles; Illustration. Looking for highly conceptual artists and established food packaging artists.
Terms: Rep receives 25-30% commission. Artists billed for portfolio supplies and bulk mailings. Advertising costs are split: 70-75% paid by talent; 30-25% paid by representative. For promotional purposes, talent must provide direct mail pieces. Advertises in *American Showcase, Creative Black Book, RSVP, The Workbook.*
How to Contact: For first contact, send nonreturnable promos, direct mailers, etc. Reports only if interested. After initial contact, "I'll call." Portfolio should include tearsheets, 4 × 5 or 8 × 10 chromes.

‡MARSHA PINKSTAFF REPRESENTING PHOTOGRAPHERS (IV), Suite 1212, 136 E. 57th St., New York NY 10022. (212)799-1500. Fax: (212)721-5910. Contact: Marsha Pinkstaff. Commercial photography representative. Estab. 1981. Represents 2 photographers. Specializes in fashion/beauty/still life. Markets include: advertising agencies; design firms; editorial/magazines.
Handles: Photography.
Terms: Rep receives 25% commission. Exclusive area representation is required. Advertising costs are split: 75% paid by talent; 25% paid by representative.
How to Contact: For first contact, send direct mail flier/brochure. "I will call if I'm interested."
Tips: "Talent calls me. Establish your own vision; don't try to second guess the market."

MARIA PISCOPO (IV), 2038 Calvert Ave., Costa Mesa CA 92626-3520. (714)556-8133. Fax: (714)556-0899. Contact: Maria Piscopo. Commercial photography representative. Estab. 1978. Member of SPAR, Women in Photography, Society of Illustrative Photographers. Markets include: advertising agencies; design firms; corporations.
Handles: Photography. Looking for "unique, unusual styles; handle only established photography."
Terms: Rep receives 25-30% commission. Exclusive area representation is required. No geographic restrictions. Advertising costs are split: 75% paid by talent; 25% paid by representative. For promotional purposes, talent must provide 1 show portfolio, 3 travelling portfolios, leave-behinds and at least 6 new promo pieces per year. Advertises in *American Showcase, The Workbook, New Media.*
How to Contact: For first contact, send query letter, direct mail flier/brochure and SASE. Reports in 2 weeks, if interested.
Tips: Obtains new talent through personal referral and photo magazine articles. "Be very businesslike, organized, professional and follow the above instructions!"

‡CHRISTINE PRAPAS/ARTIST REPRESENTATIVE (V), 8402 SW Soods Creek Court, Portland OR 97219. (503)246-9511. Fax: (503)246-6016. Contact: Christine Prapas. Commercial illustration and photography representative. Estab. 1978. Member of AIGA. "Promotional material welcome."

PUBLISHERS' GRAPHICS (II, III, IV), 251 Greenwood Ave., Bethel CT 06801. (203)797-8188. Fax: (203)798-8848. Commercial illustration representative for juvenile markets. Estab. 1970. Member of Graphic Artists Guild, Author's Guild Inc.. Staff includes Paige C. Gillies (President, selects illustrators, develops talent); Susan P. Schwarzchild (sales manager). Specializes in children's book illustration. Markets include: design firms; editorial/magazines; paper products/greeting cards; publishing/books; sales/promotion firms.
Handles: Illustration.
Terms: Rep receives 25% commission. Exclusive area representation is required. For promotional purposes, talent must provide original art, proofs, photocopies "to start. The assignments generate most sample/promotional material thereafter unless there is a stylistic change in the work." Advertises in *Literary Market Place.*
How to Contact: For first contact, send résumé, photocopies and SASE. Reports in 6 weeks. After initial contact, "We will contact them. We don't respond to phone inquiries." Portfolios should include original art, tearsheets, photocopies.
Tips: Obtains new talent through "clients recommending our agency to artists. We ask for referrals from our illustrators. We receive submissions by mail."

GERALD & CULLEN RAPP, INC. (III), 108 E. 35th St., New York NY 10016. (212)889-3337. Fax: (212)889-3341. Contact: John Knepper (illustration); Donna Petrizzo (photography). Commercial illustration, photography and graphic design representative. Estab. 1945. Member of SPAR, Society of Illustrators, Graphic Artists Guild. Represents 32 illustrators, 3 photographers, 1 designer. Markets include: advertising agencies; corporations/client direct; design firms; editorial/magazines; paper products/greeting cards; publishing/books; sales/promotion firms.
Handles: Illustration, photography.
Terms: Rep receives 25-30% commission. Exclusive area representation is required. No geographic restrictions. Split of advertising costs are negotiated. Advertises in *American Showcase*, *New York Gold*, *The Workbook*, and *CA*, *Print*, *Art Director* magazines. "Conducts active direct mail program."
How to Contact: For first contact, send query letter, direct mail flier/brochure. Reports in 1 week. After initial contact, call for appointment to show portfolio of tearsheets, slides.
Tips: Obtains new talent through recommendations from others, solicitations.

‡JODI RAPPAPORT (III), #609, 5410 Wilshire Blvd., Los Angeles CA 90036. (213)934-8633. Fax: (213)934-0690. Commercial photography, graphic design, stylist and art director representative. Estab. 1987. Member of SPAR. Represents 4 photographers, 2 designers. Markets include: advertising agencies; corporations/client direct; design firms; editorial/magazines; sales/promotion firms. Clients include galleries.
Handles: Photography, design.
Terms: Rep receives 25% commission. Charges for messengers and air courier per charges incurred. Exclusive area representation is required. Advertising costs are paid by talent. For promotional purposes, talent must provide direct mail pieces, professional portfolio presentation.
How to Contact: For first contact, send direct mail flier/brochure. Reports in 1 week, only if interested. After initial contact, drop off portfolio for review. "If interested, I will call to set up meeting. Portfolio content depends upon the client and what presentation form is appropriate for the work."
Tips: "I generally only take meeting with photographers who are recommended to me. Otherwise, I keep promos on file. Books are seen on a drop-off basis only. Any photographer interested in seeking representation should research the talent the rep is working with so they have an idea if the rep is appropriate for their needs. They should be clear about their focus and direction, and know what venues they would like to explore. They should have a great, strong presentation."

REDMOND REPRESENTS (III), 7K Misty Wood Circle, Timonium MD 21093. (410)666-1916. Contact: Sharon Redmond. Commercial illustration and photography representative. Estab. 1987. Markets include: advertising agencies; corporations/client direct; design firms.
Handles: Illustration, photography.
Terms: Rep receives 30% commission. Exclusive area representation is required. No geographic restrictions. Advertising costs and expenses are split: 50% paid by talent; 50% paid by representative. For promotional purposes, talent must provide a small portfolio (easy to Federal Express) and at least 6 direct mail pieces (with fax number included). Advertises in *American Showcase*, *Creative Black Book*.
How to Contact: For first contact, send photocopies. Reports in 2 weeks. After initial contact, representative will call talent to set an appointment.
Tips: Obtains new talent through recommendations from others, advertising a "black book," etc. "Even if I'm not taking in new talent, I do want *photocopies* sent of new work. You never know when an ad agency will require a different style of illustration/photography and it's always nice to refer to my files."

‡■PAMELA REID (III), 2nd Floor, 35 E. 67th St., New York NY 10021. (212)982-2226. Fax: (212)772-6107. Contact: Pamela Reid. Commercial photography representive, fashion and beauty photography and personalities. Estab. 1982. Member of SPAR. Represents 1 photographer. Specializes in fashion, beauty, personalities. Markets include: advertising agencies; editorial/magazines; publishing books; TV/catalogs.
Handles: Photography.
Terms: Rep receives 25% commission. Charges for messengers and all promotional materials. Exclusive area representation is required in US. Advertising costs are paid by talent. For promotional purposes, "art photographers need to have a portfolio—or enough tearsheets to make one." Advertises in *American Showcase*, *Creative Black Book*, *The Workbook*.

Commercial Art and Photography Representatives 215

How to Contact: For first contact, "call me." Reporting is "always individual, usually quick." After initial contact, call for appointment to show portfolio of tearsheets and photographs.
Tips: Obtains new talent through recommendations from others or "they find me. I am not looking for talent that does not already work—Europe or here."

KERRY REILLY: REPS (II), P.O. Box 13025, Charlotte NC 28270. (704)372-6007. Fax: same. Contact: Kerry Reilly. Commercial illustration and photography representative. Estab. 1990. Represents 16 illustrators, 3 photographers. Markets include: advertising agencies; corporations/client direct; design firms; editorial/magazines.
Handles: Illustration, photography. Looking for computer graphics, freehand, etc.
Terms: Rep receives 25% commission. Exclusive area representation is required. No geographic restrictions. Advertising costs are split: 75% paid by talent; 25% paid by representative. For promotional purposes, talent must provide at least 2 pages printed leave-behind samples. Preferred format is 9 × 12 pages, portfolio work on 4 × 5 transparencies. Advertises in *American Showcase*.
How to Contact: For first contact, send direct mail flier/brochure or samples of work. Reports in 2 weeks. After initial contact, call for appointment to show portfolio or drop off or mail tearsheets, slides, 4 × 5 transparencies.
Tips: Obtains new talent through recommendations from others. "It's essential to have printed samples—a lot of printed samples."

‡REPRESENTED BY KEN MANN INC. (IV), 20 W. 46th St., New York NY 10036. (212)944-2853. Fax: (212)921-8673. Contact: Ken Mann. Commercial photography representative. Estab. 1974. Member of SPAR. Represents 3 photographers. Specializes in "highest quality work!" Markets include: advertising agencies.
Handles: Photography.
Terms: Rep receives 25% commission. Exclusive area representation is required. Advertising costs are split: 75% paid by talent; 25% paid by representative. Advertises in *Creative Black Book*.
How to Contact: For first contact, send query letter, résumé, bio, direct mail flier/brochure, photocopies, photostats, "nothing that needs to be returned." Reports in 1 week if interested. After initial contact, call for appointment to show portfolio of tearsheets and photographs.
Tips: Obtains new talent through editorial work, recommendations. "Put together the best portfolio possible because knowledgable reps only want the best!"

‡RETNA LTD. (II, III), 18 E. 17th St., New York NY 10003. (212)255-0622. Fax: (212)255-1224. Contact: Lee Marsh. Stock photo agency. Estab. 1970. Represents 1000 photographers. Specializes in music and celebrity photography. Markets include: editorial/magazines; publishing/books; record companies.
Handles: Photography. Looking for "studio photographers who shoot actors, actresses and musicians."
Terms: Rep receives 50% commission. Exclusive area representation is required. Advertising costs are paid by representative. "Any personal promotional material welcome." Advertises in *Creative Black Book*.
How to Contact: Send query letter, slides. "Phone calls welcome." Reports in 2 weeks, only if interested. Call for appointment to show portfolio of tearsheets, slides, photographs.

RIDGEWAY ARTISTS REPRESENTATIVE (III), 444 Lentz Ct., Lansing MI 48917. (517)371-3086. Fax: (517)371-5160. Contact: Edwin Bonnen. Commercial illustration and photography representative. Estab. 1984. Member of AAF, AIGA. Represents 3 illustrators, 1 photographer. Markets include: advertising agencies; corporations/client direct; design firms; editorial/magazines.
Handles: Illustration, photography, fine art. "We are primarily looking for individuals who have developed a distinctive style, whether they be a photographer or illustrator. Photographers must have an area they specialize in. We want artists who are pros in the commercial worlds; i.e., working with tight deadlines in sometimes less than ideal situations. We would consider a fine artist looking for commercial outlet if it was a good fit."
Terms: Rep receives 25% commission in the state of Michigan, 35% out of state. Exclusive area representation is required. Advertising costs are split: 75% paid by talent; 25% paid by representative. For promotional purposes, talent must provide portfolio of laminated color prints. "Direct mail is primary method of advertising; use of sourcebooks is secondary."

How to Contact: For first contact, send query letter, bio, direct mail flier/brochure. Reports in 3 weeks, only if interested. After initial contact, call for appointment to show portfolio of photographs.
Tips: "Obtains new talent through recommendations, sourcebooks and solicitations."

ARLENE ROSENBERG (II), 377 W. 11th St., New York NY 10014. (212)675-7983. Fax: (212)675-7984. Contact: Arlene Rosenberg. Commercial photography representative. Estab. 1980. Member of SPAR. Represent 2 photographers. Staff includes Erin Wilheim, assistant. Markets include: advertising agencies; design firms; editorial/magazines.
Handles: Photography.
Terms: Rep receives 25% commission. Exclusive area representation is required. Advertising costs are split: 75% paid by talent; 25% paid by representative. "Will review with talent" what to provide in portfolio. Advertises in *Creative Black Book*.
How to Contact: For first contact, send direct mail flier/brochure. Reports in 5 days on queries. After initial contact, call for appointment to show portfolio of tearsheets and chromes.
Tips: Obtains new talent through recommendations.

ROSENTHAL REPRESENTS (IV), 3443 Wade St., Los Angeles CA 90066. (213)390-9595. Fax: (213)306-6878. Commercial illustration representative and licensing agent for artists who do advertising, entertainment, action/sports, children's humorous, storyboard, animal, graphic, floral, realistic, impressionistic and game packaging art. Estab. 1979. Member of SPAR, Society of Illustrators, Graphic Artists Guild, Women in Design and Art Directors Club. Represents 100 illustrators, 3 photographers, 2 designers and 5 fine artists. Specializes in game packaging, personalities, licensing, merchandising art and storyboard artists. Markets include: advertising agencies; corporations/client direct; paper products/greeting cards; sales/promotion firms; licensees and manufacturers.
Handles: Illustration.
Terms: Rep receives 25-30% as a rep; 40% as a licensing agent. Exclusive area representation is required. No geographic restrictions. Advertising costs are paid by talent. For promotion purposes, talent must provide 1-2 sets of transparencies (mounted and labeled), 10 sets of slides of your best work (labeled with name on each slide), 1-3 promos. Advertises in *American Showcase, Creative Black Book* and *The Workbook*.
How to Contact: For first contact, send direct mail flier/brochure, tearsheets, slides, photocopies, photostats and SASE. Reports in 1 week. After initial contact, call for appointment to show portfolio of tearsheets, slides, photographs, photocopies.
Tips: Obtains new talent through seeing their work in an advertising book or at an award show.

‡LINDA RUDERMAN (III), 1245 Park Ave., New York NY 10128. (212)369-7531. Contact: Linda Ruderman. Commercial photography representative. Estab. 1988. Represents 2 photographers. Specializes in food photography, "but have repped still life, fashion, kids." Markets include: advertising agencies; corporations/client direct; design firms; sales/promotion firms.
Handles: Photography.
Terms: "12-15%, to be discussed. Depends on the entire agreement, no set policy. Each agreement is individual." For promotional purposes, talent must provide reprints from sourcebooks and/or direct mail pieces. Advertises in *Creative Black Book* and *The Workbook*.
How to Contact: For first contact send résumé, bio, direct mail flier/brochure. Reports back only if interested. Call for appointment to show portfolio of tearsheets, slides, photographs.
Tips: Obtains new talent through recommendations from others, solicitation.

S.I. INTERNATIONAL (II), 43 E. 19th St., New York NY 10003. (212)254-4996. Fax: (212)995-0911. Commercial illustration representative. Estab. 1973. Member of SPAR, Graphic Artists Guild. Represents 20 illustrators, 1 photographer. Specializes in license characters, educational publishing and

---

The needs of art and photography reps are constantly changing! If you are using this book and it is 1995 or later, buy the newest edition of Guide to Literary Agents and Art/Photo Reps *at your favorite book or art supply store or order directly from Writer's Digest Books.*

Commercial Art and Photography Representatives 217

children's illustration, mass market paperbacks. Markets include design firms; publishing/books; sales/promotion firms; licensing firms.
Handles: Illustration. Looking for artists "who have the ability to do children's illustration and to do license characters."
Terms: Rep receives 25-30% commission. Advertising costs are split: 70% paid by talent; 30% paid by representative. "Contact agency for details. Must have mailer." Advertises in *RSVP*.
How to Contact: For first contact, send query letter, tearsheets. Reports in 3 weeks. After initial contact, write for appointment to show portfolio of tearsheets, slides.

‡DARIO SACRAMONE (III), 302 W. 12th St., New York NY 10014. (212)929-0487. Fax: (212)242-4429. Commercial photography representative. Estab. 1972. Represents 2 photographers. Markets include: advertising agencies; design firms; editorial/magazines.
Handles: Photography.
Terms: Rep receives 25% commission. Exclusive area representation is required. For promotional purposes, talent must provide direct mail piece, minimum of 3 professionally put together portfolios.
How to Contact: For first contact, send bio, direct mail flier/brochure. After initial contact, drop off or mail in appropriate materials for review.
Tips: Obtains new talent through recommendations from others.

■RICHARD SALZMAN (II, III), 716 Sanchez St., San Francisco CA 94114. (415)285-8267. Fax: (415)285-8268. Contact: Richard Salzman. Commercial illustration representative. Estab. 1982. Member of SPAR, Graphic Artists Guild, AIGA, SFCA, WADC. Represents 14 illustrators. Markets include: advertising agencies; corporations/client direct; design firms; editorial/magazines; publishing books.
Handles: Illustration. "We're always looking for visionaries and are also interested in digital art or other 'new' media."
Terms: Rep receives 30% commission. Exclusive area representation in US is required. Advertising costs are split: 70% paid by talent; 30% paid by representative. "We share promotional costs." Charges for "portfolios. Talent is required to pay cost of the portfolio (6 copies) created by the representative." Advertises in *American Showcase, The Workbook* and *Creative Illustration Book*.
How to Contact: For first contact, send tearsheets, slides, photocopies. After initial contact, call for appointment to show portfolio.
Tips: "We receive 20 to 30 solicitors a week. We sign an average of one new artist a year. Solicit to reps the way you would to a client or art director."

‡■TRUDY SANDS & ASSOCIATES (III), 1350 Chemical St., Dallas TX 75207. (214)905-9037. Fax: (214)905-9038. Contact: Trudy Sands. Commercial illustration and photography representative. Estab. 1984. Member of AIGA. Represents 7 illustrators, 1 photographer. Markets include: advertising agencies; corporations/client direct; design firms; editorial/magazines; publishing/books.
Handles: Illustration.
Terms: Rep receives 25% commission. Charges 75% of Federal Express bills. Exclusive area representation is required. 25% of advertising costs is paid by representative when billing 10,000 or more a year. For promotional purposes, talent must provide "4 mailers a year with rep's name and phone number. Two new portfolio pieces a month. Certain format agreed upon by rep and illustrator." Advertises in *RSVP, The Workbook, Japanese Sourcebook*.
How to Contact: For first contact, send direct mail flier/brochure. Reports in 1 month if interested. After initial contact, call for appointment to show portfolio of 4×5 transparencies or laminated photocopies.
Tips: Obtains new talent through direct mail or sourcebooks. "Have an interesting style. Good promo pieces. Be willing to advertise. Don't expect reps to call you back long distance. Ask art directors which reps they like."

‡KEVIN R. SCHOCHAT (II), #14-N, 150 E. 18th St., New York NY 10003. (212)475-7068. Fax: (212)475-1040. Contact: Kevin R. Schochat. Commercial photography representative. Estab. 1982. Represents 4 photographers. Markets include: advertising agencies; corporations/client direct; design firms; editorial/magazines; publishing/books; sales/promotion firms.
Handles: Photography.
Terms: Rep receives 25% commission. Advertising costs are split: 75% paid by talent; 25% paid by representative. "Talent must be willing to do regular promotions and mailings. Also, portfolio must be up-to-date, with new ideas and tests added frequently. A photographer should love to take pictures,

therefore, adding new work to his/her portfolio." Advertises in *Creative Black Book, New York Gold*.
How to Contact: For first contact, "phone call is fine." Reports in 2 days. After initial contact, call for appointment to show portfolio of tearsheets, slides, photographs; "his/her best work."
Tips: Obtains new talent through "recommendations from people in my field, review of various publications, attending portfolio reviews, notice of award shows, solicitation of people that interest me, etc. Show only your best work and be truly passionate about what you do."

FREDA SCOTT, INC. (III), 244 Ninth St., San Francisco CA 94103. (415)621-2992. Fax: (415)621-5202. Contact: Wendy Fuchs or Freda Scott. Commercial illustration and photography representative. Estab. 1980. Member of SPAR. Represents 10 illustrators, 6 photographers. Markets include: advertising agencies; corporations/client direct; design firms; editorial/magazines; paper products/greeting cards; publishing/books; sales/promotion firms.
Handles: Illustration, photography.
Terms: Rep receives 25% commission. No geographic restrictions. Advertising costs are split: 75% paid by talent; 25% paid by representative. For promotional purposes, talent must provide "promotion piece and ad in a directory. I also need at least 3 portfolios." Advertises in *American Showcase, Creative Black Book, The Workbook*.
How to Contact: For first contact, send direct mail flier/brochure, tearsheets and SASE. If you send transparencies, reports in 1 week, if interested. "You need to make follow up calls." After initial contact, call for appointment to show portfolio of tearsheets, photographs, 4×5's or 8×10's.
Tips: Obtains new talent sometimes through recommendations, sometimes solicitation. "If you are seriously interested in getting repped, keep sending promos—once every 6 months or so. Do it yourself a year or two until you know what you need a rep to do."

‡SHARPE + ASSOCIATES (V), 7536 Ogelsby Ave., Los Angeles, CA 90045. (310)641-8556. Fax: (310)641-8534. Contact: John Sharpe (LA), Coleen Hedleston (NY: (212)595-1125). Commercial illustration and photography representative. Estab. 1987. Member of APA, ADLA. Represents 3 illustrators, 4 photographers. Not currently seeking new talent but "always willing to look at work." Staff includes: John Sharpe and Colleen Hedleston (general commercial—advertising and design), "both have ad agency marketing backgrounds. We tend to show more non-mainstream work." Markets include: advertising agencies; corporations/client direct; design firms; editorial/magazines; sales/promotion firms.
Handles: Illustration, photography.
Terms: Rep recieves 25% commission. Exclusive area representation is required, Advertising costs are split: 75% paid by talent; 25% paid by representative. For promotional purposes, "promotion and advertising materials are a shared responsibility, though the talent must be able to afford 75% of the material/media. The portfolios are 100% the talent's responsiblity and we like to have at least 2 complete books." Advertises in *Creative Black Book, The Workbook*, Music Industry Sourcebook, *AR Directory* and select magazines.
How to Contact: For first contact, call, then followup with printed samples. Reports in 2 weeks. Call for appointment to show portfolio of c- or r-prints of original work for illustration and transparencies or prints for photography.
Tips: Obtains new talent mostly through referrals, occasional solicitations. "Once they have a professional portfolio together and at least one representative promotional piece, they should target reps along with potential buyers of their work as if the two groups are one and the same. They need to market themselves to reps as if the reps are potential clients."

■SOLDAT & ASSOCIATES (II), Suite 1008, 307 N. Michigan, Chicago IL 60601. (312)201-9662. Fax: (312)201-9664. Contact: Rick Soldat. Commercial illustration and photography representative. Estab. 1990. Member of SPAR. Represents 4 illustrators, 4 photographers. Markets include: advertising agencies; corporations/client direct; design firms; publishing/books; sales/promotion firms.
Handles: Illustration, photography.
Terms: Rep receives 25-30% commission. Charges for postage, shipping, long-distance travel. Exclusive area representation in the Midwest is required. Advertising costs are split: 75% paid by talent; 25% paid by representative. For promotional purposes, talent must provide "a promo for direct mail and other purposes." Advertises in *The Workbook* and *Chicago Talent Sourcebook*.
How to Contact: For first contact, send query letter, tearsheets. Reports in 1 week. After initial contact, call for appointment to show portfolio of original art, tearsheets, slides, photographs.
Tips: Obtains new talent through "recommendations from others, talent search, talent calling us directly."

Commercial Art and Photography Representatives 219

‡DANE SONNEVILLE ASSOC. INC. (II), P.O. Box 155, 285 Aycrigg, Passaic NJ 07055. Phone and fax: (201)472-1225. Contact: Dane. Commercial illustration, photography and graphic design representative, illustration or photography broker, paste up, printing, hair and make up, all type stylists, computer image artists, writers. Estab. 1971. Represents 20 illustrators, 10 photographers and 10 designers. Specializes in "resourcefulness and expeditious service." Markets include: advertising agencies; corporations/client direct; design firms; editorial/magazines; publishing/books; sales/promotion firms.
Handles: Illustration, photography, design, writing, all creative support personnel.
Terms: Rep receives 25% commission. Advertising costs are paid by talent. For promotional purposes, talent must provide unlimited promo pieces (leave behind). Advertises in *American Showcase, Creative Black Book, RSVP, The Workbook.*
How to Contact: For first contact, send résumé, direct mail flier/brochure, tearsheets. Reports in 1 week if interested. After initial contact, call for appointment to show portfolio of original art, tearsheets, slides, photographs.
Tips: Obtains new talent through recommendations from others. "Knock on every door."

‡■SOODAK REPRESENTS (III, IV), 11135 Korman Dr., Potomac MD 20854. (301)983-2343. Fax: (301)983-3040. Contact: Arlene Soodak. Commercial photography representative. Estab. 1985. Represents 4 photographers. Specializes in international capabilities—photography, food, location, still life; East Coast, West Coast, Paris. Markets include: advertising agencies; design firms.
Handles: Photography. Looking for "established or award winners such as Kodak's European 'photographer of the year,' former National Geographic, etc."
Terms: Rep receives 25% commission. Exclusive area representation is required. Payment of advertising costs "depends on length of time artist is with me." For promotional purposes, talent must provide "intact portfolio of excellent quality work for promo package and direct mail campaign which I will market and help design." Advertises in *The Workbook.*
How to Contact: For first contact, send direct mail flier/brochure, tearsheets, photocopies. Reports in 10 days. After initial contact, drop off or mail in portfolio for review.
Tips: Obtains new talent through recommendations from others.

‡STORYBOARDS (III, IV), #108, 4052 Del Rey Ave., Venice CA 90292. (310)305-1998. Fax: (310)305-1810. Contact: Jennifer Morrison. Commercial illustration representative and storyboard artists for advertising, commercial production and feature films. Estab. 1979. Represents 30 illustrators. Markets include: advertising agencies; commercial productions; feature films.
Handles: Illustration, set design.
Terms: Rep receives 25% commission. Exclusive area representation is required. Advertising costs are split: 75% paid by talent; 25% paid by representative. "Talent and agency work together on promo." Advertises in *The Workbook.*
How to Contact: For first contact, send non-returnable samples or portfolio drop off and SASE. Reports in 5 days. Drop off or mail in appropriate samples for review. Portfolio should include storyboards/comp samples.
Tips: Obtains new talent through referrals.

‡SULLIVAN & ASSOCIATES (II, III), 3805 Maple Ct., Marietta GA 30066. (404)971-6782. Fax: (404)973-3331. Contact: Tom Sullivan. Commercial illustration, commercial photography and graphic design representative. Estab. 1988. Member of Creative Club of Atlanta, Atlanta Ad Club. Represents 14 illustrators, 7 photographers and 7 designers, including computer graphic skills in illustration/design/production and photography. Staff includes Tom Sullivan (sales, talent evaluation, management), Debbie Sullivan (accounting, administration). Specializes in "providing whatever creative or production resource the client needs." Markets include: advertising agencies, corporations/client direct; design firms; editorial/magazines; publishing/books; sales/promotion firms.
Handles: Illustration, photography. "Open to what is marketable; computer graphics skills."
Terms: Rep receives 25% commission. Exclusive area representation in Southeastern US is required. Advertising costs are split: 75-100% paid by talent; 0-25% paid by representative. "Negotiated on individual basis depending on: (1) length of time worked with; (2) area of representation; (3) scope of exclusive representation." For promotional purposes, talent must provide "direct mail piece, portfolio in form of 8½×11 (8×10 prints) pages in 22 ring presentation book." Advertises in *American Showcase, The Workbook.*

How to Contact: For first contact, send bio, direct mail flier/brochure; "follow up with phone call." Reports in 2 weeks if interested. After initial contact, call for appointment to show portfolio of tearsheets, photographs, photostats, photocopies, "anything appropriate in nothing larger than 8½×11 print format."
Tips: Obtains new talent through referrals and direct contact from creative person. "Have direct mail piece or be ready to produce it immediately upon reaching an agreement with a rep. Be prepared to immediately put together a portfolio based on what the rep needs for that specific market area."

‡**T & M ENTERPRISES (II)**, Suite 2020, 270 N. Canon Dr., Beverly Hills CA 90210. (310)281-7504. Fax: (310)274-7957. Contact: Tony Marques. Commercial photography representative and photography broker. Estab. 1985. Represents 50 photographers. Specializes in women photography only: high fashion, swimsuit, lingerie, glamour and fine (good taste) *Playboy*-style pictures. Markets include: advertising agencies; corporations/client direct; editorial/magazines; paper products/greeting cards; publishing/books; sales/promotion firms; medical magazines.
Handles: Photography.
Terms: Rep receives 50% commission. Exclusive area representation is not required. Advertising costs are paid by representative. "We promote the standard material the photographer has available, unless our clients request it." Advertises in Europe, South and Central America and magazines not known in the US.
How to Contact: For first contact, send slides, photographs, transparencies and printed work, if any. Reports in 2 days. After initial contact, drop off or mail in appropriate materials for review. Portfolio should include slides, photographs, transparencies, printed work.
Tips: Obtains new talent through worldwide famous fashion shows in Paris, Rome, London and Tokyo; participating in well-known international beauty contests; recommendations from others. "Send your material clean. Send your material organized (neat). Do not borrow other photographers' work in order to get representation. Protect—always—yourself by copyrighting your material. Get releases from everybody that is in the picture (or everything owned by somebody)."

‡**TONAL VALUES, INC. (V)**, 111 NE 42nd St., Miami FL 33137. Representative not currently seeking new talent.

JOSEPH TRIBELLI DESIGNS, LTD. (II, IV), 254-33 Iowa Rd., Great Neck NY 11020. (516)482-2699. Contact: Joseph Tribelli. Representative of textile designers only. Estab. 1988. Member of Graphic Artists Guild. Represents 9 designers. Specializes in textile surface design for apparel (women and men). "All designs are on paper."
Handles: Textile design for apparel and home furnishings.
Terms: Rep receives 40% commission. Exclusive area representation is required.
How to Contact: "Telephone first." Reports back in 2 weeks. After initial contact, drop off or mail appropriate materials. Portfolio should include original art.
Tips: Obtains new talent through "placing ads, recommendations. I am interested in only textile designers who can paint on paper. Do not apply unless you have a flair for fashion."

‡■**TWO STEPS UP, INC. (II, III)**, #1A, 26 Bedford St., New York NY 10014. (212)675-1892. Fax: (212)691-3627 ("write my name and phone on fax"). Contact: Amy Cohen. Commercial photography representative. Estab. 1989. Represents a food photographer and a romance cover photographer. Markets include: advertising agencies; corporations/client direct; design firms (least); editorial/magazines.
Handles: Photography. "I am looking to take on 2-3 more photographers; anything except food or fashion: portrait, still life, lifestyle, kids; open to other categories."
Terms: Rep receives 25% commission and a monthly draw. Exclusive area representation is required. Advertising costs are paid by talent (at present only). For promotional purposes, "need minimum 2 portfolios with cases, tearsheets optional, and at least 4 leave-behinds. Direct mail not mandatory. Must supply a minimum of 3 new printed promo pieces and shoot at least 4 new portfolio pieces annually." Advertises in *The Workbook*, *Single Image*.
How to Contact: For first contact, send query letter, direct mail flier/brochure; "no originals." Reports in 1 week. After initial contact, call for appointment.
Tips: Obtains new talent through recommendations from *The Workbook*, recommendations from art directors, solicitation from sourcebooks. "As repping someone is very much like a marriage, it is of utmost importance to establish clear and direct communication with my talent. Talent must be willing to test all the time, to keep the portfolio fresh and current. As I frequently work with a consultant, it

We've just made getting your words published a little easier

Subscribe to WRITER'S DIGEST now, and get this invaluable guide, *Getting Published: What Every Writer Needs to Know*, FREE with your paid subscription.

SPECIAL FREE GIFT OFFER!

INSIDE: How to write irresistible query letters and prepare polished manuscripts. How to give an editor nothing to do—except buy your work. Where to find ideas. And the "test" every editor gives...14 questions you can use to evaluate your freelancing savvy.

Use the card below to start your subscription today!

Subscription Savings Card

☐ **Yes!** I want professional advice on how to write publishable material and sell it to the best-paying markets. Start my 1-year (12 issues) subscription to WRITER'S DIGEST for just $18.97... **a 46% savings off the newsstand price.**

Name _____

Address _____

City _____

State _____ Zip _____

☐ Payment enclosed. Send my FREE gift right away!
☐ Bill me, and send my free gift upon payment.
Charge my ☐ Visa ☐ MasterCard

Card # _____ Exp. _____

Signature _____

Guarantee: If you aren't completely satisfied with your subscription at any time, simply cancel and receive a full refund on all unmailed issues due you.
Outside the U.S. add $7 (includes GST) and remit in U.S. funds. Newsstand rate $35.40.

JPLA9

No other source offers so much information and instruction...

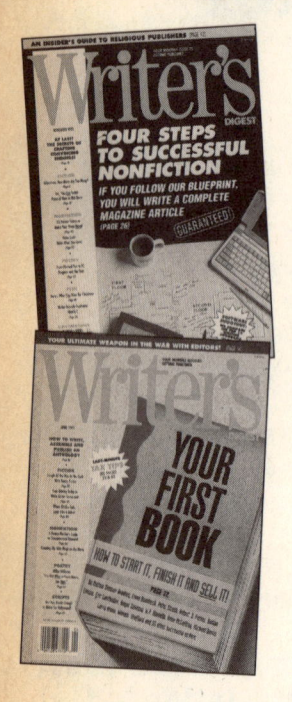

on writing...

WRITER'S DIGEST is packed with advice from the experts that can make you a better writer. Whatever your challenge...from generating plot ideas to overcoming writer's block. Whatever your specialty...from writing poetry to children's stories.

and selling what you write!

Learn the secrets of top-dollar freelancers. How to slant your writing for multiple sales and negotiate contracts with editors and publishers. How to make and keep contacts that help your career. Find out what markets are hot for your work right now, how much they're paying, and how to get in touch with the right people.

Subscribe today and save 46% off the newsstand price!

BUSINESS REPLY MAIL
FIRST CLASS MAIL   PERMIT NO. 76   HARLAN, IA

POSTAGE WILL BE PAID BY ADDRESSEE

NO POSTAGE
NECESSARY
IF MAILED
IN THE
UNITED STATES

Writer's DIGEST

PO BOX 2124
HARLAN IA 51593-2313

would be helpful for talent to be open to bi- or triannual meetings with the consultant and myself to discuss the portfolio. I am not interested in someone who expects instant fame and fortune. My best working relationship is honest, with equal amounts of energy expended on both sides. Growth is a continual process for both of us."

‡■SUSAN P. URSTADT INC. WRITERS AND ARTISTS AGENCY (II), P.O. Box 1676, New Canaan CT 06849. (203)966-6111. Contact: Susan Urstadt. Illustration and photography representative. Estab. 1975. Member of AAR. Specializes in illustrated books.
Handles: Photography and illustration for children's books; adult books on lifestyle, gardening, food; botanical and zoological illustration.
Terms: Rep receives 25% commission. Advertising costs are negotiable. Charges for out of pocket expenses. Exclusive area representation is required. For promotional purposes, talent is required to provide oversize color postcard with 4 different images and artist bio on back.
How to Contact: For first contact, send query letter, résumé, bio, direct mail/flier and SASE. "No original art, no oversize submissions." Reports in 1 month. After initial contact, "We'll call you if we fall in love with it." Portfolio should include appropriate materials as advised.
Tips: Obtains clients through word of mouth. "Good luck!"

URSULA INTERNATIONAL CREATIVES, (V), Ottostrasse 92, 26135 Oldenburg Germany. Specializing in the European markets.

PHILIP M. VELORIC, ARTIST REPRESENTATIVE (II), 128 Beechtree Dr., Broomall PA 19008. (215)356-0362. Fax: (215)353-7531. Contact: Philip M. Veloric. Commercial illustration representative. Estab. 1963. Member of Art Directors Club of Philadelphia. Represents 22 illustrators. "Most of my business is from textbook publishing, but not all of it." Markets include: advertising agencies; design firms; publishing/books; collectibles.
Handles: Illustration. "Artists should be able to do (and have samples to show) all ethnic children (getting ages right; tell a story; develop a character); earth science, life and physical science; some trade books also."
Terms: Rep receives 25% commission. Exclusive area representation is required. Advertising costs are split: 75% paid by talent; 25% paid by representative. Advertises in *RSVP*.
How to Contact: For first contact, call. After initial contact, call for appointment to show portfolio of original art, tearsheets, photocopies, laser copies.
Tips: Obtains new talent through recommendations from others.

‡JAE WAGONER, ARTIST REPRESENTATIVE (II, IV), Unit #C, 654 Pier Ave., Santa Monica CA 90405. (310)392-4877. Contact: Jae Wagoner "by mail only—send copies or tear sheets only for us to keep—do not call!" Commercial illustration representative. Estab. 1975. Represents 12 illustrators. Markets include: advertising agencies; corporations/client direct; design firms; editorial/magazines; paper products/greeting cards; publishing/books; sales/promotion firms.
Handles: Illustration.
Terms: Rep receives 25% commission locally; 30% outside of Los Angeles. Exclusive area representation required. Advertising costs depend. For promotional purposes talent must advertise once a year in major promotional book (ex: *Workbook*) exclusively with us. "Specifications and details are handled privately." Advertises in *American Showcase* and *The Workbook*.
How to Contact: When making first contact, send: query letter (with other reps mentioned), photocopies ("examples to keep only. No unsolicited work returned.") Reports in weeks only if interested. After initial contact, talent should "wait to hear from us."
Tips: "We select first from 'keepable' samples mailed to us. The actual work determines our interest, not verbal recommendation or résumés. Sometimes we search for styles we are lacking. It is *not* a good idea to call a rep out of the blue. You are just another voice on the phone. What is important is your work, *not* who you know, where you went to school, etc. Unsolicited work that needs to be returned creates a negative situation for the agent. It can get lost, and the volume can get horrendous. Also— do your homework—do not call and expect to be given the address by phone. It's a waste of the rep's

---

To find a rep located near you or one who handles a region in which you need representation, check the Art and Photography Reps Geographic Index.

time and shows a lack of effort. Be brief and professional. Do not call for advice or referrals. That's not the rep's function and we get countless requests."

WARNER & ASSOCIATES (IV), 1425 Belleview Ave., Plainfield NJ 07060. (908)755-7236. Contact: Bob Warner. Commercial illustration and photography representative. Estab. 1986. Represents 4 illustrators, 4 photographers. "My specialized markets are advertising agencies that service pharmaceutical, medical, health-care clients."
Handles: Illustration, photography. Looking for medical illustrators: microscope photographers (photomicrography), science illustrators, special effects photographers.
Terms: Rep receives 25% commission. "Promo pieces and portfolios obviously are needed; who makes up what and at what costs and to whom, varies widely in this business."
How to Contact: For first contact send query letter "or phone me." Reports back in days. Portfolio should include "anything that talent considers good sample material."
Tips: Obtains new talent "by hearsay and recommendations. Also, specialists in my line of work often hear about my work from art directors and they call me."

WARSHAW BLUMENTHAL, INC. (III), 104 E. 40th St., New York NY 10016. (212)867-4225. Fax: (212)867-4154. Contact: Andrea Warshaw. Commercial illustration representative. Estab. 1988. Member of SPAR. Represents 26 illustrators. "We service the ad agencies in offering high-tech storyboard, comp art and animatic art for testing. Currently looking for finished artists. We also represent letters' and a Macintosh computer artist who animates on the system."
Terms: No information provided.
How to Contact: For first contact, send résumé, direct mail flier/brochure, photocopies. Reports in 2 days. After initial contact, call for appointment or drop off or mail portfolio of "finished-looking animatic art and/or a reel."
Tips: Obtains new talent through word of mouth and recommendations.

WASHINGTON-ARTISTS' REPRESENTATIVES (II), Suite 152, 4901 Broadway, San Antonio TX 78209. (210)822-1336. Fax: (210)822-1375. Contact: Dick Washington. Commercial illustration and photography representative. Estab. 1983. Member of CASSA. Represents 10 illustrators, 2 photographers.
Terms: No information provided.
How to Contact: For first contact, send tearsheets. Reports in 2 weeks, only if interested. After initial contact, call for appointment to show portfolio of original art, tearsheets, slides.
Tips: Usually obtains, new talent through recommendations and solicitation. "Make sure that you are ready for a real commitment and relationship. It's an important step for an artist, and should be taken seriously. Don't allow an art rep to sign you to an exclusive contract. You will want representation in all the major markets eventually."

‡**THE WEBER GROUP (II)**, 125 W. 77 St., New York NY 10024. (212)799-6532. Fax: (212)874-9488. Contact: Tricia Weber. Commercial illustration representative. Estab. 1984. Represents 7 illustrators. Group includes Abe Gurvin and Bill Mayer (humorous); Raul Colon and Bruno Pacuilli (conceptual/editorial); David McKelvey (realistic airbrush); Burton Morris; Marti Shohet (graphic line). Specializes in advertising illustration, publishing and design firm work. Markets include: advertising agencies; corporations/client direct; design firms; editorial/magazines; book publishers.
Handles: Illustration.
Terms: Rep receives 25% commission. Advertising costs are split: 75% paid by talent; 25% paid by representative. For promotional purposes, talent must provide "a portfolio (transparencies or color prints to be determined after meeting) of 10-15 quality pieces; advertise in at least 1 top directory once a year and participate in direct mail with group." Advertises in *American Showcase, The Workbook*.
How to Contact: For first contact, send tearsheets, slides, photographs, photocopies or photostats. Reports in 2 weeks. "Will return anything if requested." After initial contact, drop off or mail in appropriate materials for review. Portfolio should include tearsheets, slides and/or photographs. "Good quality reproductions are necessary to show care about presentation."
Tips: "Usually referred by other reps, art buyers, art directors. Attends shows to see new talent. My job as a rep is to seek new talent, and see who is out there with an exciting 'new' style (new approach to an old style). Presentation is important. 'Neat,' but not necessarily in the traditional sense of the word, is important."

Commercial Art and Photography Representatives 223

ELYSE WEISSBERG (II,III), 299 Pearl St., New York NY 10038. (212)406-2566. Fax: (212)571-7568. Contact: Elyse Weissberg. Commercial photography representative. Estab. 1982. Member of SPAR. Represents 3 photographers. Markets include: advertising agencies; corporations/client direct; design firms; editorial/magazines; publishing/books; sales/promotion firms.
Handles: Photography. "I'm not looking for talent now, but I'm always interested in seeing what's out there."
Terms: "Each of my contracts are negotiated separately." No geographic restrictions. No specific promotional requirements. "My only requirement is ambition." Advertises in *American Showcase, Creative Black Book, The Workbook.*
How to Contact: For first contact, send direct mail flier/brochure. Reports in 1 week, if interested. After initial contact, drop off or mail in portfolio for review.
Tips: Obtains new talent through recommendations, direct mail. "Don't give up! Someone is always looking for new talent. Elyse is available on a conslultation basis. She reviews photography portfolios and gives direction in marketing and promotion."

SUSAN WELLS & ASSOCIATES, INC. (V), 5134 Timber Trail NE, Atlanta GA 30342. Representative not currently seeking new talent.

‡PAUL WILLARD ASSOCIATES, LTD. (II, III), 10415 N. 38th St., Phoenix AZ 85028. (602)257-0097. Fax: (602)996-5459. Contact: Paul Willard. Commercial illustration, photography and film producer/director (commercial) representative. Estab. 1983. Markets include: advertising agencies; corporations/client direct; design firms; editorial/magazines.
Handles: Illustration, photography, commercial film directors' reels. Looking for "unique conceptual illustration for corporate communications, car photography/film."
Terms: Rep receives 30% commission on illustration and photography. Exclusive area representation is required in most cases. Advertising costs are paid by talent. For promotional purposes, talent must provide direct mail tearsheets, portfolio of 4×5 or 8×10 transparencies (usually 2-20 pieces). Advertises in *American Showcase* and other publications.
How to Contact: For first contact, send query letter, tearsheets or reel. Reports in 3 weeks. Portfolio should include tearsheets, slides, 4×5 or 8×10 transparencies.
Tips: "I may call directly from ads or by recommendations from my clients. Solicitation by mail can sometimes result in a successful relationship. We use a rating of marketability of style, consistency shown in work throughout and personality as a guide while selecting. All must be unique and show enthusiasm and competence."

■WINSTON WEST, LTD. (III, IV), 195 S. Beverly Dr., Beverly Hills CA 90213. (212)275-2858. Fax: (213)275-0917. Contact: Bonnie Winston. Commercial photography representative (fashion/entertainment). Estab. 1986. Represents 8 photographers. Specializes in "editorial fashion and commercial advertising (with an edge)." Markets include: advertising agencies; client direct; editorial/magazines.
Handles: Photography.
Terms: Rep receives 25% commission. Charges for courier services. Exclusive area representation is required. No geographic restrictions. Advertising costs are split: 75% paid by talent; 25% paid by representative. Advertises by direct mail.
How to Contact: For first contact, send direct mail flier/brochure, photographs, photocopies, photostats. Reports in days, only if interested. After initial contact, call for appointment to show portfolio of tearsheets.
Tips: Obtains new talent through "recommendations from the modeling agencies. If you are a new fashion photographer or a photographer that's relocated recently, develop relationships with the modeling agencies in town. They are invaluable sources for client leads and know all the reps."

DEBORAH WOLFE LTD., 731 N. 24th St., Philadelphia PA 19130. (215)232-6666. Fax: (215)232-6585. Contact: Deborah Wolfe. Commercial illustration representative. Estab. 1978. Represents 25 illustrators. Markets include: advertising agencies; corporations/client direct; design firms; editorial/magazines; publishing/books.
Handles: Illustration.
Terms: Rep receives 25% commission. Advertises in *American Showcase* and *Creative Black Book.*
How to Contact: For first contact, send direct mail flier/brochure, tearsheets, slides. Reports in 3 weeks.
Tips: "Artists usually contact us through mail or drop off at our office. If interested, we ask to see more work (including originals)."

‡**WORLDWIDE IMAGES (II)**, Suite 112, 805 E St., San Rafael CA 94901. (415)892-6708. Contact: Norman Buller. Commercial photography representative. Estab. 1988. Represents 16 photographers. Specializes in nudes, all pro sports, celebrities, rock stars, men's magazine layouts, calendars, posters. Markets include: advertising agencies; corporations/client direct; design firms; editorial/magazines; paper products/greeting cards; publishing/books; sales/promotion firms.
Handles: Photography (all formats).
Terms: Rep receives 50% commission.
How to Contact: For first contact, send slides, photographs and SASE. Reports immediately. Portfolio should include slides, photographs.
Tips: Obtains new clients through recommendations from others, solicitation, at conferences.

‡**JIM ZACCARO PRODUCTIONS INC. (III)**, 315 E. 68th St., New York NY 10021. (212)744-4000. Fax: (212)744-4442. Contact: Jim Zaccaro. Commercial photography and fine art representative. Estab. 1961. Member of SPAR, DGA. Represents 4 photographers.
How to Contact: For first contact, send query letter, direct mail flier/brochure. Call for appointment to show portfolio.

‡**DAVID ZAITZ ARTIST REPRESENTATIVE (III)**, #10, 11830 Darlington Ave., Los Angeles CA 90049. (310)207-4806. Fax: (310)207-6368. Contact: D. Zaitz. Commercial photo rep. Estab. 1985. Represents 5 photographers. Specializes in advertising. Markets include: advertising agencies; design firms.
Handles: Photography.
Terms: Rep receives 25% commission. Exclusive area representation is required, Advertising cost split varies. For promotional purposes, talent must provide promo cards and/or sourcebook ad reprints to use as leave-behinds or mailers. Advertises in *The Workbook*.
How to Contact: For first contact, send direct mail flier/brochure. Reports in 7 days. Call for appointment to show portfolio of photographs.
Tips: Obtains new talent through referral through art directors, contact from photographers. "Learn to represent yourself *first*, then delegate that responsibility to a rep that best reflects your personal/business style. A rep should augment, embellish and help direct your business—not a quick fix to the problem: 'no work.'"

Additional Art and Photography Reps

The following reps have full listings in other sections of this book, but are also interested in illustrators or photographers. After reading the listing (find the page number in the Listings Index), send a query for more information on needs and submission policies.

Arts Counsel Inc.
Andrea Brown Literary Agency, Inc.
Pema Browne Ltd.
Corporate Art Associates, Ltd.
The Charlotte Gusay Literary Agency
The Hamersfield Agency
Kirchoff/Wohlberg, Inc., Authors' Rep Division
Gina Maccoby Literary Agency
Ruth Nathan
Northwest Literary Services
William Pell Agency
Pesha Rubenstein Literary Agency, Inc.
Lynn Seligman, Literary Agent
Jeanne Toomey Associates
Susan P. Urstadt Inc. Writers and Artists Agency
Wecksler-Incomco

Commercial Art/Photo Reps/'93-'94

The following reps appeared in the last edition of this book but are absent from this edition. These reps failed to respond to our request for an update of their listing, or were left out for the reasons indicated in parentheses following the rep name.

Ivy Bernhard (no longer represents photography)
Tania Kimcie
Frank Meo
Pamela Neail Associates (out of business)
Pacific Design Studio
Parallax (out of business)
Photo Agents Ltd. (out of business)
Kay Reese & Associates, Inc. (out of business)
Repertoire
David Scroggy Agency (no longer represents artists)
Studio Artists/Don Pepper

Fine Art Reps

While much of what we've said in the Commercial Art/Photo Reps section holds true for fine art reps as well, there are some differences. First of all, there are fewer "official" fine art reps. Yet many gallery owners, art consultants, art publishers and art distributors also act as reps for the artists they handle.

Since there are fewer fine art reps, there are also fewer established norms. And fewer norms mean more room for variety in the way reps work. Some promote their talent by presenting portfolios or slide shows to clients; others hold exhibitions; others maintain extensive slide files. It's important to ask a potential rep for as much information as possible about how he works so that you can make the best informed decision.

What do fine art reps do?

Fine art reps promote the work of fine artists, sculptors, craftspeople and fine art photographers to galleries and museums, but they also sell to corporate art collectors, developers, interior designers, art publishers and even some book publishers. They may also operate their own gallery or be in the art publishing or other art-related business.

In general, fine art reps call on clients with your portfolio or other promotional material. Like commercial reps, they may have certain promotional requirements. Most do not advertise in commercial talent books, but do advertise in art publications—those seen by decorators, gallery owners and collectors.

Although some fine art reps' terms are identical to those of a commercial rep, most take a higher commission and do not charge talent for advertising costs. Most require an exclusive area of representation. In addition to selling the work you've already created, many arrange commission work for you.

Why get a fine art rep?

Reps can help by taking over the sales, marketing and other business aspects of your work so you can devote more time to the creative process. They can handle the recordkeeping, billing and other paper work—keeping track of the money owed you and the particulars of who is considering your work.

Most galleries do an excellent job of promoting and selling work within their immediate areas. Those situated to attract tourists help "spread the word" about your work across the country, but a rep can broaden your exposure considerably. Depending on the rep, you may find yourself working with clients on a national or even international level.

Reps cultivate contacts. They watch the market carefully and can advise you on trends and prices. They may be able to get you into shows, help get you your own or even put one on for you.

A few considerations

Before approaching a rep, make sure you are ready. You must be willing to make a commitment to your career as an artist. You should have a sizable body of work ready to show and sell. Consider carefully the idea of doing commissioned work—can you do work "on demand" and deliver it on time?

Prepare your portfolio with care. Include slides and other material for promotion. When sending slides, make sure they are labeled individually with your name and address. Also indicate directions on your slides. For finished work, include a price list with your slides. Make sure your pricing is consistent and logical. One artist suggests pricing by size only. She feels pricing by other, less tangible, considerations puts out signals that you feel some of your work is not as good as your other work. Your rep should be able to advise you on prices or check out your competition at local galleries.

For more information on working with reps see Finding and Working with Art/Photo Reps by Barbara Gordon and the books listed in the Resources section. *Artist's Market* and *Photographer's Market* include more in depth information on the business of art or photography and are a must for your business bookshelf.

Help with your search

To help you with your search for representation, we've included a Geographic Index in the back of this book, divided by state and province. The Agents and Representatives Index on page 270 will help locate individual reps. Often you will read about a rep, but if he is an employee of a large agency, you may not be able to find his business number. We asked agencies to list representatives on their staffs. In the index we list the names in alphabetical order along with the name of their agency. Find the name of the person you would like to contact and then check the listing for that agency.

A few of the commercial illustration and photography representatives are also interested in fine artists. This is especially true of reps who work with book publishers. If a rep's *primary* function is selling illustration, but is also interested in handling some fine artists or fine art photographers, we've listed them in Additional Fine Art Reps at the end of this section.

In addition to the listings in this section, word-of-mouth and referrals are still an important way to find representation. You may also be able to meet a rep at a show or workshop. Artist and photographer organizations provide information on reps to members through newsletters and meetings.

About the listings

Most fine art representatives do not charge for additional expenses beyond those incurred in preparing your portfolio. Depending on the arrangement, you may have to help pay for shipping of your work to the rep. A few reps require you to pay for special portfolios or other advertising materials. A handful also charge monthly retainers to cover marketing expenses. Where possible, we've indicated these listings with a solid box (■) symbol.

We've ranked the agencies listed in this section according to their openness to submissions. Below is our ranking system:

I Newer representative actively seeking clients.
II Representative seeking both new and established artists or photographers.
III Representative prefers to work with established artists or photographers, mostly through referrals.
IV Representative handling only certain types of work or work by artists or photographers under certain circumstances.
V Representative not currently seeking new clients. We have included mention of reps rated V to let you know they are currently not open to new clients. *Unless you have a strong recommendation from someone in the field, our advice is to approach only those reps ranked I-IV.*

ADMINISTRATIVE ARTS, INC. (II), P.O. Box 547935, Orlando FL 32854-1266. Contact: Brenda B. Harris. Fine art advisor. Estab. 1983. Registry includes 1,000 fine artists (including fine art crafts). Markets include: architects; corporate collections; developers; private collections; public art. Staff includes Brenda B. Harris (public and private art collecting, marketing and business management); Susan A. Gillen (public art collecting).
Handles: Fine art. "We prefer artists with established regional and national credentials. We also support emerging talent."
Terms: "Trade discount requested varies from 15-50% depending on project and medium. Submissions must include: 1) complete résumé; 2) artist's statement or brief profile; 3) labeled slides (artist's name, title of work, date, medium, image size and *retail price*); 4) availability of works submitted." No geographic restrictions.
How to Contact: For first contact, send cover letter, résumé, profile, labeled slides (including pricing), tearsheets, copies of reviews, etc. and SASE. Reports in 1-3 weeks.
Tips: "Artists are generally referred by their business or art agent, another artist or art professional, educators, or art editors who know our firm. A good impression starts with a cover letter and a well organized, typed résumé. *Always place your name and slide identification on each slide.* Make sure that slides are good representations of your work. Know your retail and net pricing and the standard industry discounts. Invite the art professional to visit your studio. To get placements, be cooperative in getting art to the art professional when and where it's needed."

‡ALBRECHT & JENNINGS ART ENTERPRISES (II, IV), 3546 Woodland Trail, Williamsburg MI 49690. (616)938-2163. Contact: Tom Albrecht. Fine art representative. Estab. 1991. Represents 60 fine artists (includes 15 sculptors). Staff includes Tom Albrecht, Karen Jennings. Specializes in Michigan and Midwest art, especially by emerging artists. Markets include: corporate collections; private collections.
Handles: Fine art.
Terms: Rep receives 40% commission. Advertising costs are paid by representative. For promotional purposes, talent must provide slides and photographs of artwork, and up to date résumés.
How to Contact: For first contact, send query letter, résumé, bio, slides, photographs and SASE. Reports in 2 weeks. After initial contact, call for appointment to show portfolio of slides and photographs.
Tips: Obtains talent "by referral from other artists, looking at galleries, and solicitation."

JACK ARNOLD FINE ART (II, IV), 5 E. 67 St., New York NY 10021. (212)249-7218. Fax: (212)249-7232. Contact: Jack Arnold. Fine art representative. Estab. 1979. Represents 15 fine artists (includes 1 sculptor). Specializes in contemporary graphics and paintings. Markets include: galleries; museums; private collections; corporate collections.
Handles: Looking for contemporary impressionists and realists.
Terms: Rep receives 50% commission. Exclusive area representation preferred. No geographic restrictions. For promotional purposes, talent must provide color prints or slides.
How to Contact: For first contact, send bio, photographs, retail prices and SASE. Reports in days. After initial contact, drop off or mail in portfolios of slides, photographs.
Tips: Obtains new talent through referrals.

‡ART EMOTION CORP. (II), 24 E. Piper Lane, Prospect Heights IL 60070. (708)459-0209. Contact: Gerard V. Perez. Estab. 1977. Represents 45 fine artists. Specializes in "selling to art galleries." Markets include: corporate collections; galleries; interior decorators.
Handles: Fine art.
Terms: "We buy for resale." Exclusive area representation is required. For promotional purposes talent must provide slides, color prints, "any visuals." Advertises in *Art News, Decor, Art Business News.*
How to Contact: For first contact, send tearsheets, slides, photographs and SASE. Reports in 1 month, only if interested. "Don't call us—if interested, we will call you." Portfolio should include slides, photographs.
Tips: Obtains new talent "through recommendations from others and word of mouth."

---

‡ *The double dagger before a listing indicates the listing is new in this edition.*

ART SOURCE L.A. (II), 1416 Sixth St., Santa Monica CA 90401. (310)917-6688. Fax: (310)917-6685. Contact: Francine Ellman. Fine art representative. Estab. 1980. Member of Architectural Design Council. Represents 10 photographers, 30 fine artists (includes 4 sculptors). Specializes in fine art consulting and curating; creative management, exhibition and design. Markets include: architects; corporate collections; developers; public space galleries; interior decorators; museums; private collections; publishing/books; film industry.
Handles: Fine art, fine photography.
Terms: Rep receives commission, amount varies. Exclusive area representation required in some cases. No geographic restrictions. "We request artists or photographers to submit a minimum of 5 slides/visuals, bio and SASE. Advertises in *Art News*, *Artscene*, *Art in America*, *Blue Book*, *Gallery Guide*, *Vision*.
How to Contact: For first contact, send résumé, bio, slides or photographs and SASE. Reports in 1-2 months. After initial contact, "we will call to schedule an appointment" to show portfolio of original art, slides, photographs.
Tips: Obtains new talent through recommendations, artists' submission and trade shows.

ARTCO INCORPORATED (II, III), 3148 RFD Cuba Rd., Long Grove IL 60047. (708)438-8420. Fax: (708)438-6464. Contact: Sybil Tillman. Fine art representative. Estab. 1970. Member of International Society of Appraisers. Represents 60 fine artists. Specializes in contemporary artists' originals and limited edition graphics. Markets include: architects; art publishers; corporate collections; galleries; private collections.
Handles: Fine art.
Terms: "Each commission is determined mutually. For promotional purposes, I would like to see original work or transparencies." No geographic restrictions. Advertises in newspapers, magazine, etc.
How to Contact: For first contact, send query letter, résumé, bio, slides, photographs or transparencies. Reports in 2 weeks. After initial contact, call for appointment to show portfolio of original art, slides, photographs.
Tips: Obtains new talent through recommendations from others, solicitation, at conferences, advertising.

ARTS COUNSEL INC. (V), 12th Floor, 116 E. 27th St., New York NY 10016, (212)725-3806. Fax: (212)779-9589. Contact: Fran Black. Fine art, commercial illustration, commercial photography representative. Estab. 1985. Represents 4 illustrators, 5 photographers, 12 fine artists (includes 4 sculptors). Specializes in marketing, proposal and guide writing, presentation techniques and public relations. Markets include: advertising agencies; corporations/client direct; design firms; art publishers; corporate collections; interior decorators; museums, private collections.
Handles: Fine art, illustration, photography. "We are not actively looking, but we will review the work of artists with museum credentials."
Terms: Rep receives 25% commission. Charges 5% for long-distance calls. Promotional material done cooperatively. For promotional purposes, talent must provide "promotional materials on hand as well as 3-4 complete portfolios." Advertises in *Creative Black Book*, *The Workbook*, *Graphis*.
How to Contact: For first contact, send query letter, bio, direct mail flier/brochure. Reports in 5 days. After initial contact, call for appointment to show portfolio of original art, tearsheets, photographs, laminates.
Tips: Obtains new talent through recommendations from others as well as through select advertising and promotion materials. "Know what you want to achieve in the commercial world. Be open to growth and development while maintaining a distinctive style."

CATHY BAUM & ASSOCIATES, 384 Stevick Dr., Atherton CA 94027. (415)854-5668. Fax: (415)854-8522. Contact: Cathy Baum or Kris Hartman. Art advisory firm. Estab. 1976. Member of National Association for Corporate Art. "Cathy Baum & Associates is a fine arts advisory firm. We do not represent artists, but will work directly with artists, if their work is appropriate for our client's art program. We have slide files on artists in all visual media of the fine arts." Markets include: architects; corporate collections; developers; interior designers.
Handles: Fine art media—painting, sculpture, prints, photography.
Terms: Rep receives 20-50% commission. For promotional purposes, talent must provide slides of artwork, prices, bio.
How to Contact: For first contact, send bio, slides, price list. Reports in 2 weeks. After initial contact, firm will request additional material. Portfolio should include slides.
Tips: Obtains new talent through "contacts in the arts, artists sending slides, galleries, etc."

Fine Art Reps 229

CORCORAN FINE ARTS LIMITED, INC. (II), 2341 Roxboro Rd., Cleveland OH 44106. (216)397-0777. Fax: (216)397-0222. Contact: James Corcoran. Fine art representative. Estab. 1986. Member of NOADA (Northeast Ohio Dealers Association); ISA (International Society of Appraisers). Represents 5 photographers, 11 fine artists (includes 3 sculptors). Staff includes Meghan Wilson (gallery associate); Bill Haak (office administrator); James Corcoran (owner/manager). Specializes in representing high-quality contemporary work. Markets include: architects; corporate collections; developers; galleries; interior decorators; museums; private collections.
Handles: Fine art.
Terms: Rep receives 50% commission. Exclusive area representation is required. Advertising costs are "decided case by case."
How to Contact: For first contact send a query letter, résumé, bio, slides, photographs, SASE. Reports back within 1 month. After initial contact, drop off or mail in appropriate materials for review. Portfolio should include slides, photographs.
Tips: Usually obtains new talent by solicitation.

CORPORATE ART ASSOCIATES, LTD. (II), Suite 402, 270 Lafayette St., New York NY 10012. (212)941-9685. Director: James Cavello. Fine art representative. Also handles commercial illustration and photography, graphic design. Art consultant. Estab. 1987. Represents 15 illustrators, 50 photographers, 20 designers, 2,000 fine artists (includes 40 sculptors). Markets include: advertising agencies; corporations/client direct; design firms; editorial/magazines; paper products/greeting cards; publishing/books; sales/promotion firms; architects; art publishers; corporate collections; developers; galleries; interior decorators; private collections.
Handles: Fine art, illustration, photography, design.
Terms: Rep receives 50% commission. No geographic restrictions. Advertising costs are paid by talent.
How to Contact: For first contact, send query letter, résumé, bio, direct mail flier/brochure, tearsheets, slides, photographs, photocopies, photostats and SASE. Reports in days. After initial contact, drop off or mail in portfolio of thumbnails, roughs, original art, tearsheets, slides, photographs, photostats, photocopies.
Tips: Obtains new talent through recommendations from others.

ROBERT GALITZ FINE ART/ACCENT ART (II), 166 Hilltop Ct., Sleepy Hollow IL 60118. (708)426-8842. Fax: (708)426-8846. Contact: Robert Galitz. Fine art representative. Estab. 1985. Represents 100 fine artists (includes 2 sculptors). Specializes in contemporary/abstract corporate art. Markets include: architects; corporate collections; galleries; interior decorators; private collections.
Handles: Fine art.
Terms: Rep receives 25-40% commission. No geographic restrictions; sells mainly in Chicago, Illinois, Wisconsin, Indiana and Kentucky. For promotional purposes talent must provide "good photos and slides." Advertises in monthly art publications and guides.
How to Contact: For first contact, send query letter, slides, photographs. Reports in 2 weeks. After initial contact, call for appointment to show portfolio of original art.
Tips: Obtains new talent through recommendations from others, solicitation, at conferences. "Be confident, persistent. Never give up or quit."

ICEBOX, 2401 Central Ave. NE, Minneapolis MN 55418. (612)788-1790. Contact: Howard Christopherson. Fine art representative. Estab. 1988. Represents 4 photographers, 6 fine artists (includes 2 sculptors). Specializes in "thought-provoking art work and photography, predominantly Minnesota artists." Markets include: corporate collections; interior decorators; museums; private collections.
Handles: Fine art and fine art photographs. Looking for "new photography and thought-provoking works."
Terms: Rep receives 33-50% commission. Exclusive representation in Minnesota is required. For promotional purposes, talent must provide slides. Advertises in *Art Paper* and local newspapers and magazines.

Reps ranked I and II are most open to new, as well as established, talents. Those ranked III prefer established talent with references from others in the art or photography field.

How to Contact: For first contact, send résumé, bio, slides and SASE. Reports in 2 months. After initial contact, drop off or mail in appropriate materials for review. Portfolio should include slides.

L.A. ART EXCHANGE (II), 2451 Broadway, Santa Monica CA 90404. (310)828-6866. Fax: (310)828-2643. Contact: Jayne Zehngut. Fine art representative. Estab. 1987. Member of Professional Picture Framers Assoc. Represents 20 fine artists. "We deal with retail, wholesale and corporate accounts." Markets include: corporations/client direct design firms; architects; corporate collections; developers; galleries; interior decorators.
Handles: Fine art, photography, design.
Terms: No information provided. Exclusive area representation is "preferred." No geographic restrictions.
How to Contact: For first contact, send résumé, bio, slides, photographs and SASE. Reports in 1 week. After initial contact, write for appointment or drop off or mail in appropriate materials for review.
Tips: Obtains new talent through "advertising in *Decor* magazine and *Art Business News* and local newspapers. Primary businesses are custom picture framing; fine art and poster sales; art consulting (corporate and residential)."

NELDA LEE INC. (III), 2610 21st St., Odessa TX 79761. (915)366-8426. Fax: (915)550-2830. President: Nelda Lee. Member agent: Vice President: Cory Ricot. Fine art representative. Estab. 1967. Senior member of American Society of Appraisers, President of Texas Association of Art Dealers. Represents 50-60 artists (includes 4 sculptors). Markets include: corporate collections; developers; galleries; interior decorators; museums; private collections.
Handles: Fine art, illustration.
Terms: Rep receives 40-50% commission. Exclusive area representation is required. No geographic restrictions. Advertising costs are paid by representative. Advertises in *Texas Monthly, Southwest Art*, local TV and newspapers.
How to Contact: For first contact, send query letter and photographs ("include phone number"). Reports in 10 days. After initial contact, call for appointment to show portfolio of original art and photographs.
Tips: Obtains new talent through "direct contact from talent. Don't give up. Keep contacting—about every six months to a year."

LESLI ART, INC. (II), Box 6693, Woodland Hills CA 91365. (818)999-9228. Contact: Stan Shevrin. Fine art representative. Estab. 1965. Represents 28 fine artists. Specializes in "artists painting in oil or acrylic, in the manner of the impressionists. Also represent illustrators whose figurative work can be placed in art galleries."
Terms: Negotiable.
How to Contact: For first contact, send bio, slides, photographs and SASE. Reports in 2 weeks.
Tips: Obtains new talent through "reviewing portfolios. Artists should show their most current works and state a preference for subject matter and medium."

LONDON CONTEMPORARY ART (II), (formerly Fine Art Representative), 729 Pine Crest, Prospect Heights IL 60070. (708)459-3990. Contact: Nancy Rudin. Fine art representative. Estab. 1977. Represents 45 fine artists. Specializes in "selling to art galleries." Markets include: galleries; corporate collections; interior decorators.
Handles: Fine art.
Terms: Publisher of original art. Exclusive representation is required. For promotional purposes talent must provide slides, color prints, "any visuals." Advertises in *Decor, Art Business News, Art & Antiques, Preview, Sunstorm*.
How to Contact: For first contact, send tearsheets, slides, photographs and SASE. Reports in 1 month, only if interested. "Don't call us—if interested, we will call you." Portfolio should include slides, photographs.
Tips: Obtains new talent through recommendations from others and word of mouth.

MEDIA GALLERY/ENTERPRISES (II), 145 W. Fourth Ave., Garnett KS 66032-1313. (913)448-5813. Contact: Robert Cugno. Fine art representative. Estab. 1963. Number of artists and sculptors represented varies. Specializes in clay—contemporary and modern. Markets include: galleries; museums; private collections.

Fine Art Reps 231

Handles: Fine art, clay.
Terms: Rep receives 40-60% commission. For promotional purposes, talent must provide photos and slides.
How to Contact: For first contact, send bio, slides, SASE. Reports in 1-2 weeks. After initial contact, drop off or mail in appropriate materials for review.
Tips: Obtains new talent through recommendations from other artists, collectors, art consultants and gallery directors.

■**PENNAMENITIES (IV),** R.D. #2, Box 1080, Schuylkill Haven PA 17972. (717)754-7744. Fax: (717)754-7744. Contact: Deborah A. Miller. Fine art representative. Estab. 1988. Member of Summit Arts Fellowship. Represents 35 fine artists. Specializes in "arranging New York City art exhibits." Markets include: galleries; private collections.
Handles: Fine art (originals and prints).
Terms: Rep receives 30-50% commission. Charges $350 annual fee which covers correspondence, copies, phone and fax or services involved in setting up NYC exhibit.
How to Contact: For first contact send résumé, bio, slides, price list, SASE required. After initial contact, drop off or mail in appropriate materials for review. Portfolio should include transparencies, photographs or slides.
Tips: "Initial contact is usually made by artist seeking representative's services."

‡**JOAN SAPIRO ART CONSULTANTS (II, IV),** 4750 E. Belleview Ave., Littleton CO 80121. (303)793-0792. Fax: (303)721-1401. Fax: (303)290-9204. Contact: Joan Sapiro or Jennifer Kalin. Art consultants. Estab. 1980. Specializes in "corporate art with other emphasis on hospitality and health care."
Handles: All mediums of artwork and all prices if applicable for clientele.
Terms: "50/50. Artist must be flexible and willing to ship work on consignment. Also must be able to provide sketches etc. if commission piece involved." No geographic restrictions.
How to Contact: For first contact, send résumé, bio, direct mail flier/brochure, tearsheets, slides, photographs, price list—net (wholesale) and SASE. Reports in 2 weeks. After initial contact, drop off or mail in appropriate materials for review. Portfolios should include tearsheets, slides, price list and SASE.
Tips: Obtains new talent through recommendations, publications, travel and research.

‡**SEIFFER & ASSOCIATES, (II),** 19 Stony Hill Rd., Bethel CT 06801. (203)794-9550. Fax: (203)794-9054. Contact: Wendy Seiffer. Licensing agency. Estab. 1987. "We license artwork to be reproduced on posters and prints, collectible plates, apparel, mugs, music boxes, puzzles, cards, calendars and other gift and stationery items. We're a full-scale licensing agency specializing in fine art. Collectibles and apparel are our strongest areas. Posters and stationery products are our next strongest areas. Our licensed products are featured at The Nature Company, Spiegel, L.L. Bean and at fine shops worldwide. Our clients include Turner Publications, Lenox, The Danbury Mint, The Franklin Mint." Staff includes Wendy Seiffer, President (marketing); Barbara Chriswell (artist relations); Kim Pfitzner (account executive); Deb Serkin (Director of creative services); John Seiffer, Vice President (international sales, operations, contracts).
Handles: Fine art and exceptional illustration. Looking for "colorful, well-executed and realistic or photorealistic work. Purely decorative is fine as well."
Terms: Rep receives 50% commission. Exclusive worldwide representation is usually required. No geographic restrictions of representation and sales. For promotional purposes, "great visuals are essential. Photographs or tearsheets, and reproduction-quality transparencies (supplied by the artist) are required."
How to Contact: For first contact, send résumé, comprehensive portfolio (no originals) and SASE. Reports in 2 months. Portfolio should include at least 12-24 images presenting a wide range of work.
Tips: "Have great visuals—at least 12-24 images to show consistency. Include a bio/artist's statement. For successful licensing, artist should have a healthy inventory of work, including work done in series. Reproduction quality transparencies (4×5 or bigger) are required."

NICKI SHEARER ART SOURCE (II), 6101 Walhonding Rd., Bethesda MD 20816. (301)320-2211. Fax: (301)320-2210. Contact: Nicki Shearer. Fine art representative. Estab. 1979. Represents "many" fine artists (several are sculptors). Specializes in art for hotels, hospitals, other commercial space (law firms, etc.). Markets include: architects; corporate collections; developers; interior decorators.

Handles: Fine art.
Terms: Rep receives 40-50% commission. Exclusive area representation is not required, however, "I would like to represent artists who are not represented in this area." Advertising costs are paid by representative. For promotional purposes, talent must provide slides, photographs, résumé, "any other promotional materials" and SASE.
How to Contact: For first contact, send résumé, bio, direct mail flier/brochure, 2 or 3 slides, photographs—"call first, if possible." Reports in 1 month, if interested. After initial contact, drop off or mail in appropriate materials for review.
Tips: Obtains new talent through "recommendations from others, museum shows, other exhibits, as well as juried shows."

SIMPATICO ART & STONE (II), 1221 Demaret Lane, Houston TX 77055-6115. (713)467-7123. Contact: Billie Blake Fant. Fine art broker/consultant/exhibitor. Estab. 1973. Specializes in unique fine art, sculpture and Texas domestic stone furniture, carvings, architectural elements. Market includes: corporate, institutional and residential clients.
Handles: Looking for unique fine art and sculpture not presently represented in Houston, Texas.
Terms: Standard commission. Exclusive area representation required.
How to Contact: For first contact, send query letter, résumé, slides.
Tips: Obtains new talent through travel, publications, exhibits and referrals.

Additional Fine Art Reps

The following reps have full listings in other sections of this book. These reps and agents have indicated they are *primarily* interested in handling book manuscripts, but are also interested in fine artists. After reading the listing (you can find the page number in the Listings Index), send them a query to obtain more information on their needs and submission policies.

Artists Associates
Carolyn Brindle Inc.
Kathy Bruml/Artists Representative
Stephen Gill

Jedell Productions, Inc.
Frank & Jeff Lavaty And Associates
McConnell McNamara & Co.
Colleen Mackay Photography

Ridgeway Artists Representative
Rosenthal Represents
Jim Zaccaro Productions Inc.

Fine Art Reps/'93-'94 changes

The following agencies appeared in the last (1993) edition of *Guide to Literary Agents & Art/Photo Reps* but are absent from the 1994 edition. These agencies failed to respond to our request for an update of their listing, or were left out for the reason indicated in parentheses following the agency name.

International Art Connection and Art Connection Plus (unable to contact)
Madrazo Arts (unable to contact)
Tolease Lautrec

Resources

Recommended Books & Publications

For writers and scriptwriters

ADVENTURES IN THE SCREEN TRADE, by William Goldman, published by Warner Books, 666 Fifth Ave., New York NY 10103. An insider's view of screenwriting and the entertainment business.

AGENT & MANAGER, 7th Floor, 650 First Ave., New York NY 10016. Monthly trade magazine for all types of agents and managers. Information on new agents, news and deals.

BEYOND THE BESTSELLER: A LITERARY AGENT TAKES YOU INSIDE PUBLISHING, by Richard Curtis, published by NAL, 375 Hudson St., New York NY 10014. The "inside story" on publishing by a New York agent.

BUSINESS & LEGAL FORMS FOR AUTHORS AND SELF-PUBLISHERS, by Tad Crawford, published by Allworth Press, c/o Writer's Digest Books, 1507 Dana Ave., Cincinnati OH 45207. Forms for all types of agreements and contracts needed in the publishing business.

CHILDREN'S WRITER'S & ILLUSTRATOR'S MARKET, edited by Christine Martin, published by Writer's Digest Books, 1507 Dana Ave., Cincinnati OH 45207. Annual market directory for children's writers and illustrators. Includes information on writing and art business.

THE COMPLETE BOOK OF SCRIPTWRITING, by J. Michael Straczyniski, published by Writer's Digest Books, 1507 Dana Ave., Cincinnati OH 45207. How to write and sell all types of scripts.

THE COMPLETE GUIDE TO STANDARD SCRIPT FORMAT (Parts 1 and 2), by Hillis Cole and Judith Haag, published by CMC Publishing, 11642 Otsego St., N. Hollywood CA 91601. Standard script formats and other information for scriptwriters.

DAILY VARIETY, 5700 Wilshire Blvd., Los Angeles CA 90036. Publication featuring information on the entertainment business, trade oriented.

DRAMATISTS SOURCEBOOK, edited by Angela E. Mitchell and Gilliam Richards, published by Theatre Communications Group, Inc., 355 Lexington Ave., New York NY 10017. Directory listing opportunities for playwrights. Includes agents.

GETTING YOUR SCRIPT THROUGH THE HOLLYWOOD MAZE, by Linda Stuart, published by Acrobat Books, P.O. Box 870, Venice CA 90294. An insider's guide to writing and marketing movie scripts.

THE GUIDE TO WRITERS CONFERENCES, published by ShawGuides, Suite 1406, Biltmore Way, Coral Gables FL 33134. Directory of writers' conferences.

HOLLYWOOD REPORTER, Billboard Publications, Inc., 6715 Sunset Blvd., Hollywood CA 90028. Publication covering news and information on the entertainment industry. Includes information on scriptwriters and sales of scripts.

HOLLYWOOD SCRIPTWRITER, #385, 1626 N. Wilcox, Hollywood CA 90028. Newsletter featuring information for scriptwriters. Includes an annual agents issue.

HOW TO BE YOUR OWN LITERARY AGENT, by Richard Curtis, published by Houghton Mifflin Company, 2 Park St., Boston MA 02108. An insider's guide to contract negotiations, deal-making and the business of publishing.

HOW TO PITCH & SELL YOUR TV SCRIPT, by David Silver, published by Writer's Digest Books, 1507 Dana Ave., Cincinnati OH 45207. Information on marketing your television scripts. Includes information on working with script agents.

HOW TO SELL YOUR SCREENPLAY, by Carl Sautter, published by New Chapter Press, Suite 1122, 381 Park Ave. S., New York NY 10016. Tips on selling screenplays.

HOW TO WRITE A BOOK PROPOSAL, by Michael Larsen, published by Writer's Digest Books, 1507 Dana Ave., Cincinnati OH 45207. How to put together a professional-quality book proposal package.

HOW TO WRITE IRRESISTIBLE QUERY LETTERS, by Lisa Collier Cool, published by Writer's Digest Books, 1507 Dana Ave., Cincinnati OH 45207. How to write professional, effective queries.

THE INSIDER'S GUIDE TO BOOK EDITORS, PUBLISHERS & LITERARY AGENTS, by Jeff Herman,

published by Prima Communications, Box 1260, Rocklin CA 95677-1260. An inside look at the publishing industry. Includes information on agents.
LITERARY AGENTS: A WRITER'S GUIDE, by Adam Begley, published by Poets & Writer's, 72 Spring St., New York NY 10012. Directory of literary agents. Includes articles on working with agents. Published every five years.
LITERARY AGENTS: HOW TO GET AND WORK WITH THE RIGHT ONE FOR YOU, by Michael Larsen, published by Writer's Digest Books, 1507 Dana Ave., Cincinnati OH 45207. How to approach and work with an agent.
LITERARY MARKET PLACE (LMP), R.R. Bowker Company, 121 Chanlon Road, New Providence NJ 07974. Book publishing industry directory. In addition to publishing companies, includes a list of literary agents and a list of art representatives.
MAKING A GOOD SCRIPT GREAT, by Dr. Linda Seger, published by Samuel French Trade, 7623 Sunset Blvd., Hollywood CA 90046. Information on improving your script.
MANUSCRIPT SUBMISSION, by Scott Edelstein, published by Writer's Digest Books, 1507 Dana Ave., Cincinnati OH 45207. How to prepare submissions for publishers and agents, especially for the fiction writer.
NOVEL & SHORT STORY WRITER'S MARKET, edited by Robin Gee, published by Writer's Digest Books, 1507 Dana Ave., Cincinnati OH 45207. Annual market directory for fiction writers. Includes information on the writing business, organizations and conferences for fiction writers.
POETS AND WRITERS, 72 Spring St., New York NY 10012. Magazine for writers. Includes interviews and articles of interest to poets and literary writers. Poets and Writers also publishes several books and directories for writers.
PROFESSIONAL WRITER'S GUIDE, revised and expanded edition, edited by Donald Bower and James Lee Young, National Writers Press, Suite 424, 1450 S. Havana, Aurora CO 80012. The basics of starting and building a writing career.
PUBLISHERS WEEKLY, 249 W. 17th St., New York NY 10011. Weekly magazine covering industry trends and news in the book publishing industry. Contains announcements of new agencies.
SUCCESSFUL SCRIPTWRITING, by Jurgen Wolff and Kerry Cox, published by Writer's Digest Books, 1507 Dana Ave., Cincinnati OH 45207. Includes information on the movie and television business, as well as tips on marketing and selling scripts.
THEATRE DIRECTORY, Theatre Communications Group, Inc., 355 Lexington Ave., New York NY 10017. Directory listing theaters in the U.S.
THE TV SCRIPTWRITER'S HANDBOOK, by Alfred Brenner, published by Writer's Digest Books, 1507 Dana Ave., Cincinnati OH 45207. Includes all aspects of writing for television including marketing scripts.
THE WRITER, 120 Boylston St., Boston MA 02116. Magazine for writers. Includes articles on technique and writing issues.
WRITER'S DIGEST, 1507 Dana Ave., Cincinnati OH 45207. Monthly magazine for writers. Includes technique, lifestyle, business and market information.
THE WRITER'S DIGEST GUIDE TO MANUSCRIPT FORMATS, by Dian Dincin Buchman and Seli Groves, published by Writer's Digest Books, 1507 Dana Ave., Cincinnati OH 45207. Models for all types of manuscript formats including query and cover letters to editors, publishers and agents.
WRITER'S ESSENTIAL DESK REFERENCE, edited by Glenda Tennant Neff, published by Writer's Digest Books, 1507 Dana Ave., Cincinnati OH 45207. Reference guide for writers including business, tax and legal information for both U.S. and Canadian writers.
A WRITER'S GUIDE TO CONTRACT NEGOTIATIONS, by Richard Balkin, published by Writer's Digest Books, 1507 Dana Ave., Cincinnati OH 45207. Written by an agent, this is an insider's view of book contract negotiations.
THE WRITER'S LEGAL COMPANION, by Brad Bunnin and Peter Beren, published by Addison Wesley, Jacob Way, Reading MA 01867. Legal guide for writers. Bunnin is a publishing-industry lawyer.
WRITER'S MARKET, edited by Mark Garvey, published by Writer's Digest Books, 1507 Dana Ave., Cincinnati OH 45207. Annual market directory for writers and scriptwriters. Includes information on the writing business.
WRITING SCRIPTS THAT SELL, by Michael Hauge, published by McGraw-Hill, 1221 Avenue of the Americas, New York NY 10020. Technique information for scriptwriters.

For artists and photographers

ADVERTISING AGE, 740 Rush St., Chicago IL 60611-2590. Weekly advertising and marketing tabloid.
ADWEEK, A/S/M Communications, Inc., 49 E. 21st St., New York NY 10010. Weekly advertising and marketing magazine.
AMERICAN ARTIST, P.O. Box 1944, Marion OH 43306-2044. Magazine featuring instructional articles, profiles and technique information for artists.

Recommended Books & Publications 235

AMERICAN PHOTO, *43rd Floor, 1633 Broadway, New York NY 10019. Monthly magazine emphasizing the craft and philosophy of photography.*

AMERICAN SHOWCASE, *14th Floor, 915 Broadway, New York NY 10010. Annual talent sourcebook featuring illustrators, photographers and designers.*

ART DIRECTION, *6th Floor, 10 E. 39th St., New York NY 10016-0199. Monthly magazine featuring art directors' views on advertising and photography.*

ART IN AMERICA, *575 Broadway, New York NY 10012. Features in-depth articles on art issues, news and reviews. August issue includes an annual guide to artists, galleries and museums.*

THE ARTIST'S FRIENDLY LEGAL GUIDE, *by Floyd Conner, Peter Karlan, Jean Perwin & David M. Spatt, published by North Light Books, 1507 Dana Ave., Cincinnati OH 45207. Tips on taxes and legal matters by tax experts and lawyers familiar with the art business.*

THE ARTIST'S MAGAZINE, *1507 Dana Ave., Cincinnati OH 45207. Monthly art magazine featuring how-to technique and business information for artists.*

ARTIST'S MARKET, *edited by Jenny Pfalzgraf, published by Writer's Digest Books, 1507 Dana Ave., Cincinnati OH 45207. Annual markets directory for artists. Includes art business information.*

ASMP BULLETIN, *monthly newsletter of American Society of Media Photographers, Suite 502, Washington Park, 14 Washington Rd., Princeton Junction NJ 08550-1033. Subscription comes with membership in ASMP.*

BUSINESS AND LEGAL FORMS FOR FINE ARTISTS, *by Tad Crawford, published by Allworth Press, % North Light Books, 1507 Dana Ave., Cincinnati OH 45207. Forms for agreements and other contracts for fine artists.*

BUSINESS AND LEGAL FORMS FOR ILLUSTRATORS, *by Tad Crawford, published by Allworth Press, c/o North Light Books, 1507 Dana Ave., Cincinnati OH 45207. Forms for agreements and contracts for illustrators.*

CHICAGO CREATIVE DIRECTORY, *Suite 810, 333 N. Michigan Ave., Chicago IL 60610. Annual talent sourcebook featuring illustrators and designers in the Chicago area.*

CHICAGO MIDWEST FLASH, *Alexander Communications, Suite 203, 212 W. Superior, Chicago IL 60610. Quarterly magazine including articles and news on graphic art and advertising in the Midwest.*

COMMUNICATIONS ARTS, *410 Sherman Ave., Box 10300, Palo Alto CA 94303. Magazine covering design, illustration and photography. Published 8 times a year.*

CREATIVE BLACK BOOK, *3rd Floor, 115 Fifth Ave., New York NY 10003. Annual talent sourcebook featuring illustrators, photographers and designers.*

CREATIVE ILLUSTRATION BOOK, *3rd Floor, 115 Fifth Ave., New York NY 10003. Annual directory of illustration.*

CREATIVE SOURCE, *Wilcord Publications Ltd., Suite 110, 511 King St. West, Toronto, Ontario M5V 2Z4. Annual talent sourcebook featuring illustrators and designers in Canada.*

DECOR, *Commerce Publications, 330 N. 4th St., St. Louis MO 63102. Monthly magazine covering trends in art publishing, home accessories and framing.*

THE DESIGNER'S COMMONSENSE BUSINESS BOOK, *by Barbara Ganim, published by North Light Books, 1507 Dana Ave., Cincinnati OH 45207. Includes information on business matters for graphic designers.*

EDITOR & PUBLISHER, *The Editor & Publisher Co., Inc., 11 W. 19th St., New York NY 10011. Weekly magazine covering latest developments in journalism and newspaper production.*

FINE ART INDEX, *International Art Reference, 159 W. Burton Place, Chicago IL 60610. Annual directory listing contemporary fine artists and galleries.*

THE FINE ARTIST'S GUIDE TO SHOWING & SELLING YOUR WORK, *by Sally Prince Davis, published by North Light Books, 1507 Dana Ave., Cincinnati OH 45207. Information on developing a marketing plan for fine artists.*

FOLIO, *Box 4949, Stamford CT 06907-0949. Monthly magazine featuring trends in magazine circulation, production and editorial.*

GETTING STARTED AS A FREELANCE ILLUSTRATOR OR DESIGNER, *by Michael Fleishman, published by North Light Books, 1507 Dana Ave., Cincinnati OH 45207. Book presenting information on promotion, portfolios and markets open to freelancers.*

THE GRAPHIC ARTIST'S GUIDE TO MARKETING & SELF-PROMOTION, *by Sally Prince Davis, published by North Light Books, 1507 Dana Ave., Cincinnati OH 45207. Contains information on marketing and promotion for graphic artists and designers.*

GRAPHIC ARTISTS GUILD HANDBOOK PRICING & ETHICAL GUIDELINES, *by the Graphic Artists Guild, distributed by North Light Books, 1507 Dana Ave., Cincinnati OH 45207. Guidebook for pricing and business standards for graphic artists and their clients.*

GRAPHIS, *Graphis U.S. Inc., 141 Lexington Ave., New York NY 10016. Bimonthly international journal of the graphic design industry.*

GUILFOYLE REPORT, *% AG Editions, 142 Bank St., New York NY 10014. Quarterly market tips newsletter for nature and stock photographers.*

HOW, *1507 Dana Ave., Cincinnati OH 45207. Bimonthly magazine featuring trends in graphic design and illustration.*

HOW TO SELL YOUR PHOTOGRAPHS AND ILLUSTRATIONS, *by Elliott and Barbara Gordon, published by Allworth Press, % North Light Books, 1507 Dana Ave., Cincinnati OH 45207. Business-building tips from commercial reps Elliott and Barbara Gordon. Contains information on working with art/photo reps.*

INTERIOR DESIGN, *249 W. 17th St., New York NY 10011. Monthly magazine featuring industry news and trends in furnishing and interior design.*

LEGAL GUIDE FOR THE VISUAL ARTIST, *by Tad Crawford, published by Allworth Press, c/o North Light Books, 1507 Dana Ave., Cincinnati OH 45207. Guide to art law covering copyright and contracts.*

MAGAZINE DESIGN AND PRODUCTION, *Suite 106, 8340 Mission Road, Prairie Village KS 66206. Monthly magazine with information on all aspects of magazine design and production.*

NEW YORK GOLD, *10 E. 21st St., New York NY 10010. Annual talent sourcebook featuring photographers.*

THE PERFECT PORTFOLIO, *by Henrietta Brackman, published by Amphoto Books, c/o Watson Guptill Publishing, 1515 Broadway, New York NY 10036. Information on how to develop and improve your photography portfolio.*

PHOTO DISTRICT NEWS, *49 East 21st St., New York NY 10010. Monthly trade magazine for the photography industry.*

PHOTO/DESIGN, *1515 Broadway, New York NY 10036. Monthly magazine emphasizing photography in the advertising/design fields.*

THE PHOTOGRAPHER'S BUSINESS & LEGAL HANDBOOK, *by Leonard Duboff, published by Images Press, c/o Writer's Digest Books, 1507 Dana Ave., Cincinnati OH 45207. A guide to copyright, trademarks, libel law and other legal concerns for photographers.*

PHOTOGRAPHER'S MARKET, *edited by Michael Willins, published by Writer's Digest Books, 1507 Dana Ave., Cincinnati OH 45207. Annual market directory for photographers. Includes photography business information.*

PHOTOGRAPHING YOUR ART WORK, *by Russell Hart, published by North Light Books, published by Writer's Digest Books, 1507 Dana Ave., Cincinnati OH 45207. How to photograph all types of artwork to create the best slides for your portfolio.*

PRINT, *RC Publications, 9th Floor, 104 5th Ave., New York NY 10011. Bimonthly magazine focusing on creative trends and technological advances in illustration, design, photography and printing. Also publishes Regional Design Annual featuring the year's best in design and illustration.*

THE PROFESSIONAL DESIGNER'S GUIDE TO MARKETING YOUR WORK, *by Mary Yeung, published by North Light Books, 1507 Dana Ave., Cincinnati OH 45207. Tips on marketing for graphic designers. Includes information on finding a rep.*

PROMO, *by Rose DeNeve, published by North Light Books, 1507 Dana Ave., Cincinnati OH 45207. A collection of outstanding promo pieces that have worked for illustrators and graphic designers.*

RSVP, *Box 050314, Brooklyn NY 11205. Annual talent sourcebook featuring illustrators and designers.*

STEP-BY-STEP GRAPHICS, *Dynamic Graphics, Inc., 6000 N. Forest Park Drive, Peoria IL 61614-3597. Bimonthly magazine featuring instruction for graphic design and illustration projects.*

U&lc, *Upper and Lower Case, 866 Second Ave., New York NY 10017. Newspaper format quarterly featuring news and information for the graphic artist.*

THE ULTIMATE PORTFOLIO, *by Martha Metzdorf, published by North Light Books, 1507 Dana Ave., Cincinnati OH 45207. A showcase of some of the best and most successful portfolios by illustrators and graphic designers.*

WOMEN'S WEAR DAILY, *Fairchild Publications, 7 West 34th St., New York NY 10001. Tabloid (Monday through Friday) focusing on women's and children's apparel.*

THE WORK BOOK, *Scott & Daughters Publishing, Suite A, 940 N. Highland Ave., Los Angeles CA 90038. Annual talent sourcebook listing illustrators, photographers and designers primarily in the Los Angeles area.*

Professional Organizations

Organizations for agents and reps

ASSOCIATION OF AUTHORS' REPRESENTATIVES (AAR), *3rd Floor, 10 Astor Place, New York NY 10003. A list of member agents is available for SAE with 52 cents for postage.*
SOCIETY OF PHOTOGRAPHERS' AND ARTISTS' REPRESENTATIVES, *Suite 1166, 60 E. 42nd St., New York NY 10165. A membership directory is available for about $35 (check for current price).*

Organizations for writers, artists and photographers

The following professional organizations publish newsletters and hold conferences and meetings in which they often share information on agents or reps.

ADVERTISING PHOTOGRAPHERS OF AMERICA (APA), *Room 601, 27 W. 20th St., New York NY 10011.*
AMERICAN INSTITUTE OF GRAPHIC ARTS, *1059 Third Ave., New York NY 10021.*
AMERICAN SOCIETY OF JOURNALISTS & AUTHORS, *Suite 302, 1501 Broadway, New York NY 10036.*
AMERICAN SOCIETY OF MEDIA PHOTOGRAPHERS, *Suite 502, Washington Park 14 Washington Rd., Princeton Junction NJ 08550-1033.*
THE AUTHORS GUILD INC., *330 W. 42nd St., New York NY 10036.*
COUNCIL OF WRITERS ORGANIZATIONS, *% Michigan Living, 1 Auto Club Dr., Dearborn MI 48126.*
GRAPHIC ARTIST GUILD, *8th Floor, 11 W. 20th St., New York NY 10011.*
HORROR WRITERS OF AMERICA, *V. Aalko, Executive Secretary, 5336 Reef Way, Oxnard CA 93035.*
THE INTERNATIONAL WOMEN'S WRITING GUILD, *P.O. Box 810, Gracie Station, New York NY 10016. Provides a literary agent list to members and holds "Meet the Agents and Editors" for members in April and October.*
MYSTERY WRITERS OF AMERICA (MWA), *6th Floor, 17 E. 47th St., New York NY 10017.*
NATIONAL LEAGUE OF AMERICAN PEN WOMEN, *1300 17th St. NW, Washington DC 20036.*
NATIONAL WRITERS ASSOCIATION, *Suite 424, 1450 S. Havana, Aurora CO 80012. In addition to agent referrals, also operates an agency for members.*
NATIONAL WRITERS UNION, *Suite 203, 873 Broadway, New York NY 10003-1209. A trade union, this organization has an agent data base available to members.*
PEN AMERICAN CENTER, *568 Broadway, New York NY 10012.*
PROFESSIONAL PHOTOGRAPHERS OF AMERICA, INC. (PPA), *1090 Executive Way, Des Plaines IL 60018.*
ROMANCE WRITERS OF AMERICA, *#315, 13700 Veterans Memorial Dr., Houston TX 77014. Publishes an annual agent list for members for $10.*
SCIENCE FICTION AND FANTASY WRITERS OF AMERICA, *#1B, 5 Winding Brook Dr., Guilderland NY 12084.*
SOCIETY OF CHILDREN'S BOOK WRITERS & ILLUSTRATORS, *P.O. Box 66296, Mar Vista Station, Los Angeles CA 90066. Provides a literary agents list to members.*
SOCIETY OF ILLUSTRATORS, *128 E. 63rd St., New York NY 10021.*
VISUAL ARTISTS & GALLERIES ASSOCIATION, *Suite 2626, Rockefeller Plaza, New York NY 10020.*
WASHINGTON INDEPENDENT WRITERS, *Room 220, 733 15th St. NW, Washington DC 20005.*
WOMEN IN COMMUNICATIONS, INC., *Suite 417, 2101 Wilson Blvd., Arlington VA 22201.*
WRITERS GUILD OF AMERICA-EAST, *555 W. 57th St., New York NY 10019. Provides list of WGA signatory agents for $1.29.*
WRITERS GUILD OF AMERICA-WEST, *8955 Beverly Blvd., West Hollywood CA 90048. Provides a list of WGA signatory agents for $2 and SASE sent to Agency Department.*

Key to Symbols and Abbreviations

‡ *A listing new to this edition*
* *Agents who charge fees to previously unpublished writers only*
□ *Script agents who charge reading or other fees*
■ *Art/photo representatives who charge a one-time or monthly fee for handling, marketing or other services in addition to commission and advertising costs*
● *Comment from the editor of* Guide to Literary Agents & Art/Photo Reps
ms — manuscript; mss — manuscripts
SASE — self-addressed, stamped envelope
SAE — self-addressed envelope
IRC — International Reply Coupon, for use on reply mail in countries other than your own.
The Glossary contains definitions of words and expressions used throughout the book. The Table of Acronyms translates acronyms of organizations connected with agenting, writing or art.

Table of Acronyms

The organizations and their acronyms listed below are frequently referred to in the listings and are widely used in the industries of agenting, writing, art and photography.

AAP	American Association of Publishers
AAR	Association of Author's Representatives (1991 merger of ILAA and SAR)
ABA	American Booksellers Association
ABWA	Associated Business Writers of America
ADC	Art Directors Club
AEB	Association of Editorial Businesses
AFTRA	American Federation of TV and Radio Artists
AGVA	American Guild of Variety Artists
AIGA	American Institute of Graphic Artists
AMWA	American Medical Writer's Association
APA	Advertising Photographers of America
ASJA	American Society of Journalists and Authors
ASMP	American Society of Media Photographers
ASP	American Society of Photographers
ASPP	American Society of Picture Professionals
ATA	Association of Talent Agents
AWA	Aviation/Space Writers Association
CAA	Canadian Authors Association
DGA	Director's Guild of America
GWAA	Garden Writers Association of America

Table of Acronyms

HWA	Horror Writers of America
IACP	International Association of Culinary Professionals
ILAA	Independent Literary Agents Association (see AAR)
MWA	Mystery Writers of America, Inc.
NASW	National Association of Science Writers
NLAPW	National League of American Pen Women
NWA	National Writers Association
OWAA	Outdoor Writers Association of America, Inc.
PAI	Photo Administrators, Inc.
PPA	Professional Photographers of America
RWA	Romance Writers of America
SAG	Screen Actor's Guild
SAR	Society of Authors' Representatives (see AAR)
SATW	Society of American Travel Writers
SCBWI	Society of Children's Book Writers & Illustrators
SFWA	Science Fiction and Fantasy Writers of America
SPAR	Society of Photographers and Artists Representatives
VAGA	Visual Artists & Galleries Association
WGA	Writers Guild of America
WIA	Women in the Arts Foundation, Inc.
WIF	Women in Film
WICI	Women in Communications, Inc.
WIW	Washington Independent Writers
WNBA	Women's National Book Association
WRW	Washington Romance Writers (chapter of RWA)
WWA	Western Writers of America

Glossary

Advance. Money that a publisher pays a writer prior to publication of a book, usually paid in installments, such as one-half upon signing the contract; one-half upon delivery of the complete, satisfactory manuscript. An advance is paid against the royalty money to be earned by the book. Agents take their percentage off the top of the advance as well as from the royalties earned.
Advertising costs. Costs incurred by placing advertisements in newspapers or magazines, purchasing pages in industry talent books, promoting a show or exhibition, creation and mailing of direct mail or other promo pieces, list rental, slide copying—anything that promotes the work of the talent and may lead to sales.
Bio. Brief (usually one page) background information about an artist, writer or photographer. Includes work and educational experience.
Book. When used in commercial art circles, it refers to a portfolio. See *portfolio*.
Broker. A situation in which a rep handles only some of the work of an artist or photographer or in which the rep sells just what the talent has brought to sell. A percentage is taken from each sale. The rep is not handling the talent's career, only certain work.
Business-size envelope. Also known as a #10 envelope.
Category fiction. A term used to include all various types of fiction. See *genre*.
Cibachrome. Trademark for a full-color positive print made from a transparency.
Client. When referring to a literary or script agent "client" is used to mean the writer whose work the agent is handling, but when referring to art or photography representation, "client" refers to the art/photo buyer. The word "talent" is used to refer to the artist or photographer whose work is handled by the rep.
Client direct. Sales directly to a corporate client instead of to a middle person such as a developer, architect or interior decorator.
Clips. Writing samples, usually from newspapers or magazines, of your published work.
Collaterals. Accompanying or auxiliary pieces, such as brochures, especially used in advertising. Samples of these may be included in a portfolio.
Commercial novel. A novel designed to appeal to a broad audience. It often falls into a category or genre such as western, romance, mystery, science fiction and horror. See also *genre*.
Concept. A statement that summarizes a screenplay or teleplay—before the treatment is written.
Contributor's copies. Copies of the author's book sent to the author. The number of contributor's copies is often negotiated in the publishing contract.
Copyediting. Editing of a manuscript for writing style, grammar, punctuation and factual accuracy. Some agents offer this service.
Cover letter. A brief descriptive letter sent with a manuscript submitted to an agent or publisher.
C-print. Any enlargement printed from a negative. Any enlargement from a transparency is called an R-print.
Creative sourcebook. Also known as creative or talent directory. An annual book sent to art directors and others who buy the work of illustrators or photographers. Each page is an advertisement for the work of a talent or a group of talents and includes a representation of their style and contact information. Pages may be purchased by the rep or talent.
Critiquing service. A service offered by some agents in which writers pay a fee for comments on the saleability or other qualities of their manuscript. Sometimes the critique includes suggestions on how to improve the work. Fees vary, as do the quality of the critiques.
Direct mail package. Sales or promotional material distributed by mail. Usually consists of an outer envelope, a cover letter, brochure or flier, SASE or postpaid reply card.
Direct mail piece. A flier or brochure used in advertising the work of an artist, designer or photographer. The piece usually includes more than one image or one striking image that best shows the artist's or photographer's style.
Division. An unincorporated branch of a company.
Editing service. A service offered by some agents in which writers pay a fee—either lump sum or per-page—to have their manuscript edited. The quality and extent of the editing varies from agency to agency.
El-hi. Elementary to high school. A term used to indicate reading or interest level.
Evaluation fees. Fees an agent may charge to evaluate material. The extent and quality of this evaluation varies, but comments usually concern the saleability of the manuscript.
Exclusive. Offering a manuscript, usually for a set period of time, to just one agent and guaranteeing that agent is the only one looking at the manuscript.

Exclusive area representation. Requirement that an artist's or photographer's work be handled by only one rep within a given area.

Floor bid. If a publisher is very interested in a manuscript he may offer to enter a floor bid when the book goes to auction. The publisher sits out of the auction, but agrees to take the book by topping the highest bid by an agreed-upon percentage (usually 10 percent).

Foreign rights agent. An agent who handles selling the rights to a country other than that of the first book agent. Usually an additional percentage (about 5 percent) will be added on to the first book agent's commission to cover the foreign rights agent.

Genre. Refers to either a general classification of writing such as a novel, poem or short story or to the categories within those classifications, such as problem novels or sonnets. Genre fiction is a term that covers various types of commercial novels such as mystery, romance, western, science fiction or horror.

Ghosting or ghost writing. When a writer puts into literary form the words, ideas or knowledge of another person under that person's name it is called ghostwriting. Some agents offer this service. Others will pair ghostwriters with celebrities or experts.

Glossy. A black and white photograph with a shiny surface as opposed to a non-shiny matte finish.

IRC. International Reply Coupons; purchased at a post office to enclose with material sent outside your country to cover the cost of return postage. The recipient can turn in the coupons for stamps in their own country.

Leave-behinds. Promotional or direct mail fliers, brochures or other information about a talent designed to be left with a prospective buyer.

Mainstream fiction. Fiction on subjects or trends that transcend popular novel categories such as mystery or romance. Using conventional methods, this kind of fiction tells stories about people and their conflicts.

Marketing fee. Fee charged by some agents to cover marketing expenses. It may be used to cover postage, telephone calls, faxes, photocopying or any other expense incurred in marketing a manuscript.

Mass market paperbacks. Softcover book, usually around 4 × 7, on a popular subject directed at a general audience and sold in groceries and drugstores as well as bookstores.

MFTS. Made for TV series. A series developed for television also known as episodics.

Middle reader. The general classification of books written for readers 9-11 years old.

Mini-series. A limited dramatic series written for television, often based on a popular novel.

MOW. Movie of the week. A movie script written especially for television, usually seven acts with time for commercial breaks. Topics are often contemporary, sometimes controversial, fictional accounts. Also known as a made-for-TV-movie.

Net receipts. One method of royalty payment based on the amount of money a book publisher receives on the sale of the book after the booksellers' discounts, special sales discounts and returned copies.

Novelization. A novel created from the script of a popular movie, usually called a movie "tie-in" and published in paperback.

Novella. A short novel or long short story, usually 7,000 to 15,000 words. Also called a novelette.

Option clause. A contract clause giving a publisher the right to publish an author's next book.

Outline. A summary of a book's contents in 5 to 15 double-spaced pages; often in the form of chapter headings with a descriptive sentence or two under each one to show the scope of the book. A screenplay's or teleplay's outline is a scene-by-scene narrative description of the story (10-15 pages for a ½-hour teleplay; 15-25 pages for 1-hour; 25-40 pages for 90 minutes and 40-60 pages for a 2-hour feature film or teleplay).

Over-the-transom. Slang for the path of an unsolicited manuscript into the slush pile.

Photostats. Black-and-white copies produced by an inexpensive photographic process using paper negatives; only line values are held with accuracy. Also called a stat.

Picture book. A type of book aimed at the preschool to 8-year-old that tells the story primarily or entirely with artwork. Agents and reps interested in selling to publishers of these books often handle both artists and writers.

PMT. Photomechanical transfer, photostat produced without a negative.

Portfolio. Photographs or artwork samples (slides, originals, tearsheets, photocopies) assembled to demonstrate an artist's or photographer's style and abilities, often presented to clients.

Promotional piece. Also called promo piece. Material designed to promote an artist's or photographer's work. Usually more expensively produced and elaborate than a direct-mail or leave-behind, a promo piece can be colorful and include special printing techniques or folds.

Proofreading. Close reading and correction of a manuscript's typographical errors. A few agents offer this service for a fee.

Proposal. An offer to an editor or publisher to write a specific work, usually a package consisting of an outline and sample chapters.

Prospectus. A preliminary, written description of a book, usually one page in length.

Query. A letter written to an agent, rep, or a potential market, to elicit interest in a writer's, artist's or photographer's work.

Release. A statement that your idea is original, has never been sold to anyone else and that you are selling negotiated rights to the idea upon payment.

Remainders. Leftover copies of an out-of-print or slow-selling book, which can be purchased from the publisher at a reduced rate. Depending on the author's contract, a reduced royalty or no royalty is paid on remaindered books.

Reporting time. The time it takes the agent or rep to get back to you on your query or submission.

Roughs. Preliminary sketches or drawings.

Royalties. A percentage of the retail price paid to the author for each copy of the book that is sold. Agents take their percentage from the royalties earned as well as from the advance.

SASE. Self-addressed, stamped envelope. This or a self-addressed, stamped postcard should be included with all correspondence with reps or agents.

Scholarly books. Books written for an academic or research audience. These are usually heavily researched, technical and often contain terms used only within a specific field.

Screenplay. Script for a film intended to be shown in movie theaters.

Script. Broad term covering teleplay, screenplay or stage play. Sometimes used as a shortened version of the word "manuscript" when referring to books.

Simultaneous submission. Sending the same manuscript to several agents or publishers at the same time. Simultaneous query letters are common, but simultaneous submissions are unacceptable to many agents or publishers.

Sitcom. Situation comedy. Episodic comedy script for a television series. Term comes from the characters dealing with various situations with humorous results.

Slides. Usually called transparencies; positive color slides.

Slush pile. A stack of unsolicited submissions in the office of an editor, agent or publisher.

Standard commission. The commission an agent or rep earns on the sales of a manuscript, illustration or photograph. For literary agents, this commission percentage (usually between 10 and 20 percent) is taken from the advance and royalties paid to the writer. For script agents, the commission is taken from script sales; if handling plays, agents take a percentage from the box office proceeds. For art and photo reps the commission (usually 25 to 30 percent) is taken from sales.

Stock photo agency. A business that maintains a large collection of photos which it makes available to clients such as advertising agencies and periodicals. These agencies (not listed in this book) take a percentage from work sold for the photographer. Unlike photo reps, these agencies do not handle the careers of individual photographers, but sell the work of various photographers to clients looking for specific images. Stock agency listings may be found in *Photographer's Market*.

Storyboards. Series of panels which illustrates a progressive sequence or graphics and story copy for a TV commercial, film or filmstrip. Serves as a guide for an eventual finished product. Some artists specialize in doing storyboard work.

Subagent. An agent who handles certain subsidiary rights. This agent usually works in conjunction with the agent who has handled the book rights and the percentage paid the book agent is increased to cover paying the subagent.

Subsidiary. An incorporated branch of a company or conglomerate (e.g. Alfred Knopf, Inc., is a subsidiary of Random House, Inc.)

Subsidiary rights. All rights other than book publishing rights included in a book publishing contract, such as paperback rights, bookclub rights, movie rights. Part of an agent's job is to negotiate those rights and advise you on which to sell and which to keep.

Synopsis. A brief summary of a story, novel or play. As a part of a book proposal, it is a comprehensive summary condensed in a page or page and a half, single-spaced. See also *outline*.

Talent. When used in commercial art circles, talent refers to the artist or photographer. See *client*.

Tearsheet. Published samples of your work, usually pages torn from a magazine.

Textbook. Book used in a classroom on the elementary, high school or college level.

Thumbnail. A rough layout in miniature, usually used in reference to a book or other large project.

Trade book. Either a hard cover or soft cover book; subject matter frequently concerns a special interest for a general audience; sold mainly in bookstores.

Trade paperback. A softbound volume, usually around 5 × 8, published and designed for the general public, available mainly in bookstores.

Transparencies. Positive color slides; not color prints.

Treatment. Synopsis of a television or film script (40-60 pages for a 2-hour feature film or teleplay).

Unsolicited manuscript. An unrequested manuscript sent to an editor, agent or publisher.

Young adult. The general classification of books written for readers age 12-18.

Young reader. Books written for readers 5-8 years old, where artwork only supports the text.

Indexes

Subject Index

The following subject index is divided into nonfiction and fiction subject categories for each of three sections—Nonfee-charging Literary Agents, Fee-charging Literary Agents and Script Agents. To find an agent who is interested in the type of manuscript you've written, see the appropriate sections under subject headings that best describe your work. Check the Listings Index for the page number of the agent's listing. Agents who said they were open to most nonfiction or fiction subjects appear in the "Open" heading.

Nonfee charging agents/Fiction

Action/adventure Acton, Dystel, Leone & Jaffe; Allan, Lee; Amsterdam, Marcia; Appleseeds Management; Authors' Literary Agency; Baldi Literary Agency, Malaga; Behar, Josh; Bernsen, Jamail & Goodson, L.L.P.; Brandt & Brandt; Carvainis, Maria; Chadd-Stevens; Curtis Assoc., Richard; Dark Horse Group; Diamant, The Writer's Workshop, Inc., Anita; Diamond Literary Agency, Inc.; Dijkstra, Sandra; Doyen Literary Services; Ducas, Robert; Dupree/Miller and Assoc.; Ellenberg, Ethan; Esquire Literary Productions; Farber; Frontier Talents; Garon-Brooke Assoc., Jay; Geiger, Ellen; Greenburger Assoc., Sanford J.; Gusay, Charlotte; Hawkins & Assoc., John; Klinger, Inc., Harvey; Lampack, Peter; Lantz-Joy Harris Literary Agency Inc., The Robert; Lincoln, Ray; Literary Bridge; Literary Group; Love, Nancy; Lyceum Creative Properties; Madsen, Robert; Naggar, Jean V.; Otitis Media; Parks Agency, The Richard; Pelter, Rodney; Perkins Associates, L.; Picard Literary Agent, Alison J.; Renaissance: A Literary/Talent Agency; Rock Literary Agency; Schmidt Literary Agency, Harold; Seymour Agency, The; Siegel Literary Agency, Bobbe; Wald Associates, Inc., Mary Jack; Waterside Productions, Inc.; Weiner Literary Agency, Cherry; Westchester Literary Agency, Inc.; Zeckendorf Assoc. Inc., Susan

Cartoon/comic Axelrod Agency; Baldi Literary Agency, Malaga; Dark Horse Group; Dupree/Miller and Assoc.; Ellenberg, Ethan; Frontier Talents; Gusay, Charlotte; Hawkins & Assoc., John; Lantz-Joy Harris Literary Agency Inc., The Robert; Lyceum Creative Properties; Pelter, Rodney; Rock Literary Agency; Van Der Leun & Associates; Gusay, Charlotte; Lantz-Joy Harris Literary Agency Inc., The Robert; Pelter, Rodney; Rock Literary Agency

Contemporary issues Acton, Dystel, Leone & Jaffe; Agents Inc. for Medical and Mental Health Professionals; Authors' Literary Agency; Baldi Literary Agency, Malaga; Bartczak Assoc., Gene; Bernsen, Jamail & Goodson, L.L.P.; Blassingame Spectrum Corp.; Boates, Reid; Bova, Barbara; Brandt, Joan; Brandt & Brandt; Brown Assoc., Marie; Cantrell-Colas; Dark Horse Group; de la Haba Agency Inc., The Lois; Diamant, The Writer's Workshop, Inc., Anita; Diamond Literary Agency, Inc.; Dijkstra, Sandra; Doyen Literary Services; Ducas, Robert; Dupree/Miller and Assoc.; Esquire Literary Productions; Farber; Flaherty, Joyce A.; Fogelman; Garon-Brooke Assoc., Jay; Geiger, Ellen; Greenburger Assoc., Sanford J.; Gusay, Charlotte; Hardy Agency; Hawkins & Assoc., John; Kouts, Barbara S.; Kroll Literary Agency, Edite; Lampack, Peter; Lantz-Joy Harris Literary Agency Inc., The Robert; Lincoln, Ray; Literary Bridge; Los Angeles Literary Assoc.; Love, Nancy; Lyceum Creative Properties; McGrath, Helen; Markowitz, Barbara; Marmur Assoc., Mildred; Miller Assoc., Roberta D.; Naggar, Jean V.; Novak III, Edward A.; Parks Agency, The Richard; Pelter, Rodney; Picard Literary Agent, Alison J.; Quicksilver Books-Literary Agents; Raymond, Literary Agent, Charlotte Cecil; Rees Literary Agency, Helen; Riverside Literary Agency; Rock Literary Agency; Rose Literary Agency; Roth Agency, The ; Schmidt Literary Agency, Harold; Schwartz Agency, Laurens R.; Seligman, Literary Agent, Lynn; Shepard Agency, The; Siegel Literary Agency, Bobbe; Singer Literary Agency Inc., Evelyn; Spitzer Literary Agency, Philip G.; Stauffer Associates, Nancy; Stepping Stone; Stern Literary Agency, Gloria; Van Der Leun & Associates; Wald Associates, Inc., Mary Jack; Waterside Productions, Inc.; Watkins Loomis Agency, Inc.; Weiner Literary Agency, Cherry; Weingel-Fidel Agency, The; Westchester

Literary Agency, Inc.; Witherspoon & Associates, Inc.; Zeckendorf Assoc. Inc., Susan

Detective/police/crime Acton, Dystel, Leone & Jaffe; Allan, Lee; Allen, James; Amsterdam, Marcia; Appleseeds Management; Authors' Literary Agency; Axelrod Agency; Baldi Literary Agency, Malaga; Behar, Josh; Bernsen, Jamail & Goodson, L.L.P.; Boates, Reid; Brandt, Joan; Brandt & Brandt; Cantrell-Colas; Carvainis, Maria; Clark, SJ; Cohen, Ruth; Collin, Frances; Curtis Assoc., Richard; Dark Horse Group; de la Haba Agency Inc., The Lois; Diamant, The Writer's Workshop, Inc., Anita; Diamond Literary Agency, Inc.; Dijkstra, Sandra; Doyen Literary Services; Ducas, Robert; Dupree/Miller and Assoc.; Ellenberg, Ethan; Esquire Literary Productions; Farber; Flaherty, Joyce A.; Flaming Star Literary Enterprises; Frontier Talents; Garon-Brooke Assoc., Jay; Geiger, Ellen; Greenburger Assoc., Sanford J.; Gusay, Charlotte; Hawkins & Assoc., John; Hull House; IMG-Julian Bach; J de S Assoc.; Kidde, Hoyt & Picard; Klinger, Inc., Harvey; Lampack, Peter; Lantz-Joy Harris Literary Agency Inc., The Robert; Lincoln, Ray; Literary Bridge; Literary Group; Love, Nancy; Lyceum Creative Properties; Maass, Donald; McGrath, Helen; Markowitz, Barbara; Marmur Assoc., Mildred; Miller Assoc., Roberta D.; Morhaim, Howard; Multimedia Product Development; Naggar, Jean V.; Novak III, Edward A.; Otitis Media; Parks Agency, The Richard; Pelter, Rodney; Perkins Associates, L.; Picard Literary Agent, Alison J.; Rees Literary Agency, Helen; Renaissance: A Literary/Talent Agency; Riverside Literary Agency; Rock Literary Agency; Rubenstein Literary Agency, Inc., Pesha; Schmidt Literary Agency, Harold; Seligman, Literary Agent, Lynn; Siegel Literary Agency, Bobbe; Singer Literary Agency Inc., Evelyn; Spitzer Literary Agency, Philip G.; Steele & Co., Ltd., Lyle; Stepping Stone; Stern Literary Agency, Gloria; Targ Literary Agency, Inc., Roslyn; Wald Associates, Inc., Mary Jack; Wallace Literary Agency, Inc.; Waterside Productions, Inc.; Weiner Literary Agency, Cherry; Weingel-Fidel Agency, The; Westchester Literary Agency, Inc.; Wieser & Wieser, Inc.; Witherspoon & Associates, Inc.; Zeckendorf Assoc. Inc., Susan

Erotica Agency Chicago; Baldi Literary Agency, Malaga; Bernsen, Jamail & Goodson, L.L.P.; Brandt & Brandt; Chadd-Stevens; de la Haba Agency Inc., The Lois; Geiger, Ellen; Gusay, Charlotte; Lantz-Joy Harris Literary Agency Inc., The Robert; Lyceum Creative Properties; Pelter, Rodney; Rock Literary Agency

Ethnic Acton, Dystel, Leone & Jaffe; Baldi Literary Agency, Malaga; Bernsen, Jamail & Goodson, L.L.P.; Brandt & Brandt; Brown Assoc., Marie; Cantrell-Colas; Cohen, Ruth; Collin, Frances; Crown International Literature and Arts Agency, Bonnie R.; de la Haba Agency Inc., The Lois; Dijkstra, Sandra; Doyen Literary Services; Esquire Literary Productions; Geiger, Ellen; Greenburger Assoc., Sanford J.; Gusay, Charlotte; Hawkins & Assoc., John; Lantz-Joy Harris Literary Agency Inc., The Robert; Lincoln, Ray; Love, Nancy; Lyceum Creative Properties; Naggar, Jean V.; Pelter, Rodney; Perkins Associates, L.; Picard Literary Agent, Alison J.; Raymond, Literary Agent, Charlotte Cecil; Renaissance: A Literary/Talent Agency; Riverside Literary Agency; Rock Literary Agency; Rose Literary Agency; Roth Agency, The ; Schmidt Literary Agency, Harold; Seligman, Literary Agent, Lynn; Stepping Stone; Stern Literary Agency, Gloria; Van Der Leun & Associates; Wald Associates, Inc., Mary Jack; Witherspoon & Associates, Inc.; Zeckendorf Assoc. Inc., Susan

Experimental Agency Chicago; Baldi Literary Agency, Malaga; Bernsen, Jamail & Goodson, L.L.P.; Brandt & Brandt; Cantrell-Colas; Chadd-Stevens; de la Haba Agency Inc., The Lois; Diamant, The Writer's Workshop, Inc., Anita; Doyen Literary Services; Frontier Talents; Gusay, Charlotte; Hawkins & Assoc., John; Lantz-Joy Harris Literary Agency Inc., The Robert; Lyceum Creative Properties; Pelter, Rodney; Rock Literary Agency; Stern Literary Agency, Gloria; Wald Associates, Inc., Mary Jack

Family saga Acton, Dystel, Leone & Jaffe; Axelrod Agency; Boates, Reid; Brandt & Brandt; Brown Assoc., Marie; Cantrell-Colas; Carvainis, Maria; Cohen, Ruth; Collin, Frances; Crown International Literature and Arts Agency, Bonnie R.; Curtis Assoc., Richard; Diamant, The Writer's Workshop, Inc., Anita; Diamond Literary Agency, Inc.; Dijkstra, Sandra; Doyen Literary Services; Ducas, Robert; Ellenberg, Ethan; Esquire Literary Productions; Flaherty, Joyce A.; Garon-Brooke Assoc., Jay; Geiger, Ellen; Greenburger Assoc., Sanford J.; Gusay, Charlotte; Hawkins & Assoc., John; Klinger, Inc., Harvey; Kouts, Barbara S.; Lampack, Peter; Lantz-Joy Harris Literary Agency Inc., The Robert; Lincoln, Ray; Literary Bridge; Maass, Donald; McGrath, Helen; Marmur Assoc., Mildred; Morhaim, Howard; Naggar, Jean V.; Parks Agency, The Richard; Pelter, Rodney; Rees Literary Agency, Helen; Renaissance: A Literary/Talent Agency; Rock Literary Agency; Roth Agency, The ; Schmidt Literary Agency, Harold; Shepard Agency, The; Siegel Literary Agency, Bobbe; Steele & Co., Ltd., Lyle; Wald Associates, Inc., Mary Jack; Weiner Literary Agency, Cherry; Westchester Literary Agency, Inc.; Wieser & Wieser, Inc.; Witherspoon & Associates, Inc.; Zeckendorf Assoc. Inc., Susan

Fantasy Allan, Lee; Allen, James; Appleseeds Management; Behar, Josh; Bernsen, Jamail & Goodson, L.L.P.; Butler, Art and Literary Agent, Jane; Carvainis, Maria; Chadd-Stevens; Collin, Frances; Curtis Assoc., Richard; de la Haba Agency Inc., The Lois; Dijkstra, Sandra; Doyen Literary

Subject Index: Nonfee charging/Fiction 245

Services; Ellenberg, Ethan; Esquire Literary Productions; Garon-Brooke Assoc., Jay; Goodman Literary Agency, Irene; Gusay, Charlotte; Lincoln, Ray; Literary Bridge; Lyceum Creative Properties; Maass, Donald; Naggar, Jean V.; Otitis Media; Pelter, Rodney; Renaissance: A Literary/Talent Agency; Rock Literary Agency; Schwartz Agency, Laurens R.; Seligman, Literary Agent, Lynn; Siegel Literary Agency, Bobbe; Smith, Literary Agent, Valerie; Wald Associates, Inc., Mary Jack; Weiner Literary Agency, Cherry; Westchester Literary Agency, Inc.

Feminist Baldi Literary Agency, Malaga; Bernsen, Jamail & Goodson, L.L.P.; Brandt & Brandt; Brown Assoc., Marie; Cantrell-Colas; Curtis Assoc., Richard; de la Haba Agency Inc., The Lois; Diamant, The Writer's Workshop, Inc., Anita; Diamond Literary Agency, Inc.; Dijkstra, Sandra; Dupree/Miller and Assoc.; Esquire Literary Productions; Flaherty, Joyce A.; Geiger, Ellen; Greenburger Assoc., Sanford J.; Gusay, Charlotte; Hawkins & Assoc., John; IMG-Julian Bach; Kidde, Hoyt & Picard; Kouts, Barbara S.; Kroll Literary Agency, Edite; Lantz-Joy Harris Literary Agency Inc., The Robert; Lincoln, Ray; Literary Bridge; Lyceum Creative Properties; Marmur Assoc., Mildred; Naggar, Jean V.; Pelter, Rodney; Picard Literary Agent, Alison J.; Rees Literary Agency, Helen; Riverside Literary Agency; Rock Literary Agency; Rose Literary Agency; Roth Agency, The ; Schmidt Literary Agency, Harold; Seligman, Literary Agent, Lynn; Siegel Literary Agency, Bobbe; Stern Literary Agency, Gloria; Wald Associates, Inc., Mary Jack; Witherspoon & Associates, Inc.

Gay Bernsen, Jamail & Goodson, L.L.P.; Brandt & Brandt; Brown Assoc., Marie; de la Haba Agency Inc., The Lois; Diamant, The Writer's Workshop, Inc., Anita; Dupree/Miller and Assoc.; Esquire Literary Productions; Garon-Brooke Assoc., Jay; Geiger, Ellen; Greenburger Assoc., Sanford J.; Gusay, Charlotte; Hawkins & Assoc., John; Kidde, Hoyt & Picard; Lantz-Joy Harris Literary Agency Inc., The Robert; Lincoln, Ray; Lyceum Creative Properties; Naggar, Jean V.; Parks Agency, The Richard; Picard Literary Agent, Alison J.; Raymond, Literary Agent, Charlotte Cecil; Riverside Literary Agency; Rock Literary Agency; Rose Literary Agency; Steele & Co., Ltd., Lyle; Wald Associates, Inc., Mary Jack; Witherspoon & Associates, Inc.

Glitz Acton, Dystel, Leone & Jaffe; Amsterdam, Marcia; Carvainis, Maria; de la Haba Agency Inc., The Lois; Diamond Literary Agency, Inc.; Doyen Literary Services; Dupree/Miller and Assoc.; Ellenberg, Ethan; Esquire Literary Productions; Flaming Star Literary Enterprises; Garon-Brooke Assoc., Jay; Geiger, Ellen; Greenburger Assoc., Sanford J.; Gusay, Charlotte; Hawkins & Assoc., John; Klinger, Inc., Harvey; Lampack, Peter; Lantz-Joy Harris Literary Agency Inc., The Robert; Literary Bridge; Morhaim, Howard; Multimedia Product Development; Naggar, Jean V.; Parks Agency, The Richard; Pelter, Rodney; Picard Literary Agent, Alison J.; Rees Literary Agency, Helen; Riverside Literary Agency; Rock Literary Agency; Rubenstein Literary Agency, Inc., Pesha; Schmidt Literary Agency, Harold; Siegel Literary Agency, Bobbe; Teal Literary Agency, Patricia; Wald Associates, Inc., Mary Jack; Waterside Productions, Inc.; Weiner Literary Agency, Cherry; Witherspoon & Associates, Inc.; Zeckendorf Assoc. Inc., Susan

Historical Acton, Dystel, Leone & Jaffe; Allan, Lee; Allen, James; Amsterdam, Marcia; Appleseeds Management; Axelrod Agency; Baldi Literary Agency, Malaga; Bernsen, Jamail & Goodson, L.L.P.; Blassingame Spectrum Corp.; Brandt & Brandt; Brown Assoc., Marie; Butler, Art and Literary Agent, Jane; Cantrell-Colas; Carvainis, Maria; Cohen, Ruth; Collin, Frances; Crown International Literature and Arts Agency, Bonnie R.; Curtis Assoc., Richard; Dark Horse Group; Davie, Elaine; de la Haba Agency Inc., The Lois; Diamant, The Writer's Workshop, Inc., Anita; Diamond Literary Agency, Inc.; Doyen Literary Services; Ducas, Robert; Dupree/Miller and Assoc.; Ellenberg, Ethan; Elmo, Ann; Esquire Literary Productions; Farber; Flaherty, Joyce A.; Fogelman; Frontier Talents; Garon-Brooke Assoc., Jay; Geiger, Ellen; Greenburger Assoc., Sanford J.; Gusay, Charlotte; Hawkins & Assoc., John; J de S Assoc.; Kouts, Barbara S.; Lampack, Peter; Lantz-Joy Harris Literary Agency Inc., The Robert; Lincoln, Ray; Literary Bridge; Lyceum Creative Properties; Maass, Donald; Morhaim, Howard; Multimedia Product Development; Naggar, Jean V.; Novak III, Edward A.; Otitis Media; Parks Agency, The Richard; Pelter, Rodney; Picard Literary Agent, Alison J.; Rees Literary Agency, Helen; Renaissance: A Literary/Talent Agency; Riverside Literary Agency; Rock Literary Agency; Rubenstein Literary Agency, Inc., Pesha; Seligman, Literary Agent, Lynn; Shepard Agency, The; Siegel Literary Agency, Bobbe; Singer Literary Agency Inc., Evelyn; Steele & Co., Ltd., Lyle; Van Der Leun & Associates; Wald Associates, Inc., Mary Jack; Wecksler-Incomco; Weiner Literary Agency, Cherry; Westchester Literary Agency, Inc.; Witherspoon & Associates, Inc.; Zeckendorf Assoc. Inc., Susan

Humor/satire Agency Chicago; Ajlouny, Joseph S.; Allan, Lee; Amsterdam, Marcia; Appleseeds Management; Baldi Literary Agency, Malaga; Brandt & Brandt; Brown Assoc., Marie; Cantrell-Colas; Carvainis, Maria; de la Haba Agency Inc., The Lois; Diamond Literary Agency, Inc.; Doyen Literary Services; Dupree/Miller and Assoc.; Ellenberg, Ethan; Esquire Literary Productions; Farber; Frontier Talents; Geiger, Ellen; Greenburger Assoc., Sanford J.; Gusay, Charlotte; Hawkins & Assoc., John; Kidde, Hoyt & Picard; Lantz-Joy Harris Literary Agency Inc., The Robert; Lincoln, Ray; Literary Group; Lyceum Creative Properties; Madsen, Robert; Markowitz, Barbara;

Miller Assoc., Roberta D.; Otitis Media; Pelter, Rodney; Picard Literary Agent, Alison J.; Rees Literary Agency, Helen; Renaissance: A Literary/Talent Agency; Rock Literary Agency; Rose Literary Agency; Seligman, Literary Agent, Lynn; Seymour Agency, The; Shepard Agency, The; Wald Associates, Inc., Mary Jack; Westchester Literary Agency, Inc.; Witherspoon & Associates, Inc.; Wohl Literary Agency, Gary S.

Juvenile Allan, Lee; Bartczak Assoc., Gene; Bernsen, Jamail & Goodson, L.L.P.; Brown Assoc., Marie; Brown, Andrea; Butler, Art and Literary Agent, Jane; Butler, Art and Literary Agent, Jane; Cantrell-Colas; Carvainis, Maria; Clark, SJ; Cohen, Ruth; Dark Horse Group; de la Haba Agency Inc., The Lois; Diamant, The Writer's Workshop, Inc., Anita; Dijkstra, Sandra; Doyen Literary Services; Elek Assoc., Peter; Ellenberg, Ethan; Farber; Gotham Art & Literary Agency; Greenburger Assoc., Sanford J.; Gusay, Charlotte; Hawkins & Assoc., John; J de S Assoc.; Kirchoff/Wohlberg, Authors' Representation Div.; Kouts, Barbara S.; Lincoln, Ray; Lyceum Creative Properties; Maccoby, Gina; Markowitz, Barbara; Marmur Assoc., Mildred; MGA Agency; Multimedia Product Development; Naggar, Jean V.; Picard Literary Agent, Alison J.; Rubenstein Literary Agency, Inc., Pesha; Seymour Agency, The; Targ Literary Agency, Inc., Roslyn; Wald Associates, Inc., Mary Jack; Wasserman Literary Agency Inc., Harriet; Westchester Literary Agency, Inc.

Lesbian Baldi Literary Agency, Malaga; Bernsen, Jamail & Goodson, L.L.P.; Brandt & Brandt; Geiger, Ellen; Greenburger Assoc., Sanford J.; Gusay, Charlotte; Hawkins & Assoc., John; Kidde, Hoyt & Picard; Lantz-Joy Harris Literary Agency Inc., The Robert; Lincoln, Ray; Lyceum Creative Properties; Naggar, Jean V.; Parks Agency, The Richard; Pelter, Rodney; Picard Literary Agent, Alison J.; Raymond, Literary Agent, Charlotte Cecil; Riverside Literary Agency; Rock Literary Agency; Schmidt Literary Agency, Harold; Steele & Co., Ltd., Lyle; Witherspoon & Associates, Inc.

Literary Acton, Dystel, Leone & Jaffe; Agents Inc. for Medical and Mental Health Professionals; Allan, Lee; Authors' Literary Agency; Axelrod Agency; Baldi Literary Agency, Malaga; Behar, Josh; Bernsen, Jamail & Goodson, L.L.P.; Blassingame Spectrum Corp.; Borchardt Inc., Georges; Brandt, Joan; Brandt & Brandt; Brown Assoc., Marie; Cantrell-Colas; Carvainis, Maria; Cohen, Ruth; Collin, Frances; Congdon Assoc., Don; Crown International Literature and Arts Agency, Bonnie R.; Darhansoff & Verrill; de la Haba Agency Inc., The Lois; Diamant, The Writer's Workshop, Inc., Anita; Dijkstra, Sandra; Ducas, Robert; Dupree/Miller and Assoc.; Ellenberg, Ethan; Ellison, Nicholas; Flaherty, Joyce A.; Frontier Talents; Fuhrman, Candice; Garon-Brooke Assoc., Jay; Geiger, Ellen; Gotham Art & Literary Agency; Greenburger Assoc., Sanford J.; Gregory Assoc., Maia; Gusay, Charlotte; Hardy Agency; Hawkins & Assoc., John; Herner, Susan; Hull House; IMG-Julian Bach; J de S Assoc.; Kidde, Hoyt & Picard; Klinger, Inc., Harvey; Kouts, Barbara S.; Kroll Literary Agency, Edite; Lampack, Peter; Lantz-Joy Harris Literary Agency Inc., The Robert; Levine, Ellen; Lincoln, Ray; Love, Nancy; Lyceum Creative Properties; Maass, Donald; Maccoby, Gina; McGrath, Helen; Mann, Carol; Markson, Elaine; Marmur Assoc., Mildred; Miller Assoc., Roberta D.; Naggar, Jean V.; Nine Muses and Apollo; Novak III, Edward A.; Otitis Media; Parks Agency, The Richard; Paton Literary Agency, Kathi J.; Pelter, Rodney; Perkins Associates, L.; Picard Literary Agent, Alison J.; Pryor, Inc., Roberta; Quicksilver Books-Literary Agents; Raymond, Literary Agent, Charlotte Cecil; Renaissance: A Literary/Talent Agency; Riverside Literary Agency; Rock Literary Agency; Rose Literary Agency; Roth Agency, The ; Sandum & Associates; Schaffner Agency, Inc.; Schmidt Literary Agency, Harold; Schwartz Agency, Laurens R.; Seligman, Literary Agent, Lynn; Shepard Agency, The; Siegel Literary Agency, Bobbe; Smith, Literary Agent, Valerie; Snell Literary Agency, Michael; Spitzer Literary Agency, Philip G.; Stauffer Associates, Nancy; Steele & Co., Ltd., Lyle; Stepping Stone; Stern Literary Agency, Gloria; Van Der Leun & Associates; Wald Associates, Inc., Mary Jack; Wallace Literary Agency, Inc.; Waterside Productions, Inc.; Watkins Loomis Agency, Inc.; Wecksler-Incomco; Weingel-Fidel Agency, The; Westchester Literary Agency, Inc.; Wieser & Wieser, Inc.; Witherspoon & Associates, Inc.; Writers' Productions; Writers' Representatives, Inc.; Zeckendorf Assoc. Inc., Susan

Mainstream Acton, Dystel, Leone & Jaffe; Allan, Lee; Allen, James; Amsterdam, Marcia; Appleseeds Management; Authors' Literary Agency; Axelrod Agency; Baldi Literary Agency, Malaga; Bernsen, Jamail & Goodson, L.L.P.; Blassingame Spectrum Corp.; Boates, Reid; Bova, Barbara; Brandt, Joan; Brandt & Brandt; Brown Assoc., Marie; Cantrell-Colas; Carvainis, Maria; Cleaver, Diane; Cohen, Ruth; Collin, Frances; Columbia Literary Assoc.; Curtis Assoc., Richard; Dark Horse Group; de la Haba Agency Inc., The Lois; Diamant, The Writer's Workshop, Inc., Anita; Diamond Literary Agency, Inc.; Dijkstra, Sandra; Doyen Literary Services; Ducas, Robert; Dupree/Miller and Assoc.; Eisenberg, Vicki; Ellenberg, Ethan; Ellison, Nicholas; Esquire Literary Productions; Farber; Flaherty, Joyce A.; Flaming Star Literary Enterprises; Fogelman; Frontier Talents; Fuhrman, Candice; Garon-Brooke Assoc., Jay; Gartenberg, Max; Geiger, Ellen; Goodman Literary Agency, Irene; Gotham Art & Literary Agency; Greenburger Assoc., Sanford J.; Gusay, Charlotte; Hawkins & Assoc., John; Herner, Susan; Hull House; IMG-Julian Bach; International Publisher Assoc.; J de S Assoc.; Kidde, Hoyt & Picard; Klinger, Inc., Harvey; Kouts, Barbara

S.; Kroll Literary Agency, Edite; Lantz-Joy Harris Literary Agency Inc., The Robert; Levant & Wales; Lincoln, Ray; Lipkind, Wendy; Literary Bridge; Lord Literistic, Sterling; Los Angeles Literary Assoc.; Love, Nancy; Lowenstein Associates, Inc.; Lyceum Creative Properties; Maass, Donald; Maccoby, Gina; McGrath, Helen; Markson, Elaine; Marmur Assoc., Mildred; Miller Assoc., Roberta D.; Morhaim, Howard; Multimedia Product Development; Naggar, Jean V.; Nine Muses and Apollo; Novak III, Edward A.; Otitis Media; Parks Agency, The Richard; Paton Literary Agency, Kathi J.; Pelter, Rodney; Perkins Associates, L.; Picard Literary Agent, Alison J.; Quicksilver Books-Literary Agents; Raymond, Literary Agent, Charlotte Cecil; Rees Literary Agency, Helen; Renaissance: A Literary/Talent Agency; Riverside Literary Agency; Rock Literary Agency; Roth Agency, The ; Sandum & Associates; Schmidt Literary Agency, Harold; Schwartz Agency, Laurens R.; Seligman, Literary Agent, Lynn; Siegel Literary Agency, Bobbe; Sierra Literary Agency; Smith, Literary Agent, Valerie; Spitzer Literary Agency, Philip G.; Stauffer Associates, Nancy; Stepping Stone; Stern Literary Agency, Gloria; Teal Literary Agency, Patricia; Van Der Leun & Associates; Wald Associates, Inc., Mary Jack; Wallace Literary Agency, Inc.; Ware Literary Agency, John A.; Waterside Productions, Inc.; Watkins Loomis Agency, Inc.; Weiner Literary Agency, Cherry; Weingel-Fidel Agency, The; Westchester Literary Agency, Inc.; Wieser & Wieser, Inc.; Witherspoon & Associates, Inc.; Wreschner, Authors' Representative, Ruth; Zeckendorf Assoc. Inc., Susan

Mystery/suspense Acton, Dystel, Leone & Jaffe; Agents Inc. for Medical and Mental Health Professionals; Allan, Lee; Allen, James; Amsterdam, Marcia; Appleseeds Management; Authors' Literary Agency; Axelrod Agency; Baldi Literary Agency, Malaga; Bernsen, Jamail & Goodson, L.L.P.; Blassingame Spectrum Corp.; Boates, Reid; Bova, Barbara; Brandt, Joan; Brandt & Brandt; Brown Assoc., Marie; Butler, Art and Literary Agent, Jane; Cantrell-Colas; Carvainis, Maria; Chadd-Stevens; Ciske Literary Agency, Francine; Clark, SJ; Cleaver, Diane; Cohen, Ruth; Collin, Frances; Columbia Literary Assoc.; Curtis Assoc., Richard; Dark Horse Group; Davie, Elaine; de la Haba Agency Inc., The Lois; Diamant, The Writer's Workshop, Inc., Anita; Diamond Literary Agency, Inc.; Dijkstra, Sandra; Doyen Literary Services; Ducas, Robert; Dupree/Miller and Assoc.; Ellenberg, Ethan; Esquire Literary Productions; Farber; Flaherty, Joyce A.; Flaming Star Literary Enterprises; Frontier Talents; Garon-Brooke Assoc., Jay; Gartenberg, Max; Geiger, Ellen; Goodman Literary Agency, Irene; Greenburger Assoc., Sanford J.; Gusay, Charlotte; Hawkins & Assoc., John; Herner, Susan; Hull House; J de S Assoc.; Kidde, Hoyt & Picard; Klinger, Inc., Harvey; Kouts, Barbara S.; Kroll Literary Agency, Edite; Lampack, Peter; Lantz-Joy Harris Literary Agency Inc., The Robert; Lincoln, Ray; Lipkind, Wendy; Literary Bridge; Literary Group; Love, Nancy; Lyceum Creative Properties; Maass, Donald; Maccoby, Gina; McGrath, Helen; Madsen, Robert; Markowitz, Barbara; Marmur Assoc., Mildred; MGA Agency; Morhaim, Howard; Morrison, Henry; Multimedia Product Development; Naggar, Jean V.; Novak III, Edward A.; Otitis Media; Parks Agency, The Richard; Pelter, Rodney; Perkins Associates, L.; Picard Literary Agent, Alison J.; Protter Literary Agent, Susan Ann; Rees Literary Agency, Helen; Renaissance: A Literary/Talent Agency; Riverside Literary Agency; Rock Literary Agency; Rosenthal Literary Agency, Jean; Rubenstein Literary Agency, Inc., Pesha; Schmidt Literary Agency, Harold; Seligman, Literary Agent, Lynn; Siegel Literary Agency, Bobbe; Singer Literary Agency Inc., Evelyn; Snell Literary Agency, Michael; Spitzer Literary Agency, Philip G.; Steele & Co., Ltd., Lyle; Stepping Stone; Stern Literary Agency, Gloria; Targ Literary Agency, Inc., Roslyn; Teal Literary Agency, Patricia; Wald Associates, Inc., Mary Jack; Wallace Literary Agency, Inc.; Ware Literary Agency, John A.; Waterside Productions, Inc.; Watkins Loomis Agency, Inc.; Weiner Literary Agency, Cherry; Weingel-Fidel Agency, The; Westchester Literary Agency, Inc.; Wieser & Wieser, Inc.; Witherspoon & Associates, Inc.; Wohl Literary Agency, Gary S.; Wreschner, Authors' Representative, Ruth; Zeckendorf Assoc. Inc., Susan

Open to all fiction categories Barrett Books, Loretta; Brown Ltd., Curtis; Buck, Howard; Cohen, Hy; Collier Assoc.; Congdon Assoc., Don; Goldfarb & Assoc., Ronald; Goodman Assoc.; Hamilburg, Mitchell J.; Hoffman Literary Agency, Berenice; Larsen/Elizabeth Pomada, Michael; Lazear Agency; MacCampbell, Donald; Madsen, Robert; Martell Agency; Ober Associates, Harold; Picard Literary Agent, Alison J.; Spieler Literary Agency, Gretchen; Writers House

Picture book Axelrod Agency; Brown Assoc., Marie; Brown, Andrea; Cohen, Ruth; Dark Horse Group; Dijkstra, Sandra; Doyen Literary Services; Elek Assoc., Peter; Ellenberg, Ethan; Greenburger Assoc., Sanford J.; Gusay, Charlotte; Hawkins & Assoc., John; Kouts, Barbara S.; Kroll Literary Agency, Edite; Lantz-Joy Harris Literary Agency Inc., The Robert; Lyceum Creative Properties; MGA Agency; Naggar, Jean V.; Otitis Media; Rubenstein Literary Agency, Inc., Pesha; Wald Associates, Inc., Mary Jack

Psychic/supernatural Allan, Lee; Appleseeds Management; Behar, Josh; Bernsen, Jamail & Goodson, L.L.P.; Brandt & Brandt; Cantrell-Colas; Chadd-Stevens; Clark, SJ; Collin, Frances; Dark Horse Group; Diamant, The Writer's Workshop, Inc., Anita; Doyen Literary Services; Dupree/Miller and Assoc.; Flaherty, Joyce A.; Greenburger Assoc., Sanford J.; Gusay, Charlotte; Hawkins

& Assoc., John; Lantz-Joy Harris Literary Agency Inc., The Robert; Lincoln, Ray; Literary Bridge; Lyceum Creative Properties; Maass, Donald; McGrath, Helen; Naggar, Jean V.; Otitis Media; Parks Agency, The Richard; Pelter, Rodney; Perkins Associates, L.; Picard Literary Agent, Alison J.; Riverside Literary Agency; Rock Literary Agency; Schmidt Literary Agency, Harold; Siegel Literary Agency, Bobbe; Steele & Co., Ltd., Lyle; Wald Associates, Inc., Mary Jack; Weiner Literary Agency, Cherry

Regional Baldi Literary Agency, Malaga; Brandt & Brandt; Brown Assoc., Marie; Collin, Frances; Geiger, Ellen; Greenburger Assoc., Sanford J.; Gusay, Charlotte; Hawkins & Assoc., John; Lantz-Joy Harris Literary Agency Inc., The Robert; Lincoln, Ray; Naggar, Jean V.; Otitis Media; Pelter, Rodney; Raymond, Literary Agent, Charlotte Cecil; Rock Literary Agency; Shepard Agency, The

Religious/inspiration Bernsen, Jamail & Goodson, L.L.P.; Ciske Literary Agency, Francine; de la Haba Agency Inc., The Lois; Diamant, The Writer's Workshop, Inc., Anita; Diamond Literary Agency, Inc.; Gusay, Charlotte; Hawkins & Assoc., John; Lantz-Joy Harris Literary Agency Inc., The Robert; Multimedia Product Development; Pelter, Rodney; Rock Literary Agency; Westchester Literary Agency, Inc.

Romance Acton, Dystel, Leone & Jaffe; Allan, Lee; Allen, James; Amsterdam, Marcia; Axelrod Agency; Behar, Josh; Bernsen, Jamail & Goodson, L.L.P.; Blassingame Spectrum Corp.; Brandt & Brandt; Carvainis, Maria; Ciske Literary Agency, Francine; Collin, Frances; Columbia Literary Assoc.; Curtis Assoc., Richard; Davie, Elaine; Diamant, The Writer's Workshop, Inc., Anita; Diamond Literary Agency, Inc.; Doyen Literary Services; Dupree/Miller and Assoc.; Ellenberg, Ethan; Elmo, Ann; Esquire Literary Productions; Farber; Flaherty, Joyce A.; Fogelman; Garon-Brooke Assoc., Jay; Goodman Literary Agency, Irene; Herner, Susan; Kidde, Hoyt & Picard; Klinger, Inc., Harvey; Kouts, Barbara S.; Lantz-Joy Harris Literary Agency Inc., The Robert; Lincoln, Ray; Lowenstein Associates, Inc.; Lyceum Creative Properties; MGA Agency; Morhaim, Howard; Multimedia Product Development; Novak III, Edward A.; Picard Literary Agent, Alison J.; Rock Literary Agency; Rubenstein Literary Agency, Inc., Pesha; Seymour Agency, The; Siegel Literary Agency, Bobbe; Stern Literary Agency, Gloria; Teal Literary Agency, Patricia; Wald Associates, Inc., Mary Jack; Waterside Productions, Inc.; Weiner Literary Agency, Cherry; Westchester Literary Agency, Inc.; Wieser & Wieser, Inc.; Witherspoon & Associates, Inc.; Wohl Literary Agency, Gary S.; Zeckendorf Assoc. Inc., Susan

Science fiction Agents Inc. for Medical and Mental Health Professionals; Allan, Lee; Allen, James; Amsterdam, Marcia; Appleseeds Management; Behar, Josh; Bernsen, Jamail & Goodson, L.L.P.; Blassingame Spectrum Corp.; Bova, Barbara; Brandt & Brandt; Brown Assoc., Marie; Butler, Art and Literary Agent, Jane; Cantrell-Colas; Collin, Frances; Curtis Assoc., Richard; Dijkstra, Sandra; Doyen Literary Services; Dupree/Miller and Assoc.; Ellenberg, Ethan; Garon-Brooke Assoc., Jay; Goodman Literary Agency, Irene; Hawkins & Assoc., John; Herner, Susan; Lincoln, Ray; Literary Bridge; Lyceum Creative Properties; Maass, Donald; McGrath, Helen; Madsen, Robert; MGA Agency; Morrison, Henry; Naggar, Jean V.; Protter Literary Agent, Susan Ann; Rees Literary Agency, Helen; Renaissance: A Literary/Talent Agency; Riverside Literary Agency; Rock Literary Agency; Schmidt Literary Agency, Harold; Siegel Literary Agency, Bobbe; Smith, Literary Agent, Valerie; Targ Literary Agency, Inc., Roslyn; Wald Associates, Inc., Mary Jack; Weiner Literary Agency, Cherry

Sports Acton, Dystel, Leone & Jaffe; Bernsen, Jamail & Goodson, L.L.P.; Brandt & Brandt; Dijkstra, Sandra; Ducas, Robert; Dupree/Miller and Assoc.; Ellenberg, Ethan; Greenburger Assoc., Sanford J.; Gusay, Charlotte; Hawkins & Assoc., John; Lantz-Joy Harris Literary Agency Inc., The Robert; Lincoln, Ray; Literary Bridge; Literary Group; McGrath, Helen; Novak III, Edward A.; Pelter, Rodney; Picard Literary Agent, Alison J.; Rees Literary Agency, Helen; Rock Literary Agency; Shepard Agency, The; Spitzer Literary Agency, Philip G.; Wald Associates, Inc., Mary Jack; Wohl Literary Agency, Gary S.

Thriller/espionage Acton, Dystel, Leone & Jaffe; Allan, Lee; Amsterdam, Marcia; Appleseeds Management; Authors' Literary Agency; Axelrod Agency; Baldi Literary Agency, Malaga; Behar, Josh; Bernsen, Jamail & Goodson, L.L.P.; Boates, Reid; Brandt, Joan; Brandt & Brandt; Cantrell-Colas; Carvainis, Maria; Ciske Literary Agency, Francine; Clark, SJ; Cleaver, Diane; Columbia Literary Assoc.; Curtis Assoc., Richard; Darhansoff & Verrill; Diamant, The Writer's Workshop, Inc., Anita; Diamond Literary Agency, Inc.; Dijkstra, Sandra; Doyen Literary Services; Ducas, Robert; Dupree/Miller and Assoc.; Ellenberg, Ethan; Esquire Literary Productions; Farber; Flaherty, Joyce A.; Flaming Star Literary Enterprises; Frontier Talents; Geiger, Ellen; Greenburger Assoc., Sanford J.; Gusay, Charlotte; Hawkins & Assoc., John; Herner, Susan; Kidde, Hoyt & Picard; Klinger, Inc., Harvey; Lampack, Peter; Lantz-Joy Harris Literary Agency Inc., The Robert; Levine, Ellen; Lincoln, Ray; Literary Bridge; Literary Group; Los Angeles Literary Assoc.; Love, Nancy; Lyceum Creative Properties; Maass, Donald; Maccoby, Gina; McGrath, Helen; Marmur Assoc., Mildred; Morhaim, Howard; Morrison, Henry; Multimedia Product Development; Naggar, Jean V.; Novak III, Edward A.; Otitis Media; Parks Agency, The Richard; Pelter, Rodney; Perkins

Associates, L.; Picard Literary Agent, Alison J.; Protter Literary Agent, Susan Ann; Rees Literary Agency, Helen; Renaissance: A Literary/Talent Agency; Riverside Literary Agency; Rock Literary Agency; Rose Literary Agency; Schmidt Literary Agency, Harold; Shepard Agency, The; Siegel Literary Agency, Bobbe; Singer Literary Agency Inc., Evelyn; Snell Literary Agency, Michael; Steele & Co., Ltd., Lyle; Stepping Stone; Stern Literary Agency, Gloria; Targ Literary Agency, Inc., Roslyn; Wald Associates, Inc., Mary Jack; Ware Literary Agency, John A.; Waterside Productions, Inc.; Wecksler-Incomco; Weiner Literary Agency, Cherry; Weingel-Fidel Agency, The; Westchester Literary Agency, Inc.; Wieser & Wieser, Inc.; Witherspoon & Associates, Inc.; Zeckendorf Assoc. Inc., Susan

Westerns/frontier Allan, Lee; Amsterdam, Marcia; Bernsen, Jamail & Goodson, L.L.P.; Brandt & Brandt; Carvainis, Maria; Ciske Literary Agency, Francine; Curtis Assoc., Richard; Davie, Elaine; Diamant, The Writer's Workshop, Inc., Anita; Doyen Literary Services; Ducas, Robert; Dupree/Miller and Assoc.; Ellenberg, Ethan; Flaherty, Joyce A.; Frontier Talents; Goodman Literary Agency, Irene; Gusay, Charlotte; Hawkins & Assoc., John; J de S Assoc.; Literary Bridge; Lyceum Creative Properties; Maass, Donald; McGrath, Helen; Madsen, Robert; Multimedia Product Development; Parks Agency, The Richard; Pelter, Rodney; Picard Literary Agent, Alison J.; Rock Literary Agency; Schmidt Literary Agency, Harold; Targ Literary Agency, Inc., Roslyn; Wald Associates, Inc., Mary Jack; Weiner Literary Agency, Cherry; Westchester Literary Agency, Inc.

Young adult Allan, Lee; Amsterdam, Marcia; Bernsen, Jamail & Goodson, L.L.P.; Brandt & Brandt; Brown, Andrea; Butler, Art and Literary Agent, Jane; Cantrell-Colas; Carvainis, Maria; Chadd-Stevens; Clark, SJ; Cohen, Ruth; de la Haba Agency Inc., The Lois; Diamant, The Writer's Workshop, Inc., Anita; Dijkstra, Sandra; Doyen Literary Services; Ellenberg, Ethan; Farber; Gusay, Charlotte; J de S Assoc.; Kirchoff/Wohlberg, Authors' Representation Div.; Kouts, Barbara S.; Lantz-Joy Harris Literary Agency Inc., The Robert; Lincoln, Ray; Maccoby, Gina; Marmur Assoc., Mildred; MGA Agency; Miller Assoc., Roberta D.; Naggar, Jean V.; Parks Agency, The Richard; Picard Literary Agent, Alison J.; Raymond, Literary Agent, Charlotte Cecil; Seymour Agency, The; Smith, Literary Agent, Valerie; Stern Literary Agency, Gloria; Wald Associates, Inc., Mary Jack; Wasserman Literary Agency Inc., Harriet; Westchester Literary Agency, Inc.

Nonfee charging agents/Nonfiction

Agriculture/horticulture Baldi Literary Agency, Malaga; Brandt & Brandt; Casselman Literary Agent, Martha; de la Haba Agency Inc., The Lois; Dijkstra, Sandra; Ellison, Nicholas; Fogelman; Gartenberg, Max; Geiger, Ellen; Hawkins & Assoc., John; Levant & Wales; Lincoln, Ray; Multimedia Product Development; Parks Agency, The Richard; Roth Agency, The ; Shepard Agency, The; Urstadt Inc. Writers and Artists Agency, Susan P.

Animals Acton, Dystel, Leone & Jaffe; Baldi Literary Agency, Malaga; Balkin Agency; Bernsen, Jamail & Goodson, L.L.P.; Boates, Reid; Brandt & Brandt; Brown, Andrea; Crown International Literature and Arts Agency, Bonnie R.; de la Haba Agency Inc., The Lois; Diamant, The Writer's Workshop, Inc., Anita; Ducas, Robert; Ellison, Nicholas; Flaherty, Joyce A.; Fuhrman, Candice; Gartenberg, Max; Geiger, Ellen; Hawkins & Assoc., John; Lincoln, Ray; Literary Bridge; Literary Group; Multimedia Product Development; Nine Muses and Apollo; Parks Agency, The Richard; Riverside Literary Agency; Rosenthal Literary Agency, Jean; Shepard Agency, The; Stepping Stone; Urstadt Inc. Writers and Artists Agency, Susan P.; Writers House

Anthropology Baldi Literary Agency, Malaga; Balkin Agency; Bernsen, Jamail & Goodson, L.L.P.; Boates, Reid; Borchardt Inc., Georges; Brandt & Brandt; Cantrell-Colas; Casselman Literary Agent, Martha; Collin, Frances; Coover Agency, Doe; Darhansoff & Verrill; de la Haba Agency Inc., The Lois; Dijkstra, Sandra; Educational Design Services; Ellison, Nicholas; Fuhrman, Candice; Geiger, Ellen; Hawkins & Assoc., John; Hochmann Books, John L.; Hull House; IMG-Julian Bach; Kellock Co.; Ketz, Louise B.; Lincoln, Ray; Literary Bridge; Lyceum Creative Properties; Mann, Carol; Otitis Media; Parks Agency, The Richard; Peter Associates, Inc., James; Quicksilver Books-Literary Agents; Rose Literary Agency; Rosenthal Literary Agency, Jean; Schmidt Literary Agency, Harold; Seligman, Literary Agent, Lynn; Siegel Literary Agency, Bobbe; Singer Literary Agency Inc., Evelyn; Steele & Co., Ltd., Lyle; Stepping Stone; Stern Literary Agency, Gloria; Urstadt Inc. Writers and Artists Agency, Susan P.; Wallace Literary Agency, Inc.; Ware Literary Agency, John A.; Waterside Productions, Inc.; Wecksler-Incomco; Weingel-Fidel Agency, The; Witherspoon & Associates, Inc.

Art/architecture/design Agency Chicago; Axelrod Agency; Baldi Literary Agency, Malaga; Boates, Reid; Brandt & Brandt; Brown Assoc., Marie; Cantrell-Colas; de la Haba Agency Inc., The Lois; Diamant, The Writer's Workshop, Inc., Anita; Dijkstra, Sandra; Ellison, Nicholas; Fuhrman, Candice; Gartenberg, Max; Geiger, Ellen; Gregory Assoc., Maia; Hawkins & Assoc., John; Hochmann Books, John L.; Hull House; Kellock Co.; Kidde, Hoyt & Picard; Lincoln, Ray; Lyceum Creative Properties; Mann, Carol; Miller Assoc., Roberta D.; Nathan, Ruth; Novak III, Edward A.; Parks

Agency, The Richard; Perkins Associates, L.; Peter Associates, Inc., James; Picard Literary Agent, Alison J.; Rose Literary Agency; Rosenthal Literary Agency, Jean; Schmidt Literary Agency, Harold; Seligman, Literary Agent, Lynn; Stepping Stone; Stern Literary Agency, Gloria; Swamy Literary Agent, Maya; Urstadt Inc. Writers and Artists Agency, Susan P.; Waterside Productions, Inc.; Watkins Loomis Agency, Inc.; Wecksler-Incomco; Weingel-Fidel Agency, The; Writers House; Zeckendorf Assoc. Inc., Susan

Biography/autobiography Acton, Dystel, Leone & Jaffe; Adler & Robin Books; Ajlouny, Joseph S.; Allan, Lee; Andrews & Assoc., Bart; Appleseeds Management; Authors' Literary Agency; Baldi Literary Agency, Malaga; Balkin Agency; Bartczak Assoc., Gene; Behar, Josh; Bernsen, Jamail & Goodson, L.L.P.; Blassingame Spectrum Corp.; Boates, Reid; Borchardt Inc., Georges; Brandt & Brandt; Brown Assoc., Marie; Cantrell-Colas; Carvainis, Maria; Casselman Literary Agent, Martha; Clausen Assoc., Connie; Collin, Frances; Coover Agency, Doe; Curtis Assoc., Richard; Darhansoff & Verrill; Dark Horse Group; de la Haba Agency Inc., The Lois; Diamant, The Writer's Workshop, Inc., Anita; Dijkstra, Sandra; Ducas, Robert; Ellenberg, Ethan; Flaherty, Joyce A.; Fogelman; Fuhrman, Candice; Garon-Brooke Assoc., Jay; Gartenberg, Max; Geiger, Ellen; Hardy Agency; Hawkins & Assoc., John; Hochmann Books, John L.; Holub & Assoc.; Hull House; IMG-Julian Bach; J de S Assoc.; Jordan Literary Agency, Lawrence; Kellock Co.; Ketz, Louise B.; Kidde, Hoyt & Picard; Klinger, Inc., Harvey; Kouts, Barbara S.; Lampack, Peter; Levine, Ellen; Lincoln, Ray; Lipkind, Wendy; Literary Bridge; Literary Group; Los Angeles Literary Assoc.; Love, Nancy; Lyceum Creative Properties; McCauley, Gerard; Maccoby, Gina; McGrath, Helen; Mann, Carol; Markowitz, Barbara; Marmur Assoc., Mildred; Miller Assoc., Roberta D.; Multimedia Product Development; Naggar, Jean V.; Nathan, Ruth; New England Publishing Assoc.; Nine Muses and Apollo; Novak III, Edward A.; Otitis Media; Parks Agency, The Richard; Peter Associates, Inc., James; Picard Literary Agent, Alison J.; Protter Literary Agent, Susan Ann; Quicksilver Books-Literary Agents; Raymond, Literary Agent, Charlotte Cecil; Rees Literary Agency, Helen; Renaissance: A Literary/Talent Agency; Riverside Literary Agency; Rose Literary Agency; Rosenthal Literary Agency, Jean; Roth Agency, The ; Schaffner Agency, Inc.; Schmidt Literary Agency, Harold; Seligman, Literary Agent, Lynn; Shepard Agency, The; Siegel Literary Agency, Bobbe; Singer Literary Agency Inc., Evelyn; Spitzer Literary Agency, Philip G.; Stauffer Associates, Nancy; Steele & Co., Ltd., Lyle; Stepping Stone; Stern Literary Agency, Gloria; Swamy Literary Agent, Maya; Teal Literary Agency, Patricia; 2M Communications Ltd.; Urstadt Inc. Writers and Artists Agency, Susan P.; Wald Associates, Inc., Mary Jack; Wallace Literary Agency, Inc.; Ware Literary Agency, John A.; Waterside Productions, Inc.; Wecksler-Incomco; Weingel-Fidel Agency, The; Westchester Literary Agency, Inc.; Witherspoon & Associates, Inc.; Writers House; Zeckendorf Assoc. Inc., Susan

Business Acton, Dystel, Leone & Jaffe; Adler & Robin Books; Agents Inc. for Medical and Mental Health Professionals; Allan, Lee; Appleseeds Management; Authors' Literary Agency; Axelrod Agency; Baldi Literary Agency, Malaga; Behar, Josh; Bernsen, Jamail & Goodson, L.L.P.; Blassingame Spectrum Corp.; Boates, Reid; Brandt & Brandt; Brown Assoc., Marie; Carvainis, Maria; Clausen Assoc., Connie; Collin, Frances; Coover Agency, Doe; Curtis Assoc., Richard; Dark Horse Group; de la Haba Agency Inc., The Lois; Diamant, The Writer's Workshop, Inc., Anita; Diamond Literary Agency, Inc.; Dijkstra, Sandra; Ducas, Robert; Educational Design Services; Ellenberg, Ethan; Ellison, Nicholas; Flaherty, Joyce A.; Fogelman; Fuhrman, Candice; Geiger, Ellen; Hawkins & Assoc., John; Herman, Jeff; Hull House; IMG-Julian Bach; J de S Assoc.; Jones, Lloyd; Jordan Literary Agency, Lawrence; Kellock Co.; Ketz, Louise B.; Kouts, Barbara S.; Lampack, Peter; Levant & Wales; Lincoln, Ray; Literary and Creative Artists; Literary Bridge; Literary Group; Los Angeles Literary Assoc.; Lyceum Creative Properties; McGrath, Helen; Mann, Carol; Marmur Assoc., Mildred; Multimedia Product Development; Naggar, Jean V.; New England Publishing Assoc.; Nine Muses and Apollo; Novak III, Edward A.; Parks Agency, The Richard; Paton Literary Agency, Kathi J.; Peter Associates, Inc., James; Picard Literary Agent, Alison J.; Quicksilver Books-Literary Agents; Rees Literary Agency, Helen; Riverside Literary Agency; Rock Literary Agency; Rose Literary Agency; Schmidt Literary Agency, Harold; Seligman, Literary Agent, Lynn; Shepard Agency, The; Singer Literary Agency Inc., Evelyn; Spitzer Literary Agency, Philip G.; Steele & Co., Ltd., Lyle; Stepping Stone; Stern Literary Agency, Gloria; Swamy Literary Agent, Maya; Urstadt Inc. Writers and Artists Agency, Susan P.; Waterside Productions, Inc.; Wecksler-Incomco; Westchester Literary Agency, Inc.; Wieser & Wieser, Inc.; Witherspoon & Associates, Inc.; Wohl Literary Agency, Gary S.; Writers House; Zeckendorf Assoc. Inc., Susan

Child guidance/parenting Acton, Dystel, Leone & Jaffe; Agents Inc. for Medical and Mental Health Professionals; Allan, Lee; Authors' Literary Agency; Blassingame Spectrum Corp.; Boates, Reid; Brandt & Brandt; Brown Assoc., Marie; Cantrell-Colas; Coover Agency, Doe; Curtis Assoc., Richard; Diamant, The Writer's Workshop, Inc., Anita; Dijkstra, Sandra; Educational Design Services; Ellenberg, Ethan; Ellison, Nicholas; Esquire Literary Productions; Flaherty, Joyce A.; Fogelman; Fuhrman, Candice; Garon-Brooke Assoc., Jay; Gartenberg, Max; Hawkins & Assoc.,

Subject Index: Nonfee charging/Nonfiction

John; Kellock Co.; Kouts, Barbara S.; Lincoln, Ray; Literary Group; Love, Nancy; Lyceum Creative Properties; Mann, Carol; Multimedia Product Development; Naggar, Jean V.; New England Publishing Assoc.; Novak III, Edward A.; Parks Agency, The Richard; Peter Associates, Inc., James; Picard Literary Agent, Alison J.; Quicksilver Books-Literary Agents; Raymond, Literary Agent, Charlotte Cecil; Riverside Literary Agency; Rose Literary Agency; Rosenthal Literary Agency, Jean; Roth Agency, The ; Seligman, Literary Agent, Lynn; Shepard Agency, The; Siegel Literary Agency, Bobbe; Singer Literary Agency Inc., Evelyn; Steele & Co., Ltd., Lyle; Stepping Stone; Stern Literary Agency, Gloria; Swamy Literary Agent, Maya; Teal Literary Agency, Patricia; 2M Communications Ltd.; Urstadt Inc. Writers and Artists Agency, Susan P.; Waterside Productions, Inc.; Westchester Literary Agency, Inc.; Writers House; Zeckendorf Assoc. Inc., Susan

Computers/electronics Allan, Lee; Authors' Literary Agency; Axelrod Agency; Baldi Literary Agency, Malaga; Bernsen, Jamail & Goodson, L.L.P.; Ellison, Nicholas; Geiger, Ellen; Herman, Jeff; Jordan Literary Agency, Lawrence; Lyceum Creative Properties; Moore Literary Agency; Shepard Agency, The; Swamy Literary Agent, Maya; Waterside Productions, Inc.

Cooking/food/nutrition Acton, Dystel, Leone & Jaffe; Adler & Robin Books; Agents Inc. for Medical and Mental Health Professionals; Ajlouny, Joseph S.; Allan, Lee; Authors' Literary Agency; Baldi Literary Agency, Malaga; Bernsen, Jamail & Goodson, L.L.P.; Brandt & Brandt; Brown Assoc., Marie; Cantrell-Colas; Casselman Literary Agent, Martha; Ciske Literary Agency, Francine; Clausen Assoc., Connie; Columbia Literary Assoc.; Coover Agency, Doe; de la Haba Agency Inc., The Lois; Diamant, The Writer's Workshop, Inc., Anita; Dijkstra, Sandra; Ellenberg, Ethan; Ellison, Nicholas; Elmo, Ann; Fogelman; Geiger, Ellen; Hawkins & Assoc., John; Hochmann Books, John L.; IMG-Julian Bach; Klinger, Inc., Harvey; Lincoln, Ray; Literary and Creative Artists; Love, Nancy; Lyceum Creative Properties; Marmur Assoc., Mildred; Multimedia Product Development; Naggar, Jean V.; Otitis Media; Parks Agency, The Richard; Picard Literary Agent, Alison J.; Pryor, Inc., Roberta; Quicksilver Books-Literary Agents; Riverside Literary Agency; Rose Literary Agency; Roth Agency, The ; Seligman, Literary Agent, Lynn; Shepard Agency, The; Siegel Literary Agency, Bobbe; Steele & Co., Ltd., Lyle; Stepping Stone; Stern Literary Agency, Gloria; Urstadt Inc. Writers and Artists Agency, Susan P.; Wieser & Wieser, Inc.; Wohl Literary Agency, Gary S.; Writers House

Crafts/hobbies Adler & Robin Books; Bernsen, Jamail & Goodson, L.L.P.; Brandt & Brandt; Diamant, The Writer's Workshop, Inc., Anita; Ellenberg, Ethan; Ellison, Nicholas; Flaherty, Joyce A.; Hawkins & Assoc., John; Kellock Co.; Lincoln, Ray; Parks Agency, The Richard; Peter Associates, Inc., James; Shepard Agency, The; Urstadt Inc. Writers and Artists Agency, Susan P.; Wohl Literary Agency, Gary S.

Current Affairs Acton, Dystel, Leone & Jaffe; Allan, Lee; Authors' Literary Agency; Baldi Literary Agency, Malaga; Balkin Agency; Boates, Reid; Borchardt Inc., Georges; Brandt & Brandt; Cantrell-Colas; Carvainis, Maria; Clausen Assoc., Connie; Darhansoff & Verrill; de la Haba Agency Inc., The Lois; Diamant, The Writer's Workshop, Inc., Anita; Dijkstra, Sandra; Ducas, Robert; Educational Design Services; Ellenberg, Ethan; Ellison, Nicholas; Flaming Star Literary Enterprises; Fogelman; Fuhrman, Candice; Gartenberg, Max; Geiger, Ellen; Hardy Agency; Hawkins & Assoc., John; Hochmann Books, John L.; Hull House; IMG-Julian Bach; J de S Assoc.; Jones, Lloyd; Kellock Co.; Ketz, Louise B.; Kidde, Hoyt & Picard; Kouts, Barbara S.; Kroll Literary Agency, Edite; Lampack, Peter; Levine, Ellen; Lincoln, Ray; Lipkind, Wendy; Literary Group; Love, Nancy; Lyceum Creative Properties; McCauley, Gerard; Maccoby, Gina; McGrath, Helen; Mann, Carol; Marmur Assoc., Mildred; Miller Assoc., Roberta D.; Multimedia Product Development; Naggar, Jean V.; Nine Muses and Apollo; Novak III, Edward A.; Parks Agency, The Richard; Perkins Associates, L.; Peter Associates, Inc., James; Picard Literary Agent, Alison J.; Raymond, Literary Agent, Charlotte Cecil; Rees Literary Agency, Helen; Rose Literary Agency; Roth Agency, The ; Schaffner Agency, Inc.; Schmidt Literary Agency, Harold; Seligman, Literary Agent, Lynn; Shepard Agency, The; Singer Literary Agency Inc., Evelyn; Spitzer Literary Agency, Philip G.; Stauffer Associates, Nancy; Steele & Co., Ltd., Lyle; Stepping Stone; Stern Literary Agency, Gloria; Swamy Literary Agent, Maya; Urstadt Inc. Writers and Artists Agency, Susan P.; Wald Associates, Inc., Mary Jack; Wallace Literary Agency, Inc.; Ware Literary Agency, John A.; Wecksler-Incomco; Wieser & Wieser, Inc.; Witherspoon & Associates, Inc.

Ethnic/cultural interests Acton, Dystel, Leone & Jaffe; Agency Chicago; Baldi Literary Agency, Malaga; Bernsen, Jamail & Goodson, L.L.P.; Boates, Reid; Brandt & Brandt; Brown Assoc., Marie; Cantrell-Colas; Clausen Assoc., Connie; Cohen, Ruth; Coover Agency, Doe; Crown International Literature and Arts Agency, Bonnie R.; de la Haba Agency Inc., The Lois; Dijkstra, Sandra; Educational Design Services; Ellison, Nicholas; Frontier Talents; Fuhrman, Candice; Geiger, Ellen; Hawkins & Assoc., John; Hull House; J de S Assoc.; Jones, Lloyd; Kidde, Hoyt & Picard; Kouts, Barbara S.; Lincoln, Ray; Love, Nancy; Lyceum Creative Properties; Maccoby, Gina; Mann, Carol; Marmur Assoc., Mildred; Miller Assoc., Roberta D.; Nine Muses and Apollo; Novak III, Edward A.; Otitis Media; Parks Agency, The Richard; Perkins Associates, L.; Peter

Associates, Inc., James; Picard Literary Agent, Alison J.; Raymond, Literary Agent, Charlotte Cecil; Rees Literary Agency, Helen; Rose Literary Agency; Roth Agency, The ; Schmidt Literary Agency, Harold; Seligman, Literary Agent, Lynn; Siegel Literary Agency, Bobbe; Spitzer Literary Agency, Philip G.; Stauffer Associates, Nancy; Steele & Co., Ltd., Lyle; Stepping Stone; Stern Literary Agency, Gloria; Swamy Literary Agent, Maya; 2M Communications Ltd.; Wald Associates, Inc., Mary Jack; Waterside Productions, Inc.; Witherspoon & Associates, Inc.

Gay/Lesbian issues Acton, Dystel, Leone & Jaffe; Baldi Literary Agency, Malaga; Brandt & Brandt; Brown Assoc., Marie; Clausen Assoc., Connie; de la Haba Agency Inc., The Lois; Ducas, Robert; Garon-Brooke Assoc., Jay; Geiger, Ellen; Hawkins & Assoc., John; Hochmann Books, John L.; Kidde, Hoyt & Picard; Lincoln, Ray; Literary Group; Lyceum Creative Properties; Naggar, Jean V.; Nine Muses and Apollo; Novak III, Edward A.; Otitis Media; Parks Agency, The Richard; Picard Literary Agent, Alison J.; Raymond, Literary Agent, Charlotte Cecil; Riverside Literary Agency; Rose Literary Agency; Schmidt Literary Agency, Harold; Steele & Co., Ltd., Lyle; Stepping Stone; 2M Communications Ltd.; Witherspoon & Associates, Inc.

Government/politics/law Acton, Dystel, Leone & Jaffe; Allan, Lee; Authors' Literary Agency; Axelrod Agency; Baldi Literary Agency, Malaga; Bernsen, Jamail & Goodson, L.L.P.; Black, David; Boates, Reid; Brandt & Brandt; Cantrell-Colas; Carvainis, Maria; Dark Horse Group; de la Haba Agency Inc., The Lois; Diamant, The Writer's Workshop, Inc., Anita; Dijkstra, Sandra; Ducas, Robert; Educational Design Services; Ellenberg, Ethan; Ellison, Nicholas; Flaming Star Literary Enterprises; Fogelman; Geiger, Ellen; Hardy Agency; Hawkins & Assoc., John; Herman, Jeff; Hochmann Books, John L.; Hull House; IMG-Julian Bach; J de S Assoc.; Kellock Co.; Lampack, Peter; Lincoln, Ray; Literary and Creative Artists; Literary Bridge; Love, Nancy; Lyceum Creative Properties; Madsen, Robert; Mann, Carol; Marmur Assoc., Mildred; Naggar, Jean V.; New England Publishing Assoc.; Nine Muses and Apollo; Novak III, Edward A.; Otitis Media; Parks Agency, The Richard; Peter Associates, Inc., James; Picard Literary Agent, Alison J.; Rees Literary Agency, Helen; Rose Literary Agency; Roth Agency, The ; Schmidt Literary Agency, Harold; Seligman, Literary Agent, Lynn; Shepard Agency, The; Singer Literary Agency Inc., Evelyn; Spitzer Literary Agency, Philip G.; Steele & Co., Ltd., Lyle; Stepping Stone; Stern Literary Agency, Gloria; Swamy Literary Agent, Maya; Westchester Literary Agency, Inc.; Witherspoon & Associates, Inc.

Health/medicine Acton, Dystel, Leone & Jaffe; Adler & Robin Books; Agents Inc. for Medical and Mental Health Professionals; Ajlouny, Joseph S.; Allan, Lee; Appleseeds Management; Authors' Literary Agency; Axelrod Agency; Baldi Literary Agency, Malaga; Balkin Agency; Bernsen, Jamail & Goodson, L.L.P.; Blassingame Spectrum Corp.; Boates, Reid; Brandt & Brandt; Cantrell-Colas; Carvainis, Maria; Casselman Literary Agent, Martha; Clausen Assoc., Connie; Collin, Frances; Columbia Literary Assoc.; Coover Agency, Doe; Darhansoff & Verrill; de la Haba Agency Inc., The Lois; Diamant, The Writer's Workshop, Inc., Anita; Dijkstra, Sandra; Ducas, Robert; Ellenberg, Ethan; Ellison, Nicholas; Flaherty, Joyce A.; Flaming Star Literary Enterprises; Fuhrman, Candice; Garon-Brooke Assoc., Jay; Gartenberg, Max; Geiger, Ellen; Hardy Agency; Hawkins & Assoc., John; Herman, Jeff; Hochmann Books, John L.; J de S Assoc.; Jones, Lloyd; Jordan Literary Agency, Lawrence; Kellock Co.; Klinger, Inc., Harvey; Kouts, Barbara S.; Lampack, Peter; Levant & Wales; Lincoln, Ray; Lipkind, Wendy; Literary and Creative Artists; Literary Bridge; Literary Group; Love, Nancy; Lowenstein Associates, Inc.; McGrath, Helen; Mann, Carol; Marmur Assoc., Mildred; Multimedia Product Development; Naggar, Jean V.; New England Publishing Assoc.; Nine Muses and Apollo; Novak III, Edward A.; Otitis Media; Parks Agency, The Richard; Peter Associates, Inc., James; Picard Literary Agent, Alison J.; Protter Literary Agent, Susan Ann; Quicksilver Books-Literary Agents; Rees Literary Agency, Helen; Riverside Literary Agency; Rose Literary Agency; Rosenthal Literary Agency, Jean; Roth Agency, The ; Schmidt Literary Agency, Harold; Seligman, Literary Agent, Lynn; Shepard Agency, The; Siegel Literary Agency, Bobbe; Singer Literary Agency Inc., Evelyn; Spitzer Literary Agency, Philip G.; Steele & Co., Ltd., Lyle; Stepping Stone; Stern Literary Agency, Gloria; Swamy Literary Agent, Maya; Teal Literary Agency, Patricia; 2M Communications Ltd.; Urstadt Inc. Writers and Artists Agency, Susan P.; Wald Associates, Inc., Mary Jack; Ware Literary Agency, John A.; Waterside Productions, Inc.; Weingel-Fidel Agency, The; Wieser & Wieser, Inc.; Witherspoon & Associates, Inc.; Wreschner, Authors' Representative, Ruth; Writers House; Zeckendorf Assoc. Inc., Susan

History Acton, Dystel, Leone & Jaffe; Ajlouny, Joseph S.; Allan, Lee; Authors' Literary Agency; Axelrod Agency; Baldi Literary Agency, Malaga; Balkin Agency; Bernsen, Jamail & Goodson, L.L.P.; Blassingame Spectrum Corp.; Boates, Reid; Borchardt Inc., Georges; Brandt & Brandt; Brown Assoc., Marie; Cantrell-Colas; Carvainis, Maria; Collin, Frances; Coover Agency, Doe; Curtis Assoc., Richard; Darhansoff & Verrill; Dark Horse Group; de la Haba Agency Inc., The Lois; Diamant, The Writer's Workshop, Inc., Anita; Dijkstra, Sandra; Ducas, Robert; Educational Design Services; Ellenberg, Ethan; Ellison, Nicholas; Flaherty, Joyce A.; Fuhrman, Candice; Garon-Brooke Assoc., Jay; Gartenberg, Max; Geiger, Ellen; Gregory Assoc., Maia; Hawkins & Assoc.,

This Could Be The Most Important Decision Of Your Career!

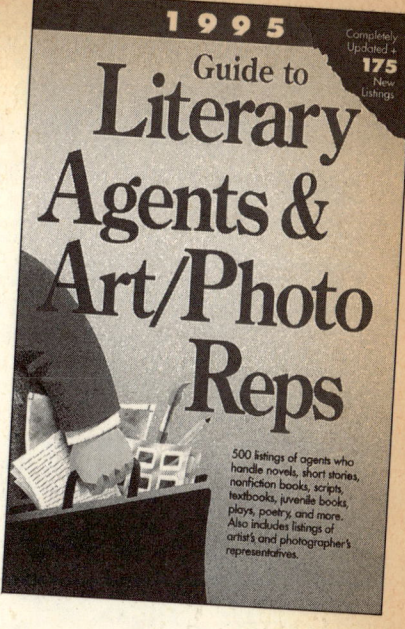

You already know an agent or rep can be the key to successfully selling your work. But, how do you know when you're ready to obtain one? And, how do you go about selecting an agent or rep that's right for you and your work? You've got to make an informed decision and the only way to do that is to get current information on the agents and reps that are out there, and what they have to offer you. All of this information is included in *Guide to Literary Agents & Art/Photo Reps*. It's updated annually to keep up with this fast changing industry.

You can make sure you have the latest marketing information available by ordering the next edition of *Guide to Literary Agents & Art/Photo Reps* now. When you do, we'll guarantee your cost will not go up from the current edition.

That's right, we'll send you the 1995 edition of *Guide to Literary Agents & Art/Photo Reps* at the same low price as the 1994 edition — just $18.95 (plus postage and handling costs). Use the order form below to be sure you get the price guarantee, and we'll reserve your copy of *1995 Guide to Literary Agents & Art/Photo Reps*.

(The 1995 edition will ship in February 1995.)
See other side for more books to help you sell your work!

30-DAY MONEY BACK GUARANTEE

To order, drop this postpaid card in the mail.

OFFER EXPIRES DECEMBER 31, 1995!

☐ **YES!** I want the most current edition of *Guide to Literary Agents & Art/Photo Reps*. Please send me the 1995 edition at the 1994 price -- $18.95.* (NOTE: The 1995 Edition will be ready for shipment in February 1995.) #10407
Also send me the following books NOW:
____(#10339) *1994 Writer's Market* $26.95*
____(#10361) *1994 Novel & Short Story Writer's Market* $19.95*
____(#10362) *1994 Children's Writer's & Illustrator's Market* $19.95*
____(#10340) *1994 Photographer's Market* $22.95*
____(#10380) *Mystery Writer's Market Place and Sourcebook* $17.95*

*Plus postage & handling: $3.00 for one book, $1.00 for each additional book. Ohio residents add 5.5% sales tax.

☐ Please send me a FREE catalog of your books for writers.

Visa/MasterCard Orders Call Toll-Free 1-800-289-0963
☐ Payment enclosed (Slip this card and payment into an envelope)
☐ Please charge my:
☐ Visa ☐ MasterCard Exp._____
Acct #_____
Signature_____
Name_____
Address_____
City_____
State _____ Zip _____

#6545

THESE BUYERS WANT TO PURCHASE YOUR WORK!

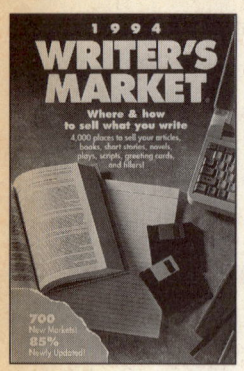

1994 WRITER'S MARKET®

This new edition contains up-to-date information on 4,000 buyers of freelance materials, as well as listings of workshops, contests and awards. Helpful articles and interviews with top professionals make this the source for your marketing efforts.
1056 pages/$26.95/hardcover

1994 Children's Writer's & Illustrator's Market®

The two key aspects of children's publishing are brought together in this handy volume, offering hundreds of outlets for your work, along with professional guidance from those who have already succeeded in this lucrative field. 256 pages/$19.95/paperback

1994 Photographer's Market®

The most comprehensive book of its kind, this directory contains 2,500 up-to-date listings of U.S. and international buyers of freelance photos, coupled with advice from top professionals in the field.
608 pages/$22.95/hardcover

1994 Novel & Short Story Writer's Market®

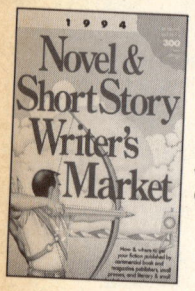

This exclusive market guide for novel and short story writers includes complete information on 1,900 fiction publishers, coupled with helpful articles and interviews with notable fiction writers.
624 pages/$19.95/paperback

Mystery Writer's Marketplace and Sourcebook

This new directory/resource guide takes you inside the mystery field offering a select list of those mystery publishers, magazines and agents that handle a large volume of mysteries and are most open to new writers.
336 pages/$17.95/hardcover

Use the coupon on the other side to order these books today!

BUSINESS REPLY MAIL
FIRST CLASS MAIL   PERMIT NO. 17   CINCINNATI, OH

NO POSTAGE
NECESSARY
IF MAILED
IN THE
UNITED STATES

POSTAGE WILL BE PAID BY ADDRESSEE

WRITER'S DIGEST BOOKS
1507 DANA AVENUE
CINCINNATI OH 45207-9965

John; Herman, Jeff; Hochmann Books, John L.; Hull House; IMG-Julian Bach; J de S Assoc.; Kellock Co.; Ketz, Louise B.; Kidde, Hoyt & Picard; Kouts, Barbara S.; Lampack, Peter; Lincoln, Ray; Lipkind, Wendy; Literary Bridge; Literary Group; Los Angeles Literary Assoc.; Love, Nancy; Lyceum Creative Properties; McCauley, Gerard; McGrath, Helen; Madsen, Robert; Mann, Carol; Marmur Assoc., Mildred; Multimedia Product Development; Naggar, Jean V.; New England Publishing Assoc.; Nine Muses and Apollo; Novak III, Edward A.; Otitis Media; Parks Agency, The Richard; Peter Associates, Inc., James; Picard Literary Agent, Alison J.; Raymond, Literary Agent, Charlotte Cecil; Rees Literary Agency, Helen; Renaissance: A Literary/Talent Agency; Riverside Literary Agency; Rock Literary Agency; Rose Literary Agency; Rosenthal Literary Agency, Jean; Roth Agency, The ; Schmidt Literary Agency, Harold; Seligman, Literary Agent, Lynn; Shepard Agency, The; Siegel Literary Agency, Bobbe; Spitzer Literary Agency, Philip G.; Steele & Co., Ltd., Lyle; Stepping Stone; Stern Literary Agency, Gloria; Swamy Literary Agent, Maya; Wald Associates, Inc., Mary Jack; Wallace Literary Agency, Inc.; Ware Literary Agency, John A.; Watkins Loomis Agency, Inc.; Wecksler-Incomco; Westchester Literary Agency, Inc.; Wieser & Wieser, Inc.; Witherspoon & Associates, Inc.; Writers House; Zeckendorf Assoc. Inc., Susan

Interior design/decorating Baldi Literary Agency, Malaga; Brandt & Brandt; Ellison, Nicholas; Geiger, Ellen; Hawkins & Assoc., John; Kellock Co.; Lincoln, Ray; Mann, Carol; Naggar, Jean V.; Peter Associates, Inc., James; Picard Literary Agent, Alison J.; Seligman, Literary Agent, Lynn; Shepard Agency, The; Stepping Stone; Urstadt Inc. Writers and Artists Agency, Susan P.; Writers House

Juvenile nonfiction Allan, Lee; Authors' Literary Agency; Bartczak Assoc., Gene; Brandt & Brandt; Brown Assoc., Marie; Brown, Andrea; Cantrell-Colas; Cohen, Ruth; Dark Horse Group; de la Haba Agency Inc., The Lois; Diamant, The Writer's Workshop, Inc., Anita; Educational Design Services; Elek Assoc., Peter; Ellenberg, Ethan; Elmo, Ann; Feiler, Florence; Hawkins & Assoc., John; Jones, Lloyd; Kellock Co.; Kirchoff/Wohlberg, Authors' Representation Div.; Kouts, Barbara S.; Lincoln, Ray; Literary Bridge; Lyceum Creative Properties; Maccoby, Gina; Markowitz, Barbara; Marmur Assoc., Mildred; Multimedia Product Development; Naggar, Jean V.; Picard Literary Agent, Alison J.; Raymond, Literary Agent, Charlotte Cecil; Rubenstein Literary Agency, Inc., Pesha; Shepard Agency, The; Singer Literary Agency Inc., Evelyn; Targ Literary Agency, Inc., Roslyn; Wald Associates, Inc., Mary Jack; Wasserman Literary Agency Inc., Harriet; Westchester Literary Agency, Inc.; Writers House

Language/literature/criticism Ajlouny, Joseph S.; Baldi Literary Agency, Malaga; Balkin Agency; Boates, Reid; Brandt & Brandt; Cantrell-Colas; Coover Agency, Doe; Darhansoff & Verrill; Dijkstra, Sandra; Educational Design Services; Ellison, Nicholas; Fuhrman, Candice; Geiger, Ellen; Gregory Assoc., Maia; Hawkins & Assoc., John; IMG-Julian Bach; Lincoln, Ray; Lyceum Creative Properties; Miller Assoc., Roberta D.; New England Publishing Assoc.; Nine Muses and Apollo; Otitis Media; Parks Agency, The Richard; Quicksilver Books-Literary Agents; Riverside Literary Agency; Rose Literary Agency; Roth Agency, The ; Schmidt Literary Agency, Harold; Seligman, Literary Agent, Lynn; Shepard Agency, The; Siegel Literary Agency, Bobbe; Stern Literary Agency, Gloria; Swamy Literary Agent, Maya; Wald Associates, Inc., Mary Jack; Wallace Literary Agency, Inc.; Westchester Literary Agency, Inc.

Military/war Acton, Dystel, Leone & Jaffe; Allan, Lee; Authors' Literary Agency; Baldi Literary Agency, Malaga; Bernsen, Jamail & Goodson, L.L.P.; Brandt & Brandt; Cantrell-Colas; Carvainis, Maria; Curtis Assoc., Richard; Dijkstra, Sandra; Ducas, Robert; Educational Design Services; Ellenberg, Ethan; Ellison, Nicholas; Esquire Literary Productions; Flaherty, Joyce A.; Garon-Brooke Assoc., Jay; Gartenberg, Max; Geiger, Ellen; Hawkins & Assoc., John; Hochmann Books, John L.; Hull House; IMG-Julian Bach; J de S Assoc.; Kellock Co.; Ketz, Louise B.; McCauley, Gerard; McGrath, Helen; Madsen, Robert; Marmur Assoc., Mildred; New England Publishing Assoc.; Novak III, Edward A.; Otitis Media; Parks Agency, The Richard; Peter Associates, Inc., James; Picard Literary Agent, Alison J.; Riverside Literary Agency; Rose Literary Agency; Schmidt Literary Agency, Harold; Spitzer Literary Agency, Philip G.; Swamy Literary Agent, Maya; Urstadt Inc. Writers and Artists Agency, Susan P.; Wald Associates, Inc., Mary Jack; Wallace Literary Agency, Inc.; Westchester Literary Agency, Inc.; Writers House

Money/finance/economics Acton, Dystel, Leone & Jaffe; Allan, Lee; Appleseeds Management; Authors' Literary Agency; Axelrod Agency; Baldi Literary Agency, Malaga; Behar, Josh; Brandt & Brandt; Brown Assoc., Marie; Cantrell-Colas; Carvainis, Maria; Clausen Assoc., Connie; Coover Agency, Doe; Curtis Assoc., Richard; de la Haba Agency Inc., The Lois; Diamant, The Writer's Workshop, Inc., Anita; Diamond Literary Agency, Inc.; Dijkstra, Sandra; Ducas, Robert; Educational Design Services; Ellenberg, Ethan; Ellison, Nicholas; Flaherty, Joyce A.; Fogelman; Fuhrman, Candice; Gartenberg, Max; Geiger, Ellen; Hawkins & Assoc., John; Hull House; Jones, Lloyd; Kellock Co.; Ketz, Louise B.; Lampack, Peter; Lincoln, Ray; Literary Bridge; Los Angeles Literary Assoc.; Mann, Carol; Marmur Assoc., Mildred; Multimedia Product Development; Naggar, Jean V.; New England Publishing Assoc.; Nine Muses and Apollo; Novak III, Edward A.;

Parks Agency, The Richard; Peter Associates, Inc., James; Riverside Literary Agency; Rose Literary Agency; Schmidt Literary Agency, Harold; Seligman, Literary Agent, Lynn; Shepard Agency, The; Singer Literary Agency Inc., Evelyn; Steele & Co., Ltd., Lyle; Stern Literary Agency, Gloria; Swamy Literary Agent, Maya; Urstadt Inc. Writers and Artists Agency, Susan P.; Wald Associates, Inc., Mary Jack; Waterside Productions, Inc.; Wieser & Wieser, Inc.; Witherspoon & Associates, Inc.; Writers House

Music/dance/theater/film Acton, Dystel, Leone & Jaffe; Agency Chicago; Allan, Lee; Andrews & Assoc., Bart; Appleseeds Management; Axelrod Agency; Baldi Literary Agency, Malaga; Balkin Agency; Bernsen, Jamail & Goodson, L.L.P.; Brandt & Brandt; Brown Assoc., Marie; Clausen Assoc., Connie; Curtis Assoc., Richard; de la Haba Agency Inc., The Lois; Dijkstra, Sandra; Ellison, Nicholas; Fuhrman, Candice; Garon-Brooke Assoc., Jay; Gartenberg, Max; Geiger, Ellen; Gregory Assoc., Maia; Hawkins & Assoc., John; Hochmann Books, John L.; Hull House; IMG-Julian Bach; Kellock Co.; Kouts, Barbara S.; Lincoln, Ray; Literary Group; Lyceum Creative Properties; Maccoby, Gina; Marmur Assoc., Mildred; Naggar, Jean V.; Nathan, Ruth; Novak III, Edward A.; Otitis Media; Parks Agency, The Richard; Perkins Associates, L.; Picard Literary Agent, Alison J.; Renaissance: A Literary/Talent Agency; Riverside Literary Agency; Rose Literary Agency; Roth Agency, The ; Schaffner Agency, Inc.; Schmidt Literary Agency, Harold; Seligman, Literary Agent, Lynn; Shepard Agency, The; Spitzer Literary Agency, Philip G.; Swamy Literary Agent, Maya; 2M Communications Ltd.; Urstadt Inc. Writers and Artists Agency, Susan P.; Wald Associates, Inc., Mary Jack; Waterside Productions, Inc.; Wecksler-Incomco; Weingel-Fidel Agency, The; Witherspoon & Associates, Inc.; Writers House; Zeckendorf Assoc. Inc., Susan

Nature/environment Acton, Dystel, Leone & Jaffe; Agency Chicago; Allan, Lee; Authors' Literary Agency; Axelrod Agency; Baldi Literary Agency, Malaga; Balkin Agency; Bernsen, Jamail & Goodson, L.L.P.; Boates, Reid; Brandt & Brandt; Cantrell-Colas; Clausen Assoc., Connie; Collin, Frances; Coover Agency, Doe; Crown International Literature and Arts Agency, Bonnie R.; Darhansoff & Verrill; de la Haba Agency Inc., The Lois; Diamant, The Writer's Workshop, Inc., Anita; Diamond Literary Agency, Inc.; Dijkstra, Sandra; Ducas, Robert; Ellenberg, Ethan; Ellison, Nicholas; Flaherty, Joyce A.; Flaming Star Literary Enterprises; Fuhrman, Candice; Gartenberg, Max; Geiger, Ellen; Hawkins & Assoc., John; IMG-Julian Bach; Kellock Co.; Kouts, Barbara S.; Levant & Wales; Lincoln, Ray; Literary Group; Love, Nancy; Lyceum Creative Properties; Marmur Assoc., Mildred; Multimedia Product Development; New England Publishing Assoc.; Novak III, Edward A.; Parks Agency, The Richard; Picard Literary Agent, Alison J.; Pryor, Inc., Roberta; Quicksilver Books-Literary Agents; Raymond, Literary Agent, Charlotte Cecil; Riverside Literary Agency; Rose Literary Agency; Roth Agency, The ; Rubenstein Literary Agency, Inc., Pesha; Schaffner Agency, Inc.; Schmidt Literary Agency, Harold; Seligman, Literary Agent, Lynn; Shepard Agency, The; Siegel Literary Agency, Bobbe; Spitzer Literary Agency, Philip G.; Stauffer Associates, Nancy; Steele & Co., Ltd., Lyle; Stepping Stone; Swamy Literary Agent, Maya; Urstadt Inc. Writers and Artists Agency, Susan P.; Wald Associates, Inc., Mary Jack; Waterside Productions, Inc.; Wecksler-Incomco; Westchester Literary Agency, Inc.; Wieser & Wieser, Inc.; Writers House

New Age/metaphysics Behar, Josh; Bernsen, Jamail & Goodson, L.L.P.; Brown Assoc., Marie; Cantrell-Colas; Clark, SJ; Dark Horse Group; de la Haba Agency Inc., The Lois; Diamant, The Writer's Workshop, Inc., Anita; Ellenberg, Ethan; Ellison, Nicholas; Flaming Star Literary Enterprises; Hardy Agency; Hawkins & Assoc., John; J de S Assoc.; Lyceum Creative Properties; Naggar, Jean V.; Picard Literary Agent, Alison J.; Quicksilver Books-Literary Agents; Rees Literary Agency, Helen; Riverside Literary Agency; Schmidt Literary Agency, Harold; Steele & Co., Ltd., Lyle; Stepping Stone; Swamy Literary Agent, Maya; Waterside Productions, Inc.

Open to all nonfiction categories Barrett Books, Loretta; Brown Ltd., Curtis; Buck, Howard; Bykofsky Assoc., Sheree; Cleaver, Diane; Cohen, Hy; Collier Assoc.; Congdon Assoc., Don; Doyen Literary Services; Dupree/Miller and Assoc.; Eisenberg, Vicki; Fleming, Peter; Goldfarb & Assoc., Ronald; Goodman Assoc.; Gotham Art & Literary Agency; Greenburger Assoc., Sanford J.; Hamilburg, Mitchell J.; Hoffman Literary Agency, Berenice; International Publisher Assoc.; Larsen/Elizabeth Pomada, Michael; Lazear Agency; Madsen, Robert; Martell Agency; MGA Agency; Ober Associates, Harold; Pelter, Rodney; Picard Literary Agent, Alison J.; Rock Literary Agency; Sandum & Associates; Snell Literary Agency, Michael; Spieler Literary Agency, Gretchen; Van Der Leun & Associates

Photography Baldi Literary Agency, Malaga; Brown Assoc., Marie; Diamond Literary Agency, Inc.; Ellison, Nicholas; Geiger, Ellen; Hawkins & Assoc., John; Kellock Co.; Otitis Media; Swamy Literary Agent, Maya; Urstadt Inc. Writers and Artists Agency, Susan P.; Wald Associates, Inc., Mary Jack; Wecksler-Incomco; Westchester Literary Agency, Inc.

Psychology Acton, Dystel, Leone & Jaffe; Agents Inc. for Medical and Mental Health Professionals; Allan, Lee; Appleseeds Management; Baldi Literary Agency, Malaga; Boates, Reid; Brandt & Brandt; Brown Assoc., Marie; Cantrell-Colas; Carvainis, Maria; Clausen Assoc., Connie; Coover Agency, Doe; Diamant, The Writer's Workshop, Inc., Anita; Diamond Literary Agency, Inc.;

Dijkstra, Sandra; Ellenberg, Ethan; Ellison, Nicholas; Esquire Literary Productions; Flaherty, Joyce A.; Fuhrman, Candice; Garon-Brooke Assoc., Jay; Gartenberg, Max; Geiger, Ellen; Hawkins & Assoc., John; Herman, Jeff; IMG-Julian Bach; Jones, Lloyd; Kellock Co.; Kidde, Hoyt & Picard; Klinger, Inc., Harvey; Kouts, Barbara S.; Levant & Wales; Lincoln, Ray; Literary Bridge; Literary Group; Love, Nancy; Lyceum Creative Properties; McGrath, Helen; Mann, Carol; Naggar, Jean V.; New England Publishing Assoc.; Nine Muses and Apollo; Parks Agency, The Richard; Paton Literary Agency, Kathi J.; Peter Associates, Inc., James; Picard Literary Agent, Alison J.; Protter Literary Agent, Susan Ann; Quicksilver Books-Literary Agents; Raymond, Literary Agent, Charlotte Cecil; Rees Literary Agency, Helen; Riverside Literary Agency; Rose Literary Agency; Roth Agency, The ; Schmidt Literary Agency, Harold; Seligman, Literary Agent, Lynn; Shepard Agency, The; Siegel Literary Agency, Bobbe; Spitzer Literary Agency, Philip G.; Steele & Co., Ltd., Lyle; Stepping Stone; Stern Literary Agency, Gloria; Swamy Literary Agent, Maya; Teal Literary Agency, Patricia; Ware Literary Agency, John A.; Waterside Productions, Inc.; Weingel-Fidel Agency, The; Westchester Literary Agency, Inc.; Wieser & Wieser, Inc.; Writers House; Zeckendorf Assoc. Inc., Susan

Religious/inspirational Brandenburgh & Assoc.; Brown Assoc., Marie; Ciske Literary Agency, Francine; Coover Agency, Doe; de la Haba Agency Inc., The Lois; Diamant, The Writer's Workshop, Inc., Anita; Diamond Literary Agency, Inc.; Donlan, Thomas C.; Ellenberg, Ethan; Ellison, Nicholas; Fuhrman, Candice; Geiger, Ellen; Holub & Assoc.; Jordan Literary Agency, Lawrence; Los Angeles Literary Assoc.; Marmur Assoc., Mildred; Naggar, Jean V.; Quicksilver Books-Literary Agents; Rees Literary Agency, Helen; Shepard Agency, The; Stepping Stone; Swamy Literary Agent, Maya; Westchester Literary Agency, Inc.

Science/technology Acton, Dystel, Leone & Jaffe; Agents Inc. for Medical and Mental Health Professionals; Allan, Lee; Axelrod Agency; Baldi Literary Agency, Malaga; Balkin Agency; Bernsen, Jamail & Goodson, L.L.P.; Boates, Reid; Bova, Barbara; Brandt & Brandt; Brown, Andrea; Cantrell-Colas; Carvainis, Maria; Coover Agency, Doe; Curtis Assoc., Richard; Darhansoff & Verrill; Diamant, The Writer's Workshop, Inc., Anita; Dijkstra, Sandra; Ducas, Robert; Educational Design Services; Ellenberg, Ethan; Ellison, Nicholas; Flaming Star Literary Enterprises; Fuhrman, Candice; Gartenberg, Max; Geiger, Ellen; Hawkins & Assoc., John; Jordan Literary Agency, Lawrence; Ketz, Louise B.; Klinger, Inc., Harvey; Levant & Wales; Levine, Ellen; Lincoln, Ray; Lipkind, Wendy; Love, Nancy; Lowenstein Associates, Inc.; Madsen, Robert; Marmur Assoc., Mildred; Multimedia Product Development; New England Publishing Assoc.; Nine Muses and Apollo; Novak III, Edward A.; Parks Agency, The Richard; Picard Literary Agent, Alison J.; Protter Literary Agent, Susan Ann; Rees Literary Agency, Helen; Riverside Literary Agency; Rose Literary Agency; Schmidt Literary Agency, Harold; Seligman, Literary Agent, Lynn; Singer Literary Agency Inc., Evelyn; Steele & Co., Ltd., Lyle; Stern Literary Agency, Gloria; Swamy Literary Agent, Maya; Wald Associates, Inc., Mary Jack; Wallace Literary Agency, Inc.; Ware Literary Agency, John A.; Watkins Loomis Agency, Inc.; Weingel-Fidel Agency, The; Witherspoon & Associates, Inc.; Writers House; Zeckendorf Assoc. Inc., Susan

Self-help/personal improvement Acton, Dystel, Leone & Jaffe; Adler & Robin Books; Agents Inc. for Medical and Mental Health Professionals; Ajlouny, Joseph S.; Allan, Lee; Appleseeds Management; Authors' Literary Agency; Baldi Literary Agency, Malaga; Behar, Josh; Boates, Reid; Brandt & Brandt; Brown Assoc., Marie; Cantrell-Colas; Ciske Literary Agency, Francine; Clausen Assoc., Connie; Columbia Literary Assoc.; Curtis Assoc., Richard; Dark Horse Group; Davie, Elaine; de la Haba Agency Inc., The Lois; Diamant, The Writer's Workshop, Inc., Anita; Diamond Literary Agency, Inc.; Dijkstra, Sandra; Ellenberg, Ethan; Esquire Literary Productions; Flaherty, Joyce A.; Flaming Star Literary Enterprises; Fogelman, Evan; Fuhrman, Candice; Garon-Brooke Assoc., Jay; Gartenberg, Max; Geiger, Ellen; Hawkins & Assoc., John; Herman, Jeff; Holub & Assoc.; IMG-Julian Bach; J de S Assoc.; Jones, Lloyd; Jordan Literary Agency, Lawrence; Kellock Co.; Klinger, Inc., Harvey; Kouts, Barbara S.; Lincoln, Ray; Literary and Creative Artists; Literary Bridge; Literary Group; Los Angeles Literary Assoc.; Love, Nancy; McGrath, Helen; Madsen, Robert; Mann, Carol; Multimedia Product Development; Naggar, Jean V.; New England Publishing Assoc.; Nine Muses and Apollo; Novak III, Edward A.; Otitis Media; Parks Agency, The Richard; Peter Associates, Inc., James; Picard Literary Agent, Alison J.; Quicksilver Books-Literary Agents; Rees Literary Agency, Helen; Riverside Literary Agency; Rose Literary Agency; Roth Agency, The ; Schmidt Literary Agency, Harold; Seligman, Literary Agent, Lynn; Shepard Agency, The; Siegel Literary Agency, Bobbe; Sierra Literary Agency; Singer Literary Agency Inc., Evelyn; Stauffer Associates, Nancy; Steele & Co., Ltd., Lyle; Stepping Stone; Stern Literary Agency, Gloria; Swamy Literary Agent, Maya; Targ Literary Agency, Inc., Roslyn; Teal Literary Agency, Patricia; 2M Communications Ltd.; Urstadt Inc. Writers and Artists Agency, Susan P.; Weiner Literary Agency, Cherry; Westchester Literary Agency, Inc.; Witherspoon & Associates, Inc.; Writers House

Sociology Agents Inc. for Medical and Mental Health Professionals; Ajlouny, Joseph S.; Baldi Literary Agency, Malaga; Balkin Agency; Brandt & Brandt; Brown Assoc., Marie; Cantrell-Colas; Coover Agency, Doe; Dijkstra, Sandra; Educational Design Services; Ellison, Nicholas; Geiger, Ellen; Hawkins & Assoc., John; Hochmann Books, John L.; Hull House; J de S Assoc.; Kellock Co.; Lincoln, Ray; Lipkind, Wendy; Literary Group; Love, Nancy; Lyceum Creative Properties; Mann, Carol; Multimedia Product Development; Naggar, Jean V.; New England Publishing Assoc.; Parks Agency, The Richard; Paton Literary Agency, Kathi J.; Raymond, Literary Agent, Charlotte Cecil; Rees Literary Agency, Helen; Rose Literary Agency; Roth Agency, The ; Schmidt Literary Agency, Harold; Seligman, Literary Agent, Lynn; Shepard Agency, The; Spitzer Literary Agency, Philip G.; Stauffer Associates, Nancy; Steele & Co., Ltd., Lyle; Stern Literary Agency, Gloria; Swamy Literary Agent, Maya; Wald Associates, Inc., Mary Jack; Waterside Productions, Inc.; Weiner Literary Agency, Cherry; Weingel-Fidel Agency, The; Zeckendorf Assoc. Inc., Susan

Sports Acton, Dystel, Leone & Jaffe; Agency Chicago; Agents Inc. for Medical and Mental Health Professionals; Allan, Lee; Bernsen, Jamail & Goodson, L.L.P.; Black, David; Boates, Reid; Brandt & Brandt; Curtis Assoc., Richard; Diamant, The Writer's Workshop, Inc., Anita; Dijkstra, Sandra; Ducas, Robert; Ellenberg, Ethan; Flaming Star Literary Enterprises; Gartenberg, Max; Geiger, Ellen; Hawkins & Assoc., John; IMG-Julian Bach; J de S Assoc.; Jones, Lloyd; Jordan Literary Agency, Lawrence; Kellock Co.; Ketz, Louise B.; Klinger, Inc., Harvey; Lincoln, Ray; Literary Bridge; Literary Group; McCauley, Gerard; McGrath, Helen; Marmur Assoc., Mildred; Novak III, Edward A.; Otitis Media; Picard Literary Agent, Alison J.; Rees Literary Agency, Helen; Rose Literary Agency; Seymour Agency, The; Shepard Agency, The; Siegel Literary Agency, Bobbe; Spitzer Literary Agency, Philip G.; Steele & Co., Ltd., Lyle; Stern Literary Agency, Gloria; Urstadt Inc. Writers and Artists Agency, Susan P.; Wald Associates, Inc., Mary Jack; Ware Literary Agency, John A.; Waterside Productions, Inc.; Wohl Literary Agency, Gary S.

Translations Balkin Agency; Crown International Literature and Arts Agency, Bonnie R.; Dijkstra, Sandra; Donlan, Thomas C.; Ellison, Nicholas; J de S Assoc.; Lyceum Creative Properties; Raymond, Literary Agent, Charlotte Cecil; Schmidt Literary Agency, Harold; Seligman, Literary Agent, Lynn; Stauffer Associates, Nancy; Swamy Literary Agent, Maya; Wald Associates, Inc., Mary Jack; Watkins Loomis Agency, Inc.; Wieser & Wieser, Inc.

True crime/investigative Acton, Dystel, Leone & Jaffe; Allan, Lee; Appleseeds Management; Authors' Literary Agency; Baldi Literary Agency, Malaga; Balkin Agency; Bernsen, Jamail & Goodson, L.L.P.; Boates, Reid; Brandt & Brandt; Cantrell-Colas; Carvainis, Maria; Ciske Literary Agency, Francine; Clausen Assoc., Connie; Cohen, Ruth; Collin, Frances; Coover Agency, Doe; Curtis Assoc., Richard; Dark Horse Group; Davie, Elaine; Diamant, The Writer's Workshop, Inc., Anita; Diamond Literary Agency, Inc.; Diamond Literary Agency, Inc.; Dijkstra, Sandra; Ducas, Robert; Ellenberg, Ethan; Ellison, Nicholas; Esquire Literary Productions; Flaherty, Joyce A.; Fogelman; Fuhrman, Candice; Garon-Brooke Assoc., Jay; Gartenberg, Max; Geiger, Ellen; Hawkins & Assoc., John; Hull House; IMG-Julian Bach; Jones, Lloyd; Ketz, Louise B.; Klinger, Inc., Harvey; Lampack, Peter; Literary Bridge; Literary Group; Love, Nancy; Madsen, Robert; Mann, Carol; Marmur Assoc., Mildred; Multimedia Product Development; Naggar, Jean V.; New England Publishing Assoc.; Nine Muses and Apollo; Novak III, Edward A.; Otitis Media; Parks Agency, The Richard; Picard Literary Agent, Alison J.; Quicksilver Books-Literary Agents; Rees Literary Agency, Helen; Renaissance: A Literary/Talent Agency; Riverside Literary Agency; Rose Literary Agency; Roth Agency, The ; Rubenstein Literary Agency, Inc., Pesha; Schmidt Literary Agency, Harold; Seligman, Literary Agent, Lynn; Siegel Literary Agency, Bobbe; Spitzer Literary Agency, Philip G.; Steele & Co., Ltd., Lyle; Stepping Stone; Stern Literary Agency, Gloria; Swamy Literary Agent, Maya; Teal Literary Agency, Patricia; Wald Associates, Inc., Mary Jack; Wallace Literary Agency, Inc.; Ware Literary Agency, John A.; Waterside Productions, Inc.; Weingel-Fidel Agency, The; Westchester Literary Agency, Inc.; Wieser & Wieser, Inc.; Witherspoon & Associates, Inc.; Writers House; Zeckendorf Assoc. Inc., Susan

Women's issues/women's studies Acton, Dystel, Leone & Jaffe; Adler & Robin Books; Authors' Literary Agency; Baldi Literary Agency, Malaga; Bartczak Assoc., Gene; Behar, Josh; Boates, Reid; Borchardt Inc., Georges; Brandt & Brandt; Brown Assoc., Marie; Cantrell-Colas; Carvainis, Maria; Casselman Literary Agent, Martha; Ciske Literary Agency, Francine; Clausen Assoc., Connie; Cohen, Ruth; Coover Agency, Doe; Crown International Literature and Arts Agency, Bonnie R.; Dark Horse Group; Davie, Elaine; de la Haba Agency Inc., The Lois; Diamant, The Writer's Workshop, Inc., Anita; Diamond Literary Agency, Inc.; Dijkstra, Sandra; Educational Design Services; Ellison, Nicholas; Elmo, Ann; Flaherty, Joyce A.; Fogelman; Fuhrman, Candice; Gartenberg, Max; Geiger, Ellen; Hawkins & Assoc., John; IMG-Julian Bach; Jones, Lloyd; Kellock Co.; Kidde, Hoyt & Picard; Klinger, Inc., Harvey; Kouts, Barbara S.; Kroll Literary Agency, Edite; Lampack, Peter; Levine, Ellen; Lincoln, Ray; Literary Bridge; Literary Group; Love, Nancy; Maccoby, Gina; McGrath, Helen; Mann, Carol; Marmur Assoc., Mildred; Naggar, Jean V.; New England Publishing Assoc.; Nine Muses and Apollo; Novak III, Edward A.; Otitis Media; Parks Agency, The Richard; Paton Literary Agency, Kathi J.; Picard Literary Agent, Alison J.; Raymond,

Literary Agent, Charlotte Cecil; Rees Literary Agency, Helen; Riverside Literary Agency; Rose Literary Agency; Roth Agency, The ; Schmidt Literary Agency, Harold; Seligman, Literary Agent, Lynn; Shepard Agency, The; Siegel Literary Agency, Bobbe; Stauffer Associates, Nancy; Stepping Stone; Stern Literary Agency, Gloria; Swamy Literary Agent, Maya; Teal Literary Agency, Patricia; 2M Communications Ltd.; Waterside Productions, Inc.; Weingel-Fidel Agency, The; Witherspoon & Associates, Inc.; Writers House; Zeckendorf Assoc. Inc., Susan

Fee-charging agents/Fiction

Action/Adventure A & R Burke Corp.; Ace Consultants; Ahearn Agency; Alden–Literary Service, Farel T.; Anthony, Joseph; Ashby Literary Agency; Authors' Marketing Services Ltd.; Browne Ltd., Pema; Castiglia Literary Agency, Julie; Cook Agency, Bruce; Dorese Agency Ltd.; Eden; Film & Fiction; Fishbein, Frieda; Flannery White and Stone; ForthWrite; Fran; Gislason Agency; Gladden Unlimited; Hamilton, Andrew; Hubbs, Yvonne Trudeau; Independent Publishing; Jenks, Carolyn; Kaltman, Larry; Kellock & Assoc. Ltd., J.; Kern, Natasha; Keyser Literary Agency; Klausner International; Law Offices of Robert L. Fenton PC; McKinley, Virginia C.; Marshall, Evan; Merhige-Merdon Marketing/Promo Co. Inc., Greg; Nelson Literary Agency & Lecture Bureau, BK; Northwest Literary Services; Olesha Agency, Andrea; Pen & Ink Literary Agency; PMA Literary and Film Management, Inc.; QCorp Literary Agency; Rose Agency; Southern Literary Agency; Steinberg Literary Agency, Michael; Stern Agency, Gloria; Wallerstein Agency, The Gerry B.; West Coast Literary Associates; Wildstar Associates; Write Designs Literary Agency; Writer's Advocate, The

Cartoon/comic Colby: Literary Agency; Cook Agency, Bruce; Eden; Fran; Hamilton, Andrew; Independent Publishing; Klausner International; Merhige-Merdon Marketing/Promo Co. Inc., Greg; Pen & Ink Literary Agency; Singer Media Corporation

Confessional Ackerman Literary Services; Anthony, Joseph; Eden; Gislason Agency; Hamilton, Andrew; Independent Publishing; Jenks, Carolyn; Kaltman, Larry; Merhige-Merdon Marketing/Promo Co. Inc., Greg; Northwest Literary Services; Pen & Ink Literary Agency; QCorp Literary Agency; Visions Press; Writer's Advocate, The; Zelasky Literary Agency, Tom

Contemporary issues A & R Burke Corp.; Ahearn Agency; Browne Ltd., Pema; Castiglia Literary Agency, Julie; Dorese Agency Ltd.; Fishbein, Frieda; Flannery White and Stone; Gislason Agency; Hamilton, Andrew; Heacock Literary Agency; Hubbs, Yvonne Trudeau; Independent Publishing; Jenks, Carolyn; Kaltman, Larry; Kellock & Assoc. Ltd., J.; Keyser Literary Agency; Klausner International; Law Offices of Robert L. Fenton PC; Levine Communications, James; Lopopolo, Toni; McKinley, Virginia C.; Marshall, Evan; Nelson Literary Agency & Lecture Bureau, BK; Northwest Literary Services; Olesha Agency, Andrea; Pen & Ink Literary Agency; QCorp Literary Agency; Rose Agency; State of the Art Ltd.; Steinberg Literary Agency, Michael; Stern Agency, Gloria; Visions Press; Wallerstein Agency, The Gerry B.; West Coast Literary Associates; Writer's Advocate, The; Zelasky Literary Agency, Tom

Detective/police/crime A & R Burke Corp.; Ackerman Literary Services; Ahearn Agency; Alden–Literary Service, Farel T.; Anthony, Joseph; Authors' Marketing Services Ltd.; Browne Ltd., Pema; Castiglia Literary Agency, Julie; Colby: Literary Agency; Dorese Agency Ltd.; Eden; Film And Fiction Agency, The; Fishbein, Frieda; Gislason Agency; Goddard: Book Development, Connie; Hamilton, Andrew; Independent Publishing; Jenks, Carolyn; Kaltman, Larry; Kellock & Assoc. Ltd., J.; Law Offices of Robert L. Fenton PC; Lopopolo, Toni; M.H. International; McKinley, Virginia C.; Marshall, Evan; Merhige-Merdon Marketing/Promo Co. Inc., Greg; Northwest Literary Services; Oceanic Press; Pell Agency, William; Pen & Ink Literary Agency; QCorp Literary Agency; Russell-Simenauer Literary Agency Inc.; Sebastian Literary Agency; Singer Media Corporation; Southern Literary Agency; State of the Art Ltd.; Steinberg Literary Agency, Michael; Stern Agency, Gloria; Toomey Associates, Jeanne; Wallerstein Agency, The Gerry B.; Watt & Associates, Sandra; West Coast Literary Associates; Wildstar Associates; Write Designs Literary Agency; Writer's Advocate, The; Zelasky Literary Agency, Tom

Erotica Ace Consultants; Anthony, Joseph; Eastwind Writers; Hamilton, Andrew; Hubbs, Yvonne Trudeau; Independent Publishing; Kaltman, Larry; Northwest Literary Services; Oceanic Press; QCorp Literary Agency; Singer Media Corporation; Steinberg Literary Agency, Michael; Stern Agency, Gloria; Visions Press; Writer's Advocate, The

Ethnic A & R Burke Corp.; Ace Consultants; Ahearn Agency; Castiglia Literary Agency, Julie; Dorese Agency Ltd.; Eastwind Writers; Flannery White and Stone; Hamilton, Andrew; Independent Publishing; Kaltman, Larry; Kellock & Assoc. Ltd., J.; Keyser Literary Agency; Klausner International; Law Offices of Robert L. Fenton PC; Lopopolo, Toni; McKinley, Virginia C.; Merhige-Merdon Marketing/Promo Co. Inc., Greg; Northwest Literary Services; Olesha Agency, Andrea; QCorp Literary Agency; Sebastian Literary Agency; Visions Press; Writer's Advocate, The

Experimental Eden; Flannery White and Stone; Gislason Agency; Independent Publishing; Kellock & Assoc. Ltd., J.; Keyser Literary Agency; Klausner International; Northwest Literary Services; Oceanic Press; Olesha Agency, Andrea; QCorp Literary Agency; West Coast Literary Associates; Writer's Advocate, The

Family saga A & R Burke Corp.; Ackerman Literary Services; Ahearn Agency; Alden—Literary Service, Farel T.; Castiglia Literary Agency, Julie; Cook Agency, Bruce; Dorese Agency Ltd.; Fishbein, Frieda; Flannery White and Stone; ForthWrite; Hamilton, Andrew; Hubbs, Yvonne Trudeau; Jenks, Carolyn; Kellock & Assoc. Ltd., J.; Keyser Literary Agency; Klausner International; Lopopolo, Toni; McKinley, Virginia C.; Marcil, Denise; Marshall, Evan; Merhige-Merdon Marketing/Promo Co. Inc., Greg; Nelson Literary Agency & Lecture Bureau, BK; Northwest Literary Services; Oceanic Press; Olesha Agency, Andrea; Pen & Ink Literary Agency; QCorp Literary Agency; Russell-Simenauer Literary Agency Inc.; Sebastian Literary Agency; Wallerstein Agency, The Gerry B.; Writer's Advocate, The; Zelasky Literary Agency, Tom

Fantasy A & R Burke Corp.; Ahearn Agency; Anthony, Joseph; Cook Agency, Bruce; Eden; Fishbein, Frieda; Fran; Gislason Agency; Hubbs, Yvonne Trudeau; Independent Publishing; Jenks, Carolyn; Kellock & Assoc. Ltd., J.; Keyser Literary Agency; Klausner International; McKinley, Virginia C.; Northwest Literary Services; Olesha Agency, Andrea; Pen & Ink Literary Agency; QCorp Literary Agency; Singer Media Corporation; Stern Agency, Gloria; Wildstar Associates; Writer's Advocate, The

Feminist A & R Burke Corp.; Ahearn Agency; Browne Ltd., Pema; Castiglia Literary Agency, Julie; Dorese Agency Ltd.; Fishbein, Frieda; Flannery White and Stone; Gislason Agency; Hubbs, Yvonne Trudeau; Independent Publishing; Jenks, Carolyn; Kellock & Assoc. Ltd., J.; Keyser Literary Agency; Klausner International; Lopopolo, Toni; McKinley, Virginia C.; Merhige-Merdon Marketing/Promo Co. Inc., Greg; Nelson Literary Agency & Lecture Bureau, BK; Northwest Literary Services; Olesha Agency, Andrea; PMA Literary and Film Management, Inc.; QCorp Literary Agency; Russell-Simenauer Literary Agency Inc.; State of the Art Ltd.; Stern Agency, Gloria; Writer's Advocate, The; Zelasky Literary Agency, Tom

Gay Ace Consultants; Ahearn Agency; Castiglia Literary Agency, Julie; Dorese Agency Ltd.; Flannery White and Stone; Jenks, Carolyn; Klausner International; Lopopolo, Toni; Olesha Agency, Andrea; Pen & Ink Literary Agency; QCorp Literary Agency; Sebastian Literary Agency; Visions Press; Writer's Advocate, The

Glitz Ackerman Literary Services; Ahearn Agency; Browne Ltd., Pema; Castiglia Literary Agency, Julie; Dorese Agency Ltd.; Hubbs, Yvonne Trudeau; Kellock & Assoc. Ltd., J.; Law Offices of Robert L. Fenton PC; Marshall, Evan; Olesha Agency, Andrea; Pen & Ink Literary Agency; QCorp Literary Agency; Sebastian Literary Agency; Singer Media Corporation; Stern Agency, Gloria; Wallerstein Agency, The Gerry B.; Watt & Associates, Sandra; Wildstar Associates; Writer's Advocate, The

Historical A & R Burke Corp.; Ackerman Literary Services; Ahearn Agency; Alden—Literary Service, Farel T.; Ashby Literary Agency; Browne Ltd., Pema; Cook Agency, Bruce; Dorese Agency Ltd.; Eden; Fishbein, Frieda; Flannery White and Stone; ForthWrite; Fran; Goddard: Book Development, Connie; Hubbs, Yvonne Trudeau; Independent Publishing; Kellock & Assoc. Ltd., J.; Kern, Natasha; Keyser Literary Agency; Klausner International; Law Offices of Robert L. Fenton PC; Lee Shore Agency; Lopopolo, Toni; M.H. International; Marcil, Denise; Marshall, Evan; Northwest Literary Services; Pen & Ink Literary Agency; QCorp Literary Agency; Rose Agency; Sebastian Literary Agency; Wallerstein Agency, The Gerry B.; West Coast Literary Associates; Wildstar Associates; Write Designs Literary Agency; Writer's Advocate, The; Zelasky Literary Agency, Tom

Humor/satire A & R Burke Corp.; Ace Consultants; Ahearn Agency; Browne Ltd., Pema; Colby: Literary Agency; Cook Agency, Bruce; Eastwind Writers; Eden; Film & Fiction; Fishbein, Frieda; Flannery White and Stone; Hamilton, Andrew; Independent Publishing; Kaltman, Larry; Kellock & Assoc. Ltd., J.; Keyser Literary Agency; Klausner International; Law Offices of Robert L. Fenton PC; Lopopolo, Toni; McKinley, Virginia C.; Merhige-Merdon Marketing/Promo Co. Inc., Greg; Northwest Literary Services; Olesha Agency, Andrea; Pell Agency, William; Pen & Ink Literary Agency; QCorp Literary Agency; Rose Agency; Southern Literary Agency; Wallerstein Agency, The Gerry B.; Writer's Advocate, The

Juvenile A & R Burke Corp.; Ahearn Agency; Browne Ltd., Pema; Catalog™, The; Cook Agency, Bruce; Eden; Flannery White and Stone; ForthWrite; Fran; Hamersfield Agency; Hamilton, Andrew; Independent Publishing; Kellock & Assoc. Ltd., J.; Klausner International; Levine Communications, James; McKinley, Virginia C.; Merhige-Merdon Marketing/Promo Co. Inc., Greg; Northwest Literary Services; Olesha Agency, Andrea; Pen & Ink Literary Agency; Popkin, Julie; QCorp Literary Agency; Rose Agency; Russell-Simenauer Literary Agency Inc.; Writer's Advocate, The

Lesbian Ace Consultants; Ahearn Agency; Dorese Agency Ltd.; Flannery White and Stone; Hamil-

Subject Index: Fee-charging/Fiction 259

ton, Andrew; Jenks, Carolyn; Klausner International; Lopopolo, Toni; Olesha Agency, Andrea; Pen & Ink Literary Agency; QCorp Literary Agency; Visions Press; Writer's Advocate, The

Literary A & R Burke Corp.; Acacia House Publishing Services; Ahearn Agency; Ashby Literary Agency; Becker, Maximilian; Browne Ltd., Pema; Castiglia Literary Agency, Julie; Cook Agency, Bruce; Dorese Agency Ltd.; Eastwind Writers; Flannery White and Stone; ForthWrite; Gislason Agency; Heacock Literary Agency; Independent Publishing; Kaltman, Larry; Kellock & Assoc. Ltd., J.; Keyser Literary Agency; Klausner International; Levine Communications, James; Lopopolo, Toni; McKinley, Virginia C.; Merhige-Merdon Marketing/Promo Co. Inc., Greg; Nelson Literary Agency & Lecture Bureau, BK; Northwest Literary Services; Olesha Agency, Andrea; Popkin, Julie; QCorp Literary Agency; Sebastian Literary Agency; Wallerstein Agency, The Gerry B.; West Coast Literary Associates; Wildstar Associates; Write Designs Literary Agency; Writer's Advocate, The; Zelasky Literary Agency, Tom

Mainstream A & R Burke Corp.; Acacia House Publishing Services; Ace Consultants; Ackerman Literary Services; Ahearn Agency; Alden—Literary Service, Farel T.; Ashby Literary Agency; Becker, Maximilian; Browne Ltd., Pema; Castiglia Literary Agency, Julie; Catalog™, The; Dorese Agency Ltd.; Film & Fiction; Fishbein, Frieda; Flannery White and Stone; ForthWrite; Fran; Gislason Agency; Gladden Unlimited; Goddard: Book Development, Connie; Hubbs, Yvonne Trudeau; Independent Publishing; Kaltman, Larry; Kellock & Assoc. Ltd., J.; Kern, Natasha; Keyser Literary Agency; Klausner International; Law Offices of Robert L. Fenton PC; Lee Shore Agency; Levine Communications, James; Lopopolo, Toni; Marshall, Evan; Merhige-Merdon Marketing/Promo Co. Inc., Greg; Nelson Literary Agency & Lecture Bureau, BK; Northwest Literary Services; Oceanic Press; Olesha Agency, Andrea; Pen & Ink Literary Agency; Popkin, Julie; QCorp Literary Agency; Rose Agency; Russell-Simenauer Literary Agency Inc.; Sebastian Literary Agency; Southern Literary Agency; Steinberg Literary Agency, Michael; Stern Agency, Gloria; TARC Literary Agency; Visions Press; Wallerstein Agency, The Gerry B.; Watt & Associates, Sandra; West Coast Literary Associates; Wildstar Associates; Write Designs Literary Agency; Writer's Advocate, The; Writer's Consulting Group; Zelasky Literary Agency, Tom

Mystery/suspense A & R Burke Corp.; Ace Consultants; Ackerman Literary Services; Ahearn Agency; Alden—Literary Service, Farel T.; Anthony, Joseph; Ashby Literary Agency; Author Author; Authors' Marketing Services Ltd.; Becker, Maximilian; Browne Ltd., Pema; Castiglia Literary Agency, Julie; Colby: Literary Agency; Cook Agency, Bruce; Dorese Agency Ltd.; Eastwind Writers; Film & Fiction; Fishbein, Frieda; Flannery White and Stone; ForthWrite; Fran; Gislason Agency; Goddard: Book Development, Connie; Hamilton, Andrew; Hubbs, Yvonne Trudeau; Independent Publishing; Jenks, Carolyn; Kaltman, Larry; Kellock & Assoc. Ltd., J.; Kern, Natasha; Klausner International; Law Offices of Robert L. Fenton PC; Lee Shore Agency; Lopopolo, Toni; M.H. International; McKinley, Virginia C.; Marshall, Evan; Merhige-Merdon Marketing/Promo Co. Inc., Greg; Nelson Literary Agency & Lecture Bureau, BK; Northwest Literary Services; Oceanic Press; Oceanic Press Service; Olesha Agency, Andrea; Pen & Ink Literary Agency; PMA Literary and Film Management, Inc.; Popkin, Julie; Porcelain, Sidney E.; QCorp Literary Agency; Rose Agency; Russell-Simenauer Literary Agency Inc.; Sebastian Literary Agency; Singer Media Corporation; Southern Literary Agency; State of the Art Ltd.; Steinberg Literary Agency, Michael; TARC Literary Agency; Wallerstein Agency, The Gerry B.; Watt & Associates, Sandra; West Coast Literary Associates; Wildstar Associates; Write Designs Literary Agency; Writer's Advocate, The; Zelasky Literary Agency, Tom

Open to all fiction categories Bernstein, Meredith; Brinke Literary Agency; Curtis Bruce; Follendore, Joan; Glenmark; Morgan, David H.; Neighbors, Charles; New Writers Literary Project; New Writing Agency; Northeast Literary Agency; Rhodes Literary Agency; Sullivan Associates, Mark

Picture book A & R Burke Corp.; Acacia House Publishing Services; Browne Ltd., Pema; Castiglia Literary Agency, Julie; Eastwind Writers; Eden; Flannery White and Stone; ForthWrite; Fran; Independent Publishing; Kellock & Assoc. Ltd., J.; Klausner International; Merhige-Merdon Marketing/Promo Co. Inc., Greg; Northwest Literary Services; Pen & Ink Literary Agency; QCorp Literary Agency; Singer Media Corporation; Writer's Advocate, The

Psychic/supernatural Ace Consultants; Ackerman Literary Services; Ahearn Agency; Alden—Literary Service, Farel T.; Anthony, Joseph; Browne Ltd., Pema; Dorese Agency Ltd.; Flannery White and Stone; Gislason Agency; Hamilton, Andrew; Heacock Literary Agency; Hubbs, Yvonne Trudeau; Independent Publishing; Jenks, Carolyn; Keyser Literary Agency; Klausner International; Marshall, Evan; Northwest Literary Services; Oceanic Press; Olesha Agency, Andrea; Pen & Ink Literary Agency; QCorp Literary Agency; Russell-Simenauer Literary Agency Inc.; Singer Media Corporation; Toomey Associates, Jeanne; Wildstar Associates; Writer's Advocate, The

Regional Ahearn Agency; Castiglia Literary Agency, Julie; Cook Agency, Bruce; Dorese Agency Ltd.; Flannery White and Stone; Fran; Jenks, Carolyn; Keyser Literary Agency; Klausner International; Merhige-Merdon Marketing/Promo Co. Inc., Greg; Northwest Literary Services; Olesha

Agency, Andrea; QCorp Literary Agency; West Coast Literary Associates; Writer's Advocate, The

Religious/inspiration Browne Ltd., Pema; Cook Agency, Bruce; Hamilton, Andrew; Keyser Literary Agency; Klausner International; McKinley, Virginia C.; Merhige-Merdon Marketing/Promo Co. Inc., Greg; Olesha Agency, Andrea; Pen & Ink Literary Agency; QCorp Literary Agency; Rose Agency; Write Designs Literary Agency; Writer's Advocate, The

Romance A & R Burke Corp.; Ackerman Literary Services; Ahearn Agency; Anthony, Joseph; Ashby Literary Agency; Author Author; Authors' Marketing Services Ltd.; Browne Ltd., Pema; Castiglia Literary Agency, Julie; Eastwind Writers; Eden; Fishbein, Frieda; Flannery White and Stone; ForthWrite; Gislason Agency; Hamilton, Andrew; Haynes, Elizabeth; Hubbs, Yvonne Trudeau; Jenks, Carolyn; Kaltman, Larry; Kellock & Assoc. Ltd., J.; Kern, Natasha; Keyser Literary Agency; Klausner International; Law Offices of Robert L. Fenton PC; Lee Shore Agency; M.H. International; McKinley, Virginia C.; Marcil, Denise; Marshall, Evan; Merhige-Merdon Marketing/Promo Co. Inc., Greg; Nelson Literary Agency & Lecture Bureau, BK; Northwest Literary Services; Oceanic Press; Oceanic Press Service; Pen & Ink Literary Agency; Popkin, Julie; QCorp Literary Agency; Rose Agency; Russell-Simenauer Literary Agency Inc.; Singer Media Corporation; Visions Press; Wallerstein Agency, The Gerry B.; Warren Literary Agency, James; West Coast Literary Associates; Wildstar Associates; Writer's Advocate, The; Zelasky Literary Agency, Tom

Science fiction A & R Burke Corp.; Ahearn Agency; Anthony, Joseph; Ashby Literary Agency; Author Author; Becker, Maximilian; Browne Ltd., Pema; Cook Agency, Bruce; Eastwind Writers; Eden; Fishbein, Frieda; Flannery White and Stone, Fran; Gislason Agency; Hubbs, Yvonne Trudeau; Jenks, Carolyn; Kellock & Assoc. Ltd., J.; Keyser Literary Agency; Klausner International; Law Offices of Robert L. Fenton PC; Northwest Literary Services; Oceanic Press; Olesha Agency, Andrea; Pen & Ink Literary Agency; Popkin, Julie; QCorp Literary Agency; Rhodes Literary Agency; Singer Media Corporation; State of the Art Ltd.; Steinberg Literary Agency, Michael; Stern Agency, Gloria; Wallace Literary Agency, Bess; West Coast Literary Associates; Wildstar Associates; Writer's Advocate, The; Zelasky Literary Agency, Tom

Sports A & R Burke Corp.; Colby: Literary Agency; Dorese Agency Ltd.; Hamilton, Andrew; Jenks, Carolyn; Kaltman, Larry; Kellock & Assoc. Ltd., J.; Klausner International; Law Offices of Robert L. Fenton PC; Merhige-Merdon Marketing/Promo Co. Inc., Greg; Nelson Literary Agency & Lecture Bureau, BK; Northwest Literary Services; Oceanic Press; QCorp Literary Agency; Writer's Advocate, The

Thriller/espionage A & R Burke Corp.; Ace Consultants; Ackerman Literary Services; Ahearn Agency; Alden—Literary Service, Farel T.; Anthony, Joseph; Ashby Literary Agency; Authors' Marketing Services Ltd.; Browne Ltd., Pema; Colby: Literary Agency; Cook Agency, Bruce; Film & Fiction; Fishbein, Frieda; Flannery White and Stone; Gislason Agency; Gladden Unlimited; Goddard: Book Development, Connie; Hamilton, Andrew; Hubbs, Yvonne Trudeau; Independent Publishing; Jenks, Carolyn; Kaltman, Larry; Kellock & Assoc. Ltd., J.; Kern, Natasha; Klausner International; Law Offices of Robert L. Fenton PC; M.H. International; Marshall, Evan; Merhige-Merdon Marketing/Promo Co. Inc., Greg; Nelson Literary Agency & Lecture Bureau, BK; Northwest Literary Services; Oceanic Press; Pell Agency, William; Pen & Ink Literary Agency; PMA Literary and Film Management, Inc.; QCorp Literary Agency; Russell-Simenauer Literary Agency Inc.; Sebastian Literary Agency; Singer Media Corporation; Southern Literary Agency; Steinberg Literary Agency, Michael; Stern Agency, Gloria; Toomey Associates, Jeanne; Wallerstein Agency, The Gerry B.; Watt & Associates, Sandra; West Coast Literary Associates; Wildstar Associates; Write Designs Literary Agency; Writer's Advocate, The; Writer's Consulting Group; Zelasky Literary Agency, Tom

Westerns/frontier Ahearn Agency; Alden—Literary Service, Farel T.; Ashby Literary Agency; Colby: Literary Agency; Eastwind Writers; Eden; Film & Fiction; Flannery White and Stone; Fran; Hamilton, Andrew; Kellock & Assoc. Ltd., J.; Kern, Natasha; Keyser Literary Agency; Klausner International; Law Offices of Robert L. Fenton PC; Lee Shore Agency; Lopopolo, Toni; McKinley, Virginia C.; Merhige-Merdon Marketing/Promo Co. Inc., Greg; Northwest Literary Services; Oceanic Press; QCorp Literary Agency; Singer Media Corporation; Stern Agency, Gloria; Wallerstein Agency, The Gerry B.; West Coast Literary Associates; Wildstar Associates; Writer's Advocate, The; Zelasky Literary Agency, Tom

Young adult A & R Burke Corp.; Acacia House Publishing Services; Ahearn Agency; Anthony, Joseph; Browne Ltd., Pema; Cook Agency, Bruce; Dorese Agency Ltd.; Eastwind Writers; Eden; Fishbein, Frieda; Flannery White and Stone; ForthWrite; Fran; Hamilton, Andrew; Independent Publishing; Kaltman, Larry; Kellock & Assoc. Ltd., J.; Kern, Natasha; Klausner International; Lee Shore Agency; Levine Communications, James; Merhige-Merdon Marketing/Promo Co. Inc., Greg; Northwest Literary Services; Oceanic Press; Olesha Agency, Andrea; Pen & Ink Literary Agency; QCorp Literary Agency; Rose Agency; Singer Media Corporation; Visions Press; Wallerstein Agency, The Gerry B.; Writer's Advocate, The; Zelasky Literary Agency, Tom

Fee-charging agents/Nonfiction

Agriculture/horticulture Acacia House Publishing Services; Catalog™, The; Eden; ForthWrite; Fran; Goddard: Book Development, Connie; Levine Communications, James; Northwest Literary Services; Toomey Associates, Jeanne; Wallace Literary Agency, Bess

Animals Acacia House Publishing Services; Ahearn Agency; Alden—Literary Service, Farel T.; Ashby Literary Agency; Castiglia Literary Agency, Julie; Eden; Fishbein, Frieda; ForthWrite; Fran; Gislason Agency; Goddard: Book Development, Connie; Hamilton, Andrew; Jenks, Carolyn; Kellock & Assoc. Ltd., J.; Levine Communications, James; Lopopolo, Toni; McKinley, Virginia C.; Merhige-Merdon Marketing/Promo Co. Inc., Greg; Nelson Literary Agency & Lecture Bureau, BK; Northwest Literary Services; Toomey Associates, Jeanne; Wallace Literary Agency, Bess; Watt & Associates, Sandra; Writer's Advocate, The

Anthropology Acacia House Publishing Services; Brinke Literary Agency; Browne Ltd., Pema; Castiglia Literary Agency, Julie; ForthWrite; Goddard: Book Development, Connie; Heacock Literary Agency; Independent Publishing; Kellock & Assoc. Ltd., J.; Nelson Literary Agency & Lecture Bureau, BK; Sebastian Literary Agency; Southern Literary Agency; Sullivan Associates, Mark; Toomey Associates, Jeanne; Wallace Literary Agency, Bess; Watt & Associates, Sandra; Writer's Advocate, The

Art/architecture/design A & R Burke Corp.; Acacia House Publishing Services; Browne Ltd., Pema; Castiglia Literary Agency, Julie; Dorese Agency Ltd.; ForthWrite; Gislason Agency; Goddard: Book Development, Connie; Heacock Literary Agency; Independent Publishing; Jenks, Carolyn; Kellock & Assoc. Ltd., J.; Levine Communications, James; Northwest Literary Services; Pen & Ink Literary Agency; Popkin, Julie; Sebastian Literary Agency; State of the Art Ltd.; Toomey Associates, Jeanne; Write Designs Literary Agency; Writer's Advocate, The

Biography/autobiography A & R Burke Corp.; Acacia House Publishing Services; Ace Consultants; Ahearn Agency; Author Aid Associates; Author Author; Authors' Marketing Services Ltd.; Becker/Aleta M. Daley, Maximilian; Browne Ltd., Pema; Castiglia Literary Agency, Julie; Cook Agency, Bruce; Curtis Bruce; Dorese Agency Ltd.; Eastwind Writers; Fishbein, Frieda; ForthWrite; Fran; Gislason Agency; Gladden Unlimited; Goddard: Book Development, Connie; Hamilton, Andrew; Heacock Literary Agency; Independent Publishing; Jenks, Carolyn; Kellock & Assoc. Ltd., J.; Kern, Natasha; Keyser Literary Agency; Law Offices of Robert L. Fenton PC; Levine Communications, James; McKinley, Virginia C.; Marshall, Evan; Merhige-Merdon Marketing/Promo Co. Inc., Greg; Nelson Literary Agency & Lecture Bureau, BK; Northwest Literary Services; Oceanic Press; Oceanic Press Service; Pen & Ink Literary Agency; PMA Literary and Film Management, Inc.; Sebastian Literary Agency; Singer Media Corporation; Southern Literary Agency; Steinberg Literary Agency, Michael; Sullivan Associates, Mark; Toomey Associates, Jeanne; West Coast Literary Associates; Wildstar Associates; Write Designs Literary Agency; Writer's Advocate, The; Zelasky Literary Agency, Tom

Business A & R Burke Corp.; Ahearn Agency; Ashby Literary Agency; Author Author; Authors' Marketing Services Ltd.; Browne Ltd., Pema; Castiglia Literary Agency, Julie; Catalog™, The; Cook Agency, Bruce; Dorese Agency Ltd.; Flannery White and Stone; ForthWrite; Fran; Gladden Unlimited; Goddard: Book Development, Connie; Hamilton, Andrew; Heacock Literary Agency; Independent Publishing; Jenks, Carolyn; Kellock & Assoc. Ltd., J.; Kern, Natasha; Law Offices of Robert L. Fenton PC; Levine Communications, James; Literary/Business Assoc.; McKinley, Virginia C.; Marcil, Denise; Marshall, Evan; Nelson Literary Agency & Lecture Bureau, BK; Oceanic Press; Pen & Ink Literary Agency; Rose Agency; Sebastian Literary Agency; Singer Media Corporation; Southern Literary Agency; Steinberg Literary Agency, Michael; Stern Agency, Gloria; Sullivan Associates, Mark; Wildstar Associates; Write Designs Literary Agency; Writer's Advocate, The

Child guidance/parenting Acacia House Publishing Services; Ahearn Agency; Author Author; Authors' Marketing Services Ltd.; Browne Ltd., Pema; Castiglia Literary Agency, Julie; Catalog™, The; Cook Agency, Bruce; Curtis Bruce; Dorese Agency Ltd.; Flannery White and Stone; ForthWrite; Gislason Agency; Goddard: Book Development, Connie; Hamilton, Andrew; Heacock Literary Agency; Independent Publishing; Kellock & Assoc. Ltd., J.; Kern, Natasha; Law Offices of Robert L. Fenton PC; Levine Communications, James; McKinley, Virginia C.; Marcil, Denise; Marshall, Evan; Merhige-Merdon Marketing/Promo Co. Inc., Greg; Nelson Literary Agency & Lecture Bureau, BK; Northwest Literary Services; Oceanic Press; Pen & Ink Literary Agency; Rose Agency; Russell-Simenauer Literary Agency Inc.; Sebastian Literary Agency; Singer Media Corporation; Southern Literary Agency; Steinberg Literary Agency, Michael; Wildstar Associates; Writer's Advocate, The

Computers/electronics A & R Burke Corp.; Acacia House Publishing Services; Ashby Literary Agency; Catalog™, The; Eden; Goddard: Book Development, Connie; Law Offices of Robert L. Fenton PC; Levine Communications, James; Nelson Literary Agency & Lecture Bureau, BK;

Oceanic Press; Pen & Ink Literary Agency; Sebastian Literary Agency; Singer Media Corporation; Steinberg Literary Agency, Michael; Write Designs Literary Agency

Cooking/food/nutrition Acacia House Publishing Services; Browne Ltd., Pema; Castiglia Literary Agency, Julie; Cook Agency, Bruce; Dorese Agency Ltd.; Eden; Fishbein, Frieda; ForthWrite; Fran; Goddard: Book Development, Connie; Hamilton, Andrew; Independent Publishing; Jenks, Carolyn; Kellock & Assoc. Ltd., J.; Kern, Natasha; Levine Communications, James; Lopopolo, Toni; Marcil, Denise; Marshall, Evan; Merhige-Merdon Marketing/Promo Co. Inc., Greg; Nelson Literary Agency & Lecture Bureau, BK; Northwest Literary Services; Olesha Agency, Andrea; Pen & Ink Literary Agency; Stern Agency, Gloria; Sullivan Associates, Mark; Wildstar Associates; Write Designs Literary Agency; Writer's Advocate, The

Crafts/hobbies Acacia House Publishing Services; Ackerman Literary Services; Catalog™, The; Dorese Agency Ltd.; Eden; ForthWrite; Fran; Goddard: Book Development, Connie; Heacock Literary Agency; Independent Publishing; Nelson Literary Agency & Lecture Bureau, BK; Northwest Literary Services; Pen & Ink Literary Agency; Sullivan Associates, Mark; Wildstar Associates; Write Designs Literary Agency; Writer's Advocate, The

Current Affairs A & R Burke Corp.; Acacia House Publishing Services; Ahearn Agency; Ashby Literary Agency; Authors' Marketing Services Ltd.; Castiglia Literary Agency, Julie; Dorese Agency Ltd.; Eden; Fishbein, Frieda; Flannery White and Stone; Gislason Agency; Goddard: Book Development, Connie; Hamilton, Andrew; Hubbs, Yvonne Trudeau; Independent Publishing; Jenks, Carolyn; Kellock & Assoc. Ltd., J.; Kern, Natasha; Keyser Literary Agency; Law Offices of Robert L. Fenton PC; Lopopolo, Toni; Marshall, Evan; Nelson Literary Agency & Lecture Bureau, BK; Sebastian Literary Agency; Steinberg Literary Agency, Michael; Stern Agency, Gloria; Sullivan Associates, Mark; Wallace Literary Agency, Bess; West Coast Literary Associates; Wildstar Associates; Writer's Advocate, The; Zelasky Literary Agency, Tom

Ethnic/cultural interests Acacia House Publishing Services; Ace Consultants; Ahearn Agency; Becker/Aleta M. Daley, Maximilian; Castiglia Literary Agency, Julie; Eastwind Writers; Flannery White and Stone; Fran; Goddard: Book Development, Connie; Hamilton, Andrew; Independent Publishing; Jenks, Carolyn; Keyser Literary Agency; Lopopolo, Toni; McKinley, Virginia C.; Merhige-Merdon Marketing/Promo Co. Inc., Greg; Olesha Agency, Andrea; Sebastian Literary Agency; Steinberg Literary Agency, Michael; Stern Agency, Gloria; Visions Press; West Coast Literary Associates; Wildstar Associates; Writer's Advocate, The

Gay/Lesbian issues Acacia House Publishing Services; Ace Consultants; Ahearn Agency; Dorese Agency Ltd.; Flannery White and Stone; Jenks, Carolyn; Levine Communications, James; Olesha Agency, Andrea; Pen & Ink Literary Agency; Visions Press; Wildstar Associates; Writer's Advocate, The

Government/politics/law A & R Burke Corp.; Acacia House Publishing Services; Ashby Literary Agency; Browne Ltd., Pema; Dorese Agency Ltd.; Eden; Flannery White and Stone; Gislason Agency; Goddard: Book Development, Connie; Hamilton, Andrew; Heacock Literary Agency; Independent Publishing; Jenks, Carolyn; Kellock & Assoc. Ltd., J.; Keyser Literary Agency; Law Offices of Robert L. Fenton PC; Marshall, Evan; Popkin, Julie; Sebastian Literary Agency; Steinberg Literary Agency, Michael; Toomey Associates, Jeanne; Wallace Literary Agency, Bess; West Coast Literary Associates; Wildstar Associates; Writer's Advocate, The; Zelasky Literary Agency, Tom

Health/medicine Acacia House Publishing Services; Ahearn Agency; Anthony, Joseph; Browne Ltd., Pema; Castiglia Literary Agency, Julie; Catalog™, The; Cook Agency, Bruce; Dorese Agency Ltd.; Flannery White and Stone; ForthWrite; Fran; Goddard: Book Development, Connie; Hamilton, Andrew; Heacock Literary Agency; Jenks, Carolyn; Kaltman, Larry; Kellock & Assoc. Ltd., J.; Kern, Natasha; Law Offices of Robert L. Fenton PC; Levine Communications, James; Literary/Business Assoc.; McKinley, Virginia C.; Marcil, Denise; Marshall, Evan; Nelson Literary Agency & Lecture Bureau, BK; Northwest Literary Services; Oceanic Press; Pen & Ink Literary Agency; Russell-Simenauer Literary Agency Inc.; Sebastian Literary Agency; Singer Media Corporation; Southern Literary Agency; Stern Agency, Gloria; Sullivan Associates, Mark; Wildstar Associates; Write Designs Literary Agency; Writer's Advocate, The

History A & R Burke Corp.; Acacia House Publishing Services; Ahearn Agency; Alden–Literary Service, Farel T.; Ashby Literary Agency; Castiglia Literary Agency, Julie; Cook Agency, Bruce; Dorese Agency Ltd.; Eden; ForthWrite; Fran; Goddard: Book Development, Connie; Hamilton, Andrew; Heacock Literary Agency; Hubbs, Yvonne Trudeau; Independent Publishing; Jenks, Carolyn; Kellock & Assoc. Ltd., J.; Keyser Literary Agency; Lopopolo, Toni; Marshall, Evan; Northwest Literary Services; Pen & Ink Literary Agency; PMA Literary and Film Management, Inc.; Popkin, Julie; Sebastian Literary Agency; Southern Literary Agency; Steinberg Literary Agency, Michael; Toomey Associates, Jeanne; Wallace Literary Agency, Bess; West Coast Literary Associates; Wildstar Associates; Write Designs Literary Agency; Writer's Advocate, The

Interior design/decorating Acacia House Publishing Services; Castiglia Literary Agency, Julie;

Dorese Agency Ltd.; ForthWrite; Goddard: Book Development, Connie; Marshall, Evan; Olesha Agency, Andrea; Pen & Ink Literary Agency; Sullivan Associates, Mark; Toomey Associates, Jeanne; Wildstar Associates; Writer's Advocate, The

Juvenile nonfiction A & R Burke Corp.; Acacia House Publishing Services; Ahearn Agency; Alden—Literary Service, Farel T.; Browne Ltd., Pema; Castiglia Literary Agency, Julie; Catalog™, The; Cook Agency, Bruce; Eden; Fishbein, Frieda; Flannery White and Stone; ForthWrite; Fran; Hamersfield Agency; Hamilton, Andrew; Independent Publishing; Jenks, Carolyn; Kellock & Assoc. Ltd., J.; Levine Communications, James; McKinley, Virginia C.; Merhige-Merdon Marketing/Promo Co. Inc., Greg; Northwest Literary Services; Pen & Ink Literary Agency; Rose Agency; Russell-Simenauer Literary Agency Inc.; Singer Media Corporation; Writer's Advocate, The

Language/literature/criticism A & R Burke Corp.; Acacia House Publishing Services; Castiglia Literary Agency, Julie; Cook Agency, Bruce; Dorese Agency Ltd.; Eden; Goddard: Book Development, Connie; Independent Publishing; Jenks, Carolyn; Kellock & Assoc. Ltd., J.; Keyser Literary Agency; Northwest Literary Services; Olesha Agency, Andrea; Popkin, Julie; Sullivan Associates, Mark; West Coast Literary Associates; Wildstar Associates; Writer's Advocate, The

Military/war A & R Burke Corp.; Acacia House Publishing Services; Anthony, Joseph; Ashby Literary Agency; Author Aid Associates; Authors' Marketing Services Ltd.; Browne Ltd., Pema; Dorese Agency Ltd.; Eden; Fishbein, Frieda; Goddard: Book Development, Connie; Heacock Literary Agency; Independent Publishing; Law Offices of Robert L. Fenton PC; Lee Shore Agency; McKinley, Virginia C.; Merhige-Merdon Marketing/Promo Co. Inc., Greg; Nelson Literary Agency & Lecture Bureau, BK; Pen & Ink Literary Agency; Sullivan Associates, Mark; Taylor Literary Agency, Dawson; Wallace Literary Agency, Bess; Wildstar Associates; Write Designs Literary Agency; Writer's Advocate, The; Zelasky Literary Agency, Tom

Money/finance/economics A & R Burke Corp.; Acacia House Publishing Services; Ashby Literary Agency; Catalog™, The; Dorese Agency Ltd.; Eden; Flannery White and Stone; ForthWrite; Goddard: Book Development, Connie; Hamilton, Andrew; Independent Publishing; Kellock & Assoc. Ltd., J.; Law Offices of Robert L. Fenton PC; Levine Communications, James; Lopopolo, Toni; McKinley, Virginia C.; Marcil, Denise; Marshall, Evan; Nelson Literary Agency & Lecture Bureau, BK; Oceanic Press; Pen & Ink Literary Agency; Russell-Simenauer Literary Agency Inc.; Sebastian Literary Agency; Singer Media Corporation; Southern Literary Agency; Steinberg Literary Agency, Michael; Stern Agency, Gloria; Sullivan Associates, Mark; Toomey Associates, Jeanne; Wildstar Associates; Write Designs Literary Agency; Writer's Advocate, The; A & R Burke Corp.; Acacia House Publishing Services; Ahearn Agency; Castiglia Literary Agency, Julie; Cook Agency, Bruce; Dorese Agency Ltd.; Eden; Flannery White and Stone; ForthWrite; Gislason Agency; Goddard, Connie: Book Development; Hamilton, Andrew; Heacock Literary Agency; Independent Publishing; Jenks, Carolyn; Kellock & Assoc. Ltd., J.; Law Offices of Robert L. Fenton PC; McKinley, Virginia C.; Marcil, Denise; Marshall, Evan; Merhige-Merdon Marketing/Promo Co. Inc., Greg; Nelson Literary Agency & Lecture Bureau, BK; Northwest Literary Services; Oceanic Press; Olesha Agency, Andrea; Sullivan Associates, Mark; West Coast Literary Associates; Wildstar Associates; Writer's Advocate, The

Nature/environment Acacia House Publishing Services; Browne Ltd., Pema; Castiglia Literary Agency, Julie; Catalog™, The; Cook Agency, Bruce; Eastwind Writers; Eden; Fishbein, Frieda; Flannery White and Stone; ForthWrite; Fran; Goddard: Book Development, Connie; Heacock Literary Agency; Independent Publishing; Kellock & Assoc. Ltd., J.; Levine Communications, James; Lopopolo, Toni; McKinley, Virginia C.; Nelson Literary Agency & Lecture Bureau, BK; Northwest Literary Services; Olesha Agency, Andrea; Pen & Ink Literary Agency; Sebastian Literary Agency; Steinberg Literary Agency, Michael; Sullivan Associates, Mark; Toomey Associates, Jeanne; West Coast Literary Associates; Wildstar Associates; Write Designs Literary Agency; Writer's Advocate, The

New Age/metaphysics Acacia House Publishing Services; Ace Consultants; Alden—Literary Service, Farel T.; Brinke Literary Agency; Browne Ltd., Pema; Castiglia Literary Agency, Julie; Dorese Agency Ltd.; Gislason Agency; Heacock Literary Agency; Jenks, Carolyn; Kellock & Assoc. Ltd., J.; Keyser Literary Agency; Levine Communications, James; Marshall, Evan; New Age World Services; Northwest Literary Services; Oceanic Press; Sullivan Associates, Mark; Watt & Associates, Sandra; Wildstar Associates; Writer's Advocate, The

Open to all nonfiction categories Authors And Artists Resource Center/Tarc; Bernstein, Meredith; Follendore, Joan; Glenmark; Klausner International; Morgan, David H.; Neighbors, Charles; New Writers Literary Project; New Writing Agency; Northeast Literary Agency; QCorp Literary Agency; Rhodes Literary Agency; Wallerstein Agency, The Gerry B.

Photography Acacia House Publishing Services; Dorese Agency Ltd.; Eden; ForthWrite; Goddard: Book Development, Connie; Hamersfield Agency; Independent Publishing; Merhige-Merdon Marketing/Promo Co. Inc., Greg; Northwest Literary Services; Pell Agency, William; Pen & Ink

Literary Agency; Sullivan Associates, Mark; Write Designs Literary Agency; Writer's Advocate, The

Psychology A & R Burke Corp.; Acacia House Publishing Services; Anthony, Joseph; Browne Ltd., Pema; Castiglia Literary Agency, Julie; Catalog™, The; Cook Agency, Bruce; Dorese Agency Ltd.; Flannery White and Stone; ForthWrite; Gislason Agency; Goddard: Book Development, Connie; Hamilton, Andrew; Heacock Literary Agency; Independent Publishing; Jenks, Carolyn; Kern, Natasha; Keyser Literary Agency; Levine Communications, James; Literary/Business Assoc.; Lopopolo, Toni; McKinley, Virginia C.; Marcil, Denise; Marshall, Evan; Nelson Literary Agency & Lecture Bureau, BK; Oceanic Press; Pen & Ink Literary Agency; Russell-Simenauer Literary Agency Inc.; Sebastian Literary Agency; Singer Media Corporation; Southern Literary Agency; Steinberg Literary Agency, Michael; Stern Agency, Gloria; Sullivan Associates, Mark; TARC Literary Agency; Wallace Literary Agency, Bess; West Coast Literary Associates; Wildstar Associates; Writer's Advocate, The

Religious/inspirational Acacia House Publishing Services; Browne Ltd., Pema; Castiglia Literary Agency, Julie; Cook Agency, Bruce; Curtis Bruce; ForthWrite; Goddard: Book Development, Connie; Hamilton, Andrew; Independent Publishing; Jenks, Carolyn; Keyser Literary Agency; Law Offices of Robert L. Fenton PC; Levine Communications, James; Literary/Business Assoc.; McKinley, Virginia C.; Nelson Literary Agency & Lecture Bureau, BK; Pen & Ink Literary Agency; Rose Agency; Russell-Simenauer Literary Agency Inc.; Sullivan Associates, Mark; Visions Press; Write Designs Literary Agency; Writer's Advocate, The

Science/technology A & R Burke Corp.; Acacia House Publishing Services; Anthony, Joseph; Browne Ltd., Pema; Castiglia Literary Agency, Julie; Catalog™, The; Eden; ForthWrite; Goddard: Book Development, Connie; Independent Publishing; Kaltman, Larry; Kern, Natasha; Keyser Literary Agency; Law Offices of Robert L. Fenton PC; Levine Communications, James; Nelson Literary Agency & Lecture Bureau, BK; Oceanic Press; PMA Literary and Film Management, Inc.; Sebastian Literary Agency; Sullivan Associates, Mark; Wildstar Associates

Self-help/personal improvement A & R Burke Corp.; Acacia House Publishing Services; Ahearn Agency; Alden–Literary Service, Farel T.; Anthony, Joseph; Author Author; Browne Ltd., Pema; Castiglia Literary Agency, Julie; Catalog™, The; Cook Agency, Bruce; Curtis Bruce; Dorese Agency Ltd.; Fishbein, Frieda; Flannery White and Stone; ForthWrite; Fran; Gislason Agency; Gladden Unlimited; Goddard: Book Development, Connie; Hamilton, Andrew; Heacock Literary Agency; Independent Publishing; Jenks, Carolyn; Kaltman, Larry; Kellock & Assoc. Ltd., J.; Kern, Natasha; Law Offices of Robert L. Fenton PC; Levine Communications, James; Literary/Business Assoc.; Lopopolo, Toni; McKinley, Virginia C.; Marcil, Denise; Marshall, Evan; Merhige-Merdon Marketing/Promo Co. Inc., Greg; Nelson Literary Agency & Lecture Bureau, BK; Northwest Literary Services; Oceanic Press; Olesha Agency, Andrea; Pen & Ink Literary Agency; Rose Agency; Russell-Simenauer Literary Agency Inc.; Sebastian Literary Agency; Singer Media Corporation; Southern Literary Agency; State of the Art Ltd.; Steinberg Literary Agency, Michael; Stern Agency, Gloria; TARC Literary Agency; Visions Press; Watt & Associates, Sandra; Wildstar Associates; Writer's Advocate, The; Zelasky Literary Agency, Tom

Sociology A & R Burke Corp.; Acacia House Publishing Services; Brinke Literary Agency; Castiglia Literary Agency, Julie; Cook Agency, Bruce; Dorese Agency Ltd.; Flannery White and Stone; ForthWrite; Goddard: Book Development, Connie; Hamilton, Andrew; Heacock Literary Agency; Independent Publishing; Jenks, Carolyn; Keyser Literary Agency; Levine Communications, James; Lopopolo, Toni; McKinley, Virginia C.; Merhige-Merdon Marketing/Promo Co. Inc., Greg; Nelson Literary Agency & Lecture Bureau, BK; Pen & Ink Literary Agency; Russell-Simenauer Literary Agency Inc.; Sebastian Literary Agency; Stern Agency, Gloria; Writer's Advocate, The

Sports A & R Burke Corp.; Acacia House Publishing Services; Ace Consultants; Browne Ltd., Pema; Castiglia Literary Agency, Julie; Dorese Agency Ltd.; Eden; Flannery White and Stone; Goddard: Book Development, Connie; Hamilton, Andrew; Heacock Literary Agency; Independent Publishing; Jenks, Carolyn; Kaltman, Larry; Kellock & Assoc. Ltd., J.; Law Offices of Robert L. Fenton PC; Levine Communications, James; McKinley, Virginia C.; Merhige-Merdon Marketing/Promo Co. Inc., Greg; Nelson Literary Agency & Lecture Bureau, BK; Northwest Literary Services; Oceanic Press; Sebastian Literary Agency; Sullivan Associates, Mark; Taylor Literary Agency, Dawson; Watt & Associates, Sandra; Wildstar Associates; Write Designs Literary Agency; Writer's Advocate, The

Translations Eastwind Writers; Eden; Goddard: Book Development, Connie; Hamersfield Agency; M.H. International; Northwest Literary Services; Singer Media Corporation; Write Designs Literary Agency; Writer's Advocate, The

True crime/investigative A & R Burke Corp.; Acacia House Publishing Services; Ace Consultants; Ackerman Literary Services; Ahearn Agency; Alden–Literary Service, Farel T.; Anthony, Joseph; Author Author; Authors' Marketing Services Ltd.; Browne Ltd., Pema; Dorese Agency Ltd.; Eden; Fishbein, Frieda; Gislason Agency; Goddard: Book Development, Connie; Hamilton, Andrew;

Heacock Literary Agency; Independent Publishing; Jenks, Carolyn; Kellock & Assoc. Ltd., J.; Law Offices of Robert L. Fenton PC; Levine Communications, James; Lopopolo, Toni; Marcil, Denise; Marshall, Evan; Merhige-Merdon Marketing/Promo Co. Inc., Greg; Nelson Literary Agency & Lecture Bureau, BK; Northwest Literary Services; Oceanic Press; Pen & Ink Literary Agency; PMA Literary and Film Management, Inc.; Russell-Simenauer Literary Agency Inc.; Sebastian Literary Agency; Singer Media Corporation; Stern Agency, Gloria; TARC Literary Agency; Toomey Associates, Jeanne; Wallace Literary Agency, Bess; Watt & Associates, Sandra; West Coast Literary Associates; Writer's Advocate, The; Writer's Consulting Group; Zelasky Literary Agency, Tom

Women's issues/women's studies A & R Burke Corp.; Acacia House Publishing Services; Ahearn Agency; Author Author; Becker/Aleta M. Daley, Maximilian; Browne Ltd., Pema; Castiglia Literary Agency, Julie; Catalog™, The; Dorese Agency Ltd.; Eden; Fishbein, Frieda; Flannery White and Stone; ForthWrite; Gislason Agency; Goddard: Book Development, Connie; Hamilton, Andrew; Heacock Literary Agency; Hubbs, Yvonne Trudeau; Independent Publishing; Jenks, Carolyn; Kellock & Assoc. Ltd., J.; Kern, Natasha; Keyser Literary Agency; Law Offices of Robert L. Fenton PC; Levine Communications, James; Lopopolo, Toni; McKinley, Virginia C.; Marcil, Denise; Merhige-Merdon Marketing/Promo Co. Inc., Greg; Nelson Literary Agency & Lecture Bureau, BK; Northwest Literary Services; Oceanic Press; Olesha Agency, Andrea; Russell-Simenauer Literary Agency Inc.; Schulman, A Literary Agency, Susan; Sebastian Literary Agency; Singer Media Corporation; State of the Art Ltd.; Stern Agency, Gloria; Visions Press; Watt & Associates, Sandra; West Coast Literary Associates; Wildstar Associates; Writer's Advocate, The; Writer's Consulting Group; Zelasky Literary Agency, Tom

Script agents/Fiction

Action/Adventure Allied Artists; All-Star Talent; Amato, Michael; Berzon, Marian; Bethel Agency; Buchwald, Don; Cameron, Marshall; Chandelyn Literary Agency; Client First—A/K/A Leo P. Haffey Agency; Coast To Coast Talent and Literary; Cyberstorm!; Douroux & Co.; Dykeman Assoc.; Earth Tracks; F.L.A.I.R.; Gardner Agency; Hodges Agency, Carolyn; International Leonards Corp.; Kay, Charlene; Kick Entertainment; Lee, L. Harry; Montgomery-West; Panda Talent; Rogers and Associates, Stephanie; Silver Screen Placements; Sobel Management Associates, Lee; Steele & Associates, Ellen Lively; Swanson Inc., H.N.; Talent Bank Agency, The; Turtle Agency, The; Wain Agency, Erika

Cartoon/comic Allied Artists; All-Star Talent; Bethel Agency; Bulger and Associates, Kelvin C.; Chandelyn Literary Agency; Client First—A/K/A Leo P. Haffey Agency; Earth Tracks; F.L.A.I.R.; International Leonards Corp.; Silver Screen Placements

Confessional Bethel Agency; Panda Talent

Contemporary issues All-Star Talent; Berzon, Marian; Bethel Agency; Bulger and Associates, Kelvin C.; Chandelyn Literary Agency; Client First—A/K/A Leo P. Haffey Agency; Diskant & Assoc.; Dykeman Assoc.; Earth Tracks; Hodges Agency, Carolyn; International Leonards Corp.; Legacies; Merrill, Helen; Rogers and Associates, Stephanie; Scribe Agency; Silver Screen Placements; Talent Bank Agency, The

Detective/police/crime Allied Artists; All-Star Talent; Beal Management, Mary; Bethel Agency; Cameron, Marshall; Client First—A/K/A Leo P. Haffey Agency; Coast To Coast Talent and Literary; Cyberstorm!; Douroux & Co.; Dykeman Assoc.; Earth Tracks; F.L.A.I.R.; Gardner Agency; Hodges Agency, Carolyn; International Leonards Corp.; Kick Entertainment; Lee, L. Harry; Montgomery-West; Palmer, Dorothy; Panda Talent; Silver Screen Placements; Steele & Associates, Ellen Lively; Swanson Inc., H.N.; Talent Bank Agency, The; Turtle Agency, The; Wain Agency, Erika

Erotica Allied Artists; Beal Management, Mary; Coast To Coast Talent and Literary; Earth Tracks; F.L.A.I.R.; Gardner Agency; Lee, L. Harry; Turtle Agency, The

Ethnic Bethel Agency; Chandelyn Literary Agency; Hodges Agency, Carolyn; Legacies; Talent Bank Agency, The

Experimental Gardner Agency; Hodges Agency, Carolyn

Family saga All-Star Talent; Berzon, Marian; Bethel Agency; Buchwald, Don; Bulger And Associates, Kelvin C.; Chandelyn Literary Agency; Client First—A/K/A Leo P. Haffey Agency; Douroux & Co.; F.L.A.I.R.; International Leonards Corp.; Kay, Charlene; Kick Entertainment; Lee, L. Harry; Legacies; Panda Talent; Silver Screen Placements; Steele & Associates, Ellen Lively; Talent Bank Agency, The; Turtle Agency, The; Wain Agency, Erika

Fantasy All-Star Talent; Berzon, Marian; Bethel Agency; Chandelyn Literary Agency; Douroux & Co.; Dykeman Assoc.; F.L.A.I.R.; Gardner Agency; Hodges Agency, Carolyn; International Leonards Corp.; Kick Entertainment; Lee, L. Harry; Silver Screen Placements; Sobel Management

Associates, Lee; Talent Bank Agency, The; Turtle Agency, The; Wain Agency, Erika
Feminist Beal Management, Mary; Bethel Agency; Hodges Agency, Carolyn; Legacies; Sorice Agency, Camille; Talent Bank Agency, The; Wain Agency, Erika
Gay Beal Management, Mary; Bethel Agency; Hodges Agency, Carolyn; Talent Bank Agency, The
Glitz Bethel Agency; Hodges Agency, Carolyn; Steele & Associates, Ellen Lively
Historical Bethel Agency; Bulger and Associates, Kelvin C.; Chandelyn Literary Agency; Client First—A/K/A Leo P. Haffey Agency; Diskant & Assoc.; Douroux & Co.; Hodges Agency, Carolyn; International Leonards Corp.; Lee, L. Harry; Legacies; Silver Screen Placements; Swanson Inc., H.N.; Talent Bank Agency, The; Turtle Agency, The
Humor/satire All-Star Talent; Berzon, Marian; Bethel Agency; Bulger and Associates, Kelvin C.; Cameron, Marshall; Chandelyn Literary Agency; Client First—A/K/A Leo P. Haffey Agency; Coast To Coast Talent and Literary; Cyberstorm!; Douroux & Co.; Earth Tracks; F.L.A.I.R.; Gardner Agency; International Leonards Corp.; Lee, L. Harry; Legacies; Palmer, Dorothy; Panda Talent; Silver Screen Placements; Steele & Associates, Ellen Lively; Swanson Inc., H.N.; Talent Bank Agency, The; Wain Agency, Erika
Juvenile Amato, Michael; Berzon, Marian; Chandelyn Literary Agency; F.L.A.I.R.; Hodges Agency, Carolyn; Panda Talent; Silver Screen Placements; Talent Bank Agency, The; Wain Agency, Erika
Lesbian Beal Management, Mary; Bethel Agency; Hodges Agency, Carolyn
Literary Beal Management, Mary; Bethel Agency; Chandelyn Literary Agency; Coast To Coast Talent and Literary; Hayes & Assoc., Gil; Hodges Agency, Carolyn; Lee, L. Harry; Merrill, Helen; Scribe Agency
Mainstream All-Star Talent; Beal Management, Mary; Berzon, Marian; Bethel Agency; Buchwald, Don; Douroux & Co.; Gardner Agency; Hayes & Assoc., Gil; Hodges Agency, Carolyn; International Leonards Corp.; Lee, L. Harry; Merrill, Helen; Scagnetti Talent & Literary Agency, Jack; Scribe Agency; Silver Screen Placements; Sobel Management Associates, Lee; Steele & Associates, Ellen Lively; Swanson Inc., H.N.; Talent Bank Agency, The; Turtle Agency, The
Mystery/suspense All-Star Talent; Beal Management, Mary; Berzon, Marian; Bethel Agency; Cameron, Marshall; Chandelyn Literary Agency; Client First—A/K/A Leo P. Haffey Agency; Coast To Coast Talent and Literary; Diskant & Assoc.; Douroux & Co.; Dykeman Assoc.; F.L.A.I.R.; Hayes & Assoc., Gil; Hodges Agency, Carolyn; International Leonards Corp.; Kick Entertainment; Lee, L. Harry; Montgomery-West; Palmer, Dorothy; Panda Talent; Scagnetti Talent & Literary Agency, Jack; Silver Screen Placements; Sobel Management Associates, Lee; Sorice Agency, Camille; Steele & Associates, Ellen Lively; Swanson Inc., H.N.; Talent Bank Agency, The; Turtle Agency, The; Wain Agency, Erika
Open to all fiction categories Agency for the Performing Arts; American Play Co.; Circle of Confusion; Dragon Literary; Raintree Agency; Total Acting Experience, A
Picture book Bethel Agency; Chandelyn Literary Agency; Talent Bank Agency, The
Psychic/supernatural Allied Artists; All-Star Talent; Beal Management, Mary; Bethel Agency; Coast To Coast Talent and Literary; F.L.A.I.R.; Gardner Agency; Hodges Agency, Carolyn; Kick Entertainment; Steele & Associates, Ellen Lively; Turtle Agency, The
Regional Bethel Agency; Hayes & Assoc., Gil; Hodges Agency, Carolyn; International Leonards Corp.
Religious/inspiration Berzon, Marian; Bethel Agency; Chandelyn Literary Agency; Dykeman Assoc.; F.L.A.I.R.
Romance Allied Artists; All-Star Talent; Berzon, Marian; Bethel Agency; Buchwald, Don; Chandelyn Literary Agency; Client First—A/K/A Leo P. Haffey Agency; Coast To Coast Talent and Literary; Douroux & Co.; Earth Tracks; Hodges Agency, Carolyn; International Leonards Corp.; Kay, Charlene; Lee, L. Harry; Montgomery-West; Palmer, Dorothy; Rogers and Associates, Stephanie; Turtle Agency, The
Science fiction Allied Artists; All-Star Talent; Beal Management, Mary; Buchwald, Don; Chandelyn Literary Agency; Client First—A/K/A Leo P. Haffey Agency; Douroux & Co.; Dykeman Assoc.; Gardner Agency; Hodges Agency, Carolyn; International Leonards Corp.; Kick Entertainment; Lee, L. Harry; Montgomery-West; Silver Screen Placements; Sobel Management Associates, Lee; Talent Bank Agency, The; Turtle Agency, The; Wain Agency, Erika
Sports Allied Artists; All-Star.Talent; Bethel Agency; Client First—A/K/A Leo P. Haffey Agency; International Leonards Corp.; Lee, L. Harry; Panda Talent; Scagnetti Talent & Literary Agency, Jack; Swanson Inc., H.N.
Thriller/espionage All-Star Talent; Beal Management, Mary; Berzon, Marian; Bethel Agency; Buchwald, Don; Cameron, Marshall; Client First—A/K/A Leo P. Haffey Agency; Coast To Coast Talent and Literary; Douroux & Co.; Dykeman Assoc.; Earth Tracks; F.L.A.I.R.; Gardner Agency; Hodges Agency, Carolyn; International Leonards Corp.; Kay, Charlene; Kick Entertainment; Lee, L. Harry; Montgomery-West; Palmer, Dorothy; Panda Talent; Rogers and Associates, Stephanie; Scagnetti Talent & Literary Agency, Jack; Silver Screen Placements; Sobel Management Associ-

Subject Index: Script agents/Nonfiction 267

ates, Lee; Steele & Associates, Ellen Lively; Swanson Inc., H.N.; Talent Bank Agency, The; Turtle Agency, The; Wain Agency, Erika
Westerns/frontier All-Star Talent; Bethel Agency; Buchwald, Don; Client First Take—A/K/A Haffey Agency; Douroux & Co.; Kick Entertainment; Lee, L. Harry; Talent Bank Agency, The; Turtle Agency, The
Young adult Amato, Michael; Berzon, Marian; Bethel Agency; Chandelyn Literary Agency; Diskant & Assoc.; Earth Tracks; F.L.A.I.R.; Lee, L. Harry; Silver Screen Placements; Turtle Agency, The

Script agents/Nonfiction
Agriculture/horticulture Bethel Agency; Chandelyn Literary Agency; Bethel Agency; Chandelyn Literary Agency; F.L.A.I.R.; Panda Talent; Waing Agency, Erika
Animals Wain Agency, Erika
Anthropology Bethel Agency; Chandelyn Literary Agency; International Leonards Corp.
Art/architecture/design Bethel Agency; Chandelyn Literary Agency
Biography/autobiography Bethel Agency; Buchwald, Don; Chandelyn Literary Agency; Circle of Confusion; Diskant & Assoc.; Dykeman Assoc.; Hayes & Assoc., Gil; International Leonards Corp.; Merrill, Helen; Sobel Management Associates, Lee
Business Bethel Agency; Chandelyn Literary Agency; Circle of Confusion; Dykeman Assoc.; Gardner Agency; International Leonards Corp.
Child guidance/parenting Bethel Agency; Chandelyn Literary Agency; F.L.A.I.R.
Cooking/food/nutrition Amato, Michael; Bethel Agency; Chandelyn Literary Agency; Palmer, Dorothy; Steele & Associates, Ellen Lively
Crafts/hobbies Bethel Agency; Chandelyn Literary Agency
Current Affairs Amato, Michael; Bethel Agency; Buchwald, Don; Bulger and Associates, Kelvin C.; Chandelyn Literary Agency; Circle of Confusion; Diskant & Assoc.; Hayes & Assoc., Gil; International Leonards Corp.; Palmer, Dorothy; Swanson Inc., H.N.
Ethnic/cultural interests Bethel Agency; Bulger and Associates, Kelvin C.; Chandelyn Literary Agency
Gay/Lesbian issues Beal Management, Mary; Bethel Agency; Circle of Confusion
Government/politics/law Allied Artists; Beal Management, Mary; Bethel Agency; Circle of Confusion
Health/medicine Amato, Michael; Bethel Agency; Chandelyn Literary Agency; Circle of Confusion; F.L.A.I.R.; Hayes & Assoc., Gil; Palmer, Dorothy; Raintree Agency; Scagnetti Talent & Literary Agency, Jack
History Bethel Agency; Buchwald, Don; Bulger and Associates, Kelvin C.; Chandelyn Literary Agency; Circle of Confusion; Diskant & Assoc.; International Leonards Corp.; Kohner, Paul; Lee, L. Harry
Interior design/decorating Bethel Agency; Chandelyn Literary Agency
Juvenile nonfiction Bethel Agency; Chandelyn Literary Agency; Circle of Confusion; F.L.A.I.R.
Language/literature/criticism Bethel Agency; Chandelyn Literary Agency
Military/war Bethel Agency; Kick Entertainment; Kohner, Paul; Lee, L. Harry; Panda Talent; Scagnetti Talent & Literary Agency, Jack; Wain Agency, Erika
Money/finance/economics Bethel Agency; Chandelyn Literary Agency; Dykeman Assoc.; F.L.A.I.R.; International Leonards Corp.
Music/dance/theater/film Allied Artists; Bethel Agency; Chandelyn Literary Agency; Coast To Coast Talent and Literary; F.L.A.I.R.; Gardner Agency; International Leonards Corp.; Kohner, Paul
Nature/environment Bethel Agency; Chandelyn Literary Agency; F.L.A.I.R.; Raintree Agency
New Age/metaphysics Coast To Coast Talent and Literary; Gardner Agency; International Leonards Corp.; Steele & Associates, Ellen Lively
Open to all nonfiction categories Agency for the Performing Arts; American Play Co.; Dragon Literary; Total Acting Experience, A
Photography Bethel Agency; Chandelyn Literary Agency
Psychology Beal Management, Mary; Bethel Agency; Chandelyn Literary Agency; F.L.A.I.R.; International Leonards Corp.; Panda Talent; Sorice Agency, Camille
Religious/inspiratio Bethel Agency; Chandelyn Literary Agency; Dykeman Assoc.; F.L.A.I.R.; International Leonards Corp.
Science/technology Bethel Agency; Buchwald, Don; Chandelyn Literary Agency; International Leonards Corp.; Wain Agency, Erika
Self-help/personal improvement Bethel Agency; Chandelyn Literary Agency; Coast To Coast Talent and Literary; F.L.A.I.R.; International Leonards Corp.; Scagnetti Talent & Literary Agency, Jack; Sorice Agency, Camille; Steele & Associates, Ellen Lively

Sociology Bethel Agency; Chandelyn Literary Agency; Raintree Agency
Sports Bethel Agency; Buchwald, Don; Chandelyn Literary Agency; International Leonards Corp.; Panda Talent; Scagnetti Talent & Literary Agency, Jack; Swanson Inc., H.N.
Translations Bethel Agency; Imison Playwrights, Michael
True crime/investigative Beal Management, Mary; Bethel Agency; Circle of Confusion; Coast To Coast Talent and Literary; F.L.A.I.R.; International Leonards Corp.; Kick Entertainment; Kohner, Paul; Palmer, Dorothy; Panda Talent; Scagnetti Talent & Literary Agency, Jack; Sobel Management Associates, Lee; Steele & Associates, Ellen Lively; Wain Agency, Erika
Women's issues/women's studies Amato, Michael; Bethel Agency; Chandelyn Literary Agency; Circle of Confusion; Coast To Coast Talent and Literary; F.L.A.I.R.; Palmer, Dorothy; Raintree Agency; Steele & Associates, Ellen Lively; Wain Agency, Erika

Art Reps
Children's book illustration Artists International; Asciutto Art Reps.; Bancroft & Friends, Carol; Brown, Andrea; Browne Ltd., Pema; Creative Freelancers Management; Dwyer & O'Grady; Elek Assoc., Peter; Gusay, Charlotte; HK Portfolio; Kroll Literary Agency, Edite; Maccoby, Gina; Publishers' Graphics; S.I. Interntional; Urstadt Inc. Writers and Artists Agency, Susan P.; Veloric, Artist Representative, Philip M.

Commercial Art/Photo and Fine Art Reps Geographic Index

All art/photo and fine art reps are listed together in this index by state. Some talents have just one rep to handle all their work, but many talents choose to have more than one rep covering different sections of the country.

Arizona
Asciutto Art Reps., Inc.
Willard Associates, Ltd., Paul

California
April & Wong
Art Source L.A.
Baum & Associates, Cathy
Burlingham/Artist Representation, Tricia
Campbell, Marianne
Collier Represents, Jan
Conrad Represents . . .
CVB Creative Resource
De Moreta Represents, Linda
DW Represents
Epstein/Photographer's Representative, Rhoni
Gardner & Associates, Jean
Gordon/Artist Representative, T.J.
Hall & Associates

Hauser, Another Girl Rep, Barb
Keswick Hamilton
Knable & Associates, Inc., Ellen
L.A. Art Exchange
Lee + Lou Productions Inc.
Lesli Art, Inc.
Lilie Artist's Representative, Jim
Martha Productions, Inc.
Morgan/Artist Representative, Michele
Piscopo, Maria
Rappaport, Jodi
Rosenthal Represents
Salzman, Richard
Scott, Inc., Freda
Sharpe + Associates
Storyboards
T & M Enterprises
Winston West, Ltd.

Worldwide Images
Zaitz Artist Representative

Colorado
Guenzi Agents, Inc., Carol
Sapiro Art Consultants, Joan

Connecticut
Artists International
Bancroft & Friends, Carol
Caton Artist Representative, Chip
Cornell + McCarthy
HK Portfolio
McConnell McNamara & Co.
Palulian, Joanne
Publishers' Graphics
Urstadt Inc. Writers and Artists Agency, Susan P.

Florida
Administrative Arts, Inc.

Tonal Values, Inc.

Georgia
Sullivan & Associates

Illinois
Albrecht and Associates, Anne
Art Emotion Corp.
Artco Incorporated
Donaldson Represents, Karen
Edsey & Sons, Steven
Fiat & Associates, Randi
Galitz Fine Art/Accent Art, Robert
Kuehnel & Associates, Peter
Langley Represents, Sharon
London Contemporary Art
Montagano & Associates
Soldat & Associates

Kansas
Media Gallery/Enterprises

Maryland
Giannini & Talent
Redmond Represents
Shearer Art Source, Nicki
Soodak Represents

Massachusetts
Cadenbach Associates, Marilyn
Goldstein, Gwen Walters
Kurlansky Associates, Sharon
Leighton & Company

Michigan
Albrecht & Jennings Art Enterprises
Neis Group, The
Ridgeway Artists Representative

Minnesota
Freelance Hotline, Inc.
Icebox

Missouri
Bartels Associates, Ceci
Creative Productions, Inc.
Kastaris & Associates

New Hampshire
Dwyer & O'Grady, Inc.

New Jersey
Bruml/Artists Representative, Kathy
Holt & Associates, Inc., Rita

Sonneville Assoc. Inc., Dane
Warner & Associates

New York
American Artists, Rep. Inc.
Anton, Inc., Jerry
Arnold Fine Art, Jack
Artists Associates
Arts Counsel Inc.
Barracca Assoc. Inc., Sal
Beidler Inc., Barbara
Bernstein & Andriulli Inc.
Brindle Inc., Carolyn
Brody, Artists and Photographers Representative, Sam
Browne Ltd., Pema
Bruck and Moss Associates
Carp, Inc., Stan
Chislovsky Design Inc., Carol
Collignon, Daniele
Corporate Art Associates, Ltd.
Creative Freelancers Management, Inc.
Elliott/Oreman Artists' Representatives
Foster Artist Rep., (Pat)
Ginsburg & Associates, Inc., Michael
Godfrey Representing Artists, Dennis
Goldman Agency, David
Gordon Associates Ltd., Barbara
Grien—Representing Artists, Anita
Jedell Productions, Inc.
Keating, Peggy
Kirchoff/Wohlberg, Artists Representation Division
Klimt, Bill and Maurine
Korn Associates Ltd., Elaine
Lamont, Mary
Lavaty & Associates, Frank & Jeff
Levin•Dorr
Lindgren & Smith
Locke Studios, Inc., John
Lott, Peter & George
McKay Photography, Colleen
Mattelson Associates Ltd.
Mendola Artists
Miller Represents, Susan
Morgan Associates, Vicki
Newborn Group, The
Oz New York Inc.
Page, Jackie
Penny & Stermer Group, The
Pinkstaff Representing Photographers, Marsha
Rapp, Inc., Gerald & Cullen

Reid, Pamela
Represented by Ken Mann Inc.
Retna Ltd.
Rosenberg, Arlene
Ruderman, Linda
Sacramone, Dario
Schochat, Kevin R.
Tribelli Designs, Ltd., Joseph
Two Steps Up, Inc.
Warshaw Blumenthal, Inc.
Weber Group, The
Weissberg, Elyse
Zaccaro Productions Inc., Jim

North Carolina
Reilly: Reps, Kerry

Ohio
Berendsen & Associates, Inc.
Coleman Presents Inc., Woody
Corcoran Fine Arts Limited, Inc.
Hull Associates, Scott

Oregon
Prapas/Artist Representative, Christine

Pennsylvania
Francisco Communications, Inc.
Goodman Inc., Tom
Kerr, Ralph
Knecht—Artist Representative, Cliff
Pennamenities
Veloric, Artist Representative, Philip M.

Rhode Island
Artist Development Group

Texas
Brooke & Company
Lee Inc., Nelda
Sands & Associates, Trudy
Seiffer & Associates
Simpatico Art & Stone
Washington-Artists' Representatives

Washington
Dodge and Associates, Sharon
Hackett/Artist Representative, Pat

Wisconsin
Dodge Creative Services Inc.

Agents and Reps Index

This index of agent and rep names was created to help you locate agents or reps even when you do not know for which agency they work. You may have read or heard about a particular rep, but do not know how to contact him. Agent and rep names are listed with their agencies' names. Check the Listing Index for the page number of the agency.

A

Abend, Sheldon (American Play Co.)
Abercrombie, Lisa (Lyle Steele & Co., Ltd.)
Ackerman, Sharon (Ackerman Literary Services)
Adams, Charlene (Client First-A/K/A Leo P. Haffey Agency)
Adams, Deborah (The Jeff Herman Agency Inc.)
Adler, Jr., Bill (Adler & Robin Books, Inc.)
Agarwal, Rajeev K. (Circle of Confusion)
Ahearn, Pamela G. (The Ahearn Agency, Inc.)
Ajlouny, Joe (The Joseph S. Ajlouny Agency)
Albrecht, Ann (Ann Albrecht and Associates)
Albrecht, Tom (Albrecht & Jennings Art Enterprises)
Alden, Farel T. (Farel T. Alden-Literary Service)
Allred, Robert (All-Star Talent Agency)
Amador, Mark (The Marian Berzon Agency)
Amato, Mary Ann (Legacies)
Amparan, Joann (Wecksler-Incomco)
Amsterdam, Marcia (Marcia Amsterdam Agency)
Anderson, Christine (Yvonne Trudeau Hubbs Agency)
Anderson, Jeff (M.H. International Literary Agency)
Andrews, Bart (Bart Andrews & Associates Inc.)
Andriulli, Tony (Bernstein & Andriulli Inc.)
Anthony, Joseph (Joseph Anthony Agency)
Antle, Bernadette (Forthwrite Literary Agency)
Anton, Jerry (Jerry Anton, Inc.)
Aragi, Nicole (Watkins Loomis Agency, Inc.)
Arnold, Jack (Jack Arnold Fine Art)
Asciutto, Mary Anne (Asciutto Art Reps.,Inc.)
Ashby, Ed (Ashby Literary Agency)

B

Bach, Julian (IMG-Julian Bach Literary Agency)
Baldi, Malaga (Malaga Baldi Literary Agency)
Balkin, R. (Balkin Agency, Inc.)
Bancroft, Carol (Carol Bancroft & Friends)
Bannister, Chris (The Marian Berzon Agency)
Barmeier, Jim (Writer's Consulting Group)
Barr, Hollister (L. Harry Lee Literary Agency)
Barr, Mary (Sierra Literary Agency)
Barracca, Sal (Sal Barracca Assoc. Inc.)
Barrett, Loretta (Loretta Barrett Books Inc.)
Barrick, Gail (H.N. Swanson Inc.)
Bartczak, Sue (Gene Bartczak Associates Inc.)
Bartels, Ceci (Ceci Bartels Associates)
Barvin, Jude (The Brinke Literary Agency)
Baum, Cathy (Cathy Baum & Associates)
Beavers, David (The Marian Berzon Agency)
Beghin, Caroline (Martha Productions, Inc.)
Behar, Josh (Josh Behar Literary Agency)
Beidler, Barbara (Barbara Beidler Inc.)
Bellacicco, Dan A. (A Total Acting Experience)
Bendell, Norm (David Goldman Agency)
Bendis, Keith (David Goldman Agency)
Benson, John (BK Nelson Literary Agency & Lecture Bureau)
Berendsen, Bob (Berendsen & Associates, Inc.)
Berkower, Amy (Writers House)
Berman, Lois (Lois Berman, Writer's Representative)
Bernard, Alec (Puddingtonstone Literary Agency)
Bernstein, Howard (Bernstein & Andriulli Inc.)
Bernstein, Meredith (Meredith Bernstein Literary Agency)
Bernstein, Ron (The Gersh Agency)
Bernstein, Sam (Bernstein & Andriulli Inc.)
Berry, Henry (Independent Publishing Agency)
Biggis, Charis (L. Harry Lee Literary Agency)
Birenbaum, Molly (Bernstein & Andriulli Inc.)
Bishop, David (Korman & Company)
Black, Fran (Arts Counsel Inc.)
Blackett, Donna (Andrea Brown Literary Agency, Inc.)
Blake, Laura J. (Curtis Brown Ltd.)
Blanton, Sandra (Peter Lampack Agency, Inc.)
Boals, Judy (Lois Berman, Writer's Representative)
Boates, Reid (Reid Boates Literary Agency)
Bobke, C.J. (Lee Allan Agency)
Bock, Jill (The Tantleff Office)
Boda (Oz New York Inc.)
Bohannon, Kendall (Flannery, White and Stone, The Writer's Advocate)
Bohn, Beth (The Turtle Agency)
Bonnen, Ed (Ridgeway Artists Representative)
Boorn, Joyce (Florence Feiler Literary Agency)
Boylan, B.R. (Otitis Media)

Agents and Reps Index

Boylan, Greg (Otitis Media)
Brandenburgh, Don (Brandenburgh & Associates Literary Agency)
Brandt, Carl (Brandt & Brandt Literary Agents Inc.)
Brandt, Joan (The Joan Brandt Agency)
Brenna, Vito (L. Harry Lee Literary Agency)
Brenneman, Cindy (CVB Creative Resource)
Breoge, Jane (L. Harry Lee Literary Agency)
Brindle, Carolyn (Carolyn Brindle Inc.)
Brodie, Michael (Artists International)
Brody, Sam (Sam Brody, Artists & Photographers Representative)
Brophy, Philippa (Sterling Lord Literistic, Inc.)
Broussard, Michael (Dupree/Miller and Associates Inc. Literary)
Brown, Allen Williams (Visions Press)
Brown, Andrea (Andrea Brown Literary Agency, Inc.)
Brown, Carrie (Visions Press)
Brown, Christopher (Visions Press)
Brown, Deborah (Peter Lampack Agency, Inc.)
Brown, Elizabeth (Visions Press)
Brown, Marie (Marie Brown Associates Inc.)
Brown, William C. (QCorp Literary Agency)
Brown, William H. (Joan Follendore Literary Agency)
Browne, Jane Jordan (Multimedia Product Development, Inc.)
Browne, Pema (Pema Browne Ltd.)
Browne, Perry (Pema Browne Ltd.)
Browne, Tiffany (Tricia Burlingham/Artist Representation)
Bruck, Nancy (Bruck and Moss Associates)
Bruml, Kathy (Kathy Bruml Artists Representative)
Buck, Howard (Howard Buck Agency)
Bulger, Kelvin C. (Kevin C. Bulger and Associates)
Buller, Norman (Worldwide Images)
Burke, Anna Mae (A & R Burke Corporation)
Burke, Janet (Alison J. Picard Literary Agent)
Burke, Robert (A & R Burke Corporation)
Burlingham, Tricia (Tricia Burlingham/Artist Representation)

C

Cadenbach, Marilyn (Marilyn Cadenbach Associates)
Callirgos, Cami (L. Harry Lee Literary Agency)
Campbell, Marianne (Marianne Campbell)
Campbell, Rita (Artist Development Group)
Campise, Jim (Authors' Literary Agency)
Capshaw, Genero (The Literary Bridge)
Capshaw, Rhobie (The Literary Bridge)
Caravatt, Paul (The Gary-Paul Agency)
Carbone, Peter (Oceanic Press, Singer Media Corporation)
Carp, Stan (Stan Carp, Inc.)
Carson, Heidi (Frieda Fishbein)
Carvainis, Maria (Maria Carvainis Agency, Inc.)
Casselman, Martha (Martha Casselman Literary Agent)
Castiglia, Julie (Julie Castiglia Literary Agency)
Caton, Chip (Chip Caton Artist Representative)
Catz, Robert S. (New Writers Literary Project)
Cavanaugh, Elizabeth (Meredith Bernstein Literary Agency)
Cavanaugh, Teresa (Jean V. Naggar Literary Agency)
Cavello, James (Corporate Art Associates, Ltd.)
Ceriale, Jodi (Ackerman Literary Services)
Chalker, Susan R. (New Writers Literary Project)
Chambers, Jacqulin (F.L.A.I.R.)
Chambers, Lewis R. (Bethel Agency)
Chapman, Jennifer (Northwest Literary Services)
Chislovsky, Carol (Carol Chislovsky)
Choron, Sandra (March Tenth, Inc.)
Christopherson, Howard (Icebox)

Chriswell, Barbara (Seiffer & Associates)
Chu, Lynn (Writers' Representatives, Inc.)
Ciske, Fran (Francine Ciske Literary Agency)
Clark, Sue (SJ Clark Literary Agency)
Clark, William (Loretta Barrett Books Inc.)
Clausen, Connie (Connie Clausen Associates)
Cleaver, Diane (Sanford J. Greenburger Associates)
Clough, Lynn (Rose Agency)
Coffey, Nancy (Jay Garon-Brooke Assoc. Inc.)
Cohen, Amy (Two Steps Up, Inc.)
Cohen, Eugenia (Puddingtonstone Literary Agency)
Cohen, Hy (Hy Cohen Literary Agency Ltd)
Cohen, Roberta (Richard Curtis Associates, Inc.)
Cohen, Ruth (Ruth Cohen, Inc. Literary Agency)
Cohen, Susan Lee (Riverside Literary Agency)
Cohen, Susan (Writers House)
Colas, Maryanne C. (Cantrell-Colas Inc., Literary Agency)
Colby, Pat (Colby: Literary Agency)
Colby, Richard (Colby: Literary Agency)
Coleman, Patricia (Southern Literary Agency)
Coleman, Woody (Woody Coleman Presents Inc.)
Collier, Jan (Jan Collier Represents)
Collier, Oscar (Collier Associates)
Collignon, Daniele (Daniele Collignon)
Collins, N. Rochelle (The Chandelyn Literary Agency)
Congdon, Don (Don Congdon Associates Inc.)
Congdon, Michael (Don Congdon Associates Inc.)
Conrad, James (Conrad Represents . . .)
Conway, Christopher (The Gary-Paul Agency)
Coover, Doe (The Doe Coover Agency)
Corcoran, James (Corcoran Fine Arts Limited, Inc.)
Cornell, Merial (Cornell & McCarthy)
Corona, Ana Maria (Frontier

Talents)
Craver, William (Writers & Artists Agency)
Crown, Bonnie (Bonnie R. Crown International Literature and Arts Agency)
Cugno, Robert (Media Gallery/Enterprises)
Cullen-DuPont, Kathryn (New England Publishing Associates, Inc.)
Currier, Aleita S. (State of the Art Ltd.)
Curtis, Jane (The Writer's Advocate)
Curtis, Richard (Richard Curtis Associates, Inc.)
Custer, Guy Robin (Lyceum Creative Properties, Inc.)

D

Daley, Aleta M. (Maximilian Becker/Aleta M. Daley)
Dalton, Pat (Diamond Literary Agency, Inc.)
Darhansoff, Liz (Darhansoff & Verrill Literary Agents)
Davie, Elaine (Elaine Davie Literary Agency)
Davis, Brooke (Brooke & Company)
de la Haba, Lois (The Lois de la Haba Agency Inc.)
de Moreta, Linda (Linda de Moreta Represents)
De Rogatis, Joseph (International Publisher Associates Inc.)
de Spoelberch, Jacques (J de S Associates Inc.)
Dearnaley, Carol Ann (The Jonathan Dolger Agency)
Deddens, Christie (Hall & Associates)
Deitz, Mason (New Writing Agency)
Diamant, Anita (Anita Diamant, The Writer's Workshop, Inc.)a
Diehl, Linda (Fogelman Literary Agency)
Dijkstra, Sandra (Sandra Dijkstra Literary Agency)
DiLeonardo, Ingrid (Otitis Media)
Diskant, George (Diskant & Associates)
Dixon, Esq., Sherrie R. (Esquire Literary Productions)
Dodge, Tim (Dodge Creative Services Inc.)
Dolger, Jonathan (The Jonathan Dolger Agency)
Donaldson, Karen (Karen Donaldson Represents)
Donlan, Thomas C. (Thomas C. Donlan)
Donnelly, Dave (BK Nelson Literary Agency & Lecture Bureau)
Doran, Michael (Southern Literary Agency)
Doran, Steve (Douroux & Co.)
Dorese, Alyss Barlow (Dorese Agency Ltd.)
Dorr, Chuck (Levin • Dorr)
Douroux, Michael E. (Douroux & Co.)
Doyen, B.J. (Doyen Literary Services, Inc.)
Dubuisson, Anne (Ellen Levine Literary Agency, Inc.)
Ducas, R. (Robert Ducas)
Ducat, J.P.R. (The Hamersfield Agency)
Dunham, Jennie (Mildred Marmur Associates Ltd.)
Dunow, Henry (Harold Ober Associates)
Dwiley, David (DW Represents)
Dwyer, Jeffrey (Dwyer & O'Grady, Inc.)
Dykeman, Alice (Dykeman Associates Inc.)

E

Eagle, Theodora (John L. Hochmann Books)
Eckstut, Arielle (James Levine Communications)
Eden, Karen (Eden Literary Agency)
Edmunds, Jeannine (Curtis Brown Ltd.)
Edsey, Steve (Steven Edsey & Sons)
Edwards, Libby (Bernstein & Andriulli Inc.)
Ehlers, Jennifer (Martha Productions, Inc.)
Eisenberg, Vicki (Vicki Eisenberg Literary Agency)
Ellenberg, Ethan (Ethan Ellenberg Literary Agency)
Elliott, Shannon (Elliott/Oreman Artists' Representatives)
Ellman, Francine (Art Source L.A.)
Elmo, Ann (Ann Elmo Agency Inc.)
Elwell, Jake (Wieser & Wieser, Inc.)
Emmons, Don (Northeast Literary Agency)
Engel, Anne (Jean V. Naggar Literary Agency)
Epstein, Rhoni (Rhoni Epstein/Photographers Representative)
Erickson, Joanne (Lee Allan Agency)
Erlacher, Bill (Artists Associates)
Esersky, Gareth (Carol Mann Agency)
Eth, Felicia (Felicia Eth Literary Representation)
Ettinger, Andrew (Los Angeles Literary Associates)
Evereaux, Anastassia (L. Harry Lee Literary Agency)

F

Fannin, Robert (Scribe Agency)
Fant, Billie Blake (Simpatico Art & Stone)
Farber, Ann (Farber Literary Agency, Inc.)
Faria, Judith (L. Harry Lee Literary Agency)
Fauchen, Mari (Oz New York Inc.)
Feiler, Florence (Florence Feiler Literary Agency)
Feldman, Leigh (Darhansoff & Verrill Literary Agents)
Fenton, Julia (Law Offices of Robert L. Fenton PC)
Fenton, P.C., Robert L. (Law Offices of Robert L. Fenton PC)
Fiat, Randi (Randi Fiat & Associates)
Ficco, C.J. (State of the Art Ltd.)
Fidel, Loretta (The Weingel-Fidel Agency)
Field, Genevieve (Connie Clausen Associates)
Finch, Diana (Ellen Levine Literary Agency, Inc.)
Fishbein, Janice (Frieda Fishbein)
Fisher, Steven (H.N. Swanson Inc.)
FitzGerald, Robert (Flannery, White and Stone)
Flaherty, John (Joyce A. Flaherty, Literary Agent)
Flaherty, Joyce (Joyce A. Flaherty, Literary Agent)
Fleenor, Harry (State of the Art Ltd.)
Fleming, Peter (Peter Fleming Agency)
Fogelman, Evan (Fogelman Literary Agency)
Foiles, S. James (Appleseeds Management)

Agents and Reps Index 273

Follandore, Joan (Joan Follandore Literary Agency)
Ford, Elizabeth (Kirchoff/Wohlberg, Artists Representation Division)
Fortunato, Lena (Joseph Anthony Agency)
Foss, Gwen (The Joseph S. Ajlouny Agency)
Foster, Pat ((Pat) Foster Artist Rep.)
Fournier, Ri (Sandra Dijkstra Literary Agency)
Francisco, Carol (Francisco Communications, Inc.)
Free, Jean (Jay Garon-Brooke Assoc. Inc.)
Freed, Theresa (Pen & Ink Literary Agency)
Freedman, Robert A. (Robert A. Freedman Dramatic Agency, Inc.)
Freymann, Sarah Jane (Stepping Stone)
Friedman, Sharon (John Hawkins & Associates, Inc.)
Friedrich, Molly (Aaron M. Priest Literary Agency)
Frisk, Mark (Howard Buck Agency)
Fruchter, Lev (David Black Literary Agency)
Fuchs, Wendy (Freda Scott, Inc.)
Fuhrman, Candice (Candice Fuhrman Literary Agency)

G

Galinson, Laura (Sandra Dijkstra Literary Agency)
Galitz, Robert (Robert Galitz Fine Art/Accent Art)
Gallagher, Coleen (Allied Artists)
Gardner, Anthony (The Tantleff Office)
Gardner, Jean (Jean Gardner & Associates)
Garon, Jay (Jay Garon-Brooke Assoc. Inc.)
Gartenberg, Max (Max Gartenberg, Literary Agent)
Gaylor, Mary Lee (L. Harry Lee Literary Agency)
Geddes, Ann (Geddes Agency)
Geiger, Ellen (Ellen Geiger Literary Agency)
Gelfman, Samuel W. (BDP & Associates Talent Agency)
Gelles-Cole, Sandi (Gelles-Cole Literary Enterprises)
Gerwin, Karen (Literary and Creative Artists Agency)
Giannini, Judi (Giannini & Talent)
Gilbert, Monica D. (Mary Jack Wald Associates, Inc.)
Gill, Stephen (Stephen Gill)
Gillen, Susan A. (Administrative Arts, Inc.)
Gillies, Paige C. (Publishers' Graphics)
Ginsberg, Peter L. (Curtis Brown Ltd.)
Ginsberg, Susan (Writers House)
Ginsburg, Michael (Ginsburg & Associates, Inc.)
Girand, Sally Wofford (Elaine Markson Literary Agency)
Gislason, Barbara J. (The Gislason Agency)
Gittenstein, Judy (Meredith Bernstein Literary Agency)
Gladden, Carolan (Gladden Unlimited)
Gladstone, Bill (Waterside Productions, Inc.)
Glasser, Carla (The Betsy Nolan Literary Agency)
Goddard, Connie (The Goddard Group: Book Development)
Godfrey, Dennis (Dennis Godfrey Representing Artists)
Golden, Winifred (Margret McBride Literary Agency)
Goldfarb, Ronald (Ronald Goldfarb & Associates)
Goldman, David (David Goldman Agency)
Goodman, Arnold (Goodman Associates)
Goodman, Irene (Irene Goodman Literary Agency)
Goodman, Tom (Tom Goodman Inc.)
Goodwin, Daniel (Peter Elek Associates)
Goon, Helen (Bernstein & Andriulli Inc.)
Gordon, Barbara (Barbara Gordon Associates Ltd.)
Gordon, Charlotte (Charlotte Gordon Agency)
Gordon, Tami (T.J. Gordon/Artist Representative)
Gore, Martha R. (The Authors and Artists Resource Center/TARC Literary Agency)
Grace, Audrey (Panda Talent)
Graham, Earl (Graham Agency)
Gray, Jim R. (Jeanne Toomey Associates)
Graybill, Nina (Ronald Goldfarb & Associates)
Greco, Gerardo (Peter Elek Associates)
Gregory, Maia (Maia Gregory Associates)
Grien, Anita (Anita Grien-Representing Artists)
Griffith, Valerie (Levant & Wales, Literary Agency, Inc.)
Grimes, Lew (Lew Grimes Literary Agency)
Gross, Shelley (Literary/Business Associates)
Grossman, Elizabeth (Sterling Lord Literistic, Inc.)
Guenzi, Carol (Carol Guenzi Agents, Inc.)
Gummery, Nancy (Montgomery-West Literary Agency)
Gusay, Charlotte (The Charlotte Gusay Literary Agency)

H

Haberman, Craig (Bernstein & Andriulli Inc.)
Hackett, Pat (Pat Hackett/Artist Representative)
Haffey, Jr., Leo P. (Client First-A/K/A Leo P. Haffey Agency)
Hall, Marni (Hall & Associates)
Hamilburg, Michael (The Mitchell J. Hamilburg Agency)
Hamilton, Andrew (Andrew Hamilton's Literary Agency)
Hamilton, Maggie (Keswick Hamilton)
Hamlin, Faith (Sanford J. Greenburger Associates)
Han, Katherine (Singer Media Corporation)
Hanna, Frances (Acacia House Publishing Services Ltd.)
Harbison, Lawrence (Samuel French, Inc.)
Harding, Alexandra (Georges Borchardt Inc.)
Harlor, Sally (Oz New York Inc.)
Harper, Laurie (Sebastian Literary Agency)
Harriet, Ph.D., Sydney H. (Agents Inc. for Medical and Mental Health Professionals)
Harrington, Dale (Northeast Literary Agency)
Harris, Brenda B. (Administrative Arts, Inc.)

Harris, Hannibal (Otitis Media)
Harris, Joy (The Robert Lantz-Joy Harris Literary Agency Inc.)
Hartley, Glen (Writers' Representatives, Inc.)
Hartman, Kris (Cathy Baum & Associates)
Harvey, Susan (Doyen Literary Services, Inc.)
Hauser, Barb (Barb Hauser, Another Girl Rep)
Hawkins, John (John Hawkins & Associates, Inc.)
Hawkridge, Janice (Singer Media Corporation)
Hayes, Gil (Gil Hayes & Assoc.)
Hayes, Linda (Columbia Literary Associates, Inc.)
Haynes, Elizabeth (Elizabeth Haynes, Limited)
Heacock, Jim (Heacock Literary Agency, Inc.)
Heacock, Rosalie (Heacock Literary Agency, Inc.)
Hedleston, Colleen (Sharpe + Associates)
Heifetz, Merrillee (Writers House)
Henshaw, Richard (Richard Curtis Associates, Inc.)
Herman, Jeffrey H. (The Jeff Herman Agency Inc.)
Herner, Susan (Susan Herner Rights Agency)
Hill, Chris (Lee Allan Agency)
Hiltebrand, Cyril (Lucianne S. Goldberg Literary Agents, Inc.)
Hilton, Alice (Alice Hilton Literary Agency)
Hochman, Gail (Brandt & Brandt Literary Agents Inc.)
Hochmann, John L. (John L. Hochmann Books)
Hodges, Carolyn (Carolyn Hodges Agency)
Hoffman, Berenice (Berenice Hoffman Literary Agency)
Hoffman, Larry (Authors' Marketing Services Ltd.)
Hoffstein, Michael (James Warren Literary Agency)
Hogenson, Barbara (Lucy Kroll Agency)
Holt, Rita (Rita Holt & Associates, Inc.)
Holtje, Bert (James Peter Associates, Inc.)
Holub, William (Holub & Associates)

Hoskins, Christine (Ackerman Literary Services)
Hotchkiss, Jody (Sterling Lord Literistic, Inc.)
Howard, Marilyn (Creative Freelancers Management, Inc.)
Howard, Rita (New Writing Agency)
Howell, Mary (Joan Follendore Literary Agency)
Howle, Vanessa (Coast to Coast Talent and Literary)
Hubbs, Thomas D. (Yvonne Trudeau Hubbs Agency)
Hubbs, Yvonne (Yvonne Trudeau Hubbs Agency)
Hudson, Scott (Writers & Artists Agency)
Hull, David Stewart (Hull House Literary Agency)
Hull, Scott (Scott Hull Associates)
Hyoun Soo Yun (Roslyn Targ Literary Agency, Inc.)

I
Imison, Michael (Michael Imison Playwrights Ltd.)

J
Jacobs, Elaine (Westchester Literary Agency, Inc.)
Jacobson, Emilie (Curtis Brown Ltd.)
James, Colin (L. Harry Lee Literary Agency)
Jasso, Caspar (Lyceum Creative Properties, Inc.)
Jedell, Joan (Jedell Productions, Inc.)
Jeffers, Medved (Westchester Literary Agency, Inc.)
Jenks, Carolyn (Carolyn Jenks Agency)
Jennings, Karen (Albrecht & Jennings Art Enterprises)
Jensen, Kathryn (Columbia Literary Associates, Inc.)
Jill, Jodi (Eden Literary Agency)
Johnson, Doris (Helen McGrath)
Jones, Lloyd (Lloyd Jones Literary Agency)
Jordan, Lawrence (Lawrence Jordan Literary Agency)
Jordan, Lee F. (Chadd-Stevens Literary Agency)
Jorgensen, Matt (Wildstar Associates)

K
Kalin, Jennifer (Joan Sapiro Art Consultants)
Kaltman, Larry (Larry Kaltman Literary Agency)
Kane, Jay (The Tantleff Office)
Kasak, Harriet (HK Portfolio)
Kaufman, Joshua (Ronald Goldfarb & Associates)
Keating, Peggy (Peggy Keating)
Keliher, Brian (Comedy Ink)
Kellock, Alan C. (The Kellock Company Inc.)
Kellock, Joanne (J. Kellock & Associates Ltd.)
Kelly, Martha (M.H. International Literary Agency)
Kepler, Jim (Lyle Steele & Co., Ltd.)
Kern, Natasha (Natasha Kern Literary Agency)
Kerr, Ralph (Ralph Kerr)
Ketay, Joyce (The Joyce Ketay Agency)
Ketz, Louise B. (Louise B. Ketz Agency)
Keyser, Grace R. (Keyser Literary Agency)
Keyser, John O. (Keyser Literary Agency)
Kidde, Katharine (Kidde, Hoyt & Picard)
Killeen, Frank (L. Harry Lee Literary Agency)
Klausner, Bertha (Bertha Klausner International Literary Agency, Inc.)
Klein, Cindy (Georges Borchardt Inc.)
Klein, Sam (Kick Entertainment)
Klimt, Bill (Bill and Maurine Klimt)
Klimt, Maurine (Bill and Maurine Klimt)
Klinger, Harvey (Harvey Klinger, Inc.)
Knable, Ellen (Ellen Knable & Associates, Inc.)
Knappman, Edward W. (New England Publishing Associates, Inc.)
Knappman, Elizabeth Frost (New England Publishing Associates, Inc.)
Knecht, Cliff (Cliff Knecht-Artist Representative)
Knepper, John (Gerald & Cullen Rapp, Inc.)
Knickerbocker, Andrea (Lee Allan Agency)
Knowlton, Perry (Curtis Brown Ltd.)
Knowlton, Timothy (Curtis Brown Ltd.)
Knowlton, Virginia (Curtis

Agents and Reps Index

Brown Ltd.)
Korman, Alison (Korman & Company)
Korn, Elaine (Elaine Korn Associates, Ltd.)
Kouts, Barbara (Barbara S. Kouts, Literary Agent)
Koyama, Tatsue (Ashby Literary Agency)
Kramer, Sidney B. (Mews Books Ltd.)
Krichevsky, Stuart (Sterling Lord Literistic, Inc.)
Krinsky, David (Earth Tracks Agency)
Kriton, George (Cinema Talent International)
Kroll, Edite (Edite Kroll Literary Agency)
Kuehnel, Peter (Peter Kuehnel & Associates)
Kuffel, Frances (Jean V. Naggar Literary Agency)
Kurlansky, Susan (Susan Kurlansky Associates)
Kurz, Norman (Lowenstein Associates, Inc.)

L

L'Angelle, James (Cyberstorm!)
Lamotte, Michael (Marianne Campbell)
Lampack, Peter (Peter Lampack Agency, Inc.)
Lande, Trish (IMG-Julian Bach Literary Agency)
Lange, Heidi (Sanford J. Greenburger Associates)
Langley, Sharon (Sharon Langley Represents!)
Larsen, Michael (Michael Larsen/Elizabeth Pomada Literary Agents)
Laughren, Brent (Northwest Literary Services)
Lavaty, Frank (Frank & Jeff Lavaty & Associates)
Lavaty, Jeff (Frank & Jeff Lavaty & Associates)
Lebowitz, Fran (Writers House)
Lee, Bill (The Talent Bank Agency)
Lee, Helen J. (Oceanic Press Service, Singer Media Corporation)
Lee, Kristy (Singer Media Corporation)
Lee, L. Harry (L. Harry Lee Literary Agency)
Lee, Lettie (Ann Elmo Agency Inc.)
Lee, Nelda (Nelda Lee Inc.)

Lee, Paul (Eastwind Writers)
Lehr, Donald (The Betsy Nolan Literary Agency)
Leonards, David (International Leonards Corp.)
Leone, Ralph (Wildstar Associates)
Lerman, Marvin (Artist Development Group)
Lescher, Robert (Lescher & Lescher Ltd.)
Lescher, Susan (Lescher & Lescher Ltd.)
Levant, Dan (Levant & Wales, Literary Agency, Inc.)
Levin, Bruce (Levin • Dorr)
Levin, William (Silver Screen Placements)
Levine, Ellen (Ellen Levine Literary Agency, Inc.)
Levine, James A. (James Levine Communications)
Levine, Victor A. (Northeast Literary Agency)
Lilie, Jim (Jim Lilie Artist's Representative)
Lincoln, Jerome A. (Ray Lincoln Literary Agency)
Lincoln, Mrs. Ray (Ray Lincoln Literary Agency)
Linder, Bertram L. (Educational Design Services, Inc.)
Lipkind, Wendy (Wendy Lipkind Agency)
Liss, Laurie (Harvey Klinger, Inc.)
Lloyd, Lem (Mary Jack Wald Associates, Inc.)
Lombroso, Dorit (Korman & Company)
Lopez, Lourdes (Helen Merrill Ltd.)
Lopopolo, Toni (Toni Lopopolo Literary Agency)
Lord, Sterling (Sterling Lord Literistic, Inc.)
Lott, George (Peter & George Lott)
Lott, Peter (Peter & George Lott)
Love, Nancy (Nancy Love Literary Agency)
Lowenstein, Barbara (Barbara Lowenstein Associates, Inc.)
Lucas, Ling (Nine Muses and Apollo)
Lundgren, Curtis H.C. (The Curtis Bruce Agency)
Luttinger, Selma (Robert A. Freedman Dramatic Agency, Inc.)
Lynch, Richard (New Writing Agency)

M

Maass, Donald (Donald Maass Literary Agency)
McAusland, Dennis (Frontier Talents)
McCarthy, Cheryl (Greg Merhige-Merdon Marketing/Promo Co. Inc.)
McCleary, Carol (Harvey Klinger, Inc.)
McClendon, Carole (Waterside Productions, Inc.)
McCluskey, Neil G. (Westchester Literary Agency, Inc.)
Maccoby, Gina (Gina Maccoby Literary Agency)
McDonough, Richard P. (Richard P. McDonough, Literary Agent)
McGrath, Helen (Helen McGrath)
McKay, Colleen (Colleen McKay Photography)
McKay, Meg (Executive Excellence)
McKerrow, Chris (Curtis Brown Ltd.)
Mackey, Elizabeth (The Robbins Office, Inc.)
McKinley, Catherine E. (Marie Brown Associates Inc.)
McKinley, Virginia C. (Virginia C. McKinley, Literary Agency)
McKnight, Linda (MGA Agency Inc.)
McMahon, Eileen (John Locke Studios, Inc.)
McNair, Sarah (Michael Imison Playwrights Ltd.)
McNamara, Paula B. (McConnell McNamara & Co.)
Madsen, Robert (Robert Madsen Agency)
Maley, Margot (Waterside Productions, Inc.)
Mann, Carol (Carol Mann Agency)
Mann, Ken (Represented by Ken Mann Inc.)
Manrique, Lory (PMA Literary and Film Management, Inc.)
Marcil, Denise (The Denise Marcil Literary Agency)
Markowitz, Barbara (Barbara Markowitz Literary Agency)
Markson, Elaine (Elaine Markson Literary Agency)
Marlowe, Marilyn (Curtis Brown Ltd.)
Marmur, Mildred (Mildred Marmur Associates Ltd.)

Marques, Tony (T & M Enterprises)
Marsh, Lee (Retna Ltd.)
Marshall, Evan (The Evan Marshall Agency)
Martell, Alice Fried (The Martell Agency)
Matson, Peter (Sterling Lord Literistic, Inc.)
Mattelson, Judy (Mattelson Associates Ltd.)
Matthias, Lee A. (Lee Allan Agency)
Mattis, Lawrence (Circle of Confusion)
Maynard, Gary (The Gary Paul Agency)
Mazmamian, Joan (Helen Rees Literary Agency)
Meade, Sam (New Writing Agency)
Melillo, Maria (The Writer's Advocate)
Mendola, Tim (Mendola Artists)
Merhige, Greg (Greg Merhige-Merdon Marketing/Promo Co. Inc.)
Merrill, Helen (Helen Merrill Ltd.)
Meth, David L. (Writers' Productions)
Meyst, Charles G. (The Gardner Agency)
Michael, Douglas (Frieda Fishbein)
Milburn, Patrick (Joan Follendore Literary Agency)
Miller, Deborah A. (Media Gallery/Enterprises)
Miller, Jan (Dupree/Miller and Associates Inc. Literary)
Miller, Judy (Bernstein & Andriulli Inc.)
Miller, Kristin (Don Buchwald Agency)
Miller, Peter (PMA Literary and Film Management, Inc.)
Miller, Roberta D. (Roberta D. Miller Associates)
Miller, Stuart M. (Agency for the Performing Arts)
Miller, Susan (Susan Miller Represents)
Miller, T. Patrick (The Chandelyn Literary Agency)
Minogue, Bryan (The Martell Agency)
Mohyde, Colleen (The Doe Coover Agency)
Monaco, Richard (Wildstar Associates)
Montagano, David (Montagano & Associates)
Moore, Claudette (Moore Literary Agency)
Moran, Maureen (Donald MacCampbell Inc.)
Morel, Madeleine (2M Communications Ltd.)
Morgan, David H. (David H. Morgan Literary Agency)
Morgan, Michele (Michele Morgan/Artist Representative)
Morgan, Vicki (Vicki Morgan Associates)
Morgart, Erin Jones (M.H. International Literary Agency)
Morhaim, Howard (Howard Morhaim Literary Agency)
Morrison, Jennifer (Storyboards Inc.)
Mortimer, Lydia (Hull House Literary Agency)
Morton, B. (The Film & Fiction Agency)
Mosely, Jane (Lucianne S. Goldberg Literary Agents, Inc.)
Mosgrove, Will (Marianne Campbell)
Moss, Eileen (Bruck and Moss Associates)
Mulert, Carl (The Joyce Ketay Agency)
Mullen, Allison (Howard Morhaim Literary Agency)
Murphy, David (H.N. Swanson Inc.)

N

Nadell, Bonnie (Frederick Hill Associates)
Naggar, Jean (Jean V. Naggar Literary Agency)
Neighbors, Charles (Charles Neighbors Literary Agency)
Neis, Judy (The Neis Group)
Nellis, Muriel (Literary and Creative Artists Agency)
Nelson, Bonita (BK Nelson Literary Agency & Lecture Bureau)
Nguyen, Kim Van (Robert Madsen Agency)
Nolan, Betsy (The Betsy Nolan Literary Agency)
Nolton, Gary (Marianne Campbell)
Novak, Ed (Edward A. Novak III Literary Representation)
Nusblatt, Leslie (Bernstein & Andriulli Inc.)

O

O'Connor, Leighton (Leighton & Company)
O'Grady, Elizabeth (Dwyer & O'Grady, Inc.)
Olesha, Andrea (Andrea Olesha Agency)
Olm, Sandrine (Lucianne S. Goldberg Literary Agents, Inc.)
Orr, Alice (Alice Orr Agency, Inc.)
Orrmont, Arthur (Author Aid Associates)
Ortiz, Natalie (Bernstein & Andriulli Inc.)
Osborne, Geoff (Lyceum Creative Properties, Inc.)
Otte, Jane H. (The Otte Company)
Otte, L. David (The Otte Company)

P

Page, Jackie (Jackie Page)
Palmer, Dorothy (Dorothy Palmer)
Palulian, Joanne (Joanne Palulian)
Panettiere, Vincent (Panettiere & Co.)
Pantel, Elena (The Joseph S. Ajlouny Agency)
Papadopoulous, Costas (M.H. International Literary Agency)
Parker, Stacy (L. Harry Lee Literary Agency)
Parks, Richard (The Richard Parks Agency)
Pate, Randy (Randy Pate & Associates)
Paton, Kathi (Kathi J. Paton Literary Agency)
Patrick, Jean (Diamond Literary Agency, Inc.)
Pell, William (William Pell Agency)
Pembroke, Lynne (Jack Scagnetti Talent & Literary Agency)
Pennamenities (Media Gallery/Enterprises)
Perez, Gerard V. (Art Emotion Corp.)
Perkins, Lori (L. Perkins Associates)
Perkins, M. (Acton, Dystel, Leone & Jaffe, Inc.)
Peterson, Jill (Tonal Values Inc.)
Petrizzo, Donna (Gerald & Cullen Rapp, Inc.)

Agents and Reps Index

Pfitzner, Kim (Seiffer & Associates)
Picard, Alison (Alison J. Picard Literary Agent)
Pinkstaff, Marsha (Marsha Pinkstaff Representing Photographers)
Pisarski, Lee (Lee + Lou Productions Inc.)
Piscopo, Maria (Maria Piscopo)
Polk, Katie (L. Harry Lee Literary Agency)
Pollak, Fran (Mews Books Ltd.)
Pomada, Elizabeth (Michael Larsen/Elizabeth Pomada Literary Agents)
Pool, Linda (Creative Productions, Inc.)
Popkin, Julie (Julie Popkin)
Porcelain, Sidney (Sidney E. Porcelain)
Porter, Terry D. (Agape Productions)
Powers, Jennifer (Schaffner Agency, Inc.)
Prapas, Christine (Christine Prapas/Artist Representative)
Pratt-Dewey, Beth (Adler & Robin Books, Inc.)
Prescott, Ashton (The Marshall Cameron Agency)
Prescott, Margo (The Marshall Cameron Agency)
Preston, Harry (Stanton & Associates International Literary Agency)
Priano, Timothy (Oz New York Inc.)
Priest, Aaron (Aaron M. Priest Literary Agency)
Protter, Susan (Susan Ann Protter Literary Agent)
Pryor, Roberta (Roberta Pryor, Inc.)
Pugarelli, Angela (Rhodes Literary Agency)
Pugarelli, Fred C. (Rhodes Literary Agency)
Pulitzer-Voges, Elizabeth (Kirchoff/Wohlberg, Inc., Authors' Representation Division)

R

Rabinoff, Lynne (Mary Jack Wald Associates, Inc.)
Raintree, Diane (Raintree Agency)
Ramer, Susan (Don Congdon Associates Inc.)
Rappaport, Jodi (Jodi Rappaport)
Rathmann, Fran (Fran Literary Agency)
Raymond, Charlotte Cecil (Charlotte Cecil Raymond, Literary Agent)
Redmond, Sharon (Redmond Represents)
Reed, Cliff (The Film & Fiction Agency)
Reid, Pamela (Pamela Reid)
Reilly, Kerry (Kerry Reilly: Reps)
Reiss, William (John Hawkins & Associates, Inc.)
Ricciardi, Mike (The Marian Berzon Agency)
Richardson, Bruce D. (Dragon Literary, Inc.)
Rickard, Joan (Author Author Literary Agency)
Rico't, Cory (Nelda Lee Inc.)
Robbins, Kathy P. (The Robbins Office, Inc.)
Roberts, Jane (Literary and Creative Artists Agency)
Robinson, Jennifer (PMA Literary and Film Management, Inc.)
Robinson, Linton (Frontier Talents)
Rock, Andrew T. (Rock Literary Agency)
Roenbeck, Patti (L. Harry Lee Literary Agency)
Rogers, Stephanie (Stephanie Rogers and Associates)
Romine, Charles (BK Nelson Literary Agency & Lecture Bureau)
Rose, Mitchell (Rose Literary Agency)
Rosenberg, Arlene (Arlene Rosenberg)
Rosenfeld, Arthur (Westchester Literary Agency, Inc.)
Rosenfeld, Fran (Bernstein & Andriulli Inc.)
Rosenstiel, Leonie (Author Aid Associates)
Rosenthal, Jean (Jean Rosenthal Literary Agency)
Rosenthal, Judith (Barbara Markowitz Literary Agency)
Ross, Lisa (F. Joseph Spieler)
Ross, Luna Carne (The Lois de la Haba Agency Inc.)
Roth, Shelley E. (The Roth Agency)
Rothery, Charles (L. Harry Lee Literary Agency)
Roy, Dave (Lyceum Creative Properties, Inc.)
Roy, Lesley (The Gary-Paul Agency)
Rubie, Peter (L. Perkins Associates)
Rubin, Michele (Writers House)
Rubinstein, Pesha (Pesha Rubinstein, Literary Agency, Inc.)
Ruderman, Linda (Linda Ruderman)
Rudin, Nancy (London Contemporary Art)
Rue, Robin (Anita Diamant, The Writer's Workshop, Inc.)
Rumanes, George N. (Cinema Talent International)
Russell, Margaret (Russell-Simenauer Literary Agency Inc.)
Russo, Fran (William Pell Agency)

S

Sacramone, Dario (Dario Sacramone)
Salt, Gary (Paul Kohner, Inc.)
Salzman, Richard (Richard Salzman)
Sands, Trudy (Trudy Sands & Associates)
Sandum, Howard E. (Sandum & Associates)
Sanford, Shelly A. (Bernsen, Jamail & Goodson)
Santoianni, John B. (The Tantleff Office)
Santucci, Ernest (Agency Chicago)
Sapiro, Joan (Joan Sapiro Art Consultants)
Scagnetti, Jack (Jack Scagnetti Talent & Literary Agency)
Schaeffer, Glenn (Glenmark Literary Agency)
Schaffner, Timothy (Schaffner Agency, Inc.)
Schlessiger, Charles (Brandt & Brandt Literary Agents Inc.)
Schmalz, Wendy (Harold Ober Associates)
Schmidt, Harold (Harold Schmidt Literary Agency)
Schneider, Anthony (PMA Literary and Film Management, Inc.)
Schochat, Kevin R. (Kevin R. Schochat)
Schulman, Ruth (F.L.A.I.R.)
Schulman, Susan (Susan Schulman, A Literary Agency)

Schwartz, Laurens R. (Laurens R. Schwartz Agency)
Schwarzchild, Susan P. (Publishers' Graphics)
Scott, Freda (Freda Scott, Inc.)
Seiffer, John (Seiffer & Associates)
Seiffer, Wendy (Seiffer & Associates)
Seitz, Steve (Ethan Ellenberg Literary Agency)
Seligman, Lynn (Lynn Seligman, Literary Agent)
Selzer, Edwin (Educational Design Services, Inc.)
Serkin, Deb (Seiffer & Associates)
Servis, Harold (Ellen Lively Steele & Associates)
Seymour, Mary Sue (The Seymour Agency)
Seymour, Mike (The Seymour Agency)
Shanks, Thomas J. (H.N. Swanson Inc.)
Shannon, Denise (Georges Borchardt Inc.)
Sharpe, John (Sharpe + Associates)
Shearer, Nicki (Nicki Shearer Art Source)
Sheldon, Anne (The Hardy Agency)
Shelton, Ken (Executive Excellence)
Shepard, Jean (The Shepard Agency)
Shepard, Lance (The Shepard Agency)
Shepherd, Peter (Harold Ober Associates)
Sher, Danis (Mary Jack Wald Associates, Inc.)
Shevrin, Stan (Lesli Art, Inc.)
Shreves, Richard (Richard R. Shreves Agency)
Siegel, Bobbe (Bobbe Siegel Literary Agency)
Sigman, Joan (The Newborn Group)
Silverstein, Bob (Quicksilver Books-Literary Agents)
Simenauer, Jacqueline (Russell-Simenauer Literary Agency Inc.)
Simpson, Robert (Roslyn Targ Literary Agency, Inc.)
Sinclair, Carl (Scribe Agency)
Singer, Evelyn (Evelyn Singer Literary Agency Inc.)
Singer, Katherine (Oceanic Press)
Singer, Kurt (Singer Media Corporation)

Skolnick, Irene (Curtis Brown Ltd.)
Smith, Claire (Harold Ober Associates)
Smith, Davis (Dupree/Miller and Associates Inc. Literary)
Smith, Dick (Authors' Literary Agency)
Smith, Patricia (Michael Snell Literary Agency)
Smith, Valerie (Valerie Smith, Literary Agent)
Snell, Michael (Michael Snell Literary Agency)
Sobel, Lee (Lee Sobel Management Associates)
Soldat, Rick (Soldat & Associates)
Soloweij, Constance (Flannery, White and Stone)
Sommer, Elyse (Elyse Sommer, Inc.)
Sonneville, Dane (Dane Sonneville Assoc. Inc.)
Soodak, Arlene (Soodak Represents)
Soper, Elisa (Freelance Hotline, Inc.)
Sorice, Camille (Camille Sorice Agency)
South, Davida (Sandra Watt & Associates)
Spelman, Martha (Martha Productions, Inc.)
Spieler, Gretchen (Gretchen Spieler Literary Agency)
Spieler, Joe (F. Joseph Spieler)
Spiers, Herb (S.I. International)
Spitzer, Philip (Philip G. Spitzer Literary Agency)
Stanton, Henry (Stanton & Associates International Literary Agency)
Stauffer, Nancy (Nancy Stauffer Associates)
Steele, Ellen Lively (Ellen Lively Steele & Associates)
Steele, Lyle (Lyle Steele & Co., Ltd.)
Stefanski, Lily (Peter Kuehnel & Associates)
Steinberg, Michael (Michael Steinberg Literary Agency)
Sterling, Cynthia (Lee Shore Agency)
Stermer, Carol Lee (The Penny & Stermer Group)
Stern, Gloria (Gloria Stern Agency)
Stern, Gloria (Gloria Stern Literary Agency)

Stogas, Nikki (M.H. International Literary Agency)
Stone, Ivy Fischer (Fifi Oscard Agency)
Storey, Douglas (The Catalog® Literary Agency)
Streeter, Newton E. (Ace Consultants)
Strickland, Judy (Write Designs Literary Agency)
Sturges, Frank (Scott Hull Associates)
Sullivan, Debbie (Sullivan & Associates)
Sullivan, Mark (Mark Sullivan Associates)
Sullivan, Tom (Sullivan & Associates)
Suter, Anne Elisabeth (Gotham Art & Literary Agency Inc.)
Swamy, Maya (Maya Swamy, Literary Agent)
Sweeney, Emma (Curtis Brown Ltd.)

T

Tagen, Elizabeth (Carolyn Jenks Agency)
Talbot, William (Samuel French, Inc.)
Tantleff, Jack (The Tantleff Office)
Targ, Roslyn (Roslyn Targ Literary Agency, Inc.)
Taylor, Clyde (Curtis Brown Ltd.)
Taylor, Dawson (Dawson Taylor Literary Agency)
Taylor, Jess (Curtis Brown Ltd.)
Teal, Patricia (Patricia Teal Literary Agency)
Thoma, Geri (Elaine Markson Literary Agency)
Tillman, Sybil (Artco Incorporated)
Tomkins, Susan (Michael Amato Agency)
Toomey, Jeanne (Jeanne Toomey Associates)
Toyama, Kathee (Ellen Knable & Associates, Inc.)
Tramble, Nichelle (SJ Clark Literary Agency)
Traum, Michael (Don Buchwald Agency)
Travis, Susan (Margret McBride Literary Agency)
Tribelli, Joseph (Joseph Tribelli Designs, Ltd.)
Trupin, James (Jet Literary Associates, Inc.)
Tuqeau, Chris (Carol Bancroft

Agents and Reps Index

& Friends)
Turtle, Cindy (The Turtle Agency)
Tymensky, Linda (The Dark Horse Group, Inc.)

U

Urstadt, Susan (Susan P. Urstadt Writers & Artists Agency)

V

Valenti, Miguel (The Gary-Paul Agency)
Vallely, Janis C. (Flaming Star Literary Enterprises)
Vallely, Joseph B. (Flaming Star Literary Enterprises)
Van Bomel, Ed (L. Harry Lee Literary Agency)
Van der Beets, Dr. Richard (West Coast Literary Associates)
Van der Leun, Patricia (Van der Leun & Associates)
Vandertuin, Victoria (New Age World Services)
Veloric, Philip M. (Philip M. Veloric, Artist Representative)
Verrill, Charles (Darhansoff & Verrill Literary Agents)
Vesel, Beth (Stanford J. Greenburger Associates)
Vesneske, Jr., Ed (Nine Muses and Apollo)
Vidor, Michael (The Hardy Agency)

W

Wagner, Matthew (Waterside Productions, Inc.)
Wagoner, Jae (Jae Wagoner, Artist Representative)
Wales, Elizabeth (Levant & Wales, Literary Agency, Inc.)
Wallace, Bess D. (Bess Wallace Literary Agency)
Wallace, Lois (Wallace Literary Agency, Inc.)
Wallace, Thomas C. (Wallace Literary Agency, Inc.)
Wallerstein, Gerry B. (The Gerry B. Wallerstein Agency)
Wallerstein, Michele (H.N. Swanson Inc.)
Walters Goldstein, Gwen (Gwen Walters Goldstein)
Walters, Maureen (Curtis Brown Ltd.)
Ward, Barbara (Gunther Stuhlmann, Author's Representative)
Ware, John (John A. Ware Literary Agency)
Warner, Bob (Warner & Associates)
Warren, James (James Warren Literary Agency)
Washington, Dick (Washington-Artists' Representatives)
Wasserman, Harriet (Harriet Wasserman Literary Agency)
Watt, Sandra (Sandra Watt & Associates)
Weber, Tricia (The Weber Group)
Wecksler, Sally (Wecksler-Incomco)
Weimann, Frank (The Literary Group)
Weiner, Cherry (Cherry Weiner Literary Agency)
Weissberg, Elyse (Elyse Weissberg)
Wells, Susan (Susan Wells & Associates, Inc.)
Westberg, Phyllis (Harold Ober Associates)
Western, Carole (Montgomery-West Literary Agency)
Weyr, Rhoda A. (Rhoda Weyr Agency)
Whelan, Elisabeth (Roberta D. Miller Associates)
White, Marta (Scribe Agency)
Whitman, John R. (Kirchoff/Wohlberg, Inc., Authors' Representation Division)
Wieser, George (Wieser & Wieser, Inc.)
Wieser, Olga (Wieser & Wieser, Inc.)
Willard, Paul (Paul Willard Associates, Ltd.)
Williamson, Dean (Dupree/Miller and Associates Inc. Literary)
Willig, Alan (The Tantleff Office)
Winston, Bonnie (Winston West, Ltd.)
Witherspoon, Kimberly (Witherspoon & Associates, Inc.)
Wolfe, Deborah (Deborah Wolfe Ltd.)
Wong, John (April & Wong)
Wood, Eleanor (Blassingame Spectrum Corp.)
Wood, Theron B. (Dragon Literary, Inc.)
Wreschner, Ruth (Ruth Wreschner, Authors' Representative)
Wright, Dan (Ann Wright Representatives)
Wright, Stephen (Stephen Wright Authors' Representative)
Wylegala, Wendy (Kidde, Hoyt & Picard)
Wyszaki, Kathleen (The Dark Horse Group, Inc.)

Y

Yost, Nancy (Lowenstein Associates, Inc.)
Young, Edward (Bruce Cook Agency)
Young, Elizabeth (Bruce Cook Agency)
Yuen, Sue (Susan Herner Rights Agency)

Z

Zabel, Bruce W. (The Curtis Bruce Agency)
Zaccaro, Jim (Jim Zaccaro Prod. Inc.)
Zaitz, David (David Zaitz Artist Representative)
Zeckendorf, Susan (Susan Zeckendorf Assoc. Inc.)
Zehngut, Jayne (L.A. Art Exchange)
Zelasky, Tom (Tom Zelasky Literary Agency)
Zhorne, Wendy L. (Forthwrite Literary Agency)
Ziemska, Elizabeth (Nicholas Ellison, Inc.)
Zitwer, Barbara (The Lois de la Haba Agency Inc.)
Zuckerman, Albert (Writers House)

Listing Index

A
A & R Burke Corporation 114
Acacia House Publishing Services Ltd. 115
Ace Consultants 115
Ackerman Literary Services 116
Acton, Dystel, Leone & Jaffe, Inc. 47
Adler & Robin Books Inc. 47
Administrative Arts, Inc. 227
Agape Productions 162
Agency Chicago 48
Agency for the Performing Arts 162
Agents Inc. for Medical and Mental Health Professionals 48
Ahearn Agency, Inc., The 116
Ajlouny Agency, Joseph S. 48
Albrecht and Assoc., Anne 187
Albrecht & Jennings Art Enterprises 227
Alden—Literary Service, Farel T. 116
Allan Agency, Lee 49
Allen, Literary Agency, James 49
Allied Artists 162
All-Star Talent Agency 163
Amato Agency, Michael 163
American Artists, Rep. Inc. 187
American Play Co., Inc. 163
Amsterdam Agency, Marcia 50
Andrews & Assoc., Bart 50
Anthony Agency, Joseph 117
Anton, Inc., Jerry 187
Appleseeds Management 50
April & Wong 188
Arnold Fine Art, Jack 227
Art Emotion Corp. 227
Art Source L.A. 228
Artco Incorporated 228
Artist Development Group 188
Artists Assoc. 188
Artists International 188
Arts Counsel Inc. 228
Asciutto Art Reps., Inc. 189
Ashby Literary Agency 117
Author Aid Associates 118
Author Author Literary Agency 118
Authors And Artists Resource Center/Tarc Literary Agency, The 119
Authors' Literary Agency 51

Authors' Marketing Services Ltd. 119
Axelrod Agency, The 51

B
Bach Literary Agency, Julian (see IMG-Julian Bach 75)
Baldi Literary Agency, Malaga 51
Balkin Agency, Inc. 52
Bancroft & Friends, Carol 189
Barber Literary Agency, Inc., Virginia 52
Barracca Assoc. Inc., Sal 189
Barrett Books Inc., Loretta 52
Bartczak Associates Inc., Gene 52
Bartels Associates, Ceci 189
Baum & Associates, Cathy 228
BDP & Associates Talent Agency 163
Beal Management, The Mary 163
Becker/Aleta M. Daley, Maximilian 119
Behar Literary Agency, Josh 52
Beidler Inc., Barbara 190
Berendsen & Associates, Inc. 190
Berman, Writers' Representative, Lois 164
Bernsen, Jamail & Goodson, L.L.P. 53
Bernstein & Andriulli Inc. 190
Bernstein Literary Agency, Meredith 119
Berzon Agency, Marian 164
Bethel Agency 165
Black Literary Agency, David 53
Blassingame Spectrum Corp. 53
Boates Literary Agency, Reid 53
Bond Ltd., Alison M. 54
Borchardt Inc., Georges 54
Bova Literary Agency, The Barbara 54
Brandenburgh & Associates Literary Agency 54
Brandt Agency, The Joan 54
Brandt & Brandt Literary Agents Inc. 54
Brindle Inc., Carolyn 190
Brinke Literary Agency 120

Brody, Artists and Photographers Representative, Sam 191
Brooke & Company 191
Brown Assoc., Marie 55
Brown Ltd., Curtis 55
Brown Literary Agency, Inc., Andrea 55
Browne Ltd., Pema 120, 191
Bruck and Moss Associates 191
Bruml/Artists Representative, Kathy 192
Buchwald Agency, Don 165
Buck Agency, Howard 56
Bulger and Assoc., Kelvin C. 165
Burger Assoc. Ltd., Knox 56
Burlingham/Artist Representation, Tricia 192
Butler, Art and Literary Agent, Jane 56
Bykofsky Associates, Sheree 56

C
Cadenbach Assoc., Marilyn 192
Cameron Agency, The Marshall 165
Campbell, Marianne 192
Canatella Agency, Margaret 166
Cantrell-Colas Inc., Literary Agency 56
Carp, Inc., Stan 193
Carvainis Agency, Inc., Maria 57
Casselman Literary Agent, Martha 57
Castiglia Literary Agency, Julie 120
Catalog™ Literary Agency, The 121
Caton Artist Representative, Chip 193
Chadd-Stevens Literary Agency 57
Chandelyn Literary Agency, The 166
Chislovsky Design Inc., Carol 193
Cinema Talent International 166
Circle of Confusion Ltd. 166
Ciske Literary Agency, Francine 57
Clark Literary Agency, SJ 58
Clausen Associates, Connie 58

Listing Index

Cleaver Inc., Diane 58
Client First—A/K/A Leo P. Haffey Agency 166
Coast To Coast Talent and Literary 167
Cohen, Inc. Literary Agency, Ruth 58
Cohen Literary Agency Ltd., Hy 59
Colby: Literary Agency 121
Coleman Presents Inc., Woody 193
Collier Associates 59
Collier Represents, Jan 194
Collignon, Daniele 194
Collin Literary Agent, Frances 59
Columbia Literary Assoc. 59
Comedy Ink 167
Congdon Associates, Inc., Don 60
Conrad & Assoc., James (see Conrad Represents... 194)
Conrad Represents... 194
Cook Agency, Bruce 121
Coover Agency, The Doe 60
Coppage Company, The 167
Corcoran Fine Arts Limited, Inc. 229
Cornell + McCarthy 194
Corporate Art Assoc., Ltd. 229
Creative Arts of Ventura 194
Creative Freelancers Management, Inc. 194
Creative Productions, Inc. 195
Crown International Literature and Arts Agency, Bonnie R. 60
Curtis Assoc., Inc., Richard 60
Curtis Bruce Agency, The 122
CVB Creative Resource 195
Cyberstorm! 167

D

Darhansoff & Verrill Literary Agents 61
Dark Horse Group, Inc. 61
Davie Literary Agency, Elaine 61
de la Haba Agency, Lois 62
De Moreta Represents, Linda 195
Diamant, The Writer's Workshop, Inc., Anita 62
Diamond Literary 168
Diamond Literary Agency 63
Dijkstra Literary Agency, Sandra 63
Diskant & Associates 168
Dodge and Assoc., Sharon 195
Dodge Creative Services 196
Dolger Agency, Jonathan 64
Donadio & Ashworth Inc. Literary Representatives 64

Donaldson Represents, Karen 196
Donlan, Thomas C. 64
Dorese Agency Ltd. 122
Douroux & Co. 168
Doyen Literary Services, Inc. 64
Dragon Literary, Inc. 168
Ducas, Robert 64
Dupree/Miller and Associates Inc. Literary 65
DW Represents 196
Dwyer & O'Grady, Inc. 197
Dykeman Associates Inc. 168

E

Earth Tracks Agency 169
Eastwind Writers 123
Eden Literary Agency 123
Edsey & Sons, Steven 197
Educational Design Services, Inc. 65
Eisenberg Literary Agency, Vicki 65
Elek Associates, Peter 65
Ellenberg Literary Agency, Ethan 66
Elliott/Oreman Artists' Representatives 197
Ellison Inc., Nicholas 66
Elmo Agency Inc., Ann 66
Embers Literary Agency 67
Epstein/Photographer's Representative, Rhoni 197
Esquire Literary Productions 67
Eth Literary Representation, Felicia 67
Executive Excellence 124

F

Farber Literary Agency Inc. 67
Farquharson Ltd., John 67
Feiler Literary Agency, Florence 67
Fiat & Associates, Randi 198
Fields-Rita Scott Inc., Marje 68
Film & Fiction Agency, The 124
Fine Art Representative (see London Contemporary Art 230)
F.L.A.I.R. 169
Fishbein Ltd., Frieda 124
Flaherty, Literary Agent, Joyce A. 68
Flaming Star Literary Enterprises 68
Flannery White and Stone 125
Fleming Agency, Peter 68
Fogelman Literary Agency 69
Follendore Literary Agency, Joan 125
Forbes Inc., Pat 198
ForthWrite Literary Agency 125

Foster Artist Rep., (Pat) 198
Fran Literary Agency 126
Francisco Communications, Inc. 198
Freedman Dramatic Agency, Inc., Robert A. 169
Freelance Hotline, Inc. 198
French, Inc., Samuel 170
Frontier Talents 69
Fuhrman Literary Agency, Candice 69

G

Galitz Fine Art/Accent Art, Robert 229
Gardner Agency, The 170
Gardner & Assoc., Jean 199
Garon-Brooke Assoc., Jay 70
Gartenberg, Literary Agent, Max 70
Gary-Paul Agency, The 170
Geddes Agency 170
Geiger Literary Agency, Ellen 70
Gelles-Cole Literary Enterprises 126
Gersh Agency, The 170
Giannini & Talent 199
Gill, Stephen 199
Ginsburg & Assoc., Michael 199
Gislason Agency, The 127
Gladden Unlimited 127
Glenmark Literary Agency 127
Goddard: Book Development, Connie 128
Godfrey Representing Artists, Dennis 200
Goldberg Literary Agents, Inc., Lucianne S. 128
Goldfarb & Assoc., Ronald 71
Goldman Agency, David 200
Goldstein, Gwen Walters 200
Goodman Associates 71
Goodman Inc., Tom 201
Goodman Literary Agency, Irene 71
Gordon Agency, Charlotte 71
Gordon Assoc., Barbara 201
Gordon/Artist Representative, T.J. 201
Gotham Art & Literary Agency Inc. 72
Gotler Metropolitan Talent Agency, Joel (see Renaissance: A Literary/Talent Agency 95)
Graham Agency 171
Greenburger Associates, Sanford J. 72
Gregory Associates, Maia 72
Grien—Representing Artists, Anita 201
Grimes Literary Agency, Lew

Groffsky Literary Agency, Maxine 72
Guenzi Agents, Inc., Carol 201
Gusay Literary Agency, The Charlotte 72

H
Hackett/Artist Representative, Pat 202
Hall & Associates 202
Hamersfield Agency, The 128
Hamilburg Agency, The Mitchell J. 73
Hamilton's Literary Agency, Andrew 129
Handaris, Literary Agency, Marisa (see M.H. International Literary Agency 135)
Hardy Agency, The 73
Hauser, Another Girl Rep, Barb 202
Hawkins & Assoc., John 73
Hayes & Assoc., Gil 171
Haynes Limited, Elizabeth 129
Heacock Literary Agency, Inc. 129
Herman Agency, Inc., The Jeff 73
Herner Rights Agency, Susan 73
Hill Associates, Frederick 74
Hilton Literary Agency, Alice 171
HK Portfolio 202
Hochmann Books, John L. 74
Hodges Agency, Carolyn 171
Hoffman Literary Agency, Berenice 74
Holt & Assoc., Rita 203
Holub & Associates 75
Hubbs Agency, Yvonne Trudeau 130
Hull Associates, Scott 203
Hull House Literary Agency 75

I
Icebox 229
IMG-Julian Bach Literary Agency 75
Imison Playwrights Ltd., Michael 172
Independent Publishing Agency 130
International Creative Management 75
International Leonards Corp. 172
International Publisher Associates Inc. 76

J
J de S Associates Inc. 76
Jackson Agency, Melanie 76
Janklow & Nesbit Associates 76
Jedell Productions, Inc. 203
Jenks Agency, Carolyn 131
Jet Literary Associates, Inc. 76
Jones Literary Agency, Lloyd 76
Jordan Literary Agency, Lawrence 76

K
Kaltman Literary Agency, Larry 131
Karpfinger Agency, The 77
Kastaris & Associates 203
Kay Agency, Charlene 172
Keating, Peggy 204
Kellock & Assoc. Ltd., J. 131
Kellock Company, Inc., The 77
Kellogg Creative Services 204
Kern Literary Agency, Natasha 132
Kerr, Ralph 204
Keswick Hamilton 204
Ketay Agency, The Joyce 172
Ketz Agency, Louise B. 77
Keyser Literary Agency 133
Kick Entertainment 172
Kidd, Literary Agent, Virginia 77
Kidde, Hoyt & Picard 77
Kirchoff/Wohlberg, Artists Representation Div. 204
Kirchoff/Wohlberg, Authors' Representation Div. 78
Klausner International Literary Agency, Inc. 133
Klimt, Bill and Maurine 205
Klinger, Inc., Harvey 78
Knable & Assoc., Ellen 205
Knecht—Artist Representative, Cliff 205
Kohner, Inc., Paul 173
Korman & Company 205
Korn Assoc. Ltd., Elaine 206
Kouts, Literary Agent, Barbara S. 78
Kroll Agency, Lucy 78
Kroll Literary Agency, Edite 79
Kuehnel & Assoc., Peter 206
Kurlansky Assoc., Sharon 206

L
L.A. Art Exchange 230
Lamont, Mary 206
Lampack Agency, Inc., Peter 79
Langley Represents, Sharon 206
Lantz-Joy Harris Literary Agency Inc., The Robert 79
Larsen/Elizabeth Pomada Literary Agents, Michael 79
Lavaty & Associates, Frank & Jeff 207
Law Offices of Robert L. Fenton PC 134
Lazear Agency Incorporated 80
Lazin Books, Sarah 80
Lee Inc., Nelda 230
Lee Literary Agency, L. Harry 173
Lee + Lou Productions 207
Legacies 174
Leighton & Company 207
Leone Agency, Inc., Adele (see Wildstar Associates 151)
Lescher & Lescher Ltd. 80
Lesli Art, Inc. 230
Levant & Wales, Literary Agency, Inc. 80
Levin•Dorr 208
Levine Communications, Inc., James 134
Levine Literary Agency, Inc., Ellen 80
Lewis, Robert 81
Lilie Artist's Representative, Jim 208
Lincoln Literary Agency, Ray 81
Lindgren & Smith 208
Lipkind Agency, Wendy 81
Literary and Creative Artists Agency 81
Literary Bridge, The 82
Literary Group, The 82
Literary/Business Assoc. 135
Locke Studios, Inc., John 208
London Contemporary Art 230
Lopopolo Literary Agency, Toni 135
Lord Literistic, Inc., Sterling 82
Los Angeles Literary Assoc. 82
Lott, Peter & George 208
Love Literary Agency, Nancy 83
Lowenstein Associates, Inc. 83
Lyceum Creative Properties 83

M
M.H. International Literary Agency 135
Maass Literary Agency, Donald 84
McBride Literary Agency, Margret 84
MacCampbell Inc., Donald 84
McCauley, Gerard 84
McClellan Assoc., Anita D. 85
Maccoby Literary Agency, Gina 85
McConnell McNamara & Co. 209
McDonough, Literary Agent, Richard P. 85
McGrath, Helen 85
McKay Photography, Colleen 209

Listing Index 283

McKinley, Literary Agency, Virginia C. 136
Madsen Agency, Robert 86
Mann Agency, Carol 86
March Tenth, Inc. 86
Marcil Literary Agency, The Denise 136
Markowitz Literary Agency, Barbara 86
Markson Literary Agency, Elaine 87
Marmur Associates Ltd., Mildred 87
Marshall Agency, The Evan 137
Martell Agency, The 87
Martha Productions, Inc. 209
Matson Co. Inc., Harold 87
Mattelson Associates Ltd. 210
Media Gallery/Enterprises 230
Mendola Artists 210
Meredith, Inc., Scott (see Scott Meredith Literary Agency LP 137)
Meredith, Literary Agency, LP, Scott 137
Merhige-Merdon Marketing/Promo Co. Inc., Greg 137
Merrill Ltd., Helen 174
Mews Books Ltd. 137
MGA Agency Inc. 87
Miller Associates, Roberta D. 87
Miller Represents, Susan 210
Montagano & Associates 211
Montgomery-West Literary Agency 174
Moore Literary Agency 88
Morgan Associates, Vicki 211
Morgan Literary Agency, Inc., David H. 138
Morgan/Artist Representative, Michele 211
Morhaim Literary Agency, Howard 88
Morris Agency, William 88
Morrison, Inc., Henry 88
Multimedia Product Development, Inc. 88

N
Naggar Literary Agency, Jean V. 89
Nathan, Ruth 89
Neighbors Literary Agency, Charles 138
Neis Group, The 211
Nelson Literary Agency & Lecture Bureau, BK 138
New Age World Services 139
New England Publishing Associates, Inc. 89
New Writers Literary Project 139
New Writing Agency 139

Newborn Group, The 211
Nine Muses and Apollo 90
Nolan Literary Agency, The Betsy 90
Northeast Literary Agency 140
Northwest Literary Services 140
Novak III Literary Representation, Edward A. 90

O
Ober Associates, Harold 90
Oceanic Press 141
Oceanic Press Service 141
Olesha Agency, Andrea 141
Orr Agency, Inc., Alice 91
Oscard Agency, Inc., Fifi 91
Otitis Media 91
Otte Company, The 91
Oz New York Inc. 212

P
Page, Jackie 212
Palmer, Dorothy 174
Palulian, Joanne 212
Panda Talent 174
Panettiere & Co. 175
Parks Agency, The Richard 91
Pate & Associates, Randy 212
Paton Literary Agency, Kathi J. 92
Pell Agency, William 142
Pelter, Rodney 92
Pen & Ink Literary Agency 142
Pennamenities 231
Penny & Stermer Group, 213
Perkins Associates, L. 92
Perkins' Literary Agency 93
Peter Associates, Inc., James 93
Picard Literary Agent, Alison J. 93
Pinkstaff Representing Photographers, Marsha 213
Piscopo, Maria 213
PMA Literary and Film Management, Inc. 142
Popkin, Julie 142
Porcelain, Sidney E. 143
Prapas/Artist Representative, Christine 213
Priest Literary Agency, Aaron M. 93
Protter Literary Agent, Susan Ann 93
Pryor, Inc., Roberta 94
Publishers' Graphics 213
Puddingtonstone Literary Agency 143

Q
QCorp Literary Agency 143
Quicksilver Books-Literary Agents 94

R
Raintree Agency 175
Rapp, Gerald & Cullen 214
Rappaport, Jodi 214
Raymond, Literary Agent, Charlotte Cecil 94
Redmond Represents 214
Rees Literary Agency, Helen 95
Reid, Pamela 214
Reilly: Reps, Kerry 215
Renaissance: A Literary/Talent Agency 95
Represented by Ken Mann Inc. 215
Retna Ltd. 215
Rhodes Literary Agency 95
Rhodes Literary Agency 144
Ridgeway Artists Representative 215
Riverside Literary Agency 95
Robbins Office, Inc., The 95
Rock Literary Agency 96
Rogers and Associates, Stephanie 175
Rogers, Literary Representative, Irene 96
Rose Agency 144
Rose Literary Agency 96
Rosenberg, Arlene 216
Rosenthal Literary Agency, Jean 96
Rosenthal Represents 216
Roth Agency, The 96
Rotrosen Agency, Jane 97
Rubenstein Literary Agency, Inc., Pesha 97
Ruderman, Linda 216
Russell-Simenauer Literary Agency Inc. 144

S
S.I. International 216
Sacramone, Dario 217
Salzman, Richard 217
Sands & Associates, Trudy 217
Sandum & Associates 97
Sapiro Art Consultants, Joan 231
Scagnetti Talent & Literary Agency, Jack 175
Schaffner Agency, Inc. 97
Schmidt Literary Agency, Harold 98
Schochat, Kevin R. 217
Schulman, A Literary Agency, Susan 145
Schwartz Agency, Laurens R. 98
Scott, Inc., Freda 218
Scribe Agency 175
Sebastian Literary Agency 145
Seiffer & Associates 231
Seligman, Literary Agent, Lynn

98
Seymour Agency, The 99
Sharpe + Associates 218
Shearer Art Source, Nicki 231
Sheedy Literary Agency, Inc., Charlotte 99
Shepard Agency, The 99
Sherman & Assoc., Ken 176
Shreves Agency, Richard R. 99
Siegel Literary Agency, Bobbe 99
Sierra Literary Agency 100
Silver Screen Placements 176
Simpatico Art & Stone 232
Singer Literary Agency Inc., Evelyn 100
Singer Media Corporation 145
Smith, Literary Agent, Valerie 100
Snell Literary Agency, Michael 100
Sobel Management Associates, Lee 176
Soldat & Associates 218
Sommer, Inc., Elyse 101
Sonneville Assoc., Dane 219
Soodak Represents 219
Sorice Agency, Camille 176
Southern Literary Agency 146
Spieler, F. Joseph 101
Spieler Literary Agency, Gretchen 101
Spitzer Literary Agency, Philip G. 102
Stanton & Associates International Literary Agency 177
State of the Art Ltd. 146
Stauffer Associates, Nancy 102
Steele & Associates, Ellen Lively 177
Steele & Co., Ltd., Lyle 102
Steinberg Literary Agency, Michael 147
Stepping Stone 103
Stern Agency, Gloria 147
Stern Literary Agency, Gloria 103
Sternig Literary Agency, Larry 103
Storyboards 219
Stuhlmann, Author's Representative, Gunther 103

Sullivan & Associates 219
Sullivan Associates, Mark 148
Swamy Literary Agent, Maya 103
Swanson Inc., H.N. 177

T
T & M Enterprises 220
Talent Bank Agency, The 177
Tantleff Office, The 178
TARC Literary Agency 148
Targ Literary Agency, Inc., Roslyn 104
Taylor Literary Agency, Dawson 148
Teal Literary Agency, Patricia 104
Tonal Values, Inc. 220
Toomey Associates, Jeanne 148
Total Acting Experience, A 178
Tribelli Designs, Ltd., Joseph 220
Turtle Agency, The 178
Two Steps Up, Inc. 220
2M Communications Ltd. 104

U
Urstadt Inc. Writers and Artists Agency, Susan P. 105, 221
Ursula International Creatives 221

V
Van Der Leun & Associates 105
Veloric, Artist Representative, Philip M. 221
Visions Press 149

W
Wagoner, Artist Representative, Jae 221
Wain Agency, Erika 179
Wald Associates, Inc., Mary Jack 105
Wallace Literary Agency, Bess 149
Wallace Literary Agency 106
Wallerstein Agency, Gerry 150
Ware Literary Agency, John A. 106
Warner & Associates 222
Warren Literary Agency, James 150

Warshaw Blumenthal, Inc. 222
Washington-Artists' Representatives 222
Wasserman Literary Agency, Inc., Harriet 106
Waterside Productions 106
Watkins Loomis Agency 107
Watt & Associates, Sandra 150
Weber Group, The 222
Wecksler-Incomco 107
Weil Agency, Inc., Wendy 107
Weiner Literary Agency, Cherry 107
Weingel-Fidel Agency, The 107
Weissberg, Elyse 223
Wells & Assoc., Inc., Susan 223
West Coast Literary Assoc. 151
Westchester Literary Agency, Inc. 108
Weyr Agency, Rhoda 108
Wieser & Wieser, Inc. 108
Wildstar Associates 151
Willard Assoc., Ltd., Paul 223
Windermere Agency, Julius 179
Winston West, Ltd. 223
Witherspoon & Assoc., Inc. 109
Wohl Literary Agency, Gary S. 109
Wolfe Ltd., Deborah 223
Worldwide Images 224
Wreschner, Authors' Representative, Ruth 109
Wright Authors' Representative, Stephen 152
Wright Representatives, Ann 179
Write Designs Literary Agency 152
Writer's Advocate, The 152
Writers & Artists Agency 179
Writer's Consulting Group 153
Writers House 109
Writers' Productions 110
Writers' Representatives 110

Z
Zaccaro Productions, Jim 224
Zaitz Artist Representative 224
Zeckendorf Assoc., Susan 110
Zelasky Literary Agency, Tom 153